NOBEL LAUREATES

1901-2000

Also by Alan Symons

NOBEL LAUREATES
1901-2000

ALAN SYMONS

POLO PUBLISHING
LONDON

Published by POLO PUBLISHING
PO Box 108, Hampton, Middx: TW12 3QJ
Fax No. 020 8979 9425

A catalogue record of this book is available from the
British Library.

ISBN 0-9523751-3-3

Printed and Bound in Great Britain by Bath Press

First Published in 2000 by Polo Publishing, London

Book cover design by Anthony and Patrick Maher.
Page layout design and computer work by Chris Adams
of AdSoft Solutions.

INTRODUCTION

I cannot remember a time when the announcement of the Nobel Prizes didn't give me a frisson of expectancy. I was rarely disappointed. My decision to write a book on the subject came about following the award, in 1993, of the Peace Prize to Nelson Mandela. After many years of intense research, I am most impressed by the efficiency and dedication of all the Nobel Institutions. However, even the commitment of these splendid people are shadows when compared to the master-Alfred Nobel. Here is a man with a tortured soul, who instead of being oblivious to the world's suffering, raises his sights to a post-life future in order to improve the world as he knew it. No subsequent philanthropist has come near to giving to the world the hope Alfred Nobel has achieved. It wasn't simply the amount of money Nobel left, there are many who have left far more, it was his great imagination and love of humanity.

Laureates don't set out with the idea of winning the coveted Nobel Prize, they can't, the procedures don't allow for it. They simply get on with their work, the results of which benefit mankind. This regardless of whether it is in the field of literature, physics, chemistry, economics or physiology or medicine. Only with the Peace Prize is there a dimension of possible partiality. It is this Prize that the underdogs, the tortured, and the dispossessed have come to think of as their own.. Example after example exists of the award being given to people and organisations devoted to the masses and not to parochial organizations. There have been occasions when the Prize embarrasses authority; a situation which Alfred Nobel would surely have approved .

When the Norwegian Nobel Institute in 1935 awarded their Peace Prize to the pacifist, Carl von Ossietsky, languishing in a German concentration camp, Adolph Hitler, then German Chancellor, was infuriated. He forbade any German ever to accept one in the future. In the event Nobel prizes continued to be awarded to Germans, often German Jews. Thus has the independence of the Nobel ideal been maintained as an examination of those who have been awarded a Peace Prize will appreciate. Of course there have been criticisms, four awards in relation to the troubles in Northern Island come to mind, but at the time the award is made there is an upsurge of hope and it not the fault of the Nobel Institute that events become retrogressive because of the bigotries of lesser folk. And there have been omissions. Glaring omissions such as Mahatma Ghandi not being awarded a Peace Prize or Graham Greene a prize for Literature. The scientific and medical prizes have proved to be the least controversial, while those for literature and peace, by their very nature have been the most exposed to critical expression . Perhaps an interesting list of non-receivers could well be established.

I have long been impressed by the ability of the various Nobel Committees to raise the temperature of world opinion by their independent decisions. During WW2, when Sweden could have been swept aside by German might with comparative ease, the Nobel Committees never flinched from their dedicated task of rewarding those whom their advisors counselled should be Nobel recipients. As a result, the first prizewinners during the war for Chemistry and Physics was in 1943, when two Jews; Georg von Hevesy and Otto Hahn respectively received Nobel Prizes. Post-war, former members of the Nazi party won awards, disregarded their Fuhrer's edict and accepted the Nobel Medal, the Nobel Diploma and the Nobel cheque with alacrity

Some have won awards and turned them down perhaps they (and others) should be reminded of Nobel's apt aphorism: "Second to agriculture, humbug is the biggest industry of our age". Others have used their Nobel laureate standing to join companies and thereby raise their stature.

Whilst the prize is universal, it covers 55 countries and all five continents a close examination reveals an extreme oddity, namely, that of the 703 Nobel awards awarded from 1901, 127 have been won by Jewish men and women, from all over the world, and covering all six disciplines. It means that .3% of the world's population have won 18% of all Nobel prizes.

The award of the Nobel Prize will continue as long as the funds, most wisely invested, survive. The fact that the Nobel Foundations have overcome two world wars, numerous recessions and reoccurring stock market crashes, bodes well for the future. However, so well entrenched has the Nobel prize come to mean the pinnacle of success, I believe recipients would gladly forgo the prize money, and sleep well with the gold medal and diploma tucked under their pillow.

Alan Symons, London.

Alfred Nobel-His Life and Times

Alfred Bernhard Nobel was born in Stockholm, Sweden on October 21st 1833. At the time he was the youngest of three sons born to Andrietta and Immanuel Nobel. Immanuel Nobel was an engineer who fancied himself as an entrepreneur. As a result, at the time Alfred was born, his father was a declared bankrupt. In 1837 the family was left to fend for themselves in Stockholm whilst Nobel Senior took off, first for Finland and then Russia.

Alfred's mother was descended from an intellectual family that included Olof Rudbeck, a noted Swedish naturalist and who, in the latter half of the 17th century, described, in some detail, the lymphatic vessels. In 1842, the family left Stockholm to join the father in St. Petersburg. Here Alfred was taught by tutors with the result that, at 16, he was a competent chemist and fluent in French, German, English, Russian and of course Swedish.

In 1850, at the age of 17, Alfred left Russia for Paris in order to spend a year studying chemistry. He followed this with a 4 year stint in the United States, where he worked at shipbuilding under John Ericsson. Upon his return to Russia and St. Petersburg, Alfred worked in his father's factory until the company went bankrupt in 1859.

He returned to Stockholm and there Alfred Nobel began manufacturing a liquid explosive called nitro-glycerine. In 1864 production was progressing when the factory blew up killing five people, including Alfred's younger brother, Emil. In the event the Swedish government forbade Alfred to rebuild the factory. He was now dubbed by the newspapers as 'the mad scientist'.

Heartbroken by the death of his brother but determined to continue, Alfred bought a large barge and moored it well away from any buildings. There he began experimenting to find a way to minimize the danger of handling nitro-glycerine. He chanced upon the discovery that nitro could be absorbed to dryness by kierelguhr, sometimes known as diatomite, a siliceous packing material and an absorbent filter in the manufacture of explosives so allowing the potentially lethal product to be handled relatively safely.

This resulted later in Nobel perfecting dynamite and producing a detonator cap.. He was granted patents for dynamite in 1867 in Great Britain, with the US following a year later. He went on to patent Blasting Gelatin, a more powerful form of dynamite in 1876. Some years later there followed Ballistite, a smokeless powder containing nitroglycerin and a precursor to cordite. His perfection in the field of detonators completed the cycle and led directly to his invention of gelignite so beloved by safe crackers during the first half of the 20th century.

He went on to make an immense fortune from explosive inventions much of which he spent on developing the Baku oil fields of Russia. This investment proved most productive and added to his already considerable fortune. He was a man who favoured seclusion. He never married and had an abiding interest in literature. He would write poetry in English in the style of Shelley and Byron and amongst his papers, discovered after his death, was a near complete novel.

His view of the future, as it related to mankind and nations was pessimistic. However much he became disillusioned, by what he saw and heard, he never turned his back on the world. Paris had a big influence on his life. In 1873 he settled in what he termed his favourite city. There he found a sophistication that he felt had nothing to do with social class, he once said, 'even the dogs reek of civilization in Paris', and he bought a magnificent house in Avenue Malakoff, off the Bois de Boulogne.

In 1876 he placed an advertisement in a newspaper for a private secretary. Thus he met Countess Bertha Kinsky von Chinic und Tettau. She was 33, Nobel 43. She worked for him for only a short time but they remained lifelong friends. He would spend many hours going over his plans for what would become known as 'Nobel Prizes'. Indeed, and perhaps somewhat ironical, is the fact that she would later become world famous as a pacifist writer under the name of Bertha von Suttner, whose book *Lay Down Your Arms* became a best seller and resulted in her being awarded the Nobel Peace Prize for 1905.

Early in the 1890s Nobel met the young and beautiful Sophie Hess, whilst on a trip to Vienna. He was captivated by her and leased a house for her in Avenue d'Eylau, close to where his friend Victor Hugo lived. Their on-going relationship lasted some eighteen years. Following Nobel's deal with the Italian government, that would allow them to manufacture ballistite under licence, he was accused of 'high treason' by the French government and forced to leave Paris.

He settled in San Remo on Italy's Costa d'ell Fiori and died alone on December 10th 1896. Right up to the time of his death Nobel was working on his inventions. His laboratories were busy with his ideas, many well before their time. His work in the field of weapon technology included ballistic rockets. Other inventions created manufacturing empires and ran from artificial gutta-percha to mild steel for armour plating. The synthetic transuranic element, nobelium was named after him.

His supply of aphorisms are seemingly endless and come in all shapes and sizes, they include;

'Contentment is the only real wealth'
'We build upon the sand and the older we become the more unstable this foundation becomes'
'The truthful man is usually defeated by the liar'
'Lying is the greatest of all sins'
'Justice is to be found only in imagination'
'Worry is the stomach's worst poison'
'A heart can no more be forced to love than a stomach can be forced to digest food by persuasion'
'Second to agriculture, humbug is the biggest industry of our age'
'A recluse without books and ink is a dead man before he dies'
'My home is where my work is, and I work everywhere'

The Will of Alfred Nobel

"I, Alfred Nobel, hereby declare...

The whole of my remaining realizable estate shall be dealt with in the following way: the capital, invested in safe securities by my executors, shall constitute a fund, the interest on which shall be annually distributed in the form of prizes to those who, during the preceding year, shall have conferred the greatest benefit on mankind. The said interest shall be divided into five equal parts, which shall be apportioned as follows.
One part to the person who shall have made the most important discovery or invention within the field of physics; one part to the person who shall have made the most important chemical discovery or improvement; one part to the person who shall have made the most important discovery within the domain of physiology or medicine; one part to the person who shall have produced in the field of literature the most outstanding work of an idealistic tendency; and one part to the person who shall have done the most or the best work for fraternity between nations, for the abolition or reduction of standing armies and for the holding and promotion of peace congresses. The prize for physics and chemistry shall be awarded by the Swedish Academy of Sciences; that for physiological or medical works by the Karolinska Institute in Stockholm; that for literature by the Academy in Stockholm; and that for champions of peace by a committee of five persons elected by the Norwegian Storting. It is my express wish that in awarding the prizes no consideration whatever shall be given to the nationality of the candidates, but that the most worthy shall receive the prize, whether he is Scandinavian or not"
Paris, November 27th 1895.

Thus did Alfred Nobel leave his work to posterity. He was self-effacing to the point of denial. In a letter to his brother Ludvig in 1887, he wrote what he called his 'self-portrait'

"Alfred Nobel-pitiable, half-creature, should have been stifled by a humane doctor when he made his entry yelling into life. Greatest merits: Keeps his nails clean and is never a burden to anyone. Greatest fault: Lacks family, cheerful spirits, and strong stomach. Greatest and only petition: Not to be buried alive. Greatest sin: Does not worship Mammon . Important events in his life: None "

The Nobel Foundation

The Foundation's Objects;

The Nobel Foundation is established under the terms of the will of Alfred Nobel, drawn up on the 27th November, 1895 as follows:

"The whole of my remaining realizable estate shall be dealt with in the following way: the capital, invested in safe securities by my executors, shall constitute a fund, the interest of which shall be annually distributed in the form of prizes to those who, during the preceding year, shall have conferred the greatest benefit to mankind. The said interest shall be divided into five equal parts, which shall be apportioned as follows: one part to the person who shall have made the most important discovery or invention within the field of physics;.........

Following the death of Alfred Nobel and the publication of his will the Nobel Foundation was set-up to achieve Nobel's aims. There was a certain amount of discussion, concerning the contents of the will, with members of Nobel's family and agreement was reached on June 5th 1898 when the objectors issued the following statement;
"....hereby acknowledge Dr. Nobel's will and renounce unconditionally, for themselves and their heirs, all further claims on Dr Nobel's estate and all claims to take part in its administration, and similarly every right to protest against the elucidations of, or addition to, the will as any other provisions as to its carrying into effect and the uses to which the proceeds are put, which, now or in the future, shall be enjoined by the Crown or whomsoever competent: subject, however, to the following express reservations:

a) that the basic statutes, common to the prize-awarding institutions, dealing with the manner of, and the conditions for, the award of prizes as prescribed in the will, shall be drawn up in consultation with a representative nominated by Robert Nobel's family and submitted to the approval of the Crown; and
b) that there shall be no departure from the following main principles, viz: that each of the annual prizes established by the will shall be awarded at least during each five-year period from, and including, the year immediately following that in which the Nobel Foundation commences its activities, and that the amount of a prize thus awarded shall under no circumstances be less than sixty per cent of that portion of the annual yield of the fund that shall be available for the prize award, nor shall it be divided into more than three prizes at most"

The task of designating the Nobel laureates in Literature was given to the Swedish Academy in Stockholm. The right to nominate candidates for the is wide but nominations must be submitted to the Academy's Nobel Committee no later than February 1st of each year. Further conditions for the literary prize and other subjects are as follows;

To be eligible for consideration for the award of a prize, a written work shall have been issued in print. A prize may be equally divided between two works each of which may be considered to merit a prize. If a work which is to be rewarded has been produced by two or three persons, the prize shall be awarded to the jointly. In no case may a prize be divided between more than three persons. Work produced by a person since deceased shall not be considered for an award; if, however, a prize-winner dies before he has received the prize, then the prize may be presented.

Each prize-awarding body shall be competent to decide whether the prize it is entitled to award may be conferred upon an institution or association.

A work may not be awarded a prize, unless it by experience or expert scrutiny has been found to be of such outstanding importance as is manifestly intended by the will. If none of the works under consideration is found to be of the character here indicated, the prize money shall be reserved until the following year. If, even then, the prize cannot be awarded, the amount shall be added to the main fund.

A Nobel Committee, consisting of three, four or five persons to give their opinion in the matter of the award of prizes, shall be set up for each Swedish Prize section. The award of the Peace Prize shall be carried out by the committee of the Norwegian Storting referred to in the will, which has been known as the Norwegian Nobel Committee since the 1st of January 1977.

Swedish citizenship or membership of the adjudication body shall not be necessary qualifications for election to membership of a Nobel Committee. Persons other than Norwegians may be members of the Norwegian Committee. For such work as may be involved in his task, a member of the Nobel Committee may receive reasonable remuneration the amount to be determined by the prize-awarding body. When for special reasons deemed necessary, the prize-awarding body shall be entitled to appoint experts to take part as members in the deliberations and decisions of the Nobel Committee.

No persons may be considered eligible for an award unless nominated in writing by a person competent to make such nominations. Personal applications for an award shall not be considered.

Competence to submit nominations shall be incumbent on representatives, Swedish as well as foreign, for the field of culture in question, in conformity with detailed regulations issued by the prize-awarding body.

Each year the prize adjudication shall embrace such nominations as have been submitted during the preceding twelve months up to the 1st of February. If, in addition to the prize for the current year, the prize-awarding body has at its disposal prize money that has not been allocated in a previous year(s) the question of the award of the first-mentioned prize shall be decided before a decision is taken as to the amount reserved from the preceding year.

Nominations shall be explained and accompanied by evidence in support of them. Where a nomination is couched in a language whose translation must entail particular trouble or considerable expense, or where, for the appraisement of a proposed work, the prize-awarding body make itself acquainted with the contents of writings couched in such a language, the prize-awarding body shall not be under obligation to take up the nomination for further consideration.

On the Festival Day of the Foundation, i.e. December 10th, the anniversary of Nobel's death, the prize-awarding bodies shall present to each prize-winner a cheque for the amount of the prize, a diploma and a gold medal that bears the image of Alfred Nobel with an appropriate inscription.

If a prize-winner decline the prize, or doesn't cash the cheque in the ten months following receipt, then the amount of the prize will be added to the main fund. It is expected also that a prize-winner will give a lecture upon his subject with six months of receipt of the prize.

No appeal may be made against the decision of a prize-awarding body with regard to the award of a prize. Proposals received for the award of a prize, and investigations and opinions concerning the award of a prize may not be divulged. Should divergent opinions have been expressed in connection with the decision of a prize-awarding body concerning the award of a prize, these may not be included in the record or otherwise divulged. However, a prize-awarding body may, after due consideration in each individual case, permit access to material which formed the basis for evaluation and decision concerning a prize, for purposes of historical research. Such permission may not be granted until at least 50 years have elapsed after the date on which the decision in question was taken.

For assistance with the scrutiny necessary for the prize-adjudication and the promotion in other ways of the object of the Foundation, the prize-awarding bodies shall be empowered to set up scientific institutions and other establishments. These will belonging to the Foundation, shall be called , 'Nobel Institutes'. Each Nobel Institute shall be under the direction of the prize-awarding body which has established it. Those activities of the Nobel Institutions aimed at promoting the objects of the Foundation beyond the activities necessary for the adjudication of prizes shall be pursued in consultation with the Board of the Foundation. Decisions concerning the limits on the use of available funds for these purposes shall be taken by the Board.

The institutes shall in point of organization and finance be free and independent. For this reason their assets may not be used to defray the costs of the prize-awarding bodies own establishments or those of other institutions. The prize-awarding bodies at the Nobel Institutes may also employ men or women of foreign nationality. Of that part of the revenues from the main fund places annually at the disposal of each prize section, one quarter shall be withheld from distribution. After the immediate expenses of the prize distribution have been defrayed, the remainder of the amount withheld shall be used to defray the costs of each section for the maintenance of its Nobel Institute. Such amounts as are not required for the years expenses shall be reserved for the future needs of the Institute.

Administration of the Foundation

The Foundation shall be represented by a Board, which has its seat in Stockholm and consists of seven members and two deputies, Swedish or Norwegian citizens, who shall be elected by the trustees of the prize-awarding bodies. The Board shall choose from among its own members a chairman, a Vice-Chairman and an Executive Director.
The members of the Board and the deputies shall be appointed for two years, as from May 1st. The trustees shall determine a reasonable remuneration to be paid each board member, with the exception of the Executive Director, who receives no remuneration. The trustees shall also determine a reasonable remuneration for its auditors. The salary of the Executive Director shall be determined by the Board.

The Board shall administer the property of the Foundation and to make payments to prize-winners. They also effect all disbursements necessary to prize distribution, Institutes and all other purposes. The Board are empowered to engage legal representatives and engage such assistants as they deem necessary for administration purposes and will fix their salaries and pensions.

The prize-awarding bodies shall elect, for two calender years at a time, fifteen trustees, six of whom shall be chosen by the Academy of Sciences, and three by each of the other prize-awarding bodies. Deputies shall be elected to serve in place of trustees in case of hindrance; namely, four by the Academy of Sciences and two by each of the other prize-awarding bodies. The trustees shall elect a chairman from their midst. To make this election they shall be summoned by the oldest in years among the trustees of the Academy of Sciences. A quorum of at least nine trustees is necessary for a decision to be taken. If any prize-awarding body neglects to elect trustees, this shall not constitute an obstacle to the other trustees to make decisions in matters under consideration. A trustee resident elsewhere than at the place where the meeting is held shall be entitled to receive from the common means of the Foundation reasonable reimbursement for expenses caused by attendance.

The administration of the Board and the accounts of the Foundation shall, for each calender year be examined by six auditors. Of these the Government shall appoint one, who will be chairman, the prize-awarding bodies will elect one each and the trustees one, who shall be an authorized public accountant. The auditors report is made public. On the basis of the auditor's report the trustees of the prize-awarding bodies shall have the authority to adopt the report and accounts of the Board or to take such measures against the Board or any member thereof as may be called for. If no action is taken within a year and a day from the day when the Board's report was presented to the auditors, then discharge from personal liability for their administration during the year reported shall have deemed to have been granted.
Instructions in respect to the administration, beyond what is laid down in these statutes, shall

be given in special regulations issued by the Government.

One tenth of the annual revenues derived from the main fund shall be accrued to the Main Fund. To the same fund shall be added the interest accruing from the amounts of the prizes up to the time they are paid they are paid to the prize-winners, or are carried over to the main fund because a prize is not awarded.

A brief summary of the above.

1) There are six prizes awarded annually. Each has a Nobel Committee.

2) The prize awarders are the Royal Swedish Academy of Sciences (physics, chemistry and economics), The Royal Caroline Medico-Chirurgical Institute (physiology or medicine) and the Swedish Academy (literature) all in Sweden. The Norwegian Nobel Committee (peace) in Oslo appointed by the Norwegian Storting (parliament)

3) The selection processes take place in the autumn of the year preceding the awards. Invitations are sent out to those competent under the Nobel rules to nominate candidates.

4) The basis of selection is is professional competence and international range. Self-nomination is not allowed. Prize nominations mus reach the proper committee in writing by February 1st of the year of the awards.

5) Each of the six committees has the right to call in experts, regardless of nationality. During September and early October the committees submit their recommendations. The eventual awarders must make their selection by November 15th. A committee recommendation is usually but not always followed.

6) The deliberations and voting is secret at all stages. Other than the Peace Prize prizes must only be given to individuals. No individual can be nominated posthumously. However, if nominated and accepted, a prize can be awarded after death.

7) A prize is either given in its entirety to one person or can be divided equally between two or three people. If divided then each receive a share of the prize money. Each Laureate receives a medal and diploma.

8) If a Laureate declines the award or is prevented by his government from accepting, then the money reverts to the Nobel Fund but the medal and diploma can be awarded later.

The Nobel Rules of Nominational Invitations;

The Royal Swedish Academy of Sciences send invitations to nominate Physics, Chemistry and Economic Laureates. These are sent to;

a) Swedish and foreign members of the Academy of Sciences. b)The members of the Nobel Committees for Physics and Chemistry. c) Scientists who have been awarded the Prize by the Academy of Sciences. d) Permanent and assistant professors in the sciences of physics and chemistry at the universities and institutes of technology of Sweden, Denmark, Finland,

Iceland and Norway and the Karolinska Institute. e) Holders of corresponding chairs in at least six universities or university colleges selected by the Academy of Sciences with a view to ensuring the appropriate distribution over the different and their seats of learning. f) Other scientists from whom the Academy may see fit to invite proposals.

The Nobel Assembly at the Karolinska Institute send invitations to nominate Physiology or Medicine Laureates. These are sent to;

a) Members of the Assembly; b) Swedish and foreign members of the medical class of the Royal Academy of Sciences; c) Previous recipients of the Nobel Prize in Physiology or Medicine; d) Members of the Nobel Committee not qualified under (a). e) Holders of established posts as professors at the faculties of medicine in Sweden and holders of similar posts at the faculties of medicine or similar institutions in Denmark, Finland, Iceland and Norway; f) Holders of similar posts at no fewer than six other faculties of medicine selected by the Assembly with a view to ensuring the appropriate distribution of the task among various countries and their seats of learning and, g) Practitioners of natural sciences whom the Assembly may otherwise see fit to approach.

The Swedish Academy has the right to nominate Literature candidates. Members of the Swedish Academy and of other academies, institutions and societies which are similar to it in constitution and purpose; by professors of literature and linguistics at universities and university colleges; by previous Nobel Prize Laureates for Literature and by presidents of those societies of authors that are representative of the lierary production in their respective countries.

The Norwegian Nobel Committee have responsibility for the Peace Prize and send out nomination invitations to;

a) Active and former members of the Norwegian Nobel Committee and the advisors appointed by the Norwegian Nobel Institute; b) Members of the national assemblies and governments of the different states and members of the Interparliamentary Union; c) Members of the International Court of Justice at the Hague and the International Court of Arbitration at the Hague; d) Members of the Commission of the Permanent International Peace Bureau; e) Members and associate members of the Institut de Droit International; f) University professors of political sciences and juriprudence, history and philosophy; g) Persons who have been awarded the Nobel Peace Prize.

The Royal Academy of Sciences are responsible for nominations for the Bank of Sweden Prize in Economic Sciences in Memory of Alfred Nobel. Invitations to nominate are sent to;

a) Swedish and foreign members of the Academy of Sciences; b) Members of the Prize Committee for the Alfred Nobel Memorial Prize in Economic Sciences; c) Recipients of the Prize in Economic Sciences; d) Permanent professors in relevant subjects at the universities and colleges in Sweden, Denmark, Finland, Iceland and Norway; e) Holders of corresponding chairs in at least six universities or colleges selected for the relevant year by the Academy of Sciences with a view to ensuring the appropriate distribution between different countries and their seats of learning; and f) Other scientists whom the Academy may sit fit to invite proposals.

The Nobel Week

The Prize Award Ceremonies and Banquets on December 10th.

   Starting in 1901, the Nobel Prizes have been presented to Laureates at ceremonies held on the anniversary of Alfred Nobel's death.   As per Nobel's stipulation in his will, the Nobel Prizes in Physics, Chemistry, Physiology or Medicine and Literature are awarded in Stockholm, Sweden and the Nobel Peace Prize in Oslo, Norway.
In 1968, on the occasion of the 300th anniversary of the Bank of Sweden, the bank announced that as from 1969 an additional prize to be known as The Sveriges Riksbank Prize in Economic Sciences in Memory of Alfred Nobel would be presented at ceremony held in Stockholm.

   Since 1926 the Prize Award Ceremony in Stockholm has taken place at the Stockholm Concert Hall (Stockholms Konserthus). In Oslo, the ceremony was held at the Nobel Institute until 1947 when it was held in the auditorium of Oslo University. In 1990 the event moved to Oslo Town Hall.

   At the Award ceremony in Stockholm, the King of Sweden hands each Laureate a diploma and a medal. Following the ceremony a banquet is held for some 1,300 people including students. The Festivities in Stockholm are arranged by the Nobel Foundation and are primarily an academic celebration focussing on science and literature. In addition to the Nobel Laureates and their families there are present, the King and Queen of Sweden who are the guests of honour. Present also are members of the Government and Parliament and Swedish citizens involved in some way with Nobel related functions.

   In Oslo the Nobel Peace Prize is presented by the Chairman of the Norwegian Nobel Committee. Present are the King and Queen of Norway, the Government, Storting (parliament) members and invited guests. Several hundred seats are reserved for persons with special reasons for wishing to attend the ceremony. Later that evening, the Norwegian Nobel Committee hosts a banquet in honour of the Laureate with specially invited guests.
In recent years as the Nobel Prize has become to be recognized as the most prestigious prize in the world, they are no longer local events but major international events that receive world-wide coverage by the media.

The Money

All the figures quoted are in Swedish Crowns. Between 1901 and 1920 the amount per Laureate was 150,800. Between 1920 and 1923 it was 134,000. In 1923 it fell to 115,000, the lowest amount.

This amount of prize money lasted until 1940 and probably reflected the 'Wall Street crash of 1929'. In 1940 it rose to 138,600 and stayed at this level until 1946, at that time the Foundation was granted tax exemption. Between 1946 and 1950, the prize money was 121,000. It rose in 1950 to 164,300.

Three years later, in 1953, the Foundation's investment rules were changed. The prize rose to 175,300 for the next seven years. In 1960 it was 226,000 and stayed at that level until 1969, when the Prize in Economics was added. In 1970 it was 400,000 and stayed at that level until 1980 when it rose to 880,000 where it remained until 1989.

In 1989 the prize money rose dramatically to 3,000,000. Thereafter it has increased every year as follows;
1990, 4,000,0000. 1991, 6,000,000; 1992, 6,500,000; 1993, 6,700,000; 1994, 7,000,000; 1995, 7,200,000; 1996, 7,400,000; 1997, 7,500,000; 1998, 7,600,000 and in 1999, 7,900,000 (£530.000).

1901

Death of Queen Victoria • President William McKinley assassinated succeeded by Theodore Roosevelt • The Social Revolutionary Party is organised in Russia • Marconi transmits messages by wireless telegraphy from Cornwall to Newfoundland • Edvard Munch, *Girls on the Bridge* • A. Strindberg, *Dance of Death* • Rudyard Kipling, *Kim* • Miles Franklin, *My Brilliant Career* • HG.Wells, *The First Men in the Moon* • André Malraux and Walt Disney born • Toulouse-Lautrec died.

LITERATURE

SULLY PRUDHOMME (1839-1907)

Sully Prudhomme, born in Paris, France, on March 16, 1839, was the pseudonym used by René-François-Armand Prudhomme; the son of a Parisian shopkeeper. Beside being a notable French poet, he was also a leading member of the Parnassian club, which existed in order to restore elegance, beauty and original standards, to poetry and encourage those who wished to ignore the excesses of Romanticism. Following a minimal education, that concentrated upon science, Sully found his eyesight was too poor for a career in this subject.

In 1860, he left a clerking job in a factory office and started to study law. Following a broken love affair in 1865, he began writing poetry. It was sad verse. Most melancholy. *Stances et poemes* (1865) contains probably his best known poem, *Le vase brisé*. Other books of poetry followed, all written in similar sentimental style. *Les épreuves* (1866) and *Les Solitudes* (1869). His later verse reflected a more philosophical approach, as shown in *La Justice* (1878) and *Le Bonheur* (1888). His later works became more and more obscure, as he experienced some difficulty in expressing deep philosophical postures in verse. In 1881, he was elected to the French Academy and in 1901 was awarded the first Nobel Prize for Literature; **"in special recognition of his poetic composition, which gives evidence of lofty idealism, artistic perfection and a rare combination of the qualities of both heart and intellect"**

He died in Chatenay, France in September 1907. He never married.

CHEMISTRY

JACOBUS HENRICUS VAN'T HOFF (1852-1911)

Jacobus Henricus Van't Hoff, was born in Rotterdam, Netherlands on August 30, 1852. Following his education at Leiden University in Holland, he worked in Bonn, Germany under August Kekule before moving on to Paris and the laboratory of Charles Adolphe Wurtz. In Paris he met Joseph-AchilleLeBel. Each was working independently from the other on stereochemistry, a three dimensional structure. It was a concept concerned with helping to explain optical rotation and based upon four chemical compounds, that carbon can form, and directed to the corners of a tetrahedron.

Hoff, was professor of chemistry at the University of Amsterdam (1878-96) and, in 1884, published his most important work, *Études de Dynamique Chimique*, describing the principles of chemical kinetics and how the laws of thermodynamics applied to chemical equilibriums.

In 1886, he demonstrated a similarity between the behaviour of dilute solutions and gases; this followed his historical concept of chemical affinity. He later worked on the Arrhenius theory of the dissociation of electrolytes before becoming, in 1896, professor to the Prussian Academy of Science in Berlin. It is a fact that it was Hoff's efforts, in studying and analysing salt deposits at Stassfurt, Germany, that led to that country having a chemical industry. He was married and had two sons and two daughters. In 1887 he co-founded the *Journal of Physical Chemistry*.

In 1901 Hoff, who idolised the poet Lord Byron, was awarded the first Nobel Prize for Chemistry; **"in recognition of the extraordinary services he has rendered by the discovery of the laws of chemical dynamics and osmotic pressure in solutions"**

He died in Berlin on March 1, 1911.

PHYSICS

WILHELM CONRAD ROENTGEN (1845-1923)

Wilhelm Conrad Roentgen, was born in Lennep, Prussia (Germany) on March 27, 1845. He was educated at the Polytechnic in Zurich and, following completion of his degree course, became professor of physics at Strasbourg University (1876-79). Then followed the Universities of Giessen (1879-88), Wurzburg (1888-1900) and Munich (1900-1920). During these periods he was constantly conducting research into the capillary action of fluids, the specific heat of gases, absorption of heat by gases and much else.

At some time in 1895 Roentgen, whilst experimenting with the flow of electric current in a partially empty glass tube (later to be known as cathode-ray tube), noticed that a local piece of barium platinocyanide gave off some light when the tube was in use. His on-going theories came to recognise that when the cathode rays or electrons struck the glass wall of the

tube, an unknown radiation was formed that travelled across the room, struck the chemical and caused fluorescence. Later research involving the use of paper, wood and other material showed they were transparent to this new type of radiation.

He further found that photographic plates were affected but Roentgen was of the view that these rays were unrelated to light. He went on to perfect what was to become known as X-ray photographs. He took the first ever X-ray photographs of the interior of metal objects and also inspected the bones of his wife's hand. In 1901 he was the first recipient of the Nobel Prize for Physics; **"in recognition of the extraordinary services he has rendered by the discovery of the remarkable rays subsequently named after him"**

It was the beginning of modern diagnostic medicine and heralded a new age in physics. He died from stomach cancer in Munich on February 10, 1923. He married but had no children. He did however adopt his wife's niece.

PHYSIOLOGY or MEDICINE

EMIL von BEHRING (1854-1917)

Emil von Behring, was born in Hansdorf, Prussia (Germany) on March 15, 1854. He was educated at the University of Berlin after which he served with the Army Medical Corps. In 1889, he became an assistant at the Robert Koch Institute of Hygiene in Berlin. Whilst there, he met the Japanese bacteriologist Kitasato Shibasaburo. The two men later showed how it was possible to provide an animal with immunity from tetanus, by injecting it with the blood serum of another animal already infected with the disease. They called this technique, antitoxic immunity and brought it onto the market to prevent diphtheria.

By 1892 it was a routine treatment for the disease. His further researches included work on TB and he founded a vaccine for immunising cattle. In order to further practical research, he became a financial partner in a dye-works company in Hochst. He published much including, *The Practical Goals of Blood Serum Therapy* (1892) and *The Etiology and Etiological Therapy of Tetanus* (1904). Behring, in 1901 was the first recipient of the Nobel Prize for Physiology or Medicine, **"for his work on serum therapy, especially its application against diphtheria, by which he has opened a new road in the domain of medical science and thereby placed in the hands of the physician a victorious weapon against illness and death"**

Behring has always been considered the founder of the science of immunology. He died in Marburg, Germany on March 31, 1917. Nearing middle-age, he married an 18 year old who bore him seven children.

PEACE

JEAN DUNANT (1828-1910)
and
FREDERIC PASSY (1822-1912)

Jean Henri Dunant was born on May 8, 1828 in Geneva, Switzerland. On June 24, 1859 he was an eyewitness to the Battle of Solferino, Italy, that resulted in some 40,000 casualties. He worked organising emergency services to aid the wounded Austrians and French soldiers, but it was a case of too little too late. He wrote his *Un Souvenir de Solférino* in 1862, in which he suggested the formation, in every European country, of emergency services with volunteers to prevent and alleviate suffering. It would be without taking into account class or creed. He also proposed an international agreement to cover war prisoners and war wounded. Two years later, Dunant founded The Red Cross Society and the Geneva Convention was born. Three years later in 1867, and Dunant was a bankrupt. He had devoted so much of his life to good works that he neglected his business. He left Geneva to spend the rest of his life in poverty. He continued to espouse the causes of peace and the treatment of prisoners of war, the abolition of slavery and much else.

He was particularly concerned about the establishment of a Jewish national home. He was a Christian Zionist, largely ignored by Jewish leaders of the time. It all changed, when in 1895, a Swiss journalist found Dunant living in Heiden, Switzerland. He was brought to the notice of the public and showered with annuities and honours. In 1897, Herzl, the father of modern Zionism referred to Dunant, at the First Zionist Congress in Basle, in glowing terms. Dunant also founded the World's Young Men's Christian Association and in 1901 was the co-recipient of the first Nobel Peace Prize; **"for his work in founding the committee of the Red Cross"**

He died in Heiden on October 30, 1910. He never married. He was living in a hospice at the time of his death and upon his instructions, there was no ceremony or mourners. He spent none of his Nobel money and left all he had left to the hospice.

Frederic Passy was born in Paris on May 20, 1822. Following a stint as auditor to the French Council of State (1846-49), he became involved with various economic reforms in the free trader tradition. During the Crimean War of 1853-1856, Passy worked for peace. In 1867, in the magazine *Le Temps,* he begged for peace between France and Prussia concerning Luxembourg. At the same time he founded the Ligue Internationale de la Paix. Following the Franco-Prussian War (1870-1871), he secured permanent independence and neutrality for Alsace-Lorraine. Between 1881 and 1889 he was a member of the French Chamber of Deputies.

There he argued successfully, for arbitration to settle the dispute between Holland and France, over the French Guiana-Surinam boundary. In 1888 he co-founded the Inter-Parliamentary Union. He wrote much including, *Mélanges économiques* (1857), *L'Histoire du Travail* (1873) and *Vérités en▪paradoxes* (1894). In 1901, Passy was the co-recipient of the first Nobel Peace Prize **"for his work in founding the first French peace society"**

He died in Paris on June 12, 1912. He was married and had one son.

1902

Boer War ends • Theodore Roosevelt buys rights of the French Panama Company • *The Times Literary Supplement* **issued • Monet,** *Waterloo Bridge* **• Walter de la Mare,** *Songs of Childhood* **• Arnold Bennett,** *Anna of the Five Towns* **• Joseph Conrad,** *Typhoon* **• A.Conan Doyle,** *The Hound of the Baskervilles* **• A.E.W. Mason,** *The Four Feathers* **• Beatrix Potter,** *The Tale of Peter Rabbit* **• John Steinbeck is born • Emil Zola dies • Edward VII crowned.**

LITERATURE

THEODORE MOMMSEN (1817-1903)

Christain Mathias Theodore Mommsen was born on November 30, 1817 in Garding, Germany. The son of a Protestant minister, he received a classical education in the senior classes of the Gymnasium Christianeum in Altona. Between 1838 to 1843, he was at the University of Kiel studying jurisprudence. He was a disciple of Friedrich Karl von Savigny, a founder of the historical school of jurisprudence. A research scholarship followed his doctor's degree, by courtesy of the King of Denmark. It meant he could spend three years (1844-47) in Italy.

In Rome, at the Archaeological Institute, he spent his time researching. He now planned his, *Corpus Inscriptionum Latinarum*; a detailed collection of Latin inscriptions preserved since antiquity on lasting materials that included iron and stone, all arranged according to the basic principles of philological methods. It was to become the first complete understanding of the ancient world.

On his return home from Italy, he became embroiled in the politics between Denmark and Germany. Germany wanted to take over Schleswig and Mommsen wanted it to be part of a republic. He was a liberal, and as such, became the editor of *Schleswig-Holsteinische Zeitung* until, in 1848, he was offered, and accepted, a professorship in civil law at the University of Leipzig. He was dismissed a year later, over his involvement in the Saxony uprising. He became most fortunate in being offered, in 1854, a professorship at the University of Breslau. He continued to involve himself in politics and became a deputy in the Prussian Landtag (1873-79) and later in the German Reichstag

(1881-84). He wasn't particularly effective.

He wrote much, his masterpiece being his *History of Rome*. This was in three volumes (1854-56). Many years later he contemplated writing a fourth volume, but abandoned the idea on the basis it wouldn't match the brilliance of his original work. Instead, he launched himself on Roman constitutional law which he published in three volumes between 1871 and 1888. Mommsen was quoted as saying it was for this work that he wished to be remembered; it was the first time that Roman Law was codified. His last major work was, *Roman Criminal Law* (1899). In 1902 Mommsen was awarded the Nobel Prize for Literature; **"the greatest living master of the art of historical writing with special reference to his monumental work, A History of Rome"**

He died on November 1, 1903 in Charlottenburg, Berlin. In 1854 Mommsen married the daughter of a bookseller. He and Marie Reimer spent nearly 50 years together in what was said to be an idyllic marriage that produced 16 children- 7 daughters and 9 sons.

CHEMISTRY

EMIL FISCHER (1852-1919)

Emil Hermann Fischer, was born on October 9th 1852 in Euskirchen, Prussia (Germany). Following his education at Bonn and Strasbourg universities and his PhD (1874) he had several posts before settling in at the University of Berlin in 1892. His early research work (1881), concentrated on the purines and he determined the structures of uric acid, caffeine and other related substances. He demonstrated how they were all derivatives of a single compound that he named purine.

Two years later, he began his most important work, the research into the sugar group; work of the utmost importance to organic chemistry. Previously, in 1875, Fischer had published his discovery of the compound phenyl hydrazine. He later found that this substance reacts with simple sugars to form derivatives called osazone.   Fischer was awarded the 1902 Nobel Prize for Chemistry; **"in recognition of the extraordinary services he has rendered by his work on sugar and purine syntheses"**

During WW1, he is credited with inventing a butter-like substance he called 'ester margarine'. He was married with three sons, one of whom was killed during WW1. Fischer died in Berlin on July 15, 1919, having committed suicide because of Germany's defeat.

PHYSICS

HENDRIK LORENTZ (1853-1928)
and
PIETER ZEEMAN (1865-1943)

"in recognition of the extraordinary service they rendered by their researches into the influence of magnetism upon radiation phenomena"

Hendrik Lorentz was born in Arnhem, Holland on July 18, 1853. In 1878 he was appointed professor of mathematical physics at Leiden University. For his doctoral thesis, Lorentz chose to re-define James Maxwell's theory of electromagnetics. This resulted in the easier understanding of the reflection and refraction of light. He went on to theorize that the atoms of matter might consist of charged particles and that these particles were the source of light. His work resulted in being known as the 'Lorentz Transformations'.

These are mathematical formulas that describe the increase of mass, shortening of length and dilation of time. Later these ideas formed the basis of Einstein's theory of relativity. Lorentz received a half share of the 1902 Nobel Prize for his work on the theory of electromagnetic radiation. A man of great personal charm; whilst at Leiden, he delivered a regular Monday lecture that attracted physicists from all over the world. He died in Haarlem on February 4, 1928. He was married with two daughters and a son.

Peter Zeeman was born in Zonnemaire, Holland on May 25, 1865. Zeeman was a student of Lorentz and the men were jointly awarded the 1902 Nobel Prize for Physics. Zeeman's was for his discovery of the 'Zeeman Effect'; this was the splitting of spectrum lines into a number of components by strong magnetic fields.

Zeeman was appointed professor of physics at Amsterdam University in 1900. In 1908 he became the director of the University's Physical Institute. There he remained, researching on the propagation of light in moving media in quartz and flint. He died on October 9, 1943. He was married with three daughters and a son.

PHYSIOLOGY or MEDICINE

RONALD ROSS (1857-1932)

Ronald Ross was born in Almora, India on May 13, 1857. In 1879, following graduating in medicine from St. Bartholomew in London, Ross joined the Indian Medical Service and took part in the third Anglo war to conquer Burma (1885). Whilst on leave in London, he began his researches into bacteria. Back in India, and working with Patrick Manson, Ross began a series of research on malaria. In 1897, he discovered evidence of the malarial parasite within the Anopheles mosquito.

He went on to demonstrate that birds would become infected with malaria following the single bite of a mosquito. He wrote a paper suggesting that the same means were used to infect humans. He left India for London and the Liverpool School of Tropical Medicine, followed by Liverpool University. In 1902 Ross was awarded the Nobel Prize for Physiology or Medicine; **"for his work on malaria, by which he has shown how it enters the organism and thereby has laid the foundation for successful research on this disease and methods of combatting it"**

In 1911, he was knighted and in 1912 appointed head of the Ross Institute and Hospital for Tropical Diseases, founded in his honour. In 1910 he published *The Prevention of Malaria*. He died in Putney, London, after a long illness, on September 16, 1932. He was married with two sons and two daughters.

PEACE

ELIE DUCOMMUN (1833-1906)
and
CHARLES GOBAT (1834-1914)

Elie Ducommun was born in Geneva, Switzerland on February 19, 1833. Following a classical education, Ducommun became a journalist and later an editor, working on magazines and newspapers in both Geneva and Bern. He was then appointed general secretary of the Jura-Simplon Railway. All the spare time he could muster was spent on peace activities.

As well as becoming an activist in the European Union, he was editor of, *Les état-Unis d'Europe*, the organ of the International League of Peace and Freedom (1867). From 1889, Ducommun was the director of The International Peace Bureau. Ducommun was co-awarded the 1902 Nobel Peace Prize; **"as Honorary Secretary of the Permanent International Peace Bureau in Berne, Switzerland"** He died in Bern of heart disease on December 7, 1906. He married but had no children.

Charles-Albert Gobat was born in Tramelan, Switzerland on May 21, 1834. Following a formal education Gobat became a lawyer. He began practising in Bern and later in nearby Delemont. He was also a lecturer at the Sorbonne in Paris and active in politics.

From its' inception in 1888, Gobat worked for the Inter-Parliamentary Union and in 1892 was the president of the fourth conference held in Bern. He was the director of the International Peace Bureau at the time he was co-awarded the 1902 Nobel Peace Prize; **"for his work as Secretary of the General Inter-Parliamentary Union and as Honorary Secretary of the Permanent International Peace Bureau in Berne, Switzerland"**

He wrote, *The Nightmare of Europe* in 1911; a prophetic work that became a reality in August 1914 and the start of WW1. He died a few months earlier on March 16, in Bern whilst at a Peace Conference; he rose to speak but collapsed and died. He never married.

1903

US regulation of child labour is introduced • 20 mph limit in UK for motor cars • Russian Social Democratic Party splits into Menshevists, led by Plecharoff and Bolshevists, led by Lenin and Trotsky • Emily Pankhurst founded Women's Suffragette Movement • G.E. Moore, *Principia Ethica* • George Bernard Shaw, *Man and Superman* • Erskine Childers, *The Riddle of the Sands* • Henry James, *The Ambassadors* • Jack London, *The Call of the Wild* • Louis Leakey and Evelyn Waugh born • Gauguin and Pissarro die.

LITERATURE

BJORNSTJERNE BJORNSON (1832-1910)

Bjornstjerne Martinius Bjornson was born in Kvikne, Norway on December 8, 1832. He was destined to become one of the literary giants of 19th century Norway. He was the son of a pastor and grew up in the small farming community of Romsdalen, that would feature in his future novels. Educated at Molde in Oslo, from the beginning his writings expressed a love for his country and Bjornson drew heavily on Norwegian sagas and countryside myths. Between 1857 and 1859, he was Henrik Ibsen's successor as artistic director at the Bergen Theatre. Many of his novels he turned into plays and his work generally raised the nation's morale. Indeed his poem, *Yes, We Love This Land,* is the Norwegian National Anthem. In 1859 he married the actress Karoline Reimers and began interesting himself in politics. He became the editor of the *Bergenposten* and as a result of what he wrote, concerning the daily scene, the ruling Conservative were ousted and the Liberal Party was created.

He went on to become the director of the Christiana Theatre and, from 1866-1871, he edited the *Norsk Folkeblad*. He wrote much; novels, plays and poetry. His political work, with the accompanying in-fighting, became so great and time consuming that Bjornson was forced to seek self exile in order to concentrate on his writings. Two dramas brought him international recognition; *The Bankrupt (1875)* and in the same year *The Editor*.

His writings showed a critical attitude towards the Christian belief in miracles. He believed that schools must bring about changes in society and a recognition that Socialism was the answer. He later worked for peace and understanding between nations. Although awarded the Nobel Prize for Literature in 1903; **"a tribute to his noble, magnificent and versatile poetry, which has always been distinguished by both the freshness of its inspiration and the rare purity of its spirit"**

He constantly lived under the shadow of Ibsen. He died in Paris, France on April 26, 1910. He was married with a son and daughter.

CHEMISTRY

SVANTE ARRHENIUS (1859-1927)

Svante August Arrhenius was born in Vik, Sweden on February 19, 1859. He was educated at the Cathedral School in Uppsala and then onto the County University. to study physics, chemistry and mathematics. For his doctorate he worked in Stockholm under Erik Edlund. In 1883 he published his first paper and in May 1884 his thesis. This was greeted with contempt and he was awarded the fourth class; a bare pass.

He was accused of indulging in the manipulation of imaginary data. Arrhenius accused his critics of being unable to understand what he was stating because of their lack of knowledge. He sent copies of his thesis to the famous chemists of the time and, as a result, he was offered a post by Wilhelm Ostwald of Riga University, whereupon his own university countered by offering Arrhenius a post as a lecturer in physical chemistry. However, in 1886 he was awarded a travelling scholarship from the Swedish Academy of Sciences.

He gradually refined his theories, winning over eminent scientists to his point of view. Abroad, his reputation was very high and in 1902, he was awarded the Davy Medal from the Royal Society of London. However, not until he was awarded the Nobel Prize for Chemistry in 1903; **"in recognition of the extraordinary services he has rendered to the advancement of chemistry by his electrolytic theory of dissociation"**

And the first Swede to be so honoured, did his countrymen accept him. His prize was for proving his theory, that certain substances that dissolve in water to yield a solution that conducts electricity, are separated, or dissociated, into electrically charged particles, or ions, even when there is no current flowing through the solution. In 1905, he was offered a chair at the University of Berlin.

This Arrhenius, on patriotic grounds, turned down.

He was later appointed the director of the Nobel Institute for Physical Chemistry at Stockholm. This appointment allowed him much time for travel and research and in 1911 he went to the USA where he was awarded the first Willard Gibbs Medal. He is described as a genial fellow who was only interested in science. He was however, married twice with two sons and two daughters. He died in Stockholm on October 2, 1927.

PHYSICS

PIERRE CURIE (1859-1906)
MARIE CURIE (1867-1934)
and
ANTOINE BECQUEREL (1852-1908)

"in recognition of the extraordinary services they have rendered by their joint researches on the radiation phenomena discovered by Professor Henri Becquerel"

Pierre Curie was born in Paris on May 15, 1859. He began his education at home, courtesy of his father a doctor. As a result Pierre matriculated at 16. He was graded a scientist at 18 and became a laboratory assistant at the Sorbonne. Here, he carried out experiments on the wavelengths of heat waves. Assisted now by his elder brother Jacques, the brothers associated the phenomenon of pyroelectricity with a change in the volume of the crystal in which it appears, and discovered piezoelectricity.

Pierre later formulated the principle of symmetry , and went on to define the symmetry of different physical phenomena.

Following his appointment in 1882, as supervisor at the School of Physics and Industrial Chemistry in Paris, Curie began his now famous studies on magnetism. He discovered that the magnetic coefficients of attraction of paramagnetic bodies vary in inverse proportion to the absolute imperator. This became known as Curie's Law and in 1895 Curie received his doctorate in science.

In the early part of 1894, Pierre Curie met Marie Skodowska; they married the following year. This marked the beginning of the world famous partnership that resulted in the discovery of first, polonium and then radium (1898). This discovery, and further research, led the way to produce radium therapy. Pierre refused the chair offered to him by Geneva University in order to continue his research with Marie. Pierre shared the 1903 Nobel Prize for Physics and was appointed, in 1904, a professor at the Sorbonne. The following year he was elected a member of the Academy of Sciences. On April 19, 1906, whilst out walking in the Rue Dauphine in Paris, Pierre was run over by a heavy laden dray; he died instantly. He is remembered as one the founders of modern physics.

Marie Curie was born Marie Skodowska in Warsaw, Poland on November 7, 1867. Her father, a teacher of physics, lost his savings via poor investments. Marie, now aged 16 and the holder of a gold medal in secondary education, became a teacher. She also gave reading classes to illiterate women. Two years later she became a governess in a rich household and suffered an unhappy love affair. In 1891, her sister Bronia, following her medical degree, financed Marie's medical education in Paris. There, Marie lived in a garret and survived on bread and water. In 1894 she was listed second when the mathematical results were published.

The following year she was married to Pierre Curie and the famous partnership began. Their discovery called polonium was so named by Marie to honour Poland. Marie had two daughters, Irene (1897) and Eve (1904). However, childbirth and rearing of children were not on the agenda as nothing was allowed to interfere with research. On the results of her research, Marie in 1903 received her doctorate of science. Besides the Nobel Prize of 1903 for Physics; which she shared with her husband and Antoine Becquerel, Marie was also a recipient of the Davy Medal of the Royal Society.

Following the death of Pierre in 1906, Marie turned all her attention to completing the scientific work they had begun. She was appointed to the chair left vacant at the Sorbonne and so became the first woman ever to teach there. In 1911 she received the Nobel Prize for Chemistry; this time she didn't share with anyone else. The award was given for her work in isolating pure radium. During World War One, Marie Curie, assisted by her daughter Irene, worked on the development of X-radiography. In 1918 the Radium Institute in Paris became the world centre for nuclear physics and chemistry.

In 1921 she was in the USA where she was received by President Harding. She lectured all over the States and continued this work in Europe. She is now seen as one of the foremost scientists of her day, and her work, in accumulating a stockpile of intense radioactive material, that would be used for research in nuclear physics, of the utmost importance. A great influence on future generations of nuclear physicists and chemists. There have been numerous biographies of her. Probably the best is *Madame Curie* written by her daughter Eve Curie in 1937 and reprinted in 1986. Marie Curie died in Sallanches, France on July 4, 1934 from leukemia, brought about by her work on radiation.

Antoine Henri Becquerel was born in Paris on December 15, 1852. He came from a scientific family and his grandfather was Antoine-Cesar Becquerel (1788-1878). He received his formal scientific education at the École Polytechnique (1872-74) and his engineering education at the École des Ponts et Chaussées (1874-77). Various teaching posts followed, culminating as professor of physics at the École Polytechnique in 1895. Becquerel's main area of research concerned the rotation of plane-polarized light by magnetic fields. His work on photography led to his further work on radioactivity.

His work on X-rays, included the investigation of the hypothesis that luminescent materials, however stimulated, might also yield X-rays. Antoine spent much time proving the theory, publishing the results of his research in 1896. His work on radioactivity was of the greatest importance and led to medical use. For his work on radioactivity, Becquerel shared the 1903 Nobel Prize for Physics. He later became president of the Académie des Sciènces. He died on August 25, 1908 in Le Croisic, France. He was married with a son.

PHYSIOLOGY or MEDICINE

NIELS FINSEN (1860-1904)

Niels Finsen was born on December 15, 1860 on the Faeroe Islands of Denmark. Following a basic education, he was accepted at the University of Copenhagen from where he received his MD in 1890. He became interested on the effects of light on living organisms and discovered that prolonged exposure to the red light, created by exclusion of the violet end of the spectrum, by those suffering from smallpox, prevented the bursting of the facial boils or creation of pockmarks.

He thereupon created an ultraviolet treatment for lupus vulgaris or skin TB, which was most successful.

This medical discovery became known as phototherapy and led to the use of ultraviolet sterilization methods in bacteriological research. In 1896, The Finsen Institute was founded in Copenhagen. He himself was often unwell, suffering as he did from Pick's disease. In 1903, Finsen was awarded the Nobel Prize for Physiology or Medicine; **"in recognition of his contribution to the treatment of diseases, especially lupus vulgaris, with concentrated light radiation, whereby he has opened a new avenue for medical science"**

He died in Copenhagen on September 4, 1904. He was married with four children.

PEACE

WILLIAM CREMER (1838-1908)

William Randal Cremer was born on March 18, 1838 in Fareham, England. Following a minimum education Cremer in 1860, became one of the founders of the Amalgamated Society of Carpenters and Joiners. He later became the secretary of the British section of the First International of Working Men's Association, before resigning over an internal matter of principle.

During the Franco-Prussian war of 1870-71, he created a working mens committee dedicated to keeping Britain neutral. This organization went on to become the Workmen's Peace Association with Cremer the secretary until his death. A political radical, he sat as an MP in the House of Commons from 1885-1895. He was also edited the peace journal, *Arbiter,* from 1889. In 1903, he was awarded Nobel Prize for Peace; **"for his work concerning international arbitration"** In 1907 he was knighted. He died from pneumonia on July 22, 1908 whilst living in London. He was married but had no children.

1904

Russo-Japanese war • Theodore Roosevelt wins US presidential election • safety razors introduced • The Willow Tea Rooms, Glasgow • Puccini, *Madame Butterfly***• James Barrie,** *Peter Pan* **• Abbey Theatre, Dublin founded • G.K. Chesterton,** *The Napoleon of Notting Hill* **• Joseph Conrad,** *Nostromo* **• Fr Rolfe, Graham Greene and Marlene Dietrich born • Dvorák and Chekhov die • Britain and France sign the Entente Cordiale.**

LITERATURE

FREDERIC MISTRAL (1830-1914)
and
JOSE ECHEGARAY y EIZAGUIRRE (1832-1916)

Frédéric Mistral was born in Maillane, France on September 8th 1830. He was the son of a wealthy farmer who could well afford to send his son to the expensive Collège Royal of Avignon. There, Mistral came under the influence of his teacher Joseph Roumanille, a poet. In 1851, Mistral was awarded a law degree from the University of Aix-en-Provence; however, he was wealthy enough not to have to work and decided to dedicate his life restating the life and language of Provençals.

He and others, in 1854, founded the Félibrige, an association to maintain Provençale language and customs. Following 20 years work, Mistral published a dictionary devoted to the language of Southern France that was also used by word smiths in Italy and Spain. Although he didn't succeed in having the language adopted, he did write some of the finest poetry France has ever known and even to-day, he is considered one of the greatest poets of France.

His claim to greatness relies on his poems, *Mirèjo* and *Lou Pouèmo dôu Rose* both of which are epics in 12 cantos. The first inspired an opera by Gounod (1863) whilst the latter tells of a romance cut short by tragedy. In 1904 Mistral was co-awarded the Nobel Prize for Literature; **"in recognition of the fresh originality and true inspiration of his poetic production, which faithfully reflects the natural scenery and native spirit of his people, and, in addition, his significant work as a Provencale philogist"**

He died on March 25, 1914 in the town where he was born. He married but died childless.

José Echegaray y Eizaguirre was born in Madrid, Spain on April 19, 1832. In his early twenties he was appointed professor of mathematics, before entering the civil service (1868) and rising ever upwards. In 1874, when he was 42, his first play, *El libro talonario* (The Checkbook) appeared.

From then on he produced, on average, two plays a year to become the leading Spanish dramatist of the last part of the 19th century and a revolutionist of the theatre.

In 1904 he was co-awarded the Nobel Prize for Literature; **"in recognition of the numerous and brilliant compositions which, in an individual and original manner, have revived the great traditions of the Spanish drama"**

He died In Madrid on September 4, 1916. He was married with a daughter.

CHEMISTRY

WILLIAM RAMSAY (1852-1916)

William Ramsay was born in Glasgow, Scotland on October 2,1852. At the University of Heidelberg he was a student of the analytical chemist, Robert Bunsen who invented the Bunsen burner. Between 1880-87, Ramsay was professor of chemistry at Bristol University, followed by London University (1887-1913). He spent most of his working life researching noble gases and in 1895, Ramsay freed helium from the mineral cleveite, so becoming the first person to isolate that element.

In 1903 he was able to demonstrate that helium, which is the lightest of the inert gases, is constantly produced during the radioactive decay of radium. This discovery was of the utmost importance and led to an modern understanding of nuclear reactions. In 1888 he was elected Fellow of the Royal Society and knighted in 1902.

In 1904, he received the ultimate accolade when he was awarded the Nobel Prize for Chemistry ; **"in recognition of his services in the discovery of the inert gaseous elements in air, and his determination of their place in the periodic system"**

Ramsay was considered to have extraordinary personal charm with a kindly and generous disposition. Most beloved by his students, he received the Prussian order *Pour le Merite*. He was married with a son and daughter and died on July 23, 1916 in High Wycombe, England.

PHYSICS

JOHN RAYLEIGH (1842-1919)

John **William Strutt Rayleigh** was born in Maldon, Essex, England on November 12, 1842. He suffered poor health in his early life and, as a consequence, was withdrawn from both Eton and Harrow Schools and educated at home by a tutor. In 1861, he was judged fit enough to enter Trinity College, Cambridge from where he graduated with a first class BA degree in the Mathematical Tripos. He then developed an overriding interest in both the experimental and mathematical sides of physical science. In 1869 he wrote a paper that reduced to common man proportions of understanding, the theories in electromagnetic by James Clerk Maxwell. In 1871, in order to recover from a life threatening bout of rheumatic fever, Rayleigh took his wife Evelyn on a trip up the Nile.

During this time he began writing his great work, *The Theory of Sound*. In this achievement, Rayleigh examines questions of vibrations and the resonance of elastic solids and gases. Published in two volumes, 1877 and 1878, it was the most important book on these subjects for over 50 years. In 1873, following the death of his father, he became the 3rd Baron Rayleigh. He moved into the family manor house and built a laboratory alongside the house. Rayleigh's theory explains why the sky is blue; because of the scattering of sunlight by small particles in the atmosphere.

However, Rayleigh's greatest single contribution to science is probably his discovery and isolation of argon, a rare gas of the atmosphere. His experiments were numerous and important and resulted in his being awarded the 1904 Nobel Prize; **"for his investigations of the desities of the most important gases and for his discovery of argon in connection with these studies"**

In 1905 he was elected president of the Royal Society. He married Arthur Balfour's sister and had three children. Later on in life, he was the foremost leader in British physics and in 1908 was appointed chancellor of Cambridge University. Although frail in body, his mind was strong and active and he worked up to his death on June 30, 1919, whilst living at Terling Place, Witham, Essex.

PHYSIOLOGY or MEDICINE

IVAN PAVLOV (1849-1936)

Ivan **Petrovitch Pavlov** was born in Ryazan, Russia on September 26th 1849. Pavlov's father was the village priest whilst his grandfather was the sexton. It was therefore no surprise that he studied theology. However, in 1870 he came to his senses to study chemistry and physiology at the University of St. Petersburg. He later graduated from the Imperial Medical Academy, with an MD, and later studied under Carl Ludwig in Leipzig. He learnt much and his first independent research was on the physiology of the circulatory system. He went on to investigate cardiac physiology and

the regulation of blood pressure.

Beyond the theory was his work as a brilliant surgeon. His brilliance in both fields was of the utmost importance and Pavlov led the way for much that came later. In 1904 he was awarded the Nobel Prize for Physiology or Medicine;

"in recognition of his work on the physiology of digestion, through which knowledge on vital aspects of the subject has been transformed and enlarged"

In 1890, he became professor of physiology at the Imperial Medical Academy and stayed until he resigned, in 1924, to become the first director of the Institute of Experimental Medicine. In January 1921, Lenin issued a decree noting his work. Pavlov was of course famous as the man who caused a dog to salivate. Showered with honours, he died in Leningrad on February 27, 1936. He was married with four sons and a daughter.

PEACE

INSTITUTE OF INTERNATIONAL LAW

The **Institute of International Law** was the initiative of Gustave Rolin-Jaequemyns, a Belgian jurist, who, following the Franco-Prussian war of 1870-71, assembled ten notable jurists from 10 major countries, including Tobias Asser (qv), to the town hall in Ghent, Belgium. As a result the Institute held its first public session in Geneva in 1874.

The Institute of International Law is purely a scientific and private association without any official sanction, whose objective is to promote the progress of international law as demanded by a modern civilized and democratic society. They now represent some 40 countries and their finances come from a series of legacies and bequests. The award of the 1904 Nobel Peace Prize has been a particular source of prestige and funding.

1905

Chinese boycott US goods • Mutiny on battleship *Potemkin* • Sinn Fein Party founded in Dublin • SunYat-sen organises a union of secret societies • Lenin, *Two Tactics* • Picasso, *Boy with Pipe* • Richard Strauss, *Salome* • E.M.Forster, *Where Angels Fear to Tread* • H.G.Wells, *Kipps* • Arthur Koestler and Greta Garbo born • AA founded in UK • 1,000 Jews massacred by Russian Czar • Amundsen of Norway discovers the magnetic North Pole • Dr. Barnardo dies.

LITERATURE

HENRYK SIENKIEWICZ (1846-1916)

Henryk Sienkiewicz was born in Wola Okrzejska, Poland on May 5th 1846. Although he studied literature and history at Warsaw University, he left in 1871 without taking a degree. Following his flirtation with a method of philosophy known as 'positivism', he settled down to his chosen occupation of writer, and published his first novel, *In Vain* in 1872. It didn't shake the world of literature and he journeyed to the US as special correspondent of *The Polish Gazette.* Upon his return, he published a collection of short stories and gradually became known in his native land. However, it wasn't until 1883 that he caused the public in many countries to sit up and take his writings seriously.

His trilogy of historical novels, consisting of, *With Fire and Sword* (1883), *Potop* (1886) and *Pan Michael* (1888), were very well received. These popular novels are set in the latter part of the 17th century and describe Poland's ongoing troubles with Cossacks, Tartars, Turks and Swedes. Probably his greatest work is *Quo Vadis?* (1896) which established his international reputation and would later provide Hollywood with one of its' epics. In 1905, he was awarded the Nobel Prize for Literature; **"because of his outstanding merits as an epic writer"**

He died in Vevey, Switzerland on November 15, 1916. He married three times and had a son and a daughter.

CHEMISTRY

ADOLPH von BAEYER (1835-1917)

Adolph von Baeyer was born in Berlin, the son of a Jewish mother, on October 31, 1835. At the age of twelve he discovered a new double salt of copper and sodium. Although Baeyer studied under Robert Bunsen, August Kekule was his main sphere of influence. He became professor of chemistry at Strasbourg in 1872 and transferred to Munich in 1875 remaining there until 1915. His research encompassed the chemistry of organic dyes as well as explaining the strain theory that explained why carbon rings of some five or six atoms, are so much more common than carbon rings with other numbers of atoms.

Another first was his discovery of barbituric acid as a derivative of uric acid. In 1881, The Royal Society of London awarded him the Davy medal for his work on indigo dyes. In 1905 Baeyer was awarded the Nobel Prize for Chemistry; **"in recognition of his services in the advancement of organic chemistry and chemical industry, through his work on organic dyes and hydro aromatic compounds"**

In the same year, to celebrate his 70th birthday, a collection of his papers was published. He died from a seizure in Starnberg, Munich, on August 20, 1917. He was married with 2 sons and a daughter.

PHYSICS

PHILIPP LENARD (1862-1947)

Philipp Edouard Anton Lenard was born on June 7, 1862 in Pressburg, Hungary. Lenard served as a physics professor at a number of universities including, Breslau in 1894, Aachen,1895, Heidelberg,1896 and Kiel in 1898. He then returned to the university of Heidelberg until he retired in 1931. He is particularly known for his work on the cathode-ray tube and the effects that later became known as the photoelectric effect or electron.

His experiments also included studies of ultraviolet light and phosphorescence. Much of his early work would be most important in the development of nuclear physics and electronics. In 1905 he was awarded the Noble Prize for Physics; **"for his work on cathode rays"**

Following the rise of Hitler, Lenard became an ardent Nazi party member. He was violently anti-Semitic and publicly derided what he called 'Jewish Science' including the work of Albert Einstein. As a reward, Hitler named him 'Chief Aryan of German Physics'. Lenard died in Messelhausen, Germany on May 20, 1947. He was married with a son.

PHYSIOLOGY or MEDICINE

ROBERT KOCH (1843-1910)

Robert Heinrich Hermann Koch was born in Clausthal, Germany on December 11, 1843. He graduated in medicine from the University of Göttingen in 1866. He was an army surgeon in the Franco-Prussian war of 1870-71. Following the war, he created a small laboratory. Here, in a simply equipped situation, he began his investigations into pathogenic organisms. He researched the problems of anthrax and completed the microbes life cycle in 1876.

The following year, Koch published an important paper concerning the overall investigation of bacteria. In 1878, he completed his experiments on the etiology of wound infection; by inoculating animals from various sources, Koch produced six types of infection, each due to a specific micro-organism.

He was now world famous and specialized in bacteria research. He became centred at Berlin's German Health Office. He concentrated on TB, and by 1882, had isolated and grown the tubercle bacillus, the core of TB. He later travelled to India and worked on cholera bacillus, then endemic with the disease. He discovered the cholera organism and how it was transmitted from drinking water and some foods. Koch was awarded the 1905 Nobel Prize for Physiology or Medicine; **"for his investigations and discoveries in relation to tuberculosis"**

Koch set forth four principles that became known as, ' Koch's Postulates'. He died in Baden-Baden, Germany on May 27, 1910. He married twice and had one daughter.

PEACE

BERTHA von SUTTNER (1843-1914)

Bertha Fêlicie Sophie Freifrau von Suttner was born in Prague, Czechoslovakia on June 9, 1843. She was the daughter of a Field Marshall who got himself into debt and died before she was born. Her family didn't approve of her fiancee, Arthur von Suttner, so Bertha obtained a job with Alfred Nobel as his secretary/housekeeper at his Paris residence. A little later, she left the job and married Suttner staying friendly with Nobel until his death in 1896. She became involved with the peace movement and in 1891, she founded the Austrian Pacifist Organisation.

Between 1892 and 1899, she edited the international journal devoted to pacifism. *Lay Down Your Arms;* the translated title of her most famous novel, *Die Waffen niederl* (1892), brought her considerable fame. Bertha Suttner was awarded the 1905 Nobel Prize for Peace; **"for her work on pacifism"**

1906

Alaska elects a delegate to US Congress • Alfred Dreyfus is rehabilitated • Peaceful picketing becomes legal in UK • Aga Khan founds All India Moslem League • HMS *Dreadnought* launched • First Mozart festival in Salzburg • E. Nesbit, *The Railway Children* • Upton Sinclair, *The Jungle* • Dimitry Shostakovich and Samuel Beckett born • Henri Ibsen and Paul Cézanne die.

LITERATURE

GIOSUE CARDUCCI (1835-1907)

Giosue Carducci was born in Lucca, Italy on July 27, 1835. His father was a country doctor and Carducci received his early education at the village school. He later graduated in literature from Pisa University and became a professor of Italian literature, at Bologna University, where he remained for over 40 years. His first book of poetry, *Rime,* was published in 1857. In 1863 came, *Inno a Satana*. Some of his best work appeared in *Lambics and Epodes* (1867-69).

He often wrote in Latin rather than Italian, and his *Odi barbare,* are imitative of Horace and Virgil. In 1906, Carducci, a republican and anti-Catholic, was awarded the 1906 Nobel Prize for Literature; **"not only in consideration of his deep learning and critical research, but above all as a tribute to the creative energy, freshness of style, and lyrical force which characterize his poetic masterpieces"** He died in Bologna on February 16, 1907. He was married with three children.

CHEMISTRY

HENRI MOISSAN (1852-1907)

Henri Ferdinard-Frédéric Moissan was born to a French-Jewish mother, living in Paris, on September 28, 1852. Educated at the Muséum d'Histoire Naturelle and the École de Pharmacie in Paris, where Moissan was later a professor of toxicology (1886). In 1900, he was doing the same job at the Sorbonne. He studied and experimented with fluorine products from 1884 and by 1886, he had produced gas fluorine. Now Moissan experimented and developed the electric arc furnace. It meant he was able to produce acetylene at low commercial rates.

He was a prolific writer that included *The Electric Furnace* (1897) and the five volume *Treatise on Inorganic Chemistry* (1904-06). In 1906, Moissan was awarded the Nobel Prize for Chemistry; **"in recognition of the great services rendered by him in his investigation and isolation of the element fluorine, and for the adoption in the service of science of the electric furnace called after him"**

He died in Paris, shortly after his return from receiving the prize in Stockholm, on February 20, 1907. He was married with a son.

PHYSICS

JOSEPH THOMSON (1856-1940)

Joseph John Thomson was born in Manchester, England on December 18, 1856. His father was a bookseller who ensured his son's entry to Owens College (now part of Manchester University) when he was only 14. When aged 20, he was at Cambridge University, where he would remain for the remainder of his life.

He was an early researcher into the field of electromagnetism. His work was recognised by his election in 1884, to the Royal Society of London. His most important work was the realisation that all matter, whatsoever the source, has particles of the same type that are much less massive than the atoms of which they form part. Thomson didn't exactly split the atom but he certainly chipped at it.

His discovery of the electron in 1897, revolutionised the scientific world. Beside his prior interest in physics, he also concerned himself with politics, sports and the theatre. It is considered that Thomson made atomic physics a science that later benefited the world. In 1906 he was awarded the Nobel Prize for Physics; **"in recognition of the great merits of his theoretical and experimental investigations on the conduction of electricity by gases"**

In 1918, he was made master of Trinity College, Cambridge and later, 7 Nobel Prizes would be awarded amongst his students. In 1908 he was knighted and in 1912 he received the Order of Merit. He died in Cambridge on August 30, 1940. He was married with a son and daughter. His son, George Thomson, received the Nobel Prize for Physics in 1937.

PHYSIOLOGY or MEDICINE

CAMILLO GOLGI (1843-1926)
and
SANTIAGO RAMON y CAJAL (1852-1934)

"in recognition of their work on the structure of the nervous system"

Camillo Golgi was born in Corteno, Italy on July 7, 1834. He qualified as a doctor and went to work at a home for incurables. Here, in 1873, he devised the silver nitrate method of staining tissue that was to prove such a great asset in future nerve studies. Later, whilst at the University of Pavia, Golgi in 1880, discovered and described what has become known as Golgi tendon spindle or organ; the point where sensory nerve fibres end and are caught within a tendon. Between 1885 and 1893 Golgi researched malaria.

Here he discovered two types of intermittent malarial fever; tertian, occurring daily, and quartan, occurring every third day and caused by varying species of the protozoan parasite. He further deduced, that fever convulsions happen with the release of the parasite's spores from red blood cells. In 1906, Golgi co-shared the Nobel Prize for Physiology or Medicine.

He died in Pavia on January 21, 1926. Married without issue, he adopted his niece.

Santiago y Cajal, Ramon was born in Petilla de Aragon, Spain on May 1, 1852. As a boy he was apprenticed to a barber. Following his qualifying as a doctor, he served as a professor of anatomy at the University of Valencia (1884-87), followed by the universities of Barcelona (1887-92) and Madrid (1892-1922). His researches resulted in his establishing the nerve cell as the basic unit of nervous structure.

This resulted in the modern appreciation of a nerve impulse. Using a gold stain, Ramon went on to determine the structure of the eye retina that would later be of great help in dealing with brain tumours.

In 1906, Ramon co-shared the Nobel Prize for Physiology or Medicine. In 1920, King Alfonso X111 of Spain authorised the building of the Institute Cajal in Madrid. His best known book is, *The Degeneration and Regeneration of the Nervous System* (1928). Ramon died in Madrid on October 17, 1934. He was married with four sons and four daughters.

PEACE

THEODORE ROOSEVELT (1858-1919)

Theodore Roosevelt was born in New York City on October 27, 1858 into a well-to-do family that originated in the Netherlands. His prime education was from private tutors before on-going to Harvard University, followed by Columbia University Law School. He turned from a promising law career to write on history, and later adopted a political career. He was a tough man who kept fit. At 23, he was in the New York State Assembly. He was then defeated in three successive elections to spend some years in the wilderness of Dakota.

In 1898 the US declared war on Spain. Roosevelt resigned from the government; he had been assistant secretary of the navy, and created a cavalry unit known as, The Rough Riders. He took this force to Cuba, where following the battle of Santiago, he was able to return home a hero.

In 1900, he was vice president to McKinley. Roosevelt expected to spend time in boring terms he wasn't disappointed. On September 14, 1901, it all turned upside down when McKinley was murdered and Roosevelt automatically became president of the US. He worked hard in order to get elected, in his own right, in 1904. This he achieved and set about creating a better society. In 1905, he brought about legislation to forbid any country, save the US, to intervene in Latin-American affairs. It was a high handed action that created the policy of ' Speak softly and carry a big stick'.

He generally encouraged European countries to pursue the path of peace and, as a result, was awarded the 1906 Nobel Prize for Peace; **"for mediating the Russo-Japanese War"**

During WWI, Roosevelt supported the Allies. However, he died in his sleep before the post-war election, on January 6, 1919 at Oyster Bay, New York. He was twice married and had six children.

1907

The triple alliance between Germany, Austria and Italy renewed for six years• Oklahoma is admitted as a US state • Lenin leaves Russia • Bakelite invented • Boy Scout movement founded • US restricts immigration • Elgar's *Pomp and Circumstance no.4 in G* • Hilaire Belloc, *Cautionary Tales* • J.M. Synge, *Playboy of the Western World* • Joseph Conrad, *The Secret Agent* • E.M.Forster, *The Longest Journey* • WH.Auden and Alberto Moravia born • Grieg dies • New Zealand wins autonomy.

LITERATURE

RUDYARD KIPLING (1865-1936)

Joseph **Rudyard Kipling** was born in Bombay, India on December 30, 1865. Kipling had an unhappy childhood. His family returned to the UK, when Kipling was 6 years old, and then left him with a foster mother in Southsea, a situation he describes in his story, *Baa,Baa,Black Sheep* (1888). There followed a cheap boarding school in North Devon that was quite frightful and described later in *Stalky & Co* (1899).

Kipling returned to India in 1882 and later married in America. Between 1889 and 1891, he lived in London's Strand, in a flat above a shop called,' Harris the Sausage King' who kept him supplied with sausage and mash for twopence. He spent many hours at Gatti's Music Hall.

In 1892, he went to his wife's home state of Vermont and there he wrote his *Jungle Books*. Following an argument with his in-laws, Kipling returned to Britain and a house in Sussex (1902). After his receipt of the Nobel Prize for Literature in 1907, **"in consideration of the power of observation, originality of imagination, virility of ideas and remarkable talent for narration which characterize the creations of this world-famous author"**

He went to South Africa where he was given a house by Cecil Rhodes. He gained a small reputation as a humorist with his, *The Village that Voted the Earth was Flat* (1913). He later became increasingly isolated from the liberal thought of the 20th century, and eventually returned to London where he died on January 18, 1936. He was married with three children.

CHEMISTRY

EDUARD BUCHNER (1860-1917)

Eduard Buchner was born in Munich, Germany on May 20, 1860. He received his doctorate from Munich University in 1888 and was subsequently professor at a succession of universities. In 1898, he was appointed to an agricultural professorship at Berlin University and there concentrated on research. He went on to prove that fermentation of carbohydrates results from the various enzymes within yeast and not in the yeast cell.

He was able to demonstrate that extraction from yeast cells, causes sugar to break up into carbon dioxide and alcohol. He was awarded the 1907 Nobel Prize for Chemistry; **"for his biochemical researches and his discovery of cell-free fermentation"**

During WWI he was a major in the German army and wounded in battle. He died on August 13, 1917 in Focsani, Rumania. He was married without children.

PHYSICS

ALBERT MICHELSON (1852-1931)

Albert Abraham Michelson was born in Strelno, Germany on December 19, 1852. He came from a distinguished Jewish family who emigrated to the US when Albert was two. They settled in San Francisco, where Albert's father prospered as a merchant. When Albert was 17, he enrolled at the United States Naval Academy. He graduated in science with honours and then remained at the academy as a scientific instructor(1875-79).

In 1878, he began what would become his life's work; the accurate measurement of the speed of light.

He resigned from the navy and spent the next few years travelling Europe to gain knowledge and to study the field of optics. A few years later, he returned to the US and announced that the speed of light was 299,852 kilometres per second. He later amended this figure to 299,774. In 1907 he was awarded the Nobel Prize for Physics, **"for his optical precision instruments and the spectroscope and metro logical investigations carried out with their aid"**

He was the first American ever to receive a Nobel Prize for a science subject. In 1889, he was appointed professor of physics at the newly created University of Chicago and where he remained until his retirement in 1929. In the 1970s, researchers into speed of light, using far more advanced methods, came up with a result that was just 2 kilometres difference from

Michelson's calculation. He was married with a son and three daughters. In 1973, his daughter Dorothy Livingstone, published a biography of her father entitled, *The Master of Light*. Albert Michelson died in Pasadena, US on May 9, 1931.

PHYSIOLOGY or MEDICINE

CHARLES LAVERAN (1845-1922)

Charles-Louis Alphonse Laveran was born in Paris on June 18, 1845. He graduated from the medical school of Strasbourg University and then joined the French army, serving as an army surgeon in the Franco-German War (1870-71).

Thereafter, he taught military medicine until 1897 when he joined the Pasteur Institute, Paris. Laveran later became influential in developing processes in order to research effects of tropical medicine.

In 1907 he established, at the Pasteur Institute, the Laboratory of Tropical Diseases. In 1907, Laveran was awarded the Nobel Prize for Physiology or Medicine; **"in recognition of his work on the role played by protozoa in causing diseases"**

He also discovered the parasite that causes human malaria. He died in Paris on May 18, 1922. He was married without issue.

PEACE

ERNESTO MONETA (1833-1918)
and
LOUIS RENAULT (1843-1918)

Ernesto Teodoro Moneta was born in Milan, Italy on September 20, 1833. At the age of 15 he was fighting in the streets against Austrian rule and fought with Garibaldi in the victorious war of freedom. In 1861, he was in the regular Italian army, fighting in the Battle of Custoza (1866). He resigned the army in favour of becoming editor of *Il Secolo* (1867-96), a democratic news sheet published in Milan. The war sufferings he had experienced at first hand was a lingering sore, and one which he sought to do something about. He founded ' The International Society For Peace' to work for disarmament and peace.

He was a warm, cheerful man most fond of horse riding and amateur acting. He founded an arbitration service that sought to settle disputes by discussion and debate, rather than war. He was president of the International Peace Conference held in Milan in 1906. In the following year Moneta shared the Nobel Peace Prize; **"for his work with the Lombard Union for International Peace and**

Arbitration" However, he wasn't all peace and light. In 1911 he supported Italy's incursion into Libya and, in 1915, he supported Italy entering WWI on the side of the Allies. He died of pneumonia in Milan on February 10, 1918. He was married with two sons.

Louis Renault was born in Autun, France on May 21, 1843. Following an extensive education in law, he became Professor of Law at Dijon University (1868-73). In 1890, he was working for the French foreign ministry, and set up a committee to examine foreign policy in the light of recent international agreements. He became famous as an international arbitrator.

It all resulted in his being co-awarded the 1907 Nobel Peace Prize; **"for his work with the second Hague Peace Conference"** He died at his holiday villa in Barbizon, France on February 8th 1918. He was working right to the end of his life; he never retired. He was married with four daughters and a son. He was named to the legion of Honour and to the Academy of Moral and Political Science in France as well as being awarded various decorations from some nineteen foreign countries.

1908

South Africa convention agrees on a Union of South Africa• Kaiser Wilhelm ll states 'although the German people are hostile to Britain, I am a friend' • Jacob Epstein, *Figures* **causes uproar • Béla Bartók,** *First String Quartet* **• Jack Johnson becomes first black heavyweight boxing champion • Ezra Pound,** *A Lume Spento* **• Arnold Bennett,** *The Old Wives' Tale* **• Kenneth Grahame,** *The Wind in the Willows* **• G.K.Chesterton,** *The Man Who Was Thursday* **• E.M.Forster,** *A Room With a View* **• Simone de Beauvoir, Ian Fleming born • Rimsky-Korsakov dies • Old age pension introduced in Britain.**

LITERATURE

RUDOLPH EUCKEN (1846-1926)

Rudolph Christoph Eucken was born in Aurich, Germany on January 5, 1846. Eucken studied philosophy at the University of Göttingen and was later appointed professor of philosophy at Basel University (1871-74). He then joined the university of Jena and stayed until 1920. Eucken appreciated philosophy by experience and sought a spiritual lifestyle. He caused much controversy by his anti-socialist utterings and constant attacks on natural philosophy.

However, in 1908 he was awarded the Nobel Prize for Literature; **"in recognition of his earnest search for truth, his penetrating power of thought, his wide range of vision, and the warmth**

and strength in presentation with which in his numerous works he has vindicated and developed an idealistic philosophy of life"

A great supporter of German ambitions during WWI, he died in Jena, Germany on September 14, 1926. He was married with two sons and a daughter.

CHEMISTRY

ERNEST RUTHERFORD (1871-1937)

Ernest Rutherford was born on August 30, 1871 in Spring Grove, South Island, New Zealand. His father was a wheelwright who raised 12 children. Ernest, his fourth child, received his early education at Nelson College and Christchurchs' Canterbury College, thanks to his winning scholarships. Following the success of his first research project on magnetization of iron, by high-frequency discharges (1894), followed by magnetic viscosity (1896), he was admitted to the Cavendish Laboratory at Cambridge University. He later laid the groundwork for the development of nuclear physics, following his investigation of radioactive particles and developing the nuclear theory of the structure of the atom.

In 1898 he was professor of physics at McGill University, Montreal, Canada and in 1907 was teaching at Manchester University.

Together with Niels Bohr,(qv), he developed the quantum theory and, in 1908, was awarded the Nobel Prize for Chemistry; **"for his investigations into the disintegration of the elements, and the chemistry of radioactive substances"**

His work in investigating radioactivity, discovering the alpha particle and developing the nuclear theory of atomic structure, brought him world-wide recognition. In 1914 he was knighted and during WWI, did valuable work for the Admiralty on submarine detection. He received the Copley Medal of the Royal Society in 1922. In 1925, he became president of the Royal Society and received the Order of Merit. He was created a baron in 1931 and took as his title; Baron Rutherford of Nelson.

When not working he enjoyed motoring and playing golf. Rutherford's contribution to general science, and atomic science in particular, cannot be underestimated. He died in Cambridge, England on October 19, 1937 and buried at Westminster Abbey. Although he was married with a daughter his title died with him.

PHYSICS

GABRIEL LIPPMANN (1845-1921)

Gabriel Lippman was born in Hollerich, Luxembourg, to a French-Jewish family, on August 16, 1845. Although he never obtained a teacher certificate (he failed the exam because he only liked working at subjects he enjoyed) he was appointed professor of mathematical physics at the Sorbonne, Paris in 1883. He is best known for his researches in the areas of optics and electricity. He is responsible for inventing the coelostat, a devise for long exposures of the sky whilst compensating for the Earth's movement during that process.

In 1891, he created what became known as the Lippman process; the use of natural colours of light wavelengths in place of dyes for colour photography. He went on to produce the first colour photographic plate. Lippman was awarded the 1908 Nobel Prize for Physics; **"for his method of reproducing colours photographically based on the phenomenon of interference"**

He died on July 13, 1921 whilst on board ship travelling between Canada and France. He was married without children.

PHYSIOLOGY or MEDICINE

PAUL EHRLICH (1854-1915)
and
ELIE METCHNIKOFF (1845-1916)

"in recognition of their work on immunity"

Paul Ehrlich was born in Silesia, Germany, to a middle-class German-Jewish family, on March 14, 1854. Whilst still a medical student at Leipzig University, Ehrlich was undertaking scientific experiments. It resulted in his proving that the chemical mechanism that works in therapeutic and toxic processes also determines cell nutrition. Following this work, he was asked to do research at Berlin's Charité Hospital. Here, he invented a staining method for the TB bacillus. This great advance on previous methods meant a microscope diagnosis of TB was now possible.

Between 1879 and 1883, Ehrlich published 37 papers although he considered the last one to be the most important; 'The Requirement of the Organism for Oxygen'. That year he married Hedwig Pinkus, by whom he later had two daughters. His researches continued with recognising, that chemotherapy could kill parasites or halt their growth without damaging the organism. He turned his attention to the disease, Syphilis. This had been a killer since its' identification some 400 years previously. Now Ehrlich tackled this problem and came up with Formula 606, later called Salvarsan.

This became known as the ' magic bullet' . Altogether, his work won him a half share in the 1908 Nobel Prize for Physiology or Medicine. Later he became a Privy Councillor in his native Prussia, a rare distinction for a Jew. He was awarded honorary doctorates by many of the world's universities. He died, following a stroke, in Bad Homburg, Germany on March 14, 1915. Although Britain and Germany were in the middle of WW1, the *Times* of London stated in an obituary, ' the whole world was in his debt'. In 1940 Hollywood made a film of his life, with Edward G Robinson playing the part of Paul Ehrlich, entitled, *Dr Ehrlich's Magic Bullet.*

Ilya (Elie) Ilich Mechnikov who had a Jewish mother and a Russian father was born in Kharkov, Russia on May 15, 1845. He graduated from Gorky State University in 1864 and became professor of zoology and comparative anatomy at Odessa University (1870-82). He then worked in Meesina, Italy (1882-86) and whilst there, noticed how the digestive organs in starfish larvae contained variant or splinter cells or phagocytes.

During his long sojourn at the Pasteur Institute in Paris, he established that, the phagocytes are the basic defence against severe infection in most animals, as well as humankind. The rest of his life was given over to the study of lactic acid producing bacteria as a means of increasing life. He advocated that every diet must include sour milk.

In 1908, he was co-awarded the Nobel Prize for Physiology of Medicine. Among his writings was *The Coparitive Pathology of Inflammation* (1892), *Immunity in Infectious Diseases* (1901) and in 1903, *The Nature of Man.* He died Paris on July 16, 1916. He was married twice but had no children.

PEACE

KLAS ARNOLDSON (1844-1916)
and
FREDRIK BAJER (1837-1922)

Klas Pontus Arnoldson was born in Göteborg, Sweden on October 27, 1844, the son of a caretaker. After a minimal education, Klas became a railway clerk who later rose to be a stationmaster. He then became a professional politician and elected to the Swedish parliament; The Riksdag. Arnoldson became a devotee to pacifism and worked for and supported the neutrality of Scandinavian countries. In 1883, he co-founded the Swedish Association for Peace and Conciliation.

In 1890, there was high tension between Sweden and Norway, it might have led to war save for the efforts of Arnoldson, who peacefully resolved the problems. His ongoing work led to his being co-awarded the 1908 Nobel Peace Prize; **"for his on-going work between work** to settle the dispute between Sweden and Norway" The award was not popular in Sweden. Newspapers were incensed saying the award was an outrage against Sweden. The Nobel reply was that Arnoldson's candidacy was proposed and approved by the unanimous vote of the Swedish group of the Interparliamentary Union.

Arnoldson died from a heart attack, in Stockholm on February 20, 1916. He married but had no children.

Fredrik Bajer was born in Copenhagen, Denmark on April 21, 1837. Following a minimal education, Bajer joined the Danish army for the war against Prussia. The army strength was then reduced and he joined the army of the unemployed. Following an inheritance, Fredrik was free to pursue his ideals. He worked for the emancipation of women, the peace organisations, and for co-operation between Scandinavian countries. In 1871 he was the founder of the Danish Women's Association and the Danish Peace Association in 1885.

He entered parliament as a left-wing liberal (1872-95) and advocated world arbitration treaties. It resulted in his becoming most influential in the policies of Danish foreign affairs for peace. In 1891, he co-founded the International Peace Bureau in Bern, becoming the president in 1907. In 1908 he was co-awarded the Nobel Prize for Peace; **"for his outstanding work on the board of the Peace Bureau"**

He died in Copenhagen on January 22, 1922. He was married without children.

1909

Britain alarmed as German navy grows • Japan take over Korea • German women admitted to university • Girl Guide movement founded • Sigmund Freud lectures in US on psychoanalysis • Henri Matisse, *The Dance* **• Frank Lloyd Wright, Robie House, Chicago • Diaghilev produces his Russian Ballet in Paris,** *Les Sylphides* **• Gertrude Stein,** *Three Lives* **• H.G.Wells,** *Tono-Bungay* **• Stephen Spender and Kwame Nkrumah born • Charles Swinbourne dies • Blériot flies the Channel • British Suffragettes forced fed in prison.**

LITERATURE

SELMA LAGERLÖF (1858-1940)

Selma Ottiliana Lovisa Lagerlöf was born in Mårbacka, Sweden on November 20, 1858. An early illness left her limping. With her childhood restricted, she was educated at home. Later her handicap didn't matter. She trained as a teacher in Stockholm before teaching at Landskrona (1885) Whilst there, she wrote her first novel. *Gösta Berlings saga* was published in 1891 in 2 volumes and tells the tale of 12 Cavaliers and their leader, Gösta Berling.

This work began the Swedish Romantic revival. In 1894 she wrote a book of short stories and further became famous outside of Sweden

She gave up teaching for writing, became most prolific and following publication of, *Jerusalem* (1901-92), went on to become the foremost novelist in Sweden.

She stopped writing during WW1, the facts of the brutal war disturbed her greatly. The war over, she once again took up her pen and wrote, *Mårbacka* (1922) followed by several more novels throughout the 1920s. In 1909 she was awarded the Nobel Prize for Literature; **"in appreciation of the lofty idealism, vivid imagination and spiritual perception that characterize her writings"**

With the prize money, she bought back the childhood home that had been sold to pay off her father's debts. Selma Lagerlöf was not only a great modern teller of tales she was also the first woman to receive a Nobel Prize for Literature. She died in the house in which she was born on March 16, 1940. She never married. In the 1990s, a spa in Sweden was named the Selma Lagerlöf Spa.

CHEMISTRY

WOLFGANG OSTWALD (1883-1943)

Carl Wilhelm Wolfgang Ostwald was born in Riga, Latvia on May 27, 1883. He spent most his working life at Leipzig University.

He began as a zoology student before turning to chemistry. Ostwald specialised in colloids and became an international expert.

His work on the electrical and optical properties of colloids brought him several honours. He was awarded the 1909 Nobel Prize for Chemistry; **"in recognition of his work on catalysis and for his investigations into the fundamental principles governing chemical equilibria and rates of reaction"**

He went on to discover the Ostwald Law of Dilution and invented a process for making nitric acid by the oxidation of ammonia. In 1922 he founded the Kolloid Gesellschaft. He died in Dresden, Germany during an Allied air raid on November 22,1943. He was married with 3 sons and 2 daughters.

PHYSICS

GUGLIELMO MARCONI (1874-1937)
and
KARL BRAUN (1850-1918)

"in recognition of their contribution to the development of wireless telegraphy"

Marchese Guglielmo Marconi was born in Bologna, Italy on April 25, 1874. His father was Italian his mother Irish. Marconi received his early education in Bologna, and then Florence. He was at a technical school in Leghorn, studying physics, when he started researching electromagnetic waves. He knew of the work of Heinrich Hertz and James Maxwell and Oliver Lodge. The three provided Marconi with knowledge of mathematics, radio waves and lightening and electricity. He took it in and, at his father's farm in Bologna, put his total knowledge into creating a system of radio telegraphy. For his efforts he shared the 1909 Nobel Prize for Physics.

It was due to his cousin, Jameson Davis, that Marconi's invention gathered pace and recognition. Davis financed what became known as, Marconi's Wireless Telegraph Company Limited. (1900). Gradually the telegraph became more dependable and used by increasing numbers of organisations, including the Royal Navy. During WW1, he was a Commander in the Italian Navy and awarded the Military Medal. His recreations were hunting, cycling and motoring.

The distances between sender and receiver grew to hundreds of miles; by 1910 the distances reached over 6,000 miles and, by 1918, Britain to Australia. During WW1 both sides used the invention. In April 1912, David Sarnoff, in New York, used Marconi's telegraph to communicate with the liner 'Titanic' when that ship sent out SOS messages. He stayed at his post for 72 hours communicating with other agencies and overseeing the rescue work by means of Marconi's invention.

Marconi received many honours and honorary degrees. He was president of the Royal Italian Academy and a supporter of the Italian fascist leader, Mussolini. Marconi died in Rome on July 20, 1937. He had three wives two daughters and a son.

Karl Ferdinand Braun was born in Fulda, Germany on June 6, 1850. He received a PhD from Berlin University in 1872 and worked in several German universities culminating as professor of physics at Strasbourg University (1895). Braun discovered crystalline materials act as rectifiers, to allow current to flow in one direction only. His work led to the famous crystal sets that received early radio transmissions; complete with 'cat's whiskers'.

Braun improved on Marconi's work and, as a result he shared with him, the 1909 Nobel Prize for Physics. In 1915, Braun was in New York for a patent court case. During his visit the US entered WW1 in the Allied cause. As a result Braun was prevented from returning to Germany and died in New York on April 20, 1918.

He was married with two sons and two daughters.

PHYSIOLOGY or MEDICINE

EMIL KOCHER (1841-1917)

Emil Theodor Kocher was born in Bern, Switzerland on August 25, 1841. He qualified in medicine from Bern University in 1865, and went on to study in London, Paris and Vienna. In 1872, he was professor of clinical surgery at Bern, where he stayed for 45 years. In 1876, he became the first surgeon to excise the thyroid gland in the treatment for goiter. Kocher was awarded the 1909 Nobel Prize for Physiology or Medicine; **"for his work on the physiology, pathology and surgery of the thyroid gland"**

He later found that when a total excision of the thyroid gland was undertaken, there was a much reduced mortality rate. By 1912, he had performed over 5,000 thyroid excisions and reduced the mortality from 18% to 0.5%. His method of gallbladder incision stills carries his name.

Kocher died in Bern on July 27, 1917. He was married with three sons.

PEACE

AUGUSTE BEERNAERT (1829-1912)
and
PAUL de CONSTANT ESTOURNELLES (1852-1924)

Auguste-Marie-François Beernaert was born on July 26, 1829 in Ostende, Belgium. Following graduating from university, with a degree in law, he began practising until, in 1873, he became a professional politician and a member of the Belgian Chamber of Deputies.

He became prime minister (1884-1894) and in 1895, was elected president of the Chamber of Deputies.

He was his country's first delegate to the Hague Peace Conferences of 1899 and 1907. At the age of 80, he was co-awarded the 1909 Nobel Peace Prize; **"in recognition of his work with the Hague Peace Conferences"**

He died from pneumonia in Lucerne, Switzerland on October 6, 1912. He was married without children.

Paul Henri Benjamin de Constant Estournelles was born in Fleche, France on November 22, 1852. His aristocratic family could trace its ancestry back to the time of the Crusades. Following university, he joined the French diplomatic service. Although he reached the rank of minister, he decided to give up diplomacy for politics. He was elected to the Senate in 1904. Following 9 years as a deputy, he continued being elected until 1920.

A member of several international conferences, he was the leader of the French delegation to the Hague peace conference of 1899, that led to the Permanent Court of Arbitration at the Hague. He was able to persuade President Roosevelt to submit the US Dispute with Mexico to the Hague court. This example was followed by other governments. A great organiser and publicist, he was awarded a share of the 1909 Nobel Peace Prize; **"for his work in persuading President Theodore Roosevelt to submit a US dispute with Mexico to the Hague Tribunal"**

He died in Paris on May 15, 1924. He was married with two sons and three daughters. Despite a very busy life d'Estournelle found time to take up fencing, yachting and painting. In addition he was an enthusiastic car driver and aeroplane pilot.

1910

Marie Curie, *Treatise on Radiography* **• Manhattan Bridge in New York opens • Arthur Evans excavates Knossos • Igor Stravinsky,** *The Firebird* **• John Masefield,** *Ballades and Poems* **• E.M.Forster,** *Howard's End* **• Henry Handel Richardson,** *The Getting of Wisdom* **• H.G.Wells,** *The History of Mr Polly* **• Mark Twain, Florence Nightingale and Leo Tolstoy die • George V crowned king • Halley's comet visible.**

LITERATURE

PAUL von HEYSE (1830-1914)

Luwig Paul von Heyse was born in Berlin on March 15, 1830. Heyse excelled in studying Classical and Romantic languages and, by virtue of a grant from Maximilian ll of Bavaria, was able to spend a year touring Italy. In 1854 he settled in Munich and there, published his short stories that found much favour.

In 1855, he wrote what is considered his masterpiece, *L'Arrabiata*. He became a master of that genre with the result, that his book, *Das Buch der Freundschaft* (1883-1884) was a best-seller of the time and, as a result, he was elected head of the Munich Circle of Writers.

Beside his work writing novels, plays and epic poems, he also translated the Italian poets. Heyse was dedicated to the traditionalist school of writing and would have little or nothing to do with the growing school of Naturalism. The result was that his popularity was low, at the time he received the Nobel Prize for Literature in 1910; **"as a tribute to the consummate artistry, permeated with idealism, which he has demonstrated during his long productive career as a lyric poet, dramatist, novelist and writer of world-renowned short stories"**

Heyse died in Munich on April 2, 1914. He married twice and had three sons and three daughters. His complete works, in 15 volumes, were published in 1924.

CHEMISTRY

OTTO WALLACH (1847-1931)

Otto **Wallach** was born in Königsberg, Germany, on March 27, 1847. He received his doctorate in 1869 from the University of Göttingen. He became a professor of pharmacy at Bonn University in 1876 and was later, appointed director of the Chemical Institute at Göttingen (1899-1915). Whilst still at Bonn, Wallach became interested in the composition of a group of volatile oils used in pharmaceutical preparations. His colleague, August Kekule, asserted that these oils could not be analysed.

However, Wallach, a master of experimentation, was not easily denied. By methods of repeated distillation he was able to separate the parts of complex mixtures. Wallach was awarded the 1910 Nobel Prize for Chemistry;. **"in recognition of his services to organic chemistry and the chemical industry by his pioneer work in the field of alicyclic compounds"**

Despite being Jewish, in an increasingly anti-Semitic environment, Wallach served as the president of the German Chemical Society. He died in Göttingen on February 26, 1931. He never married.

PHYSICS

JOHANNES van der WAALS (1837-1923)

Johannes **Diederik van der Waals** was born in Leiden, Netherlands on November 23, 1837. For his doctorate in 1873, Waals wrote for his thesis, *On the Continuity of the Liquid and Gaseous State*. This dissertation brought him to the notice of those who were interested in the kinetic theory of attractive forces.

In 1881, he introduced into the laws of physics, an exact formula as to size and attraction, and still known as ' van der Waals Equation'.

In 1910, Waals was awarded the Nobel Prize for Physics; **"for his work on the equation of state for gases and liquids"**

Waals' work later enabled James Dewar of England and Heike Onnes(qv) of The Netherlands, to agree the data required for the liquefaction of hydrogen and helium. In 1887, Waals was appointed professor of physics at Amsterdam University. He remained there until he retired in 1907. He died in Amsterdam on March 9, 1923. He was married with three daughters and a son.

PHYSIOLOGY or MEDICINE

ALBRECHT KOSSEL (1853-1927)

Albrecht Kossel was born in Rostock, Germany on September 16, 1853. He graduated from the Strasbourg University, in medicine, in 1878, and went on to do research at the Physiological Institute in Berlin. In 1879, he began investigating the recently isolated substances known as nucleoproteins. For the next twenty years, Kossel chemically analysed these nucleic acids, gradually breaking down their components to reveal; adenine, cytosine, guanine, thymine and uracil.

During this programme he also discovered the amino acid, histidine, thymic acid and agmatine. In 1910, Kossel was awarded the Nobel Prize for Physiology or Medicine; **"in recognition of the contributions to our knowledge of cell chemistry made through his work on proteins, including the nucleic substances"**

He died in Heidelberg, Germany on July 5, 1927. He was married with a son and daughter.

PEACE

THE INTERNATIONAL PEACE BUREAU

The International Peace Bureau (IPB) was founded following the third Universal Peace Congress in Rome in 1891. Fredrik Bajer (qv) was the first president, when it was established in Bern. In the early years, the IPB was synonymous with the peace societies, to whom it was affiliated. The Bureau arranged annual peace congresses, formulated the agendas and carried out their decisions. Information was forthcoming via its fortnightly publication, *Correspondance bimensuelle* and the year book, *Annuaire du Mouvement pacifiste.*

Funds were always difficult to raise, although the award of the 1910 Nobel Peace Prize made a big difference. The International Peace Bureau eventually gave way to the League of Nations, but not for long. The IPB eventually found its own image and concentrated its efforts on communicating ideas and proposals, more in keeping with a progressive peace movement.

In 1924, the Bureau moved to Geneva, which is still where the HQ is situated. Post WW2, the IPB became the International Liaison Committee of Organizations for Peace (ILCOP).

1911

David Lloyd George introduces National Health Insurance Bill for Britain • Kaiser speaks of 'Germany's place in the sun which her navy will secure for her' • Suffragette riots in London • US Supreme Court orders dissolution of Standard Oil Co.• Sun Yet-sen elected president of China • Amundsen reaches South Pole • Andrew Carnegie endows International Peace Foundation • Irving Berlin's, *Alexander's Ragtime Band* • Arnold Bennett, *The Card* • Frances Hodgson Burnett, *The Secret Garden* • Gustav Mahler and WS Gilbert die.

LITERATURE

MAURICE MAETERLINCK (1862-1949)

Maurice Polydore-Marie-Bernard Maeterlinck was born in Ghent, Belgium on August 29, 1862. Following his time at Ghent University, where he studied law, he went on to represent all that was fine and noble in the Symbolist tradition of poetry, drama and literature. In 1892 he wrote, *Pelléeas et Mélisande* and his reputation was assured. It was translated into many languages and became the basis upon which Debussy wrote his opera of the same name. It is set in a nebulous fairy tale past, written in prose and is extremely depressing.

In 1909, *L'Oiseau bleu* became equally popular, albeit a more cheerful piece that was influenced by Maeterlinck's mastery of Shakespeare. In 1918, his patriotic play, *The Burgomaster of Stilmonde* was very well received Further works followed but by now he was a spent force.

He had been awarded the 1911 Nobel Prize for Literature, **"in appreciation of his many-sided literary activities, and especially of his dramatic works, which are distinguished by a wealth of imagination and by a poetic fantasy, which reveals, sometimes in the guise of a fairy tale, a deep inspiration, while in a mysterious way they appeal to the readers' own feelings and stimulate their imaginations"**

The reward of being created Count of Belgium in 1932, convinced him to retire. He went to Nice in Southern France, survived WW2 and died, one of the most famous Belgian born writers, on May 6, 1949. He was married but had no surviving children.

CHEMISTRY

MARIE CURIE (1867-1934)

In 1903 **Marie Curie** shared the Nobel Prize for Physics with her husband, Pierre and Henri Becquerel (see 1903/Physics). In 1906, she succeeded her husband as professor of physics at the Sorbonne; the first woman ever to teach there. In 1911, she was awarded the Nobel Prize for Chemistry: **"in recognition of her services to the advancement of chemistry by the discovery of the elements radium and polonium, by the isolation of radium and the study of the nature and compounds of this remarkable element"**

She spent much time travelling and lecturing. She died in Sallanches, France on July 4, 1934. She was married with two daughters. Her daughter Irene, received the 1935 Nobel Prize for Chemistry, and daughter Eve wrote her mother's biography, *Madame Curie* in 1938.

PHYSICS

WILHELM WIEN (1864-1928)

Wilhelm Carl Werner Otto Fritz Franz Wien was born on January 13, 1864 in Gaffkin, Germany. He was appointed professor of physics at Giessen University in 1899 and there spent much time researching radiation of energy from blackbodys. Wien showed, that although the radiation emitted from a blackbody, is shared over a wide range of wavelengths, there is a maximum. In 1893 he determined that this maximum is inversely proportional to the absolute temperature of the body. In 1911, Wien was awarded the Nobel Prize for Physics; **"for his discoveries regarding the laws governing the radiation of heat"**

Wien's work later allowed Max Planck to arrive at his quantum theory of radiation. In 1920, Wien was appointed to the University of Munich and there, he studied and contributed to the discovery of cathode ray tubes; the essential ingredient of a TV set. Wien died in Munich on August 30, 1928. He was married with two sons and two daughters.

PHYSIOLOGY or MEDICINE

ALLVAR GULLSTRAND (1862-1930)

Allvar Gullstrand was born in Landskrona, Sweden on June 5, 1862. He studied in Austria and Sweden before arriving at his doctorate in 1890. His research area was optics. He went on to demonstrate that the eye lens increases the convexity of the surface by two thirds, with the remaining third steady. He devised what has become known as Gullstrand's slit lamp. A diagnostic aid that allows a detailed study of the eye.

He did much to expand the knowledge of the structure and function of the cornea and his work on astigmatism was invaluable. In 1911, he was awarded the Nobel Prize for Physiology or Medicine: **"for his work on the dioptrics of the eye"**

In 1913 Gullstrand was appointed professor of physical optics at Uppsala University. He died in Stockholm, Sweden on July 28, 1930. He was married with a daughter who died in childhood.

PEACE

TOBIAS ASSER (1838-1913)
and
ALFRED FRIED (1864-1921)

Tobias Michael Carel Asser was born in Amsterdam on April 28,1838 to a well established Jewish family. From 1862 to 1893, Asser was professor of international law at Amsterdam University. He was also founder of the Institute of International Law (1873). He went on to become the prime mover in the creation of the Permanent Court of Arbitration at The Hague. It was Asser who, in 1900, arbitrated between Russia and America over fishing rights in the Baring Straits.

He is noted for his work on the Hague Treaties of 1902-5, concerning family law, as well as other social legislation. Asser was the Netherlands's delegate to the 1907 Hague Peace Conference. In 1911, he shared the Nobel Peace Prize; **"for his role in the formation of the Permanent Court of Arbitration at the Hague peace conference (1899)"**

In 1904 he was appointed a Minister Without Portfolio, a post he retained until his death. He died in The Hague on July 29, 1913. He was married with three sons and a daughter.

Alfred Hermann Fried was born in Vienna, Austria on November 11, 1864 into a well known Jewish family. In 1891 Fried was living in Berlin, where he founded the pacifist magazine *Die Waffen nieder!* (Lay Down Your Arms!) The name was changed in 1899 to *Friedenswarte* (The Peacekeeper). In 1892 he founded the German Peace Society, a powerful lobby against the talk of war. Fried advocated world-wide pacifism. He was co-awarded the 1911 Nobel Peace Prize; **"for founding the German Peace Society"**

During WW1 he was forced to flee to Switzerland, having being accused of treason by the Austrians. In Switzerland he worked caring for prisoners of war. The war over, Fried returned to Austria, where he spent the remainder of his life preaching peace and the need for a European Union. He died in poverty from lung disease in Vienna on May 5, 1921. He was married three times without issue.

1912

New Mexico and Arizona become US states • House of Commons rejects women's franchise bill • Woodrow Wilson wins US presidential election • SS Titanic sinks on maiden voyage • Marcel Duchamp, *Nude Descending A Staircase* • Frederick Delius, *On Hearing the First Cuckoo in Spring* • Charles Pathe produces first news film • Saki, *The Unbearable Bassington* • Tennessee Williams born • August Strindberg and Jules Massenet die.

LITERATURE

GERHART HAUPTMANN (1862-1946)

Gerhart Johann Robert Hauptmann was born in Silesia, Germany on November 15, 1862. His father owned the main hotel, in nearby Bad Salzbrunn, and was considerably well off, certainly sufficiently so to enable his son to study sculpture at the Breslau Art Institute (1880-1882). He then spent a year at Jena University studying science and philosophy. After further study at Berlin University, he finally decided to become a writer.

Following a wealthy father Gerhart was clever enough to find a wealthy wife. The happy couple settled down in, Erkner, a wealthy suburb of Berlin. In 1889 he found overnight fame, following the production of his social drama called, *Vor Sonnenaufgang* (Before Dawn). This stark drama shocked audiences and became most controversial.

He went on to write about the underprivileged. In 1892, his *Die Weber* (The Weavers) caused further uproar; from those that had wealth whilst those that hadn't praised the work. He continued his writings, becoming a favourite of the left whilst incurring the continuing wrath of governments. In 1912, he was awarded the Nobel Prize for Literature; **"primarily in recognition of his fruitful, varied and outstanding production in the realm of dramatic art"** Hauptmann continued writing right up to the time the Nazis took over Germany. During the time of WW2, he remained in Prussia and relied upon his fame to see him safely through. The new regime made no doubts of their indifference toward him, albeit realising that Hauptmann was one of their most famous living writers. Following the war, his area came under the aegis of Russia having been liberated by the Red Army in 1945. He died in Agnetendorf, Germany on June 6, 1946. He was married twice with four sons.

CHEMISTRY

VICTOR GRIGNARD (1871-1935)
and
PAUL SABATIER (1854-1941)

Victor **Francois-Auguste-Grignard** was born in Cherbourg, France on May 6, 1871. In 1898 he began his research career studying alkylzinc compounds. His doctoral dissertation in 1901 described the preparation of alcohols, acids and hydrocarbons by means of reactions of organomagnesium compounds. In 1910 he became professor of chemistry at Nancy University and later (1919) held a similar position at Lyon University.

In 1912, Grignard shared the Nobel Prize for Chemistry;**"for the discovery of the so-called Grignard reagent, which in recent years has greatly advanced the progress of organic chemistry"**

He died in Lyon on December 13, 1935. He was married with a son and daughter.

Paul **Sabatier** was born in Carcassonne, France on November 5, 1854. He studied at the École Normale Supérieure and took his doctor's degree in 1880. He was appointed an associate professor at Toulouse University in 1882, a full professor in 1884 and the dean in 1905, retiring in 1930.

His main area of research activity was in catalytic organic synthesis. He also worked on foods and founded the basis for what became known as margarine. His work on organic synthesis was awarded with a co-share of the 1912 Nobel Prize for Chemistry:**" for his method of hydrogenating organic compounds in the presence of finely disintegrated metals whereby the progress of organic chemistry has been greatly advanced in recent years"**

He was later to demonstrate that nickel was a catalyst in hydorgenation. He retired in 1930 and died in Toulouse on August 14, 1941. He never married.

PHYSICS

NILS DALEN (1869-1937)

Nils **Gustaf Dalen** was born in Stenstorp, Sweden on November 30, 1869. The son of a farmer , he was educated at Goteborg and Zurich universities, receiving a doctorate in engineering. In 1906, he was chief engineer of the Gas Accumulator Company, which specialised in selling acetylene gas. Whilst managing director of the company,

Dalen invented Agamassan; this was a material that absorbed acetylene thereby making it possible to concentrate the gas without danger of explosion. In 1912, he was awarded the Nobel Prize for Physics; **"for his invention of automatic regulators for use in conjunction with gas accumulators for illuminating lighthouses and buoys"** .

This device turned off at dawn and on at dusk. This resulted in its' worldwide use for buoys and unmanned lighthouses. The following year, Dalen was blinded by an explosion whilst working on an experiment. This disaster however, didn't prevent him continuing with his research and he worked until he died. On December 9, 1937 in Stockholm, Sweden. He was married with two sons and a daughter. Unfortunately, his infirmity meant he was unable to attend the presentation of his award.

PHYSIOLOGY or MEDICINE

ALEXIS CARREL (1873-1944)

Alexis **Carrel** was born on June 28, 1873 at Sainte-Foy-les-Lyon, France. Carrel received his MD from Lyon University in 1900. In 1904 he left for Chicago University and later, at the Rockefeller Institute for Medical Research in New York. His work, on developing a method of suturing blood vessels, was rewarded with the 1912 Nobel Prize for Physiology or Medicine; **"in recognition of his work on vascular suture and the transplantation of blood vessels and organs"**

This work would later become the groundwork for further studies in organ transplants. During WW1, Carrel returned to his native France, where he worked developing the Carrel-Dakin method of treating wounds with antiseptic irrigations. The war over, Carrel returned to the Rockefeller Institute and stayed until the outbreak of WW2. Once again Carrel returned to France.

In 1941 he was appointed the director of the Foundation Francaise pour l'Étude des Problèmes Humains in Paris. His main writings were, *Man, the Unknown* (1935) and *Reflections on Life* (1952). Carrel died in Paris on November 5, 1944. During WW2, he headed the Vichy controlled scientific foundation. He was married without children

PEACE

ELIHU ROOT (1845-1937)

Elihu **Root** was born in Clinton, New York State on February 15, 1845. He studied law at New York University, obtained his degree in 1867, and joined a large practise of corporation lawyers. He later became involved in politics and met up with Theodore Roosevelt. As a result, he   became involved with the Republican Party. Under President McKinley, Root became secretary of war with a seat in the Cabinet (1899-1903), the latter years under Roosevelt.

Following the Spanish-American War, Root became involved in working out satisfactory arrangements for former Spanish areas now under US control. He turned his attention to events in Puerto Rico and was the author of the Foraker Act (1900), which paved the path for a civil government. In 1901, after a reshuffle, he created the Army War College. In 1904 he left the Cabinet but returned in 1905 when Roosevelt won a second term.

This time he was secretary of state. In this post he was instrumental in persuading Latin-American states to take part in the Second Hague Peace Conference. He negotiated several treaties whereby Japan agreed to control emigration into the US. In general he concluded treaties with some twenty countries, including the controversy between the US and Great Britain over North Atlantic fishery rights.   Root, in 1912, was awarded the Nobel prize for Peace, **"for his work in promoting world harmony"**

Root continued with his work but gradually fell into bad company when he sided with William Taft and the Republican Right, who openly advocated the US joining the Allies in WWI. As a US representative to the League of Nations, Root was part of the team that framed the terms of Permanent Court of International Justice. He died in New York City on February 7, 1937. He was married with two sons and a daughter.

1913

Mrs Emily Pankhurst, the suffragette leader, sent to prison for conspiracy to blow up Lloyd George's house • Reichstag passes bill to increase the size of Germany's army • First ship passes through the Panama Canal • Niels Bohr's model of the atom • Walter Sickert, *Ennui* • Alexander Scriabin, *Prometheus* • D.H.Lawrence, *Sons and Lovers* • Benjamin Britten and Albert Camus born • James Elroy Flecker, *The Golden Journey to Samarkand*.

LITERATURE

SIR RABINDRANATH TAGORE (1861-1941)

Rabindranath Tagore was born on May 7, 1861 in Calcutta, India. He was the son of Devendranath Tagore, famous as a Great Sage. The son of a wealthy father, he wasn't required to work for his daily bread. Wanting something to do, he turned his hand at writing. He gradually became accepted when, in 1890, he wrote, *Manasi.* It marked the beginning of a mature type of writing and one that reflected new types of Bengali poetry. It also reflected the current political and social problems including Indian independence. He was a most prolific writer and included plays within his sphere of writings.

Between 1902 and 1907, he suffered the loss of both his wife and daughter. He was left suffering from depressions and often unable to work. He later surfaced to write some of his best poetry ever. In 1910 he published, *Song Offering*. It won him instant fame and three years later, the 1913 Nobel Prize for Literature;**"because of his profoundly sensitive, fresh and beautiful verse, by which, with consummate skill, he has made his poetic thought, expressed in his own English words, a part of the literature of the West"**

During the last 25 years of his life, Tagore worked harder than ever before. He lectured in Europe, China, Japan and the Americas. He was knighted by a British administration in 1915. In 1919, following the Amritsar Murders of unarmed civilians, by the British Army under the command of General Dyer, a known sadist, Tagore returned his knighthood as way of protest.

Tagore was also a gifted musician who set many of his poems to music. In 1921 Tagore founded the Visva-Bharati University at Santiniketan.

He died in Calcutta on August 7, 1941. In 1913, Tagore married and he and his wife had two sons and a daughter.

CHEMISTRY

ALFRED WERNER (1866-1919)

Alfred Werner was born in Mulhouse, France on December 12, 1866. The son of a factory worker, he received his PhD from Zurich University in 1890, for his work on the oximes, a branch of organic nitrogen compounds.

This work led to an understanding of stereochemistry. His ongoing work on simplifying the classification of inorganic compounds brought him the 1913 Nobel Prize for Chemistry; **"in recognition of his work on the linkage of atoms in molecules by which he has thrown new light on earlier investigations and opened up new fields of research especially in inorganic chemistry"**

From 1893, he taught at Zurich University; he remained there until his death in Zurich on November 15, 1919. He was married with a son and daughter. He was known as an excellent speaker and a most sociable man who enjoyed playing billiards and chess.

PHYSICS

ONNES KAMERLINGH (1853-1926)

Onnes Heike Kamerlingh was born in Groningen, Holland on September 21, 1853. Between 1871 and 1873 he studied at Heidelberg University. He was awarded a doctorate by the University of Groningen and later became professor of experimental physics at Leiden University where he spent 40 years.

He worked investigating equations describing the states of matter and studying general thermodynamics. Kamerlingh, in 1913, was awarded the Nobel Prize for Physics; **"for his investigations on the properties of matter at low temperatures which led, inter alia to the production of liquid helium"**

He died in Leiden on February 21, 1926. He was married with a son. He was also the discoverer of the phenomena known as superconductivity. During WW1, although suffering from ill-health, he aided starving children from all over the world.

PHYSIOLOGY or MEDICINE

CHARLES RICHET (1850-1935)

Charles **Robert Richet** was born in Paris on August 26, 1850. His experimental work concentrated on what Richet termed, Anaphylaxis. This concerned a patient's reaction to a second injection of an antigen. Such reactions were often fatal. For this work Richet was awarded the 1913 Nobel Prize for Physiology or Medicine; **"in recognition of his work on anaphylaxis"** From 1887 and until 1927, when he retired, Richet was a professor at Paris University. His ongoing research included the area of asthma, hay fever and other allergic conditions. For a hobby he wrote plays, poetry and novels.

He died in Paris on December 4, 1935. He was married with five sons and two daughters. Richet was a keen student of aeronautics, spiritualism and was an ardent pacifist.

PEACE

HENRI-MARIE LAFONTAINE (1854-1943)

Henri-Marie **Lafontaine** was born in Brussels, Belgium on April 22, 1854. Following Brussels University, where he studied law, he was admitted to the Bar in 1877. He gradually built up a reputation in international law. As a result, he was appointed professor of international law at the Universite Nouvelle in Brussels. Two years later he turned to politics and was elected to the Belgian Senate as a Socialist.

He later became involved in the work of the International Peace Bureau and worked to bring about the Hague Peace Conferences of 1899 and 1907. He served as President of the Bureau from 1907 to 1943. Lafontaine was awarded the 1913 Nobel Prize for Peace; **"for his work as president of the International Peace Bureau"**

Following WW1, he dedicated the remainder of his life to fostering world peace. His world became devastated following the rise to power of Adolf Hitler and the Nazification of a willing German population. Lafontaine, married with no children, died in German occupied Brussels on May 14, 1943. He was a leading supporter of women's rights.

1914

Outbreak of First World War • US declares neutrality • Ernest Shackleton leads Antarctic expedition • Oskar Kokoschka, *The Vortex* • Vaughan Williams, *A London Symphony* and *Lark Ascending* • Charlie Chaplin, *Making a Living* • Robert Frost, *North of Boston*• Robert Tressell, *The Ragged Trousered Philanthropists* • Jonas Salk born • George Westinghouse dies.

LITERATURE

NOT AWARDED

CHEMISTRY

THEODORE RICHARDS (1868- 1928)

Theodore **William Richards** was born in Germantown, Pa, US on January 31, 1868. His father was a painter and his mother a poet. In 1885 he graduated and went on to take his doctorate at Harvard University, where in 1901, he was professor of chemistry. Richards spent his research years on the atomic weights of elements. He improved on previous methods of weighing and introduced quartz apparatus, a bottling device, as well as an instrument for measuring turbidity, known as a nephelometer.

In 1914 Richards was awarded the Nobel Prize for Chemistry; **"in recognition of his accurate determinations of the atomic weight of a large number of chemical elements"**

He is also known for his work in confirming the existence of isotopes. He died on April 2, 1928 at Cambridge, Mass. He was married with two sons and a daughter. When not working he enjoyed sketching and sailing.

PHYSICS

MAX LAUE (1879-1960)

Max Theodor Felix von Laue was born in Pfaffendorf, Germany on October 9, 1879. In 1912 he was professor of physics at Zurich University. There, his research into X-rays in crystals led him to be the first to discover that, by using a crystal, he was able to prove that X-rays are electromagnetic radiations, similar to light. It was for this work that Laue was awarded the 1914 Nobel Prize for Physics; **"for his discovery of the diffraction of X-rays by crystals"**

He supported Einstein's theory of relativity and researched the ongoing quantum theory. He was involved in researching the Compton effect; whereby wavelengths can change in light, under certain conditions. He survived WW1, at which time he was director of the Institute for Theoretical Physics at Berlin University, and WW2 during which time he kept his head down, and survived to become in 1951, director of the Max Planck Institute for Research in Physical Chemistry in Berlin (1951).

He died in Berlin on April 23, 1960. He was married with a son and daughter. His passion was speed and riding motorcycles or driving fast cars. He was 80 years old when, whilst driving on the autobahn, he crashed, killing a motor cyclist. His car rolled down the embankment. He was pulled from the wreckage but died soon after. It was his first accident.

PHYSIOLOGY or MEDICINE

ROBERT BARANY (1876-1936)

Robert Barany was born on April 22, 1876 in Vienna, Austria. His middle class Jewish parents, his mother was a scientist his father a farm manager, encouraged Robert to become a doctor. As a child he had TB, but he graduated in medicine in Vienna in 1900, and decided to specialise in matters concerning the inner ear. He worked in several German hospitals between 1900 and 1905 before returning to Vienna and his alma mater. He became an international expert on the working of the human ear and the diseases attached thereto.

Barany was the first to describe the condition known as 'hardening of the ear' more importantly, he created a method for dealing with it. In 1914 Barany received the Nobel Prize for Physiology or Medicine; **"for his work on the physiology and pathology of the vestibular apparatus"** .

During WW1, he was a surgeon with the Austrian Army. He was captured by the Russians who were most impressed by their prisoner's credentials and his Nobel Prize, so they released him, following the intervention of the King of Sweden.

Despite these credentials, he was refused a full professorship in Austria because he was a Jew. Instead, he accepted a full professorship at the University of Uppsala in Sweden. The rise of Nazism caused him much disquiet and as a result, he left his valuable collection of books and papers to the National Library in Jerusalem. He died in Uppsala on April 8, 1936. Married with two sons and a daughter, Barany was the first to study the brain in depth.

PEACE

NOT AWARDED

1915

Germans first use of gas on the Western Front • First Zeppelin attack on London • France and Great Britain borrow $500 million • Nurse Edith Cavell executed in Brussels by the Germans • Haig becomes British Commander-in-Chief in France and Flanders and the casualties increase • Einstein's, *Theory of Relativity* **• Marcel Duchamp,** *The Bride Stripped Bare by Her Bachelors Even* **- the first Dada painting • Rupert Brooke,** *1914 and Other Poems* **• Film,** *The Birth of a Nation* **• John Buchan,** *The Thirty-Nine Steps* **• Joseph Conrad,** *Victory,* **Ford Madox Ford,** *The Good Soldier* **• W. Somerset Maugham,** *Of Human Bondage* **• Saul Bellow and Arthur Miller born • James Keir Hardie dies.**

LITERATURE

ROMAIN ROLLAND (1866-1944)

Romain Rolland was born on January 29, 1866 in Clamecy, France. At the age of 14, Rolland was enrolled at the École Normale Supérieure in Paris. He found, what he later termed, a society in spiritual decay. He lost any religious beliefs he might have had and concentrated instead on the writings of Spinoza and Tolstoy. In 1895, he received a doctorate in art and went on to Italy and The École Français in Rome.

He was much affected by the 'Dreyfus Affair' and the exposure of anti-Semitism in the French Army. It prompted Rolland to seek formulas for world peace through Socialism. He was principally anti Fascist, and embraced Communism as the best means of combatting that evil force.

His writings sought to promote all his beliefs. By 1912 he was writing full time, having given up his teaching posts to so do. Following two cycles of short plays, he produced his best known novel, *Jean-Christophe* in ten volumes, written between 1904 and 1912. In 1915, his pamphlet, *Above the Battle'* was published. This called for France and Germany to respect truth and humanity throughout their WW1 struggle. In 1914 he moved to Switzerland, not to return to France until 1937. In 1915 Rolland was awarded the Nobel Prize for Literature; **"as a tribute to the lofty idealism of his literary production and to the sympathy and love of truth with which he has described different types of human beings"**

He later published a series of biographies including that of Beethoven and Tolstoy. In the 1920s he was in Asia, and wrote *Mahatma Gandhi* (1924). He had an ongoing correspondence with Schweitzer, Einstein, Bertrand Russell and Tagore and this correspondence was published after his death. Rolland died on December 30, 1944 in Vézelay, France. He was married twice but died without issue.

CHEMISTRY

RICHARD WILLSTATTER (1972-1942)

Richard Willstatter was born in Karlruhe, Germany on August 13, 1872, the son of Jewish parents. In 1894 he obtained his doctorate from Munich University, for his work on the structure of cocaine. In 1905, he was professor of chemistry at Zurich University and working on the properties of chlorophyll. Between 1912 and 1916, Willstatter was professor of chemistry at Berlin University and director of the Kaiser Wilhelm Institute. In 1915, he was awarded the Nobel Prize for Chemistry; **"for his researches on plant pigments, especially chlorophyll"**

During WW1 he invented a gas mask for the German army. During the 1920s, his researches showed that enzymes are chemical substances and biological organisms. In 1924, while working in Munich, he experienced such a marked increase in anti-Semitism that he left Germany for Switzerland. He never returned; dying from a heart attack in Locarno on August 3, 1942.

He was married with a son and daughter. He is credited with his work changing the course of research in organic chemistry.

PHYSICS

WILLIAM HENRY BRAGG (1862-1942)
and
WILLIAM L. BRAGG (1890-1971)

"For their services in the analysis of crystal structure by means of X-rays"

William Henry Bragg was born in Wigton, Cumberland, England on July 2, 1862. His father's family were farmers and seamen whilst his mother was the only daughter of the local vicar. His mother died when he was seven and thereafter he went to live with two of his father's brothers, who had a chemist shop in Market Harborough. There, William attended the old grammar school that still stands in the centre of the town. In 1875, his father sent him to far off Isle of Man and King William College. A religious anti-Catholic school full of hellfire and damnation. It would however cause him to later observe, ' From religion comes a man's purpose; from science his power to achieve it.'

In 1882 he was at Trinity College, Cambridge, from where he obtained his degree and third place in the Mathematical Tripos. Then came a professorship at Adelaide University in Australia. His time there was spent lecturing and researching crystal structures. Back in England by 1912, he worked on alpha, beta and gamma rays concluding that both gamma rays and X-rays have particle-like properties. It was at this time that William began working with his son, William Lawrence. The son was studying physics at Cambridge and the twosome began applying X-rays to the study of crystal structure. The result was that both father and son jointly received the 1915 Nobel Prize for Physics.

The father, during WW1, worked on anti-submarine devices. He established a school for crystallographic research at University College, London, before becoming, director of the Royal Institution as well as of the Davy Faraday Research Laboratory in London. Bragg will always be remembered for the X-ray spectrometer, an invention that allowed physicists to measure exact X-ray wavelengths. Between 1935 and 1940, he was president of the Royal Society but found time to write science books for children and proud to have been knighted in 1920.

He died in London, during a German air raid, on March 12, 1942. He was married with a son who shared the Nobel Prize with him.

William Lawrence Bragg was born in Adelaide, South Australia, on March 31, 1890, whilst his father was a professor at the university. Following an education at St. Peter's College, Adelaide and Adelaide University he travelled, in 1909, to England and Trinity College, Cambridge. William assisted his father in his research of crystals and their relationship to X-rays. It was the son who came up with what became known as, the Bragg equation, following a series of ingenious and original experiments.

As a result he shared, with his father, the 1915 Nobel Prize for Physics. Following WW1 Bragg was professor of physics at Manchester University. In 1921, he was elected a Fellow of the Royal

Society. He later became Cavendish Professor of Experimental Physics at Cambridge University. Here he founded a school to research metals, alloys and proteins. He was knighted in 1940 and became well known to radio, and later, television audiences as a popular lecturer. Married with two sons and two daughters, in 1954 he became director of the Royal Institution in London. He retired in 1965, although he kept in touch with developments in his field, until his death in Ipswich, Suffolk, on July 1, 1971.

PHYSIOLOGY or MEDICINE

NOT AWARDED

PEACE

NOT AWARDED

1916

Roger Casement executed • Easter Rebellion in Dublin • Italy declares war on Germany • First tanks in action • Woodrow Wilson re-elected US president • plastic surgery for war wounded begins • Claude Monet, *Water Lilies* • Jazz sweeps US • Robert Graves *Over the Brazier* • Film, *Intolerance* • John Buchan, *Greenmantle* • James Joyce, *A Portrait of the Artist as a Young Man* •Harold Wilson and Yehudi Menuhin born • Henry James and Sholem Aleichem die.

LITERATURE

VERNER von HEIDENSTAM (1859-1940)

Carl Gustaf Verner von Heidenstam was born in Olshammar, Sweden on July 6th 1859. A sickly child, he became a sickly teenager and spent most of his former years in Mediterranean countries. His first book of poems, *Pilgrimage and Wander Years* was published in 1888. His stories of fables in Southern Europe became most popular with the Swedish public. There followed many volumes of historical fiction, as well as further books on classical poetry. In 1916 he was awarded the Nobel Prize for Literature; **"in recognition of his significance as the leading representative of a new ear in our literature"**

Thereafter he wrote nothing . By the time he was awarded the Nobel Prize he had already outlived his popularity. He died in Ovralid, Sweden on May 20th 1940. Although he had three wives he died without having children. At various time he was a Bhuddist, a Christian, a Muslim and an Atheist. His collected works in 23 volumes was published in 1943-5.

CHEMISTRY

NOT AWARDED

PHYSICS

NOT AWARDED

PHYSIOLOGY or MEDICINE

NOT AWARDED

PEACE

NOT AWARDED

1917

US declares war on Axis Powers • Bolshevist Revolution in Russia • The Balfour Declaration promises a Jewish Homeland in Palestine • Bobbed hair sweeps Britain and US • Carl Jung, *The Unconscious* • Picasso designs set for Diaghilev's ballet, *Parade* • Pulitzer Prize introduced • Film; *The Cure, Easy Street,* • W.B.Yeats, *The Wild Swans at Coole* • P.G.Wodehouse, *Uneasy Money* • Alec Waugh, *The Loom of Youth* • John Kennedy born • Emile Durkheim, Edgar Degas, Sarah Aaronson, Auguste Rodin and Elizabeth Garrett Anderson die.

LITERATURE

KARL GJELLERUP (1857-1919)
and
HENRIK PONTOPPIDAN (1857-1943)

Karl Adolph Gjellerup was born in Roholte, Denmark on June 2, 1857. He was the son of the local parson and, as such decided, at an early age, to study theology. Then came an understanding of the theories of Charles Darwin and the radical ideas of the Danish Jew, Georg Brandes and Gjellerup began thinking of himself as an atheist. His first book, published in1878, was, *An Idealist: A description of Epignus.* He followed, in 1882 with, *TheTeutons' Apprentice.* His novels reflected the narrow world of the Danish middle-classes.

He toyed with various religions before settling on Buddhism. He wrote, *Minna* in 1889, about contemporary Germany and in 1906 an exotic novel set in India called, *The Pilgrim Kamanita*. In 1917 he shared the Nobel Prize for Literature; **"for his varied and rich poetry, which is inspired by lofty ideals"**

He died two years later in Klotzsche, Germany, on October 11, 1919. He never married and retired on a poet's pension issued by Denmark in 1889. He was later considered the dullest of writers.

Henrik Pontoppidan was born in Fredericia, Denmark, on July 24, 1857. There were remarkable similarities between the two Nobel winning Danes. They both had fathers who were clergymen, they both began by studying for the church and they both became atheists. In 1873 he began studying engineering. Six years later he was a teacher and writing in his spare time. As early as 1881 he was writing fulltime; following publication of , *Staekkede Vinger* a book of short stories that found favour.

Pontoppidan wrote many novels and short stories and although his style didn't suit everyone; being considered cold and aloof, he prospered. His tales told of everyday life in Danish life, both town and country. His five volume novel cycle, *The Empire of Death*, written between 1912 and 1918, is probably his most famous, albeit *Man's Heaven* (1927) describes neutral Denmark during WW1 and is a critic of materialism. Between 1933 and 1940, he published four volumes of his memoirs. In 1917 he shared the Nobel Prize for Literature; **"for his authentic descriptions of present-day life in Denmark"**

At the time of his death he was living in Ordrup, part of German Occupied Denmark. He died on August 21, 1943 having had two wives and no children. His collected works covers 40 volumes.

CHEMISTRY

NOT AWARDED

PHYSICS

CHARLES BARKLA (1877-1944)

Charles Glover Barkla was born in Widnes, Lancashire, England on June 7, 1877. He was educated at Cambridge (Trinity and Kings) and in 1902 was teaching at Liverpool University. His constant research was concentrated on X-rays. He was able to polarize X-rays and prove that X-rays are transverse waves and therefore like other electromagnetic radiations. For this work Barkla was awarded the 1917 Nobel Prize for Physics.; **"for his discovery of the characteristic Röntgen radiation of the elements"**

He became a professor of natural philosophy at Edinburgh and died in that city on October 23, 1944. He was married with two sons and a daughter.

One of his sons was killed whilst serving in the RAF during WW2. He enjoyed singing and was a member of the Kings College Chapel Choir.

PHYSIOLOGY or MEDICINE

NOT AWARDED

PEACE

INTERNATIONAL COMMITTEE OF THE RED CROSS

The purpose of the Red Cross in wartime is to ensure that all sides care for the war wounded and treat, in a humane fashion, prisoners-of-war. During WW1 this was largely recognised by both the Allied countries and Axis countries (unlike WW2 when the Germans refused to recognise the Red Cross unless it suited their purpose for propaganda). The international committee is an independent council of 25 Swiss citizens with their HQ in Geneva.

1918

World War ends • Women over 30 allowed to vote in Britain • New York gets traffic lights • Influenza epidemic begins • Bela Bartok opera, *Bluebeard's Castle* • Luigi Pirandello, *Six Characters in Search of an Author* • Rebecca West, *The Return of the Soldier* • Leonard Bernstein born • Claude Debussy dies.

LITERATURE

NOT AWARDED

CHEMISTRY

FRITZ HABER (1868-1934)

Fritz Haber was born in Breslau, Germany on December 9, 1868, the son of a Jewish chemical merchant. Following a university education in Berlin, Heidelberg and Zurich, Fritz joined the family firm. He didn't stay long; he preferred an academic career. He took up chemical research at Jena University but found it too confining. During the early part of the 20th century, the world had a continuing need for nitrogen fertilizer, to offset a world shortage of food.

Haber, between 1907 and 1909, invented the process of synthesis of ammonia that guaranteed an increase of nitrogen fertilizer for the world at large. He passed on his invention to a large company and concentrated on research. In 1911, he was head of the Kaiser Wilhelm Institute for Physical Chemistry in Berlin.

During WW1, he played a leading part in Germany's chemical production and in the development of mustard gas as an instrument of war. His view, as a fervent German patriot, was that as the Allies also had the gas it was a legitimate weapon to use. He never mentioned that it was the Germans, who, on April 22, 1915, first made use of gas; perhaps he didn't know.

Post-war, Germany's requirement to make reparations to the Allies disturbed Haber. He dreamed up the idea of extracting gold from seawater. Surprisingly he succeeded. However, the amounts were small and the enterprise was not considered productive, albeit positive gains were made in scientific knowledge. In 1918, Haber received the Nobel Prize Chemistry; **"for the synthesis of ammonia from its elements"** The Haber Institute became the world's leading centre for research into physical chemistry. Haber was a world renowned figure who played an important role in co-relating world needs in industry. He was made a Privy Counsellor of Germany. Then 1933 arrived and Hitler took over everything. Haber, who had never bothered himself with things Jewish, was astonished to be called,'Jew Haber'.

With his authority and influence at a low ebb and his previous work for the fatherland ignored, he resigned and went to England. Now working in Cambridge, he took some time off to go on holiday. On his way to Italy, he suffered a heart attack in Basle, Switzerland, and died there on January 29, 1934. He was married twice with two sons and a daughter.

PHYSICS

MAX PLANCK (1858-1947)

Max Karl Ernst Ludwig Planck was born in Kiel, Germany on April 3, 1858. His father was a university professor. He was educated at the Maximilian Gymnasium in Munich and chose to study science rather than his first love, music. He achieved his doctorate in 1879, his thesis being on the second law of thermodynamics.

In 1900, Planck formulated the correct mathematical description of thermal radiation, from a perfect absorber, and demonstrated that the formulation needed a discontinuous process of emission, involving discrete quantities of energy. For this work Planck was awarded the 1918 Nobel Prize for Physics; **"in recognition of the services he rendered to the advancement of Physics by his discovery of energy quanta"**

In 1930 he was president of the Kaiser Wilhelm Society in Berlin. For a short time Planck was the principle physicist that Hitler turned to in an effort to create an atomic bomb. Planck later became disillusioned with Nazism, more so when one of his sons, Erwin, was executed for being involved with the July 1944 plot against Hitler's life. Planck died in Göttingen, Germany on October 4, 1947. He was married twice and had three sons and two daughters. Following the introduction of Einstein's theory of relativity, Planck investigated that theory further.

PHYSIOLOGY or MEDICINE

NOT AWARDED

PEACE

NOT AWARDED

1919

The Versailles Peace Conference • Mussolini starts Italian Fascist Party • Nancy Astor first British woman MP • First successful helicopter flight • motor scooter invented • The Bauhaus founded by Gropus in Weimar • Rosa Luxemburg murdered in Berlin • Manuel de Falla, *Three Cornered Hat* • Siegfried Sassoon, *War Poems* • A.P. Herbert, *The Secret Battle* • Somerset Maugham, *The Moon and Sixpence* • Film, *The Cabinet of Dr Caligan* • Margot Fonteyn born • Theodore Roosevelt and Pierre Auguste Renoir die.

LITERATURE

CARL SPITTELER (1845-1924)

Carl Spitteler was born in Liestal, Switzerland on April 24, 1845. He worked for eight years as a private tutor in Russia and Finland. Whilst abroad, he wrote a great poetic work, *Prometheus and Epimetheus* (1881). He returned to Switzerland and made a living, teaching and in journalism. His next great work was, *The Olympic Spring* (1910). He found a widely expressive power that earned him fame. He was awarded the 1919 Nobel Prize for Literature; **"in special appreciation of his epic, *Olympian Spring"***

Spitteler continued writing but he became ill and, on December 29, 1924 he died, whilst recuperating in Lucern, Switzerland.

He was married with two daughters. Spitteler's work is notable for its blend of idealistic hope for the individual and a pessimistic view of the world as a whole.

CHEMISTRY

NOT AWARDED

PHYSICS

JOHANNES STARK (1874-1957)

Johannes Stark was born in Schickenhof, Germany on April 15, 1874. Following graduation in physics, he became, in 1900, a lecturer at Göttingen University. His research work concerned electricity, and in 1913 he discovered that an electric field would cause splitting of the lines in the spectrum of light, emitted by a luminous substance. This phenomenon became known at the 'Stark Effect. Stark was awarded the 1919 Nobel Prize for Physics; **for his discovery of the Doppler effect in canal rays and the splitting of spectral lines in electric fields"**

Various university posts came and went until 1933, when Hitler came to power and Stark embraced Hitler and Nazism. He became an active anti-Semite and worked on the German nuclear bomb project. His post war sentence, by the Allies, of four years in prison, testifies to his admiration of the evil cause.

Stark died in Traustein, Germany on June 21, 1957. He was married with five children. He constantly made furious attacks on Einstein, but that didn't stop him stealing Einstein's ideas for his work that resulted in the Stark Law which states that, ' each molecule involved with a photo chemical reaction absorbs only one quantum of the radiation that causes the reaction'

PHYSIOLOGY or MEDICINE

JULES BORDET (1870-1961)

Jean-Baptiste-Vincent Jules Bordet was born on June 13, 1870 in Soignies, Belgium. His ongoing research was on the destruction of bacteria and red corpuscles in blood serum, discovered whilst working at the Pasteur Institute in Paris (1894-1901). In 1895, he discovered that two components of serum are responsible for the rupture of bacterial cell walls; one is a heat-stable antibody, found only in animals, already immune to the bacterium.

The other, is a heat sensitive substance that is found in all animals, and is now known to be a compliment. Three years later, Bordet discovered that foreign red corpuscles were also ruptured in blood serum. For this work Bordet was awarded the 1919 Nobel Prize for Physiology or Medicine; **"for his discoveries relating to immunity"**

In Brussels, he directed the Pasteur Institute of Brabant (1901-1940). He continued with his research into immunology and achieved considerable success in the fight against typhoid, syphilis and TB. Married with two daughters and a son, he died in Brussels on April 6, 1961.

PEACE

WOODROW WILSON (1856-1924)

Thomas **Woodrow Wilson** was born in Staunton, Va, USA on December 28, 1856. He was the son of a parson and educated at the forerunner of Princeton College, in 1875. He then studied law at Virginia University. He attempted a legal practise but it failed. He went to John Hopkins University and there he studied government and history and received a doctorate. He accepted a teaching post at Bryn Mawr College, as a associate professor in history and political economy. In 1890 he was doing the same job at Princeton as a full professor. In 1910 the Democrats offered him the nomination to be elected governor of New Jersey. He won and in 1912 was the Democratic nomination for the presidency.

In the White House he initiated major legislation. He was responsible for foreign policy and he pursued an isolationist policy, that allowed the US to keep out of WW1, whilst at the same time equipping the Allies, so creating great profits for the US armament industries. Despite the Germans sinking the British unarmed liner, 'Lusitania', with the loss of over 1,000 people, including 128 Americans, Wilson still wouldn't get involved. In 1916 he was re-elected and his general policies continued.

Because of renewed German attacks on neutral shipping, Wilson on April 2, 1917 asked Congress to declare war on Germany. This was passed by Congress and the US spent the next 18 months fighting on the Allied side. The war over, Wilson decided to attend the peace conferences that followed. He achieved success at the conference for his proposal for a League of Nations and terms for the later held Versailles Treaty. He was awarded the 1919 Nobel Prize for Peace; **"for his work in the founding of the League of Nations"**

He died on February 3, 1924 He was married twice and had three daughters.

1920

League of Nations founded • US Prohibition• Woman given the vote in US • John Thompson invents the sub-machine gun • Jazz goes universal • Spectators at Dadaist exhibition in Cologne smash exhibits• Edith Wharton, *The Age of Innocence* • D.H.Lawrence, *Women in Love* • Sinclair Lewis, *Main Street* • Amedo Modigliani dies.

LITERATURE

KNUT HAMSUN (1859-1952)

Knut Hamsun was born Knut Pederson on August 4, 1859 at Lom, Norway. He came from peasant stock and spent most of his childhood in the remote Lofoten Islands. As a result, he had little formal education. He was a shoemaker's apprentice when, at 19, he started writing. He then spent ten years; often working at casual labouring. In 1888 he took off for the US, where he worked as a tramcar conductor in Chicago and as a farmhand in North Dakota. In 1890 he published, *Sult*; a first novel. It had an electrifying effect on readers and other authors alike.

It was a radical departure of the realism of the usual Norwegian novel, in its place was a pacey, lyrical and impulsive style. He was a success and gave a series of lectures criticising establishment writers such as Ibsen and Tolstoy. His novels flowed, often influenced by Nietzsche and Strindberg. In *Markens grode* (1917) he states a back-to-nature philosophy that is a warning of things to come. As a result in 1920 Hamsun was awarded the Nobel Prize for Literature; **"for his monumental work, *Growth of the Soil"***

He had an antipathy to modern Western culture and found a certain kinship with Hitler's philosophy. He supported Germany during their occupation of Norway but would have no truck with their anti-Jewish policies. At the end of the war Hamsun was declared a traitor and spent some time in prison; before charges were dropped because of his great age. He died in poverty on February 19, 1952 whilst living quietly near Grimstad, Norway.

Following his death came a revival of his work. Many of his books received wide translations and he came to influence such writers as, Gorky, Mann and Bashevis Singer (qv), who regarded Hamsun as a master of the novel. He was married twice with three daughters and two sons.

CHEMISTRY

WALTER NERNST (1864-1941)

Walther Hermann Nernst was born in Briesen, Germany on June 25, 1864. His father was a judge. He received a triple university education that embraced, Zurich, Graz and Wurzburg. His research was in the field of modern physical chemistry and concerned the theory of galvanic cells, the thermodynamics of chemical equilibrium, the properties of vapours at both high and low temperatures as well as the understanding of photochemistry.

His formulation of the third law of thermodynamics resulted in his being awarded the 1920 Nobel Prize for Chemistry; **"in recognition of his work in thermochemistry"**

He later became interested in applied science and astrophysical theories. He died on November 18, 1941 in Muskau, Germany. He was married with three sons and two daughters.

PHYSICS

CHARLES GUILLAUME (1861-1938)

Charles Edouard Guillaume was born in Fleurier on February 15, 1861. Following a varied education, Guillaume joined the French International Bureau of Weights and Measures. He became the director in 1915 and spent exhaustive investigations of the mercury thermometer and of the volume of the litre. The litre he found was not 1,000,000 cubic centimetres, as accepted, but rather 1,000,028 cc.

He spent much time developing invar and elinvar. Invar's low coefficient of expansion and elinvar's low coefficient of elasticity, together with low cost, resulted in their wide use in scientific instruments. For his discovery of invar or nickel steel alloy, Guillaume received the 1920 Nobel Prize for Physics; **"in recognition of the service he has rendered to precision measurements in Physics by his discovery of anomalies in nickel steel alloys"**

Married with three children, he died in Sévres, France on June 13, 1938.

PHYSIOLOGY or MEDICINE

AUGUST KROGH (1874-1949)

Schack August Steenberg Krogh was born in Grena, Denmark on November 15, 1874. He studied zoology at Copenhagen University and researched the capillaries or small blood vessels in humans. He later found that the capillaries contract or dilate in proportion to the tissue's requirement for blood; and that active muscles have a greater number of open capillaries than do those who are less active.

For this work Krogh was awarded the 1920 Nobel Prize for Physiology or Medicine.; **"for his discovery of the capillary motor regulating mechanism"** Earlier, in 1906, he received an award from the Vienna Academy of Science for his theories as described in his book, *Mechanism of Gas Exchange in Lungs.* He wrote much and *The Anatomy and Physiology of Capillaries* (1922) is still a source.

He died in Copenhagen on September 13, 1949. He was married with two daughters and a son.

PEACE

LÉON BOURGEOIS (1851-1925)

Léon- Victor Auguste Bourgeois was born in Paris on May 21, 1851. Following the receipt of a law degree, Bourgeois decided upon the civil service and entered in 1876. He received rapid advancement but decided to turn to politics. In 1888, he was elected to the National Assembly, becoming prime minister in 1895. He lasted five months. He later became head of the Radical-Socialist Party and served as president of the Senate 1920-23. In 1899 he was the French delegate to the Hague Conference and argued for European co-operation.

In 1919 he became France's delegate to the League of Nations, becoming its' most popular champion. He became a leading spokesman for the theory of solidarism; that stressed the quasi contractual nature of society and the essential obligations owed to it. He was awarded the 1920 Nobel Peace Prize; **"for his work with the League of Nations"**

He died of uranic poisoning at Château d'Oger, France on September 29, 1925. He was given a public funeral. He never married.

1921

President Harding rules out US role in League of Nations • Germany declares state of economic emergency • Britain signs peace treaty with Ireland • BBC founded • Lytton Strachey, *Queen Victoria* • Eugene O'Neil, *The Emperor Jones* • Camille Saint-Saens and Engelbert Humperdinck die.

LITERATURE

ANATOLE FRANCE (1844-1924)

Jacques-Anatole-Francois Thibault was born in Paris on April 16, 1844. Surrounded by books from the time he could crawl around his father's bookshop, he decided, at an early stage in his life, to dedicate his life to literature. He wrote poetry and novels and gradually found much fame and some fortune. In 1888, came his second marriage and his new wife, Madame Arman de Caillavet filled him with a new inspiration.

This is marked by, *L'Histoire contemporaine.* (1897-1901), a four volume work, inspired by his support of Alfred Dreyfus, the French-Jewish army officer, falsely convicted of treason. Further novels brought further exposes of French life that Anatole France found unacceptable in a modern society. In 1921 he was awarded the Nobel Prize for Literature; **"in recognition of his brilliant literary achievements, characterized as they are by a nobility of style, a profound human sympathy, grace, and a true Gallic temperament"**

He wrote much and influenced a whole generation of 20th century writers. He died on October 12, 1924 at Saint-Cyr-sur-Loire. He was married three times and had a daughter. One scholar refers to his work, ' he offers an interesting case of fame followed by abrupt decline' His collected works in 25 volumes were published in 1925-35. His character of professor Bergeret is his most famous creation.

CHEMISTRY

FREDERICK SODDY (1877-1956)

Frederick Soddy was born in Eastbourne, England on September 2, 1877. He was educated at Oxford University and later worked under Sir Ernest Rutherford at McGill University, Montreal. He became a professor of chemistry at Oxford University (1919-36). His field of research was the theory of isotopes and radioactive substances. Soddy was among the first to realise that, certain elements might exist in forms, that differ in atomic weight, while being indistinguishable and inseparable chemically.

These he called isotopes. Soddy, in 1921, received the Nobel Prize for Chemistry; **"for his contributions to our knowledge of the chemistry of radioactive substances, and his investigations into the origin and nature of isotopes"**

He spent his later years lecturing. He was highly critical of the inability of the world's economic systems to make full use of scientific and technological advances. He died in Brighton, Sussex, on September 22, 1956. He was married with three children.

In 1936 Soddy was most outspoken regarding social uses. He blamed scientists for their disregard for the social consequences of their work, including radioactivity.

PHYSICS

ALBERT EINSTEIN (1879-1955)

Albert Einstein was born in Ulm, Germany on March 14, 1879. He attended the local school and, whilst still a teenager, his headmaster told Einstein's father, who had gone to see the teacher to enquire what sort of work his son might train for; only to be told, 'It doesn't matter, Albert will never make a success of anything'!

In the event, Einstein earned a doctorate at the Polytechnic Academy in Zurich, when aged 26, and at the same time published four research papers, each containing a great discovery in physics. International fame came to Einstein when his theory of relativity was verified. That was in 1919. He once explained his theory as follows; "Sit on a hot stove for a minute and it seems like an hour, sit with a pretty girl for an hour and it seems like a minute–that's relativity" In 1921 he was awarded the Nobel Prize for Physics; **"for his services to Theoretical Physics, and especially for his discovery of the law of the photoelectric effect"**

Subsequently, the name of Einstein has passed into legend. Following the rise of Hitler and the crushing of everything Jewish, Einstein left for the US becoming a citizen in 1940. He continued with his research, particularly the interpretation of the quantum theory. Meanwhile, back in Ulm, the people there held a special ceremony in honour of their most famous son. and burned his books. They also burned the synagogue and murdered 400 hundred of the 500 Jews living there.

In the US, Einstein was one of three Jewish physicists; the other two were Leo Szilard and Eugene Wigner (qv), who persuaded President Roosevelt that the threat of Germany creating an atomic bomb was most real. The result was the Manhattan Project and the building of the world's first atomic bomb. However once Einstein, and others, could confirm that the race had been won and that Germany didn't pose an atomic threat, they urged the president not to drop the bomb on the Japanese. The letter arrived the day Roosevelt died. His successor, Truman, ignored its' contents, took a pragmatic view as to probable allied casualties if mainland Japan was to be invaded, and two atomic bombs later, World War Two came to an end. Einstein was now worried about the real possibility of WW3.

He urged the outlawing of the bomb, refused to testify before McCarthy and his Committee on Un-American Activities and urged his fellow scientists to take the same view. The right wing authorities found it impossible to pursue the man the world recognised as the greatest scientist ever, so they quietly left him to his continuing research.

Einstein, who held several academic positions and was awarded many honours from all over the world, was asked by *The New Statesman*, in an interview on April 16, 1955, about his work on the bomb, Einstein replied; 'If only had I known, I would have become a watchmaker'. He died two days later at Princeton, NJ. He was married with two sons. Except for the years 1911 and 1915, Einstein was nominated for the Nobel Prize every year from 1910-1922.

In July 1998 the long legal battle concerning Einstein's lakeside summer house at Caputh, near Berlin, was resolved in favour of his heirs. He once described the place as ' my paradise' as he walked in the surrounding pinewoods with such luminaries as Max Planck and Otto Hahn. The court verdict means the property will be restored and not become a mass tourist centre.

PHYSIOLOGY or MEDICINE

NOT AWARDED

"Sit on a hot stove for a minute and it seems like an hour, sit with a pretty girl for an hour and it seems like a minute–that's relativity"

ALBERT EINSTEIN (1879-1955)

PEACE

KARL BRANTING (1860-1925)
and
CHRISTIAN LANGE (1869-)

Karl Hjalmar Branting was born in Stockholm, Sweden on November 23, 1860. He studied science in Stockholm and Uppsala but at the age of 26 threw it up to become editor of the radical newspaper, *Tiden*. He then became the editor of the *Social-Demokraten* and a founder of the Social Democratic Party. He entered parliament in 1896, as the party's only MP. The party grew and, in 1907 Branting became its' leader. He enthused the working classes to demand equalities in life generally, and political suffrage in particular. In 1917, there was a Liberal-Socialist coalition and Branting became minister of finance. In 1918 Sweden was swept by a series of democratic reforms.

An ardent advocate of Swedish neutrality during WW1, he became a delegate to the Peace Conference in Paris in 1919. He was the first Swedish representative to the League of Nations and chairman of the Berne conference of the Second Socialist International (1919). For his work in the field of international diplomacy, between 1900 and 1920, Branting co-shared the 1921 Nobel Peace Prize; **"in recognition of his conciliatory international diplomacy in the first two decades of the 20th century"**

In March 1920, he became Sweden's first Socialist prime minister. He lost in the election held a few months later; won it again in September 1921 and remained in office until April 1923. He died in Stockholm on February 24, 1925. He never married and is known as the father of socialism in Sweden.

Christian Louis Lange was born in Stavanger, Norway, on September 17, 1869. He graduated in languages from Oslo University in 1893 and received a doctorate, for his thesis on the history of internationalism. In 1919, he was secretary to the Nobel Committee in Oslo (1900-1909) and responsible for establishing the Nobel Institute library.

In 1907, he was a delegate to the second peace conference at the Hague and, in 1909, he was secretary - general of the Inter Parliamentary Union. As Norwegian delegate, to the League of Nations specialising in disarmament, he co-shared the 1921 Nobel Peace Prize; **"his work with the Inter-Parliamentary Union"**

In 1932, he received the coveted Grotius Medal from the Netherlands.

He died in Oslo on December 12 1938. He was married twice with five children.

1922

Mussolini's march on Rome • British takeover Palestine Mandate • Permanent Court of Justice opens at The Hague • First insulin injection •Tutankhamen's tomb discovered • Ludwig Wittgenstein, *Tractatus Logico-Philosophicus* • Marc Chagall, *Dead Souls* • The 'cocktail' appears • A.E.Housman, *Last Poems* • 'Birth Control' advocated by Marie Stopes • James Joyce, *Ulysses* • Marcel Proust dies.

LITERATURE

JACINTO y MARTINEZ BENAVENTE (1866-1954)

Jacinto y Martinez Benavente was born in Madrid, Spain on August 12, 1866. His father was a doctor. Jacinto used his pen as a means of social criticism. He wrote over a 150 plays and was Spain's leading dramatist for many years. His output was most varied; political, anti-monarchist with a lot of comedy.

It is said his own favourite was, *Senora Ama* (1908) set in Castile. He was awarded the 1922 Nobel Prize for Literature; **"for the happy manner in which he has continued the illustrious traditions of the Spanish drama"**

He continued writing throughout the Civil War and during this time he was kept under house arrest, by Franco's fascists. In 1941 he re-established himself with, *Lo increible.* He died in Madrid on July 14, 1954. His collected plays in 10 volumes was published in 1946 to 1955. He never married.

CHEMISTRY

FRANCIS ASTON (1877-1945)

Francis William Aston was born in Harborne, Birmingham, England on September 1, 1877. Aston trained as a chemist but decided instead to concentrate on X-rays and study the creation of X-rays by the flow of current through a gas-filled tube (1903). In 1910 he became assistant to J.J.Thomson at Cambridge. At that time, Thomson was investigating positively charged rays emanating from gaseous discharges.

Following WW1, he created a new type of positive ray apparatus which he called 'a mass spectrograph'. It showed that not only neon but also many other elements are mixtures of isotopes. His achievement is put into perspective when considering that he discovered 212 of the 287 naturally occurring nuclides. For this work Aston was awarded the 1922 Nobel Prize for Chemistry; **"for his discovery, by means of his mass spectrograph, of isotopes, in a large number of non-radioactive elements, and for his enunciation of the whole-number rule"**

His passion was piano playing and skiing. He died in Cambridge, England on November 20, 1945. He never married.

PHYSICS

NIELS BOHR (1885-1962)

Niels Henrik David Bohr was born in Copenhagen, Denmark on October 7, 1885. He was the son of a Gentile father and Jewish mother, At school he competed academically against his younger brother, Harald, and lost. Harald went on to become a leading mathematician. However, at Copenhagen University Niels was found to be most perceptive and his first research project resulted in a gold medal from the Royal Danish Academy of Sciences. In 1911 he gained his doctorate and went to England to join Ernest Rutherford, the man who discovered the workings of the atomic nucleus.

Niels Bohr took Rutherford's work a stage further and applied the quantum theory. Rutherford, for his part, found it difficult to appreciate the logic of Bohr's assertions. He was eventually persuaded and the concept of the 'Rutherford-Bohr atom' of nuclear physics was established. Bohr continued with his work on atomic structure, which earned him the 1922 Nobel Prize for Physics; **"for his services in the investigation of the structure of atoms and of the radiation emanating from them"**

His thinking was often at odds with other scientists. Einstein, his friend for over 30 years, claimed Bohr was constantly departing from the norm and it was a matter of deep sorrow to both men that they could not come to terms with each other. Only very recently, long after the death of both of them, has Bohr's view been confirmed. By the mid 1930s the main focus of scientific interest was nuclear physics, and here Bohr played a major part with his appreciation of nuclear fission.

In September 1943, Bohr was tipped off that the Germans was about to arrest him and his family. That night they escaped the Germans by travelling to Malmo, in neutral Sweden, in an old fishing boat. Now safe in Sweden, Bohr successfully persuaded the King to offer an unconditional sanctuary to all the Jews of Denmark. Desperately wanted by the Allies to work on the Manhattan Project, the making of the atom bomb, Bohr was flown to England the following month, laying in the bomb rack of an unarmed RAF Mosquito fighter/bomber. Bohr, who was convinced that the uranium atom split by Hahn and Strassman in 1938 was the rareisotope U-235, was of major importance to the overall success of the project.

After Hiroshima, Bohr saw the atom bomb as a threat to the whole of mankind and spent the rest of his life working for peace. However, it didn't stop him seeing a positive use for atomic energy and he encouraged its development for use as a source of energy. In 1957, he was awarded the first 'Atoms for Peace' prize by the Ford Foundation. He was appointed director of the Institute of Theoretical Physics in Copenhagen in 1920 and retained it until his death on November 18, 1962 in Copenhagen.

He wrote much including, *Atomic Physics and Human Knowledge* (1958) in this book he gives an account of his discussions with Albert Einstein on quantum theory over a period of twenty years. It is worth noting that nearly all the world's leading theoretical physicists of the 1920s and 30s spent some time at the Niels Bohr Institute for Theoretical Physics. He was married with six sons. His son Aage received the Nobel Prize for Physics in 1975.

PHYSIOLOGY or MEDICINE

ARCHIBALD HILL (1886-1977)
and
OTTO MEYERHOF (1884-1951)

Archibald Vivian Hill was born in Bristol, England on September 26, 1886. Whilst at Cambridge University between 1911 and 1914 he began his researches in physiological thermodynamics of muscle and nerve tissue. Using muscles in frogs, he was able to demonstrate that oxygen is needed only for the recovery, not the contractile, phase of muscular activity.

This lay the foundation for the discovery of the series of biochemical reactions carried out in muscle cells that results in contraction. Hill received a half share of the 1922 Nobel Prize for Physiology or Medicine; **"for his discovery relating to the production of heat in the muscle"**

Following his teaching work at the universities of London and Manchester, he was appointed Foulerton research professor of the Royal Society from 1926 until he retired in 1951. Hill derived a mathematical expression; known as the 'Hill equation', for the uptake of oxygen by haemoglobin. He died in Cambridge on June 3, 1977. He was married with two sons and two daughters.

Otto Meyerhof was born In Hanover, Germany on April 12, 1884. He received an MD from Heidelberg University in 1909. Thereafter he held teaching and researching posts in physical chemistry at several German universities. Between 1929 and 1938 he headed the department of physiology at the Kaiser-Wilhelm Institute. In 1922 he shared the Nobel Prize for Physiology or Medicine; **"for his discovery of the fixed relationship between the consumption of oxygen and the metabolism of lactic acid in the muscle"**

He spent his latter years as research professor at Pennsylvania University and indulging his hobby of painting. He wrote, *The Chemical Dyanamics of Life Phenomena* (1924).

He died in Philadelphia, from a heart attack, on October 5, 1951. He was married with two sons and a daughter.

PEACE

FRIDTJOF NANSEN (1861-1930)

Fridtjof Nansen was born in Oslo, Norway on October 10, 1861, the son of a lawyer. Following a local schooling, Nansen passed to university with the intention of studying zoology. This work gave him the flavour for a future career. A specialist in skiing, hunting and fishing, he became a scientific explorer. He was the first to appreciate the future of Greenland and became the first to cross that mighty terrain. The expedition started on August 15th 1888 and returned home in triumph in May 1889. Further dangerous and exciting expeditions followed in Arctic regions and Nansen was a national hero. Many of the journeys resulted in the collection of essential scientific knowledge which Nansen had the ability to select.

He spent over 30 years voyaging, discovering, selecting items of zoology and physical oceanography. As he grew older, so did his interest in people and countries deepen. His credentials were excellent. He was an internationally regarded scientist who went out and met danger head on. The USSR didn't recognise the League of Nations; Nansen was their intermediary. He headed the Norwegian delegation to the League and organised more exchange of WW1 prisoners than the Red Cross. Over a million POWS owed their freedom to Nansen's efforts. In 1921 he directed famine relief in Russia.

On July 5th 1922, on the initiative of Nansen, an international agreement was signed in Geneva that resulted in identification cards for displaced persons. It became known as the 'Nansen passport'. In 1922, he was awarded the Nobel Prize for Peace, **"for his relief work after World War 1"**

He used his prize money for international relief work. Acknowledged by all as a great explorer and humanitarian, Nansen died in Lysaker, Norway on May 13, 1930. He married twice and had two daughters and two sons. He personally organised the repatriation of a half a million prisoners of war during and following WW1.

1923

Hitler's takeover in Munich fails • A birth control clinic opens in New York • USSR established • Stanley Spencer, *The Resurrection* • D.H.Lawrence, *Kangaroo* • Arnold Bennett, *Riceyman Steps* • Aldous Huxley, *Antic Hay* • Maria Callas born• Sarah Bernhardt dies.

LITERATURE

WILLIAM YEATS (1865-1939)

William Butler Yeats was born on June 13, 1865 in Dublin, Ireland. His father was a barrister, who later became an artist, and his mother the daughter of a prosperous merchant. Although his parents were Protestants the population was Catholic. Yeats wasn't persuaded to either dogma. When Yeats was two the family moved to London. His Irish roots were sustained by frequent trips to Sligo where his grandparents lived. He was fifteen, when the family returned to Dublin and in 1883 he was at the Metropolitan School of Art in Dublin. There he met future poets and painters.

He had started to write and his first work appeared in the *Dublin University Review* in 1885. In 1887 the family were once again on the move back to London. Here, Yeats became a professional writer and joined the Theosophical Society. His collected poetry entitled, *The Wanderings of Oisin, and other Poems* was published in 1889 and caused a ripple of interest among those Yeats was trying to reach.

He became involved in London literary life and hobnobbed with such luminaries as William Morris, Lionel Johnson and Arthur Symons. He met and fell in love with Maud Gonne. Maud was an Irish patriot, an activity in which Yeats joined more out of love for Maud, than any fervent conviction. He wrote his 1902 play for her. *Cathleen rii Houlihan* was produced in Dublin to mixed reviews. In 1898 he met Augusta Lady Gregory who became his close friend. Yeats, turned down in marriage by Gonne, returned with renewed vigour to his writings.

He was a founder member of the Irish Literary Theatre which later became The Abbey Theatre. He managed the theatre, promoted playwrights, including Synge and put on many of his own works. The height of his achievement probably came with *The Wild Swans at Coole* (1917) and ending with *The Winding Stair* published in 1929; writing much good work in between.

In 1922, following the independence of Ireland, Yeats served in the Senate for six years. In 1923 he was awarded the Nobel Prize for Literature,**"for his always inspired poetry, in a highly artistic form gives expression to the spirit of a whole nation"**

The award caused him to become an Irish hero overnight. In January 1939 he decided to spend the winter abroad in the warmer climes of Southern France. He died soon after arrival on January 28, 1939 and buried at Roquebrune, France. It was a temporary resting place whilst

WW2 intervened. That event over, his body was returned to Ireland and the Protestant churchyard in Sligo. He was married with a son and a daughter. In 1915, as an Irish Nationalist, he refused the honour of a knighthood.

CHEMISTRY

FRITZ PREGL (1869-1930)

Fritz Pregl was born in Laibach, Austria on September 3, 1869. He received his MD from Gratz University in 1893. Around the beginning of the 20th century he began his researches into bile acids and other substances. He had great difficulty obtaining certain materials in sufficient quantities, so he devised analytical methods that required tiny amounts. By 1912, he was able to reliably measure carbon, nitrogen and hydrogen, from only a few milligrams of subject material. This breakthrough enabled other scientists to work with similar minute quantities of material.

He also developed a sensitive microbalance and micromethod for quantifying atomic groups as well as discovering a simpler method of determining a kidney's functional capacity. In 1923 Pregl was awarded the Nobel Prize for Chemistry; **"for his invention of the method of micro-analysis of organic substances"**

He died in Graz, Austria on December 13, 1930. He never married.

PHYSICS

ROBERT MILLIKAN (1868-1953)

Robert Andrews Millikan was born in Morrison, Ill, US, on March 22, 1868. He later studied in Germany at Berlin and Göttingen universities. Upon his return to the US, he joined Chicago University as a teacher.

Here, in 1909, he performed his now famous oil-drop experiment to determine the value of the electronic charge. He also confirmed Einstein's photoelectric equation and acquired an exact value for the Planck constant.

In 1921 he became director of the Norman Bridge Laboratory of Physics at the California Institute of Technology. In 1923, Millikan received the Nobel Prize for Physics; **"for his work on the elementary charges of electricity and on the photoelectric effect"**.

He died on December 19, 1953 at San Marino, California. He was married with three sons.

PHYSIOLOGY or MEDICINE

FREDERICK BANTING (1891-1941)
and
JOHN MACLEOD (1876-1935)

"for the discovery of insulin"

Frederick Grant Banting was born Alliston, Ont. Canada on November 14, 1891. Whilst serving with the Canadian Army during WW1 he was awarded the MM for gallantry. He spent much time working at Toronto University researching, with John Macleod, the possible effective method of treating diabetes. They solved the great problem by obtaining a pancreatic extract of insulin. In 1923, in consideration of this most valuable find Banting was awarded, together with Macleod the Nobel Prize for Physiology or Medicine.

Banting shared his prize with Charles Best, who had greatly assisted him. He was created a knight in 1934.

During WW2 he was on war service, when his plane crashed over Newfoundland on February 21, 1941, he was killed. He was married twice and had a son.

John James Rickard Macleod was born in Perth, Scotland on September 6, 1876. Following several leading appointments at the London Hospital (1899-1902) and Cleveland University (1903-1918) he arrived at Toronto University in 1918.

Here he met up with Frederick Banting and Charles Best. Banting and Best, under the direction of Macleod, began investigating the secretions of the pancreas and eventually succeeded in isolating and preparing insulin (1921). For his part, Macleod was awarded a half share of the 1923 Nobel Prize for Physiology or Medicine. He was later appointed dean of the faculty of medicine at Toronto University.

He died in Aberdeen, Scotland on March 16, 1935. Amongst his writings best known is *Physiology and Biochemistry in Modern Medicine* (1918). He was married but had no children.

PEACE

NOT AWARDED

1924

Britain, France and China recognise USSR • Coolidge signs bill limiting immigration into US and excluding all Japanese • Rioting in Delhi between Hindus and Moslems • Insecticides appear • George Gershwin, *Rhapsody in Blue* • E.M.Forster, *A Passage to India* • Margaret Kennedy, *The Constant Nymph* • Lenin, Franz Kafka, Joseph Conrad and Puccini die.

LITERATURE

WIADYSIAW REYMONT (1867-1925)

Wiadysiaw **Stanislaw Reymont** was born in Radom, Poland, when it was part of the Greater Russian Empire, on May 7, 1867. He spent much of his youth working in a variety of jobs; from railway worker to shop apprentice to actor. With very little schooling he set out to become a writer. *The Promised Land* was published in 1899 and is set in an expanding industrial area of Lodz.

His novel, *The Peasants* (1904-9) is a history of peasant life during the four seasons of the year. It was this work that gave Reymont the 1924 Nobel Prize for Literature; **"for his great national epic, *The Peasants*"**

His later work never lived up to his earlier promise. He died in Warsaw on December 5, 1925.

CHEMISTRY

NOT AWARDED

PHYSICS

KARL SIEGBAHN (1886-1978)

Karl **Manne Georg Siegbahn** was born in Orebro, Sweden on December 3, 1886, the son of the station master At the age of 30, his ongoing research revealed the existence of a new group of wavelengths, the M-series in X-ray emission spectra. He developed equipment that enabled him to accurately determine the wavelengths of X-rays. In 1923, he became professor of physics at Uppsala University and there, in 1924, he was able to provide proof that X-rays are bent when they pass through prisms.

Siegbahn was awarded the 1924 Nobel Prize for Physics; **"for his discoveries and research in the field of X-ray spectroscopy"**

In 1937 he became professor of physics at Stockholm University. Also in that year he became director of the Nobel Institute of Physics in Stockholm, created by the Swedish Royal Academy of Sciences. He remained in that position until he retired in 1975. He died in Stockholm on September 26, 1978. He was married with two sons. He later worked on problems connected with nuclear physics.

PHYSIOLOGY or MEDICINE

WILLEM EINTHOVEN (1860-1927)

Willem **Einthoven** was born in Java, Dutch East Indies, on May 21, 1860. He graduated in medicine from Utrecht University and later, in 1886, became professor of physiology at Leiden University where he remained until his death in 1927. In 1903, he created the first string galvanometer, that became known as the Einthoven galvanometer, and was thus able to measure the changes of electrical potential caused by contractions of the heart muscle and so graphically record them.

Einthoven called this programme an ' electrocardiogram'. Between 1908 and 1913, he constantly studied patterns of records of normal heart activity and thereby gleaned the principle of recognising and interpreting deviations in heart patterns. In 1924 he was awarded the Nobel Prize for Physiology or Medicine;**"for his discovery of the mechanism of the electrocardiogram"**

He died in Leiden, Netherlands, on September 29, 1927. He was married with two sons and two daughters.

PEACE

NOT AWARDED

1925

Trotsky dismissed as chairman of Russian Revolutionary Council • Italy occupies Somaliland • Adolf Hitler, *Mein Kampf* • Tennessee in US forbids the teaching of Darwin's human evolution theory • Aaron Copland, *Symphony No.1* • *The New Yorker* appears • Sean O'Casey, *Juno and the Paycock* • Charles Chaplin, *The Gold Rush* • Anita Loos, *Gentlemen Prefer Blondes* • Film, *Battleship Potemkin* • Peter Sellers born • August von Wasserman, Rider Haggard and Karl Abraham die.

LITERATURE

GEORGE BERNARD SHAW (1856-1950)

George Bernard Shaw was born in Dublin, Ireland on July 26, 1856. He was the third child, and only son, of Protestant parents and grew up in what he later described as, 'genteel poverty'. His schooling was varied and spasmodic and, by the age of 16, he was working in an estate agent's office.

By his own devises, he gathered a wide knowledge of music, literature and art. His mother encouraged him and took him on visits to the National Gallery of Ireland. In 1872, his parents parted and his mother left for London, taking with her her two daughters. Four years later George followed suit, resolving to become a writer.

During his twenties, Shaw suffered much poverty. He spent most days in the reading room of the British Museum, keeping warm and reading and writing. He taught himself in the evenings, by attending evening classes and going to free lectures. His writing failed. In 1879, his semi autobiographical book entitled, *Immaturity* was rejected by every publisher in London (in 1930 it was published to great acclaim).

The following four novels met the same fate. Although he failed as a writer, he grew in maturity. He became a Socialist and a vegetarian and remained so all his life. In 1885 he received a break. The drama critic, William Archer, found Shaw a job on *The Pall Mall Gazette.* His journalistic work ranged from book reviews to music critic. He also wrote art reviews for *World* (1886-89). He began to get noticed when he became theatre critic on the *Saturday Review* (1895-98). It was then that Shaw began writing his own plays.

In 1892, his play, *Widowers' Houses* was given a positive reception. There followed, in 1897, *Candida* at the Royal Court Theatre and Shaw was on his way. It was followed by, *You Never Can Tell*. However, his next play would be a triumph, albeit the censor didn't allow it to be produced until 1903. *Mrs Warren's Profession* was a great success.

He continued to write much; plays, political pamphlets, screenplays. Probably Shaw's greatest success was, *Pygmalion*, first performed in the theatre in 1913. It subsequently became a stage musical and film, under the name, *My Fair Lady*. Shaw was a great character, to whom little was sacred. He loved being in the public eye and stories of him abound.

He was probably the most important playwright since Shakespeare, and only in the latter half of the 20th century would his genius be threatened. In 1925 Shaw was awarded the Nobel Prize for Literature; **"for his work which is marked by both idealism and humanity, its stimulating satire often being infused with a singular poetic beauty"**

He died in Ayot St.Lawrence, Herts, England on November 2, 1950. He was married but without children. He was offered the Order of Merit, he turned it down.

CHEMISTRY

RICHARD ZSIGMONDY (1865-1929)

Richard Zsigmondy was born on April 1, 1865, in Vienna, Austria. He received his doctorate from Munich University in 1889. He then worked in research in Berlin, before joining Graz University.   Between 1908 and 1929, he was director of the Institute for Inorganic Chemistry at Göttingen University. In 1897, whilst researching in a glassworks factory, he began working on colloidal gold which he found present in ruby glass. Here he discovered a water suspension of gold.

He reckoned he could learn a lot about the colloidal state of matter by studying the manner in which the particles scatter light. He developed the ultramicroscope in 1903, in order to investigate the various aspects of colloids. His work was rewarded by the award of the 1925 Nobel Prize for Chemistry; **"for his demonstration of the heterogenous nature of colloid solutions and for the methods he used, which have since become fundamental in modern colloid chemistry"**

The work of Zsigmondy was greatly appreciated by those working in the fields of biochemistry and bacteriology. He died in Göttingen, Germany on September 23, 1929. He was married with two daughters.

PHYSICS

JAMES FRANCK (1882-1964)
and
GUSTAV HERTZ (1887-1975)

"For their discovery of the laws governing the impact of an electron upon an atom"

James Franck was born in Hamburg, Germany, on August 26, 1882. He studied chemistry at Berlin University and spent many years researching the reaction of bombardment of electrons on the ionization of atoms. This important work won him, a half share of the 1925 Nobel Prize for Physics, and would bear much fruit during the race for the atom bomb during WW2. At Göttingen University, he was, in 1920, appointed professor of physics.

In 1933, as a Jew, Franck resigned his post in protest at Nazism and went to Denmark. Two years later he was a professor at John Hopkins University in the US In 1938 he was at Chicago University. Here he researched photochemistry used in the aircraft industry.

Franck worked on the development of the atom bomb and was one of the few who appreciated its devastating power. He urged that a demonstration of its power be given in an un-populated area of Japan. In the latter part of his life he returned to Germany and the Göttingen Institute. He died in Göttingen on May 21, 1964, whilst on a visit. He was twice married and had two daughters. He was responsible for the ' Franck Report' of 1945. This called for an open demonstration of the power of the A-Bomb before dropping it on a large Japanese city.

Gustav Ludwig Hertz was born in Hamburg, Germany, on July 22, 1887. Hertz, like Franck, was Jewish and suffered the same discrimination in obtaining a university education. In the case of Hertz, he was fortunate to be the nephew of the famous German physicist, Heinrich Hertz, so was able to study at the universities of Göttingen, Munich and Berlin; becoming assistant in physics at Berlin University in 1913. Here he met, and worked with Franck, on what happens when an electron strikes an atom.

Their measurements showed that the distinct wavelengths of light emitted, by each element, corresponded to the series of possible energy states for the atoms of that element. In 1925, Hertz shared the Nobel Prize for Physics with James Franck. In the same year, Hertz was appointed professor of physics at Halle University. In 1928 he transferred to the Technische Hochschule in Berlin. In 1932, he attracted the attention of the world's scientific press with his discovery of a method of separating the isotopes of neon.

He spent most of the Second World War working in Soviet Russia. In 1954, he returned to East Germany, and was appointed professor of physics and director of the Physics

Institute in Leipzig. He retired in 1961 and died in East Berlin on October 30, 1975. He was married twice with two sons.

PHYSIOLOGY or MEDICINE

NOT AWARDED

PEACE

CHARLES DAWES (1865-1951)
and
SIR AUSTEN CHAMBERLAIN (1863-1937)

Charles Gates Dawes was born in Marietta, Ohio, US on August 27, 1865. He was educated at Matietta College and Cincinnati Law School. Having graduated as a lawyer, he practised in Lincoln, Nebraska moving on to Evanston, Illinois. There he made his permanent home, gave up the law for private business, and ran the Central Trust Company of Illinois. During WW1, he was head of supply procurement for the US army in France. In 1923 he was appointed by the Allied Reparations Commission, to plan a solution for Germany's problem of being unable to pay the Allies the reparations due.

He came up with a plan that became known as the , 'Dawes Plan' and saved Germany, and Europe, from economic ruin for a few years. His plan bought time but it was only a partial solution; it did nothing to prevent the 'Wall Street' crash of 1929, the enormous inflation in Germany, the rise of Hitler and the eventual start of WW2. In 1925 a then grateful society awarded him a half share of the Nobel Prize for Peace; **"for his work resulting in the 'Dawes Plan'**

In 1939, he wrote, *A Journal of Reparations*. He returned to the banking business and died following a heart attack in Evanston on April 23, 1951. He was married with a son, who drowned whilst on holiday, and a daughter.

Sir **Joseph Austen Chamberlain** was born on October 16, 1863 in Birmingham, England. The eldest son of Joseph Chamberlain, he had a privileged upbringing and a rapid rise up the political ladder. He entered the House of Commons in 1892 and 10 years later was postmaster-general. He was Chancellor of the Exchequer (1903-05 and 1919-21), and was part of the Lloyd George wartime cabinet. Between 1924 and 1929, he served as foreign secretary in Baldwin's government.

It fell to Chamberlain to negotiate a group of treaties, intended to secure and maintain peace in Western Europe, by eliminating any possible border disputes involving Germany. The pact became known as, The Locarno Pact (1925) The ink was barely dry, when it was announced that for this work, Chamberlain would receive a half share in the 1925 Nobel Peace Prize; **"for his work resulting in the 'Locarno Pact'.**

Later the same year, he was knighted. He became an elder statesman, watching his half brother, Neville, climbing up the political ladder and Hitler eroding his Locarno Pact. He died in London from apoplexy, on March 16, 1937. He was married with two sons and a daughter.

1926

General Strike in Britain • Hejaz renamed Saudi Arabia •Trotsky and Zinoviev expelled from Russian Politbureau • Logie Baird demonstrates television in London • Henry Moore, *Draped Reclining Figure* **• Alban Berg,** *Wozzeck* **• A.A. Milne,** *Winnie-the-Pooh* **• Le Corbusier,** *The Coming Architecture* **• Film;** *The General* **• Harry Houdini and Claude Monet die.**

LITERATURE

GRAZIA DELEDDA (1875-1936)

Grazia **Deledda** was born in Sardinia, Italy on September 27, 1875, the daughter of a landowner. Her formal education was minimal but she was a natural storyteller and amused those around her for hours on end with her tales of Sardinian folklore. These she later retold in books and when she was 17 some were published. She married young and moved to Rome. Her heart and the foundations for her stories however, remained in her native and beloved Sardinia, the setting for most of her fiction. Probably her best known works were, *After the Divorce* (1905), and *Ashes* (1910) which became a film in 1916.

The Woman and the Priest (1922) was the story of a mother who yearns for her son to become a priest but lives to see him yield to the temptations that are all around him. She wrote some 50 novels and developed the same theme in most of them. She was awarded the 1926 Nobel Prize for Literature; **"for her idealistically inspired writings which with plastic clarity picture the life of her native island and with depth and sympathy deal with human problems in general"** .

She died in Rome on August 15, 1936. She was married with two sons.

CHEMISTRY

THE SVEDBERG (1884-1971)

The Svedberg was born Theodor Svedberg in Flerang, Sweden on August 30, 1884. He received a doctorate from Uppsala University in 1907 and stayed on to teach. He researched the chemistry of colloids and invented the ultracentrifuge (1924). By means of this instrument, later frequently updated, Svedberg was able to make precise determinations of the molecular weights of highly complex proteins of which haemoglobin was only one.

In later years, and with an updated ultracentrifuge that was capable of generating a centrifugal force of up to 5,000 times the force of gravity, he made studies in nuclear chemistry and cyclotron. In 1926 he was awarded the Nobel Prize for Chemistry; **"for his works on disperse systems"** One of his students was Arne Tiselius, who he helped in the development of electrophoresis and who would be awarded the Nobel Prize for Chemistry in 1948. Svedberg died in Orebro, Sweden, on February 25, 1971. He had a total of four wives who between them gave him 6 sons and 6 daughters. However, his hobbies were painting and botany.

PHYSICS

JEAN PERRIN (1870-1942)

Jean-Baptiste Perrin was born in Lille, France on September 30, 1870. He was educated at the École Normale Supérieure in Paris and, in 1898, he joined the teaching staff of Paris University becoming professor of physical chemistry in 1910 and remaining as such for 30 years. In 1895, he was able to establish that, cathode rays are negatively charged particles that became known as electrons. In 1908, he pondered the question concerning the way in which, colloidal particles remained suspended in a liquid in defiance of gravity.

Continued observations meant he was able to confirm Einstein's equation concerning the phenomenon and thus able to estimate the size of atoms and molecules as well as their quantity in a given volume. For this work, Perrin received the 1926 Nobel Prize for Physics; **"for his work on the discontinuous structure of matter, and especially for his discovery of sedimentation equilibrium"**

Following the German occupation of France in 1940, Perrin left for the US where, in New York he died on April 17, 1942. He was married with a son and daughter. Following the end of WW2, his remains were transferred to France on the battleship, *Jeanne d' Arc* and he was buried in the Pantheon.

PHYSIOLOGY or MEDICINE

JOHANNES FIBIGER (1867-1928)

Johannes Andreas Grib Fibiger was born on April 23, 1867 in Silkeborg, Denmark where his father was a doctor. Following a formal education, he became professor of pathological anatomy at Copenhagen University in 1900. His PhD thesis was on the work of bacteriologists, Robert Koch and Emil von Behring. Fibiger continued this branch of research and in 1907, whilst dissecting rats infected with TB, discovered tumours in their stomachs. Intensive research followed with the result that it was found that the rats had eaten infected cockroaches who in turn had eaten infected worms.

By 1913, Fibiger had demonstrated that tumours underwent metastasis. His work added importance to the concept that cancer is caused by tissue irritation. Fibiger's work led to important advances in the cure for some types of cancer. His work was a required prelude to the production of chemical carcinogens and a vital ingredient in the development of modern cancer research. Fibiger was awarded the 1926 Nobel Prize for Physiology or Medicine; **"for his discovery of the Spiroptera carcinoma"**

He died in Copenhagen on January 30, 1928. He was married without children.

PEACE

ARISTIDE BRIAND (1862-1932)
and
GUSTAV STRESEMANN (1878-1929)

Aristide Briand was born in Nantes, France on March 28, 1862. He would become prime minister of France eleven times. He trained as a lawyer and in 1904 co-founded, *L'Humanité*. In 1901 he became secretary-general of the Socialist Party.Following WW1, he became a highly vocal advocate of the League of Nations. A member of the team concerned with the Locarno Pact, Briand distinguished himself in the work he did, and which became known as the Kellog-Briand Pact (1928).

It was a short-lived agreement by which 60 countries agreed to outlaw war as an instrument of national policy. Briand shared the 1926 Nobel Prize for Peace.; **"for his work in promoting international peace"** He later bid for but lost in the race to become French president. He died in Paris on March 7, 1932. He never married. He was the man who wrote the French law that resulted in the separation of Church and State.

Gustav Stresemann was born in Berlin, Germany on May 10, 1878. He was the son of a beer salesman who had five children. Gustav was the only one who responded to schooling and went on to university. These included Berlin and Leipzig. He started by studying literature, he ended up with an economics degree, having written a thesis on, *The Growth of the Berlin Bottled-Beer Industry*. He was most interested in modern history, particularly Napoleon and Goethe. He believed in the superiority of the German Empire and, as a result, became a politician who joined the right-wing National Liberal Party.

In 1907 he was elected to the Reichstag and at 28 its' youngest member. In WW1 Stresemann wholeheartedly supported the German cause, convinced his country was fighting a defensive war. He moved further to the right and became involved in political in-fighting to get former chancellor Bulow re-elected. He failed and turned his attention to strengthening the monarchy to which end he suggested abolition of the voting system.

He was demolished, when Germany sued for peace and emotionally overcome, when the Kaiser ran off to Holland. He opposed the Versailles Treaty and spent the rest of his life seeking its' revision. However, his saving grace appears to be his brief term as chancellor- August 13 to November 23, 1923- during which time he co-ordinated various political parties in order to achieve the recovery of Germany.

A few months later, in November, he failed to survive a vote of confidence. He became foreign minister in the new government and in this position he constantly fought for his corner. He created a foreign policy, which few countries found acceptable. By his domineering manner and refusal to compromise, he is considered the person chiefly responsible for the restoration of Germany's international standing following WW1. He was however, considered worthy to receive a half share of the 1926 Nobel Prize for Peace; **"for his policy of reconciliation and negotiation"**

He died in Berlin on October 3, 1929. He was married with two sons.

1927

Geneva Economic conference attended by 52 nations including USSR • German economy collapses • Kemal Ataturk, *The New Turkey* • Lindbergh flies from New York to Paris • Eric Gill, *Mankind* • The Talkies arrive with Al Jolson's *The Jazz Singer* • Sinclair Lewis, *Elmer Gantry* • Virginia Woolf, *To The Lighthouse* • Films; *Wings, Napoleon, The Kid Brother* • Georg Brandes and Jerome K Jerome die.

LITERATURE

HENRI BERGSON (1859-1941)

Henri Louis Bergson was born in Paris on October 18, 1859. His Jewish father was a musician who came from a wealthy Polish family whilst his mother came from a English Jewish family. His upbringing and education however, was typically French. His early education was at the Lycée Condorcet in Paris and, from 1878 to 1881, he studied at École Normale Supérieure in Paris. He became a teacher at small, local schools, later becoming professor at the Còllege de France.

He became a highly original thinker who went on to become a cult figure. He demonstrated the differences between the fundamental reality of the dynamic flux of consciousness with the inert physical world of discrete objects, which was a convenient fiction for the mechanistic descriptions of science.

His writings are most literary and analogical, and he is credited with having influenced Marcel Proust, to whom he was distantly related. In 1915, he became a member of the Academie Francaise. Bergson was a most prolific writer whose most important works are, *Time and Freewill* (1889), *Matter and Memory* (1896) and *Creative Evolution* (1907). In 1927 he was awarded the Nobel Prize for Literature; **"in recognition of his rich and vitalizing ideas and brilliant skill with which they have been presented"**

There were times when Bergson flirted with the philosophy of Catholicism but he later declared; "My reflections have led me closer to Catholicism, in which I see the complete fulfilment of Judaism" He went on; "I would have become a convert, had I not foreseen for years a formidable wave of anti-Semitism about to break upon the world. I wanted to remain among those who tomorrow were to be persecuted" (*Les Deux Sources).*

89

To confirm this conviction, he left his sick bed to queue, in the cold, in order to register as a Jew in accordance with Vichy law, albeit he had been offered exemption. He died in Paris soon after, on January 4, 1941. He was married with a daughter. His books have been translated into 20 languages.

CHEMISTRY

HEINRICH WIELAND (1877-1957)

Heinrich Otto Wieland was born in Pforzheim, Germany on June 4, 1877. He was a professor at Munich University where researching resulted in his finding that different forms of nitrogen, in organic compounds, can be detected and distinguished from one another. He then worked on bile acids, that are produced by the liver and found that three acids, when isolated, were of similar structure as well as being structurally related to cholesterol.

Later work led Wieland to believe that oxidation in living tissues is a matter of removing hydrogen atoms and not of adding oxygen .

This theory became of great importance in the fields of biochemistry, physiology and medicine. For his work Wieland was awarded the 1927 Nobel Prize for Chemistry; **"for his investigations of the constitution of the bile acids and related substances"**

He died in Munich on August 5, 1957. He was married with three sons and a daughter. Wieland's son in law, Feodor Lyner, was awarded the Nobel Prize for Medicine in 1964.

PHYSICS

ARTHUR COMPTON (1892-1962)
and
CHARLES WILSON (1869-1959)

Arthur Holly Compton was born in Wooster, Ohio, US, on September 10, 1892. In 1916 he received his PhD from Princeton University and went on to become director of the physics department of Washington University in St.Louis. That was in 1920. In 1923 he transferred to Chicago University and there developed what became known as the 'Compton Effect' This represents his discovery and explanation of the change in the wavelength X-rays when they collide with electrons. In 1927, he was rewarded with a half share of the Nobel Prize for Physics; **"for his discovery of the effect named after him"**

Still at Chicago University, but now in charge of the Metallurgical Laboratory (1942-1945), he oversaw the development the first self-sustaining atomic chain reaction, thus clearing the way for the controlled release of nuclear energy. In 1945, he returned to Washington University becoming its' chancellor as well as professor of natural history (1953-1961).

He died in Berkeley, California on March 15, 1962. He was married with two sons.

Charles **Thomson Rees Wilson** was born in Glencorse, Midlothian, Scotland, on February 14, 1869. He was educated at Manchester and Cambridge universities, later becoming professor of natural philosophy at Cambridge (1925-34). In 1895, whilst studying meteorology, he devised a way of expanding moist air in a closed container. This expansion cooled the air so that it became supersaturated with moisture, condensed on dust particles.

In particular, Wilson noticed that when he used dust free air that air remained supersaturated and that clouds did not form until the degree of supersaturation reached a certain critical point. He further experimented with X-rays and eventually discovered that radiation left a trail of condensed water droplets in his cloud chamber.

This was in 1912 and his chamber proved most valuable in the study of nuclear physics and led directly to the work of Donald Glaser (qv) in 1952, and his bubble chamber. His discovery became known as the 'Wilson cloud chamber' and was widely used to study radioactivity, X-rays and cosmic rays. This chamber was known as the most original piece of apparatus in the whole of physics. For this work Wilson received a half share of the 1927 Nobel Prize for Physics; **"for his method of making the paths of electrically charged particles visible by condensation of vapour"**

In 1937 he received the coveted Copley medal. During WW2, he devised a method of protecting barrage balloons, used by the British, from being struck by lightning. He died in Carlops, Peebles, Scotland, on November 15, 1959. He was married with a son and two daughters.

PHYSIOLOGY or MEDICINE

JULIUS WAGNER-JAUREGG (1857-1940)

Julius **Wagner-Jauregg** was born in Wels, Austria on March 7, 1857. Whilst at Vienna University he noticed that people suffering from certain nervous disorders, showed a marked improvement following their contracting fever infections. In 1887 he suggested that a fever infection be deliberately given to a mental patient as a method of treating the insane. He suggested that a dose of malaria be used as that could be controlled by quinine. He introduced the programme whilst professor of psychiatry and neurology at Graz University(1889-93) but with very limited success.

In 1917 he held the same position at Vienna University and here he proved to be more successful. It led to the development of fever therapy and shock treatments for a considerable number of mental disorders. He thus became responsible for drastically reducing the number of deaths in mental patients, particularly those whose problems were brought about by a syphilitic condition. For this work he was awarded the 1927 Nobel Prize for Physiology or Medicine; **"for his discovery of the therapeutic value of malaria inoculation in the treatment of dementia paralytica"**

He died in Vienna on September 27, 1940. He was married with a son and daughter.

PEACE

FERDINAND BUISSON (1841-1932)
and
LUDWIG QUIDDE (1858-1941)

Ferdinand **Édouard Buisson** was born in Paris, France on December 20, 1841. Following his qualifying as a teacher, he refused to take the teacher's oath of loyalty to the Second Empire of Napoleon lll. He went instead to live in Switzerland. There he taught philosophy at Neufchâtel University from 1866-1870. In 1867, he was part of the first Geneva Peace Conference and there proposed a United States of Europe.

Following the fall of Paris, during the Franco-Prussian war of 1870-71, he organised an asylum for children orphaned by the war. He returned to Paris, when the Third Republic was formed, and appointed inspector general of schools in Paris. He was later forced to resign, having advocated the elimination of religious education in French schools. Later, as National Director of Elementary Education (1879-96), he became responsible for the drafting of statutes that removed public schools from the control of the church.

He was also a leading advocate of free and compulsory education and he saw this measure become law in 1882. He taught at the Sorbonne (1896-1902), leaving to sit in the national Chamber of Deputies (1902-14, 1919-23). In 1898, he co-founded the French League of Human Rights. He became the League's President and worked hard for peace from 1913 to 1926, a period that included the first World War (1914-1918). For this work Buisson received a half share of the 1927 Nobel Prize for Peace; **"for his peacemaking efforts"**

He died at Thieuloy-Saint-Antoine, France on February 16, 1932. He was married with three children. He was often referred to as ' the world's most persistent pacifist'.

Ludwig Quidde was born in Bremen, Germany on March 23, 1858. Between 1889 and 1896 , he was editor of the *Deutsche Zeitschrift für Geschichtswissenschaft,* as well as working as professor and secretary of the Prussian Historical Institute in Rome. In 1892 he was living in Munich and an active member of the German Peace Society.

The publication of a pamphlet called *Caligula* was a satire on William ll, and brought him three months in prison for the crime of 'lese majesty'. From 1907 to 1919, he was a liberal member of the Bavarian Assembly and opposed WW1. He was an avowed pacifist and chairman of the German Peace Cartel (1921-29). In 1927 he was a co-winner of the Nobel Prize for Peace; **"awarded for his long work for peace"**

When Hitler came to power in 1933, Quidde left for Geneva where he died on March 5, 1941.

1928

Women's vote in Britain reduced from 30 to 21 • Chiang Kai-shek elected president of China • Herbert Hoover becomes US president • Alexander Fleming discovers penicillin • The Geiger Counter • USSR first 5-year plan • *New English Dictionary* begun in 1884 completed • Maurice Ravel, *Bolero* • Weil and Brecht, *The Threepenny Opera*• Walt Disney produces 'Mickey Mouse' in colour • Films; *The Passion of Joan of Arc, Two Tars , Broadway Melody,* • D.H.Lawrence, *Lady Chatterley's Lover* • Alan Symons born • Italo Svevo, Thomas Hardy and Ellen Terry die.

LITERATURE

SIGRID UNDSET (1882-1949)

Sigrid Undset was born in Kalundborg, Denmark on May 20, 1882. Her father was a known Norwegian archaeologist and Sigrid was brought up in Norway midst an atmosphere of legend and folklore. As a young person, she worked in the office of an electrical engineering factory for 10 years. She then married and brought up a family. During this time she began writing. Drawing upon her life and childhood influence. Her earliest novels deal with lower class women in a working environment. However her greatest work dealt with the distant past. *Kristin Lavransdatter* (1920-22) is a trilogy concerning a woman's life as a self-sacrificing person who is proud and independent.

Between 1925 and 1927, she wrote the four volume historical novel,

The Master of Hestviken. This work reflected Sigrid's growing interest in religion. She became converted to the Catholic faith in 1924 and this became noted in her later novels. In 1928, Sigrid received the Nobel Prize for Literature; **"principally for her powerful descriptions of Northern life during the Middle Ages"**

    During the German occupation of Norway (1940-45), she was able to escape and spent the war years in the US, lecturing on behalf of the Norwegian Government in exile. She returned to a liberated Norway and went to live in Lillehammer where she died on June 10, 1949. She was married with two sons and a daughter. Throughout her writing career she continued to explore women's erotic roles in a turbulent life.

CHEMISTRY

ADOLF WINDAUS (1876-1959)

Adolf Windaus was born in Berlin, Germany on December 25, 1876. He originally studied medicine but decided to switch to chemistry. He received his PhD from Freiburg University in 1899 and later became head of the chemical institute at Göttingen University (1915-1944). His ongoing researches established the structure of cholesterol. His further research revealed the chemical origins of vitamin D.

    He also aided the research into sex hormones and encouraged the development into drugs used for heart diseases. In 1928, he was awarded the Nobel Prize for Chemistry; **"for the services rendered through his research into the constitution of the sterols and their connection with the vitamins"**

    He died in Göttingen, Germany on June 9, 1959. He was married with two sons and a daughter.

PHYSICS

OWEN RICHARDSON (1879-1959)

Owen Williams Richardson was born in Dewsbury, Yorkshire, England on April 26, 1879. He graduated from Trinity College, Cambridge and became a student of JJ.Thomson at the Cavendish Laboratory. In 1906, he crossed the Atlantic and took up an appointment as professor of physics at Princeton University, where he remained until 1913.

    In 1911, following a series of experiments, Richardson was able to prove that electrons are emitted from hot metal not as previously thought, by air. In the same year, he aired a mathematical equation that suggested that the rate of electron emission to the absolute temperature of the metal. This became known as ' Richardson's law'.

His work on electron emission by hot metals won for Richardson the 1928 Nobel Prize for Physics; **"for his work on the thermionic phenomenon and especially for the discovery of the law named after him"**

He became director of research at King's College, London University where he remained until his retirement in 1944. In 1939 he was knighted. He died in Alton, Hants, on February 15, 1959 .

He was twice married with two sons and a daughter.

PHYSIOLOGY or MEDICINE

CHARLES NICOLLE (1866-1936)

Charles-Jules-Henri Nicolle was born in Rouen, France on September 21, 1866. He spent much time researching at Rouen University, before becoming director of the Pasteur Institute in Tunis (1902-1932). During his long time in Tunis, he founded the Archives de l'Institut Pasteur de Tunis. This became a major venue for bacteriological research. Nicolle's researches had resulted in his proving that typhus is transmitted by the body louse. He was awarded the 1928 Nobel Prize for Physiology or Medicine; **"for his work on typhus"**

He went on to distinguish between, the louse-borne form of the disease and murine typhus, that is induced into humans by the rat flea. Nicolle also contributed to contemporary knowledge in the field of measles, diphtheria and TB.

He died in Tunis on February 28, 1936. He was married with two sons.

PEACE

NOT AWARDED

1929

Wall Street crash • the term 'Apartheid' used for first time • *Graf Zeppelin* **airship flies round the world • Arabs attack Jews in Jerusalem • John Galsworthy,** *The Forsyte Chronicles* **• Piet Mondrian,** *Composition with Yellow and Blue* **• Ernest Hemingway,** *A Farewell to Arms* **• J.B.Priestley,** *The Good Companions* **• Film,** *Big Business, The Divorcee* **• Audrey Hepburn born • Emile Berliner, Garrett Fawcett and Serge Diaghilev die.**

LITERATURE

THOMAS MANN (1875-1955)

Thomas Mann was born in Lubeck, Germany on June 6, 1875. When only 16, his father died and that meant Thomas had to leave school and earn a living. He moved to Munich and worked in an insurance office by day, and writing by night. He was first published in 1898, when *Der Kleine Herr Friedemann,* found much favour. His work showed the influence of the philosophers, Schopenhauer and Nietzche. This was quickly followed by *Buddenbrooks* (1900). In 1912 his novel, *Death in Venice* was published in many languages. This was followed in 1926 by, *The Magic Mountain.* These novels resulted in the award to Mann of the 1929 Nobel Prize for Literature; **"principally for his great novel,** *Buddenbrooks***, which has won steadily increased recognition as one of the classic works of contemporary literature"**

His work held much deep meaning that was constantly being analysed with differing results. He married in 1905, had six children, and an idyllic marriage. During WW1, he was an ardent nationalist and supporter of the establishment that much annoyed his elder brother, Heinrich who taking an opposite view, urged the public to protest at the war.

Later, during the Weimar Republic, Thomas began to revise his attitude. He began to espouse the democratic ideal. In 1930 he gave a speech in Berlin, in which he appealed to the cultured and the working man to unite against Hitler. During the 1930s, he repeatedly travelled the major cities of Europe attacking Nazi policy and warning about what was to come. He had now spun 180 degrees and openly supported Communist principles.

In January 1933, when Hitler became chancellor, Thomas Mann and his wife were on holiday in Switzerland. Their children warned them not to return home. They remained and travelled Europe before deciding to settle in the US. In 1938 they settled at Princeton. In 1938 he was deprived of his German citizenship and Bonn University took away the honorary doctorate it had granted in 1919.

Acknowledged as one of the greatest writers of the century, Mann was a most prolific writer. In America he published much, including, *Doktor Faustus* which he started in 1943. In 1944 he became a US citizen. Following the war, Mann visited both East and West Germany and in each country received many honours.

In 1952, he returned to his home in Switzerland and died in Zurich on August 12, 1955. He was married with three daughters and three sons.

CHEMISTRY

ARTHUR HARDEN (1865-1940)
and
HANS von EULER-CHELPIN (1873-1964)

"for their investigations on the fermentation of sugar and fermentative enzymes"

Arthur Harden was born in Manchester, England on October 12, 1865. After Manchester University he studied in Germany. Upon his return, he headed the biochemistry department at the Jenner Institute of Preventive Medicine (1907-30). He spent some 20 years researching the effects of the fermentation of sugar and the enzyme action involved.

He was rewarded by co-winning the 1929 Nobel Prize for Chemistry. He went on to pioneer investigation into metabolic processes in living animals. In 1938 he was knighted. He wrote a number of books including, *Alcoholic Fermentation* (1911).

He died on June 17, !940 whilst living in Bourne, Buckinghamshire. He was married with no children.

Hans Karl August Simon von Euler-Chelpin was born in Augsburg, Germany on February 15, 1873. He graduated from Berlin University in 1895. In 1900, he was teaching at Stockhold University, becoming professor of general and inorganic chemistry in 1906, and director of the biochemical institute in 1929.

Euler-Chelpin's work centred on coenzymes , and his work on the biochemistry of sugars and phosphates, was rewarded by co-winning the 1929 Nobel Prize for Chemistry. He died in Stockhold on November 7, 1964.

He was married twice and had nine children. A patriot in two world wars, he was an early member of Hitler's Nazi Party.

PHYSICS

LOUIS de BROGLIE (1892-1987)

Louis Victor Pierre Raymond de Broglie was born Dieppe, France on August 15, 1892. He was the second son of the 5th Duke of Broglie and born with the proverbial silver spoon in his mouth. Choosing science as a career was a distinct break with family tradition, whose members invariably went into the army. However, he wasn't the first to breakaway.

His elder brother Maurice (the 6th Duke), was a well-known scientist who did valuable work on atomic nucleus and who died in 1960, at which time Louis became the 7th Duke. Louis's brother brought to his attention the work of Max Planck and Albert Einstein and Louis decided to become a physicist. He chose to research electrons and went onto develop the theory of electron waves.

It became his thesis for his PhD He worked on a suggestion, made some twenty years previously by Einstein, that became known as the dual nature of light. Physicists generally refuted his theory, but Einstein was most enthusiastic. In 1928, Louis became professor of theoretical physics at Henri Poincare Institute and, in 1929, he was awarded the Nobel Prize for Physics; **"for his discovery of the wave nature of electrons"**

Following the recognition of his work on the research on quantum theory, and his discovery of the wave nature of electrons, he received in 1952, the Kalinga Prize, awarded by the United Nations Economic and Social Council. He was a foreign member of the British Royal Society as well as a member of the Académie Française. He was a prolific writer, the best known of which are, *The Revolution in Physics* (1953), *Physics and Microphysics* (1960) and *New Perspectives in Physics* (1962). He died in Paris on March 19, 1987. He never married.

PHYSIOLOGY or MEDICINE

FREDERICK HOPKINS (1861-1947)
and
CHRISTIAN EIJKMAN (1858-1930)

Frederick Gowland Hopkins was born in Eastbourne, England on June 20, 1861. He investigated the effect of amino acids in 1901 and five years later, he isolated the protein from amino acid tryptophan, the results becoming known as, essential amino acids. He observed that rats failed to grow, when fed on artificial milk, but thrived on cow's milk.

Hopkins now realised that animals, although on a diet of protein, fat and carbohydrate, required another essential ingredient. He called these vitamins. He worked and taught at Cambridge University from 1898 to 1943. He was knighted in 1925 and co-shared the 1929 Nobel Prize for Physiology ·

or Medicine; **"for his discovery of the growth-stimulating vitamins"**

For his work in discovering essential nutrient factors-vitamins, he received the Order of Merit in 1935. He died in Cambridge on May 16, 1947. He was married with two daughters.

Christiaan Eijkman was born in Nijerk, Netherlands on August 11, 1858. He received a medical degree from Amsterdam University in 1883 and worked as a medical officer in the Dutch East Indies (1883-1885). There, he investigated the cause of beriberi. He thought there was a bacterial reason behind the problem. In 1897, he was able to show that the condition in domestic chickens was caused by feeding them polished, rather than unpolished rice.

He became professor of public health and forensic medicine at Utrecht University (1898-1928). In 1929 he was awarded a co-share of the Nobel Prize for Physiology or Medicine; **"for his discovery of the antineuritic vitamin"**

His work, concerning beriberi and his evidence concerning poor diets and the need for vitamins, caused to him to be known all over the world. He died in Utrecht, on November 5, 1930. He was married with two daughters and a son.

PEACE

FRANK KELLOGG (1856-1937)

Frank Billings Kellogg was born in Potsdam, New York, US on December 22, 1856. He studied law and was admitted to the bar in 1877. He represented the government in anti-trust cases, served in the US Senate (1917-23) and was US ambassador to Great Britain 1923-25. Although an Isolationist by inclination, he helped to arrange the Geneva International Conference that sought to limit armaments.

He was involved, together with Aristide Briand the French foreign minister, in what would become known as the 'Kellogg-Briand Pact'. It included 62 nations in an effort to outlaw war. The Pact failed to achieve much, although it won for Kellogg the 1929 Nobel Prize for Peace; **"for his work on the 'Kellogg -Briand Pact"**

Between 1930 and 1935, he served on the Permanent Court of International Justice; watching Hitler creating great holes in his Pact. He died in St. Paul, Minn. US, on December 21, 1937. He was married without children.

1930

Gandhi commences campaign of civil disobedience in India • Constantinople becomes Istanbul • Ras Tafari becomes Emperor Haile Selassie of Abyssinia • Acrylic plastic is invented in UK • Amy Johnson flies London to Australia solo • Sigmund Freud, *Civilisation and its Discontents* • Empire State Building, New York • Noel Coward, *Private Lives* • Marlene Dietrich, *Blue Angel* • Films; *All Quiet on the Western Front,* • W.H.Auden, *Poems* • Dashiell Hammett, *The Maltese Falcon* • D.H.Lawrence and Robert Bridges and A. Conan Doyle die.

LITERATURE

SINCLAIR LEWIS (1885-1951)

Harry Sinclair Lewis was born in Sauk Centre, Minn, US, on February 7, 1885. He graduated from Yale University in 1907 and became a newspaper reporter. In 1914 he published, *Our Mr Wrenn.* The critics liked it but it didn't sell well. He was writing for the two leading magazines of the time, *The Saturday Evening Post* and *Cosmopolitan.* But he wanted to become a serious novelist. It came about in 1920, following publication of, *Main Street.* His reputation was made. He followed with, *Babbitt* in 1922 and the title word became common usage to describe a middle-aged business man with limited imagination.

He wrote, *Arrowsmith* in 1925, *Elmer Gantry* in 1927 and *Dodsworth* in 1929. He was awarded the 1930 Nobel Prize for Literature; **"for his vigorous and graphic art of description and his ability to create, with wit and humour, new types of characters"**

He was the first American to be awarded the literature prize. He later spent much time abroad, mostly in Europe. His literary output slowed and his reputation declined when, following the end of his second marriage, he turned to drink for solace. Lewis died in Rome, Italy, on January 10, 1951, acknowledged as a great novelist. He had two wives and two sons.

CHEMISTRY

HANS FISCHER (1881-1945)

Hans Fischer was born in Hochst, Germany on July 27, 1881. He obtained his PhD in chemistry from Marburg University and an MD from Munich University. He was professor of medical chemistry at Innsbruck University and later, in 1921, he was professor of organic chemistry at Munich University.

He researched the constituent parts of hemin, a crystalline product of haemoglobin. The result was that Fischer demonstrated that there is a close relationship between hemin and chlorophyll. For this work he was awarded the 1930 Nobel Prize for Chemistry; **"for his researches into the constitution of haemin and chlorophyll and especially for his synthesis of haemin"**

He spent the rest of his life attempting to complete the synthesis of chlorophyll but died before completion. He died during an Allied air-raid on Munich, on March 31, 1945. He was married but without children.

PHYSICS

CHANDRASEKHARA RAMAN (1888-1970)

Chandrasekhara Venkata Raman was born in Trichinopoly, India on November 7, 1888. Following his education at Madras University he was, by 1917, professor of physics at Calcutta University. Here he studied the scattering of light. In 1928 he found that when a substance is illuminated by a beam of light of one frequency, the beam emerging at right angles to the original direction contains other frequencies that are characteristic of the material.

For his work to science Raman was knighted by the King Emperor in 1929. A year later he received the 1930 Nobel Prize for Physics; **"for his work on the scattering of light and for the discovery of the effect named after him"**

In 1933, he was head of the physics department at the Indian Institute of Science in Bangalore. In his honour, in 1947, the Raman Research Institute was founded. He was India's outstanding scientist and contributed to the building up of India's research institutions. He founded the Indian Academy of Sciences and the *Indian Journal of Physics*. He died in Bangalore, India on November 21, 1970. He was married with two sons.

PHYSIOLOGY or MEDICINE

KARL LANDSTEINER (1868-1943)

Karl Landsteiner was born in Vienna, Austria on June 14, 1868, the son of a Jewish newspaper publisher. He qualified as a doctor with a degree from Vienna University. While working at the university's hygiene department, he became interested in immunology. In 1901, he explained that there were at least three major types of human blood, distinguished by the antigens attached to the red blood cells.

He labelled the types, A,B, and O, with an additional group, AB, in which the cells had both A and B antigens. In 1927, he followed with M & N groups. In 1923 Landsteiner joined the Rockefeller Institute of Medical Research in New York, where he remained until his death in 1943. In 1930 he was awarded the Nobel Prize for Physiology or Medicine; **"for his discovery of human blood groups"**

He was also responsible for the development of the ABO system of blood typing, which allowed blood transfusions to become a routine medical practise. He also proved that blood types are inherited through specific genes, a tool that has proven effective in studying human genetics and anthropology. In 1940 he discovered the Rhesus factor in monkeys. He died in New York on June 26, 1943. His main writings, based upon his work, were published in 1936 under the title, *The Specificity of Serological Reactions*. His work in this field led to the establishment of immunochemistry. He was married with a son.

PEACE

NATHAN SODERBLOM (1866-1931)

Nathan Soderblom was born in Trono, Sweden, on January 15, 1866. In 1893 he was ordained a minister and went on to serve seven years as chaplain to the Swedish Legation in Paris. He became professor of theology at Uppsala University in 1901 and appointed Primate of Sweden in 1914. Soderblom, an outspoken pacifist, was most vocal about the stupidity of World War One.

In 1925, he attended the first of a series of conferences known as the Universal Conference on Life and Work, organised in Stockholm. The on-going World Council of Churches grew out of these beginnings. He was awarded the 1930 Nobel Peace Prize; **"for his efforts to further international understanding through church unity"** He died in Uppsala on July 12, 1931. Although he wrote much, his most important work is thought to be, *Gudstrons Uppkomst*, an idea he expresses that holiness rather than the idea of God is the basic notion in religious thought. He was married with seven sons and three daughters.

1931

Britain and Japan abandon gold standard • Invergordon Mutiny • Financial collapse of Central Europe begins • British governments economy measures set off riots in Glasgow and London • Noel Coward, *Cavalcade* • Films; *Frankenstein* , *A Nous la Liberte, Doctor Jekyll and Mr Hyde, Little Caesar* • E.Arnot Robertson, *Four Frightened People* • Virginia Woolf, *The Waves* • General Sir John Monash, Anna Pavlova and Arnold Bennett die.

LITERATURE

ERIK KARLFELDT (1864-1931)

Erik Axel Karlfeldt was born in Folkarna, Sweden on July 20, 1864. Karlfeldt went on to become the centre of controversy. He became a poet, whom the critics disliked and the public adored. He wrote about the peasants and countryside of his native province and rarely ventured further. His most important and enduring work, was his six-volume work of verse entitled, *Vildmarks-och Karleksvisor*. In 1912, he became secretary of the Swedish Academy.

In 1918, he was nominated for the Nobel Prize for Literature, but let it be known he would refuse the honour. In the event, the Prize was not awarded. In early 1931, he was again nominated but before he could refuse or accept, he died, on April 8, 1931, in Stockholm.

Generally, Nobel Prizes are not posthumously awarded. In this case the committee took the view that as he had been nominated, the nomination should stand. Accordingly, Karlfeldt was awarded the 1931 Nobel Prize for Literature; **"for the poetry of Erik Axel Karlfeldt"**

He was married with two children.

CHEMISTRY

KARL BOSCH (1874-1940)
and
FRIEDRICH BERGIUS (1884-1949)

"in recognition of their contributions to the invention and development of chemical high pressure methods"

Karl Bosch was born in Cologne, Germany, on August 27, 1874. Educated at Leipzig University he received his PhD in 1898, for research into organic chemistry. He went on to study general engineering and went to work for a company that became I.G.Farben and of which he later became its' chairman.   Bosch's work was to transfer the laboratory experiments of Fritz Haber (qv) into industrial production. Haber was his brother-in-law and gave him much advise. The process for synthesizing ammonia, from its elements, hydrogen and nitrogen, catalytically at high pressures, meant carrying out some 20,000 experiments.

The Bosch Process, as it became known, meant preparing hydrogen on a manufacturing scale, by passing a mixture of steam and water gas over a suitable catalyst at high temperature. Bosch was awarded a half share of the 1931 Nobel Prize for Chemistry for his devising chemical high-pressure methods of manufacture.

He retired from Farbens following the death of Haber, who had been hounded to his death by his expulsion, by Hitler, calling him 'Jew Haber'. Bosch died in Heidelberg, Germany on April 26, 1940.

IG Farben later became notorious for setting up factories at concentration camps, during WW2 and using slave labour, without ever paying any compensation. He was married with a son and daughter.

Friedrich Bergius was born in Goldschmieden near Breslau, Germany on October 11, 1884. He was educated at the universities of Breslau, Berlin and Leipzig. Bergius was responsible for converting products into food. His book, published in 1913, *The Use of High Pressure in Chemical Actions* explains his work.

He was awarded a half share of the 1931 Nobel Prize for Chemistry, for his work in developing hydrogenation methods required to convert coal dust into gasoline products. His work, converting wood into sugar, and coal into petrol products as well as synthetic butter, later allowed Hitler to provide Germany with food during WW2.

After the war, he took off for Argentina and died in Buenos Aires on March 30, 1949. He was married with two sons and a daughter.

PHYSICS

NOT AWARDED

PHYSIOLOGY or MEDICINE

OTTO WARBURG (1883-1970)

Otto **Heinrich Warburg** was born in Freiburg in Breisgan, Germany, on October 8, 1883, The son of Emil Warburg, a Jewish born physicist who was baptized in order to take up a professorship appointment, Otto received a doctorate in chemistry from Berlin University (1906) and another, in medicine, from Heidelberg in 1911. He became internationally known, following his work at the Marine Biological Station in Naples, Italy.

Here, he first conducted research into respiratory enzymes. His research was rewarded by the 1931 Nobel Prize for Physiology or Medicine; **"for his discovery of the nature and mode of action of the respiratory enzyme"**

His appointment, as head of the Max Planck Institute for Cell Physiology at Berlin, followed. Here he continued his research and investigated photosynthesis, becoming the first person to discover that the growth of malignant cells requires markedly smaller amounts of oxygen than that of normal cells. Warburg never bothered overmuch about his Jewish roots, and although he had little to do with Judaism, he did visit Palestine in 1938 on the SS *Tel Aviv.*

During the Hitler purges of Jewish scientists, Warburg was left undisturbed and he remained at his post at the Max Planck Institute. Hitler noted that Otto had been baptized, although this fact didn't save other baptized Jews. In the middle of WW2, with his Jewish friends and family either abroad, dead or in concentration camps, he was being allowed to continue his work. Indeed, he was offered the 1944 Nobel Prize for Physiology or Medicine but here Hitler drew the line. It was one thing allowing a Jew to work for the German cause, quite another to allow him such a prestigious award.

They didn't dare send him to be exterminated because of his great international prestige. Hitler told the Nobel authorities, ' Warburg as a Jew would not be allowed to accept such an honour; he already has a Nobel Prize give it to someone else'. Warburg was ignored by the Gestapo, survived the war and was still in place when, on August 1, 1970, he died in Berlin. He once told a conference of Nobel prize-winners, "cancer in most of its forms could be avoided if people would take the necessary preventive measures" He never married. It is now considered he was the greatest biochemist of the century. He worked with or helped to develop three future Nobel prizewinners; Meyerhof, Krelos and Hugo Theorell.

PEACE

JANE ADDAMS (1860-1935)
and
NICHOLAS BUTLER (1862-1947)

Jane Addams was born in Cedarville, Ill. U.S. on September 6th 1860. She graduated from Rockford College, but was forced to leave the Woman's Medical College in Philadelphia, because of ill-health. She travelled much of Europe and spent many years in London. Here she noted the poverty in the East End and how the Toynbee Hall Settlement was combatting that poverty.

Upon her return to the US, she founded a 'Toynbee Hall' in Chicago. She succeeded in obtaining a building known as Hull House and enlarging it. Addams worked with reform groups to help juveniles have a law court of their own. She worked for immigrants and against colour prejudice.

In 1915, at The Hague, she was chairman of the International Congress of Women. This she followed by founding the Women's International League for Peace and Freedom. In 1930 she wrote, *The Second Twenty Years at Hull-House.* In 1931, Jane Addams was awarded a share of the 1931 Nobel Peace Prize; **"for her work in founding Hull House, Chicago"**

She died in Chicago on May 21, 1935. She never married.

Nicholas Murray Butler was born in Elizabeth, NJ. US, on April 2, 1862. Educated at Columbia, he received his PhD in philosophy in 1884. He toured Europe, staying for long periods in Berlin and Paris, returning to the US, and taking up a teaching career, in 1885, at Columbia University; here he would stay until 1945, retiring as president of the university.

He was a great supporter of international understanding and a founder of the Carnegie Endowment for International Peace, becoming president of the organisation (1925-1945). Between 1928 and 1941, he was president of the American Academy of Arts and Letters. In 1931, he received a half share of the Nobel Prize for Peace; **"for his work with the Carnegie Endowment for International Peace"**

He died in New York on December 7, 1947. He was twice married with a daughter.

1932

Japanese occupy Shanghai • F.D.Roosevelt wins US election • Catalonia becomes independent • Famine in USSR • Chadwick discovers the neutron • Karl Jansky pioneers radio-astronomy • Bertolt Brecht, *The Mother* • First 'Tarzan ' film • Stella Gibbons, *Cold Comfort Farm* • Aldous Huxley, *Brave New World* • Films; *I am a Fugitive from a Chain Gang, Trouble in Paradise, Scarface, Grand Hotel* • Florenz Ziegfield and Kenneth Grahame die.

LITERATURE

JOHN GALSWORTHY (1867-1933)

John Galsworthy was born in Kingston Hill, Surrey, England on August 14, 1867. His father was a lawyer and rich enough to send his son to Harrow and New College, Oxford. John studied to become a lawyer and was called to the bar in 1890. He half decided to become a marine lawyer and thought he would travel around the world to give him the required experience of things naval. Amongst the people he met was Joseph Conrad, then a mate on a merchant ship. The two men went on to become lifelong friends.

His meeting with Conrad and his earnestness about writing prompted the young Galsworthy to give up law and become a writer. He had little need to worry about money and could afford to indulge himself. However, his early work, *From the Four Winds* (a collection of short stories, 1897) and his novel, *Jocelyn* (1898) he published himself under a pseudonym, John Sinjohn.

These writings received sufficient favourable attention for Galsworthy te revert to his own name, when he published *The Island Pharisees* in 1904. *The Man of Property* (1906) began the series of novels that became known as, *The Forsyte Saga*. This overall work is the one for which Galsworthy is remembered. He wrote many novels but none would become as famous as 'the Saga'. He was awarded the 1932 Nobel Prize for Literature; **"for his distinguished art of narration which takes its highest form in *The Forsyte Saga*"**

His plays include, *Justice* (1910). This concerned prison life and roused so much feeling that it led directly to prison reform. However, his best known play is probably, *Loyalties* staged in 1922. Following his death in 1933, his reputation plunged. It revived in 1967, with the BBC television series, *The Forsyte Saga*. This production became a major success in the UK, the USA and many other parts of the world. He died in Hampstead, London on January 31, 1933. He was married but had no children.

CHEMISTRY

IRVING LANGMUIR (1881-1957)

Irving Langmuir was born in Brooklyn, New York, US, on January 31, 1881. He began by studying metallurgical engineering at Columbia University but switched to Göttingen University, Germany where he studied physical chemistry and obtained a PhD in 1906. Back in the United States, he worked at the General Electric Company, researching electrical discharges in gases, electron emission and various aspects of tungsten.

He became responsible for creating a longer life tungsten-filament light bulb. He also developed other items that belonged to the arena of broadcasting. In addition, an atomic hydrogen blowtorch capable of reaching temperatures in excess of 3,000 degrees centigrade. In 1932 he was awarded the Nobel Prize for Chemistry; **"for his discoveries and investigations in surface chemistry"**

He also worked in opening new fields in colloid research and biochemistry. In 1946, he was in the forefront of those trying to produce rain by seeding clouds with silver iodide and solidified carbon dioxide. He died in Falmouth, Mass, on August 16, 1957. Married with a son and daughter, his hobbies were flying and skiing.

PHYSICS

WERNER HEISENBERG (1901-1976)

Werner Karl Heisenberg was born in Wurzburg, Germany on December 5, 1901, his father a professor of languages. Werner studied theoretical physics at Munich University and obtained an MD in 1923. The following year he was appointed a lecturer at Göttingen University. He then went to Copenhagen and spent three years working with Niels Bohr (qv).

During the 1920s, Heisenberg suggested a radical reinterpretation of the basic concepts of applied mechanics. He went on to discover a way to formulate quantum mechanics in terms of matrices (1925). Heisenberg was awarded the 1932 Nobel Prize for Physics; **"for the creation of quantum mechanics, the application of which has, inter alia, led to the discovery of the allotropic forms of hydrogen"**

As a member of the Nazi Party, he continued his work and in 1942, was appointed director of the Max Planck Institute for Physics in Berlin. During WW2, he was part of the German atomic weapons research team. In 1945 he was dismissed his post by the Allies and sent, as a prisoner, to the UK. He died in Munich on February 1, 1976. He was married with seven children.

PHYSIOLOGY or MEDICINE

CHARLES SHERRINGTON (1857-1952)
and
EDGAR ADRIAN (1889-1977)

"For their discoveries regarding the functions of neurons"

Charles Scott Sherrington was born in London, England on November 27, 1857. He was educated at Caius College, Cambridge and later became a professor at various English universities, London (1891-1895), Liverpool (1895-1913) and Oxford (1913-1935). His research work dealt in reflex actions, and led to 'Sherrington's Law', which states that when one set of muscles is stimulated, muscles opposing the action of the first are simultaneously inhibited. His book, *The Integrative Action of the Nervous System*, written in 1906 is still considered a classic on the subject. His work resulted in his being knighted in 1922, and awarded with a half share of the 1932 Nobel Prize for Physiology or Medicine.

In 1932 he published, *The Reflex Activity of the Spinal Cord.* His ongoing research of all aspects of mammalian nervous functions has resulted in the development of brain surgery and the treatment of nervous disorders. He also invented the word, 'neuron and synapse', to denote the nerve cell and the point at which the nervous impulse is transmitted, respectively, from one nerve cell to another. He died of a heart attack in Eastbourne, Sussex, on March 4, 1952. He was married but had no children.

Edgar Douglas Adrian was born in London, England on November 30, 1889. He graduated with an MD from Trinity College, Cambridge and immediately went off to war, where he worked amongst the wounded in France. After WW1, he spent much of his life teaching and researching. He served as master of Trinity College (1961-1965) and chancellor of the University (1968-1975). His research included researching the nerve impulses from sense organs and recording nerve impulses from single sensory endings. He received a half share of the 1932 Nobel Prize for Physiology or Medicine for this work.

He spent the 30s researching the electrical activity of the brain and his work on the variations and abnormalities of the changes, known as the Berger rhythm, opened new fields of investigation into epilepsy and the area of cerebral lesions. In 1942, he was awarded the Order of Merit and created a Baron in 1955. He died in London on August 4, 1977. He was married with a son and two daughters.

PEACE

NOT AWARDED

1933

Hitler wins Germany • 'New Deal' in US • Japan advances in China • Further unrest in Palestine • US repeals prohibition • Leon Trotsky, *History of the Russian Revolution* • Anderson and Millikin discover positrons • Richard Strauss, *Arabella* • Walter Greenwood, *Love on the Dole* • Films; *King Kong, The Invisible Man, Duck Soup, Cavalcade, The Private Life of Henry VIII* • John Galsworthy dies.

LITERATURE

IVAN BUNIN (1870-1953)

Ivan Alekseyevich Bunin was born in Voronezh, Russia on October 22, 1870. He worked at any job he could find in order to live to write. He wrote and he translated. His first volume of poetry, written whilst working as a clerk, was published in 1891. His translation of Longfellow's *Hiawatha* won him the Pushkin Prize from the Russian Academy in 1903. Bunin made his name with short stories. The first, *The Gentleman from San Francisco* in 1916 his last, *Dark Avenues* in 1943.

Following the Russian Revolution of 1917 Bunin settled in France, retaining his Russian nationality. Thus when he was awarded the 1933 Nobel Prize for Literature; **"for the strict artistry with which he has carried on the classical Russian traditions in prose writing"**

He became the first Russian born person to receive the Nobel prize for Literature. Probably his most famous book is, *The Well of Days* (1933). His writings dealt with the decay of Russian nobility and the poor life of the peasant. Other writings included biographies of Tolstoy and Chekhov, both of whom he personally knew. Bunin died in Paris on November 8, 1953. He never married.

CHEMISTRY

NOT AWARDED

PHYSICS

PAUL DIRAC (1902-1984)
and
ERWIN SCHRODINGER (1887-1961)

"for the discovery of new productive forms of atomic theory"

Paul **Adrien Maurice Dirac** was born in Bristol, England on August 8, 1902. His father was Swiss by birth and French master at the private school Paul attended. He then had a place at Bristol University to study engineering. He received a degree in electrical engineering but wasn't able to find a job. He received a grant and began studying science at St. John's College, Cambridge.

In 1926, whilst still a student, Dirac made a contribution to physics that brought him instant fame. He devised a form of quantum mechanics that was distinguished by its generality and logical simplicity and considered far better than that pronounced by Max Planck a few months earlier. It resulted in Dirac being awarded a half share in the 1933 Nobel Prize for Physics. In his book, *The Principles of Quantum Mechanics* (1958), considered a classic on the subject, Dirac develops the theory and writes; ' control a substratum of which we cannot form a mental picture without introducing irrelevancies'. He was a solitary figure, who shunned publicity and people. His pleasure was going on solitary walks.

In 1939 he received the Royal Society Medal. He taught at Cambridge and in 1932 was appointed Lucasain Professor of Mathematics, a chair once held by Isaac Newton. He stayed until 1968, then moved westward to the US In 1971 he was appointed professor emeritus at Florida State University. He died in Tallahassee, Florida on October 20, 1984. He was married but left no issue.

Erwin **Schrodinger** was born in Vienna, Austria on August 12, 1887. He was educated at Vienna University leaving to serve in the Austrian Army during WW1. In 1921 he was at Zurich University where he remained for six years. In 1926, and working as a theoretical physicist, he importantly contributed to the wave theory of matter and to the fundamentals of quantum mechanics.

In 1927, he accepted an invitation to succeed Max Planck, the inventor of the quantum hypothesis, at Berlin University. Here Schrodinger joined such luminaries as Albert Einstein(qv). 1933 was a big year for him. He was awarded a half share in the 1933 Nobel Prize for Physics and he took a view on the Hitler regime that persecuted Jews as a national policy. He left Germany and spent seven years working in Europe's capitals. In 1940 he arrived in Dublin and stayed fifteen years; working at the Dublin Institute for Advanced Studies. He did research in physics and philosophy, as well as a history of science.

He wrote, *What is Life?* during this period, as an attempt to show how quantum physics can be used to explain the stability of genetic structure. In 1956, he returned to Vienna to become professor emeritus at Vienna University. He died in Vienna on January 4, 1961. He was part of a childless marriage.

PHYSIOLOGY or MEDICINE

THOMAS MORGAN (1866-1945)

Thomas Hunt Morgan was born in Lexington, Ky. US, on September 25, 1866. The son of a diplomat and nephew of an army general, Thomas decided to become a naturalist. He received a degree in 1886 from Kentucky University and went to John Hopkins University where he graduated in biology, obtaining a PhD in 1890.

Between 1893 and 1910, Morgan created experimental techniques to the problems of embryology. He became professor of experimental zoology at Columbia University and remained for 24 years. It was here that he conducted most of his important research into heredity.

He transferred to the California Institute of Technology (1928-45) and carried out his experiments with the *Drosophila* fruit fly, from which he established a chromosome theory of heredity involving genes for specific tasks aligned on chromosomes. This major breakthrough in the area of genetics, resulted in his being awarded the 1933 Nobel Prize for Physiology or Medicine; **"for his discoveries concerning the role played by the chromosome in heredity"** He wrote much including, *Evolution and Adaption* (1911), *The Theory of the Gene* (1926) and *Embryology and Genetics* (1933). In 1939, he received the highly prized award of the Copley Medal by the Royal Society of London. He died in harness in Pasadena, California on December 4, 1945. He was married with a son and three daughters.

PEACE

NORMAN ANGELL (1873-1967)

Ralph Norman Angell-Lane was born in Holbeach, Lincolnshire, England on December 26, 1873 and called himself Norman Angell. As such, he received an education in France, London and Geneva that well prepared him for what lay ahead. Whilst in America (1890-98), he worked as a cowboy and gold prospector as well as a journalist on the *San Francisco Chronicle.*

He returned to England and in 1910 wrote, *The Great Illusion,* which suggested that the victors of war had rewards of economic advantage and increased world trade and therefore riches. In 1933 he wrote, *The Great Illusion, 1933,* which now stated that war was futile even for the winners. He spent much time working and preaching for world peace and was rewarded by the 1933 Nobel Prize for Peace; **"in recognition of his work for peace"**

He never married and died on October 7, 1967 in the Home for the Aged in Croydon, England.

1934

Adolf Hitler declared Fuhrer • Disarmament Conference ends in failure • Germany renegs on overseas debts • London hosts fascist and anti-fascist demonstrations • Reinhold Niebuhr, *Moral Man and Immoral Society* • Agatha Christie, *Murder on the Orient Express* • Robert Graves, *I, Claudius* • James Hilton, *Goodbye Mr Chips* • Henry Miller, •*Tropic 0f Cancer* • Films, *David Copperfield, The Gay Divorcee, Sons of the Desert, It Happened One Night,* • Sophia Loren born • Elgar, Holst, Delius and Marie Curie die.

LITERATURE

LUIGI PIRANDELLO (1867-1936)

Luigi Pirandello was born in Agrigento, Sicily, on June 28, 1867. He was the son of a merchant who wanted Luigi to follow him into commerce. Luigi, however, was interested in study, and took himself off first to Palermo and then Rome University. He quarrelled with his tutor and went off to Bonn University in Germany. There he obtained a doctorate in philology, for a thesis on the dialect of Agrigento. In 1894, he became a victim of an arranged marriage which gave him financial independence and a home in Rome. There he began to write. His most significant and popular medium was short stories.

In 1903 his fortunes changed when his wife's father went bankrupt. Luigi turned to teaching. His wife developed mental illness and went into a sanatorium in 1919, and there she stayed until she died in 1959.

Fame came with his third novel, generally considered his best, *Il fu Mattia Pascal* (1904).   His is a realistic style often reflecting political attitudes as well as expressing theories of the personality. Generally his writing is an acquired taste and this is evident from his plays. However, it his playwriting that brought him fame and riches.

These plays, *Sei personaggi* and *Enrico 1V* toured the world between 1925-27, with Pirandello's own company. In 1934, he was awarded the Nobel Prize for Literature; **"for his bold and ingenious revival of dramatic and scenic art"**

Married with three children, he died in Rome on December 10, 1936.

CHEMISTRY

HAROLD UREY (1893-1981)

Harold Clayton Urey was born on April 29, 1893 in Walkerton, Ind. US. In 1917 he received a BS degree from Montana State University and in 1923, his PhD from the University of California at Berkeley, at which place of learning he was a teacher. He then spent a couple of years in Copenhagen taking part in Niels Bohr's basic research on the theory of atomic structure. He returned to the US where he spent various times at various universities including, John Hopkins, Baltimore; Institute for Nuclear Studies; Chicago University and California University, San Diego, from where he retired in 1981.

In the 1920's he began deuterium research. He distilled a sample of liquid hydrogen and by so doing, he concentrated its deuterium form thus demonstrating its presence by light emission studies.   For this work he was rewarded with the 1934 Nobel Prize for Chemistry; **"for his discovery of heavy hydrogen"**

In 1931, he was able to announce his team's discovery of heavy water, composed of an atom of oxygen and two atoms of deuterium. During WW2, Urey directed a research programme at Columbia University, that was part of the Manhattan Project, that resulted in the A-Bomb. Urey's team provided the basic knowledge for the separation of the fissionable isotope uranium-238

.   The war over, Urey turned his attention to the ocean and ways of devising methods for estimating temperatures as far back as 180 million years ago.

This work led him to theorize on the early atmosphere of Earth and suggested that the planets of the solar system may have originated from a gaseous disk rotating about the Sun and that the disk, in combination with gases from the Sun, may have broken into fragments and begun to condense.

He elaborated on this theory in his book, *The Planets: Their Origin and Development* (1952).

He died in La Jolla, Calif. on January 5, 1981. He was married with three daughters and a son.

PHYSICS

NOT AWARDED

PHYSIOLOGY or MEDICINE

GEORGE MINOT (1885-1950), WILLIAM MURPHY (1892-1987)
and
GEORGE WHIPPLE (1878-1976)

"for their discoveries concerning liver therapy in cases of anaemia"

George Richards Minot was born in Boston, US, on December 2, 1885. He obtained his MD from Harvard University in 1912. His research into the malfunction of the human liver began in 1915 and continued until 1948. He worked at Massachusetts General Hospital, Boston (1915-23) and Harvard University (1922-28). He served as director of the the the Thorndike Memorial Laboratory, Boston City Hospital from 1928 to 1950 He and William Murphy, discovered that anaemia in humans, previously a usual fatal condition, would respond to a diet of raw liver. Minot, for this work, received a third share of the 1934 Nobel Prize for Physiology or Medicine.

Minot later succeeded in preparing effective oral- taking liver extracts, which reversed pernicious anaemia.

Minot died in Brookline, Mass. on February 25, 1950.

William Parry Murphy was born in Stoughton, Wis. US, on February 6, 1892. He obtained his MD from Harvard University in 1920 and taught at Brigham Hospital, Boston from 1923 to 1958 by which time he was a consultant in haematology.

In 1934, he was awarded a third share of the Nobel Prize for Physiology or Medicine for his share of the work in the treatment of pernicious anaemia by way of a liver diet. His textbook on the subject, *Anaemia in Practise* was published in 1939.

He was married with a son and daughter. He died on January 18, 1987.

George Hoyt Whipple was born in Ashland, NH,US, on August 28, 1878. He came from a family of doctors. It was research originated by Whipple that led to Minot and Murphy being able to conclude that a diet of raw liver was a recipe for the treatment of pernicious anaemia.

Whipple demonstrated in 1920, that liver as a dietary factor, greatly enhances haemoglobin regeneration in dogs. He later carried out experiments in artificial anaemia which established iron as the most potent inorganic factor in the creation of red blood cells. He was the third member of the trio who were jointly awarded the 1934 Nobel Prize for Physiology of Medicine. He died on February 1, 1976 in Rochester, New York. He was married with a son and daughter.

PEACE

ARTHUR HENDERSON (1863-1935)

Arthur Henderson was born in Glasgow, Scotland on September 13, 1863. After minimal schooling, he found work in a foundry in Newcastle-upon-Tyne, making railway engines. He turned to politics as a possible panacea to the problems of the working classes who generally found living conditions poor, demoralizing and often primitive.

Following years in local politics, serving as a counsellor, he found himself in parliament as a Labour MP. He became chief party whip in 1914, 1921-23 and 1925-27. Although he served as chairman of the Labour Party in 1908-10 and 1914-17 he found the office of party secretary which he held from 1911 to 1934, a tougher post. He did much important party work including re-writing most of the party constitution.

He also resigned from the war-time five man cabinet following Lloyd George changing his mind about Kerensky's plan for a socialist conference in Stockholm. This was the beginning of Henderson's work for peace.

He became the foreign secretary in MacDonald's second Labour government and as such, was a great supporter of the League of Nations.

In May 1931 he was chosen as head of the World Disarmament Conference held in Geneva in 1932. When MacDonald formed a national coalition in August 1931 Henderson resigned and became wholly concerned with matters of disarmament. He was awarded the 1934 Nobel Prize for Peace; **"for his work on disarmament"**

Married with three sons and a daughter, he died in London on October 20, 1935.

1935

Germany reneges on Versailles Treaty • Anti Catholic riots in Belfast • Italy invades Abyssinia • Persia becomes Iran • Kodak devise 35mm film • Salvador Dali, *Giraffe on Fire* **• George Gershwin,** *Porgy and Bess* **• T.S.Eliot,** *Murder in the Cathedral* **• Graham** *Greene, England Made Me* **• George Orwell,** *A Clergyman's Daughter* **• Enid Bagnold,** *National Velvet* **• Films,** *Les Miserables, A Night at the Opera, The Thirty-Nine Steps , Top Hat* **• Francoise Sagan born • Alfred Dreyfus, T.E.Lawrence and André Citroen die.**

LITERATURE

NOT AWARDED

CHEMISTRY

IRENE JOLIOT-CURIE (1897-1956)
and
FRÉDÉRIC JOLIOT-CURIE (1900-1958)

"in recognition of their synthesis of new radioactive elements"

Irène Curie was born on September 12, 1897 in Paris, the daughter of Nobel Prize winners, Pierre and Marie Curie. She was educated at the Collège Sévigné and Paris University, where she assisted her mother at the Institut du Radium. Her thesis, for her PhD, was on the alpha rays of polonium. That was in 1925, the same year she met Frédéric. They researched independently from each other until, in 1928, they jointly signed their work.

      Jean-Frédéric Joliot was born in Paris on March 19, 1900 and educated in the free public system. He succeeded in winning a scholarship, to the prestigious École de Physique at de Chimie Industrielle, from where he graduated with a degree in engineering. Upon completion of military service, he was in receipt of a research scholarship and hired by Marie Curie as an assistant. That was in 1925, the year he met his future wife, Irène.

      Together, they researched bombarded boron, aluminum and magnesium with alpha particles and obtained radioactive isotopes of elements, not normally radioactive, in particular nitrogen, phosphorus and aluminum. These discoveries showed the possibility of using artificially produced radioactive elements to follow chemical changes. The absorption of radio iodine, by the thyroid

gland, was also discovered.

It all resulted in the husband and wife team being awarded the 1935 Nobel Prize for Chemistry, for the synthesis of new radioactive elements. With the prize money, the couple were able to move. They bought a house on the edge of the Parc de Screaux in Paris and divided their time, here and at their country home, in Brittany. Frédéric was appointed professor at the Collège de France in 1937 and later supervised the construction of electrostatic accelerators at Arcueil-Cachan, as well as a cyclotron of seven million electron volts, at the Collège de France.

Irène, meanwhile, was at home raising their three children. However she, like her husband, were most political. Irene was one of only three women who participated in the Popular Front government of 1936 and made no secret of their support for the Republican cause in Spain. They were most circumspect regarding publishing anything that might aid Germany in their search for an atomic weapon.

The Joilet-Curies recorded the principle of nuclear reactors and deposited their findings in a sealed envelope and left it with the Académie des Sciences. There it remained secret until 1949. Frédéric remained in occupied France to make sure the Germans didn't steal anything from his laboratory. The couple continued to research, notably in the area of biology, where they demonstrated the use of radioactive iodine as a tracer in the thyroid gland. The German occupation continued to worry them. In June 1941, Frédéric became president of the National Front Committee.

Following the murder of the physicist. J.Solomon, by the Germans, Frédéric joined the Communist Party. He did much good work in preventing French scientists from being deported to Germany and most relieved, when Irène and the children left for Switzerland, and safety. Frédéric changed his name to Jean-Pierre Gaumont and remained in Paris. His laboratory, at the Collége de France, became the production centre for the making of explosives and was an arsenal for the liberation of Paris. For this work he received the Croix de Guerre and created a commander of the Legion of Honour. In 1944 he was elected to the Académie des Sciences.

During the 1950s, Irene's health deteriorated. A series of operations didn't help. Frédéric developed hepatitis that gradually worsened. Despite these set backs the couple continued with their work and were responsible for the creation of the nuclear physics laboratory at, d'Orsay University in South Paris. Following Irène's death in 1956, Frédéric, despite his illness and grief, became professor at Paris University in place of Irène. He also continued with his other work. Irène died in Paris on March 17, 1956 and Fredéric on August 14, 1958, also in Paris.

PHYSICS

JAMES CHADWICK (1891-1974)

James Chadwick was born in Manchester, England on October 20, 1891. He was educated at the universities of Manchester and Cambridge. He also studied at the Technische Hochschule in Berlin. From 1923 he was working with Ernest Rutherford, at the Cavendish Laboratory at Cambridge. There they studied the transmutation of elements, by bombarding them with alpha particles and investigating the nature of the atomic nucleus.

They also identified the proton as a constituent of the nuclei of other atoms. In 1932, Chadwick observed that beryllium, when exposed to bombardment by alpha particles, released an unknown radiation that, in turn, ejected protons from the nuclei of various substances .

Chadwick reckoned this radiation as being composed of particles of mass, roughly equal to the proton but without electrical charge, i.e. neutrons. It was a discovery that provided an additional tool for inducing atomic disintegration. Chadwick was awarded the 1935 Nobel Prize for Physics; **"for the discovery of the neutron"**

He was knighted in 1945 and died on July 24, 1974 in Cambridge. He was married with twin daughters.

PHYSIOLOGY or MEDICINE

HANS SPEMANN (1869-1941)

Hans Spemann was born in Stuttgart, Germany on June 27, 1869. He was educated at the universities of Heidelberg, Munich and Wurzburg and graduated in zoology, botany and physics. Whilst occupying the chair of zoology, at Freiburg University (1919-35), he conceived the concept of induction.

This is now known as embryonic induction and is the influence exercised by various parts of the embryo that directs the development of groups of cells into particular tissues and organs. The results of his work is summarized in his book, *Embryonic Development and Induction* (1936).

His work was rewarded by the award of the 1935 Nobel Prize for Physiology or Medicine; **"for his discovery of the organizer effect in embryonic development"**

Married with two sons, he died in Freiburg im Breisgau, Germany, on September 12, 1941.

PEACE

CARL von OSSIETZKY (1889-1938)

Carl von Ossietzky was born in Hamburg, Germany on October 3, 1889. A member of the German Peace Society, he was conscripted into the German Army for the duration of WW1. In 1920, whilst secretary of the society's Berlin office, he co-founded the Nie Wieder Krieg (No More War) society. In 1922, he was editor of the, *Weltbuhne,* a weekly left-wing journal, that unmasked a plan for German re-armament.

He was accused of treason and in November 1931 was sentenced to 18 months imprisonment, serving 13 months. At the time of Hitler's election as chancellor, Ossietzky was once again the editor of the paper that was anti-Nazi. He refused to flee Germany and was arrested in February 1933 and sent to Papenburg concentration camp. From there he was transferred to the prison hospital, when diagnosed with TB. During this time Ossietzky was awarded the 1935 Nobel Prize for Peace; **"for his work for peace"**

The award left little doubt that this was a demonstration of worldwide censure on Hitler and his policies. It resulted in Hitler forbidding Germans ever to accept a Nobel Prize and to removing Ossietzky to a private clinic in Berlin, where he died of TB on May 4, 1938.

1936

Spanish Civil War begins • German troops enter Rhineland • Abdication of Edward V111 • China declares war on Japan • John Maynard Keynes, *General Theory of Employment, Interest and Money* **• Penquin Books launch 'paperbacks' • Olympic Games in Berlin • Siegfried Sassoon,** *The Complete Memoirs of George Sherston* **• Cyril Connolly,** *The Rock Pool* **• Films;** *Rembrandt, San Francisco, Things to Come, The Great Ziegfeld, Mr Deeds Goes to Town,* **• Irving Thalberg, Rudyard Kipling, Houseman, Grigory Zinoviev, Maxim Gorky and Luigi Pirandello die.**

LITERATURE

EUGENE O'NEILL (1888-1953)

Eugene Gladstone O'Neill was born in New York City, US, on October 16, 1888. His father James, was a successful actor who spent most of his life touring. Eugene was born in a hotel room and spent his childhood experiencing a variety of hotels all over America. It all resulted in his growing up resenting his forced lifestyle and seeing his mother becoming an alcoholic and drug taker, as an escape from her unsettled lifestyle. Eugene saw all this as well as his mother's addiction to religion; shared by his father. Later Eugene went to boarding schools and prospered, gaining a place at Princeton University, albeit he only stayed for a year.

He then spent six years working around the world, first as a seaman, later living as a derelict on the waterfronts of Buenos Aires, London and New York. He contemplated suicide, by drinking himself to death. At 24, he decided on a different route and got himself a job as a reporter only to come down with TB, a condition that had been aggravated by his extreme life styles. He was sent to a sanitarium in Wallingford, Conn. where he spent six months. Then began what he would later term his 'rebirth'. His first efforts at play writing were clumsy and awkward but they were about real people and of sufficient interest for a critic to persuade O'Neill senior to pay for his son to go to Harvard on a play writing course.

The first result was in 1916, when a small group of players working in summer stock in Provincetown, Mass. produced O'Neills one act play, *Bound East for Cardiff.* It was produced at the Playwright's Theatre in Greenwich Village on November 3rd 1916. *Beyond the Horizon* in 1920, resulted in high praise from the critics and the Pulitzer Prize for Drama.(one of four).

His reputation grew nationally and internationally resulting in the 1936 award of the Nobel Prize for Literature; **"for the power, honesty, and deep-felt emotions of his dramatic works, which embody an original concept of tragedy"**

He married three times and had three children. He was twice divorced, his eldest son committed suicide at the age of 40, his youngest son became mentally unstable and his only daughter Oona, married Charles Chaplin when she was 18 and Chaplin was the same age as O'Neill. He never spoke to Oona again and cut her out of his life. O'Neill, one of the greatest literary figures of the 20th century, died a broken and tragic figure in a Boston hotel on November 27, 1953.

CHEMISTRY

PETER DEBYE (1884-1966)

Peter **Joseph William Debye** was born in Maastricht, Holland on March 24, 1884. He obtained his PhD in physics from Munich University in 1910 and then taught physics at the universities of Zurich, Utrecht, Göttingen and Leipzig. He then settled down to become director of the Kaiser Wilhelm Institute for Theoretical Physics in Berlin.

That was in 1935. Unhappy at the events taking place in Germany, he accepted an invitation in 1940 from Ithaca University, following his award of the 1936 Nobel Prize for Chemistry; **"for his contributions to our knowledge of molecular structure through his investigations on dipole moments and on the diffraction of X-ray and electrons in gases"**

His work on X-rays and light scattering in gases, contributed to his ability to lecture on his subjects. He became a US citizen in 1946, and was in charge of the chemistry department of Cornell University. Probably his most notable achievement came in 1923, when he extended Svante Arrhenius's theory of the dissociation of the positively and negatively charged atoms of salts in solution, thus proving that the ionization is complete and not partial. Debye died in Ithaca, New York, on November 2, 1966. He was married with a son and daughter.

PHYSICS

CARL ANDERSON (1905-1991)
and
VICTOR HESS (1883-1964)

Carl **David Anderson** was born in New York on September 3, 1905. He received his PhD from the California Institute of Technology in 1930, where he spent the rest of his working life ending as professor emeritus in 1976. In between, he researched gamma-rays and cosmic rays, using the magnetic cloud chamber.

In 1932 he discovered the positron in the course of cosmic-ray interaction study and, in 1933, he succeeded in producing positrons by gamma irradiation. In 1936, he was involved in the discovery of the muon, a basic particle some 207 times as massive as the electron. In the same year he was awarded a half share of the 1936 Nobel Prize for Physics; **"for his discovery of the positron"**

He spent a long and happy retirement in San Marino, California where he died on January 11, 1991. He was married with two sons.

Victor **Francis Hess** was born in Waldstein, Austria on June 24, 1883. Educated at Grazversity he received his PhD from Vienna University in 1906. His research centred mainly on radioactivity and atmospheric electricity.

In 1911, he experimented on altitudes and the effects of atmosphere that proved that an extremely penetrating radiation of extraterrestrial origin, permeates the atmosphere. This discovery allowed Anderson to go on and discover the positron. In 1936, Hess received a half share of the Nobel Prize for Physics; **"for his discovery of cosmic radiation"**

He left Nazi Austria in 1938, for the US where he became professor of physics at Fordham University, New York. He died in Mount Vernon, New York on December 17, 1964.

PHYSIOLOGY or MEDICINE

HENRY DALE (1875-1968)
and
OTTO LOEWI (1873-1961)

"for their discoveries relating to chemical transmission of nerve impulses"

Henry **Hallett Dale** was born in London on June 9, 1875. He graduated in medicine from Cambridge University in 1909. In 1914 he was on the staff of the Medical Research Council and from 1928 to 1942, he was director of the National Institute for Medical Research. Dale was the first to identify, in 1911, the compound histamine in animal tissues. He went on to conclude that histamine is responsible for some allergic and anaphylactic reactions. In 1930 he demonstrated how histamine is released at nerve endings in the parasympathetic nervous system.

For his work Dale was awarded a co-share of the 1936 Nobel Prize for Physiology or Medicine. He was knighted in 1932 and, during WW2, was chairman of the Scientific Advisory Committee to the War Cabinet. He received the Order of Merit in 1944. He died in Cambridge, on July 23, 1968. He never married.

Otto **Loewi** was born in Frankfurt-am-Main, Germany, on June 3, 1873. He graduated in medicine in 1896 from Strasbourg (German) University. He then became professor of pharmacology at Graz University in 1909.

His neurological researches in the 1920s, provided the first proof that chemicals were involved in the transmission of impulses from one nerve cell to another, and from neuron to the responsive organ. Further investigations followed that related to the chemical transmission of nerve impulses and won for Loewi a half share of the 1936 Nobel Prize for Physiology or Medicine.

In 1938, when the Germans marched into a welcoming Austria, they arrested Nobel Laureate Professor Otto Loewi, now aged 65, took away all his possessions and put him into prison for the offence of being Jewish. An international protest followed that resulted in his release and permission to leave the new Greater Germany. However, he wasn't allowed to leave until he had handed over, for safe keeping by the Nazis, all of the Nobel prize money he had recently received. He spent a year in Brussels and a year in London before shipping out to the US in 1940. He became research professor at the School of Medicine at New York University where he remained until his death 21 years later.

He was a most humorous man who failed to be concerned that he had been stripped of all his worldly goods and not even allowed the use of his Nobel Prize money. In addition to his work on the nervous system, he researched diabetes and the action of the drug digitalis. He created a test for detecting pancreatic disease now known as the Loewi Test. He died in New York City on December 25, 1961. He was married with three sons and a daughter.

PEACE

CARLOS LAMAS SAAVEDRA (1878-1959)

Carlos **Lamas Saavedra** was born in Buenos Aires, Argentina on November 1, 1878. He was educated as a lawyer and went on to teach law at La Plata University and Buenos Aires University where he was rector between 1941-43.

He was part of the government and in 1915 became minister of justice. Between 1932 and 1938 he was minister of foreign affairs. He was president of the International Labour Congress, Geneva (1928), the Pan-American Conference, Buenos Aires (1936) and the League of Nations Assembly (1936).

He worked on an anti-war treaty that between 1933 and 1934 was signed by the US, Italy and 14 Latin American countries. In 1936 he received the Nobel Peace Prize; **"for his part in ending the Chaco War between Bolivia and Paraguay"**

He died in Buenos Aires on May 5, 1959.

1937

Japan take Peking, Shanghai and Nanking • Fascist victories in Spain • Purge of USSR generals • US has Neutrality Act • Italy joins Germany and Japan anti-Comintern Pact • Martin Buber, *I and Thou* **• Nazi exhibition of 'Degenerate Art' in Munich • Paris World Fair • Jean Renoir,** *The Great Illusion* **• Isaac Rosenberg,** *Collected Works* **• John Steinbeck,** *Of Mice and Men* **• J.R.Tolkien,** *The Hobbit* **• Films;** *The Life of Emile Zola, The Good Earth, A Day at the Races, Snow White and the Seven Dwarfs, The Prisoner of Zenda* **• Vanessa Redgrave born • Lilian Baylis, George Gershwin, Marconi, Maurice Ravel and J.M.Barrie die.**

LITERATURE

ROGER MARTIN du GARD (1881-1958)

Roger **Martin du Gard** was born in Neuilly-sur-Seine, France, on March 23, 1881. He was originally trained as an archivist but decided instead to become a writer. He first attracted notice with his, *Jean Barois* (1913). This traced the development of an intellectual torn between the Catholic religion and a scientific life; it also examined The Dreyfus affair and examined its effect on the French population. During WW1 he was in the French Army serving in a transport division.

Then between the two world wars he produced his most important work and for which he is best known. *Les Thibaults* (1922-40) and *The Thibaults*(1939-41) is an eight part novel cycle and is a record of a family's development from the early 19th century to the end of the 1914-18 war. It resulted in his being awarded the 1937 Nobel Prize for Literature; **"for the artistic power and truth with which he has depicted human conflict as well as some fundamental aspects of contemorary life in his novel-cycle** *Les Thibault"*

Although he achieved a high literary output nothing was as successful. Married with a daughter, he died in Bellême, France on August 22, 1958.

CHEMISTRY

WALTER HAWORTH (1883-1950)
and
PAUL KARRER (1889-1971)

Walter **Norman Haworth** was born in Chorley, Lancs; England on March 19, 1883. He graduated from Manchester University in 1906 and received a PhD from Göttingen University in 1910. He taught at the universities of St.Andrews (1912-20) and Durham (1920-25). Whilst at St. Andrews he worked on carbohydrates generally and sugars in particular.

He found that sugars have a ringlike appearance, rather than a straight-line type of their carbon atoms. These ringlike characteristics have come to be known as 'Haworth Formulas'. It resulted in his book, *The Constitution of Sugars* (1929) becoming a standard text. In 1937 Haworth was awarded a half share of the Nobel Prize for Chemistry; **"for his investigations on carbohydrates and vitamin C"**

In 1934 he succeeded in synthesizing vitamin C. This work allowed for the mass production of the vitamin for medical purposes. He was knighted in 1947 and died in Birmingham on March 19, 1950. He was married with two sons.

Paul **Karrer** was born in Moscow, Russia on April 21, 1889. Educated in Switzerland (his parents were Swiss), he received his PhD from Zurich University in 1911. He spent six years working at the Georg Speyer Haus in Frankfurt-am-Main with Paul Ehrlich (qv). In 1918 he was back in Zurich as professor of chemistry. A year later, he was director of the Chemical Institute. His research speciality was on plant pigments. He was not only able to discover the chemical structure of the carotenoids but demonstrated how they formed part of vitamin A.

He later confirmed the structure of vitamin C and spent considerable time in the study of vitamin E. His book, *Organic Chemistry* (1928) was popular throughout the 1930s and 40s. He was awarded a half share of the 1937 Nobel Prize for Chemistry; **"for his investigations on carotenoids, flavins and vitamins A and B2"**

He died in Zurich on June 18, 1971.

PHYSICS

CLINTON DAVISSON (1881-1958)
and
GEORGE THOMSON (1892-1975)

"for their experimental discovery of the diffraction of electrons by crystals"

Clinton Joseph Davisson was born in Bloomington, Ill. US, on October 22, 1881. He received his PhD from Princeton University after which he spent most of his working career with Bell Telephones. His research there, centred on the emissions of electrons from a metal in the presence of heat. He later helped develop the electron microscope. In 1927 he was instrumental in finding that a beam of electrons, when reflected from a metallic crystal, shows a diffraction patterns similar to those of X-rays and other electromagnetic waves.

This discovery created greater understanding of the dual nature of subatomic particles and passably useful in the study of nuclear, atomic and molecular structure. He was awarded a half share of the 1937 Nobel Prize for Physics for discovering that electrons can be diffracted like light waves.

He died in February 1, 1958 whilst living in Charlottesville, Va. US. He was married with three sons and a daughter.

George Paget Thomson was born in Cambridge, England on May 3, 1892. He was the only son of Sir Joseph Thomson, the noted physicist and winner of the Nobel Prize for Physics in 1906. Following a stint of work at the Cavendish Laboratory he was, in 1922, appointed professor of natural philosophy at Aberdeen University.

There he conducted experiments demonstrating that a beams of electrons is diffracted upon passage through a crystalline substance. This confirmed Louis de Broglie's theory concerning particles displaying the properties of waves that have a wavelength. In 1930 he became professor of physics at the Imperial College of Science, London.

In 1937 he received a half share of the Nobel Prize for Physics for demonstrating that electrons undergo diffraction. In 1943 he was knighted and in 1952 became Master of Corpus Chrisit College where he remained until his retirement in 1962. He died in Cambridge on September 10, 1975. He was married with two sons and two daughters.

PHYSIOLOGY or MEDICINE

ALBERT SZENT- GYORGYI von NAGYRAPOLT (1893-1986)

Albert Szent-Gyorgyi was born in Budapest, Hungary on September 16, 1893. He received an MD from Budapest University in 1917 and became interested in biochemistry. He studied in Germany, Holland, England and the US He later found and isolated an organic reducing agent which named, hexuronic acid; now universally known as ascorbic acid, from plants and adrenal gland extracts.

Whilst professor at Szeged University (1931-45), he proved the acid identical to Vitamin C. His investigations on organic compounds laid the foundation for the Kreb cycle two years later. He was awarded the 1937 Nobel Prize for Physiology or Medicine; **"for his discoveries in connection with the biological combustion processes, with special reference to vitamin C ad catalysis of fumaric acid"** .

An anti-Nazi activist, he went to Sweden before emigrating to the US in 1947. There he was appointed director of the Institute for Muscle Research in Wood Holes, Mass. Here, he researched in depth, the causes of cancer. He wrote several books on his subject, including the best known, *Introduction to a Sub molecular Biology* (1960). He died in Woods Hole, on October 22, 1986. He was married with a daughter.

PEACE

EDGAR CECIL (1864-1958)

Edgar Algernon Robert Gascoyne Cecil was born in London on September 14, 1864. He was the third son of the 3rd marquess of Salisbury; three times British prime minister. Edgar, who was also a politician, was one of the main draftsmen of the League of Nations and, in 1919, was present at the 1919 Paris Peace Conference. He showed the arrogance of his class and family by inviting only the white nations who believed in their idea of a world order.

Cecil, often known as Lord Robert, opposed a provision for absolute racial equality among League member states. To his later credit, Cecil promoted disarmament and voted against Japanese aggression in Manchuria and by Italy in Ethiopia. In 1937 he was awarded the Nobel Peace Prize; **"for his work with the League of Nations"**

In 1938, he was one of few parliamentarians who voted against concessions to Germany at the Munich conference in 1938. Married without children, he died in Tunbridge Wells, England on November 24, 1958.

1938

Germany annexes a willing Austria • The 'Munich crisis' • Ball-point pen invented • British war service register • Benny Goodman star of Broadway • Thornton Wilder, *Our Town* **• New York World Fair •** *Picture Post* **starts • Samuel Beckett,** *Murphy* **• Graham Greene,** *Brighton Rock* **• Films;** *The Adventures of Robin Hood, Alexander Nevsky, Angels With Dirty Faces, Pygmalion, You Can't Take It With You* **• Constantin Stanislavsky and Kemal Ataturk die.**

LITERATURE

PEARL BUCK (1892-1973)

Pearl **Buck** was the pseudonym of Pearl Sydenstricker, born in Hillsborough, West Virginia, US on June 26, 1892. She grew up in China, where her parents were Presbyterian missionaries. She was educated in Shanghai and the US. She was working as a teacher at Nanking University, when she started to write books and articles concerning life in China. That was 1923. Some of her articles were published in US magazines but it wasn't until 1931 that fame and fortune came her way with, *The Good Earth*.

In 1937 the book became a feature film that resulted in two Academy Awards. More books followed, *Sons* (1932), *A House Divided* (1935). She wrote, *Dragon Seed* in 1942 which became a feature film in 1944.

In 1917 she married John Buck and in 1934 they divorced. A year later she married Richard Walsh, a New York publisher. Following WW2, she instituted the Pearl Buck Foundation and gave it $7,000,000. She published her autobiography, *My Several Worlds* in 1954. In 1938 she received the Nobel Prize for Literature; **"for her rich and truly epic descriptions of peasant life in China and for her biographical masterpieces"**

She died in Dalby, Vermont on March 6, 1973. Married twice she had ten children.

CHEMISTRY

RICHARD KUHN (1900-1967)

Richard Kuhn was born in Vienna, Austria on December 3, 1900. He received his doctorate from Munich University in 1922 for his work on enzymes. Between 1926 and 1929 he was at Zurich Technical School, before becoming a professor at Heidelberg University.

Kuhn investigated the structure of compounds related carotenoids. He discovered eight carotenoids, and put them into a pure form to determine their constitution. This work led to his isolating the constitution of vitamin B and he was the first to isolate a gram of it. He was awarded the 1938 Nobel Prize for Chemistry; **"for his work on carotenoids and vitamins"**

Hitler however, vetoed the award. In the event Kuhn had to wait for the end of WW2 before receiving his diploma, gold medal and financial reward. In 1948, he was appointed editor of, *Justus Liebigs Annalen der Chemie.* Married, with two sons and four daughters, he died in Heidelberg on August 1, 1967.

PHYSICS

ENRICO FERMI (1901-1954)

Enrico Fermi was born in Rome, Italy on September 29, 1901. He received his doctorate from Pisa University when he was 21, for his thesis on X-rays. He later studied, under Max Born at Göttingen University, and upon his return, he taught mathematics at Florence University. In 1926 he published a paper on the behaviour of a perfect, hypothetical gas. It impressed the physics department at Rome University and resulted in his being invited to become professor of theoretical physics.

In 1926 he developed a statistical method for predicting the characteristics of electrons. He married Laura Capon in 1928 and had two children. The Royal Academy of Italy elected him to membership in 1929; their youngest member ever. He turned to experimental physics. Following the discovery of the neutron by Chadwick (qv), Fermi had the idea of inducing artificial radioactivity, by using neutrons obtained from radioactive beryllium but reducing their speed by passing them through paraffin.

His further works culminated in sufficient knowledge being obtained that would result in understanding nuclear fission. He was awarded the 1938 Nobel Prize for Physics; **"for his demonstrations of the existence of new radioactive elements produced by neutron irradiation, and for his related discovery of nuclear reactions brought about by slow neutrons"**

Fermi had to receive permission from the dictator, Mussolini, to travel to Sweden in order to receive his award. He took his family with him, picked up the award and never returned to Fascist Italy. This was essential, because his wife was Jewish and his two children were deemed likewise and the Italians had by now, albeit encouraged by Hitler, anti-Jewish measures in place. They voyaged to the US where, in 1944, they became American citizens. At Chicago University, Fermi continued his studies on the basic properties of nuclear particles. In 1950 he was elected a foreign member of the Royal Society of London. The Enrico Fermi Award was created in his honour in 1954.

Fermi was the founder of the atomic pile, following his finding of the chain reaction. This find led directly to the creation of the A-Bomb which changed the course of the world for ever. Following WW2, he created the modern nuclear reactor. The element fermium was named after him. Married with a son and daughter, he died in Chicago on November 28, 1954.

PHYSIOLOGY or MEDICINE

CORNEILLE HEYMANS (1892-1968)

Jean **Francois Corneille Heymans** was born in Ghent, Belgium on March 28th 1892. He worked at Ghent University with his father, Jean-Francois Heymans and later succeeded him as professor of pharmacology (1930).

Heymans, demonstrated how the regulatory effect on respiration of sensory organs, associated with the carotid artery, in the neck, and with the aortic arch, leading from the heart. For this he was awarded the 1938 Nobel Prize for Physiology or Medicine; **"for the discovery of the role played by the sinus and aortic mechanisms in the regulation of respiration"**

In 1950 he discovered that pressoreceptors or special nerve endings, monitor blood pressure. He died in the seaside town of Knokke, Belgium on July 18th,1968. He was married with two sons and two daughters.

PEACE

NANSEN INTERNATIONAL OFFICE FOR REFUGEES

The Nansen International Office for Refugees was created in Geneva in 1931 and named after Fridtjof Nansen who won the 1922 Nobel Prize for Peace. The office aided 'White Russians' Armenians from Turkey and the Jews from German persecution.

1939

Britain and France declare war on Germany, following the German invasion of Poland • Spanish Civil War ends with Fascist victory • Allies allowed to purchase arms in US • DDT invented and Polythene produced • George Kaufman and Moss Hart, *The Man Who Came to Dinner* **• Films;** *Gone With the Wind, The Four Feathers, The Hunchback of Notre Dame, Stagecoach* **• Christopher Isherwood,** *Goodbye to Berlin* **• James Joyce,** *Finnegans Wake* **• John Steinbeck,** *The Grapes of Wrath* **• Nathanael West,** *The Day of the Locust* **• W.B.Yeats, Isaac Babel, Ford Madox Ford, Havelock Ellis and Sigmund Freud die.**

LITERATURE

FRANS SILLANPAA (1888-1964)

Frans Eemil Sillanpaa was born in Hameenkyro, Finland on September 16, 1888. He was the son of a peasant farmer and began by studying natural science. In 1913, he left university, returned to the rural life, married and began to write. He started with short stories that were published in magazines. Between 1924 and 1927, he worked for a firm of publishers in Porvoo. He wrote his best work during the 1930s. He first came to notice in 1916, with his first novel, *Life and the Sun*, the story of young love.

In 1918 he was shocked by the civil war being waged in Finland. The following year he published, *Meek Heritage,* a forceful work depicting how a peasant is caught up with events he cannot understand.

Most of his work concerns country people and their surroundings. His last work was the well received, *The High Moment of the Day,* published in 1956. Sillanpaa was awarded the 1939 Nobel Prize for Literature; **"for his deep understanding of his country's peasantry and the exquisite art with which he has portrayed their way of life and their relationship with Nature"**

His work became established world wide. Married twice he had eight children and died in Helsinki on June 3, 1964.

CHEMISTRY

ADOLF BUTENANDT (1903-1995)
and
LEOPOLD RUZICKA (1887-1976)

Adolf Friedrich Johann Butenandt was born on March 24, 1903, in Brehen-Lehe, Germany. He was educated at Marburg and Göttingen universities and received his PhD from the latter in 1927. In 1929, he was able to isolate estrone, one of the hormones females have in their sexual function and development. In 1931, he identified androsterone, a male sex hormone. In 1934, he explained the function of progesterone, a hormone that is an important part in the female reproductive cycle.

He continued by undertaking continuous experiments of the sex hormones and their possible link with carcinogenic properties. His work led to the manufacture of cortisone. In 1939, Butenandt was awarded a half share of the Nobel Prize for Chemistry; **"for his work on sex hormones"**

However, due to the opposition of Hitler to Nobel Awards (because of the large number of Jewish Nobel laureates) he was unable to accept. In 1949, Butenandt advised the Nobel authorities he was now able to accept the award. Between 1960 and 1972, he was the elected president of the Max Planck Institute for the Advancement of Science. He was married with seven children and died on January 18, 1995.

Leopold Stephen Ruzicka was born in Vukovar, Croatia, on September 13, 1887. Between 1911 and 1916, he was working as an assistant to the German chemist, Hermann Staudinger. During this time he investigated the composition of the insecticides in pyrethrum. He followed this principle in Zurich, where he went to take up an appointment at the Federal Institute of Technology.

Ruzicka became a Swiss citizen and also lectured at the Institute. In 1926 he was professor of organic chemistry at Utrecht University.

Three years later, he left Holland and returned to Switzerland and the Institute in Zurich, as professor of Chemistry. His earlier research resulted in the discovery that, the molecules of muskone and civetone contained rings of 15 and 17 carbons respectively.

Before this time, rings with more than 8 atoms was unknown. This discovery greatly developed the research on these and other compounds. During the 1930s, he discovered the molecular structure of male hormones and in particular, testosterone, which he subsequently synthesized. For this work, Ruzicka was awarded a co-share of the 1939 Nobel Prize for Chemistry; **"for his work on polymethylenes and higher terpenes"**

Married twice, but without children, he died in Zurich, Switzerland on September 26, 1976.

PHYSICS

ERNEST LAWRENCE (1901-1958)

Ernest Orlando Lawrence was born in Canton, SD, US, on August 8, 1901. He became an assistant professor of physics at Yale University in 1927 and the following year he switched to the University of California at Berkeley where, in 1930, he became a full professor. Lawrence conceived the idea for a cyclotron in 1929. By 1936, he had built the Radiation Laboratory at Berkeley, becoming its first director. His work meant he had created a working ability to accelerate hydrogen ions or protons.

He went on to create a facility to cause nuclear disintegration. One of his cyclontrons produced technetium, the first element that does not occur in nature. His work generally was particularly responsible for the great advances in the area of particle physics, and Lawrence was awarded the 1939 Nobel Prize for Physics; **"for the invention and development of the cyclotron and for results obtained with it, especially with regard to artificial radioactive elements"**

He later instituted the use of neutron beams in the treatment of cancer. During WW2, he was part of the 'Manhattan Project', working as a programme chief in charge of the development of the electromagnetic process of separating uranium-235; ready for the first atomic bomb. In 1957 he received the Fermi Award and acknowledged as having invented, and patented a colour television tube. Married with four daughters and two sons, he died on August 27, 1958 in Palo Alto, California, US.

PHYSIOLOGY or MEDICINE

GERHARD DOMAGK (1895-1964)

Gerhard Domagk was born in Lagow, Germany on October 30, 1895. Whilst working as a research director at IG.Farben, following teaching at the universities of Grefswald (1924) and Munich (1925), he was engaged on a survey for new dyes and drugs. He realised there was an antibacterial of one of the dyes, against streptococcal infection in mice.

Later the dye, Prontosil red, was tried clinically, and the first of the sulfonamide drugs was available. He was awarded the 1939 Nobel Prize for Physiology or Medicine; **"for the discovery of the antibacterial effects of prontosil"**

However, because of the edicts of Hitler, Domagk was not allowed to accept the award. He waited until 1947, before collecting the gold medal, the diploma and the cheque. Married with a daughter and three son, he died on April 24, 1964 in Burberg, Germany.

PEACE

NOT AWARDED

1940

Germany invades Norway and Denmark • Winston Churchill becomes Prime Minister • France falls • Dunkirk • Battle of Britain • The Blitz on London • Howard Florey develops penicillin as an anti-biotic • Michael Tippert, *A Child of Our Time*• Charlie Chaplin, *The Great Dictator* • C Day Lewis, *Poems in Wartime* • Raymond Chandler, *Farewell My Lovely* • Graham Greene, *The Power and the Glory* • Ernest Hemingway, *For Whom the Bell Tolls* •Arthur Koestler, *Darkness at Noon* • Films; *Fantasia, Foreign Correspondent, The Grapes of Wrath, Pinocchio, The Thief of Baghdad, Rebecca* • Leon Trotsky, Neville Chamberlain and Eric Gill die.

LITERATURE

NOT AWARDED

CHEMISTRY

NOT AWARDED

PHYSICS

NOT AWARDED

PHYSIOLOGY or MEDICINE

NOT AWARDED

PEACE

NOT AWARDED

1941

Germany invades Russia • Japan bombs Pearl Harbour and US joins the Allies • Manhattan Project to create Atom Bomb begins •Utility label appears on clothing and furniture in Britain • Noel *Coward, Blithe Spirit* • Orsen Welles, *Citizen Kane* • Benjamin Britten, *Violin Concerto* • Films: *Citizen Kane, The Maltese Falcon, Target for Tonight, How Green Was My Valley,* • El Lissitzky, Amy Johnson, James Joyce, Virginia Woolf die.

LITERATURE

NOT AWARDED

CHEMISTRY

NOT AWARDED

PHYSICS

NOT AWARDED

PHYSIOLOGY or MEDICINE

NOT AWARDED

PEACE

NOT AWARDED

1942

Singapore falls • Battle for Stalingrad begins • Battle of El Alamein • Germans launch V-2 rocket • William Beveridge, *Report on Social Security* **• Dmitry Shostakovich,***7th Symphony(*Leningrad) **• T.S. Eliot,** *Four Quartets* **• Jean Anouilh,** *Antogone* **• Films:** *Bambi, Casablanca, King's Row, The Magnificent Ambersons, To Be or Not To Be, Mrs. Miniver,* **• Edith Stein, Walter Sickert and Michel Fokine die.**

LITERATURE

NOT AWARDED

CHEMISTRY

NOT AWARDED

PHYSICS

NOT AWARDED

PHYSIOLOGY or MEDICINE

NOT AWARDED

PEACE

NOT AWARDED

1943

Russians defeat Germans at Stalingrad • Germans surrender in North Africa • Allies invade Italy • Mussolini retires • The Warsaw Ghetto Uprising • Streptomycin discovered • Aram Khachaturian, *Ode to Stalin* • Henry Moore, *Madonna and Child* • Rodgers and Hammerstein, *Oklahoma* • Frank Sinatra is top pop idol • Nigel Balchin, *The Small Back Room* • Films: *Watch on the Rhine, For Whom the Bell Tolls,* • Rachmaninov, Max Reinhardt, Leslie Howard, Mordecai Anielewicz and Beatrice Webb die.

LITERATURE

NOT AWARDED

CHEMISTRY

GEORG von HEVESY (1885-1966)

George Charles de Hevesy was born in Budapest, Hungary on August 1, 1885. Following an education at the universities of Berlin and Freiburg, he went to Manchester University in England to work under Ernest Rutherford on the chemical separation of radium. This work, although a failure, encouraged Hevesy to concentrate on the use of radioactive isotopes as tracers.

In 1920 he was in Copenhagen, at the invitation of Niels Bohr (qv); here he discovered hafinum, a metallic element in the fourth group of the periodic system among ores of zirconium. He went on to become professor of Freiburg (1926) where he began to calculate the relative abundance of the chemical elements. In 1934, his research revealed the dynamic state of the body constituents by tracing the course of radioactive phosphorus through the body.

As a Jew, von Hevesy left Germany for Copenhagen in 1935. With Denmark occupied by the Germans he fled and, like Niels Bohr (qv) escaped by fishing boat to Sweden in 1943. There he became professor at the Institute of Organic Chemistry in Stockholm. In the same year, he was awarded the 1943 Nobel Prize for Chemistry; **"for his work on the use of isotopes as tracers in the study of chemical processes"**

He was also instrumental in explaining the chemical changes in life's processes. Hitler was said to be outraged by the award; the first Nobel award since the start of WW2. After the war Hevesy remained in Stockholm. In 1959 President Heuss of Germany awarded him the, ' Pour le Merite', this encouraged Hevesy to later return to Germany for a visit, and during that time he died in Freiburg on

July 5, 1966. He was married with three daughters and a son.

PHYSICS

OTTO STERN (1888-1969)

Otto Stern was born in Sohrau, Germany (now Zory, Poland), on February 17, 1888. Following the award of his PhD, he worked under Albert Einstein (qv) and taught at several universities. His research work was related to the development of the molecular beam as a tool to study molecular construction and to measure the magnetic moment of the proton. He subsequently discovered it was two and a half times the theoretical notion.

In 1933 the Germans, more concerned about racial matters than scientific ones, requested Jewish Otto Stern to leave.

He journeyed to the US, where he was welcomed by the Carnegie Institute of Technology at Pittsburgh (1933-45). In 1943, he was awarded the Nobel Prize for Physics; **"for his contribution to the development of the molecular ray method and his discovery of the magnetic moment of the proton"**

Hitler was said to be more than a little annoyed, when he learned of a second Jewish Laureate in the same year. Stern retired to Berkeley, California where he died on August 17, 1969. He never married.

PHYSIOLOGY or MEDICINE

EDWARD DOISY (1893-1985)
and
CARL DAM (1895-1976)

Edward Adelbert Doisy was born in Hume, Ill, US, on November 13, 1893. He received his BA and MA at Illinois University and his PhD from Harvard University. He taught at the Washington University School of Medicine (1919-23) and at St. Louis University (1923-1986); his last 21 years as emeritus professor. His research work on various vitamins and sex hormones resulted in his being awarded a half share of the 1943 Nobel Prize for Physiology or Medicine; **"for his discovery of the chemical nature of vitamin K"**

In recognition of his contributions to the knowledge of vitamins, antibiotics, hormones and blood buffer systems, St. Louis University's department of biochemistry was named in his honour (1955). He died in St. Louis, Mo. On October 23, 1985. Married, he had no children.

Carl Peter Henrik Dam was born in Copenhagen, Denmark on February 21, 1895. He graduated from the Polytechnic Institute of Copenhagen in 1920 and afterwards taught at the School of Agriculture and Veterinary Medicine and later, at the Physiological Laboratory of Copenhagen University. Dam left Europe for the US in 1940 and Rochester University, NY.There he continued his research work into vitamin deficiencies in general and vitamin K in particular. In 1943 Dam was awarded a half share of the Nobel Prize for Physiology or Medicine **"for his discovery of vitamin K"**

He also did research into antihemorrhagic substances. The war in Europe over, Dam returned to Copenhagen and the Polytechnic Institute. He died in Copenhagen on April 7, 1976. Married he had no children.

PEACE

NOT AWARDED

1944

'D'-Day • Germans retreat in panic from Russia • V-bombs on England • Roosevelt US President for 4th term • Jean-Paul Sartre, *Huis Clos* **• Tennessee Williams,** *The Glass Menagerie* **• H.E.Bates,** *Fair Stood the Wind for France* **• W.H.Auden,** *For the Time Being* **• Films:** *Going My Way, Double Indemnity, Henry V,* **• Edvard Munch and Ethel Smyth die.**

LITERATURE

JOHANNES JENSEN (1873-1950)

Johannes Vilhelm Jensen was born in Farso, Denmark on January 20, 1873. Of old peasant stock his father was a veterinarian. Following local schooling, Johannes left for Copenhagen to study medicine. After a short while he turned instead to writing and gradually made an impression as a storyteller. Between 1900 and 1901, he wrote the historical trilogy, *The Fall of the King*, a fictional story of King Christian ll of Denmark, that was translated into English in 1933. He travelled a great deal and the result was evident in his writings; *Myths* that dealt with the Far East.

Madame d'Ora and *The Wheel* reflected his trip to the US, *The Long Journey* (1922-24), are six novels that tells the story of the rise of man, from the most primitive times to the discovery of America by Columbus. This shows both his imagination and skill as an amateur anthropologist. He was awarded the 1944 Nobel Prize for Literature; **"for the rare strength and fertility of his poetic imagination with which is combined an intellectual curiosity of wide scope and a bold, freshly creative style"**

Although Denmark was occupied by Germany, Hitler was advised to ignore the award. Jensen now turned to poetry and *Digte* was the result. Married with three sons, he died in Copenhagen on November 25, 1950.

CHEMISTRY

OTTO HAHN (1879-1968)

O tto Hahn was born on March 8, 1879 in Frankfurt-am-Main, Germany. He was the son of a glazier who wanted Otto to be an architect. Otto however, decided he wanted to study chemistry and in 1901 he obtained his doctorate from Marburg University. Then came a year in the army followed by an assistant lectureship at Marburg. In 1904 he was in London, at University College, under Sir William Ramsay. There, the study was on radioactivity, then in its' infancy. Working on a sample radium preparation Hahn was able to show that a new radioactive substance, which he called radiothorium, was present.

Hahn, much encouraged, decided to continue with research rather than go into industry. He spent some time in Montreal, under Ernest Rutherford, before taking up a post at Berlin University. There he was joined by Lise Meitner an Austrian physicist who found that being a woman and a Jewess worked against her. A situation that Hahn would later take advantage of. Head of the radiochemistry department at the Kaiser Wilhelm Institute of Chemistry in Berlin, Hahn thought he was financially secure enough to get married. He chose Edith Junghans, the daughter of a wealthy man. WWI now entered his life and Otto was called up into the army. In 1915 he was a chemical warfare expert

The war over, he and Meitner isolated an isotope of the recently discovered radioactive element protactinium. In 1934 Hahn became most interested in the work of the Italian physicist, Enrico Fermi (qv) and took his theories further. Then in July 1938, Lise Meisner was forced to flee Germany because of Jewish persecution. Hahn remained and assisted by Strassman, continued their research. By the end of that year they had conclusive evidence that one of the products of uranium was a radioactive form of the much lighter element, barium. This indicated that the uranium atom had split two lighter atoms. Hahn, not quite appreciating what he had found, wrote of his problems to Lise Meitner, now living in Sweden and working with her nephew, Otto Frish, who was also there because of Jewish persecution.

Aunt and nephew were surprised to hear from Hahn, who had made no attempt to interfere on her behalf with the SS, however, they decided to assist. They formulated a plausible explanation of the process, to which they gave the name of nuclear fission.

Hahn remained in Germany throughout WW2, at times advising on the production of a possible German A-Bomb. The war over, he was taken to England for security purposes. There he discovered he had been awarded the 1944 Nobel Prize for Chemistry; **"for his discovery of heavy nuclei"**

He was returned to Germany, now in his late sixties, and elected president of the Max Planck Society. He rapidly became a public figure, a spokesman for science and a friend of President Heuss of post-war Germany. The trio of Hahn, Meisner and Strassman, once again met up when the three were jointly awarded the Enrico Fermi Award(1966). Following the death of his only son and daughter-in-law in a road accident in 1960, Hahn never fully recovered from the shock. He and his wife spent much time at their house in Göttingen, Germany where he died on July 28, 1968. His wife died two weeks later.

PHYSICS

ISIDOR RABI (1898-1988)

Isidor **Isaac Rabi** was born in Rymanow, Poland on July 29, 1898. A year later he was breathing the air of New York's Lower East Side; a Jewish Ghetto. Rabi received a BA from Cornell University in 1919 and his PhD from Columbia University in 1927. Here he would return as a professor of physics ten years later. In between he studied and worked in Europe, and invented the magnetic resonance spectroscopy.

During WW2 he was leader of a group who were developing radar, following its invention in the UK. A member of the committee advising the Atomic Energy Commission, he succeeded Robert Oppenheimer as its' chairman in 1952. One of the founders of the Brookhaven National Laboratory in Upton, New Jersey, he went on to develop what is claimed to be the world's finest physics department, at Columbia University.

Rabi was only able to achieve what he did because of the reputation he earned during the 1930s. His researches became of the utmost importance as they provided the central method for all future molecular and atomic beam experimentation. His work resulted in his being awarded the 1944 Nobel Prize for Physics; **"for his resonance method for recording the magnetic properties of atomic nuclei"**

He died in New York on January 11, 1988. He was married with two daughters.

PHYSIOLOGY or MEDICINE

JOSEPH ERLANGER (1874-1965)
and
HERBERT GASSER (1888-1963)

"For their discoveries relating to the highly differentiated functions of single nerve fibres"

Joseph Erlanger was born in San Francisco, California, US: on January 5, 1874. Born into a well known Jewish family, he graduated from John Hopkins University in 1900. He later became professor of physiology at the Washington School of Medicine in St. Louis. There he did much of his research work. The results of this work greatly contributed to what was then known in the field of cardiovascular understanding.

Erlanger invented a graphic method for measuring blood pressure and did pioneer work on what is to-day known as a fibrillator. He received a half share of the 1944 Nobel Prize for Physiology or Medicine for his work concerning nerve fibres and impulse transmission.

Married with two daughters and a son, he died in St.Louis, Missouri on December 5, 1965.

Herbert Spencer Gasser was born in Platteville, Wis. US, on July 5, 1888. The son of an established Jewish family, he was appointed professor of pharmacology at Washington University in St.Louis. Here he met Joseph Erlanger (qv). The two men collaborated in the study of very slight electrical impulses, carried by rare mammalian nerve fibres.

In 1924, they adapted the oscillograph, which allowed them to see amplified nerve impulses on a fluorescent screen. They were thus able to demonstrate that different nerve fibres exist for the specific transmission of impulses, such as cold, heat and pain. In addition, their work paved the way for medical machinery that was needed for diagnostic purposes.

In 1935, Gasser was appointed director of the Rockefeller Institute in New York; he stayed until 1953. He was awarded a half share of the 1944 Nobel Prize for Physiology or Medicine for fundamental discoveries concerning the functions of different kinds of nerve fibres. Gasser, a bachelor, died in New York on May 11, 1963.

PEACE

INTERNATIONAL COMMITTEE OF THE RED CROSS

The purpose of the Red Cross in wartime is to ensure that all sides care for the war wounded and treat, in a humane fashion, prisoners-of-war. During WW1 this was largely recognised by both the Allied countries and Axis countries (unlike WW2 when the Germans refused to recognise the Red Cross unless it suited their purpose for propaganda). The international committee is an independent council of 25 Swiss citizens with their HQ in Geneva.

1945

Germany surrenders • The German Death Camps revealed • Atom Bomb dropped on Japan • Roosevelt dies, replaced by Harry Truman • France enfranchises women • Karl Popper, *The Open Society and its Enemies* • Marc Chagall designs, *Firebird ballet* • Benjamin Brittain, *Peter Grimes* • Films, *Brief Encounter, Les Enfants du Paradis, The Lost Weekend, The Way to the Stars* • George Orwell, *Animal Farm* • Evelyn Waugh, *Brideshead Revisited* • Vietnam becomes independent under Ho Chi Minh • Mussolini, William Rothenstein, Jerome Kern, Hitler, Anne Frank, Lloyd George and Bela Bartok die.

LITERATURE

GABRIELA MISTRAL (1889-1957)

Gabriela Mistral was born Lucila Goddy Alcayaga, in Vicuna, Chile, on April 7, 1889. Her forebears were a mixture of Spanish, Basque and Indian. For her part, she grew up in a small village in Northern Chile, and was the village school-mistress at only 15. There is no record of her receiving any teacher training, but she became a college professor and later a diplomat, with posts in Madrid, Lisbon and Genoa.

Her reputation as a writer began slowly, and was established when she won a prize in 1914 for, *Sonnets of Death*. To distinguish her writing from her professional career as teacher and diplomat, she used the pseudonym of Gabriela Mistral. It was by this name that she received considerable fame, especially with her collection of early works entitled, *Desolation* (1922). This book included the poem 'Dolor', that deals with the aftermath of an ended love affair, that ends in suicide.

Her writings show a love of children and a broad tenderness. She never married, and this appears to be long regretted. *Ternura* (1924) and *Tala* (1938) are probably her best known novels, although her best work is in poetic form. She published *Lagar* in 1954. In 1945 she became the first woman in South America to be awarded the Nobel Prize for Literature; **"for her lyric poetry which, inspired by powerful emotions, has made her name a symbol of the idealistic aspirations of the entire Latin American world"**

She continued in her diplomatic work, travelling widely and finding time to be an envoy for various committees of the United Nations. She died in Hempstead, NY, US on January 10, 1957. She never married but adopted a child.

CHEMISTRY

ARTTURI VIRTANEN (1895-1973)

Artturi Ilmari Virtanen was born in Helsinki, Finland, on January 15, 1895. He was a chemistry instructor at Helsinki University (1924-39) and professor of biochemistry there (1939-48). Whilst at the university, Virtanen studied the fermentation processes that spoil stores of silage. He developed a procedure to take advantage of the fermentation process of lactic acid that increases the acidity of silage to a point, at which destructive fermentation ceases. This became known by the inventor's initials; AIV. The process includes, adding dilute hydrochloric or sulfuric acid to newly stored silage.

This increases the acidity of the fodder beyond that point. In a series of experiments (1928-29), he was able to show that acid treatment has no adverse effect on the nutritive value and edibility of the fodder, nor that of animals who feed off the fodder. For this work Virtanen was awarded the 1945 Nobel Prize for Chemistry; **"for his research and inventions in agricultural and nutrition chemistry, especially for his fodder preservation method"**

This award reflected the fact that Virtanen's work improved the production and storage of protein bearing green fodder, essential in the aftermath of WW2. He also conducted research on the nitrogen fixing bacteria, found in the root nodules of leguminous plants. Married with two sons, he died in Helsinki on November 11, 1973.

PHYSICS

WOLFGANG PAULI (1900-1958)

Wolfgang Pauli was born in Vienna, Austria, on April 25, 1900. At the age of 20, he wrote a 200 page article, for an encyclopaedia, on the theory of relativity that resulted in his appointment as a lecturer at Hamburg University, three years later. In 1924, he proposed that a fourth quantum number, which take on the numerical values + ½ or - ½, was required to specify electron energy states.

In 1925 he went further, with what has become known as, ' the Pauli exclusion principle'. This states, ' that in an atom no two electrons can have the same energy'. This principle clearly relates to the quantum theory , as well as to the observed properties of atoms, and resulted in the award of the 1945 Nobel Prize for Physics; **"for the discovery of the Exclusion Principle, also called the Pauli Principle"**

In 1940, Pauli was appointed professor of theoretical physics, at the Institute for Advanced Study at Princeton University. In 1946 he took US citizenship, only to return to Switzerland shortly after. There, in Zurich, he died on December 15, 1958. He married twice but had no children.

PHYSIOLOGY or MEDICINE

ALEXANDER FLEMING (1881-1955), ERNST CHAIN (1906-1979)
and
HOWARD FLOREY (1898-1968)

"For the discovery of penicillin and curative effect in various infectious diseases"

Alexander Fleming was born in Ayr, Scotland on August 6, 1881. He took his medical degree in 1906, at St. Mary's Hospital Medical School in London. There he conducted research on antibacterial substances that would be non-toxic to human tissue. During WW1, he was in the Royal Army Medical Corps , returning in 1918, to St. Mary's to become Hunterian professor (1918), as well as Arris and Gale lecturer, at the Royal College of Surgeons. In 1921, he was able to identify and isolate lysozyme, an enzyme found in certain animal tissues, i.e. tears, saliva etc. that exhibits antibiotic activity.

Fleming was working with the bacteria 'Staphyloccus' in 1928, when he noticed a bacteria-free circle around a mould growth that was contaminating a culture of staphylococci. Further investigation showed a substance in the mould that prevented growth of the bacteria, even when diluted 800 times. Fleming called it penicillin, from *Penicillium notatum*. In 1929, Fleming published his findings in the *British Journal of Experimental Pathology*. In 1943, he was elected a Fellow of the Royal Society, knighted in 1944 and awarded a third part of the Nobel Prize for Physiology or Medicine in 1945.

He retired, but lived long enough to see how his discovery worked for humanity. Married twice with a son, he died in London on March 11, 1955.

Ernst Boris Chain was born in Berlin, Germany on June 19, 1906. His family were prominent Jews and his father a chemical engineer. Ernst grew up in an atmosphere which insisted, that the only worthwhile occupation in life was the pursuit of intellectual activity. Moreover, any career that wasn't university-based was unthinkable. Ernst wanted to be a musician but was persuaded into a career of science. He received his PhD from the Pathological Institute of Berlin in 1927. In 1929 he became interested in Fleming's discovery of what would later become known as penicillin.

This interest, plus Hitler's wish to be rid of Jews, gave Chain the impetus to go to England. He taught at Cambridge University for two years, after which time, he joined Howard Florey at Oxford. Chain is acknowledged as the key figure in the isolation and purification of penicillin. Because Britain was concentrating on WW2, it was left to three American companies to mass-produce, by arrangement, what would become known as a 'miracle drug'; the first anti-biotic.

Chain's discovery and Florey's commercialism, made it possible for hundreds of thousands of Allied personnel to be treated for wounds, that would otherwise probably have killed them. After the war, the drug gradually became available for civilian use all over the world. Chain was awarded a third share of the 1945 Nobel Prize for Physiology or Medicine. From 1963 to 1971, he was professor of biochemistry at Imperial College London.

In 1969, he was knighted. Married with two sons and a daughter, he died on August 12, 1979, whilst on holiday in Ireland.

Howard Walter Florey was born in Adelaide, Australia on September 24, 1898. He studied medicine at both Adelaide and Oxford universities, from where he graduated in 1924. Florey's researches centred upon tissue inflammation and secretion of mucous membranes. He was successful in purifying lysozyme, a bacteria destroying enzyme found in tears and saliva; a character of the enzymes. In 1939, he concentrated with penicillin.

However, it wasn't until Ernst Chain entered into the equation that penicillin became the anti-biotic of the century. Florey was awarded a third share of the 1945 Nobel Prize for Physiology or Medicine. He was made a life peer in 1965.

At the time of his death on February 2, 1968 in Oxford, he was provost of Queen's College, Oxford and chancellor of the Australian National University in Canberra. He was married twice with a son and daughter.

PEACE

CORDELL HULL (1871-1955)

Cordell Hull was born Overton County, Tenn. US, on October 2, 1871. He trained as a lawyer and became a politician. A member of the Democratic Party, he served in the House of Representatives, between 1907-21 and 1923-31, a total of 22 years. He followed with a stint in the Senate (1931-33). He was installed as secretary of state by President Roosevelt and spent much time and effort, initiating a reciprocal trade programme designed to lower tariffs and so expand world trade. He was awarded the 1945 Nobel Peace Prize; **"for his work of 'bipartisanship'**

Other works of note was his work in improving relations between North and South America, by implementing what has become known as, the Good Neighbour Policy. His work had important and favourable repercussions when Japan attacked the US, without warning, on December 7th 1941, since many countries supported the US, who might otherwise not have done so.

Hull warned the world about Japanese aggression in China. During the war, Hull was busy preparing for the peace to follow and was a prime originator of what became the United Nations. Roosevelt described Hull as, the 'father' of the UN and his Nobel Prize reflected that view. He retired at the end of the war to write his memoirs; *Memoirs of Cordell Hull* (1950). Married without children, he died in Bethesda, Md. US, on July 23, 1955.

1946

UN meets in General Assembly • The Nuremberg Trials • Argentine elects Peron • National Health Service in Britain • Xerography invented • Bertrand Russell, *History of Western Philosophy* **• Frederick Ashton Ballet,** *Symphonic Variations* **• Eugene O'Neil,** *The Iceman Cometh* **• Eric Linklater,** *Private Angelo* **• Film:** *The Best Years of Our Lives, Great Expectations, It's A Wonderful Life, The Jolson Story, A Matter of Life and Death* **• Sir Louis Barnett, Gertrude Stein, John Maynard Keynes and Damon Runyon die.**

LITERATURE

HERMANN HESSE (1877-1962)

Hermann Hesse was born in Calw, Germany on July 2, 1877. His father urged his son to become a priest and enrolled him into the Maulbronn seminary. However, Hermann wasn't happy there and instead became apprenticed to a clock maker. He later found employment in a bookshop. There he stayed until his first book was published, *Peter Camenzind* (1904), a story about a disappointed writer. He had never been a happy schoolboy and this attitude was expressed in his novel, *Beneath the Wheels* (1906). Further books followed until in 1915, he journeyed to India.

During WW1 Hesse, lived in Switzerland and wrote about pacifism. He became a permanent resident and a citizen in 1923. He underwent psychoanalysis by JB.Lang to allay a personal problem. This experience he draws upon in his book *Demian* (1919); a book that brought him much fame. Other writings show his interest in Jungian concepts. *Steppenwolf* (1927) demonstrates the conflict between bourgeois acceptance and the spiritual self belief in a middle-aged man. In 1930 he published, *Narziss und Goldmund* regarded at Hesse's greatest novel, that deals with the friendship between two medieval priests.

His last novel was *The Glass Bead Game* (1943). He was awarded the 1946 Nobel Prize for Literature; **"for his inspired writings which, while growing in boldness and penetration, exemplify the classical humanitarian ideals and high qualities of style"**

He later became a cult figure amongst young people in the English speaking world. He lived quietly in Montagnola, Switzerland and died there on August 9, 1962. He was married three times and had three sons.

CHEMISTRY

JOHN NORTHROP (1891-1987), JAMES SUMNER (1887-1955)
and
WENDELL STANLEY (1904-1971)

John Howard Northrop was born in Yonkers, New York, US: on July 5, 1891. He was educated at Columbia University and received a doctorate in chemistry in 1915. He was invited to join the US Army and during WW1 was a captain in the US Army Chemical Warfare Service. During this time he researched the fermentation processes possible for the industrial production of acetone and ethyl alcohol.

The war over, his research, now at the Rockefeller Institute, was a study of enzymes essential for digestion, respiration as well as general life processes. In 1930 he was able to announce that enzymes obey the laws of chemical reactions. In 1938 he isolated the first bacterial virus; bacteriophage. This he proved to be a nucleoprotein. For this work and general work on pepsins he was awarded a third share of the 1946 Nobel Prize for Chemistry; **"for his work on the preparation of enzymes and virus proteins in a pure form"**

He remained at the Rockefeller Institute until 1961 when he retired. In 1934, he was elected to the National Academy of Sciences and his book, *Crystalline Enzymes* (1939) was required reading. He died in Wickenberg, Arizona on May 27, 1987.

James Batcheller Sumner was born in Canton, Mass: US, on November 19, 1887. Following a formal education in the States, where in 1926 he became the first biochemist ever to crystallize an enzyme, he journeyed to Stockholm to work with Hans von Euler-Chelpin and Theodor Svedberg.

His work there enabled Sumner, upon his return to the US, to further research with the result, that, in 1937, he crystallized the enzyme catalase. Between 1929 and 1955 he was a professor at the Cornell University Medical School, Ithaca, NY As a result, Sumner was awarded a third share of the 1946 Nobel Prize for Chemistry; **"for his discovery that enzymes can be crystallized"**

In 1947, a laboratory of enzyme chemistry was established at Cornell in his honour. He died in Buffalo, NY, on August 12, 1955. He was married three times and had five sons and two daughters.

Wendell Meredith Stanley was born in Ridgevill, Indiana, US, on August 16, 1904. Following a regular education he decided to become a biochemist. His researches, into the purification and crystallization of viruses, so demonstrated their molecular structure, it enabled later researchers to progress in this field. For his work Stanley was awarded a third share of the 1946 Nobel Prize for Chemistry; **"for the preparation of enzymes and virus proteins in a pure form"**

He was professor of biochemistry at the University of California in Berkeley from 1948 to 1971 and during this time worked on influenza viruses resulting in a preventive vaccine.

He died whilst on holiday in Salamanca, Spain, on June 15, 1971. He was married with three daughters and a son.

PHYSICS

PERCY BRIDGMAN (1882-1961)

Percy Williams Bridgman was born in Cambridge, Mass. US, on April 21, 1882. He was the son of a journalist who decided to become a physicist. Percy received his MA from Harvard University in 1905 and his PhD in 1908. He then began experimental work on static high pressures, confining himself to around 6,500 atmospheres. He gradually increased this to 100,000 and then to 400,000 atmospheres. This was an area never previously researched and caused Bridgman to create much of his equipment.

Probably his best gadget was a special type of seal, in which the pressure in the gasket always exceeds that in the pressurized fluid, ensuring that the closure is self-sealing. Most of his work dealt with the measurements of the compressibilities of liquids and solids.

His work meant he was for ever extending his range, resulting in new discoveries including high pressure forms of ice and conformation that electrons in cesium undergo a rearrangement at a certain transition pressure. This work later led to the synthesization of diamonds. In 1919 he was a professor at Harvard and Higgins Professor there in 1950. This was after he was awarded the 1946 Nobel Prize for Physics; **"for the invention of an apparatus to produce extremely high pressures, and for the discoveries he made therewith in the field of high pressure physics"**

He was a prolific writer. Besides 260 papers he published several books including *The Physics of High Pressure* (1931) and *Reflections of a Physicist* (1950). In 1961 he discovered he had cancer. With little time left and not wishing to burden others, he took his own life on August 20, in Randolph, NH. He was married with a son and daughter.

PHYSIOLOGY or MEDICINE

HERMANN MULLER (1890-1967)

Hermann **Joseph Muller** was born in New York City on December 21, 1890. The son of a prominent Jewish family, Muller was educated at Columbia University. Whilst there he became interested in the subject of genetics. In 1912 he began studying zoology. Following his classic paper in 1916, on the mechanics of crossing over genes, which established the principle of the linear linkage of genes in heredity, he obtained a PhD In 1920, he became a professor at the University of Texas in Austin and stayed for twelve years.

This was possibly the most satisfying and professional period of his life, as he studied and researched all possible biological mutations and established that these mutations were the result of chemical changes and that those changes could be artificially induced. His work provided the foundations for future discoveries in molecular biology.

In 1931 he was elected to the US National Academy of Sciences. In 1932 however, as a result of personal problems, he had a nervous breakdown. As part of a rehabilitation programme he spent a year at the Kaiser Wilhelm Institute in Berlin. A year later Hitler was on the scene and Muller left for Moscow, to continue his research into genetics at the laboratory of N.I.Vavilov. It was at this time that a Russian biologist, T. Lysenko, was hitting the headlines. Lysenko and Muller constantly battled with each other. Muller calling Lysenko's doctrines false.

However, Lysenko had powerful political friends and in 1937 Muller left Russia. On his way back to the US, he stopped off at Edinburgh University, stayed for two years and arrived home in August 1940. He spent WW2 researching at Amherst College in Mass. In 1945, he became professor of zoology at Indiana University, Bloomington (1945-67). In 1946 he was awarded the Nobel Prize for Physiology or Medicine; **"for the discovery of the production of mutations by means of X-ray irradiation"** .

The resulting publicity allowed him to promote his warning concerning radiation dangers for present and future generations. He died in Indianapolis on April 5, 1967, content that Lysenko's theories had been demolished. He was twice married with a son and daughter.

PEACE

JOHN MOTT (1865-1955)
and
EMILY BALCH (1867-1961)

John Raleigh Mott was born in Livingstone Manor, New York, US, on May 25, 1865. From 1888 to 1915, Mott was international secretary of the YMCA and one of the organizers of the World Missionary Conference held in Edinburgh in 1910. This marked the start of the ecumenical movement that later became the World Council of Churches.

He was chairman of the Student Volunteer Movement for Foreign Missions (1915-28) and of the International Missionary Council (1921-42). He was also president of the World's Alliance of YMCA (1926-37). He was awarded a half share of the 1946 Nobel Prize for Peace; **"for his work in international church and missionary movements"**

Among his writings, was *The Furore Leadership of the Church* (1909) and *The Larger Evangelism* (1944). He died on January 31, 1955 in Orlando, Florida. He married twice and had two sons and two daughters.

Emily Greene Balch was born in Boston, US, on January 8, 1867. She was in the first graduating class at Bryn Mawr College and taught at Wellesley College from 1897. She did much good work, in and around Boston, and served on several committees dedicated to helping the poor. In 1910 she lived in Slavic neighbourhoods, both in the US and Eastern Europe, in order to write her book *Our Slavic Fellow Citizens*. She was a member of the Quakers and a delegate to the International Congress of Women, (The Hague, 1915).

She was a founder of the Women's International League for Peace and Freedom and secretary-treasurer 1919-1922 and 1934-35. She opposed the US entry into WW1 and, as a result, was dismissed from her professorship at Wellesley in 1918. However, because Germany and Japan became defilers of democracy, Balch approved US participation in WW2. For her work for peace, prior, during and after WW1, she was awarded a half share of the 1946 Nobel Prize for Peace; **"in recognition of her work for women's causes"**

Her writings included *Approaches to the Great Settlement* (1918). She died in Cambridge, Mass on January 9, 1961. She never married.

1947

Marshall Aid • India and Pakistan become independent • Palestine question goes to UN • First supersonic air flight • Dead Sea Scrolls discovered • Alberto Giacometti, *Man Pointing* • Tennessee Williams, *A Streetcar Named Desire* • Philip Larkin, *A Girl in Winter* • Compton Mackenzie, *Whisky Galore* • Film: *Crossfire, In Which We Serve, Gentleman's Agreement,* • Ernst Lubitsch, Max Planck, Bronislaw Huberman, Fiorello La Guardia and Sydney Webb die.

LITERATURE

ANDRÉ GIDE (1869-1951)

André Paul-Guillaume Gide was born in Paris, France on November 22, 1869. His father came from Huguenot peasantry, his mother a Norman heiress was brought up in the Protestant tradition. At the age of eight, André was at the École Alsacienne in Paris however, poor health, considered to be neurotic, often interrupted his education. He was 11 when his father died and his mother now had him educated at home by an ever changing series of tutors. André returned to his Paris school and there passed his baccalauréate in 1889. He then decided that as he didn't need to work at a regular job, his mother had now inherited her fortune, he would therefore spend his life writing, listening to music and travelling. His first writing effort was *The Notebooks of Andre Walter* (1891) written like many of his works in the first person. He then became involved with the writer Pierre Louys, who introduced him to the French Symbolist movement and it was in this style that he wrote in the 1890s.

In 1893 he visited North Africa and there found a source for his homosexuality as well as an escape from the strict confines of Protestantism. The following year he again returned to North Africa and this time met up with Oscar Wilde together with Lord Alfred Douglas. Andre had to leave the trio to return home because of the serious illness of his mother who died in May 1895. This event appeared to regularise his position. He married his cousin Madeleine, who had previously refused him, became elected mayor of the commune of La Roque, thus becoming at 27 the youngest ever mayor in France.

Fruits of the Earth was published in 1897 and was a failure, only to become one of his most popular books after WW1. Many of his works reflect the harmony required to advance through marriage and life generally. However, his writings were to reflect several different styles during his lifetime. In the early 1900s, he worked as a literary critic and in 1908 was a joint founder of *La Nouvelle Revue Francaise.* During WW1, he worked for the Red Cross and later, in a soldier's nursing home. After the war, he worked to provide shelter for war victims. In 1916 he started to write again and his work now questioned the work of God. He coined the expression "Catholicism is inadmissible, Protestantism is intolerable; and I feel profoundly Christian"

In 1918 he published *Corydon*. This was a defence of homosexual life and caused a considerable furore. In 1926 he wrote the only book he considered a pure novel; *The Counterfeiters*. Following his travels in French Equatorial Africa, he wrote *Travels in the Congo* (1927). Here he criticized the French Colonial Administration for a lack of humanity. This is an important work as it marks the start of the final phase of his life which he expresses in political activity. He preached and wrote concerning more humane conditions in the prisons, equality for women and more.

In 1936 he visited Russia and for a while toyed with the idea of Communism but rejected the idea in *Afterthought on the USSR* (1937). In 1938 his wife died and André declared she had been the only love of his life. From 1942 to the end of WW2, Gide lived in North Africa. There he wrote *Theseus* in which he explores the past. In June 1947 he received his first honour; Doctor of Letters of Oxford University. In November he was awarded the 1947 Nobel Prize for Literature; **"for his comprehensive and artistically significant writings, in which human problems and conditions have been presented with a fearless love of truth and keen psychological insight"**

In 1950 he published the final edition of *Journal*. He had started it in 1889. It is a unique work of over a million words and is a work that traces an ever changing world. Married with a daughter, André died the following year in Paris on February 19, 1951.

CHEMISTRY

ROBERT ROBINSON (1886-1975)

Robert Robinson was born in Chesterfield, Derbys. England on September 13, 1886. Educated at Manchester University, he later became a professor at Liverpool, London and Sydney universities, as well as Waynflete professor at Oxford University (1930-55)

His research work dealt with the structure and synthesis of several organic compounds and he is noted for having formulated a qualitive electronic theory of organic molecular structure which contributed significantly to science. He was awarded the 1947 Nobel Prize for Chemistry; **"for his investigations on plant products of biological importance, especially the alkaloids"**

In 1939 he had been knighted and he was president of the Royal Society 1945 to 1950. Married twice with a son and daughter, he died in Great Missenden, near London, on February 8, 1975.

PHYSICS

EDWARD APPLETON (1892-1965)

Edward Victor Appleton was born in Bradford, England on September 6,th 1892. Educated at Cambridge University, he worked at the Cavendish Laboratory, Cambridge, from 1920 to 1924. He was then appointed Wheatstone professor of physics at King's College, London University, where he spent much time researching the propagation of electromagnetic waves and the aspects of the ionosphere.

He was able to demonstrate that radio waves of wavelength, sufficiently short to penetrate the lower region of the ionosphere, are reflected by an upper region. This has become known as the Appleton layer. It also laid the foundations for radar.

Appleton now gained an international reputation and, in 1936, became Jacksonian Professor of Natural Philosophy at Cambridge University. During WW2, he worked on the continuing research on radar and in 1941 was knighted. He was awarded the 1947 Nobel Prize for Physics; **"for his investigations of the physics of the upper atmosphere especially for the discovery of the so-called Appleton layer"**

He was appointed vice-chancellor of Edinburgh University in 1949 and died in that city on April 21, 1965. He married twice and had two daughters.

PHYSIOLOGY or MEDICINE

CARL CORI (1896-1984), GERTY CORI (1896-1957)
and
BERNADO HOUSSAY (1887-1971)

Carl Ferdinand Cori and Gerty Theresa Cori (née Radnitz) were a husband and wife team whose lives and careers were inseparable. Carl was born in Prague, Czechoslovakia on December 5, 1896 and Gerty, also born in Prague in 1896, on August 15th. He a Protestant, she Jewish. They met whilst students at the German University in Prague and married in 1920; immediately following the receipt of their medical degrees. Two years later, they were in the US on the staff of the Institute for the study of Malignant Disease in Buffalo. NY, (1922-31).

Later, at the Washington University Medical School, St. Louis, they discovered, in 1936, the activated intermediate glucose 1-phosphate, known as the 'Cori ester'.

They were able to show that this discovery represented the first step, in the conversion into glucose, of the animal storage carbohydrate glycogen, large amounts of which are found in the liver and also (because the reaction is reversible) sometimes the

final step in the blood conversion of blood glucose to glycogen.

In 1943, they were able to isolate and purify the enzyme responsible for catalysing the glycogen-Cori ester reaction, thereby achieving the test-tube synthesis of glycogen. Proof of their earlier work, now allowed them to formulate the 'Cori cycle', suggesting that liver glycogen is converted to blood glucose that is now reconverted to glycogen in muscle, and on-going to lactic acid, to reform glycogen in the liver.

This led the Coris to appreciate how insulin causes the removal of sugar from the blood, by promoting the addition of phosphate to glucose. In 1947 the husband and wife team each received a third share of the Nobel Prize for Physiology of Medicine; **"for their discovery of the course of the catalytic conversion of glycogen"**

Gerty Cori died in St. Louis on October 26, 1957. Carl found life difficult without her. He threw himself back into work, researching the physico-chemical action of enzymes involved in the breakdown of glycogen to lactic acid. He later retired to Cambridge, Mass. and died there on October 20, 1984. The couple had a daughter.

Bernardo **Alberto Houssay** was born in Buenos Aires, Argentine on April 10, 1887. In 1910 he was professor of physiology at Buenos Aires University. His research work explored the world of diabetic conditions and Houssay found, following experimental work on dogs, that the injection of pituitary extracts into normal animals induces diabetes by increasing the amount of sugar in the blood so indicating that the secretions of the gland oppose the action of insulin.

In 1943, General Peron, the fascist dictator , removed Houssay (and 150 other professors) from their posts. Houssay now founded the Institute of Biology and Experimental Medicine in Buenos Aires. This became a leading research centre in physiological medicine. In 1947 Houssay received a third share of the Nobel Prize for Physiology or Medicine; **"for his discovery of the part played by the hormone of the anterior pituitary lobe in the metabolism of sugar"** .

Peron now wanted him back at the University of Buenos Aires but Houssay rejected him out of hand. Married with three sons, he died in Buenos Aires on September 21, 1971.

PEACE

FRIENDS SERVICE COUNCIL (British)
and AMERICAN FRIENDS SERVICE COMMITTEE

Both of these organisations are branches of the Society of Friends; the Quakers. In recognition of their work during two world wars the 1947 Nobel Prize for Peace was awarded. A unique part of their work was providing conscientious objectors to killing, with an alternative. So they became ambulance drivers and non-medical hospital workers thus performing most needed tasks.

1948

The State of Israel founded • Berlin Blockade • Mahatma Gandhi assassinated • Truman wins US presidential election • Long-playing record invented • Alfred Kinsey, *Sexual Behaviour in the Human Male* • Jackson Pollock, *Composition No.1* • Christopher Fry, *The Lady's Not For Burning* • Norman Mailer, *The Naked and the Dead* • Alan Paton, *Cry, the Beloved Country* • Films; *The Naked City, Oliver Twist, The Red Shoes, Whiskey Galore, Hamlet, The Treasure of Sierra Madre, Key Largo,* • Richard Tauber, Sergi Eisenstein, Ali Jinnah and Orville Wright die.

LITERATURE

T.S. ELIOT (1888-1965)

Thomas Stearns Eliot was born in St. Louis, Mo; US, on September 26, 1888. He was fortunate not to have a father who insisted he learn a trade or profession. Instead, Eliot had the widest education possible. He started at Smith Academy in St. Louis, then onto Milton, Mass: then to Harvard. He arrived there in 1906 and left in 1909 with a BA. The following year found him at the Sorbonne in Paris and the lectures of Henri Bergson(qv) on philosophy. He returned to Harvard and spent 1911 to 1914, reading Indian philosophy and studying Sanskrit. In 1914 he met and became influenced by the American poet Ezra Pound. Eliot's first published work was *Prufrock and Other Observations* (1917).

He was now living in London and teaching French and Latin at Highgate School. He then had a brief period working as a bank clerk, and writing criticisms for small magazines. In 1919, he published *Poems,* it included a blank verse entitled ' Gerontion' in a most radical style. 1922 brought his poem *The Waste Land,* to public notice and an international reputation was made. It is a vast work in five sections and possibly Eliot's most famous work.

In 1925 Eliot became a British subject and confirmed in the Church of England. He was now known not only as a poet of distinction, but considered the greatest poet writing in the English language. He was also a critic of some note and essayist, whose work on Dante appeared in 1929. *Ash Wednesday,* a poem concerning his religious beliefs, was not well received on the basis that poetry should be secular in outlook. It is considered that *Four Quartets* (!943) is a masterpiece. Although a book, each quartet is a complete poem. It was this work that led directly to his being awarded the 1948 Nobel Prize for Literature; **"for his outstanding, pioneer contribution to present-day poetry"** Eliot was also a considerable playwright. Although many of his plays have a religious background, they are nevertheless well considered. Amongst these, *Murder in the Cathedral*, a story of Thomas à Becket, was most successful and caught the public's imagination. It was after WW2 that Eliot found a mass audience for his plays. The best known being *The Cocktail Party* (1949). It was followed by *Confidential Clerk* (1953) and *The Elder Statesman* (1958). Eliot wrote these plays as comedies, deriving his plots from Greek drama.

Eliot also worked as a publisher, he was a director of Faber and Faber, and greatly assisted young poets. He married twice. The first time was in 1915 , when he married Vivian Haigh-Wood, who died in 1947, and the second in 1957, when he married Valerie Fletcher. There were no children and Eliot died in London, on January 4, 1965.

CHEMISTRY

ARNE TISELIUS (1902-1971)

Arne **Wilhelm Kaurin Tiselius** was born in Stockholm, Sweden on August 10, 1902. Educated at Uppsala University, he was awarded a doctorate in 1930. His thesis had been the developing use of electrophoresis, for the difficult task of separating proteins in suspension, on the basis of their electrical charge.

He became a lecturer at Uppsala, after which he was in the US conducting research at Princeton University. He returned to Uppsala in 1937 to become professor of biochemistry. He later researched methods to separate the chemically similar proteins of blood serum. For this work Tiselius was awarded the 1948 Nobel Prize for Chemistry; **"for his research on electrophoresis and absorption analysis, especially for his discoveries concerning the complex nature of the serum proteins"**

Between 1946 and 1950, he was Chairman of the Swedish Natural Science Research Council and vice-president of the council 1947 to 1960. From 1960 to 1964, he was president of the Nobel Foundation. Married with a son and daughter, he died in Uppsala, Sweden on October 29, 1971.

PHYSICS

PATRICK BLACKETT (1897-1974)

Patrick **Maynard Stuart Blackett** was born in London, England on November 18, 1897. He graduated from Cambridge University in 1921 and then spent the next ten years as a researcher at the Cavendish Laboratory. Whilst there, he began developing the Wilson cloud chamber; a device that detects the path of ionizing particles into an automatic method for the study of cosmic radiation.

Blackett was awarded the 1948 Nobel Prize for Physics; **"for his development of the Wilson cloud chamber method, and his discoveries therewith in the fields of nuclear physics and cosmic radiation"**

He was professor of physics at London University (1933) and at Manchester University (1937). He occupied the first chair in radio astronomy and was involved in the Jodrell Bank Experimental Station for Radio Astronomy. He became a senior research fellow at Imperial College, London in 1965 and created a life peer in 1969. Married with a son and daughter, he died in London on July 13, 1974.

PHYSIOLOGY or MEDICINE

PAUL MULLER (1899-1965)

Paul Hermann Muller was born in Olten, Switzerland on January 12, 1899. He was working for the Geigy Company in Basle, when he began his researching career in the field of dyes and tanning agents. In 1935, he switched to the researching of an ideal agent in the field of insecticides. He wanted a chemical that would destroy insects, but leave plants and animals in no danger. The substance would have to have a stable chemical ability and a long shelf life, and be cheap to manufacture.

In 1939, Muller successfully synthesized and tested a substance already known; it was discovered in 1874 by Othmar Zeidler, who did nothing with it. Dichlorodiphenyltrichloroethane (DDT) that had lain dormant for so long, was now brought back into the world of science, by Paul Muller. It was first tried out by the Swiss government in the fight against the Colorado potato beetle, then in the US in 1943. In January 1944, it was found to effective against lice bearing typhus in Naples, Italy, and for the first time a winter typhus epidemic was halted   In 1948 Muller was awarded the Nobel Prize for Physiology or Medicine; **"for his discovery of the efficiency of DDT as a contact poison against several arthropods"**

His work in preparing a non-toxic insecticide increased food production worldwide.

Gradually however, DDT began to have detrimental effects upon wildlife and it was suspected that is was disrupting the ecological food chains. By 1970, less toxic products were on the market and a number of countries now banned the use of DDT. Married with two sons and a daughter, Muller died in Basle on October 12, 1965.

PEACE

NOT AWARDED

Although no Peace Prize has been awarded, it is clear that had Mahatma Gandhi not have been murdered two days before the deadline for nominations, he would have been nominated and awarded the Prize.

1949

North Atlantic Treaty • Mao Tse-tung Chairman of the Peoples Republic of China • Transjordan becomes Jordan • Britain recognises the independence of Eire but re-confirms Northern Ireland part of UK • Cortisone discovered • Arthur Miller, *Death of a Salesman* **• Films,** *The Third Man, On The Town, Passport to Pimlico* **• George Orwell,** *Nineteen Eighty-Four* **• Nancy Mitford,** *Love in a Cold Climate* **• Jankel Adler, Maurice Maeterlinck and Richard Strauss die.**

LITERATURE

WILLIAM FAULKNER (1897-1962)

William Cuthbert Faulkner was born in New Albany, Miss; US on September 25, 1897. His original surname was Falkner, why he should want to change it by adding the letter U, other than wanting to distinguish himself from others of the same name, no one appears to know.

He was the eldest of three sons born to Murray and Maud Falkner. Murray and his family moved around a lot, before settling in Oxford, 50 miles from William's birthplace. There, Murray ran a livery stable, before going bust and starting up a hardware store that also failed. He then became business manager of the state university.

William would later attend this educational establishment by way of, 'special dispensation for returned troops' This related to WW1, when William travelled to Canada and their joined the Royal Air Force of Canada, as a cadet pilot; the war over before he finished basic training.

William was constantly reading and his was a catholic taste. It included learning French in order to read the works of Stephane Mallarme in the original. He didn't stay long at university; he wrote and published some poems in the literary magazine and he was off.

During the next few years he took a variety of jobs that would keep body and soul in tobacco, paper and whiskey. He spent time in New York, working in a bookstore, and then back to Oxford as a postmaster. His first novel was, *Soldier's Pay* (1925) and well received. With the royalty he obtained from his publisher, Faulkner bought a ticket on a slow boat to Italy. However, it wasn't long before he was in Paris, living alone on the traditional Left Bank. His next novel, *Mosquitoes* (1927) was a satirical piece on New Orleans literary circles.

Despite this early success, Faulkner was constantly having his stories returned by magazines. His third novel, *Flags in the Dust,* written in 1927, was refused by both his previous publishers. He changed the title to *Sartoris* and it was accepted by another publisher. In 1929, he married his schoolgirl sweetheart, Estelle Oldham, who had returned from China following a marriage failure.

Again Faulkner was working during the day and writing at night. He was a prodigious writer and gradually becoming known. *As I Lay Dying* (1930), *Sanctuary* (1931), *Light in August* (1932), *Pylon* (1935) were all examples of his maturing as a writer. With *Absalom, Absalom* in 1936, he achieved wide recognition. Fame however, didn't come until *Intruder* was published in 1948. He was awarded the 1949 Nobel Prize for Literature; **"for his powerful and artistically unique contribution to the modern American novel"**

Collected Stories, published in 1950, won the National Book Award. Faulkner was now an international public figure with happy readers worldwide. He was however, a contradiction within the fight for Negro emancipation. He felt for the Negro but supported the South's right to come to its own conclusions. He therefore managed to offend both liberals and conservatives. His drinking was becoming a problem although it didn't affect his output. In 1951, he wrote his play, *Requiem for a Nun* and in 1954 his longest novel, *A Fable,* was published. His last novel was *The Reivers* (1962), both of these won the Pulitzer Prize. He died in Oxford, Miss; on July 6, 1962. He left two daughters.

CHEMISTRY

WILLIAM GIAUQUE (1895-1982)

William Francis Giauque was born in Niagara Falls, Canada on May 12, 1895. He received his PhD from the University of California, Berkeley in 1922 and became associated with the university all his life, becoming professor emeritus in 1962. Giauques researched properties of matter at temperatures close to zero.

For his research he was awarded the 1949 Nobel Prize for Chemistry; **"for his contributions in the field of chemical thermodynamics, particularly concerning the behaviour of substances at extremely low temperatures"**

He established a basis for quantum statistics and the third law of thermodynamics. He discovered the oxygen isotopes of mass 17 and 18. In 1926, he had proposed a method for obtaining temperatures well below -457.87 degrees F. In 1935 he, and his research assistant, D.P.MacDougall, first successfully employed it. Married with two sons, he died in Berkeley, California on March 28, 1982.

PHYSICS

HIDEKI YUKAWA (1907-1981)

Hideki Yukawa was born in Tokyo, Japan on January 23, 1907. He graduated from Kyoto Imperial University in 1929 and later became a lecturer there, before moving to Osaka Imperial University in 1933, from there he obtained his PhD He then returned to Kyoto University as professor of theoretical physics (1939-1950). Following a couple of breaks at Princeton and Columbia universities, Yukawa returned to Kyoto University as director of the Research Institute for Fundamental Physics (1953-70).

In 1935, he proposed a new theory of nuclear forces and predicted the existence of mesons, i.e. particles that have masses between those of the electron and the proton. In 1947, he began work on a more comprehensive theory of elementary particles, based on his notion of the nonlocal field. He received the 1949 Noble Prize for Physics; **"for his prediction of the existence of mesons on the basis of theoretical work on nuclear forces"**

Married with two sons, he died in Kyoto, Japan on September 8, 1981.

PHYSIOLOGY or MEDICINE

MONIZ EGAS (1874-1955)
and
WALTER HESS (1881-1973)

Antonio Caetano de Abreu Freire Egas Moniz was born in Avanca, Portugal on November 29, 1874 and thereafter known as, Moniz Antonio Egas. He became Lisbon University's first professor of neurology (1911-44). There he introduced and developed, arteriography, a method of making visible, brain blood vessels by injecting into the carotid artery, substances that become opaque to X rays. This method later became essential, in diagnosing intracranial diseases, particularly tumours of the pituitary gland.

By this method, Egas observed that certain psychoses involve recurrent thought patterns, dominating normal psychological processes. This resulted in the first operations that would become known as prefrontal leucotomy or lobotomy operations. Now it is known that these operations often have serious side effects and tranquillizing drugs do the job as well; but not at that time. Then it was regarded as most useful in combatting incurable psychoses.

He was awarded a half share of the 1949 Nobel Prize for Physiology or Medicine; **"for his discovery of the therapeutic value of leucotomy in certain psychoses"**

Besides his work in medical research, Egas was a politician who served in the Portuguese parliament on several occasions, between 1903 and 1917. He also led the Portuguese delegation to the Paris Peace Conference of 1918. Married without children, he died in Lisbon on December 13, 1955.

Walter **Rudolph Hess** was born in Frauenfeld, Switzerland on March 17, 1881. Between 1906 and 1912 he worked as an ophthalmologist. He then turned to physiology at Bonn University. and later became director of the Physiological Institute at Zurich University (1917-51). Here; he became interested in the autonomic nervous system; the nerves that originate at the base of the brain and extending, via the spinal cord, to control automatic functions such as, digestion and excretion.

This and further research, into areas of the brain, particularly the seat of autonomous function, lies at the base of the brain or interbrain, and resulted in Hess being awarded a half share in the 1949 Nobel Prize for Physiology or Medicine; **"for his discovery of the functional organization as a co-ordinator of the activities of the internal organs"**

His best known book is *The Biology of the Mind* (1964). Married with a son and daughter, Hess died in Locarno, Switzerland on August 12, 1973.

PEACE

JOHN BOYD ORR (1880-1971)

John **Boyd Orr** was born Kilmaurs, Scotland on September 23, 1880. He was educated at Glasgow University, beginning as a theology student before switching to nutrition. He achieved a modicum of fame, following the publication of *Food, Health and Income* (1936). This showed how over half the British public could not afford to eat foods, required for a healthy diet, and 10% were undernourished. This work was a considerable influence in determining the basis of food rationing in the UK during WW2. He was professor of agriculture at Aberdeen University, before becoming Rector of Glasgow University and an Independent MP (1945). He then became director general of the UN Food and Agricultural Organization until 1948.

He was awarded the 1949 Nobel Prize for Peace; **"for his work on economic and political nutrition"**

He later concentrated on his writings. These include *Food and the People* (1943), *Food-The Foundation of World Unity* (1948) and *As I Recall* (1966). He served in the British House of Lords from 1949 until his death on June 25, 1971, whilst living in Angus, Scotland. He was married with two sons and a daughter.

1950

United States instigates Korean war • Race riots in Johannesburg • USSR has atomic bomb • Great Britain commences legal aid • Thor Heyerdahl, *The Kon-Tiki Expedition* • UN building in New York completed • Akira Kurosawa, *Rashomon* • Tennessee Williams, *The Roman Spring of Mrs Stone* • Films; *All About Eve, Born Yesterday, Sunset Boulevard, The Asphalt Jungle* • Al Jolson, George Orwell, Kurt Weill, Leon Blum, Harold Laski and George Bernard Shaw die.

LITERATURE

BERTRAND RUSSELL (1872-1970)

Bertrand **Arthur William Russell** was born in Trelleck, England in the county of Monmouth, on the border of England and Wales, on May 18, 1872. He was the second son of Viscount Amberley. His mother, Katherine, daughter of Baron Stanley of Alderley, died of diphtheria in 1874 and his father died just 18 months later. Bertram and his elder brother Frank were brought up by their strict paternal grandmother and educated privately. This would later lead to Russell's intense desire for privacy and imbue him with strong emotional feelings and a great inner strength. In 1890, he entered Trinity College, Cambridge thirsting for knowledge. Seen as an intellectual, he stood out and soon invited to become a member of the exclusive society known as, 'The Apostles'. In 1893, he won first-class honours in the Mathematical Tripos, and then turned to philosophy.

A year later, he took a first class degree in moral sciences. It was in 1894 that he married Alys Pearsall Smith, a Quaker from Philadelphia, US, with greatly advanced views. In Germany on a lecture tour he discovered Marxism. Upon his return, he was appointed first lecturer at the London School of Economics and Political Science (LSE). In 1896, the first of his many books appeared, *German Social Democracy.* In 1903, the first work was published in the trio known as, *Principia Mathematica.* It brought him much acclaim.

In 1914, Russell joined the Labour Party and in the same year won a fellowship at Trinity. During the Boer War, in the early part of the 20th century, Russell became a pacifist and pro-Boer. He viewed British actions in South Africa, which included concentration camps, as horrendous. About the same time he and his wife 'fell out of love' and Lady Ottoline Morrell became his constant companion. (The Russells divorced in 1921). In 1908 he was elected a fellow of the Royal Society.

During World War One, Russell so angered the Establishment with his pacifism, that he was prosecuted in 1916 and fined and again in 1918 when he was jailed for six months. During his incarceration, Russell busied himself with his writings and published his *Introduction to Mathematical*

Philosophy , upon his release. In 1919 he met Dora Black and they married in 1921. In 1920, following a visit to the USSR, Russell wrote a critical book , *The Practise and Theory of Bolshevism,* predicting much that would happen later under Stalin. As a pacifist, he approved of the British policy toward Hitler, as evidenced by the 1938 Munich Agreement.

When war followed, Russell, now Lord Russell following his brother's death in 1931, stated that Hitler had to be defeated as, ' a necessary prelude to anything good'. In 1945, his best-seller, *History of Western Philosophy* was published. He frequently undertook lecture tours all over the world and he frequently appeared on television and radio. In 1949, he was awarded the Order of Merit and in 1950, was awarded the Nobel Prize for Literature; **"in recognition of his varied and significant writings in which he champions humanitarian ideals and freedom of thought"**

From 1952, he began an active political life appealing to young left wingers for whom he was an icon. He was president in 1958, of the newly launched Campaign for Nuclear Disarmament. Later, he was involved in the sit-ins for which he was sentenced to two months in prison, later reduced to seven days. During the latter 1960s, he strongly attacked US policy in Vietnam and publicised US atrocities there. He died on February 2, 1970 at Penrhyndeudraeth, Merioneth, Wales. He was married four times and had two sons and a daughter.

CHEMISTRY

OTTO DIELS (1876-1954)
and
KURT ALDER (1902-1958)

"for their discovery and development of the diene synthesis"

Otto **Paul Hermann Diels** was born in Hamburg, Germany on January 23, 1876. He studied chemistry at Berlin University and made professor of chemistry at Kiel University in 1916. In 1906 he discovered carbon suboxides, a highly reactive substance. He also discovered an easily controlled method of removing certain hydrogen atoms from specific organic molecules, via the use of metallic selenium.

In 1928, together with his pupil, Kurt Alder, he produced his most important work concerned with the diene synthesis; organic compounds with carbon double bonds used to create syntheses of some cyclic organic substances under controlled conditions. This work proved important in the onward production of synthetic rubber and plastics. His work became an important ingredient for Hitler's war machine during WW2. In 1950 Diels, an ex- Nazi party member, was awarded a half share of the Nobel Prize for Chemistry.

Diels, married with three sons and two daughters, died in Kiel, Germany on March 7, 1954.

Kurt Alder was born in Konigshutte, Germany on July 10, 1902. He studied chemistry at Berlin and Kiel Universities and received a doctorate in 1926. He and Otto Diels (qv) worked on the synthesis of a wide range of cyclic organic compounds. Between 1934 to 1936 he was a professor at Kiel University and between 1936-1940, by now an active Nazi party member, was research director of IG Farben. He was one of Hitler's scientists who developed Zyclon B gas used in the death camps.

In 1940, he took up the appointment as professor of chemistry and director of the chemical institute at Cologne University. In 1950 he was awarded a half share of the Nobel Prize for Chemistry for development of a widely used method of synthesizing cyclic organic compounds.

Alder, a bachelor, died in Cologne, Germany on June 20, 1958.

PHYSICS

CECIL POWELL (1905-1969)

Cecil Frank Powell was born in Tonbridge, Kent, England on December 5, 1905. Powell in 1928 was appointed an assistant researcher at the Henry Herbert Wills Physical Laboratory at Bristol University, becoming professor of physics there in 1948, and in 1964, its' director. During WW2, Powell developed special techniques for using sensitive photographic emulsions in order to record the paths of cosmic rays. Using plates exposed on mountain tops, or in high altitude balloons, he was able to record cosmic-ray interactions.

In 1947, his data showed the existence of the pion and the process whereby it decays into two other particles, an antimuon and a neutrino. Powell, in 1950, was awarded the Nobel Prize for Physics; **"for his development of the photographic method of studying nuclear processes and his discoveries regarding mesons made with this method"**

He later became part of a group of scientists set up to increase the social responsibilities of scientists. He died, whilst on holiday in Milan, Italy on August 9, 1969. He was married with two daughters.

PHYSIOLOGY or MEDICINE

PHILIP HENCH (1896-1965), EDWARD KENDALL (1886-1972)
and
TADEUS REICHSTEIN (1897-1996)

"for their discoveries relating to the hormones of the adrenal cortex, their structure and biological effects"

Philip Showalter Hench was born in Pittsburgh, US: on February 28, 1896. Whilst working at the Mayo Clinic in Rochester, Minn. Hench noticed that during pregnancy, a woman suffering from arthritis would often be pain-free. Hench, together with Edward Kendall, studied endocrinologic factors present in rheumatic diseases.

The result of their studies led to their use of cortisone, a hormone of the pituitary gland, that was found to alleviate the worst effects of rheumatoid arthritis. For this work Hench received a third share of the 1950 Nobel Prize for Physiology or Medicine. Hench, married with two sons and two daughters, died whilst on holiday in Ocho Rios, Jamaica on March 30, 1965.

Edward Calvin Kendall was born in South Norwalk, Conn. US, on March 8, 1886. He graduated from Columbia University with a PhD in 1910, and joined the staff of the Mayo Foundation, Rochester, Minn. There he met Philip Hench. For his part in the research on the structure and biological effects of adrenal cortex hormones, he won a third share of the 1950 Nobel Prize for Physiology or Medicine.

Kendall was head of the biochemistry laboratory at Mayo from 1945 to 1951. Later he became visiting professor of chemistry, at Princeton University. Married with three sons and a daughter, Kendall died in Princeton, NJ, on May 4, 1972.

Tadeus Reichstein was born in Wiociawek, Poland on July 20, 1897 to a middle class Jewish family and brought up in Switzerland. In 1933 he synthesized ascorbic acid (vitamin C) and, in the same year, began his work of isolating hormones manufactured by the cortex of the adrenal gland, the basis of cortisone.

In 1938 he was appointed head of the Institute of Pharmacy at Basle University. In 1950, he received a third share of the Nobel Prize for Physiology or Medicine, for his work on adrenal cortex hormones.

From 1946 to 1957, he was professor of organic chemistry at Basle University and in 1968, was awarded the Copley Medal of the British Royal Society. Reichstein, married with a daughter. He died in Basle,

Switzerland on August 1, 1996.

PEACE

RALPH BUNCHE (1904-1971)

Ralph Johnson Bunche was born in Detroit, US, on August 7, 1904. The grandson of a slave, in 1928 he received his first degree from Harvard University on government and international relations. Thereafter, he joined the teaching staff of Howard University in Washington, DC. and set up a department of political science. He received a Rosenwald scholarship, which enabled him to travel to French West Africa, Togoland and Dahomey, studying local administration methods. Between 1938 and 1940, he studied American race relations, leading to the publication of *An American Dilemma* (1944). During WW2, he served in the Office of Strategic Services and was present at the early planning meetings of the United Nations.

In 1948, Bunche was asked by Trygve Lie, the Secretary General of the UN to head a committee trying to organise a settlement between Jews and Arabs in the new State of Israel. He became chief mediator, when Folke Bernadotte was assassinated and he finally achieved a negotiated armistice by May 1949. Bunche received the 1950 Nobel Prize for Peace; **"for his successful negotiation of an Israeli-Arab truce"**

He was married with two daughters and a son. His later work for the United Nations took the shape of representing the then Secretary General, Dag Hammarskjold, in the world's trouble spots. These included the UN programme for the peaceful uses of atomic energy; and the deployment of 6,000 UN troops in the region of the Suez Canal, following the invasion of Egypt by British, French and Israeli forces. In 1960, he was in charge of enforcing the peace in Cyprus between Greeks and Turks.

Bunche was late entering the race issues of the US, but he participated in the 1965 civil rights marches and was a member of the National Association for the Advancement of Coloured People. He died in New York, US, on December 9, 1971.

1951

Truman sacks General MacArthur in Korea • de Valera resumes power in Eire • Burgess and Maclean flee to Russia • Electric power produced from atomic energy • David Riesman, *The Lonely Crowd* • Stravinsky, *The Rakes Progress* • Rodgers and Hammerstein, *South Pacific* • Films, *The Africa Queen, The Lavender Hill Mob, An American in Paris* • Robert Frost, *Complete Poems* • James Jones, *From Here to Eternity* • J.D.Salinger, *The Catcher in the Rye* • Sigmund Romberg, Serge Koussevitsky, Fanny Brice, Artur Schnabel, Andre Gide and Arnold Schonberg die.

LITERATURE

PAR LAGERKVIST (1891-1974)

Par Fabian Lagerkvist was born in Vaxjo, Sweden on May 23, 1891. His parents were religious people who lived the narrow life of a small town. It was many years before he broke the yoke of religion, and became a socialist and lead a radical, artistic and literary life. A writer in the pessimist mould, as evident in *Anguish* (1916). *Chaos* (1918) is a poem dedicated to the catastrophe of war. His play, *The Man Without a Soul* (1936), was his protest with Fascism.

However, it was not until 1944, that he achieved a best-seller, *The Dwarf* , a novel. With that, and *Barabbas* in 1950, he became world renowned. In 1949, his play, *Let Man Live,* was considered most unusual as it deals with terrorists judging each other. In 1951, Lagerkvist was awarded the Nobel Prize for Literature; **"for the artistic vigour and true independence of mind with which he endeavours in his poetry to find answers to the eternal questions confronting mankind"**

He died in Stockholm, Sweden on July 11, 1974. Twice married, he had no children.

CHEMISTRY

GLENN SEABORG (1912-1999)
and
EDWIN McMILLAN (1907- 1991)

"for their discoveries in the chemistry of the transuranium elements"

Glenn Theodore Seaborg was born in Ishpeming, Mich. US, on April 19, 1912. His parents were Swedish immigrants. Seaborg was educated at the University of California in Los Angeles, and at Berkeley, from where he received a PhD in 1937. He then taught at Berkeley from 1937 to 1945, becoming professor of chemistry in 1946 and chancellor from 1958 to 61.

Between 1940-55, he headed the team that added nine new elements, encompassing atomic numbers 94-102, the best known of which is 94-plutonium. During WW2, he was section chief at Chicago University's Metallurgical Laboratory. There the first industrial production of plutonium, used as a nuclear explosive, was undertaken. It was Seaborg who isolated plutonium from the reaction products.

The other new elements were; americium (95), curium (96), berkelium (97), californium (98), einsteinium (99), fermium (100), mendelevium (101), and nobelium (102). The work Seaborg did, leading to the periodic table of the elements, became known in 1944 as the actinide concept, which states that; ' 14 elements heavier than actinium belong in a separate group in the periodic table'. For his work in isolating and identifying elements heavier that uranium, Seaborg was co- awarded the 1951 Nobel Prize for Chemistry.

Between 1961 and 1971, he was chairman of the Atomic Energy Commission. Seaborg was one of a group of scientists who made an effort to persuade President Truman to demonstrate the power of an atomic weapon before using it on an innocent population.

In 1997, Seaborg achieved what neither Einstein or Fermi had managed when element 106 was named seaborgium. It was the first time a living scientist had an element named after him. Amongst his many writings is, *Man and Atom* (1971). He died in Lafayette, California on February 25, 1999. He was married with four sons and two daughters.

Edwin **Mattison McMillan** was born in Redondo Beach, Calif. US, on September 18, 1907. The only son of a physician, he was educated at the California Institute of Technology and received his PhD from Princeton University. Whilst studying nuclear fission, he discovered neptunium (93), a decay product of uranium-239.

In 1940, he collaborated with Philip Abelson and isolated the new element obtaining final proof of his earlier discovery. Neptunium is important, because it was the first of a group of transuranium elements that provide important nuclear fuels and contribute to nuclear knowledge and theory. For this work he was awarded a co-share of the 1951 Nobel Prize for Chemistry. In 1945, he was able to discover a method of maintaining synchronization for indefinite speeds, these accelerators became most important in later scientific discovery. McMillan enjoyed mountaineering and amongst these achievements he climbed the Matterhorn.

He died on September 7, 1991 in El Cerrito, California, from complications caused by diabetes. He was married with a daughter and two sons. Not shy from saying what he thought he once stated, "The way our government deals with the question of disarmament is shameful-a disgrace to our nation"

PHYSICS

JOHN COCKCROFT (1897-1967)
and
ERNEST WALTON (1903-1995)

"For their pioneer work on the transmutation of atomic nuclei by artificially accelerated atomic particles"

John **Douglas Cockcroft** was born in Todmorden, Yorkshire, England on May 27, 1897. He was educated at Manchester University and St. John's College, Cambridge, where he was later Jacksonian professor of natural history (1939-1946). In 1936, together with Ernest Walton, he designed what came to be called, the Cockcroft-Walton generator.

This was used to disintegrate lithium atoms by bombarding them with protons. The two men conducted further research, on the splitting of other atoms and created the importance of accelerators, of which theirs was by far the best, as essential for nuclear research.

During WW2, Cockcroft was director of the Atomic Energy Division for the National Research Council of Canada. In 1946, he undertook much the same job in Britain. He was knighted in 1948. For his pioneer work in the field of accelerators he was a awarded a half share of the 1951 Nobel Prize for Physics. In 1953, he was created Knight Commander of the Bath and in 1960, became master of Churchill College, Cambridge. He died in Cambridge, England on September 18, 1967. He was married with four daughters and a son.

Ernest Thomas Sinton Walton was born Dungarvan, Co.Waterford, Ireland on October 6, 1903. He was educated at Methodist College, Belfast and Trinity College, Dublin. In 1927, he went to Trinity College, Cambridge and there met John Cockcroft. The two worked at the Cavendish Laboratory, under Rutherford, and there, conducted their experiments into accelerators. In 1931 they met with the first of their successes and in 1934 Walton, complete with a PhD returned to Trinity College, Dublin in 1934. There he remained, as a fellow , for some 40 years.

He was Erasmus Smith's Professor of Natural and Experimental Philosophy between 1946 and 1974. In 1952 he was chairman of the School of Cosmic Physics at the Dublin Institute for Advanced Studies.

In 1951 he was awarded a half share of the Nobel Prize for Physics, for the development of the first nuclear particle accelerator, that became known as the Cockcroft-Walton generator. Walton married with two sons and two daughters, died on June 26, 1995.

PHYSIOLOGY or MEDICINE

MAX THEILER (1899-1972)

Max Theiler was born in Pretoria, South Africa on January 30, 1899. He received his medical training at St. Thomas' Hospital in London and at the London School of Hygiene and Tropical Medicine, from where he graduated in 1922. He crossed the Atlantic and took up a post with the department of tropical medicine at the Harvard Medical School in Boston.

There he studied the influence of infectious diseases and in particular, yellow fever. He discovered that mice are susceptible to yellow fever. His research led to a vaccine for humans against that disease. For this work, Theiler was awarded the 1951 Nobel Prize for Physiology of Medicine; **"for his discoveries concerning yellow fever and how to combat it"**

He continued researching at the Rockefeller Institute for Medical Research in New York, until his death in New Haven, Conn. US, on August 11, 1972. He was married with a daughter.

PEACE

LEON JOUHAUX (1879-1954)

Leon Jouhaux was born in Paris, France on July 1, 1879. At the age of 16, he was working in a Paris match factory and experiencing, at first hand, the terrible working conditions workers had to put up with. In 1906, he was national secretary of the Matchworkers Union. In 1909, he was secretary-general of the French General Confederation of Labour (CGT).

Before WW1 he worked, together with German trade union leaders, to avert war but once it began he supported the French war effort. He was present at the 1919 Versailles Peace Conference and a member of the Labour Legislation Commission. He believed that trade unionism should have a part in formulating the economy but be separate from political action.

During WW2, the French government in Vichy, banned the CGT, arrested Jouhaux and turned him over to the Gestapo. The Germans ordered him to a concentration camp, where he spent the rest of the war. He eventually returned to France and, in 1947, resumed control of the reformed CGT.

However, he and the Communist majority fell out and Jouhaux formed a breakaway movement known as , Force Ouvrière (Workers Force) as a hedge between Communist and Roman Catholic workers' unions. He was awarded the 1951 Nobel Prize for Peace; **"for his work in founding the International Confederation of Free Trade Unions"**

Married without children, he died in Paris on April 28, 1954.

1952

Eisenhower elected US President • Queen Elizabeth II on British throne • Mau Mau causes state of emergency in Kenya • Contraceptive tablets made • The H-bomb • Agatha Christie, *The Mousetrap* opens • John Steinbeck, *East of Eden* • Angus Wilson, *Hemlock and After* • Films: *High Noon, Singin' in the Rain, The Quiet Man, Viva Zapata!, Detective Story* • Jo Davidson, Sir Montague Burton, John Garfield, Eva Peron, Rudolf Slansky and Chaim Weizmann die.

LITERATURE

FRANCOIS MAURIAC (1885-1970)

Francois Mauriac was born in Bordeaux, France on October 11, 1885. He came from a deeply religious Catholic family and his major novels are now considered dreary and tense. He studied at Bordeaux University and the École Nationale des Chartes in Paris, but left to take up writing. His first work was a book of poems, *Les Mains Jointes* (1909). In 1913, he published his first novel, *L'Enfant chargé de chaînes,* followed by *La Robe prétexte* a year later.

It wasn't until 1923 and his novel *The Kiss to the Leper,* was he established as a major novelist. His, *Le Désert de l'amour* resulted in the 1925 Grand Prix du Roman of the Académie Française. However, it is *Le Noeud de vipères*, written in 1932 that is considered his masterpiece. The following year he was elected to the Académie Françaises.

He continued writing throughout the thirties and forties. He also wrote against Fascism in Italy and Spain. During WW2, he remained in France and fought with the Resistance. He worked with De Gaulle after the war and wrote a biography of him, *De Gaulle* (1964). In 1952 Mauriac, regarded as the greatest French novelist since Marcel Proust, was awarded the Nobel Prize for Literature; **"for the deep spiritual insight and the artistic intensity with which he has in his novels penetrated the drama of human life"**

Married with two sons and two daughters, he died in Paris on September 1, 1970.

CHEMISTRY

ARCHER MARTIN (1910-)
and
RICHARD SYNGE (1914-1994)

"for their invention of partition chromatography"

Archer John Porter Martin was born in London, England on March 1, 1910. He was educated at Bedford School and Peterhouse College, Cambridge. His work on nutrition led him to the study of protein structure and the development of partition chromatography, i.e. to separate and analyse proteins.

This work was rewarded by a half share in the 1952 Nobel Prize for Chemistry. From 1948 he spent several years working for the British Medical Research Council. From 1953, he worked on gas liquid chromatography.

The widespread use of chromatographic methods revolutionised analytical chemistry. He is married with two sons and three daughters.

Richard Laurence Millington Synge was born in Liverpool, England on October 28, 1914. His father was a stockbroker and Richard was educated at Winchester School and Trinity College, Cambridge. He spent much of his career at the Rowett Research Institute in Aberdeen (1948-67) and the Food Research Institute at Norwich (1967-76).

Whilst working at the Wool Industry Research Association in Leeds (1941-43), he met Archer Martin. Together they worked on the development of partition chromatography. Later, Synge received a half share of the 1952 Nobel Prize for Chemistry.

From 1968, he was an honorary professor of biological sciences at the University of East Anglia. In 1951, Synge and four other scientists formed a 'science for peace' committee. Married with three sons and two daughters he died on August 18, 1994.

PHYSICS

FELIX BLOCH (1905-1983)
and
EDWARD PURCELL (1912-1997)

"for their development of new methods for nuclear magnetic precision measurements and discoveries in connection therewith"

Felix Bloch was born in Zurich, Switzerland on October 23, 1905; the son of a Jewish wholesale grain merchant. In 1924, he started to study engineering but soon decided on a career in physics instead.

In his new department he met Erwin Schrodinger who, at that time, was in the throes of formulating quantum physics. Bloch worked at Leipzig University for some years, but with the arrival of Hitler he left for the US.

A year later he was professor of theoretical physics at Stamford University, a post he held from 1934 to 1971. Although Bloch never contributed to the formulation of quantum physics, all his work was in that direct application and to-day's students learn about ' Bloch states' and 'Bloch functions'.

At Stamford, Bloch conceived a method for detecting neutrons. During WW2, he worked on the early stages of the atomic bomb, but then switched to work on methods of countering radar detection of aircraft. In 1952, Bloch received a half-share of the Nobel Prize for Physics for his work on nuclear magnetic resonance. He was the first director-general of the European Commission for Nuclear Research, based in Geneva.

Over the last four decades, nuclear magnetic resonance techniques have become increasingly important in diagnostic medicine. Bloch died in Zurich on September 10, 1983. He was married with three sons and a daughter.

Edward Mills Purcell was born in Taylorville, Ill. US, on August 30, 1912. During WW2, he was head of a group studying radar problems at the Massachusetts Institute of Technology. He was professor of physics at Harvard University in 1949 and in 1952, he detected the 21 centimetre-wavelength radiation emitted by neutral atomic hydrogen in interstellar space. This enabled astronomers to determine the distribution, and location of hydrogen clouds, in galaxies and thereby to measure the rotation of the Milky Way.

In 1960, Purcell became the Gerhard Gade professor at Harvard. In 1980, he became professor emeritus; the same year he received the National Medal of Science. Married with two sons, Purcell was awarded a half-share of the 1952 Nobel Prize for Physics for his independent discovery in 1946 of nuclear magnetic resonance in liquids and solids. He died in 1997

PHYSIOLOGY or MEDICINE

SELMAN WAKSMAN (1888-1973)

Selman Abraham Waksman was born in Priluka, Russia on July 22, 1888, to a religious Jewish family. In 1910, to escape the anti-Semitism that followed the failed 1905 revolution, the family moved to the US, and in 1916, Selman became a US citizen. Two years later he obtained his PhD from the University of California. From then on, most of his career was spent at Rutgers University, New Jersey. Here he was professor of soil microbiology (1930-40) and director of the department (1940-58). During WW2, there was a continuous search for new anti-bacterial substances extracted from the soil.

From these actinomycetes, he took out what he called 'antibiotics'. These were valuable for their effects in killing off gram-negative bacteria. In 1943 he discovered, from a strain of fungus, streptomycin, which has since become a major factor in combatting disease. Waksman went on to isolate several other antibiotics, of which neomycin is the best known. In 1952 he was awarded the Nobel Prize for Physiology or Medicine; **"for his discovery of streptomycin, the first antibiotic effective against tuberculosis"**

His published writings *include, Principles of Soil Microbiology* (1927) and his autobiography, *My Life With the Microbes* (1954). Married with a son, he died on August 16, 1973 in Hyannis, Mass. US.

PEACE

ALBERT SCHWEITZER (1875-1965)

Albert Schweitzer was born in Kaysersberg, Germany on January 14, 1875. He was the eldest son of Lutheran pastor and educated at Strasbourg University, where he studied philosophy and received a doctorate in 1899. He later achieved a doctorate in theology. His book, *The Quest of the Historical Jesus* (1906) established him internationally.

An accomplished musician, he was a church organist when his teacher in Paris, suggested he write on the life and works of JS Bach; the result was *J.S.Bach: le musicien-poète* (1905).

In the same year, Schweitzer announced he was to be a mission doctor and devote himself to philanthropic work. He became a medical doctor in 1913 and together with his nurse-wife, Helen Breslau, went to Lambarene in the Gabon province of French Equatorial Africa.

On the banks of the Ogowe River, Schweitzer, aided by financial donations from many sources, built his hospital. An enemy alien in French territory during WW1, he was interned. He began writing his *Philosophy of Civilization* (1923), in which he explains his belief of ' reverence for life'. He returned to Africa in 1924 and rebuilt his hospital, adding a wing for lepers. By 1963 there were 350 patients in the main building and a 150 lepers in a separate colony. It was staffed mostly by white doctors and nurses with the mundane work being carried out by natives. In 1952 he was awarded the Nobel Peace Prize; **"for his efforts in behalf of the Brotherhood of Nations"** .

Described as autocratic and lacking in medical expertise, Schweitzer nevertheless exercised a strong moral appeal and exposed the lack of facilities on the African continent, becoming an example of self-denial. He died where he worked, in Lambarene, Gabon on September 4, 1965. He was married with a daughter.

1953

Stalin dies • Korean armistice • Egypt becomes a republic • Edmund Hilary and Sherpa Tenzing climb Everest • USSR test an H-bomb • Julius and Ethel Rosenberg murdered by US decree • BF Skinner, *Science and Human Behaviour* • Barbara Hepworth, *Monolith Empyrean* • LP Hartley, *The Go-Between* • Rosamond Lehmann, *The Echoing Grove* • Films: *Genevieve, Monsieur Hulot's Holiday, From Here to Eternity, A Streetcar Named Desire,* • Hilaire Belloc and Arnold Bax die.

LITERATURE

WINSTON CHURCHILL (1874-1965)

Winston Leonard Spencer Churchill was born at Blenheim Palace, Oxfordshire, England on November 30, 1874. He was the eldest son of Lord Randolph Churchill; his mother an American. Winston was educated at Harrow School and later graduated from the Royal Military College at Sandhurst. He later saw service either as an army officer or newspaper correspondent, in Cuba, India and South Africa. In 1900, he entered Parliament as a Conservative but, by 1906, had crossed the house to become a Liberal and a member of that government. In 1908 he was a member of the Cabinet, first at the Board of Trade then as Home Secretary.

The Churchill that is now praised only came about in the late thirties. Prior to that time he was a failure. He did badly at school, was a poor soldier and, during the Boer war, his reports from South Africa, ill considered. During WW1, his failure concerning the ill-fated and ill conceived Dardanelles campaign, left him discredited. His confrontation with the coal miners, during the twenties, over their strike for a living wage, did nothing to endear him to the working class. His influence in hiving off part of Palestine, to form Trans-Jordan, leads directly to the problems existing to-day in the Middle East.

Then came Hitler and Churchill became 'Winnie'. The past was put to one side. Here was the man who had opposed appeasement and was now Britain's wartime leader. Following the end of WW2, he was defeated in the general election of 1945. He turned to writing and the result was , *The Second World War,* published in 6 volumes. In 1953, Churchill was awarded the Nobel Prize for Literature; **"for his mastery of historical and biographical description as well as for brilliant oratory in defending exalted human values"**

He also received a knighthood. At this time he was once again Prime Minister. He retired in 1955 to write his, *History of the English Speaking Peoples* in 4 volumes. He died in London on January 24, 1965 and given a state funeral. He was married with four daughters and a son.

CHEMISTRY

HERMANN STAUDINGER (1881-1965)

Hermann Staudinger was born in Worms, Germany on March 23, 1881. In 1903 he received his PhD from Halle University, becoming professor of Chemistry at Freiburg University in 1926 and research director 1940-51. His area of research was in polymers and he was able to show that small molecules, form long chainlike structures by chemical interaction, and not just by physical aggregation.

He went on to demonstrate how it was possible to build up high-polymer networks, and he established the relationship between the molecular weight of a high polymer, and its viscosity. For the work he did in contributing to the development of plastics, Staudinger was awarded the 1953 Nobel Prize for Chemistry; **"for his discoveries in the field of macromolecular chemistry"**

Married without children, he died in Freiburg, Germany on September 8, 1965.

PHYSICS

FRITS ZERNIKE (1888-1966)

Frits Zernike was born in Amsterdam, Holland on July 16, 1888. Following receipt of his PhD, he joined the teaching staff of Gröningen University, becoming professor of mathematical physics and theoretical mechanics in 1915. He became a full professor in 1920 and remained so until his retirement in 1958. His area of research was in optics and astronomical telescopes. Whilst studying the flaws that occur in some diffraction gratings, because of imperfect spacing of engraved lines, he discovered the phase-contrast principle.

He discovered he could distinguish the light rays that passed through different transparent materials. Using these principles, he built a microscope in 1938. In 1952, Zernike was awarded the Rumford Medal of the Royal Society in London and the following year he was awarded the 1953 Nobel Prize for Physics; **"for his demonstration of the phase contrast method, especially for his invention of the phase contrast microscope"**

His invention of the phase-contrast microscope, permitted the study of internal cell structures. He died in Groningen, Holland on March 10, 1966. He was married twice and had two children.

PHYSIOLOGY or MEDICINE

FRITZ LIPMANN (1899-1986)
and
HANS KREBS (1900-1981)

Fritz Albert Lipmann was born on June 12, 1899 in Konisberg, Germany to a middle-class Jewish family. He received his MD in 1924 and his PhD in 1927, both from Berlin University. Between 1932 and 1939, he did research at the Biological Institute of the Carlsberg Foundation in Copenhagen. With Hitler now on the scene in his native Germany, Lipmann accepted a teaching offer from Cornell Medical School in New York (1939-41).

In 1941, he moved to the Massachusetts General Hospital in Boston, where he stayed until 1957. Whilst there, he discovered, together with Hans Kreb (qv), coenzyme A, an essential catalytic substance present in the cellular conversion of food into energy. For this work Lipmann received a half share of the 1953 Nobel Prize for Physiology or Medicine; **"for his discovery of co-enzyme A and its importance for intermediary metabolism"** From 1957 and until his death on July 24, 1986 in Poughkeepsie, NY, Lipmann taught at the Rockefeller University in New York. He was married with a son.

Hans Adolf Krebs was born in Hildesheim, Germany on August 25, 1900. The son of a Jewish physician, he obtained an MD from Hamburg University in 1925 and joined the Kaiser Wilhelm Institute. There he worked under Otto Warburg (qv), at that time researching metabolism. In 1932, Krebs was at Freiburg University, when he discovered a series of chemical reactions known as the urea cycle, showing how ammonia is converted in mammalian to urea and excreted by way of the urinary system. In 1933 Krebs was forced to leave Germany and found a ready place at Cambridge University (1933-35). He became a British subject in 1939.

From 1935 to 1943, he was at Sheffield University where he did important research especially in the field of carbohydrate metabolism. In 1937, he proved the existence of a chemical reaction cycle known as the tricarboxylic cycle, sometimes known as the 'Krebs cycle'. In 1953, he was awarded a half share of the Nobel Prize for Physiology or Medicine; **"for his discovery of the citric acid style"**

From 1954 to 1967, Krebs held the Whitley chair of biochemistry at Oxford University. He was knighted in 1958 for services to science. He was a Fellow of the Royal Society and awarded its Copley Medal in 1961. Married with two sons and a daughter, he retired in 1967 and died in Oxford on November 22, 1981.

PEACE

GEORGE MARSHALL (1880-1959)

George Catlett Marshall was born in Uniontown, PA. US, on December 31, 1880. His father was a merchant who later fell upon hard times. Marshall was educated at the Virginia Military Institute in Lexington (1897-1901). An army officer, he first saw service in the Philippines. During WW1, he was in France in 1917, with the 1st Army during the Meuse-Argonne offensive. In 1927 his wife of twenty five years died and three years later he re-married. Marshall became chief of staff of the army. From December 7th 1941, when America joined the Allied war effort, following the Japanese raid on Pearl Harbour, Marshall was the chief organiser both of manpower and equipment

He was in the forefront of those advocating a Second Front in France, to alleviate the pressure on Russian forces, at that time taking the brunt of the German army. He resigned on November 21, 1945, but allowed himself to be persuaded by President Truman to mediate in the Chinese Civil War; he was singularly unsuccessful in this endeavour. However, in January 1947 he was appointed secretary of state. He became internationally known when, in June 1947, he proposed a European Recovery Plan, known as the 'Marshall Plan"

During his term of office, the US aided both Greece and Turkey, recognised the new State of Israel and the origins of NATO. Retired because of ill health, he was recalled to run the ill-considered Korean war. (at the end of the 20th century there is still no peace treaty in force). For his work in helping in the rehabilitating of Europe, Marshall was awarded the 1953 Nobel Peace Prize.; **"for the Marshall Plan"**

A condition of the plan however, was that capital goods had to be purchased from US suppliers. The Plan wasn't a gift. All supplies had to be eventually paid for. It meant that the US had full employment and grew rich. Marshall died at the Walter Reed Hospital in Washington DC on October 16, 1959. Although twice married he had no children.

1954

Nasser becomes President of Egypt • The French defeated at Dien Bien Phu • The French send 20,000 troops to Algiers • Richard Wright, *Black Power* • Cancer caused by cigarette smoking announced • Paul Tillich, *Love, Power and Justice* • Dylan Thomas, *Under Milkwood* • Kingsley Amis, *Lucky Jim* • William Golding, *Lord of the Flies* • Films: *On The Waterfront, Rear Window, Seven Samurai,* • Robert Capa and Henri Matisse die.

LITERATURE

ERNEST HEMINGWAY (1899-1961)

Ernest **Miller Hemingway** was born in Oak Park, Ill. US, on July 21, 1899. His father was a medical doctor with a passion for killing fish and animals. Ernest graduated from high school in 1917 and obtained a job as a reporter on a Kansas City newspaper. Rejected for military service during WW1, because of a defective eye, he joined the ambulance service. He was wounded, whilst on service in Italy, on the Austro-Italian front at Fossalta di Oiave. He was hospitalized in Milan, decorated for gallantry and fell in love with his nurse, who turned down his proposal of marriage. Back in the US, he married Hadley Richardson and took a job as foreign correspondent on the *Toronto Star.*

In Paris, among the ex-pats literary group he describes so vividly in *A Movable Feast,* he attempted to survive. He published *Three Stories and Ten Poems* in 1923, in Paris, to a minimal response. The following year, *In Our Time* met with critical approval in the US, *The Sun Also Rises* (1926) and *Men Without Women* (1927) increased a growing reputation. He divorced Hadley and married Pauline Pfeiffer. He moved to Key West in Florida, followed by a lot of reports to confirm Hemingway was a variety of different personalities; myth and reality mixed.

A Farewell to Arms was published in 1929, as well as the bull fighting epic, *Death in the*

Afternoon. Probably his best known novel is *For Whom the Bell Tolls* (1940). Hemingway worked as a journalist in Spain, making no secret of his support for the Socialist cause, albeit this was against his government's neutral policy.

During WW2, he flew with the RAF in a reporting capacity and attached himself to the 22nd regiment of the 4th American Infantry Division on D-Day. He was present at the liberation of Paris and the Battle of the Bulge *The Old Man and the Sea* (1950) was probably his best work, following the end of WW2. He was awarded the Pulitzer Prize in 1953 and awarded the 1954 Nobel Prize for Literature; **"for his mastery of the art of narrative, most recently demonstrated in *The Old and the Sea*, and for the influence that he has exerted on contemporary style"** .

The father of three sons and husband to four wives, Hemingway, following hospitalisation for depression, was allowed home to his newly acquired house in Ketchum, Idaho. There, on July 2, 1961 he shot himself.

CHEMISTRY

LINUS PAULING (1901-1994)

Linus Carl Pauling was born in Portland, Oregon, US, on February 28, 1901. His father was a pharmacist and Linus received his BS in chemical engineering in 1922. At the California Institute of Technology he took his PhD in physical chemistry in 1925. He then took off for Europe to meet, and sometimes work with such luminaries as, Niels Bohr (qv) in Copenhagen; Erwin Schrodinger in Zurich; Arnold Sommerfeld in Munich and William Bragg (qv) in London. Between 1936 and 1958, he was director of the Gates and Crellin Laboratories of Chemistry at the California Institute of Technology.

His research work dealt mainly with aspects of molecular structures. He was amongst the first to apply the principles of quantum mechanics to his work, and successful in relating the distances and angles between chemical bonds to molecular characteristics, as well as interaction between molecules. For his discoveries Pauling received the 1954 Nobel Prize for Chemistry; **"for his research into the nature of the chemical bond and its application to the elucidation of the structure of complex substances"**

His continuous research work included nutritional defects and possible cures in the human condition. His enthusiasm for Vitamin C, to combat non nutritional diseases is well known.

His work in the field of nuclear disarmament was monumental. In January 1958, he presented to the United Nations, a petition signed by 11,021 scientists from all over the world, urging an end to nuclear testing. His views were well expressed in his book *No More War* (1958).

He now declared himself a pacifist, and even handed, in his opposition to nuclear testing by both the USSR and US. US right-wingers, backed by the nuclear industry, questioned his loyalty to the US. They were forced into silence when Pauling received his second Nobel Prize. This time in 1962 for Peace.

In 1963, he left the California Institute of Technology to join the Centre for the Study of

Democratic Institutions at Santa Barbara, Calif. here he devoted his talents to the study of problems of peace and war. He resigned in 1969, in protest at the educational policies of the then Governor of California, one Ronald Reagan. In 1972, he received the International Lenin Peace Prize. He joined Stamford University in California and became emeritus professor in 1974. All his working life, Pauling has received the admiration of scientists from all over the world. He was married with three sons and a daughter. He died on August 9, 1994.

PHYSICS

MAX BORN (1882-1970)
and
WALTER BOTHE (1891-1957)

Max Born was born in Breslau, Germany on December 11, 1882. His father was a professor of anatomy at Breslau University. Max received his PhD from Göttingen University in 1907 and he became a teacher in Berlin. He was a lecturer of physics at Frankfurt, before being appointed a professor of theoretical physics at Göttingen in 1921. Here was the centre, where the theory of quantum mechanics was being formulated. It was propounded in 1927, by which time Born was already a respected physicist, who had written over a thousand research papers on the subject as well as six books. His contribution to the appreciation of quantum physics cannot be overestimated, and he is generally acknowledged as the originator in this field of physics.

The theory was centrally concerned with the essence of probability, which Born introduced as an inherent feature of physics. It represented a departure from current thinking; Albert Einstein (qv) was never able to agree with this formula and a correspondence ensued between the two men. Niels Bohr (qv) however, gave Born's theory guarded acceptance. In 1933, Born was described by Adolf Hitler, as a practitioner of 'Jewish Physics' and dismissed him from his post at Göttingen.

As a Jew, he and his family were in considerable danger and forced to flee Germany. The family went to Britain, where he continued to teach; at Edinburgh and Cambridge universities. His home at Cambridge became the gathering place for scientific minds and here he indulged his passion for art and literature. It was also the place where his daughter later gave birth to his granddaughter, who grew up to become the singer, Olivia Newton John. In 1953, Born returned to Germany and retired in Heidelberg. In 1954, he was awarded a half share of the Nobel Prize for Physics; **"for his fundamental research in quantum mechanics, especially for his statistical interpretation of the wave function"**

The award was for work done in 1926. It would appear he couldn't keep away from Göttingen and he died there on January 5, 1970. He was married with two daughters and a son.

Walther **Wilhelm Georg Bothe** was born in Oranienburg, Germany on January 8, 1891. Following receipt of his PhD, Bothe taught at Berlin University (1920-31), Giessen University (1931-34) and Heidelberg (1934-57). In 1925 he and others (notably Hans Geiger of Geiger Counter fame) gathered data that allowed them to pronounce on what was termed the 'Comton effect'- the dependance of the increase in the wavelength of a beam of X-rays upon the angle through which the beam is scattered as a result of collision with electrons.

In 1930, Bothe discovered an unusual radiation, emitted by beryllium, when bombarded by alpha particles. This was later identified by Sir James Chadwick (qv) as the neutron. A leading member of the Nazi party, Bothe during WW2, led the German research for an A-Bomb. He was responsible for the planning and building of Germany's first cyclotron completed in 1943. It is perhaps ironic that when Bothe received his share of the 1954 Nobel Prize for Physics; **"for the coincidence method and his discoveries made therewith"** He shared it with the Jewish physicist Max Born, exiled from his homeland by Bothe's master and patron, Adolf Hitler. Bothe died in Heidelberg on February 8, 1957. He was un-married.

PHYSIOLOGY or MEDICINE

JOHN ENDERS (1897-1985), THOMAS WELLER (1915-)
and
FREDERICK ROBBINS (1916-)

"for their discoveries of the ability of poliomyelitis viruses to grow in cultures of various types of tissue"

John **Franklin Enders** was born in West Hartford, Conn; US, on February 10, 1897. He received an MA from Harvard University before switching to bacterial studies in which he received a PhD in 1930. He remained at Harvard and became a part of the teaching staff there. His work during WW2, when he was a civilian consultant to the US War Department, allowed him to continue his research on infectious diseases.

Much of his research was conducted at the Children's Hospital in Boston, where he established a laboratory in 1946 and where he discovered a measles vaccine. Together with Weller and Robbins, he considered the problems associated with cultivating the poliomyelitis virus in non-nervous tissue cultures prior to the development of the polio vaccine.

For this work he was awarded a third share of the 1954 Nobel Prize for Physiology or Medicine. Enders died in Waterford, Conn. on September 8 1985. He was married twice and had a son and daughter.

Thomas **Hackle Weller** was born in Ann Arbor, Mich. US, on June 15, 1915. Educated at Harvard and Michigan University, he was a teacher at the Harvard Medical School (1940-42) and served in the US Army Medical Corps during WW2. An assistant director at the Children's Medical Centre in Boston (1949-55) he, together with Enders and Robbins, achieved propagation of poliomyelitis virus in laboratory suspensions of human embryonic skin, together with muscle tissue.

He was also the first to achieve a laboratory culture of German measles virus and isolate chicken pox virus from human cell cultures. In 1954 Welder became professor of tropical public health at Harvard University and from 1968 to 1981, was also director of the Centre for the Prevention of Infectious Diseases.

In 1954 he received a third share of the Nobel Prize for Physiology or Medicine, for the part he played in the cultivation of poliomyelitis virus in tissue culture, a procedure that led to the development of polio vaccination. He is married with two sons and two daughters.

Frederick **Chapman Robbins** was born in Auburn, Ala; US, on August 25, 1916. He graduated from Harvard University Medical School in 1940 and served, during WW2 , as chief of the US Army's 15th medical general laboratory virus and rickets section, investigating epidemics of infectious hepatitis, typhus and Q fever. This experience stood him in good stead as the third member of the trio who met up at the Children's Hospital in Boston and collectively sought a cultivating poliomyelitis virus in tissue cultures, so adding to what Jonas Salk had pioneered.

Robbins was director of the pediatric department of the Cleveland Metropolitan General Hospital (1952-66), and professor of pediatrics (1952-80) as well as dean (1966-80) of the Case Western Reserve University School of Medicine, Cleveland, Ohio. For his part in the cultivation of the poliomyelitis virus in tissue cultures, Robbins was awarded a third share of the 1954 Nobel Prize for Physiology or Medicine. He is married with two daughters.

PEACE

UNITED NATIONS HIGH COMMISSIONER FOR REFUGEES.

The **office of the High Commissioner for Refugees (UNHCR)** was established by the UN, as the successor to the International Refugee Organisation, by the UN General Assembly on January 1, 1951. Their aim is to provide legal and political protection for refugees until they can acquire nationality in new countries of residence. The main office is in Geneva, with branch offices in important countries with a history of providing asylum. The UNHCR is prepared to intervene on behalf of refuges to ensure minimal rights for freedom from arbitrary expulsion, access to courts of justice, the right to work and for educational opportunities as well as ensuring there is provision for travel and ID documents. The efforts of UNHCR were rewarded when they were awarded the 1954 Nobel Peace Prize.

1955

West Germany joins NATO • Jonas Salk's anti-polio vaccine • 'flying saucers' attract attention • John Bratby, *Still Life with Chip-Fryer* • Frederick Gibberd, London Airport Buildings • Samuel Beckett, *Waiting for Godot* • Nicholas Ray, *Rebel Without a Cause* • Bill Haley, *Rock Around the Clock* • Graham Greene, *The Quiet American* • Vladimir Nabokov, *Lolita* • J.R.Tolkien, *The Lord of the Rings* • Films, *Bad Day at Black Rock, The Ladykillers, Richard lll, Marty, Pather Panchali* • Albert Einstein, Thomas Mann and Alexander Fleming die.

LITERATURE

HALLDOR LAXNESS (1902-1998)

Halldor Laxness was born Halldor Kiljan Gudjonsson in Reykjavik, Iceland on April 23, 1902. After spending most of his early years on the family farm, he commenced his era as a young man travelling Europe. His first major novel, *The Great Weaver from Kashmir* (1927), coincided with him becoming a Roman Catholic. His book is about a young man torn between religion and the pleasures of the world. Whilst in the US, he gave up religion for Socialism.

This is reflected in his novels of the1930s and '40s. He returned home to write novels that reflected Icelandic life. *Salka Valka* (1932) is about workers in a fishing village. *Independent People* (1935) is the story of a farmer fighting for his independence, whilst *World Light* (1937-40) is a novel in four volumes about a peasant poet.

The trilogy, written between 1943-46, is set in the 17th and 18th centuries and ensured Laxness as Iceland's foremost writer. His novels, during the 1950s and 60s, left social issues to become lyrical and philosophical. They include, *The Fish Can Sing* (1957), *Paradise Reclaimed* (1960) and *Christianity at Glacier* (1968). Laxness also published plays, short stories and poetry. In 1955 he received the Nobel Prize for Literature; **"for his vivid epic power which has renewed the great narrative art of Iceland"**

In 1969, he received the coveted Sonning Prize. He was twice married with two daughters and died on February 10,1998 in Leikjalundur, Iceland.

CHEMISTRY

VINCENT Du VIGNEAUD (1901-1978)

Vincent du Vigneaud was born in Chicago, US, on May 18, 1901. He studied at Illinois University, Urbana, and received his PhD from Rochester University, Rochester, NY (1927). He then studied further at John Hopkins University, Baltimore; the Kaiser Wilhelm Institute, Berlin and Edinburgh University. Between 1932 and 38, he was head of the biochemistry department of the George Washington University Medical School in Washington, DC, professor of biochemistry at the Cornell University Medical College (1938-67), and professor of Chemistry at Cornell University, Ithaca, NY (1967-75).

His research, was in the area of the isolation and synthesis of two pituitary hormones: vasopressin, which acts on the muscles of the blood vessels to create elevation of blood pressure, and oxytocin, the main agent causing contraction of the uterus and secretion of milk. du Vigneaud was awarded the 1955 Nobel Prize for Chemistry; **"for his work on biochemically important sulphur compounds, especially for the first synthesis of a polypeptide hormone"**

He also contributed to the synthesis of penicillin as well as the isolation and structure of the vitamin, biotin. Married with a son and daughter, he died in White Plains, NY; on December 11, 1978.

PHYSICS

WILLIS LAMB (1913-)
and
POLYKARP KUSCH (1911-1993)

Willis Eugene Lamb was born in Los Angeles, Calif. US, on July 12, 1913. In 1938, he joined the staff of Columbia University and, during WW2, worked in the radiation laboratory. Lamb applied new methods to measure the lines that appear in the spectrum, as defined through established quantum mechanics, only to discover in 1947, that their positions were slightly different from what had been predicted. While professor of physics at Stanford University in California (1951-56), Lamb created microwave techniques for examining the hyperfine structure of the spectral lines of helium.

His experimental work, in refining the quantum theories of electromagnetic phenomena, brought him international fame. He was awarded a co-share of the 1955 Nobel Prize for Physics; **"for his discoveries concerning the fine structure of the hydrogen spectrum"**

Until 1962, he was professor of theoretical physics at Oxford University, later switching to do the same job at Yale University. In 1974 he became professor of physics and optical sciences at Arizona University. He is married.

Polykarp Kusch was born in Blankenburg, Germany on January 26, 1911. He arrived in the United States a few months later, becoming a citizen in 1922. In 1937 he was at Columbia University, working with Isadore Rabi (qv), on the effects of magnetic fields on beams of atoms. During WW2, he was researching the improvements of radar. He returned to Columbia in 1946 as professor of physics, a post that lasted until 1972. He then became a professor at Texas University, Dallas, where he remained until his retirement in 1982. Thin and a wearer of glasses, he was a witty and dedicated teacher, beloved by his students. He received the 'The Great Teacher Award' in 1959, from Columbia.

In 1947, via precise atomic beam studies, Kusch was to demonstrate that the magnetic properties of the electron were not in agreement with existing theories. Thereafter, he made accurate measurements of the magnetic moment of the electron and its behaviour in hydrogen. His work is characterised by great accuracy and considered most reliable. In this regard, he measured numerous atomic, molecular and nuclear properties, by radio frequency beam techniques. He was awarded a co-share of the 1955 Nobel Prize for Physics; **"for his precision determination of the magnetic moment of the electron"**

He died in Dallas, Texas on March 20th 1993 from a series of strokes. He was married with three daughters.

PHYSIOLOGY or MEDICINE

HUGO THEORELL (1903-1982)

Axel Hugo Teodor Theorell was born in Linkoping, Sweden on July 6, 1903. He was an assistant professor of biochemistry at Uppsala University when, in 1932, he was the first to isolate crystalline myoglobin, an oxygen bearing protein found in red muscle. Whilst working with Otto Warburg (qv) at the Kaiser Wilhelm Institute in Berlin (1933-35), they were able to isolate from yeast, a pure sample of that found to be instrumental in the oxidative interconversion of sugars by the cell. Theorell later discovered that the enzyme is made up of two parts; non-protein coenzyme and a protein apoenzyme. This discovery in 1934, was the first time that the effect of an enzyme was attributed to the chemical activity of specific atoms.

He was director of the biochemical department of the Nobel Medical Institute in Stockholm (1937-70), and there, studied the precise nature of the chemical link between coenzyme and apoenzyme. This later led to the development of sensitive blood tests used in many spheres including, determining legal definitions of drunkenness. For his work, leading to the understanding of enzyme action, Theorell was awarded the 1955 Nobel Prize for Physiology or Medicine; **"for his discoveries concerning the nature and mode of action of oxidation enzymes"** He also served as president of the Swedish Royal Academy of Science. Married with three sons, he died in Stockholm on August 15, 1982.

PEACE

NOT AWARDED

1956

Suez crisis • Hungarian uprising• Eisenhower re-elected US President • Transatlantic telephone link • CND Aldermaston march against the A-bomb • Colin Wilson, *The Outsider* • John Osborne, *Look Back in Anger* • Ingmar Bergman, *The Seventh Seal* • Allen Ginsberg, *Howl* • Films: *Aparajito, The Searchers, Around the World in Eighty Days, The King and I,* • Sir Alexander Korda, Max Beerbohm, Julien Benda and Walter de la Mare die.

PHYSIOLOGY or MEDICINE

JUAN JIMENEZ (1881-1958)

Juan Ramon Jimenez was born in Moguer, Spain on December 24, 1881. He enjoyed a life of ill-health and a limited education, so having a wealthy father was most necessary. He published two books of poetry in 1900; printed in violet and green they were the subject of derision. In 1916 he journeyed to New York and there married Zenobia Aymar, the Spanish translator of Rabindranath Tagore,(qv) the Hindu poet.

A poet of some note in Spain, Jimenez joined forces with the Republicans during the Civil War (1936-39) and, as a result, became a marked man when Franco became the Fascist dictator. He exiled himself to Puerto Rico where he would spend the rest of his life.

His prose work *Platero y Yo,* a delightful tale of the young poet and his donkey, originally published in 1917, was later translated and well received in the US. Between 1903 and 1953, he wrote and published some 300 poems. He was in poor health when awarded the 1956 Nobel Prize for Literature; **"for his lyrical poetry, which in Spanish language constitutes an example of high spirit and artistic purity"**

He died in San Juan on May 29, 1958. Although married he had no children.

CHEMISTRY

CYRIL HINSHELWOOD (1897-1967)
and
NIKOLAI SEMENOV (1896-1986)

"for their researches into the mechanism of chemical reactions"

Cyril Norman Hinshelwood was born in London, England on June 19, 1897. Educated at Oxford University, he later became a professor there (1937). Around 1930, he began learning how water is formed. This research led him to a greater appreciation of how chain and branched chain reactions occur in explosions.

Then came his work understanding molecular kinetics within a bacterial cell. Here he observed the biological reaction to bacteria and resulting environmental changes. He concluded that more or less a permanent change in a cell's resistance to a drug might be achieved.

This was important in the area of bacterial resistance to antibiotic and similar agents. He wrote on his subject in 1926, *The Kinetics of Chemical Change* and in 1946, *The Chemical Kinetics of the Bacterial Cell*. He was knighted in 1948. For his work on the combination of hydrogen and oxygen to form water, he was awarded a co-share of the 1956 Nobel Prize for Chemistry.
He died a bachelor in London, on October 9, 1967.

Nikolai Nikolayevich Semenov was born Saratov, Russia on April 15, 1896. He was educated at Leningrad University and graduated in 1917. He taught for some time at Tomsk University in Siberia. He became assistant director and later professor, at the Leningrad Physical Technical Institute (1920-31) and director of Chemical Physics at the Academy of Sciences in Moscow , remaining until shortly before his death.

He was an acknowledged expert in molecular physics and carried out important research on the kinetics of gas reactions. His work on the mechanisms of chain and branched-chain chemical reactions, led to him being awarded a co-share of the 1956 Nobel Prize for Physics.

He was the first Soviet citizen ever to win a Nobel Prize. He wrote much on his subject including the influential book, *Some Problems in Chemical Kinetics and Reactivity* (1954). Married with a son and daughter, he died in Saratov, Russia on September 25, 1986.

PHYSICS

WILLIAM SHOCKLEY (1910-1989), WALTER BRATTAIN (1902-1987)
and
JOHN BARDEEN (1908-1991)

"for their researches on semiconductors and their discovery of the transistor effect"

William Bradford Shockley was born in London, England on February 13, 1910. His parents were US mining engineers and William was brought up in California. He was educated at the California Institute of Technology, from where he received a BS in 1932; Harvard University followed, from where he received a PhD in 1936. He then joined Bell Telephone Laboratories in 1936 where he conducted experiments that would lead to the invention of the junction transistor.

During WW2 he was in the US Navy, in charge of the anti-submarine warfare research unit. He returned to Bell Telephone as director of transistor physics research. Between 1963-74, he was professor of engineering at Stanford University. There he gave much cause for controversy with his assertions that, following standardized intelligence tests, it proved that Blacks were inferior to Whites.

Although he continued to defend his assertions that there were intellectual differences between races, it didn't appear to end his association with Stanford. In 1956 Shockley was awarded a co-share of the Nobel Prize for Physics for his part in the development of the radio transistor.

Married twice with two sons and a daughter, he died in Palo Alto, Calif. US, on August 12, 1989.

Walter Houser Brattain was born in Amoy, China on February 10, 1902. He grew up on a cattle ranch in Washington State and educated at Oregon University. He joined Bell Telephone in 1929 and there met William Shockley and John Bardeen. He worked researching the surface properties of solids.

In the main, the atomic structure of a material at the surface which usually differs from its atomic structure in the interior. He was awarded a third share of the 1956 Nobel Prize for Physics, for his work on the development of the transistor which replaced the bulky vacuum tube.

He wrote much upon his subject and, between 1967 and 1972, was a professor at Whitman College, Walla Walla, Wash.
Married twice with a son, he died in Seattle, Wash; on October 13, 1987.

John **Bardeen** was born in Madison, Wis. US, on May 23, 1908. He received his BS and MS in electrical engineering from Wisconsin University (where his father was the Dean). In 1938 he obtained his PhD, in mathematical physics, from Princeton University. During WW2, he was principal physicist at the US Naval Ordnance Laboratory in Washington, DC.

The war over, he joined Bell Telephones and, at their laboratories, met up with Shockley and Brattain. All three worked on varying aspects of what would later be termed the transistor, a conjunction of *trans*fer and re*sistor*. Bardeen's main area of expertise, was the electron-conducting properties of the semiconductors.

In 1956 he was the third Bell Telephone employee to share that years Nobel Prize for Physics. Between 1951 and 1975, Bardeen was professor of electrical engineering and physics at Illinois University. He, together with Cooper (qv) and Schrieffer (qv), worked on what is now termed the, BCS theory. These were the forerunners in superconductivity. Bardeen was later awarded a third share of the 1972 Nobel Prize for Physics.

He was married with three children and received honours from institutions all over the world. He died in Boston, Mass. on January 30, 1991 in hospital, having undergone exploratory surgery for possible lung cancer. He was an expert on transistors but, on the day of his Nobel presentation, he couldn't get his garage door open; the electric switch had let him down! He was married with two sons and a daughter.

PHYSIOLOGY or MEDICINE

DICKINSON RICHARDS (1895-1973), ANDRE COURNAND (1895-1988)
and
WERNER FORSSMANN (1904-1979)

"for their discoveries concerning heart catherization and pathological changes in the circulatory system"

Dickinson **Woodruff Richards** was born in Orange, NJ: US, on October 30, 1895. He received degrees from Yale and Columbia universities and, following an internship and further study in England, qualified as a doctor of medicine. Between 1945 and 1961, he taught at Columbia University.

He also worked at New York's Bellevue Hospital and there met Andre Cournand. They worked together, perfecting Werner Forssmann's theory of what was known as cardiac catheterization. This technique, was of using a flexible tube or catheter conducted from an elbow vein to the heart as a probe to investigate the heart.

For his part in this radical work, Richards was awarded a third share of the 1956 Nobel Prize for Physiology or Medicine. Married with four daughters, he died in Lakeville, Conn. on February 23, 1973.

Andre Frederic Cournand was born in Paris, France on September 24, 1895. His medical studies were interrupted by the advent of WW1. He was educated at the Sorbonne in Paris and emigrated to the US in 1930, becoming a citizen in 1941. Between 1934 and 1964, he was attached, in one function or another, to Columbia University and continued lecturing there after he retired.

He met Richards whilst studying at Bellevue Hospital. They decided to collaborate in clinical lung and heart research and went on to perfect Forssmann's procedure, now known as cardiac catheterization. This resulted, in being able to make more accurate diagnoses of the heart. The method was also used to examine the pulmonary artery, enabling great improvement in the diagnosis of lung diseases. For this work, Cournand was awarded a third share of the 1956 Nobel Prize for Physiology or Medicine.

He died in Great Barrington, Mass. on February 19, 1988. He was married three times, had three daughters and adopted a son.

Werner Forssmann was born in Berlin, Germany on August 20, 1904. He was a junior doctor in a Berlin hospital when, in 1929, he used himself as a human subject and watching himself in a mirror, held in front of a fluoroscope screen, whilst using a catheter.

Critics called him foolhardy and his experiment dangerous, and Forssmann was forced to abandon cardiology for urology. However, his procedures became known and, in 1941, put into practise by Richards and Cournand. Forssmann was included as the third awardee of the 1956 Nobel Prize for Physiology or Medicine.

In 1958 he was chief of the surgical division of the Evangelical Hospital in Dusseldorf. Married with five sons and a daughter, he died in Schopfheim, Germany on June 1, 1979.

PEACE

NOT AWARDED

1957

Rome Treaty for Common Market • Russia launches Sputnik 1 • Harold Macmillan succeeds Eden as British Prime Minister • Francis Bacon, *Screaming Nurse* • Lerner and Loewe, *My Fair Lady* • Stevie Smith, *Not Waving But Drowning* • John Braine, *Room at the Top* • Jack Kerouac, *On the Road* • Bernard Malamud, *The Assistant* • Film: *The Bridge on the River Kwai, Paths of Glory, Sweet Smell of Success, Twelve Angry Men, Wild Strawberries,* • Toscanini, Louis B. Mayer, Lord Hore-Belisha, Sholem Asch, Eric von Stroheim, Umberto Saba, Max Ophuls, Sibelius and Dorothy L. Sayers die.

LITERATURE

ALBERT CAMUS (1913-1960)

Albert Camus was born Mondovi, in Algiers on November 7, 1913. His father died before he was born, whilst fighting for France during WW1. His Spanish born mother worked as a charwoman, in order to provide for her two sons, widowed mother and paralysed brother. Camus describes the scene, centred in a working class area of Algiers, in his first collection of essays published in 1937 entitled, *L'Envers et l'endroit.*

In 1918, he entered primary school, where his teacher, Louis Germain, encouraged him. It resulted in Albert entering the Algiers High School in 1923. His 1938 collection of essays, *Noces*, describes the beauty of the Algerian countryside. Although a student of intellectual pursuits, he was a great fan and participant in all sorts of sport. A bout of TB put an end to his playing sport and interrupted his studies.

Camus left his mother's unhealthy flat, deciding to support himself by undertaking a variety of jobs. He became a student of philosophy at Algiers University. A professor there, Jean Grenier, was also an aficionado of football and it was because of his teaching that Camus obtained a *diplôme d'études supérieures* in 1936. Another bout of TB forced him to seek the mountain air of Europe. He read and wrote and argued politics. A member of the Algiers Communist Party, he became involved in the Socialist theatre. A reporter in the late 1930s for *Alger-Républicain,* he became a literary reviewer and was early admirer of Sartre.

During WW2, Camus published a Resistance news sheet and, following the war, became editor of *Combat,* an independent left wing journal. He became disillusioned by politics and left the paper. He had become a literary figure by the publication in 1942, of *L'Etrange. La Peste* (The Plague), followed in 1947.

His feature length essay, *L'Homme révolté* (1951) brought him into conflict with Jean-Paul Sartre. *La Chute* (1956) was considered a brilliant novel, followed in 1957, by a collection of short stories, *L'Exit et le royaume.* In the same year, aged only 44, Camus was awarded the Nobel Prize for Literature; **"for his important literary production, which, with clear-sighted earnestness, illuminates the problems of the human conscience in our times"**

His acceptance speech was dedicated to his primary school teacher, Louis Germain. He died a few months later, on January 4, 1960 as a result of a car crash. Camus was the post war spokesman for a generation emerging from the horrors of war. He married twice and had a son and daughter.

CHEMISTRY

ALEXANDER TODD (1907-1997)

Alexander **Robertus Todd** was born in Glasgow, Scotland on October 2, 1907. He received his doctorate from Oxford University in 1931 and became professor of organic chemistry at Manchester University (1938-44) and Cambridge University (1944-71). At Manchester, he worked on nucleosides, compounds that form the structural units of nucleic acids (DNA and RNA). In 1949, he reported he had synthesized a related substance namely, adenosine triphosphate (ATP). This is essential to energy utilization in living organisms. He went on to synthesize in 1949, flavin adenine dinucleotide (FAD) and, in 1955, he revealed the structure of vitamin B.

During his long career Todd worked on the structure of other vitamins, especially vitamin E, as well as alkaloids found in marijuana and other plants. In 1975, he was elected president of the Royal Society. In 1954 he was knighted and in 1962 created a life peer. He became a member of the Royal Order of Merit in 1977. He was master of Christ's College, Cambridge (1963-78) and was visiting professor at Hatfield Polytechnic (1978-86). In 1957 he was awarded the Nobel Prize for Chemistry; **"for his work on nucleotides and nucleotide co-enzymes"**

His research on the structure and synthesis of compounds, were considered vital in understanding the working of genes. Married with a son and two daughters, he died on January 10, 1997 whilst living in Cambridge, England.

PHYSICS

TSUNG LEE (1926-)
and
CHEN YANG (1922-)

"for their penetrating investigation of the so-called parity laws which has led to important discoveries regarding the elementary particles"

Tsung-Dao Lee was born in Shanghai, China on November 25, 1926. He was 20 years old when he arrived in the US and enrolled at Chicago University. Here he first met Chen Yang. They worked together at the Institute for Advanced Study at Princeton University. Lee was appointed assistant professor of physics at Columbia University in 1953.

In 1956, they decided that the theta-meson and tau-meson were not separate, but the same particle and now known as the K-meson. The law on parity conservation prohibits a single particle from having decay modes exhibiting opposite parity, it therefore followed that parity is not conserved.

It was a hypothesis that required experiments and, in 1957, their theories were confirmed. That same year Lee was awarded a half share of the 1957 Nobel Prize for Physics, for research that brought about major refinements in particle-physics theory. In 1960, Lee was professor of physics at the Institute of Advanced Physics. In 1963, he returned to Columbia University to become the first holder of the Enrico Fermi chair in physics. He is married with two sons.

Chen Ning Yang was born in Hofei, China on September 22, 1922. His father was a professor of mathematics at Tsinghua University.

Chen received his BSC. in 1942 and his Masters in 1944, both from Southwest Associated University in K'unming. He received a fellowship that allowed him into the US where, at Chicago University, he worked for his PhD His future development was due to the year he spent as an assistant to Enrico Fermi (qv). In 1955 he was a professor at Princeton University, becoming a US citizen in 1964.

From 1965, Yang was Albert Einstein professor, at the Institute of Science at New York State University. During the 1970s, Yang was a board member of Rockefeller University. He was on the board of Ben-Gurion University in Israel and Salk Institute in San Diego, Calif. In 1957, he received the Einstein Award and, in 1980, the Rumford Prize. The Liberty Award and the National Medal of Science followed in 1986.

In 1957, Yang received a half share of the Nobel Prize for Physics for his work, in association with Tsung Lee, on parity and studies in particle physics. He is married with two sons and a daughter.

PHYSIOLOGY or MEDICINE

DANIEL BOVET (1907-1992)

Daniel Bovet was born in Neuchatel, Switzerland on March 23, 1907. He studied at Geneva University from where he graduated with an MD. in 1929. He went to the Pasteur Institute in Paris, becoming head of his department in 1937. In 1944, he discovered the first antihistamine effective against certain allergic conditions. In 1947, he discovered gallamine, a muscle relaxant. He was also the first to recognise that within these products are derivatives of succinylcholine with curare, used now in light anaesthesia during surgery to induce muscle relaxation.

In 1947, Bovet was invited to set-up a laboratory of chemotherapeutic at the Superior Institute of Health in Rome; he accepted and eventually took Italian citizenship. In 1964, he was professor of pharmacology at Sassari University and, between 1971 and 1982, was professor of psycho biology at Rome University. He was awarded the 1957 Nobel Prize for Physiology or Medicine; **"for his discoveries relating to synthetic compounds that inhibit the action of certain body substances, and especially their action on the vascular system and the skeletal muscles"** Responsible for the discovery of certain chemotherapeutic agents, he died from cancer in Rome, Italy on April 8, 1992. He was married with three sons. He was someone who never wanted to profit from his work and never took out any patents on his discoveries. His one desire was to alleviate poverty and sickness.

PEACE

LESTER PEARSON (1897-1972)

Lester Bowles Pearson was born in Toronto, Canada on April 23, 1897. He studied history at Toronto University and later lectured there (1924-28). In 1928 he joined Canada's foreign department, serving in various departments both home and abroad. Between 1945-46, he was ambassador to the United States and headed the Canadian delegation to the UN from 1948 to 1956. He served as president of the UN General Assembly (1952-3).

He entered parliament in 1948 and represented Canada at the founding of NATO in 1949 becoming chairman in 1951. The Suez war, that involved Egypt, France Israel and Britain was a most testing time for Pearson. He succeeded in obtaining a cease fire and an end to all hostilities. He was awarded the 1957 Nobel Peace Prize; **"for his efforts to solve the Suez crisis of 1956"** Pearson became leader of the Liberal Party in 1958 and, following the general election of 1963, became prime minister. He resigned in 1968 and retired. Married with a son and daughter he died in Ottawa, Canada on December 27, 1972.

1958

Khrushchev takes over in Russia • De Gaulle elected President of France • Race riots in London • J K Galbraith, *The Affluent Society* • The Beatnik Movement spreads • Leonard Bernstein, *West Side Story* • HE Bates, *The Darling Buds of May* • Truman Capote, *Breakfast at Tiffany's* • Alan Sillitoe, *Saturday Night and Sunday Morning* • Films: *Touch of Evil, Vertigo, Ashes and Diamonds, Gigi, Separate Tables* • *Black Orpheus*, • Ralph Vaughen Williams, Louis Golding, Lion Feuchtwanger and Marie Stopes die.

LITERATURE

BORIS PASTERNAK (1890-1960)

Boris Leonidovich Pasternak was born in Peredelkino near Moscow, Russia on February 10, 1890. His father was the painter Leonid Pasternak and his mother the professional pianist Rosa Kaufman. Boris was brought up in a cultured Jewish atmosphere and his early ambition was to be a musician. However, a love of poetry took over and he chose to study philosophy at Moscow University.   During WW1 he was a factory worker, but, following the Revolution of October 1917, he worked in a Moscow library.

His book of poetry, *Over the Barriers* (1917), symbolized the New Russia. In a country of poetry lovers, the people loved Pasternak. His, *My Sister: Life* (1922) and *Themes and Variations* (1923) were greeted with acclaim by critics and public alike. Then, gradually, his popularity waned as his poetry, now often politically incorrect, failed to get published. He relied on translation work as a means of earning his livelihood.

In 1956 he presented the manuscript of *Dr Zhivago*, his first full length novel, for publication in a leading magazine. It was rejected as being incompatible with the structure of the Soviet Union. By 1958, via an Italian publisher, *Dr Zhivago* was selling around the world in eighteen languages and hailed as a masterpiece: but it was not available in Russia. The award of the 1958 Nobel Prize for Literature; **"for his important achievement both in contemporary lyrical poetry and in the field of the great Russian epic tradition"** only added to his problems.

Now his membership of the Union of Soviet Writers was revoked, and there were even orchestrated public meetings, calling for his deportation and telling him to 'go back to Israel.' Pasternak wrote to Soviet leader Khrushchev, declaring, ' Leaving the Motherland will equal death for me '. Suffering from cancer and heart disease, he returned to the village of his birth and died there on May 30, 1960.

His funeral was attended by thousands and his dacha and grave remain places of pilgrimage. He was married twice with two sons. In 1987, the Writer's Union rehabilitated Pasternak and the Russian people were at last permitted to read his book, and see the film, that had excited the world and won three Academy Awards. The absurd treatment of Pasternak was the direct result of the jealousy those in power had over those with talent.

In 1996 Olga Ivinskaya died. She was the role model for the character Lara, in *Dr Zhivago*; she was also Pasternak's mistress, and she suffered for her love of the author. She was twice sent to labour camps and, as a result, their baby was stillborn. The pair had met in 1946 and although Pasternak refused to divorce his wife, he spent every day with Olga, only going home to sleep. When Boris was dying, the Pasternak family refused to allow Olga to say 'goodbye'. She spent the next 35 years living on memories and fighting through the courts for the return of her love letters. She lost after many years of bitter wrangling; now it no longer matters.

CHEMISTRY

FREDERICK SANGER (1918-)

Frederick Sanger was born in Rendcombe, Glos. England, on August 13, 1918. He was educated at St. John's College, Cambridge from where, in 1943, he received a doctorate in biochemistry. He then worked continuously on research at Cambridge until 1951, thereafter at the Medical Research Council for the next decade.

His research was establishing the structure of the bovine insulin molecule, determining in 1955, the exact order of molecule's amino acids. This work was a vital preliminary to the laboratory synthesis of insulin, as well as to determine the structure of other complex proteins. His work led to the award of the 1958 Nobel Prize for Chemistry; **"for his work on the structure of proteins, especially that of insulin"**

Sanger in the 1970s, established the sequences of nucleotides in the DNA molecule of a small virus, and this achievement brought him a third share of the 1980 Nobel Prize for Chemistry, thus becoming only the fourth person ever to be awarded a second Nobel Prize. He was created a Companion of Honour in 1981, and made a member of the Order of Merit in 1986. He is married with two sons and a daughter.

PHYSICS

PAVEL CHERENKOV (1904-1990), ILYA FRANK (1908-1990)
and
IGOR TAMM (1895-1971)

"for the discovery and the interpretation of the Cherenkov effect"

Pavel Alekseyevich Cherenkov was born Novaya Chigla, Russia on July 28, 1904. He graduated in 1928 from Voronezh University. In 1934, he noted the emission of blue light from water and other transparent media when atomic particles are passed through them at a speed greater than light. This became known as the ' Cherenkov effect'. Later, Ilya Frank and Igor Tamm would further investigate.

For his preliminary work, Cherenkov was awarded a third share of the 1958 Nobel Prize for Physics. Cherenkov's principle was adapted in constructing a cosmic-ray counter and mounted on *Sputnik III*.

Married with a son and daughter, he died in Russia on January 6, 1990.

Ilya Mikhaylovich Frank was born in St. Petersburg, Russia on October 23, 1908. He was educated at Moscow State University and, in 1944, was appointed its' professor of physics, following four years at the State Optical Institute. Frank, together with Igor Tamm, provided the theoretical interpretation of the 'Cherenkov effect'. They showed that the effect arises when a charged particle traverses a medium, when moving at a greater speed of light in that medium. For this contribution, Frank received a third share of the 1958 Nobel Prize for Physics. He also worked on electron radiation with Cherenkov and Tamm and all three received the Stalin Prize in 1946.

In the same year, Frank was made a member of the USSR Academy of Sciences. Married with a son he died in Russia on June 22, 1990.

Igor Yevgenyevich Tamm was born in Vladivostok, Russia on July 8, 1895 into an old established Jewish family. Whilst a professor at Moscow University, he studied the quantum theory of diffused light in solid bodies. His method of interpreting the interaction of elementary nuclear particles is now known as the ' Tamm method'.

He was passionate concerning nuclear energy for peaceful purposes, and his later work centred on the control of thermonuclear reactions. He even went so far as to appeal for international disarmament, on US television in 1963.

For his work in interpreting the 'Cherenkov effect' Tamm was

202

awarded a share of the 1958 Nobel Prize for Physics. Married with a son and daughter, he died in Moscow on April 12, 1971.

PHYSIOLOGY or MEDICINE

GEORGE BEADLE (1903-1989), JOSHUA LEDERBERG (1925-)
and
EDWARD TATUM (1909-1975)

George Wells Beadle was born in Wahoo, Neb. US, on October 22, 1903. He received a PhD in genetics from Cornell University in 1931, and joined the laboratory of Thomas Morgan at the California Institute of Technology. There, Beadle soon realised genes chemically influence heredity. At the Institut de Biologie Physico-Chimique in Paris, Beadle designed a technique to understand the nature of the chemical effects in *Drosophila.*

These results showed that something as simple as eye colour, is the product of a long series of chemical reactions and that somehow genes affect these. He spent a year at Harvard, before going on to Stanford University where, in 1937, he, together with Edward Tatum, found that the total environment of bread mold, *Neurospora,* could be varied in such a way that the researchers could find and identify genetic changes or mutants, with ease.

After exposing these molds to X-rays, he studied the altered nutritional requirements of the mutants so produced. For his work in demonstrating that genes affect heredity by determining enzyme structure, Beadle was awarded a third share of the 1958 Nobel Prize for Physiology or Medicine.

Between 1946 and 1960, he was professor and chairman of the biology department at the California Institute of Technology. He later became chancellor of Chicago University. His publications include, *An Introduction to Genetics* (1939) and in 1963, *Genetics and Modern Biology.* He married twice, had a son, and died in Pomona, Calif. on June 9, 1989.

Joshua Lederberg was born in Montclair, NJ. US, on May 23, 1925.into a religious Jewish family. He obtained his PhD from Yale University in 1948, and established a department of medical genetics at Wisconsin University, where he taught from 1947 to 1959. He went on to Stanford Medical School and the Kennedy Laboratories of Molecular Medicine (1962-78). Subsequently, he was president of Rockefeller University, New York. As a result of his 1946 researches, he was able to confirm that the association of two different strains of bacteria resulted in genetic recombination, and therefore a new crossbreed strain of the bacteria.

In 1952, whilst his earlier findings were still being considered by his colleagues, Lederberg came up with another 'first'. His paper, *Genetic*

Exchange in Salmonella, revealed that certain types of virus were able to carry a bacterial gene from one bacterium to another. This discovery was of the greatest importance in the field of genetic research and was awarded with a share of the 1958 Nobel Prize for Physiology of Medicine. He is married twice and has a son and daughter.

Edward Lawrie Tatum was born in Boulder, Colo. US, December 14, 1909. His research work was mainly allied with that of George Beadle. He was educated at Wisconsin University and later taught at Stanford University where he met Beadle, (1937-45). He then taught at Yale University (1945-48) and Rockefeller University (1957-75). He was able to show that bacteria reproduce by a sexual process so founding the science of bacterial genetics.

For his work in creating the field of molecular genetics, Tatum was awarded a third share of the 1958 Nobel Prize for Physiology or Medicine. He was still teaching when he died suddenly in New York, on November 5, 1975. He was married three times and had two daughters.

PEACE

DOMINIQUE PIRE (1910-1969)

Dominique Georges Pire was born in Dinant, Belgium on February 10, 1910. He entered the Dominican Monastery of La Sarte in Huy in 1928, and ordained in 1934. He obtained his doctorate from the Dominican University in Rome in 1936. He returned to La Sarte to teach moral philosophy (1937-47). He was active in the Belgian Resistance movement during WW2 and later became involved with the resulting refugee movement. In 1949 he founded the Aide aux Personnes Déplacées, regardless of nationality or religion.

Branches were created all through Europe as well as special 'homes of welcome' for the aged. Pire also founded a system of sponsors, that allowed a refugee to be aided by a person in another country. He was awarded the 1958 Nobel Peace Prize; **"for his aid to displaced persons in Europe after World War ll"**

In 1960, he created in Huy, the Mahatma Gandhi International Peace Centre that later became known as the Peace University. Its purpose is to instruct youths in the principles and practise of peace. He was also the founder of the World Friendships in order to promote understanding between races.

Pire, a bachelor, died in Louvain, Belgium on January 30, 1969.

1959

Fidel Castro liberates Cuba • Hawaii is 50th US state • USSR sends dogs into orbit • Pope John XXIII announces the first Vatican Council since 1870 • Frank Lloyd Wright, Guggenheim Art Museum, New York • Shelagh Delaney, *A Taste of Honey* • Arnold Wesker, *Roots* • Jean Cocteau, *Le Testament d'Orphee* • Laurie Lee, *Cider with Rosie* • Keith Waterhouse, *Billy Liar* • Film: *Some Like it Hot, North by Northwest, The World of Apu, Ballada a Soldate, Ben-Hur, Room at the Top,* • Jacob Epstein and Stanley Spencer die.

LITERATURE

SALVATORE QUASIMODO (1901-1968)

Salvatore Quasimodo was born in Modica, Sicily, Italy on August 20, 1901. The son of a railway worker, he was educated in Messina and Syracuse. At Palermo University he studied engineering and mathematics, before going to Rome University where he graduated as an engineer. He then spent the next ten years working for the government and writing in his spare time. His first poetry appeared in Florence's *Solaria,* and considered Hermetic in style. In 1935, he left engineering to teach Italian, at a conservatory in Milan. *Suddenly it's Evening* (1942) saw an end to his Hermetic writing.

Much of his poetry shows the injustice of the Fascist regime, the horrors of war and resulting Italian guilt. He undertook much translation work and edited anthologies of Italian poetry. His work was not international, and not popular during his lifetime, in a country with a high illiteracy rate. It is therefore perhaps a little strange, that he was awarded the 1959 Nobel Prize for Literature; **"for his lyrical poetry, which, with classical fire, expresses the tragic experience of life in our own times"**

His work is described as elitist. Married twice with a son and daughter, he died in Naples on June 14, 1968.

CHEMISTRY

YAROSLAV HEYROVSKY (1890-1967)

Yaroslav Heyrovsky was born in Prague, Czechoslovakia, on December 20, 1890. He was educated at the Charles University of Prague and London University, where he worked under William Ramsey (qv). He was professor and director of physical medicine at Charles University (1926-54).

His research, that would lead to his discovery of polarographs, began whilst he was in London. He gave the first demonstration in 1924, and within a decade, his method was in common use. His instrument measures the current that flows when a predetermined potential is applied to two electrodes, immersed in the solution to be analysed. For his work, Heyrovsky was awarded the 1959 Nobel Prize for Chemistry.;**"for his discovery and development of the polarographic methods of analysis"**

Married with a son and daughter he died in Prague on March 27th 1967.

PHYSICS

EMILIO SEGRE (1905-1989)
and
OWEN CHAMBERLAIN (1920-)

"for their discovery of the antiproton"

Emilio Gino Segre was born in Tivoli, Italy on February 1, 1905, into a Jewish family. In 1922 he was studying engineering at Rome University, when he switched to physics, to study under Enrico Fermi (qv), obtaining a PhD in 1928. He became assistant professor of physics at Rome University (1932-37).   Segre and Fermi, experimenting on the effects of the neutron in relation to uranium bombardment, the following year, discovered that slow neutrons had important properties in relation to the operation of nuclear reactors.

In 1937, while at Palermo University, Segre discovered technetium, a radioactive element found, not in ores, but among fission products of uranium. This most important find caused Segre to be invited to lecture in the US. Whilst there Mussolini, the Italian Fascist leader, announced his anti-Jewish laws and, as a result, Segre decided to remain in America. (In October 1943, Segre's father-in-law, Admiral Augusto Capon and other relatives, were rounded up by the Germans taken away and murdered).

Further research by Segre, contributed to the Manhattan Project that led to the A-bomb and the end of WW2. In 1944, he became a US citizen and professor of Physics at the University of California at Berkeley (1946-72). For his part in the discovery of the antiproton, Emilio Segre was co-awarded, in 1959, a Nobel Prize for Physics.

He wrote much upon his subject, including, *Nuclei and Particles* (1964), *Enrico Fermi: Physics* (1970) and *From Falling Bodies to Radio Waves* (1984). In 1974 he returned to Italy to become professor of physics at Rome University. Married twice, he had two daughters and a son and died in Lafayette, California on April 22, 1989.

Owen Chamberlain was born in San Francisco, US, on July 10, 1920. Before receiving his PhD from Chicago University, he was working on the Manhattan Project (1942-46). In 1948, he joined the teaching staff of the University of California at Berkeley, becoming a full professor in 1958. Whilst at Berkeley, he conducted research on alpha particle decay, neutron diffraction in liquids, and high energy nuclear particle reactions.

In 1955, he, together with Segre, used a powerful particle accelerator (bevatron) to produce antiprotons. In 1956, they were able to confirm the existence of the antineutron. For his share in the project Chamberlain received, in 1959, a co-share of the Nobel Prize for Physics. He is twice married with three daughters and a son.

PHYSIOLOGY or MEDICINE

SEVERO OCHOA (1905-1993)
and
ARTHUR KORNBERG (1918-)

"for their discovery of the mechanisms in the biological synthesis of ribonucleic acid and deoxyribonucleic acid"

Severo Ochoa was born in Luarca, Spain on September 24, 1905. He was educated at Madrid University where, in 1929, he received his MD. Further education followed at Glasgow, Berlin and London universities. He was head of the physiology department for medical research at Madrid University (1935).

Between 1938-41, whilst at Oxford University, he began investigating vitamin B (thiamine). In 1946, he was professor of pharmacology at New York University and chairman of the department in 1954. From 1974, he was associated with the Roche Institute of Molecular Biology.

He was co-awarded, in 1959, a Nobel Prize for Physiology or Medicine, for his discovery of an enzyme in bacteria that allowed him to synthesize ribonucleic acid (RNA). He named the enzyme, polynucleotides phosphorylates. It has been valuable in enabling scientists to understand, and re-create the process, whereby the hereditary information contained in genes is translated, via RNA, into enzymes that determine the function and character of each cell.

Married without children, Ochoa died in Madrid on January 11, 1993.

Arthur Kornberg was born in Brooklyn, New York, US, on March 3, 1918 into a Jewish family. Having gained his PhD, he was appointed to the US National Institute of Health in Bethesda, where he was involved in, and later headed, the research into enzymes and intermediary metabolism.

During this period, which spanned the years 1942-53, he was also responsible for the research, concerning chemical reactions in cells, that result in the making of flavins adenine: essential hydrogen, containing intermediaries in biological reductions.

In 1953, he was appointed professor of microbiology at Washington University at St. Louis, where he stayed until 1959. In that year he was co-awarded a Nobel Prize for Physiology or Medicine for his work on the synthesis of the nucleic acid, DNA, which he discovered to be responsible for forming heredity-transmitting genes.

Between 1959 and 69, he was chairman of the department of biochemistry at Stanford University in Palo Alto, California. He has published several books, the best known being, *Enzymatic Synthesis of DNA* (1961). Married twice he has three sons.

PEACE

PHILIP NOEL-BAKER (1889-1982)

Philip John Noel-Baker was born in London, England, on November 1, 1889. His parents were Quakers from Canada. He studied at several universities including King's College, Cambridge, Munich and Paris. He was a noted athlete who competed in the 1912 , 1920 and 1924 Olympic Games, winning a silver medal in 1920 in the 1,500 metres. During WW1, as a Quaker, he refused to join the army but served instead, in an ambulance unit, receiving several awards for bravery under fire.

In 1919, he was a member of the British delegation to the Paris Peace Conference, later joining the League of Nations secretariat. Between 1924 and 1929 he was professor for International Relations at London University. He was a Labour MP from 1929-31 and again from 1936-70. He held several government posts and helped to draft the United Nations Charter.

From 1960-82, he was president of the International Council on Sport and Physical Recreation at UNESCO. He wrote several books amongst which, *The Arms Race* (1960) is best known and for which Noel-Baker received the, 'Albert Schweitzer Prize'. He was awarded a life peerage in 1977 and spent his retirement working for world disarmament. In 1981, aged 91, he wrote a popular song supporting the cause of peace. In 1959, he was awarded the Nobel Peace Prize; **"for his work in furthering the cause of peace through multilateral disarmament"**

Married with a son, he died in London on October 8, 1982.

1960

Sharpeville massacre in South Africa • Congo Crisis • Kennedy narrowly wins US Presidential election • Surgeons develop heart pacemaker • Harold Pinter, *The Caretaker* • Sylvia Plath, *The Colossus* • Harper Lee, *To Kill a Mockingbird* • David Storey, *This Sporting Life* • Lawrence Durrell, *The Alexandria Quartet* • Film: *Saturday Night and Sunday Morning, A Bout de Souffle, Psycho, La Dolce Vita, The Apartment,* • Vicki Baum, Boris Pasternak and Sylvia Pankhurst die.

LITERATURE

SAINT- JOHN PERSE (1887-1975)

Saint-John Perse was born Marie-René-Auguste-Aléxis-Saint-Léger Léger in Guadeloupe on May 31st 1887. He was educated at Bordeaux and Paris universities, before entering the diplomatic service and a posting in China. Here he was the French consul in Shanghai and secretary in Peking. In 1933, he was secretary-general at the Foreign Ministry, but in 1940, was dismissed his post and deprived of French citizenship by the Fascist Vichy government, who ruled part of France and overseas territories, by the grace of Adolph Hitler. He went to the United States and worked in the French Department of the Library of Congress, before returning to France in 1957.

The language of his poetry, admired by poets for its precision and purity, is a specialist affair with little appeal to the general public. He has been compared with Rimbaud and credited with a hypnotic vision, conveyed by liturgical metre and exotic phrases. For some, he is a reflection of the French national spirit, conscious of the tragedy of life as reflected in WW2, yet with the feeling of an artist for perfection and symmetry.

Amongst his better known works are, *Exile: and other poems* (1942), *Seamarks* (1957), *Chronique* (1960) and *Oiseaux* (1962). He was awarded the 1960 Nobel Prize for Literature; **"for the soaring flight and the evocative imagery of his poetry which in a visionary fashion reflects the conditions of our time"**

Married without children, he died in Presqu'île-de-Giens, France on September 20, 1975.

CHEMISTRY

WILLARD LIBBY (1908-1980)

Willard Frank Libby was born in Grand Valley, Colorado, US, on December 17, 1908. He received his PhD from the University of California where, between 1933-45, he was a member of the teaching staff. He was part of the Manhattan Project between 1941-45 and helped develop a method for separating uranium isotopes, an essential step in the manufacture of the A-bomb. He joined the Institute for Nuclear Studies at Chicago University in 1945 and stayed until 1959. In 1946, Libby was able to demonstrate that tritium, the heaviest isotope of hydrogen, was produced by cosmic radiation.

In 1947 he developed the carbon-14 dating technique. Before becoming professor of chemistry at the University of California, he served on the US Atomic Energy Commission (1955-59). In 1952 he wrote, *Radiocarbon Dating.* He was awarded the 1960 Nobel Prize for Chemistry; **"for his method to use carbon-14 for age determination in archaeology, geology, geophysics, and other branches of science"**

Libby, married twice with two daughters, died in Los Angeles on September 8, 1980.

PHYSICS

DONALD GLASER (1926-)

Donald Arthur Glaser was born in Cleveland, Ohio, US, on September 21, 1926 into an educated Jewish family. He needed the services of a child analyst in order to create an atmosphere of study. Whatever method the analyst used must have worked, because Glaser went on to take a degree in physics at the Californian Institute of Technology. He then moved to Michigan University and taught physics.

During his research work with nuclear physics, Glaser discovered limitations surrounding the cloud chamber apparatus that was used to record very high speed nuclear particles. He therefore designed what he came to call a ' bubble chamber', and in effect reversed the process previously used. He implemented the idea in 1952, and it became the foundation as an essential aid in nuclear research. It also won him the 1960 Nobel Prize for Physics; **"for the invention of the bubble chamber"**

He was 34 years of age. He later became professor of molecular biology at the University of California. He is married with a son and daughter.

PHYSIOLOGY or MEDICINE

MACFARLANE BURNET (1899-1985)
and
PETER MEDAWAR (1915-1987)

"for discovery of acquired immunological tolerance"

Frank **Macfarlane Burnet** was born in Traralgon, Australia on September 3, 1899. He obtained his medical degree from Melbourne University in 1923, before working as a research fellow at the Lister Institute of Preventative Medicine in London (1926-27). He returned to Australia in 1928, to become a director of medical research at Royal Melbourne Hospital.

Although mainly involved in researching methods of human transplants, he discovered a method for identifying bacteria by the viruses that attack them. He then developed a technique (now standard laboratory practise) of culturing viruses in living chick embryos. He went on to explain the way in which influenza viruses cause infection.

He was knighted in 1951. His many books include, *Viruses and Man* (1953), *Immunological Surveillance* (1970) and *Credo and Comment: A Scientist Reflects* (1979) In 1960, he was awarded a Nobel Prize for Physiology or Medicine for his discovery of acquired immunological tolerance to tissue transplants. Burnet, married twice with a son and two daughters, died in Melbourne on August 31, 1985.

Peter **Brian Medawar** was born in Rio de Janeiro, Brazil on February 28, 1915. He was educated at Magdalen College, Oxford, from where he received a degree in zoology. He became involved with transplant research in 1949, when he suggested that during embryonic life and immediately after birth, cells gradually acquire the ability to distinguish between their own tissue substances and unwanted cells and foreign material.

In a series of experiments on mice, he produced evidence, indicating that each animal cell contains certain genetically determined antigens that were essential to the immunity process.   He became professor of zoology at Birmingham University (1947-51) and London University (1951-62). Director of the National Institute for Medical Research, London (1962-71), professor of experimental medicine at the Royal Institution(1977-83) and president of the Royal Postgraduate Medical School (1981-87). He was knighted in 1965 and received the Order of Merit in 1981. He was awarded, in 1960, a Nobel Prize for Physiology or Medicine for his discovery of acquired immunological tolerance. He published his autobiography, *Memoir of a Thinking Radish* in 1986. Married with a son and 2 daughters, he died in London on October 2, 1987.

PEACE

ALBERT LUTHULI (1898-1967)

Albert **John Mvumbi Luthuli** was born in Rhodesia sometime in 1898. His father was a missionary interpreter from Zululand. Albert was 10 when his father died. He returned to South Africa, learned about Zulu traditions and duties, whilst in the house of his uncle, the chief of Groutville in Natal. His mother, a washerwoman, saw him through school to win a scholarship from a mission school in Adams, near Durban. After graduating, he stayed and taught others.

In 1936, he left to become the elected chief of his community of 5,000 people, who were constantly faced with hunger, poverty and with no voice in their political future. Luthuli joined the African National Congress (ANC) in 1945; it was the time when police and soldiers were crushing the strike of unarmed African miners, killing and wounding them. He was invited by the Congregational Board of Missions to tour America in 1948. He warned Americans that Christianity was facing a severe test in South Africa because of Nationalist apartheid. Luthuli returned home to become elected president of the Natal African National Congress.

In 1952, various native movements joined to protest at their country's unjust laws. It resulted in 8,500 men and women going to prison. As a result, Luthuli was ordered to resign from the ANC or his chieftainship; he refused to do either stating, ' the road to freedom is via the cross' The ANC response was to elect him president -general. Despite a serious illness in 1954 and repeated bans of where he could live or go, Luthuli constantly toured the country to address mass meetings.

In 1956 he and 155 others were rounded up and charged with high treason. In 1957 he was released when the charges could not be substantiated.

In 1960, at what became known throughout the world as the Sharpeville Massacre, Luthuli called for national mourning and publicly burnt his infamous pass. The government responded by banning the ANC. However, they were too embarrassed to forbid him to leave the country for Oslo, Norway , in order to receive the award of the 1960 Nobel Peace Prize; **"in recognition of his non-violent struggle against racial discrimination"**

His acceptance speech paid tribute to his people's nonviolence and rejection of racialism. A week following his return home, a sabotage group, subsequently identified as off-duty police, began a policy of burning and murder. Luthuli was now in enforced isolation, an honoured man working on his writings and receiving only those friends and relations, authorised by the police.

His autobiography, *Let My People Go* was published in 1962 and banned. On July 21st 1967, whilst making his usual railway bridge crossing close to his small farm, he was struck by a train and died. He was married with two sons and five daughters.

1961

South Africa leaves the Commonwealth • Berlin Wall completed • Yuri Gagarin orbits in space • DNA Structure determined • *Beyond the Fringe* **• Francois Truffaut,** *Jules et Jim* **• Joseph Heller,** *Catch-22* **• Muriel Spark,** *The Prime of Miss Jean Brodie* **• Films:** *Viridiana, The Hustler, West Side Story, Yojimbo, Judgement at Nuremberg* **• Leonard 'Chico' Marx, Moss Hart, Carl Jung and Ernest Hemingway die.**

LITERATURE

IVO ANDRIC (1892-1975)

Ivo **Andric** was born in Dolac, Bosnia on October 10, 1892. He studied at Zagreb, Krakow, Vienna and Graz universities, where his abilities as a writer of prose and verse, were soon recognised. His reputation was established in 1918, with the publication of, *Ex Ponto,* written whilst he was interned, during WW1, by the Axis powers for anti-war activities. From then onwards, there were books of short stories published at regular intervals.

After the war, Andric joined the Yugoslav diplomatic service and his new career took him to Rome, Bucharest, Berlin, Madrid and Geneva. During WW2, when Bosnia was pro-Nazi and Andric a nationalist, he wrote several novels on Bosnia.

It is said that his writings reveal a sense of compassion, and are written objectively, with a great beauty of language. However, his books did not travel well internationally, nor were they particularly welcomed in parts of Yugoslavia, where Croats were actively disliked.

For reasons best known to the Nobel Prize committee, they ignored writers of the calibre of Graham Greene, William Burroughs, Laurie Lee, Mervyn Peake, Alan Sillitoe or Muriel Spark. Instead, they honoured Andric with the 1961 Nobel Prize for Literature; **"for the epic force with which he has traced themes and depicted human destinies drawn from the history of his country"**

Married without children, he died in Belgrade, Yugo. on March 13, 1975.

CHEMISTRY

MELVIN CALVIN (1911-1997)

Melvin Calvin was born in St. Paul, Minn. US, on April 8, 1911 to Russian-Jewish parents. After receiving his doctorate from Michigan University, Calvin decided to teach. He joined the faculty of the University of California and stayed, in one position or other, until 1971. During WW2, he worked on the Manhattan Project, in the field of atomic fission. After the war, he spent considerable time away from teaching, researching the role of chlorophyll in photosynthesis.

During his studies, he developed a system of using the radioactive isotope carbon-14, as a tracer element and, as a result, could stop the growth of plants at various stages. He was awarded the 1961 Nobel Prize for Chemistry; **"for his research on the carbon dioxide assimilation in plants"**

He continued to work on photosynthesis. He later researched aspects of life, based on radiation chemistry and, in 1963, joined the US Academy of Science. He was also a foreign member of the British Royal Society. An experienced and popular lecturer, constantly expressing new ideas, he was also a prolific writer, who published some 500 papers and books. He died in Berkeley, Calif. on January 8, 1997.   He was married with two daughters and a son.

PHYSICS

ROBERT HOFSTADTER (1915-1990)
and
RUDOLF MOSSBAUER (1929-)

Robert Hofstadter was born in New York, US on February 5th 1915 to Jewish parents who emphasised the importance of education.

Robert graduated from Princeton University, with a PhD, in 1938. During WW2, he worked on scientific research for the US Air Force. In 1946 he joined the staff of Princeton, where his research work was in the field of infra-red rays. He moved to Stanford University in 1950, and stayed until 1985.

At Stanford, he was able to use a linear electron accelerator to measure the structure of atomic nuclei. He discovered that both proton and neutron have a central core, positively charged, that is encompassed by a double cloud of p1-mesons. In 1961, Hofstadter received a co-share of the Nobel Prize for Physics; **"for his pioneering studies of electron scattering in atomic nuclei and for his thereby achieved discoveries concerning the structure of the nucleons".** Married with a son and two daughters he died in

Stanford, Calif. on November 17th 1990.

Rudolph Ludwig Mossbauer was born in Munich, Germany on January 31, 1929. Whilst studying at the Technical Academy of Munich, from where he received his doctorate in 1958, he discovered the ' Mossbauer effect', concerning gamma radiation in crystals.

For his research into atomic structure he was awarded, in 1961, a co-share of the Nobel Prize for Physics; **"for his researches concerning the resonance absorption of gamma radiation and his discovery in this connection of the effect which bears his name"**

He became professor of physics at the California Institute of Technology in 1961. In 1964, he returned to Munich, to take up the same post at the Technical Academy. He is married with a son and two daughters.

PHYSIOLOGY or MEDICINE

GEORG von BEKESY (1899-1972)

Georg von Bekesy was born in Budapest, Hungary on June 3, 1899. His researches took him to various educational establishments, from Budapest University (1939-46) to Karolinska Institute, Stockholm (1946-47) and Harvard University (1947-66). He conducted intensive research that led to the possible understanding of the hearing process.

Bekesy found that sound travels along the basilar membrane, in a series of waves and he showed that these waves peak at different places on the membrane: low frequencies toward the end of the cochlea and high frequencies near its entrance. He discovered that the location of the nerve receptors and the number of receptors involved, are the most important factors in determining pitch and volume. He was awarded the 1961 Nobel Prize for Physics; **"for his discoveries of the physical mechanism of stimulation within the cochlea"**

He became professor of sensory sciences at Hawaii University in 1966. He wrote several books including, *Experiments in Hearing* (1960) and *Sensory Inhibition* (1967). He died in Hawaii on June 13, 1972.

He never married.

PEACE

DAJ HAMMARSKJOLD (1905-1961)

Dag Hjalmar Agne Carl Hammarskjold was born Jonkoping, Sweden on July 29, 1905. He was the son of Hjalmar Hammarskjold, who was prime minister of Sweden (1914-17) and later chairman of the Nobel Prize Foundation (1929-1947). Dag studied law and economics at Uppsala and Stockholm Universities. He then joined the civil service and was secretary to the Ministry of Finance, before eventually going on to become Bank of Sweden president. In 1947, he was at the Foreign Affairs Ministry until 1951, when he became assistant chairman of the Swedish delegation to the United Nations.

Following the resignation of Norway's Trygve Lie, in 1952, Hammarskjold was elected as the UN secretary-general, on April 10th 1953, for a 5 year period and subsequently re-elected in September 1957, for a further 5 year term.

During his terms of office, he had to deal with on-going problems in the Middle East, including the Suez crisis, the war in the Belgian Congo and the accusations from the USSR concerning his actions and demanding his resignation. It all ended on September 18, 1961, when the aeroplane carrying him to meet Moise Tshombe in Katanga, crashed with the loss of all aboard, at Ndola, Northern Rhodesia.

It is thought the crash was as a result of an on-board explosion. A forceful man, he often incurred the wrath of many when insisting he be able to take emergency action, without prior approval by the Security Council or General Assembly.   He was awarded the 1961 Nobel Peace Prize. **"for enhancing the prestige and effectiveness of the UN"**

He never married.

1962

Algerian Independence • US establish military unit in South Vietnam • de Gaulle escapes assassination • Britain agrees to stock US Polaris missile • *Private Eye* is published in the UK • Anthony Sampson, *The Anatomy of Britain* • Edward Albee, *Who's Afraid of Virginia Woolf* • James Baldwin, *Another Country* • Anthony Burgess, *A Clockwork Orange* • Ken Kesey, *One Flew Over the Cuckoo's Nest* • Film: *Lawrence of Arabia, A Kind of Loving, The Manchurian Candidate, To Kill a Mockingbird,* • Eleanor Roosevelt and Niels Bohr died.

LITERATURE

JOHN STEINBECK (1902-1968)

John Ernest Steinbeck was born in Salinas, California, US, on February 27, 1902. He was educated at Stanford University, at various times, between 1920 and 1926 finally leaving without taking a degree. He became a labourer by day and a writer by night, all the time gaining experience of life in general and of the working man in particular. His first novel was *Cup of Gold,* written in 1929 about Henry Morgan, the British pirate. This was followed by *The Pastures of Heaven* (1932) and, *To a God Unknown* (1933). All were unsuccessful.

In 1935 came *Tortilla Flat* and a modicum of popularity. His next, in 1936, was the grim relentless story of a labour strike; *In Dubious Battle.* In 1937 he published *Of Mice and Men* and the following year, *The Grapes of Wrath.* This book won for Steinbeck the Pulitzer Prize, The National Book Award, and financial freedom. His story of Norwegian resistance to Germany during WW2, *The Moon Is Down* (1942), became a major film.

Several of his other books also went on to become feature films. During WW2, Steinbeck was a war correspondent. The war over, he went on to achieve further success with such novels as, *Cannery Row* (1945), *Burning Bright* (1950), *East of Eden* (1952) and *The Winter of Our Discontent* (1961).

He also wrote directly for the screen and amongst his efforts *Forgotten Village* (1941) and *Viva Zapata* (1952) stand out. Steinbeck's reputation was built in the 30s, when his books reflected the trials and tribulations of ordinary people trying to survive. He was awarded the 1962 Nobel Prize for Literature; **"for his realistic and imaginative writings, combining as they do sympathetic humour and keen social perception"**

He died in New York on December 20, 1968. He was married three times and had two sons.

CHEMISTRY

MAX PERUTZ (1914-)
and
JOHN KENDREW (1917-1997)

"for their studies of the structures of globular proteins"

Max Ferdinand Perutz was born in Vienna, Austria on May 19, 1914. He was receiving an education at Vienna University when, in 1936, he was advised that, as a Jew, it would be better for his ongoing health if he left Austria. He continued his studies at Cambridge University and his research at the Cavendish Laboratory.

Here he took his first X-ray diffraction pictures of haemoglobin crystals. In 1947 he and John Kendrew, set up the Medical Research Unit for molecular biology at Cambridge. Their research into the structure of haemoglobin, led to the co- award, in 1962, of a Nobel Prize for Chemistry that included work on the X-ray diffraction, the protein that transports oxygen from the lungs to the tissues via blood cells.

Between 1962 and 1979, when he retired, Perutz was chairman of the Medical Research Centre at Cambridge. A Fellow of the Royal Society, he was also an authority in the field of crystallography and in 1938, whilst measuring the flow of glaciers, proved for the first time that the fasted flows occurs at the surface and the slowest near the bed of the glacier. He is married with a son and daughter.

John Cowdery Kendrew was born in Oxford, UK, on March 24, 1917. He was educated at Trinity College, Cambridge, receiving his PhD in 1949. He was a Fellow of Peterhouse College, Cambridge, (1947-1975) . He was also deputy chairman of the Medical Research Council and in 1981, became president of St. John's College, Oxford.

For his work in determining the structure of the muscle protein myoglobin, which stores oxygen and gives it up to the muscle cells when needed, Kendrew, in 1962, received a co-share of the Nobel Prize for Chemistry for his work on special X-ray diffraction techniques. He died in 1997. He was un-married.

PHYSICS

LEV LANDAU (1908-1968)

Lev **Davidovich Landau** was born in Baku, Russia, on January 22, 1908. His father was a engineer, his mother a doctor, both middle-class Jews. At thirteen, Lev graduated from the Gymnasium and, too young for university, went to the Baku Technical School. In 1922 he did go to Baku University and two years later the Leningrad State University, the centre of Russian physics. He graduated in 1927, and began a research programme at the Leningrad Physico-Technical Institute.

In 1929, Landau was offered the opportunity to study with Niels Bohr (qv) in Copenhagen. Following Copenhagen, Landau looked in at Cambridge and Zurich before returning to the USSR. In 1932, he was head of the Theoretical Division of the Ukrainian Physico-Technical Institute. In 1937 he moved to Moscow, to head the new theory division of the Institute of Physical Problems. There, he researched the thermal conductivity of liquid helium, work which resulted in his receiving the 1962 Nobel Prize for Physics; **"for his pioneering theories for condensed matter, especially liquid helium"**

Landau was a tough no-nonsense scientist who said what he thought. People either adored or hated him and Landau couldn't care less. On January 7th 1962 he was the victim of a car accident. He was unconscious for six weeks and several times declared clinically dead. Specialists world-wide, helped to save his life and he gradually regained the use of his faculties. However, he never returned to his normal self. Landau received awards and honours from many countries.

At home, he received the Lenin Prize and was elected to the Academy of Sciences. He was a foreign member of the Royal Society in London and of the academies of The Netherlands, Denmark and US. Married with a son, Landau died in Moscow on April 1, 1968.

PHYSIOLOGY or MEDICINE

HARRY CRICK (1916-), JAMES WATSON (1928-)
and
MAURICE WILKINS (1916-)

"for their discoveries concerning the molecular structure of nuclear acids and its significance for information transfer in living material"

Francis **Harry Compton Crick** was born in Northampton, England, on June 8, 1916. During WW2 his education was halted, to allow him to work as a physicist in the development of magnetic mines for use by the Royal Navy. The war over, he switched to biology and the Strangways Research Laboratory at Cambridge (1947). He was a pioneer in determining the three dimensional structures of large molecules, found in living organisms. He then, in 1949, transferred to the Research Council Unit at the Cavendish Laboratories.

In 1951, James Watson arrived at the unit and he and Crick were able to construct a molecular model consistent with known physical and chemical properties of DNA. This model was made up from two intertwined helical strands of sugar-phosphate, bridged horizontally by flat organic bases. Crick and Watson theorized, that if the strands were separated, each would serve as a clone. For his part in the determination of the molecular construction of DNA, the chemical substance ultimately responsible for the hereditary control of life functions, Crick was awarded in 1962, a co-share of the Nobel Prize for Physiology or Medicine.

From 1977, he was a professor at the Salk Institute for Biological Studies in California. A considerable writer, he published *What Mad Pursuit: A Personal View of Scientific Discovery* in 1988. He is twice married and has a son and two daughters.

James **Dewey Watson** was born in Chicago, US, on April 6, 1928. He was only 15 when he joined Chicago University, graduating in 1947. From his research into viruses, whilst at Indiana University, where he received a PhD in 1950, and other factors, Watson became convinced that the gene could only be understood after knowing about nucleic acid molecules. This research was being carried out in Britain at the Cavendish Laboratories in Cambridge. There, between 1951-53, he did research and worked with Crick on DNA structure.

His discovery in the spring of 1953, that the essential DNA components of four organic bases must be linked in definite pairs, was the key discovery and everything proceeded from there. In 1962, he was awarded a co-share of the Nobel Prize for Physiology or Medicine, for the important part he played in the accomplishment of one of the 20th century's most important discovery.

Between 1955 and 76, Watson was professor of biology at Harvard University. There he conducted research on nucleic acid in the synthesis of proteins. He published many books including; *Molecular Biology of the Gene* (1965) and *The Double Helix* (1968). Between 1988 and 1992 whilst at the National Institutes of Health, he helped direct a project aimed to map and decipher all of the genes in the human chromosomes; eventually resigning because of a conflict of interests with his private biotechnology companies. He is married with two sons.

Maurice **Hugh Frederick Wilkins** was born in Pongaroa, New Zealand on December 15, 1916. He was the son of a doctor from Ireland and educated at King Edward's School, Birmingham and St. John's College, Cambridge. During WW2, he spent two years working on the Manhattan Project, working on mass spectrograph separation of uranium isotopes for use in the atomic bomb, later dropped on Japan. In 1946, he joined the Medical Research Council's Biophysics Unit at King's College, London. In 1955 he was a deputy director.

There he began a series of investigations that ultimately led to his X-ray diffraction studies in DNA. This work was crucial in determining DNAs molecular structure by Crick and Watson. It resulted in Wilkins, in 1962, being awarded a co-share of the Nobel Prize for Physiology or Medicine.

However, the main work done in this field at Kings College was achieved by Rosalind Franklin (1920-58). Unfortunately the Nobel Prize is not awarded posthumously. Wilkins is married with two sons and two daughters.

PEACE

LINUS PAULING (1901-1994)

Linus **Carl Pauling** was born in Portland, Oregon, US, on February 28, 1901. A Nobel Prize winner for Chemistry in 1954, he received the Nobel Peace Prize in 1962; **"in recognition of his efforts on behalf of the international control of nuclear weapons and his campaigns against nuclear testing"**

He was deeply concerned about the possible hazards to health as a result of atomic testing and radiation fallout. His views were brilliantly expressed in his 1958 book, *No More War!*. In January 1958 he brought to the United Nations a petition signed by over 11,000 scientists from all over the world, urging an end to nuclear weapons testing. In 1963 he left the California Institute of Technology to become a staff member of the Centre for the Study of Democratic Institutions at Santa Barbara, Calif. There he largely devoted himself to the problems of peace and war. It is assumed the award of the Nobel Peace Prize was in connection with the test ban treaty of 1962.

He was estranged from many scientists in the US and there were some, urged on by commercial interests, who accused Pauling of being disloyal to the US. In 1969, he had spent some time at California University when he suddenly resigned as a protest against the educational policies of the governor, one Ronald Reagan. He joined the chemistry department of Stanford University and became professor emeritus in 1974. Pauling was honoured all over the world and in 1972, was the proud recipient of the International Lenin Peace Prize. Married with three sons and a daughter, Pauling died on August 9, 1994.

1963

Kennedy assassinated • Test Ban Treaty • Britain refused entry to Common Market • Profumo Affair • Beeching Report on British Rail • Benjamin Britten, *War Requiem* **• Joseph Mankiewicz,** *Cleopatra* **• The Beatles go international • Ian Fleming,** *On Her Majesty's Secret Service* **• Kurt Vonnegut,** *Cat's Cradle* **• Films:** *Dr. Strangelove, Eight and a Half, Hud, Tom Jones, The Leopard,* **• Herbert Samuel, Clifford Odets, Tristan Tzara, Robert Frost and Aldous Huxley die.**

LITERATURE

GEORGE SEFERIADES (1900-1971)

Giorgios Stylianou **Seferiades** was born in Smyrna, part of the Ottoman Empire and now in Turkey, on March 13, 1900. He would later write under the name of **George Seferis.** He studied law in Paris and then joined the Greek diplomatic service, serving in London and Albania, prior to WW2. During that war he was part of the Greek government in exile and post war was Greek ambassador in London (1957-62).

He published several books of poetry prior, during and post WW2, and some were translated into English. In 1931, he published *Turning Point* and followed this with *The Cistern* in 1932. *Poiimata* (1924-46 is probably his best known and *Imeroloyion katastromatos* published in 1955, his last.

He was elected to the Academy of Athens in 1947 and called the 'most distinguished Greek poet of the 'generation of the 30s'. It is said his refined lyricism and the freshness of his diction brought a new breath of life to Greek poetry. He was awarded the 1963 Nobel Prize for Literature; **"for his eminent lyrical writing, inspired by a deep feeling for the Hellenic world of culture"**

He died in Athens on September 20, 1971. He was married but had no children.

CHEMISTRY

KARL ZIEGLER (1898-1973)
and
GIULIO NATTA (1903-1979)

"for their discoveries in the field of the chemistry and technology of high polymers"

Karl Ziegler was born in Helsa, Germany on November 26, 1898. He received a doctorate from Munich University in 1923 and held various academic appointments at the universities of Frankfurt-am Main, Heidelberg and Halle. In 1928 he became the first scientist to explain the synthesis of rubber. An early member of the Nazi party, he was appointed director of the Kaiser Wilhelm Institute for Coal Research at Mulheim an der Ruhr in 1943. Here he researched lithium in organic chemistry and on cyclic carbon compounds.

After WW2, he concentrated on organoaluminum compounds. In 1953 he made his most important discovery. Ziegler, with the help of his students, was able to establish development of long-chain polymers of hydrocarbons from olefines, such as ethylene and butadiene, that led to new developments in industrial materials. In particular plastics. For this work he received a half share of the 1963 Nobel Prize for Chemistry.

He died in Mulheim, Germany on August 12, 1973. He was married with two children and 10 grandchildren.

Giulio Natta was born in Imperia, Italy on February 26, 1903. He received a doctorate in chemical engineering from Milan Polytechnic in 1924 and held chairs in chemistry at the universities of Pavia, Rome and Turin. Thereafter, in 1938, he returned to the Polytechnic as research director of industrial chemistry.

In 1953, he began intensive research of macromolecules and experimented with the polymerization of propylene. He eventually obtained polypropylene of a highly regular molecular structure. It was soon apparent that the high temperature and high strength of these polymers would prove most important in commercial processes. For his work Natta received a half share of the 1963 Nobel Prize for Chemistry.

Married with a son and daughter, he died in Bergamo, Italy on May 2, 1979.

PHYSICS

EUGENE WIGNER (1902-1995), MARIA MAYER (1906-1972)
and
JOHANNES JENSEN (1907-1973)

Eugene Paul Wigner was born in Budapest, Hungary on November 17, 1902 to middle-class Jewish parents. He was educated at the Berlin Technische Hochschule, obtaining a PhD in engineering. Then followed a period at Göttingen University until 1930, when he received an invitation to teach at Princeton University in the US. With violent anti-Semitism rife in Germany, Wigner took up the appointment. In 1938 he was appointed Thomas D Jones Professor of Mathematical Physics, a position he held until he retired. He was an early pioneer of nuclear power and from 1942-48 worked on the Manhattan Project and the aftermath.

His speciality was nuclear chain reactions connected with the atomic bomb. Wigner was one of the three Hungarian physicists, along with Szilard and Teller, who persuaded Einstein (qv) to write his now famous letter to President Roosevelt, concerning Germany's potential to manufacture nuclear weapons.

In 1956, Wigner received the Enrico Fermi Award and in 1960, the 'Atoms for Peace' award. In 1963, he was one of three to receive the Nobel Prize for Physics; **"for his contributions to the theory of the atomic nucleus and the elementary particles, particularly through the discovery and application of fundamental symmetry principles"**

He achieved international fame for his introduction of the concept of parity into nuclear physics. His *Symmetries and Reflections: Scientific Essays* was published in 1967.

Married twice with two children, Wigner died on January 1st 1995.

"for their discoveries concerning nuclear shell structure"

Maria Goeppert Mayer was born in Kattowitz, Germany on June 28, 1906. She received her doctorate from Göttingen University in 1930 and married the US physicist Joseph Mayer. Together, they further studied at John Hopkins University, Baltimore. In 1939 she was at Columbia University and there worked on the separation of uranium isotopes for the atomic bomb project.

In 1945 she was at Chicago University, working at the Institute for Nuclear Studies. In 1949 she was able to explain the nuclear shell theory. In 1963, she was joint winner of the Nobel Prize for Physics, for her explanation of the detailed properties of atomic nuclei in terms of structure of shells occupied by the protons and neutrons.

She died in San Diego, US on February 20, 1972. She was married with a daughter and son.

Johannes Hans Daniel Jensen was born in Hamburg, Germany on June 25, 1907. An early member of the Nazi party, he was professor at Hamburg University (1936-41) and at Hanover University (1941-49). In 1949 he became professor of theoretical physics at Heidelberg University. Together with Maria Mayer, he wrote *Elementary Theory of Nuclear Shell Structure* (1955).

In 1963, he was a joint winner of the Nobel Prize for Physics, for proposing the shell theory; that an atomic nucleus should be though of not as a random aggregation of neutrons and protons, but rather as a structure of shells each filled with neutrons and protons.

Jensen never married and died in Heidelberg, Germany on February 11, 1973.

PHYSIOLOGY or MEDICINE

ALAN HODGKIN (1914-1998), ANDREW HUXLEY (1917-)
and
JOHN ECCLES (1903-1997)

"for their discoveries concerning the ionic mechanisms involved in excitation and inhibition in the peripheral and central portions of the nerve cell membrane"

Alan Lloyd Hodgkin was born in Banbury, Oxon, England, on February 5, 1914. He was educated at Trinity College, Cambridge. During WW2, he worked for the Air Ministry on radar research. He then joined the teaching staff at Cambridge (1945-52), and researched the measurements of the chemical and electrical behaviour of individual nerve fibres. Together with his student, Andrew Huxley, they came to the conclusion that the activity of a nerve fibre depends on the fact that a large concentration of potassium ions is maintained inside the fibre.

He went on to discover the chemical processes responsible for the passage of impulses along individual nerve fibres. For this work Hodgkin was one of three to be awarded the 1963 Nobel prize for Physiology or Medicine.

He was a research professor for the Royal Society (1952-69), professor of biophysics at Cambridge from 1970 and chancellor of Leicester University from 1971. Among his publications is, *Conduction of the Nerve Impulse* (1964).

He was knighted in 1972. He died on December 21, 1998 . He was married with three daughters and a son.

Andrew Fielding Huxley was born in London, England on November 22, 1917. Andrew, grandson of TH. Huxley and son of Leonard Huxley received an MA from Trinity College, Cambridge. (Where he would later serve in various posts from 1941-1960 ending up as a reader in experimental biophysics in the Physiology Department). He spent many years at University College, London, first as Jodrell professor and finally as Royal Society Research Professor in the Physiology Department.

Working with his teacher, Alan Hodgkin, on researching nerve and muscle fibres he was co-awarded the 1963 Nobel Prize for Physiology or Medicine.

However, Huxley, on his own, is responsible for work of fundamental importance in the understanding of the process of contraction by a muscle fibre. He published many important findings in the *Journal of Physiology*. He was knighted in 1974. He is married and has five daughters and a son.

John Carew Eccles was born in Melbourne, Australia on January 27, 1903. Educated in Melbourne and England, Eccles between 1951-66, worked at the Australian National University in Canberra. Here he demonstrated that the excitement of a nerve cell by an impulse, causes one kind of synapse to release, into the neighbouring cell, a substance that expands the pores in nerve membranes.

Thus the expanded pores then allow free passage of sodium ions into the neighbouring nerve cell and reverses the polarity of electric charge. This wave of electric charge or impulse, is conducted from one cell to another. His discovery of the chemical means, by which impulses are communicated or repressed by nerve cells, won for Eccles a co- share of the 1963 Nobel Prize for Physiology or Medicine.

Eccles work, which took off from that of Hodgkin and Huxley, had an important influence on the medical treatment of nervous diseases. He was knighted in 1976 and awarded the AC in 1990.

Amongst his many publications are: *The Understanding of the Brain* (1973) and *The Human Psyche* (1980). Married twice, he had five daughters, four sons and died on May 2,1997, whilst living in Contra, Switzerland.

PEACE

INTERNATIONAL COMMITTEE of the RED CROSS

The purpose of the Red Cross in wartime is to ensure that all sides care for the war wounded and treat, in a humane fashion, prisoners-of-war. During WW1 this was largely recognised by both the Allied countries and Axis countries (unlike WW2 when the Germans refused to recognise the Red Cross unless it suited their purpose for propaganda). The international committee is an independent council of 25 Swiss citizens with their HQ in Geneva.

1964

US Civil Rights Bill defeated • China explodes atom bomb • Nelson Mandela given life imprisonment • British brain drain • Pope says 'no' to contraceptive pill • Cassius Clay defeats Sonny Liston • Saul Bellow, *Herzog* • Norman Mailer, *An American Dream* • Hubert Selby, *Last Exit to Brooklyn* Christopher Isherwood, *A Single Man* • Films: *A Hard Day's Night, Kwaidan, My Fair Lady, Zorba the Greek, Mary Poppins* • Eddie Cantor, Brendon Behan, Ben Hecht, Adolph 'Harpo' Marx, Peter Lorre, Cole Porter, Ian Fleming and Edith Sitwell die.

LITERATURE

JEAN-PAUL SARTRE (1905-1980)

Jean-Paul Sartre was born in Paris, France on June 21, 1905. Jean-Paul was only two, when his father died and he grew up in the home of his maternal grandfather, Carl Schweitzer, a professor of German at the Sorbonne and uncle of the missionary Albert Schweitzer (qv). A small boy with a cross eye, he was a lonely child. He went to the Lycée Henri IV in Paris and, following his mother's remarriage, to the lycée in La Rochelle. Then came the prestigious École Normale Supérieure in Paris. He graduated in 1929. It was from this time that he formed his lifetime partnership with Simone de Beauvoir and the friendships he made at the school would stand him in good stead for the rest of his life.

In 1939 Sartre was called to serve in the French Army. He saw some action and was captured by the Germans in 1940 and released a year later.

He returned to the teaching post he had from 1931, at Le Havre. In 1938 he had published *La Nausée* which brought him a modicum of success. It is fiercely anti-social and most individualistic. It was the setting for many of his future novels and the basis of his philosophy. This was revealed in 1943 in *L'Etre et le néant*. Here Sartre shows himself as a master of outstanding talent, as he places human consciousness, or nothingness, in opposition to being. It is at once a tragic and hopeful message. Conceived in wartime under a vicious occupier, it has an additional dimension.

Sartre had dramatically shown his need of individual freedom and dignity. Following WW2, he swung his attention to the needs of the poor. He turned to the medium of the theatre to get his message across. Some ten plays in some 15 years. Mostly pessimistic and often not good theatre. His politics reflected much of his new writing. He was a supporter of the Soviet Union, but never joined the Communist Party. His support crumbled when Russian tanks entered Budapest to crush the right wing led uprising.

He wrote a piece in *Les Temps Modernes* condemning Soviet intervention, disregarding the fact that the legitimate Hungarian government had requested it. He tried to find a political substitute and his new work, *Critique de la raison dialectique* (1960) was termed ' Sartrian Socialism'.

He would complain that a dichotomy meant that whilst Marxism was the only practical philosophy for the modern era, it had become ossified and expected times to fit in with it, rather than fit in and adapt itself as society changed.

In 1964 Sartre was awarded the Nobel Prize for Literature; **"for his work which, rich in ideas and filled with the spirit of freedom and the quest for truth, has exerted a far-reaching influence on our age"**

In the event, Sartre declined to accept the award. He spent the whole of the 1960s working on a four volume study called, *Flaubert*. In 1971, the first two volumes appeared. It was meant to be a complete biography of the French novelist. It is a very revealing book and brings in a mixture of Karl Marx and Sigmund Freud. It has over 2,000 pages. The third volume appeared in 1972 subtitles, *L'Idiot de la Famille*. It is considered very deep and only really appreciated for intellectual study. There was no fourth volume.

Although he continued to give interviews and write for the screen, Sartre's health was in decline. He became blind and his dependence on others angered him. A further serious illness, that led to a lung tumour, resulted in his death in Paris on April 15, 1980. His funeral was attended by some 25,000 people. Ordinary people, whose rights Sartre had always defended. Sartre never married, he did however, legally adopt his editorial assistant.

CHEMISTRY

DOROTHY HODGKIN (1910-1994)

Dorothy Mary Hodgkin *nee* Crowfoot was born in Cairo, Egypt on May 12, 1910. During her time at Somerville College, Oxford, 1928-31, she began her study of crystallography. She was working at Cambridge, 1932-34, when she took the first X-ray diffraction photograph of the protein, pepsin. She returned to Oxford as a tutor in chemistry, still only in her mid-twenties, and continued research of the sterols.

In 1937 she married writer Thomas Hodgkin, continuing her association with Oxford where she eventually became emeritus professor. She was also a professor of the Royal Society (1960-77), Chancellor of Bristol University (1970- as well as professor of Wolfson College, Oxford from 1977.

Between 1942 and 1949, Dorothy Hodgkin worked on the structural analysis of penicillin. She went on to make the first X-ray of vitamin B 12; a very complex non-protein compound. She was eventually able to determine its atomic arrangement. For this work she was awarded the Nobel Prize for Chemistry in 1964; **"for her determinations by X-ray techniques of the structures of important biochemical substances"**

Married with two sons and a daughter, she died in Shipston-on-Stour on July 29, 1994.

PHYSICS

CHARLES TOWNES (1915-), NIKOLAI BASOV (1922-)
and
ALEXANDER PROCHOROV (1916-)

"for fundamental work in the field of quantum electronics, which has led to the construction of oscillators and amplifiers based on the maser-laser principle"

Charles Hard Townes was born in Greenville, SC.US, on July 28, 1915. He studied at Furman University, from where he obtained a BA and BS in 1935; Duke University resulted in an MA in 1937 and a PhD in 1939 from the California Institute of Technology. He worked with the technical branch of Bell Telephone Laboratories until 1948, at which time he joined Columbia University.

There in 1953, he had the idea that culminated in the construction of the maser. In 1967, he was a professor at the University of California in Berkeley, there he started a programme of radio and infrared astronomy, that led to the discovery of complex molecules in the interstellar medium. He was a joint winner of the 1964 Nobel Prize for Physics, for his part in the invention of the maser and the laser.

He was confirmed into the national Inventors Hall of Fame in 1976 and awarded the Niels Bohr International Gold Medal in 1979. He is married with four daughters.

Nikolay Gennadiyevich Basov was born in Leningrad, Russia on December 14, 1922. He graduated from the Moscow Engineering Physics Institute in 1950. In the same year he started working at the Institute of Physics of the Academy of Sciences of the USSR. In 1962 he was heading the Institute. In 1959, he and Prokhorov shared the Lenin Prize for their theory of the maser principle.

For his basic work in quantum electronics, that would lead to the maser and laser, devices that produce respective monochromatic, parallel, coherent beams of microwaves and light, Basov was declared a joint winner of the 1964 Nobel Prize for Physics. He is married with two sons.

Aleksandr Mikhaylovich Prokhorov was born in Atherton, Queensland, Australia on July 11, 1916. His parents were refugees from Tsarist aggression. Following the Revolution, they returned to what had now become the USSR. In 1954 Prokhorov was head of the Institute's Oscillation Laboratory and was later professor at Moscow MV Lomonosov State University. In 1946 he became a senior associate at the P.N. Lebedev Physical Institute in Moscow.

His work with Nikolay Basov, on the maser and laser resulted in Prokhorov becoming joint winner of the 1964 Nobel Prize for Physics. He received a half share of the Lenin Prize of 1959 and in 1971 was elected corresponding member of the American Academy of Arts and Sciences. He is married with a son.

PHYSIOLOGY or MEDICINE

KONRAD BLOCH (1912-)
and
FEODOR LYNEN (1911-1979)

"for their discoveries concerning the mechanism and regulation of the cholesterol and fatty acid metabolism"

Konrad Emil Bloch was born in Neisse, Germany on January 21, 1912 and educated at the Technische Hochschule in Munich, graduating in 1934. Although most Aryan looking, with fair hair, blue eyes, regular features and an athletic bearing, Bloch the Jew, was unwanted by the new, democratically elected regime of Hitler He took off, first to Switzerland and then to the US and Columbia University.

Here in 1938 he obtained his doctorate. He remained as a member of staff and began his long affair with the biological origins of cholesterol. Between 1946 -54, he taught at Chicago University. In 1954 he was professor of biochemistry at Harvard University, but still found time to pursue his research.

His work on cholesterol, and its relation to fatty acids, led to his discovering the complex sequence of the molecule in the human body; a discovery that had an important bearing on finding a cure for arterio-sclerosis or hardening of the arteries. This most important advance in medical knowledge resulted in Bloch being awarded a co- share of the 1964 Nobel Prize for Physiology or Medicine. He is married with a son and daughter.

Feodor Lynen was born in Munich, Germany on April 6, 1911. He was educated at Munich University and eventually became a professor there, (1942-47). His research was on the intermediary metabolism of the living cell. This research would later result in his demonstrating the first steps in a chain of reactions resulting in the biosynthesis of sterols and fatty acids. For this work he was awarded a co- share of the 1964 Nobel Prize for Physiology or Medicine.

It is a further example of the paradox, in as much as the two awardees were one a Jew, and the other a card carrying member of the Nazi party.

In 1954, Lynen became director of the Max Planck Institute for Cell Chemistry in Munich. Married with three sons and two daughters, Lynen died in Munich on August 8, 1979.

PEACE

MARTIN LUTHER KING (1929-1968)

Martin Luther King was born in Atlanta, Georgia, US, on January 15, 1929. Both his father and grandfather were Baptist preachers. At the age of 15, Martin entered Morehouse College in Atlanta, graduating with a BA in 1948. Originally intending to become a doctor of medicine he decided instead on the ministry. He spent the next three years at the Crozer Theological Seminary in Chester, Pa. receiving a BA in theology in 1951.

He went on to Boston University and picked up a PhD in 1955. He began taking notice of the philosophy of non-violence, as preached by Gandhi. It is when King becomes politically active that he begins to become his own man. He met Coretta Scott and they married in 1953, going on to have 4 children.

On December 1, 1955, in Montgomery, a black woman, named Rosa Parks, refused to give up her bus seat to a white person. This contravened that city's segregation law and Rosa was arrested. The local blacks chose King to voice their protests. It took the form of a boycott and the bus company lost much money during the year it lasted. It also resulted in King's home being blown up without any interference from the white police

In 1960, he was back in Atlanta and co-minister, with his father, of the Ebenezer Baptist Church. Now head of the Southern Christian Leadership Conference (SCLC), he spent much time working on behalf of the Civil Rights Movement.

His statement, that the ' psychological moment has come when a concentrated drive against in-justice can bring great, tangible gain', launched the great civil rights campaign that continued until Blacks had full civil rights. It resulted in Kennedy winning the 1960 presidential election. The narrowness of his victory is reflected in the Black vote following his support of the civil rights fight. Although great strides had been made that allowed public opinion to support the issues King stood for, he was a long way from full integration when he was awarded the 1964 Nobel Prize for Peace; **"for his work that resulted in the Civil Rights Act of 1964"** The Act did however make a great difference, and although there would be set backs such as Selma, Alabama and the rioting in the Watts district of LA, as well as the riots in Chicago protesting at slum housing, the movement gathered momentum, culminating in King's great 'I have a dream ' speech that spun around the world.

In Memphis, Tenn, at a meeting in support of a strike by sanitation workers, King was killed by a sniper, while standing talking on a hotel balcony. It was April 4, 1968. His killer was said to be James Earl Ray who, on March 10th 1969, was sentenced to 99 years imprisonment. He protested his innocence right up until 1998 when he died. The contribution of Martin Luther King to the protest movements of the world, cannot be underestimated. His non-violent actions appealed to the consciences of the world.

He wrote a number of books including; *Stride Toward Freedom: The Montgomery Story* (1958), *Why We Can't Wait* (1964) and *Where Do We Go From Here: Chaos or Community* (1967).

Begun in 1986, the third Monday in January of each year, is a US public holiday known as 'Martin Luther King Day'. He was married with two sons and two daughters.

1965

US invades Vietnam • Race riots in Los Angeles • Winston Churchill has State Funeral • Edward White walks in space • Soviet AN-22 flies with 720 passengers • Jerzy Kosinski, *The Painted Bird* • Wole Soyinka, *The Interpreters* • Films, *Battle of Algiers, The Knack, The Sound of Music, Dr Zhivago, Shakespeare Wallah* • Helena Rubenstein, Judy Holliday, Dame Myra Hess, David Selznick, T.S.Eliot, Nat 'King' Cole, and Albert Schweitzer die.

LITERATURE

MIKHAIL SHOLOKHOV (1905-1984)

Mikhail Aleksandrovich Sholokhov was born in Veshenskaya, Russia on May 24, 1905. Following a brief education, he was fifteen when he joined the Red Army, he spent his service days in Moscow. He later left to return to his Cossack village in the Don region of Southern Russia. His later trips abroad included accompanying Khrushchev to the US in 1959. He was a Party member from 1932 and on the Central Committee from 1961. He began writing whilst in the army and his collection of short stories, *Tales of the Don* was published in 1926. *The Silent Don* followed next. *And Quiet Flows the Don* was published in two volumes in 1934; it is his greatest work.

Other writing followed, all eagerly welcomed. His *They Fought for their Country* (1959) is an epic of the Russian people's bravery during the

German invasion of 1941. Although his *The Silent Don* was considered most controversial, telling as it did the fight between traditional Don Cossacks and the Bolsheviks for independence, Sholokhov nevertheless was awarded the Stalin Prize in 1941. He was awarded the 1965 Nobel Prize for Literature; **"for the artistic power and integrity with which, in his epic of the Don, he has given expression to a historic phase in the life of the Russian people"**
.   At that time the Russian writers, Aleksander Solzhenitsyn and Roy Medvedev and others, claimed that much of *The Silent Don* was plagiarized from the Cossack writer Fyodor Kryukov who had died in 1920. They claim Sholokhov had neither the experience or maturity to produce such a work. Sholokhov, married with four children, died in the village of his birth, on February 21, 1984.

CHEMISTRY

ROBERT WOODWARD (1917-1979)

Robert Burns Woodward was born in Boston, US, on April 10, 1917. Following a traditional education, he went to the Massachusetts Institute of Technology to study chemistry in 1933. He received his PhD in 1937. He switched to Harvard and became a professor there in 1950, remaining until 1960. He then became Donner Professor (1960-69). Two wives and three children later, he was working on the synthesis of complex organic substances including quinine, cholesterol, cortisone and vitamin B12.

For this work he was awarded the 1965 Nobel Prize for Chemistry; **"for his outstanding achievements in the art of organic synthesis"**
Woodward, during his lifetime, was widely considered the father of modern organic synthesis and the most accomplished synthesist of complex molecules. The required intellectual discipline was initiated by him, in order for organic chemistry to be recognised as a major factor.

He was awarded many honorary degrees as well as awards from all over the world. These included the Davy Medal from the English Royal Society, the US National Medal of Science and, from Japan, the Order of the Rising Sun. Woodward died in Cambridge, Mass. on July 8, 1979.

PHYSICS

JULIAN SCHWINGER (1918-1994), RICHARD FEYNMAN (1918-1988)
and
SHIN TOMONAGA (1906-1979)

"for their fundamental work in quantum electrodynamics, with deep-ploughing consequences for the physics of elementary particles"

Julian Seymour Schwinger was born into a poor Jewish family, living in New York, on February 12, 1918. He was a child prodigy who graduated from Columbia University with a PhD, whilst just 21. He then spent two years working under Robert Oppenheimer, at Berkeley's University of California.

In 1945, researching the theory of quantum physics, he was able to reconcile Einstein's special theory of relativity. At this time he was teaching at Harvard University , formulating his theory of quantum electrodynamics, unaware that Feynman and Tomonaga were doing much the same. Schwinger was joint winner of the 1965 Nobel Prize for Physics for his work on formulating quantum electrodynamics.

In 1972, he was appointed professor of physics at the University of California in LA. Married without children, he died in Los Angeles on July 16, 1994.

Richard Phillips Feynman was born in New York City on May 11, 1918. He was the son of Jewish parents who set great faith in education. Accordingly, Feynman was educated at Massachusetts Institute of Technology, from where he graduated in 1939, and at Princeton University, from where he received his PhD in 1942. Whilst at Princeton, Feynman was recruited to work on the Manhattan Project, designed to create an A-Bomb. A year later, he was at Los Alamos, New Mexico, where he remained until the atom bomb had become part of post-war life.

As a professor at Cornell University, he worked on a revised theory relating to quantum electrodynamics. He started from a base structure, so disregarding existing theories. The work he did is covered by the diagrams he invented, and which later became known as ' Feynman Graphs'. From 1950 until he died, he was professor of physics at the California Institute of Technology. During this period, Feynman researched various physical phenomena and published his results. Although a man who didn't care much for rewards, he won the Einstein Award in 1954 and the Niels Bohr Gold Medal in 1973. He was a joint winner of the Nobel Prize for Physics in 1965 and commented, ' I won the prize for shoving a great problem under the carpet'.

Feynman was a character much beloved by his students and much given to practical jokes. During his time at Los Alamos, if he wanted a report out of office hours, he would crack open the combination locks-all nine of them- take what he wanted and return the file with a note,' I borrowed document No. LA 4321-Thanks-Feynman the safe cracker' He died in Los Angeles on February 15, 1988. He was married three times and had a daughter and son.

Shin'ichiro Tomonaga was born in Kyoto, Japan on March 3, 1906. Following his degree from Kyoto University, Tomonaga became professor of physics at Tokyo University in 1941. It was the year that he began his research into the problems of quantum electrodynamics, quite unaware of the same work being done in the US, with whom Japan was at war. In 1947, his work came to the notice of the West. It was then found that he, together with Schwinger and Feynman, had accomplished the same results from different approaches and had resolved the inconsistencies of the old theory without making any drastic changes.

Tomonaga was president of the Tokyo University of Education between 1956 and 62. He was most active in the campaign against the spread of nuclear weapons, urging that resources be spent to harness nuclear energy for peaceful purposes. He was a joint winner of the 1965 Nobel Prize for Physics.

His publications include; *Quantum Mechanics* (1962) and his Nobel lecture; *Development of Quantum Electrodynamics: Personal Recollections* (1966). Married with two sons and a daughter, he died in Tokyo on July 8, 1979.

PHYSIOLOGY or MEDICINE

FRANCOIS JACOB (1920-), ANDRE LWOFF (1902-1994)
and
JACQUES MONOD (1910-1976)

"for their discoveries concerning genetic control of enzyme and virus synthesis"

Francois Jacob was born in Nancy, France on June 1, 1920. His education was interrupted by the advent of the Second World War. Following the occupation of France, Jacob, a Jew, and in danger from the Fascist French and German occupiers, made his way to Britain and there, joined the Free French Forces, earning a distinguished war record. Returning to France, he obtained an MD from the Paris Faculty of Medicine in 1947 and a doctorate in 1954 from the Faculty of Science.

He joined the Pasteur Institute, and worked as a researcher, before eventually becoming head of the department concerned with cellular genetics. Whilst there, he discovered that the genes of a bacterium are arranged linearly in a ring, that can be broken at almost any point.

From 1965, he was also professor of cellular genetics at the Collège de France. In 1965, he was co-winner of the Nobel Prize for Physiology or Medicine in respect of his work on cellular genetic function and the influences of viruses concerning regulatory activities in bacteria.

In 1977 he was a member of the Academy of Sciences. Jacob has continued to research many essential factors contained within the science of DNA. He is married with three sons and a daughter.

Andre-Michael Lwoof was born in Ainay-le-Chateau, France on May 8, 1902 to Russian-Jewish immigrant parents. Educated at Paris University, he spent his entire working career at the research department of the Pasteur Institute in Paris. His work was interrupted by the Second World War, during which, Lwoof actively fought in the French Resistance; subsequently being awarded the Medal of the Resistance and created an Officer of the Legion of Honour; following the liberation of France by the Allies in 1944.

Lwoof resumed his work and contributed to the knowledge of lysogeny, a bacterial phenomena that generates subsequent bacteria by the original cell division. For this work, Lwoof co-received the 1965 Nobel Prize for Physiology or Medicine.

He also discovered that vitamins serve both as growth factors for microbes and as coenzymes. His writings include; *Problems of Morphogenesis in Ciliates* (1950) and *Biological Order* (1962).

Married without children he died in Paris on September 30, 1994.

Jacques Lucien Monod was born in Paris, France on February 9, 1910. He graduated from Paris University and, during WW2, was part of the French Resistance, before joining the Pasteur Institute. In 1954, he became head of the cellular biochemistry department and the director in 1971. He was also professor of molecular biology, at the Collège de France. Responsible for advancing the concept of gene complexes, called operons, he and Jacob postulated the existence of a class of genes that regulate the function of other genes by affecting the synthesis of messenger RNA.

For this work, which has subsequently proven correct for bacteria, Monod was co-winner of the 1965 Nobel Prize for Physiology or Medicine.

In 1971, in an essay, he espoused the view that the origin of life and the process of evolution are the result of chance. Married with two sons he died in Cannes, France, on May 31, 1976.

PEACE

THE UNITED NATIONS CHILDREN'S FUND

The **United Nations Children's Fund** was previously known as United Nations International Children's Emergency Fund (UNICEF) (1946-53). Although the name was slightly shortened the acronym of UNICEF remained. Their activities are generally in fields of relative small expenditures, but always have significant and dramatic impact on children's lives, such as the prevention of disease, and the provision of food and shelter. In 1965 UNICEF was awarded the Nobel Prize for Peace.

1966

Cultural Revolution in China • US bombs Hanoi • France withdraws from NATO • Luna IX lands on the moon • Theodor Adorno, *Negative Dialectics* • Joe Orton, *Loot* • Films: *Un Homme et Une Femme, A Man For All Seasons, Who's Afraid of Virginia Woolf?, Persona, Andrei Rublev,* • England wins World Cup • Seamus Heaney, *Death of a Naturalist* • Jean Rhys, *Wide Sargasso Sea* • William Gass, *Omensetter's Luck* • Sophie Tucker, Lenny Bruce and Walt Disney die.

LITERATURE

SHMUEL AGNON (1888-1970)
and
NELLY SACHS (1891-1970)

Shmuel Yosef Agnon is the pseudonym of Samuel Josef Czaczes, born in Buczalz, Poland on July 17, 1888. His father was a fur merchant and the family middle class Jews. The father would tell him his rabbinical stories and his mother; German stories. Little wonder, then, that Shmuel had, by the time he was eight years old, decided to become a writer. However, he had to wait until he was fifteen before he had anything published. When he was 19 he went off to Palestine.

It was now that his story, *Agunot* was published and he henceforth took the name Agnon from the title. At that time it was the custom to work the land, or engage in other forms of physical labour. Unwilling to do manual work, Agnon moved to Jerusalem and a more intellectual way of life.

After a brief sojourn in Berlin, he returned to Jerusalem in 1924, a year in which the first of the fires that were to become a feature of his life took place. The house he had recently acquired went up in smoke, in circumstances never fully explained. He lost many books and manuscripts. The next blaze occurred during the Arab-Jewish riots of 1929, again, he lost his home and many books and papers.

Agnon is best known for his epic trilogy of novels depicting Eastern Jewry in the early 20th century: *Bridal Canopy* (1931), *A Guest For The Night* (1939) and *Days Gone By* (1945). His writings reflect the contrasting influences upon his life and this has led to comparisons with Kafka. His style is often surreal and introspective. In 1966 he received a share of the Nobel Prize for Literature; **"for his profoundly characteristic narrative art with motifs from the life of the Jewish people"**

He is generally regarded as the greatest writer in Modern Hebrew. His works have been translated into many languages and read worldwide. Married with a son and daughter, Agnon died in Jerusalem on February 17, 1970.

Nelly Leonie Sachs was born in Berlin, Germany on December 10, 1891. Nelly was her nickname coined by her father a wealthy merchant. She grew up in the very fashionable district of the Tiergarten and by the age of seventeen she was an accomplished poet. During the 1920s, her romantic and quite ordinary poems appeared in magazines and newspapers; happy to have something their minimally educated readers could easily understand.

Following the arrival of Hitler, her writings became outspokenly Jewish and it is perhaps surprising she waited as late as 1940 to leave Germany for Sweden. Her exit was assisted by the aid she received from the Swedish writer, Selma Lagerlof (qv), who in turn induced the King of Sweden to intercede with the German authorities. Now safe in Sweden, Nelly lived with her mother in a one room flat, learnt Swedish and made a precarious living undertaking translations.

In 1946, she published her first book of poetry. It was called; *In The Habitations of Death* and dedicated to ' my dead brothers and sisters'. Her now famous poem, *O The Chimneys*, describes the body of Israel in smoke, as it drifts upwards in the German death camps. It was the title she used for the 1967 collection of her work translated into English. In 1965 she was awarded the German Publishers' Peace Prize. In 1966, Nelly Sachs, on her 75th birthday, was awarded the Nobel Prize for Literature; **"for her outstanding lyrical and dramatic writing, which interprets Israel's destiny with touching strength"**

Jointly with the Israeli writer S.Y.Agnon she received her prize from King Gustav of Sweden, Nelly Sachs said, ' Agnon represents the State of Israel, I represent the tragedy of the Jewish people.' Much of her poetry reflects the horrors of the Holocaust and her style appears to be a mixture of Jewish and German passion. As a playwright, her best known work is, *Eli: A Mystery Play of the Suffering of Israel* (1943). Here she forges a link between the murder, by a German soldier, of a Polish child and the Jewish legend of the 36 saints who ensure the world's continuing existence. Nelly Sachs never married and she died in Stockholm on May 12, 1970.

CHEMISTRY

ROBERT MULLIKEN (1896-1986)

Robert Sanderson Mulliken was born in Newburyport, Mass, US, on June 7, 1896. He was a graduate of Massachusetts Institute of Technology, Cambridge. In 1921 he received his PhD from Chicago University. Between 1926-28 he taught at New York University, then he returned to Chicago where he taught until 1985. He began research into the electronic structure of molecules in the 1920s.

He departed from the accepted notion, that electron orbitals for atoms are static and that atoms combine, like building blocks, to form molecules. Instead, Mulliken suggested that when molecules are formed, the atoms' original electron configurations are changed into an overall molecular type.

During WW2, he worked on the Plutonium Project, part of the development of the atomic bomb, at Chicago University. In 1955, he switched to politics and became a scientific attache at the US embassy in London. In 1966 he was awarded the Nobel Prize for Chemistry, **"for his fundamental work concerning chemical bonds and the electric structure of molecules by the molecular orbital method"**

Married with two daughters, Mulliken died in Arlington, Va. on October 3, 1986.

PHYSICS

ALFRED KASTLER (1902-1984)

Alfred Kastler was born in Guebwiller, France on May 3, 1902. He was educated in Paris at the École Normale Supérieure and taught there between 1941 and 1968. His research allowed the study of atomic structures by means of the radiations that atoms emit under excitation by light and radio waves. This method of stimulating atoms became known as, optical pumping, so called because the light energy used to stimulate the atoms was remitted.

Later, optical pumping became an important feature of the development of the maser and laser. For this work Kastler, in 1966, was awarded the Nobel Prize for Physics; **"for the discovery and development of optical methods for studying hertian resonances in atoms"**

From this time, until 1972, he was research director at the National Centre of Scientific Research. It is said that during his long career of teaching, he taught a whole generation of French scientists. Married with two sons and a daughter, Kastler died in Bandol, France on January 7, 1984.

PHYSIOLOGY or MEDICINE

CHARLES HUGGINS (1901-1997)
and
PEYTON ROUS (1879-1970)

Charles Brenton Huggins was born in Halifax, Canada on September 22, 1901. He was educated at Acadia University and at Harvard from where he received an MD in 1924. He joined Michigan University where, between 1924-27, he undertook surgery training before joining the staff of Chicago University.

Here between, 1951 and 1969, he was the director for cancer research. His research centred on the relationship between hormones and certain types of cancer. As a result, he was co-winner of the 1966 Nobel Prize for Physiology or Medicine; **"for his discoveries concerning hormonal treatment for prostatic cancer"**

In 1963 he was awarded the Lasker Award for Clinical Research. Married with a son and daughter, he died on January 12,1997 whilst living in Chicago.

Francis Peyton Rous was born in Baltimore, US, on October 5, 1879. He was educated at John Hopkins University, Baltimore and at Michigan University. He joined the Rockefeller Institute for Medical Research in New York in 1909 and stayed throughout his career. His research was on cancer treatments, liver investigations and gallbladder physiology.

He also worked on the development of blood preserving techniques that allowed blood banks to be set-up. For his discoveries, he was co-awarded the 1966 Nobel Prize for Physiology or Medicine; **"for his discovery of tumor-inducing viruses"**

Married with three daughters, Rous died in New York on February 16, 1970.

PEACE

NOT AWARDED

1967

Israel's Six-Day War • Racial violence in US • Nigeria Civil War • Che Guevara executed • First heart transplant • Demonstrations against US war in Vietnam • Sexual relations allowed between consenting male adults in the UK • Introduction of mammography • Desmond Morris, *The Naked Ape* **• Andy Warhol,** *Marilyn Monroe* **• Anthony Caro,** *Prairie* **• Stockhausen,** *Hymnen* **• Films:** *In the Heat of the Night, Belle de Jour, The Graduate, Bonnie and Clyde* **• Margaret Drabble,** *Jerusalem the Golden* **• Angus Wilson,** *No Laughing Matter* **• Ilya Ehrenburg, Harriet Cohen, John Masefield, Mischa Elman, André Maurois, Elmer Rice, Gregory Pincus, Dorothy Parker, Paul Muni, Robert Oppenheimer, Paul Whiteman, Anton Walbrook, Siegfried Sassoon, Clement Attlee and Joe Orton die.**

LITERATURE

MIGUEL ASTURIAS (1899-1974)

Miguel Angel Asturias was born in Guatemala City, Guatemala, on October 19, 1899. He received a law degree from San Carlos University in 1923 and decided to settle in Paris. There he studied ethnology at the Sorbonne and became a militant Surrealist. His first major work was ,*Legends of Guatemala* (1930) He describes the life and culture of the Maya, prior to the arrival of the Spanish.

This brought him critical acclaim in France and South America. He returned home, founded a radio magazine and wrote poetry. In 1946, he was invited by the then government to join their diplomatic department.

Asturias served in several of the countries of Central and South America and he was afforded the time and opportunity to develop his novel writing. *The President* in 1946 was a denunciation of the Guatemalan dictator Manuel Cabrera.

His masterpiece is perhaps, *Men of Maize*. Written in 1949 it tells of the terrible life endured by the Indian peasant. His epic trilogy, *The Cyclone* 1950; *The Green Pope* 1954 and *The Eyes of the Interred* 1960, was about the subjugation of the peasant banana workers. He was Guatemalan ambassador to France between 1966 and 70, at which time he took permanent residence in France.

In 1966, he was awarded the Lenin Peace Prize and awarded the 1967 Nobel Prize for Literature; **"for his vivid literary achievement, deep-rooted in the national traits and traditions of Indian peoples of Latin America"**

He was noted for awakening the moral and social aspirations of his people. Asturias died in Madrid, Spain on June 9th 1974. He was twice married and had two sons.

CHEMISTRY

MANFRED EIGEN (1927-), RONALD NORRISH (1897-1978)
and
GEORGE PORTER (1920-)

"for their studies of extremely fast chemical reactions, effected by disturbing the equilibrium by means of very short pulses of energy"

Manfred Eigen was born in Bochum, Germany on May 9th 1927. At Göttingen University he studied chemistry and physics and obtained his doctorate in 1951. At that time he joined the university's Institute of Physical Chemistry. In 1953 he began his long association with the Max Planck Institute of Physical Chemistry, winding up as chairman in 1968.

Eigen's studies involved a variety of methods known as relaxation techniques that comprised application of bursts of energy to a given solution. An example is his investigation of the rate of hydrogen ion formation through dissociation in water, diffusion-controlled proteolytic reactions and kinetics of keto-enol tautomerism. For his work on extremely rapid chemical reactions, Eigen was awarded a third share of the 1967 Nobel Prize for Chemistry. He is married with a son and daughter.

Ronald George Wreyford Norrish was born in Cambridge, England, on November 9th 1897. He was a student of Emmanuel College, Cambridge University, from where he obtained his doctorate, and later became a research fellow there. In 1963 he was elevated to Emeritus. He directed the university's physical chemistry department for nearly 30 years. His research was involved in the field of fast chemical reactions.

He worked with George Potter and together they, between 1949 and 1955, were able to stop chemical reactions at intervals approaching one-thousandth of a millionth of a second and to study the intermediate stages of progressive changes.

For this work Norrish was awarded a third share of the 1967 Nobel Prize for Chemistry. Married with two daughters, he died in Cambridge on June 7th 1978.

George Porter was born in Stainforth, Yorks; England on December 6th 1920. An undergraduate at Leeds University it was from Cambridge that Porter received his doctorate in 1949. He worked with Ronald Norrish on fast chemical reactions but specialized on studying the equilibrium of chlorine atoms and molecules. He taught at Sheffield University from 1955 to 1966 when he was appointed director of the Royal Institution of Great Britain and Fullerian Professor of Chemistry.

He was awarded a third share of the 1967 Nobel Prize for Chemistry for his work on flash photolysis a required technique in the field of fast chemical reactions. He was knighted in 1972.

He is married with two sons.

PHYSICS

HANS BETHE (1906-)

Hans Albrecht Bethe was born in Strassburg, Germany (before it lost an 's', gained an 'o' and became French), on July 2nd 1906. He studied physics at Frankfurt University and did research work on theoretical physics at Munich University, from where he obtained a PhD in 1928, on a thesis on the theory of electron diffraction. His work on crystal splitting in 1929, illustrated how the symmetrical electric field, by which an atom in a crystal is surrounded, affects its energy condition. In 1931, he worked with Enrico Fermi (qv) in Rome returning to Germany in 1932 to lecture at the University of Tubingen.

In 1933, as the son of a Jewish mother, he was forced out of his job and advised to leave the country. He spent a year in England before emigrating, in 1935, to America where he was appointed a professor of physics at Cornell University. There he remained until 1975.

A US citizen in 1941, he was appointed to the Manhattan Project at Los Alamos, New Mexico. After the atomic bomb was dropped on Japan, he was one of the scientists who keenly felt their responsibility in ensuring that an atomic war never happened. Bethe was one of the contributors to the *Bulletin of the Atomic Scientists*.

In addition, he lectured and wrote on the danger of the nuclear threat, thereby increasing public awareness. Beside being awarded the Max Planck Medal in 1955, he was a foreign member of the Royal Society of London and a member of the US National Academy of Sciences. In 1967 he was awarded the Nobel Prize for Physics; **"for his contributions to the theory of nuclear reactions, especially his discoveries concerning the energy production in stars"**

He wrote his autobiography, *Hans Bethe: Prophet of Energy*. He is married with a son and daughter.

PHYSIOLOGY or MEDICINE

RAGNAR GRANIT (1900-1991), HALDON HARTLINE (1903-1983)
and
GEORGE WALD (1906-1997)

"for their discoveries concerning the primary physiological and chemical visual processes in the eye"

Ragnar Arthur Granit was born in Helsinki, Finland on October 30th 1900. He received his MA from Helsinki University in 1927 and then proceeded to the US and Pennsylvania University to conduct research in optics. A short while later he was doing the same at Oxford University. He then became professor of physiology at Helsinki University in 1937. He later decided to live and work in Sweden and become a Swedish citizen.

In 1940, he was working at the medical department of the Caroline Institute in Stockholm. In 1946, he was chairman of the neurophysiology section. In 1945, he was appointed director of the Nobel Institute for Neurophysiology in Stockholm. His research on the optic nerve formed his 'dominator-modulator' theory of colour vision.

This theory suggests that in addition to the three kinds of photosensitive cones or colour receptors various lights respond to different portions of the light spectrum. He went on to prove that light could inhibit as well as stimulate impulses along the optic nerve. For this work he was awarded a third share of the 1967 Nobel Prize for Physiology or Medicine. Among his writings is the classic, *Sensory Mechanisms of the Retina* (1947). Married with a son, Granit died in Helsinki in 1991.

Haldan Keffer Hartline was born in Bloomsburg, Pa. US, on December 22nd 1903. Whilst at Johns Hopkins University in Baltimore, from where he received an MA in 1927, he was busy researching retinal electro physiology. In 1949, he was professor of biophysics at Johns Hopkins and in 1953 professor of neurophysiology at Rockefeller University, New York.

Hartline researched the electrical responses of the retinas of certain arthropods, vertebrates and mollusks, because their visual systems resemble that of humans, albeit simpler and therefore easier to understand. He concentrated on the eye of the horseshoe crab, and discovered and recorded, electrical impulses sent by a single optic nerve fibre when the receptors connected to it are stimulated by light. This discovery and future work was rewarded by a third share of the 1967 Nobel Prize for Physiology or Medicine. Married with three sons Hartline died in Fallston, Md. on March 17, 1983.

George Wald was born in New York, on November 18, 1906. Whilst doing postgraduate work in Berlin on a National Research Council scholarship, Wald discovered that vitamin A is a vital ingredient of the pigment of the retina and therefore essential for vision. He researched further at Heidelberg leaving in 1933 when Hitler arrived, and Jews were no longer welcome. He was briefly at the universities of Zurich and Chicago, before joining the staff at Harvard University in 1934.

In the 1940s Wald further discovered that people with cataracts, who have had the lenses of their eyes removed, can see ultraviolet light. He therefore concluded that the lens filters out the ultraviolet. He later succeeded in discovering the chemical reactions involved in the principle of sight, as applied to the way the retina is used for night vision.

In the late 1950s, he and Paul Brown, identified the pigments of the eye that were sensitive to yellow-green-light and red light; and then the pigment sensitive to blue light. They also discovered the role of vitamin A, in forming the colour pigments and showed that colour blindness is caused by the absence of these pigments. It led to Wald receiving a third share of the 1967 Nobel Prize for Physiology or Medicine.

In 1977 he was professor emeritus at Harvard University. Married twice with three sons and a daughter, during the Vietnam war Wald was an outspoken critic of American involvement. He died on April 12, 1997 whilst living in Cambridge, Mass.

PEACE

NOT AWARDED

1968

Soviet invasion of Czechoslovakia • Abortion legal in Britain • Martin Luther King assassinated • Manned mission to the moon • Jurgen Habermas, *Knowledge and Human Interests* **• Richard Hamilton,** *Swinging London* **• British censorship of theatre ends • *Cabaret, Hair* • Allen Ginsberg,** *Planet News* **• Costa-Gavras,** *Z* **• Gore Vidal,** *Myra Breckinridge* **• Films:** *Z, 2001: Space Odyssey, Weekend, If, The Producers, Oliver!,* **• Sydney Silverman, Fannie Hurst, Ziggy Elman, Tony Hancock, Bud Flanagan, Enid Blyton, Chana Orloff, Upton Sinclair and John Steinbeck die.**

LITERATURE

YASUNARI KAWABATA (1899-1972)

Yasunari Kawabata was born in Osaka, Japan on June 11, 1899. He graduated from Tokyo Imperial University in 1924 and two years later his first literary effort, *The Izu Dancer* appeared in a magazine, co-founded by Kawabata and the organ of the Neosensualist movement.

His best known novel, *The Snow Country* published in 1948, was begun in 1935. The sequel provisionally entitled, *Thousand Cranes*, began in 1949 but never completed.

The Sound of the Mountain (1949-54) is a complicated view of life in general. He attempted to put into a modern context an ancient Japanese writing tradition By and large he failed. Awarded the 1968 Nobel Prize for Literature; **"for his narrative mastery, which, with great sensibility, expresses the essence of the Japanese mind"**

He was the first Japanese writer to receive the honour. He stated at his acceptance speech, that in his work he tried to, beautify death and to seek harmony among man, nature and emptiness and that he had been striving for beauty all his life. He committed suicide on April 16, 1972 in Zushi, Japan; it was a few days after the death of his life-long friend Mishima Yukio. He was married with a daughter.

CHEMISTRY

LARS ONSAGER (1903-1976)

Lars Onsager was born in Kristiania (Oslo), Norway on November 27, 1903. He studied at the Norwegian Institute of Technology, before going to the Federal Institute of Technology in Zurich, to study under Peter Debye, the Dutch chemist (qv) (1926-28) He then went to the US and taught at Johns Hopkins University in Baltimore and Brown University in Providence. In 1935, he received his PhD from Yale, where in 1945, he became professor of theoretical chemistry.

His research work resulted in his explanation of the movement of ions in solution as related to turbulence and fluid densities. This had a major effect on the development of physical chemistry and described as 'providing the fourth law of thermodynamics '. He was awarded the 1968 Nobel Prize for Chemistry; **"for the discovery of the reciprocal relations bearing his name, which are fundamental for the thermodynamics of irreversible processes"**

Married with three sons and a daughter, Onsager died in Florida, US, on October 5, 1976.

PHYSICS

LUIS ALVAREZ (1911-1988)

Luis Walter Alvarez was born in San Francisco, US, on June 13, 1911. He studied physics at Chicago University, collecting an BS in 1932, an MS in 1934, and a PhD in 1936. Thereafter he was long associated with the University of California at Berkeley. There he was professor of physics in 1945 and professor emeritus in 1978.

In 1938 he discovered that some radioactive elements, decay by orbital-electron, capture, or put simply an orbital electron merges with its nucleus, thus producing an element with an atomic number smaller by one. A year later, together with Felix Bloch (qv), the first measurement of the magnetic moment of the neutron.

Alvarez, during WW2, became part of the organisation at Los Alamos, New Mexico, that designed and developed the atomic bomb. He also worked on the technique for detonating the bomb. Following the war, he helped construct the first proton linear and developed the liquid hydrogen bubble chamber in which subatomic particles and their reactions are discovered. Later, in the early 1980s, he assisted his son Walter, establish the theory that climatic explosions, some 60 million years ago, brought about the extinction of the dinosaur.

In 1968 Alvarez received the Nobel Prize for Physics; **"for his decisive contributions** to elementary particle physics, in particular the discovery of a large number of resonance states, made possible through his development of the technique of using hydrogen bubble chamber and data analysis"

He died in California on September 1, 1988. Married twice, he had two sons and two daughters.

PHYSIOLOGY or MEDICINE

ROBERT HOLLEY (1922-1993), HAR KHORANA (1922-)
and
MARSHALL NIRENBERG (1927-)

"for their interpretation of the genetic code and its function in protein synthesis"

Robert **William Holley** was born in Urbana, Illinois, US, on January 28, 1922. He was educated at Illinois University and obtained his PhD from Cornell University in 1947. Between 1948 and 1957, he was an associate professor at Cornell, before joining the New York State Agricultural Department. He later became professor of biochemistry (1964-69)

He was a resident fellow at the Salk Institute at La Jolla 1968-93. By 1960 Holley (and others) had shown that small molecules of ribonucleic acids, named transfer RNA, were involved in the assembly of amino acids into proteins. By 1965, Holley had determined the composition of the transfer RNA, that includes the amino acid alanine into protein molecules. For this work he co-shared the 1968 Nobel Prize for Physiology or Medicine.

He died from lung cancer, in Los Gatos, Calif; on February 11, 1993. He was married with one son.

Har **Gobind Khorana** was born in Raipur, India on January 9, 1922. He was born into a poor family, who made a lot of sacrifices, in order to send their son to Punjab University, and later to Liverpool University, albeit Har won government scholarships. In 1948, at Liverpool, he obtained his PhD. He then went to Cambridge University where he began his research work on nucleic acids, under Alexander Todd. He was later a professor at the Swiss Federal Institute of Technology and between 1952-59, he was at the British Columbia University in Canada.

Khorana's scientific contribution was, in the early 1960s, to synthesize small nucleic acid molecules whose exact structure was known. Together with the proper materials, his synthetic nucleic acids caused proteins to be synthesized, just as in the cell. In 1968, he was awarded a co-share of the Nobel prize for Physiology or Medicine.

In 1970 he prepared the first artificial copy of a yeast gene. The following year he was teaching at the Massachusetts Institute of Technology. He is married with two daughters and a son.

Marshall Warren Nirenberg was born in New York on April 10, 1927, the son of working class Jewish parents. The family moved to Florida in 1939. In 1948 he received a BSc and in 1952 a MSc in Zoology both from the University of Florida. He received his PhD from Michigan University in 1957 and joined the staff of the National Institutes of Health in Bethesda, Md.

His research, in deciphering the genetic code, and his ability to demonstrate that, with the exception of what he termed ' nonsense codons', each codon ultimately causes the incorporation of a specific amino acid into a cell protein. This research earned him the National Medal of Science in 1965 and a co- share of the 1968 Nobel Prize for Physiology or Medicine.

Nirenberg is a member of the American Academy of Arts and Sciences and the National Academy of Sciences. He married Perola Zaltzman in 1961, a chemist from the University of Brazil, Rio de Janeiro. She later became a biochemist at the National Institute of Health.

PEACE

RENÉ CASSIN (1887-1976)

René Samuel Cassin was born in Bayonne, France on October 5, 1887, the son of a well-known French Jewish family that had links with pre-Inquisition Spain. He was educated at Aix and Paris universities and studied law. During the First World War he served in the French army, was badly wounded, and decorated with the Croix de Guerre, as well as the Medaille Militaire. In 1920 he became professor of law at Lille University, where he stayed until 1929. He then went to Paris University, taking time off to be part of the French delegation to the League of Nations.

At the beginning of the Second World War, Cassin was involved, at the highest possible level, in discussions with foreign governments prior to the collapse of France. During the war years he was in London, serving in the French government-in-exile. He represented France at the founding of the United Nations, later becoming, together with Eleanor Roosevelt, the first president of the UN Commission on Human Rights. He went on to hold many public posts. In 1968 Rene Cassin was awarded the Nobel Peace Prize; **"for his work with the European Court of Human Rights"**

The large cash prize that accompanies this honour, he donated to the work of the Human Rights Institute in Strasbourg. He died in Paris on October 5, 1976. In October 1987 his remains were transferred to the Pantheon in Paris : a signal honour.

Married twice, he left no children.

1969

Charles de Gaulle resigns • Disturbances in Northern Ireland • First Men on the moon • Richard Nixon becomes US President • Human egg cell fertilised in vitro • Kenneth Clark, *Civilisation* **• Isaiah Berlin,** *Four Essays on Liberty* **• Ezra Pound,** *Cantos* **• Woodstock Music and Arts Fair • Booker Prize for fiction awarded in Britain • John Fowles,** *The French Lieutenant's Woman* **• Graham Greene,** *Travels with My Aunt* **• Philip Roth,** *Portnoy's Complaint* **• Bernice Rubens,** *The Elected Member* **• Films,** *Kes,* *Butch Cassidy and the Sundance Kid, Easy Rider, Midnight Cowboy, The Wild Bunch* **• Walter Gropius, Theodor Adorno, Rocky Marciano, Robert Briscoe, Ludwig Mies van der Rohe and Ho Chi Minh die.**

LITERATURE

SAMUEL BECKETT (1906-1989)

Samuel Barclay Beckett was born in Foxrock, Co. Dublin, Ireland on April 13, 1906. Like his fellow writers, Bernard Shaw, Oscar Wilde and William Yeats, Beckett came from an Anglo-Saxon middle-class Protestant background. At the age of 14, he was at the Portora Royal school and, between 1923 and 27, he was studying romantic languages at Trinity College, Dublin. Following his degree, he spent a brief while teaching in Belfast. He then switched to Paris, where he became a Reader in English at the École Normale Supérieure in 1928. There, he met the 'master'.

James Joyce invited Beckett to join his circle. A little while later Beckett returned to Dublin to teach French at Trinity College. This didn't last very long. Beckett was restless and began travelling much, in England, France, Italy and Germany. In 1937, he finally settled in Paris. During WW2 and the German Occupation, he was allowed by the Germans to remain. Ireland was neutral. He flirted with the French Resistance but panicked when some associates were arrested by the Gestapo. He decided to hide in the unoccupied part of France (Vichy) and worked as an agricultural labourer until the liberation.

Beckett is probably best known for his plays, including the absurdist, *Waiting for Godot* (1953), *Krapp's Last Tape* (1958 and *Happy Days* (1961). However, he considered himself first and foremost a novelist. *Murphy* (1938) and the trilogy of novels beginning with, *Molly* (1955).

In both his drama and fiction, his vision is bleak but enlivened sometimes with the injection of black humour. For a long time misleadingly associated with existentialism, Beckett is now regarded as being one of the most important early post-modernists; just behind James Joyce. An introvert in the extreme, Beckett, whilst agreeing to accept the award of the 1969 Nobel Prize for Literature; **"for his writing, which-in new forms for the novel and drama-in the destitution of modern man acquires** its elevation" he declined the trip to Stockholm in order to avoid having to make a speech.

He rarely, if ever, appeared on radio, TV or in public or gave interviews. He lived in a small house in the Marne valley near Paris. Married without children, he wrote little of importance in later life and died in Paris on December 22, 1989.

CHEMISTRY

DEREK BARTON (1918-1998)
and
ODD HASSEL (1897-1981)

"for their contributions to the development of the concept of conformation and its application in chemistry"

Derek Harold Richard Barton was born in Gravesend, Kent, England on September 8, 1918. He was educated at Imperial College, London and, following receipt of his degree, joined the College staff, first as an assistant lecturer and later as a research fellow. He was at Harvard University in the US as a visiting professor (1949-50). Here he began work that led to his seminal publication on conformation analysis. This work came to the attention of the scientific community and later revolutionized organic chemistry.

It also brought him a joint award of the 1969 Nobel Prize for Chemistry for his research that helped establish the study of the three-dimensional geometric structure of complex molecules. From 1950, he was associated with Birbeck College, London and he was professor of chemistry at Glasgow University 1955-57. In 1960, he discovered what came to be called, ' The Barton Reaction', a process that led to an easier means of synthesizing the hormone aldosterone.

Following 21 years at Imperial College, Barton retired at the age of 60 and became director of L' Institut de Chimie des Substances Naturelles at Gifsur-Yvette in France. Here he studied the invention of new chemical reactions, especially using radicals, so opening up a whole new area of organic synthesis.

In 1986 he moved to a third career, at Texas A & M University as Distinguished Professor and later Dow Professor of Chemical Invention. He continued to work on novel reactions involving the oxidation of hydrocarbons, jokingly termed Gif and Go-Agg oxidations.

Married three times with a son, he died in College Station, Texas on March 16, 1998.

Odd Hassel was born in Kristiania, Norway on May 17, 1897. Educated at Oslo University, Hassel received his doctorate from Berlin University in 1924. He returned to Norway and joined the staff of Oslo University in 1925 as an assistant professor, becoming a full professor in 1934 and until 1964. At that time he was appointed director of the physical chemistry department.

In 1930, he began his research on the structure of cyclohexane and its derivatives and discovered the existence of two types of cyclohexane. In *Crystal Chemistry* (1934) he set down the principles of conformation analysis.

During WW2, when Norway was occupied by Germany, Hassel was imprisoned, together with other university workers (1943-45).

Following liberation, Hassel's research concentrated on the structure of organic halogen compounds. In 1969, he received a co- share of the Nobel Prize for Chemistry for his work on the study of the three dimensional geometric structure of molecules.

This was an important force in revolutionizing the modern concepts of molecular structure. Hassel never married. He died in Oslo on May 11, 1981.

PHYSICS

MURRAY GELL-MANN (1929-)

Murray Gell-Mann was born in New York City on September 15, 1929. He was the son of an Austrian-Jewish immigrant. At the age of fifteen he was at Yale University, receiving a BS in physics at nineteen and a PhD, from the Massachusetts Institute of Technology, in 1951. The work he did for his doctorate, was later influential in Eugene Wigner's (qv) work on subatomic particles, for which he was awarded the 1963 Nobel Prize.

In 1952, Gell-Mann was at the Institute for Nuclear Studies at Chicago University and in 1953 introduced the idea of ' strangeness', which he adopted , as a quantum property, that accounted for previously puzzling decay patterns of certain mesons or unstable subatomic particles. Gell-Mann explained, that the ' strangeness' binds the components of the atomic nucleus.

In 1961, together with Yuval Ne'eman, an Israeli physicist, he suggested a scheme for classifying previously discovered interacting particles, into an orderly and simple arrangement, which they published under the title, *Eightfold Way* (1965). This title recalled Buddha's eightfold route to nirvana or heavenly bliss. Gell-Mann later suggested it should be practical to explain certain known particles in terms of building blocks.

These they later called , ' quarks', from James Joyce's, *Finnegan's Wake*. Of the six quarks so far predicted, five have indirectly been detected. Murray Gell-Mann was awarded the 1969 Nobel Prize for Physics. **"for his contributions and discoveries concerning the classification of** elementary particles and their interactions"

He is married with a son and daughter. At a conference Gell-Man once said "It isn't difficult to stand tall when you're surrounded by intellectual pygmies"

PHYSIOLOGY or MEDICINE

MAX DELBRUCK (1906-1981), ALFRED HERSHEY(1908-1997)
and
SALVADOR LURIA (1912-1991)

"for their discoveries concerning the replication mechanism and the genetic structure of viruses"

Max Delbruck was born in Berlin, Germany on September 4, 1906. He received his PhD in physics from Göttingen University in 1930. Whilst a research assistant at the Kaiser Wilhelm Institute for Chemistry in Berlin, his interests in bacteriophages came to the fore. An anti-Nazi, Delbruck left Germany for the US in 1937, becoming a US citizen in 1945. With a brief period; 1940-47, at Vanderbilt University, he would be associated with the California Institute of Technology until 1981.

In 1939, he discovered a one-step process for growing bacteriophages that, after a one hour latent period, would multiply to produce several hundred thousands of progeny. For his work on viruses that infect bacteria, he was awarded in 1969, a third share of the Nobel Prize for Physiology or Medicine.

Married with two sons and two daughters, Delbruck died in Pasadena, Calif. on March 9, 1981.

Alfred Day Hershey was born in Lansing, Michigan, US, on December 4, 1908. He was educated at Michigan State College and, from 1950 to 1974, he worked at the Carnegie Institution in Washington.

During the early 1940s, all three later recipients of the Nobel Prize, were regularly exchanging information on the 'phage'.

In 1945, Hershey working independently, discovered the occurrence of genetic recombination in phages. He went on to prove his theory by showing that the genetic processes in question, correspond with the crossing-over of parts of similar chromosomes, observed in cells of higher organisms.

Hershey is also noted for the work he did in the 1950s, and known as ' the Blender experiment'. Assisted by Martha Chase, he showed that phage DNA, is the principal component entering the host cell during infection. He proved that DNA, rather than protein, is the genetic material of the phage. For his discoveries, Hershey won the Albert Lasker Award in 1958, the Kimber Genetics Award in 1965 and, in 1969, a third share of the Nobel Prize for Physiology or Medicine.   He is married with a son.

Salvador **Edward Luria** was born in Turin, Italy on August 13, 1912. In 1935, he graduated in medicine from Turin University. Between 1935 and 38, he was a medical officer in the Italian Army. He witnessed Mussolini's fascist dictatorship at first hand and didn't like what he saw. By now a radiology specialist, he went to France in 1938. When the Germans arrived, he left for the US. As a Jew, he had little alternative.

While in Paris, he worked at the Curie Laboratory. Now his considerable knowledge and experience was much in demand at American universities. Although he became professor of bacteriology at Illinois University in 1950, it was not until he was professor of microbiology at the Massachusetts Institute of Technology (1959-64), that he really came into his own. He organised a new teaching and research programme, that in 1972, founded the MIT Centre for Cancer Research, with himself serving as its director until 1985.

Luria's particular field was bacteriophages (phages), sub-microscopic viruses that make-up bacteria. His work led him to DNA research, and he contributed to the discovery that viruses mutate, changing their form from one generation to another.

Luria was also a political being, often a vocal one. He criticized the Vietnam War, biological weaponry and the Lunar Programme, in terms of expense incurred for very little return. In 1969 he won a third share of the Nobel Prize for Physiology or Medicine.

He donated $25,000 from his prize money to anti-war groups. He was considered a remarkable man and an inspirational teacher. It was therefore all the more upsetting when, in 1969, his named appeared on a federal blacklist in the US because of his outspoken support for the peace movement. The government of Richard Nixon in general, and the FBI of Edgar Hoover in particular, appeared unable to accept that Professor Salvador Luria was a scientific genius with a social conscience.

In 1974 he won the National Book Award for his first non-academic book, *Life: The Unfinished Experiment.* He died of a heart attack in Lexington on February 6, 1991. He was married to Zella Hurwitz, a professor of psychology. They had one son.

ECONOMICS

(first time awarded)

RAGNAR FRISCH (1895-1973)
and
JAN TINBERGEN (1903-1994)

"for having developed and applied dynamic models for the analysis of economic processes"

Ragner **Anton Frisch** was born in Oslo, Norway on March 19, 1895. He was educated at Oslo University, obtaining his PhD in 1926. In 1931, a specially created professorship at Oslo University was awarded to Frisch and he filled this appointment until his retirement in 1965. He

was a pioneer of econometrics or the application of mathematical models in association with statistical techniques to economic data. He invented the word 'econometrics' and founded that Society, as well as serving for 21 years as editor of, *Econometrica*.

He is particularly well-known for the development of large-scale econometric modelling, linked to economic planning and national income accounting. He therefore dealt with the training of academically trained economists into key civil-service positions. Much of his published work is regarded as classics.

In 1969, he was co-awarded one of the two first-time Nobel Prizes for Economics. He died in Oslo on January 31, 1973. He was married twice and had a daughter.

Jan Tinbergen was born in The Hague, Holland on April 12, 1903. He was the brother of Nikolaas Tinbergen, the zoologist and Nobel Prizewinner. Jan was educated at Leiden University and, from 1929 to 1945, was a business-cycle statistician with the Central Bureau of Statistics.

Between 1945 and 1955, he was director of the Central Planning Bureau. He was also professor of economics at the Netherlands School of Economics (1933-73).

Between 1936 and 38, he was an economic advisor to the League of Nations in Geneva. There, he completed his now famous analysis of the economic development of the United States, from 1919 to 1932. He later built an econometric model of The Netherlands, applicable to both short and long term political-economic planning. He published much including, *Shaping the World Economy* (1962) and *Income Distribution* (1975). In 1969 he was co-winner of the first Nobel Prize for Economics. Married with four daughters, he died in Holland on June 9, 1994.

PEACE

INTERNATIONAL LABOUR ORGANISATION

The ILO was created in 1919, following the end of WW1, by the Treaty of Versailles. It became an affiliated agency of the League of Nations. In 1946, The ILO went on to become the first specialised agency to be affiliated to the United Nations. The functions of the ILO is the development and promotion of standards to protect and improve conditions of work and standards of living. It compiles statistics and deals with un-employment, labour relations, trade-union rights and human rights all over the world.

The 1969 Nobel Peace Prize was awarded to the ILO in recognition of its activities .The ILO publishes much, including *The International Labour* Review (monthly) and *The Year Book of Labour Statistics*.

1970

US offensive in Cambodia • Four anti-war students killed by US State police at Kent State University • Salvador Allende wins democratic Chilean election • 747 jumbo jet airliners begin schedule services • The 'floppy disc' is introduced • Kate Millet, *Sexual Politics* **• Yukio Mishima commits ritual suicide • Dario Fo,** *Accidental Death of an Anarchist* **• The Beatles split up • Dan Jacobson,** *The Rape of Tamar* **• Iris Murdoch,** *A Fairly Honourable Defeat* **• Peter Porter,** *The Last of England* **• Films:** *Patton, Ryan's Daughter, M*A*S*H, Walkabout, Tristana* **• Bertrand Russell, Marc Rothko, E.M. Forster, Jimi Hendrix, Abdel Nasser and Charles de Gaulle die.**

LITERATURE

ALEKSANDR SOLZHENITSYN (1918-)

Aleksandr Isayevich Solzhenitsyn was born in Kislovodsk, Russia on December 11, 1918. His father having been killed in an accident, prior to Aleksandr's birth, he was brought up by his mother and her family of intellectual Cossacks. He was educated at Rostov-na-Donu University and graduated in mathematics. A love of literature caused him to undertake correspondence courses and an external degree from Moscow State University was the result. During WW2, he was a captain of artillery until in 1945, he was sent to a labour camp for 8 years for criticizing Joseph Stalin. He was rehabilitated in 1956, and became a teacher of mathematics in central Russia; whilst writing in his spare time.

In 1962 his short novel, *One Day in the Life of Ivan Denisovich* was published and became instantly popular. Further writings met with increasing criticism that resulted in Solzhenitsyn publishing his own work and circulating them at home and abroad. *The First Circle* appeared in 1968 followed by, *Cancer Ward*. This was autobiographical, telling as it did, the story behind the diagnosis he received advising him he had terminal cancer. He disliked the Soviet Government and they disliked him. In 1970 he was awarded the Nobel Prize for Literature; **"for the ethical force with which he has pursued the indispensable traditions of Russian literature"**

Solzhenitsyn declined to go to Stockholm to receive his prize on the unsubstantiated belief that he wouldn't be allowed to return to Russia. His next novel, *August 1914*, an historical novel of WW1, was also published abroad and well received. *The Gulag Archipelago* (1973) is probably his best known book .and is his attempt to create a literary-historical record of the vast systems of prisons and labour camps existing in the USSR. Published abroad, the book caused much anger at home, resulting in an accord for Solzhenitsyn to go on a lecture tour of the US and not return. In 1990 his Soviet citizenship was restored following his book, *The Mortal Danger* that exposed the American misconceptions concerning the USSR. In 1998 he published *Russia in Collapse*. There is now a paradox, insofar that in post Soviet Russia, he is free to speak his mind-and few want to listen. He is un-married.

CHEMISTRY

LUIS LELOIR (1906-1987)

Luis Federico Leloir was born in Paris, France on September 6, 1906. His parents returned to their home in Argentina and there, Luis received his education. He worked for a period at Cambridge University and then spent 1934-35 as an assistant at the Institute of Physiology at Buenos Aires University.

He set up his own research institute in 1947 and researched into the oxidation of fatty acids, including the formation and breaking down of lactose in the body. This work ultimatly led to his discovery of sugar nucleotides, elements in the natural processes of carbohydrate metabolism. For this work Leloir was awarded the 1970 Nobel Prize for Chemistry; **"for his discovery of sugar nucleotides and their role in the biosynthesis of carbohydrates"**

He died in Buenos Aires, Argentine on December 2, 1987. Married in 1943, he had a daughter.

PHYSICS

HANNES ALFVÉN (1908-1995)
and
LOUIS NÉEL (1904-)

Hannes Olof Gosta Alfvén was born in Norrköping, Sweden on May 30, 1908. He was educated at Uppsala University and in 1940, he joined the staff of the Royal Institute of Technology in Stockholm. His research into space physics included the theorem frozen-in flux. This means that under certain circumstances, a plasma is bound to the magnetic lines of flux that pass through it. Alfven later used this concept to explain the origin of cosmic rays. In 1939 he published his theory of magnetic storms and wrote of the aurora influencing the modern concept of the Earth's magnetic field.

The study of plasmas in magnetic fields was pioneered by Alfven and this work has become fundamental in controling nuclear fusion. He later divided his teaching time between the University of California and the Royal Institute in Oslo. An early supporter of the concept that challenges the 'big-bang' model of the origin of the universe; known as ' plasma cosmology', this holds that the universe had no begining or forseeable end. Alfvén was awarded a 1970

Nobel Prize for Physics; **"for fundamental work and discoveries in magno-hydrodynamics with fruitful applications in different parts of plasma physics"**

Alfvén has written much upon his subject including, *On the Origin of the Solar System* (1954), *Worlds-Antiworlds* (1966) and *Cosmic Plasma* (1981). In 1935 Alfvén married Maria Kerstin, they had five children. He died on April 2,1995 in Norrköping, Sweden.

Louis-Eugène Félix Néel was born in Lyon, France on November 22, 1904. He graduated from the École Normale Supérieure and became professor at Strasbourg University in 1937, and at Grenoble (1946-76). During the thirties, he researched, on the molecular level, the forms of magnetism as against those of ferromagnetism.

He went on to discover that in certain substances alternating groups of atoms, align their electrons in opposite directions, thereby neutralising the net magnetic effect. This is known as antiferromagnetism. His work has provided much information on changes in the direction and strength of the Earth's magnetic field. His pioneering work in the studies of the magnetic properties of solids, became internationally known. He received a 1970 Nobel Prize for Physics; **"for fundamental work and discoveries concerning antiferromagnetism and ferrimagnetism which have led to important applications in solid state physics"**

Between 1971 and 76, Neel was director of the Polytechnic Institute in Grenoble. Married in 1931, he has three children.

PHYSIOLOGY or MEDICINE

JULIUS AXELROD (1912-), ULF von EULER (1905-1983)
and
BERNARD KATZ (1911-)

"for their discoveries concerning the humoral transmittors in the nerve terminals and the mechanism for their storage, release and inactivation"

Julius Axelrod was born in New York, US, on May 30, 1912. His efforts to receive a university education was beset with difficulties, due to his poverty and having to fight the Jewish quota system operated by some establishments. Refused admission to medical school, he instead took a degree in chemical pharmacology and received a BS from the College of the City of New York in 1933.

He followed with an MS from New York University in 1941, and a PhD from George Washington University in 1955. By this time he was head of the pharmacology department at the National Institute of Mental Health. He worked on the research division of Goldwater Memorial Hospital leaving in 1949 to join the chemical pharmacology department at the

National Heart Institute in Bethesda, Md.

Axelrod went on to discover that noradrenaline could be neutralized by an enzyme, catechol-o-methyl transferase, which he isolated and named. This enzyme proved critical in appreciating the entire nervous system and useful in dealing with effects from certain drugs in the research on hypertension and schizophrenia. For this work he was awarded a third share of the 1970 Nobel Prize for Physiology or Medicine. Axelrod is married with two children

Ulf Svante von Euler-Chelpin was born in Stockholm, Sweden on February 7, 1905. His father was the 1929 Nobel Prize winner Hans von Euler-Chelpin (qv). Ulf graduated from the Karolinska Institutet in Stockholm and went on to join the teaching staff in 1930 staying until 1971. He joined the Nobel Committee for Physiology or Medicine in 1953 and was president of the Nobel Foundation (1966-75).

His main achievement was his identification of noradrenaline, a key neurotransmitter in the sympathetic nervous system. He also discovered that noradrenaline was stored within nerve fibres. Euler-Chelpin also discovered the hormones known as prostaglandins, important in the regulation of the cardiovascular and nervous systems. For his work on the mechanics of nerve impulses he was awarded a third share of the 1970 Nobel Prize for Physiology or Medicine.

He died in Stockholm on March 9, 1983. He was married with four children

Bernard Katz was born in Leipzig, Germany on March 26, 1911. He received a medical degree from Leipzig University in 1934 and decided, as a Jew, he would leave Germany for Britain. At London University he studied for his PhD, which he obtained in 1938. He received a Carnegie Fellowship and went off to study in Australia (1939-42). There he joined the Royal Australian Air Force and served for the remainder of WW2.

He returned to University College London as a professor, and head of the biophysics department (1952-78). Whilst there, he discovered matters concerning the release of the neurotransmitter, acetylcholine, which carries impulses from nerve fibres to muscle fibre. This work won him the award of a third share of the 1970 Nobel Prize for Physiology or Medicine.

Katz was made a Fellow of the Royal Society in 1965 and knighted in 1969. In 1978 he became emeritus professor at University College. Among his writings are; *Electric Excitation of Nerves* (1939), *Nerve, Muscle and Synapse* (1966) and *Transmitter Substances* (1969). Katz is married with two children.

ECONOMICS

PAUL SAMUELSON (1915-)

Paul **Anthony Samuelson** was born in Gary, Indiana, US, on May 15, 1915, into a middle class Jewish family. He was educated at Chicago University, from where he obtained a BA, and at Harvard, from where he received his PhD in 1941. Known as an outstanding economic theorist, he established a mathematical technique which became his problem solver.

In 1947, he produced his *Foundations of Economic Analysis,* which explained his thinking concerning the universal features of consumer habits, as the mainspring of economic theory, and in particular, his mathematical formulation of the interaction of the multiplier and accelerator effects on economics.

His best-selling textbook, *Economics*, originally published in 1948, was updated in 1980. Besides serving as a government advisor on occasions, he was professor of economics at the Massachusetts Institute of Technology from 1940. His contributions to world economics was recognized when he was awarded the 1970 Nobel Prize for Economics; **"for the scientific work through which he has developed static and dynamic economic theory and actively contributed to raising the level of analysis in economic science"**

He was the first American to win a Nobel prize for Economics. He is unmarried.

PEACE

NORMAN BORLAUG (1914-)

Norman **Ernest Borlaug** was born in Cresco, Iowa, US, on March 25, 1914. At Minnesota University, he studied plant biology and forestry, earning a PhD in 1941. Between 1944 and 1960, he was a research scientist at the Rockefeller Foundation's Co-operative Mexican Agricultural Program in Mexico. There, he developed a strain of grain that substantially increased crop yields three fold.

He went on to be responsible for the increase in crop yields in India and Pakistan by some 60%. It all promised to alleviate world hunger but famine is still a regular feature in parts of the world. In constant demand as a consultant, Borlaug was awarded the 1970 Nobel Peace Prize; **"for his work with the Food Crop Program, 1960-63"**

He was un-married.

1971

War in Pakistan • China admitted to UN • Indira Gandhi wins India's general election • Over 45,000 US servicemen killed in Vietnam • First space station in orbit • 'Greenpeace' founded • First computer'chip' makes appearance • Germaine Greer, *The Female Eunuch* • Marvin Gaye, *What's Goin' On* • Films, *Death in Venice, A Clockwork Orange, The Last Picture Show, The French Connection* • E.M.Forster, *Maurice* • Tom Sharpe, *Riotous Assembly* • Coco Chanel, Arne Jacobson, Edward Andrade, Stevie Smith, Stravinsky and Nikita Khrushchev die.

LITERATURE

PABLO NERUDA (1904-1973)

Pablo Neruda was born Ricardo Reyes Basoalto Neftali in Parrel, Chile, on July 12, 1904. He was the son of a railway worker, his mother dying shortly after Pablo's birth. The family moved southwards and settled in Temuco where his father re-married. At the age of six, Pablo was at Temuco Boys School and writing poetry at the age of ten. In 1920 he left school and legally adopted his new name. Influenced by the great Chilean poet, Gabriela Mistral, he read the great classic writers who would later influence his writings. He also became a militant anarchist. In 1921, he was at a teachers training college in Santiago. However, writing poetry got in the way of his studies. Wearing a cape around his shoulders and a large sombrero on his head, Pablo invaded the cafes of literary society.

A member of the Federation of Chilean Students, he won their poetry award. In 1923 he published, *Crepusculario* at his own expense; financed by selling his furniture. For his next publication he found a publisher and *Twenty Love Poems and a Song of Despair* was published in 1924, to critical and public acclaim. He was now only 20 and one of the best known poets in Chile.

He now left college and concentrated on writing poetry. In 1927 he was appointed honorary consul in Rangoon, Burma, and spent five years there and in other parts of Asia. During this time he married a Dutch girl and wrote, *Residence on Earth*. In 1933 he was recalled to become consul in Buenos Aires. There he met the Spanish poet, Federico Garcia Lorca. Later, as consul in Madrid, he met his second wife. The outbreak of the Spanish Civil War interrupted his work. The execution of Lorca by Fascist rebels in Granada affected him badly. He published, *Spain in the Heart* during the war, returning to Chile in 1938.

He was consul in Mexico during WW2 and, influenced by the news in general and the battle for Stalingrad in particular, he produced some of his greatest poetry. In 1945 he was elected a Senator in Chile until, in 1948, a right wing coup forced Neruda and other Communists into hiding. During this time he wrote his epic poem, *General Song.*

In 1948 he was to be found in Paris, attending the Congress of Supporters of Peace and in 1949, he was in the USSR. In 1952 he was permitted to return to Chile and there he married his third wife. In 1953 he was awarded the Lenin Prize for peace and in 1971 was awarded the Nobel Prize for Literature; **"for a poetry that, with the action of an elemental force, brings alive a continent's destiny and dreams"**

He spent many years travelling throughout North and South America, continuously writing, with force and feeling. He died in Santiago on September 23, 1973. He was without children.

CHEMISTRY

GERHARD HERZBERG (1904-1999)

Gerhard Herzberg was born in Hamburg, Germany on December 25, 1904. He was educated at Göttingen and Berlin. An anti-Nazi, with a Jewish wife, he left Germany in 1935 and found a teaching post at Saskatchewan University in Saskatoon, Canada, before eventually joining the National Research Council in Ottawa. He had spent some time in Chicago, at the Yerkes Observatory but found the atmosphere of McCarthy America, too reminiscent of prewar Germany. His research into spectroscopic studies, proved essential to physical chemistry and quantum mechanics.

They also helped stimulate a resurgence of investigation into the chemical reactions to gases. He was awarded the 1971 Nobel Prize for Chemistry; **"for his contributions to the knowledge of electronic structure and geometry of molecules, particularly free radicals"**

Herzberg especially examined free radicals- groups of atoms that contain odd numbers of electrons and he was the first to identify the spectra of certain free radicals in interstellar gas. He later contributed considerable spectrographic information on the atmospheres of the outer planets and the stars, and his three volume *Molecular Spectra and Molecular Structure* (1936-66) is of particular importance. He continued work past the official age of 65 and didn't retire until he was 90.

He died in Ottawa on March 3, 1999. He was married twice with a son and daughter.

PHYSICS

DENNIS GABOR (1900-1979)

Dennis Gabor was born on June 5, 1900 in Budapest, Hungary. Educated at Budapest University, he later spent two years teaching at Berlin University. Between 1926 and 1933, he worked as a research engineer at Siemens. With the arrival of Hitler, Gabor, as a Jew, was forced to flee and he made his way to England where he later became a British citizen. In London he joined the company of Thomson-Houston.

In 1947, he had the notion of holography; by using filtered light sources, he developed the notion to a basic technique. Holography was not, however, really feasible until the laser was demonstrated in 1960. In 1958 Gabor was professor of applied electron physics at Imperial College, London.

Here he carried out research into high-speed oscilloscopes, physical optics and television. In this field he invented a colour television tube of greatly reduced depth, so making colour TV sets for the home, a practical proposition. During his career, Gabor was granted some 100 patents and awarded the 1971 Nobel Prize for Physics; **"for his invention and development of the holographic method"**

His invention of holography, a system of lensless, three dimensional photography has proven to have many applications. He died in London on February 8th 1979. In 1936 he married Marjorie Butler of Rugby. He received a CBE in 1970. The Albert Michelson Medal of the Franklin Institute, Philadelphia in 1968 and became a Fellow of the Royal Society in 1956.

PHYSIOLOGY or MEDICINE

EARL SUTHERLAND (1915-1974)

Earl Wilbur Sutherland was born in Burligame, Kan. US, on November 19, 1915. He graduated from Washburn College, Kansas in 1937, and received an MD from Washington University Medical School in 1942. Following service with the US Army during WW2 , he joined the staff of Washington University. In 1953 he became director of the department of medicine at Western Reserve University in Cleveland.

There, in 1956, he discovered cyclic AMP. In 1971 he was awarded the Nobel Prize for Physiology or Medicine; **"for his discoveries concerning the mechanisms of the action of hormones"**

He was responsible for the isolation of cyclic adenosine mono-phosphate, and the demonstration of its involvement in numerous metabolic processes that occur in animals. From 1973 and until his death, he was a member of the faculty of the University of Miami Medical School. He died on

March 9, 1974 in Miami, Florida. He married in 1963 and had two sons and two daughters.

ECONOMICS

SIMON KUZNETS (1901-1985)

Simon Kuznets was born in Kharkov, Russia on April 30, 1901. In 1907, in order to escape the Jewish persecution ordered by the Tsar, Kuznets senior emigrated to the US, where he changed the family name to Smith. Simon however, remained in Russia with his grandparents until he was 21. At that time he followed the family to the US but refused to change his name.

Knowing little English, he completed his education at Columbia University, picking up a PhD in 1926. A year later, following publication of his thesis on the repeated cycle of retail business, he was working at the National Bureau of Economic Research. While at the Bureau, he did exceptional work concerning US national income, especially during the years of depression when government required economic information upon which to base forecasts and policy. He was able to define distinctly, the relation of national product to national income, and this formed the basis of future economic structure. His book, *National Income and its Composition 1919-1938,* was published in 1941 and became the bible for economists worldwide.

He was professor of Economics at Pennsylvania University (1930-54) and during WW2, was Director of the Bureau of Planning and Statistics on the War Production Board. He taught at John Hopkins University (1954-60) and at Harvard University (1961-71). He emphasized the complexity of gathering data and the relation of that data to historical situations. He explained the existence of cyclical variations, in a growth rate, and the factors that make-up that menu, known as the Kuznets Cycle. In 1971, Kuznets received the Nobel Prize for Economics; **"for his empirically founded interpretation of economic growth which has led to new and deepened insight into the economic and social structure and process of development"**

He died on July 8, 1985 in Cambridge, Massachusetts. He was married with a son, daughter and four grandchildren.

PEACE

WILLY BRANDT (1913-1992)

Willy Brandt, was born Herbert Ernst Karl Frahm, in Lubeck, Germany on December 18th 1913. He entered university in 1932 and a year later, following the Nazis coming to power, he was forced to flee the country because of his activities with the Social Democrats. He adopted the name of Willy Brandt and went to Norway. There he attended Oslo University and later worked as a journalist. When the Germans arrived in Norway, Brandt took off for Sweden where he remained for the duration

of WW2. The war over, he returned to Germany as a Norwegian citizen and worked in the Norwegian mission in Berlin as a press attache. He returned to politics and resumed his German citizenship. Between 1957 and 1966, he was mayor of Berlin and one of the very few acceptable Germans around. He became world famous and campaigned to be chancellor of West Germany three times- 1961, 1965 and, 1969 at which time he was the winner.

He encouraged good relations with the Soviet Union and had a special policy with regard to East Germany. He resigned in 1974 because a senior aide, Gunther Guillaume was revealed as an East German spy. In 1971 he was awarded the Nobel Peace Prize **"for his continuing work toward reconciliation between West Germany and the Soviet bloc"**

He died from cancer, on October 8/9, 1992 in Unkel, near Bonn, Germany. He was married three times and had a daughter and three sons.

1972

East-West Detente • Tate exhibits Anre's bricks • Tutankhamun exhibition at the British Museum • USSR beats US in Olympic basketball final • Samuel Beckett, *Not I* • Tom Stoppard, *Jumpers* • Films; *The Discreet Charm of the Bourgeoisie, The Godfather, Cabaret, Cries and Whispers, Deliverance* • Reggae spreads from Jamaica • Bobby Fischer beats Boris Spassky in World Chess Championship • Chaim Potok, *My Name is Asher Lev* • Maurice Chevalier, Kwame Nikrumah, C.Day Lewis, Louis Leakey, Victor Barna, Ezra Pound and Harry S Truman die.

LITERATURE

HEINRICH BOLL (1917-1985)

Heinrich Theodor Boll was born in Cologne, Germany on December 21st 1917. He was the son of a furniture maker. He graduated from senior school in 1937 and was called into labour service before serving in the German Army throughout WW2. The war over, he returned to Cologne and began writing of his war-time experiences. He took as his themes an anti-war and nonconformist attitude. It suited the time.

His books generally present a panorama of German life from the two world wars to the 1970s. This is illustrated by his novel, *Group Portrait with Lady* (1971). His books have little appeal for those outside Germany. His works failing to come to terms with the revelations that

Germans had lost their right to be considered a cultured and civilised nation. He was awarded the Nobel Prize for Literature in 1972; **"for his writing, which, through its combination of a broad perspective on his time and a sensitive skill in characterization, has contributed to a renewal of German literature"**

He died in Bonn on July 16th 1985. He was married with two sons.

CHEMISTRY

STANFORD MOORE (1913-1982), WILLIAM STEIN (1911-1980)

"for their contribution to the understanding of the connection between chemical structure and catalytic activity of the active centre of the ribonuclease molecule"

and
CHRISTIAN ANFINSEN (1916-1995)

Stanford Moore was born in Chicago, US, on September 4, 1913. He received his PhD from Wisconsin University in 1938 and joined the staff of Rockefeller University in New York in 1938. Here he became a professor in 1952.

He is best known for his applications of the technique of chromatography to the analysis of amino acids and peptides. In 1972, he was awarded a share of the Nobel Prize for Chemistry for his research on the molecular structures of proteins.

He died in New York on August 23, 1982. He never married.

William Howard Stein was born in New York, US, on June 25, 1911. His parents were victims of Eastern European anti-Semitism. He received his PhD from Columbia College of Physicians and Surgeons in 1938. He joined the staff of the Rockefeller Institute for Medical Research and made a professor in 1954. Stein spent the period between 1949 and 1963 working out how ribonuclease catalyses the digestion of food.

He discovered new methods of analysing amino-acids obtained from proteins, and used the same method to determine the structure of ribonuclease. He was awarded a share of the Nobel Prize for Chemistry in 1972, for his study of the composition and functioning of the pancreatic enzyme ribonuclease. Later, Stein and Moore worked out the complete sequence of deoxyribonuclease; a molecule twice as complex as ribonuclease. Stein died in New York on February 2, 1980.

He was still only a graduate student when, in 1936, he married Phoebe Hockstader. They had three sons.

Christian **Boehmer Anfinsen** was born in Monessen, Pa: US, on March 26, 1916. He received his PhD from Harvard University in 1943 and, after teaching stints at Pennsylvania and Harvard universities, he joined the Nobel Medical Institute in Stockholm. His research centred on the adaption of the structure of enzymes and other proteins to their physiological activities.

He received in 1972, a share of the Nobel Prize for Chemistry; **"for his work on ribonuclease, especially concerning the connection between the amino acids sequence and the biologically active conformation"**

His work also included research on the relationships between molecular structure and biological function of proteins. His writings include the important, *The Molecular Basis of Evolution* (1959). He died on May 14, 1995 in Randallstown, MD. He was un-married.

PHYSICS

JOHN BARDEEN (1908-1991), LEON COOPER (1930-)
and
JOHN SCHRIEFFER (1931-)

"for their jointly developed theory of superconductivity, usually called the BCS-theory"

John **Bardeen** was born in Madison, Wis: US, on May 23, 1908. He earned his BA and MA in electrical engineering from Wisconsin University and received his PhD in 1936 in mathematical physics, from Princeton University. He became a principle physicist to the US Navy during WW2. He later joined Bell Telephone Laboratories and did research work on the electron-conducting properties of semi-conductors. This led, in 1947, to the invention of the transistor that ushered in the age of microminiature electronic parts.

Bardeen was a professor of engineering and physics at Illinois University between 1951 and 1975. The theory of superconductivity is now called the BCS Theory; this is from the initials of the three men whose theory it was. Bardeen, who in 1956 shared the Nobel Prize for Physics with Schockley and Brattain for their invention of the transistor, was a joint winner of the 1972 Nobel Prize for Physics, for his part in the development of the theory of superconductivity. A keen golfer, he was married with three children and died from lung cancer in Boston on January 30, 1991.

On the day he was to be awarded his 1972 Nobel Prize, Bardeen, the discoverer of the transistor, found he couldn't get his garage door open because the transistor wouldn't operate.

Leon N. Cooper was born in New York on February 28, 1930. He was educated at Columbia University and received his PhD in 1954. He taught at Ohio State University, before joining the staff at Brown University in Providence. There, he was appointed a university professor in 1966 and professor of science in 1974.

His principle contribution to the BCS theory was the discovery in 1956, that electrons, which under normal conditions repel each other, are attracted to each other in superconductors; a condition termed the Cooper electron pairs.

For this work, Cooper was a joint winner of the 1972 Nobel Prize for Physics. His writings include, *An Introduction to the Meaning and Structure of Physics* (1968) and *Methods and Applications of Linear Programming* (1974). He never married.

John Robert Schrieffer was born in Oak Park, Ill: US, on May 31 1931. He was educated at the Massachusetts Institute of Technology, Cambridge, and Illinois University, Urbana. There he received his PhD in 1957. He showed a lot of promise when, as a graduate student, he helped explain why metals lose their electrical resistance at very low temperatures. His principal contribution to the BCS theory, of which he was the S, came to him when travelling on the underground subway.

He taught at Chicago University (1957-59) and Illinois University (1959-62) before joining Cornell University (1969-75). From 1980, he has been professor of physics at the University of California in Santa Barbara.

In 1972, he was a joint winner of the Nobel Prize for Physics for his part in the first successful macroscopic theory of superconductivity. In 1964 he published, *Theory of Superconductivity*.

Schrieffer is married with three children.

PHYSIOLOGY or MEDICINE

GERALD EDELMAN (1929-)
and
RODNEY PORTER (1917-1985)

"for their discoveries concerning the chemical structure of antibodies"

Gerald Maurice Edelman was born in New York on July 1, 1929. His father, a Jewish doctor was not against his son wanting to become a violinist, but pleased when he decided to follow in his footsteps. Gerald was educated at Pennsylvania University and received his PhD from Rockefeller University in 1960. He became a full professor at Rockefeller in 1966 and organised the construction of a precise model of an entire antibody molecule. This was found to be a four-chain structure consisting

of more than 1,300 amino acids.

Edelman, and his team, was then able to identify the exact locations on the molecule where antigenic binding occurs. This work led to his receiving a co- share of the 1972 Nobel Prize for Physiology or Medicine. In 1975 he discovered the proteins called the cell-adhesion molecules, which work to attach individual cells to one another to make tissues. In 1987 he published, *Neural Darwinism: The Theory of Neuronal Group Selection.* He is married with two sons and a daughter.

Rodney Robert Porter was born in Newton-le-Willows, Lancs; England on October 8, 1917. He was educated at Liverpool University and Cambridge University. Between 1949 and 1960, he worked at the Medical Research Institute at Mill Hill in London. He was professor of immunology at St. Mary's Hospital Medical School until 1967, at which time he joined Oxford University. During WW2 Professor Porter served in the British army 1940-46.

Porter, working independently from Edelman, used a fragmentation technique to analyse the antibody structure. In this way, Porter was able to achieve a complete model of the molecule comprising more than 1,300 amino acids. For this work, Porter was co-winner of the 1972 Nobel Prize for Physiology or Medicine. He died in Winchester, Hampshire on September 7, 1985. He never married.

ECONOMICS

JOHN HICKS (1904-1989)
and
KENNETH ARROW (1921-)

John Richard Hicks was born in Leamington Spa, Warks: England on April 8, 1904. Educated at Clifton College and Balliol College, Oxford, he taught at the London School of Economics (1926-35). He was professor of political economy at Manchester (1938-46) and Oxford (1952-65). He was later, for two decades, a fellow of All Souls College, Oxford. He became a Fellow of the British Academy in 1942 and foreign member of Swedish, Italian and American academies.

He wrote a classic book on the conflict between business-cycle theory and equilibrium theory, *Value and Capital* (1939). Other works of note include, *A Theory of Economic History* (1969) and *Casualty in Economics* (1979).

He was knighted in 1964. For his contribution to the equilibrium theory, Hicks was awarded a half share of the 1972 Nobel Prize for Economics; **"for his pioneering contributions to general economic equilibrium"**

He died in Blockley, Glos; on May 20, 1989. He was married to an economist.

Kenneth Joseph Arrow was born in New York on August 23rd 1921. During WW2 he served as a captain in the US Army Air Force. In 1951 he received a PhD from Columbia University and taught at Stanford University (1949-68). From 1968 to 1979, he was professor of economics at Harvard University and there would produce a famous school of economic theorists.

In 1979 he returned to Stanford. Probably his most unusual thesis was the ' impossibility theorem' (Arrow's theorem). This holds that, under certain conditions of rationality and equality, it is impossible to guarantee that a ranking of societal preferences will correspond to rankings of individual preferences, when more than two individuals and alternative choices are involved.

An important contributor to welfare economics, he was awarded a co-share of the 1972 Nobel Prize for Economics; **"for pioneering contributions to economic and welfare theories"**

His writings include, *Social Choice and Individual Values* (1951) and *The Limits of Organization* (1974)   He is married with two sons.

PEACE

NOT AWARDED

1973

Israel's Yom Kippur War • US withdrawal from Vietnam • Britain, Ireland and Denmark join the EC • US Watergate hearings • US backed military junta murder Allende and takeover Chile • Calf produced from a frozen embryo • Peter Shaffer, *Equus* • Film, *Last Tango in Paris, Mean Streets, Badlands, Day for Night, The Sting, Don't Look Now* • Erica Jong, *Fear of Flying* • Graham Greene, *The Honorary Consul* • Noel Coward, Pablo Picasso, Otto Klemperer, David Ben-Gurion, Edward G Robinson, Jacques Lipchitz, John Cranko, Pablo Casals and WH Auden die.

LITERATURE

PATRICK WHITE (1912-1990)

Patrick Victor Martindale White was born in London, England on May 28, 1912. His Australian parents were visiting England at the time of his birth and when Mrs White was deemed able to travel, the family returned to Australia and a sheep farm. 12 years later Patrick returned to the UK and an education. He was at Kings College, Cambridge until WW2, at which time he joined the RAF. Following the war, he returned to Australia and the sheep.   His first novel was, *Happy Valley* (1939), set in New South Wales. Although his later material is largely Australian they have a wider vision.

His books often reflect a sense of isolation with a style that is dense with allegorical meaning. His novels include, *The Tree Man* (1955), *Voss* (1957), *A Fringe of Leaves* (1975) and *The Twyborn Affair* (1979). He also wrote plays that include, *Night on Bald Mountain* (1964). His autobiography, *Flaws in the Glass* (1981) is most frank.

White, who did more than any other writer to put Australia on the international map, was awarded the 1973 Nobel Prize for Literature; **"for an epic and psychological narrative art which has introduced a new continent into literature"**

He died in Sydney, NSW, on September 30, 1990. He never married.

CHEMISTRY

ERNST FISCHER (1918-)
and
GEOFFREY WILKINSON (1921-)

"for their pioneering work, performed independently, on the chemistry of the organometallic, so called sandwich compounds"

Ernst Otto Fischer was born in Munich, Germany on November 10, 1918. During WW2, Fischer served in the German army. Indeed, he was so eager, he enlisted prior to the war commencing. In 1952, he received a doctorate in natural sciences from the Technical University in Munich.

He went on to lecture there between 1954 and 57 and later became professor of the Inorganic Chemistry Institute (1964). A theoretical chemist, he received a half share of the 1973 Nobel Prize for Chemistry for his work investigating and explaining how certain metals and organic substances can merge.

He has spent much time lecturing upon his subject both in Europe and the US. He never married.

Geoffrey Wilkinson was born in Todmorden, Yorkshire, England on July 14, 1921. He studied at the Imperial College, London and between 1943 -46, worked with the Atomic Energy Project in Canada. He taught in Berkeley, at the University of California (1948-50), the Massachusetts Institute of Technology (1950-51) and Harvard University (1951-55). He returned to London University in1956.

His researches on metal to hydrogen bonding, and his discovery of chlorotris, a homogeneous hydrogenation catalyst for alkanes known as Wilkinson's catalyst, has had widespread meaning for organic and inorganic chemistry. This procedure has proven to have very important industrial applications. It all added up to his receiving a half share of the 1973 Nobel Prize for Chemistry. In 1976 he was knighted. Wilkinson is married with two daughters.

PHYSICS

LEO ESAKI (1925-), IVAR GIAEVER (1929-)

"for their experimental discoveries regarding tunneling phenomena in semiconductors and superconductors, respectively"

and
BRIAN JOSEPHSON (1940-)

Leo Esaki was born in Osaka, Japan on March 12, 1925. He graduated in physics from Tokyo University and joined the Kobe Kogyo company. In 1956 he was the chief physicist of the Sony Corporation, where he conducted his researches into superconductivity. In 1959 he received his PhD from Tokyo University.

His later work at Sony dealt with quantum mechanics and, in the main, on the phenomenon of tunneling, in which the wavelength character of matter enables electrons to pass through barriers that the laws of classical mechanics say are impenetrable.

Esaki devised ways to modify the behaviour of solid state semiconductors, by adding impurities. This work led to his invention of the double diode, which became known as the Esaki diode. In 1960 he was awarded an IBM fellowship and was able to conduct further research, this time in the US.

It led him to accept a post at the IBM research laboratories in Yorktown, NY. In 1973 he was awarded a third share of the Nobel Prize for Physics for his work on superconductivity. Esaki remains a Japanese citizen and is unmarried.

Ivar Giaever was born in Bergen, Norway on April 5, 1929. He received and engineering degree from the Norwegian Institute of Technology in Trondheim in 1952, and later became patent examiner for the Norwegian government. In 1954 he migrated to Canada and there worked as a mechanical engineer for the General Electric Company in Ontario.

Two years later, he transferred to the company's development centre in Schenectady, NY. There he developed an interest in physics and worked for his PhD which he received in 1964. Most of his experimental work was in the field of solid state physics with special emphasis on superconductivity.

His later experiments allowed him to produce superconductor devices, that allowed electrons to pass like waves of radiation, through holes in solid-state devices. His work was influenced by both Esaki and Josephson and led to his receiving a third share of the 1973 Nobel Prize for Physics. He is married with four children.

Brian **David Josephson** was born in Cardiff, Wales on January 4, 1940. He came from a middle-class Jewish family who encouraged Brian to enter Trinity College, Cambridge at a young age, and from where he obtained his PhD whilst only 24. He was only 22, when his researches resulted in a process deemed to be so important to electronic development, that it won him election as a Fellow of Trinity College. This discovery became known as, ' The Josephson Effect'.

Whilst still an undergraduate he published the results of his primary work, which dealt with certain aspects of the special theory of relativity and the Mossbauer effect. A brilliant student, no lecturer dare make a mistake in front of him; if he did, he would be gently taken to one side after the class was over, and Josephson would quietly and politely explain his error.

Further research concerned voltage applications and in 1970 he was elected a Fellow of the Royal Society. His work on the Josephson Effect, twinned with his theories of superconductivity, resulted in his being awarded a third share of the 1973 Nobel Prize for Physics; **"for his theoretical predictions of the properties of a supercurrent through a tunnel barrier, in particular those phenomena which are generally known as the Josephson effects"**

He was 33 and one of the youngest persons ever to be awarded a Nobel prize. In 1974 he was appointed professor of physics at Cambridge. For physical recreation, Josephson had taken to mountain walking, this later developed his interest in Eastern mysticism as it refers to scientific understanding. It led to his co-writing, with V.S. Ramachandran, *Consciousness and the Physical World* (1980). In 1980, using Josephson's discoveries, scientists made an experimental computer with switch structures 100 times faster than previously possible with silicon-based chips. He is un-married.

PHYSIOLOGY or MEDICINE

KARL FRSICH (1886-1982), KONRAD LORENZ (1903-1989)
and
NIKO TINBERGEN (1907-1988)

"for their discoveries concerning organization and elicitation of individual and social behaviour patterns"

Karl **von Frisch** was born in Vienna, Austria on November 20, 1886. He received his PhD from Munich University in 1910 and went to work at the Zoological Institution of Rostock University; in 1921 he was appointed its' director. In 1923, he was doing the same thing at Breslau University. In 1925, he was back at Munich University where he established a zoological department. The zoo was destroyed during WW2 and Frisch didn't return until 1950. He then stayed until his retirement in 1958.

In 1910, he was able to prove that fish could distinguish colour and brightness differences. He later proved that their hearing was superior to that of humans. Frisch is however, best known for his work on the behaviour of bees. In 1919, he was able to demonstrate that bees can be trained to distinguish between various tastes and odours. He found that bees can communicate the distance and direction of a food supply to other members of the colony, by two types of rhymic movements or dances; circling and wagging.

The circling dance indicates food is within about 75m of the hive, whilst the wagging dance indicates a greater distance. In 1949 Frisch established that bees, via their perception of polarized light, use the Sun as a compass. He also found that they are capable of using this method of navigation when the Sun is not visible, thus proving they remember patterns of polarization presented by the sky at differing times of the day, and the location of previously met landmarks.

For his work in advancing our knowledge of the chemical and visual sensors of insects, Frisch was awarded a third share of the 1973 Nobel Prize for Physiology or Medicine. He died in Munich on June 12, 1982. He never married.

Konrad Lorenz was born in Vienna, Austria on November 7, 1903. He was the son of an orthopaedic surgeon and showed an early interest in the behaviour pattern of animals. He kept many species; fish, birds, monkeys, rabbits, cats and dogs. A local zoo entrusted him to look after their sick animals and write up a daily report. In 1922, he graduated from secondary school and followed this by studying medicine at Columbia University in New York. He later returned to Vienna University, from where he received his MD in 1928. Zoology was however his greater interest and in which he received a PhD in 1933.

He established colonies of birds that included jackdaws and greylag goose, and published research papers based upon his observations, thus gaining an international reputation. A rather spectacular experiment, to prove bird fostering, was when a newly hatched mallard duck heard Lorenz imitating his mother's quacking sounds, and promptly adopted him as his father.

In 1936, Lorenz convinced Hitler to allow the founding of the German Society for Animal Psychology. Between 1940 and 42, he was a professor at the Albertus University at Konigsberg. In 1942 he was called to serve as a doctor in the German Army and sent to the Russian Front. There he was captured by the Russians and held until 1948. Following various posts at various universities, Lorenz was appointed, in 1961, the director of the Max Planck Institute, retiring in 1973. He was awarded a third share of the 1973 Nobel Prize for Physiology or Medicine for his work in modern ethology and the study of animal behaviour by means of comparitive zoological methods.

He died in Altenburg, Austria on February 27, 1989. Amongst his writings, *On Aggression* (1963) he argues that whilst aggression behaviour in man is inborn, it may be modified or channelled into other forms of activity. He was married without children.

Nikolaas Tinbergen was born in The Hague, Netherlands, on April 15,1907. He is the brother of Jan Tinbergen, the economist and co-recipient of the first Nobel Prize for Economics (1969). Nikolaas received a PhD in 1932 from Leiden University and taught there until 1949. He then joined Oxford University (1949-1974), where he founded a research department on animal behaviour.

He became a British citizen in 1955. In the early 1970s, he began studying and comparing human behaviour and behavioral disorders particularly autism.   He maintained that infantile autism, characterized by extreme self-absorption and withdrawal from reality, is primarily emotional, and the result of severely overestimated anxiety. His writings on this subject include, *Early Childhood Autism; An Ethological Approach* (1972)

In 1973 Tinbergen received a third share of the Nobel Prize for Physiology or Medicine for his work in revitalizing the science of ethology. His writings on the subject include, *Social Behaviour of Animals* (1953) and *Animal Behaviour* (1965). Probably his most important work was, *The Study of Instinct* (1951) that explores the work of the European ethological school up to that time. He died in Oxford, England on December 21, 1988. He was married without children.

ECONOMICS

WASSILY LEONTIEF (1906-1999)

Wassily Leontief was born in Leningrad, Russia on August 5,1906. He was a student at Leningrad University (1921-25) and at Berlin University (1925-28). He went to the US in 1931 and taught at Harvard University (1931-1975). Between 1948 and 1975, he was also director of the Harvard Economic Research Project on the Structure of the American Economy.

In 1975, he was appointed professor of economics at New York University. At the heart of his complex input-output system, is a grid-like table showing what individual industries buy from and sell to one another. With the additon of government, consumers, foreign countries and other elements, there emerges a general outline of the goods and services circulating in a national economy. This method, originated by Leontief, is used, in some form or other, by some 50 industrialized countries for planning and forecasting.

He is also known for developing linear programming, a mathematical technique for solving complex problems of economic operations. He created what has become known as the 'Leontief Paradox', namely that the number one capitalist country, the US, finds it harder to secure finance than labour. In 1973 Leotief was awarded the Nobel Prize for Economics; **"for the development of the input-output method and for its application to important economic problems"**

He died in 1999. He was married with a daughter.

PEACE

HENRY KISSINGER (1923-)
and
LE DUC THO (1911-1990)

Henry Alfred Kissinger was born in Fuerth, Germany on May27, 1923. His father was a schoolteacher and the Kissingers, father and two sons, had the odd distinction of being expelled from school on the same day. Their common offence was being Jewish. By 1938 the family had seen the light, left Germany for the US and settled in New York. Henry combined working with learning and eventually graduated from high school at the top of his year. During WW2, he served in the US Army winding up with the occupation forces in Germany. Here he worked as an administrator and interpreter.

In 1954 he obtained a PhD from Harvard University and stayed on to teach. He subsequently held a series of government posts and eventually appeared to specialize in the role of peace negotiator.

In 1972, he was instrumental in organizing President Nixon's historic visits to Moscow and Peking. Whilst these visits were considered by some, to take the heat off Nixon and distract from the Watergate affair, they did open the door that led to better relations between the Cold War superpowers.

In 1973, Kissinger, following his appointment as US Secretary of State, concluded the Vietnam war settlement. His opposite number was Le Duc Tho. Both men were awarded the 1973 Nobel Prize for Peace. Tho declined to accept his award.

Kissinger continued his shuttle diplomacy concerned with the Middle East process. In the 1950s and 60s, Kissinger appears to have been the voice of reason among the hawks in American politics. However, in the film, *Nixon*, Oliver Stone has Kissinger as a hawk advocating an extension to the Vietnam bombing campaign. The exact extent of Kissinger's possible involvement in the Watergate scandal has never been fully explored; perhaps he was 'Deep Throat'! In 1971, in an interview with the *New York Times*, he said, ' Power is the ultimate aphrodisiac'.

His writings include, *American Foreign Policy* (1969), *The White House Years* (1979) and *For the Record* (1981). He now appears to enjoy a lifestyle with an emphasis on parties, to which he escorts attractive ladies of the moment. It is said that his humour is at the root of his appeal. However, his involvement in backing Suharto, the Indonesian despot, in the takeover of East Timor has never satisfactorily been explained. In a live BBC radio programme in the summer of 1999, he had a flaming row with the well regarded presenter, Jeremy Paxman and walked out of the studio.

Married twice he has two children.

Le Duc Tho, whose original name was Phan Dinh Khai, was born in Nam Ha province, Vietnam, on October 14,1911. He was one of the founders of the Indochinese Communist Party of 1930. For his part in this work he was imprisoned by the French in two distinct periods; 1930-36 and 1939-44. Following his second release he returned to Hanoi in 1945 and helped lead the Viet Minh, a militant independence party, and the Vietnam Workers' Party. He was the senior party official in South Vietnam when the country was liberated from French control and split North and South. The Communist Party, dominant in the North and a right wing government, backed by the US, in the South.

The Vietnam war of 1955-75 saw Tho directing operations against the US puppet government, whilst living in hiding in South Vietnam. He came into prominence whilst acting as an advisor to the North Vietnam delegation at the Paris Peace Conferences (1968-73), eventually becoming his delegation's principal spokesman. As such, he negotiated the cease-fire agreement that led to the withdrawal of remaining US troops from Vietnam.

For this work Tho was awarded a half share of the 1973 Nobel Prize for Peace. He declined to accept. He remained a member of the Politburo until his retirement in 1986. He died in Hanoi on October 13, 1990.

1974

Nixon resigns US presidency • Cyprus Partitioned • Chinese emperor's 'terracotta army' discovered • Warning that chlorofluorocarbons might damage the atmosphere's ozone layer • The first Grand Unified Theory about the origins of the Universe • Films: *Chinatown, Last Tango in Paris, The Enigma of Kaspar Hauser, Lacombe , Lucien* • Nadine Gordimer, *The Conservationist,* Jennifer Johnston, *How Many Miles to Babylon?* • Philip Larkin, *High Windows* • Jack Benny, David Oistrakh, Darius Milhaud, Walter Lippmann, Sam Goldwyn, Jacob Bronowski and Duke Ellington die.

LITERATURE

EYVIND JOHNSON (1900-1976)
and
HARRY MARTINSON (1904-1978)

Eyvind Johnson was born in Svartbjornsbyn, Sweden on July 29, 1900. He lived close to the region of the Arctic Circle. It was a hard life and he suffered a grim boyhood. He had little schooling but a lot of imagination. Thus armed, he travelled south into an area that was slowly recovering from a world war, a war that had centred upon Europe. His early novels, said to be influenced by Proust and Joyce, are mostly concerned with man's frustration.

In *Bobinack* (1932), he exposes the machinations of capitalism. In *Rain at Daybreak*

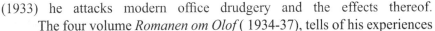

(1933) he attacks modern office drudgery and the effects thereof.

The four volume *Romanen om Olof* (1934-37), tells of his experiences as a logger working in the sub-arctic. His later novels attack totalitarian terror and neutralism.

Return to Ithaca (1952) and *The Days of his Grace* (1960), have been translated into many languages. He received a co- share of the 1974 Nobel Prize for Literature; **"for a narrative art, farseeing in lands and ages, in the service of freedom"**

He was one of the few working class writers to be so honoured. He died in Stockholm on August 25, 1976. He was married twice and had three children.

Harry Edmund Martinson was born in Jamshog, Sweden on May 6, 1904. He spent his childhood in a series of foster homes receiving little love and much punishment. He spent his youth, and early adulthood, as a merchant seaman and, when he couldn't get work as a labourer, as a vagrant. He wrote of his experiences. First in poetry, *Ghost Ship* (1929) and later in his autobiographical novels, *Flowering Nettle* (1935) and *The Way Out* (1936).

In *The Road* (1948), he sympathetically examines the life of tramps and other social outcasts. He was also responsible for the poem that became an opera, *Aniara, A Review of Man in Time and Space (1956).* Martinson, a self taught working class writer, was awarded a co- share of the 1974 Nobel Prize for Literature; **"for writings that catch the dewdrop and reflect the cosmos"**

He died in Stockholm on February 11,1978. Between 1929 and 1940, he was married to the writer, Moa Martinson.

CHEMISTRY

PAUL FLORY (1910-1985)

Paul John Flory was born in Sterling, Ill, US, on June 19,1910. He was educated at Manchester College, North Manchester, Ind, and Ohio State University from where in 1934, he obtained his PhD.

Thereafter, he worked at the universities of Cincinnati and Cornel and in industry, with Standard Oil and the Goodyear Tyre Company. Between 1961 and 1976, he was a professor of chemistry at Stanford University becoming, Emeritus in 1976

His scientific researches included polymers and the eventual production of nylon and synthetic rubber. His further researches included an appreciation of these flexible products and the importance of establishing a relationship between their chemical structures and their physical properties.

For his work on synthetics, Flory was awarded the 1974 Nobel Prize for Chemistry.; **"for his fundamental achievements, both theoretical and experimental, in the physical chemistry of the macromolecules"**

He died in Big Sur, Calif. on September 9, 1985. He married Emily Tabor in 1936 and had three children.

PHYSICS

ANTONY HEWISH (1924-)
and
MARTIN RYLE (1918-1984)

"for their pioneering research in radio astrophysics: Ryle for his observations and inventions, in particular of the aperture synthesis technique, and Hewish for his decisive role in the discovery of pulsars"

Antony Hewish was born in Fowey, Cornwall, England on May 11,1924. He was educated at Cambridge University and, in 1946, joined the university's radio astronomy group led by Martin Ryle. Hewish was director of a research project at Mullard Radioastronomy Observatory, Cambridge, when he realised the significance of an observation, made by Jocelyn Bell, a graduate assistant.

Hewish concluded that the regularly patterned radio signals, that Bell had detected, were not caused by earthly interference, or perhaps by intelligent life on another planet, but from energy emissions from certain stars.

In 1971, he was appointed professor of radio astronomy at the Cavendish Laboratory, Cambridge. As a result of his discovery of pulsars, Hewish was awarded a co- share of the 1974 Nobel Prize for Physics, the first time the prize was awarded for observational astronomy.

He is married with a son.

Martin Ryle was born in Brighton, Sussex, England, on September 27, 1918. The nephew of the philosopher, Gilbert Ryle, Martin was educated at Oxford University from where in 1939, he received a degree in physics. During WW2, he was occupied in developing radar equipment so essential to the RAF and Royal Navy. Following the war, Ryle received a fellowship at the prestigious Cavendish Laboratory. There he researched extraterrestrial radio sources and, using the principles of radar, developed an advanced radio telescope.

In 1957, he was director of the Mullard Radio Astronomy Observatory. He was elected to the Royal Society in 1952 and knighted in 1966 and served as Astronomer Royal (1972-82). His work on the study of radio waves of the Sun, sunspots and local stars allowed him to guide the Cambridge radio astronomy group and produce radio source guides. The *Third Cambridge Catalogue* (1959), helped lead to the discovery of the first quasar. In order to map quasars, Ryle developed a technique he called aperture synthesis, a process that called into use the aid of two radio telescopes.

For his work in developing the revolutionary radio telescope systems and using them for the accurate location of weak radio sources, Ryel was awarded a co- share of the 1974 Nobel Prize for Physics. He died in Cambridge on October 14, 1984. He married in 1947 and had three children. His hobby was sailing small boats which he designed and built.

PHYSIOLOGY or MEDICINE

ALBERT CLAUDE (1898-1983), CHRISTAIN du DUVE (1917-)
and
GEORGE PALADE (1912-)

"for their discoveries concerning the structural and functional organization of the cell"

Albert Claude was born in Longlier, Belgium, on August 24, 1898. He was educated at Liege University from where, in 1928, he obtained his PhD Awarded a research scholarship, he continued at Rockefeller University in New York. There he was trying to isolate the Rous sarcoma virus from chicken tumours. The virus was in centrifuges which when he spun them sent the heavier particles to the bottom and the lighter particles settled in layers above.

To make the comparison he centrifuged normal cells. Thus Claude was able to deduce that separated particles consisted of distinct organelles. This analysis allowed him to discover the endoplasmic reticulum and to understand the function of the mitochondria, as the centre of respiratory activity.

He then took to the electron microscope and his demonstration into the activity of cell-life, allowed scientists to correlate the biological activity of each cellular part, with its structure and its place in the cell. For this work, upon which modern biology is partly based, Claude was awarded a third share of the 1974 Nobel Prize for Physiology or Medicine. Although becoming a US citizen in 1941 he never gave up his Belgian nationality. He has dual citizenship and this allows him to hold professorships in both Rockefeller and Brussels universities.

Between 1948 to 1971, he was also director of the Jules Bordet Institute. He died in Brussels on May 22, 1983. He was un-married.

Christian Rene de Duve was born in Thames Ditton, Surrey, England on October 2, 1917. His parents were Belgians, but Christian received his early education in Surrey. In 1941 he received his MD from the Catholic Louvain University. He returned there to teach in 1947.

Whilst researching the effect of insulin on liver tissue in 1949, he noticed a delay in the action of enzymes that break down cell material, suggesting the enzymes were enclosed within a membranous envelope. He reckoned the possible size of this organelle, christened it the lysosome, and later identified it in electron microscope pictures.

He refined the cell fractionation techniques of Albert Claude, in order to isolate the lysosomes and peroxisomes for study. From 1962, de Duve simultaneously headed research laboratories at Louvain and at the Rockefeller University in New York. For his work in discovering lysosomes, or the digestive organelles of the cell and peroxisomes, or organelles that are the site of metabolic processes, de Duve was awarded a third share of the 1974 Nobel Prize for Physiology or Medicine. He is married with four children.

George Emil Palade was born in Lasi, Romania on November 19, 1912. He received his PhD from Bucharest University in 1940 and remained there as a professor until the end of WW2. He then left for the US and Rockefeller University in New York.

Palade's most important discovery was that microsomes, or bodies formerly thought to be fragments of mitochondria, are actually parts of the endoplasmic reticulum and have a high ribonucleic acid content (RNA). These became known as ribosomes. In 1952, Palade became a US citizen and in 1958 was professor of cytology at the Rockefeller Institute until 1972, at which time he left for Yale University Medical School.

He was awarded a third share of the 1974 Nobel Prize for Physiology or Medicine, for his work in conducting electron microscopy studies resulting in the discovery of several cellular structures. Married twice he has two children.

ECONOMICS

GUNNAR MYRDAL (1898-1987)
and
FRIEDRICH von HAYEK (1899-1992)

"For their pioneering work in the theory of money and economic fluctuations and for their penetrating analysis of the interdependence of economic, social and institutional phenomena"

Gunnar Karl Myrdal was born in Gustafs, Dalecarlia, Sweden on December 6,1898. He was educated at Stockholm University from where he gained a PhD in economics in 1927. He received a Rockefeller travelling scholarship which took him to the US and, upon his return to Sweden, he was appointed professor of political economy at Stockholm University (1933-1967). He was later Emeritus professor of International Economy. At the invitation of the Carnegie Corporation, NY, Myrdal explored the social and economic problems of blacks in the US, 1938-40 and as a result wrote, *An American Dilemma: The Negro Problem and Modern Democracy* (1944).

Here Myrdal presented his theory of cumulative causation, i.e. poverty breeding poverty. This idea became a feature of his writings and lectures on economic developments. He argues that rather than rich and poor countries converging with economic development, they might well diverge with the poor countries becoming poorer, as the rich countries enjoyed economies of scale, whilst the poor ones were forced to rely upon primary products. Between 1947 and 1957, Myrdal was secretary-general of the United Nations Economic Commission for Europe. He published many works upon his subject including, *The Political Element in the Development of Economic Theory* (1930 and 1953), *Beyond the Welfare State : Economic Planning and its International Implications* (1960) and *Asian Drama: An Inquiry into the Poverty of Nations* (1968). His innovative ideas on economic and social growth for underdeveloped nations, created world-wide reassessment of the existing economics system. As a result, Myrdal was awarded a half share of the 1974 Nobel Prize for Economics. He died in Stockholm on May 17, 1987.

He was married and had three children.

Friedrich August von Hayek was born in Vienna, Austria on May 8,1899. The son of a professor of botany at Vienna University, Friedrich served in the Austrian Army during WW1. He studied a mixture of law, psychology and economics and received a doctorate from Vienna University in 1923. He took a year off, to study at New York University, following which he returned to Vienna to become director of the Austrian Institute of Economic Research. In 1931 he moved to the UK becoming a British citizen in 1938. During WW2, he taught at London University and at the London School of Economics.

Between 1950-62, he was professor of social and moral science at

Chicago University.   Hayek's view was that governmental control of, or intervention in a free market, only forestalls such economic ailments as inflation, unemployment, recession and depression. His published works include, *The Road to Serfdom* (1944), *The Constitution of Liberty* (1960) and *Unemployment and Monetary Policy: Government as Generator of the Business Cycle* (1979).

A critic of Keynes and his welfare state, Hayek, an admitted conservative, was praised by Margaret Thatcher when he stated ' You can't buck the market" He was awarded a co- share of the 1974 Nobel Prize for Economics, probably as a counter to Gunner Myrdal an economic liberal. Hayek died in Freiburg, Germany on March 23, 1992. He was married with a son and daughter.

PEACE

SEAN MacBRIDE (1904-1988)
and
EISAKU SATO (1901-1975)

Sean MacBride was born in Paris, France on January 26, 1904. His father was executed by the British, for the part he played in the Easter Uprising in Dublin of 1916. His mother was the Irish actress and patriot, Maud Gonne. Sean followed in his parents footsteps and by the age of 24, was chief of staff of the IRA. He worked as a journalist and later qualified as a lawyer.

Following partition, MacBride continued to fight for a united Ireland until 1947, when he accepted the situation that warfare was futile. He become a member of the House of Representatives for the party he founded in 1936, the Republican Party. He was minister of external affairs (1948-51) and in 1950 was president of the Council of Foreign Ministers of the Council of Europe.

He was most active in the field of human rights and chairman of Amnesty International between 1961 and 1975. In 1973 he was the United Nations assistant secretary-general and in 1977 was appointed president of the International Commission for the Study of Communication Problems that was started by UNESCO.

For his continuing work, MacBride was awarded a half share of the 1974 Nobel Peace Prize; **"for his efforts on behalf of human rights"**
He died in Dublin, Eire on January 15, 1988. He never married.

Eisaku Sato was born in Tabuse, Japan on March 27, 1901. He graduated in 1924 with a law degree from Tokyo University. He joined the Ministry of Railways becoming its bureau control chief in 1941. In 1948 he was vice-minister for transport and joined the Liberal Party. A year later he was an MP.

In 1953 he resigned from his post as minister of construction, to become chief secretary of the Liberal Party. A year later, his party merged with the Democratic Party and Sato was a leading member and cabinet member of the government of Ikeda Hayato. When Ikeda announced his resignation, because of ill-health, he named Sato his successor.

Now prime minister, Sato oversaw his country reach an era of prosperity, previously

unknown. He undertook the improvement of Japanese-Asian relations.

However, the People's Republic of China mistrusted him. They disliked Japanese support for American aggression in Vietnam. In 1969, Sato reached agreement with US President Nixon, for the return of Ryukyu Islands and this was effected in 1972. In the early 1970s, problems arose over the huge surpluses as a result of one-sided trading between the US and Japan. Sato needed new markets and sought these in Europe and the USSR. However, he became increasingly unpopular and, in June 1972, he resigned.

Sato was awarded a half-share of the 1974 Nobel Peace; **"for his work on nuclear weapons, leading to Japan signing the Treaty on the Non-proliferation of Nuclear Weapon"**

He died in Tokyo on June 3,1975. He married in 1926 and had two sons.

1975

North Vietnamese triumphant • British North Sea Oil begins • Civil war in Lebanon • Spanish monarchy restored • The first monoclonal antibodies produced • 'Lucy' discovered, the remains of a hominid some 3 million years old found in Ethiopia • Films; *One Flew Over the Cuckoo's Nest, Picnic at Hanging Rock* • Bob Dylan, *Blood on the Tracks* • Arthur Ashe wins Wimbledon-the first black Men's singles champion • Saul Bellow, *Humboldt's Gift* • E.L.Doctorow, *Ragtime* • Ruth Prawer Jhabvala, *Heat and Dust* • Julian Huxley, Chiang Kai-shek, de Valera, Franco, Haile Selassie, Hannah Arendt, Josephine Baker, Barbara Hepworth and Dmitry Shostakovich die.

LITERATURE

EUGENIO MONTALE (1896-1981)

Eugenio Montale was born in Genoa, Italy on October 12, 1896. A veteran of WW1, he became an immediate opponent of Fascism, when it made an appearance in the early 1920s. Co-founder in 1922 of *Primo tempo*, a literary journal, he published his first book of poetry, *Cuttlefish Bones,* in 1925. Further works included, *The House of the Custom's Officer and other Poems* (1932), *The Occasions* (1939), The obscure, *Land's End* (1943). In 1956 his *The Storm and other Poems* won for Montale the Marzotto Prize and became a landmark for his change of style.

Now his writings showed a skill and warmth previously missing. Further works continued in this style and included , *Satura* (1962),

Harmony and Pastels (1962), *The Offender* (1966) and *Xenia* written in 1966 in memory of his wife who died in 1963.

Although principally a poet, he also worked as a translator, prose writer and editor. In 1975 he was awarded the Nobel Prize for Literature; **"for his distinctive poetry which, with great artistic sensitivity, has interpreted human values under the sign of an outlook on life with no illusions"**

He died in Milan on September 12, 1981. He never married.

CHEMISTRY

JOHN CORNFORTH (1917-)
and
VLADIMIR PRELOG (1906-)

John Warcup Cornforth was born in Sydney, Australia on September 7,1917. From an early age, Cornforth became progressively deaf, although he graduated from Sydney University in 1937 and went to England to obtain a PhD from Oxford University in 1941. During WW2, he worked to determine the structure of the central molecule of penicillin.

In 1946, he joined the staff of the National Institute for Medical Research in London and remained until 1962. He worked for Shell Research Ltd, from 1962-68 and was director 1968-75. He later became Royal Society research professor in the School of Molecular Sciences at Sussex University until 1982.

His researches resulted in a new appreciation of the stereo chemistry of enzymic processes, in particular, the biosynthesis of sterols and terpenoids. For this work he was awarded a co- share of the 1975 Nobel prize for Chemistry; **"for his work on the stereo chemistry of enzyme-catalysed reactions"**

He was knighted in 1977 and became a foreign member of the American Academy of Arts and Sciences in 1973 and of the National Academy of Sciences in 1978. He is married.

Vladimir Prelog was born in Sarajevo, Bosnia, on July 23 1906. He was educated at the Institute Technical School of Chemistry in Prague and received his doctorate in 1929. He spent some years in a commercial laboratory before teaching at Zagreb University in 1935. In 1942 he joined the faculty of the Federal Institute of Technology in Zurich, where he was head of the laboratory of organic chemistry from 1957 to 1965.

He retired in 1976. His research extended to the stereo chemistry of alkaloids, antibiotics, enzymes and other natural compounds. Probably his most important research, and one which earned him a co- share of the 1975 Nobel Prize for Chemistry; **"for his research into stereo chemistry of organic molecules and reactions"**

This was fundamentally important to the understanding of biological processes, as was his study and research into the stereo chemistry of organic molecules and reactions. He is married with a child.

PHYSICS

AAGE BOHR (1922-), BEN MOTTELSON (1926-)
and
JAMES RAINWATER (1917-1986)

"for the discovery of the connection between collective motion and particle motion in atomic nuclei and the development of the theory of the structure of the atomic nucleus based on this connection"

Aage Niels Bohr was born in Copenhagen, Denmark on June 19,1922. It was the year his father Niels Bohr was awarded the Nobel Prize for Physics. Aage would follow in his footsteps. However, in September 1943, his father was tipped off that the Germans were about to arrest him and his family because they were Jewish. That night they escaped to Malmo, Sweden in an old fishing boat.

Aage then worked as an assistant to his father in Los Alamos, US on the development of the atomic bomb. The war over, the family returned to Denmark and his education continued at Copenhagen University from where he received his doctorate in 1957. Following his father's death in 1962 he became director of the Niels Bohr Institute until 1970.

His experiments, whilst working with Ben Mottelson, in the early 1950s led to his discovering that the motion of subatomic particles can distort the shape of nucleus. This challenged the widely held theory that all nuclei are perfectly spherical. This discovery, inspired by the theories of James Rainwater, was most important for the understanding and development of nuclear fusion. He is married with three children.

Ben Roy Mottelson was born in Chicago, Ill, US, on July 9, 1926. The grandson of a rabbi, Mottelson's father was a engineer. Ben graduated during WW2 and the US Navy sent him to Purdue University for officers training and from where he received a BS. He received his PhD from Harvard University in theoretical physics in 1950. He then accepted a fellowship at the Niels Bohr Institute of Theoretical Physics in Copenhagen.

He later taught at the Nordic Institute for Theoretical Nuclear Physics and became a Danish citizen. His work with Aage Bohr, that proved that asymmetries occur in atoms of all elements resulted in his being awarded a third share of the 1975 Nobel Prize for Physics.

He married in 1948 and has three children. The family became Danish citizens in 1971.

Leo James Rainwater was born in Council, Idaho, US on December 9,1917. Educated at the California Institute of Technology and Columbia University, he received his PhD in 1946. During WW2, he worked on the development of the atomic bomb and in 1949 began working on the theory that not all atomic nuclei are spherical, as was then generally believed. However, it wasn't until Bohr and Mottelson experimented and later proved the Rainwater theory, that he would be honoured with the third share of the 1975 Nobel Prize for Physics.

He was professor of physics at Columbia from 1952 and later Pupin Professor at Columbia from 1982. He continued research especially into X-rays and was awarded the Atomic Energy Commission's Ernest Orlando Lawrence Prize for Physics in 1963. He died in New York on May 31,1986. He married in 1942 and had three sons and a daughter.

PHYSIOLOGY or MEDICINE

DAVID BALTIMORE (1938-), RENATO DULBECCO (1914-)
and
HOWARD TEMIN (1934-)

"for their discoveries concerning the interaction between tumour viruses and genetic material of the cell"

David Baltimore was born in New York, US, on March 7,1938. The son in a middle class Jewish family, he graduated from Swarthmore College, Pennsylvania and received his PhD from Rockefeller Institute, New York, in 1964. He later did post graduate work at the Massachusetts Institute of Technology. He met Dulbecco, when they were both at the Salk Institute in La Jolla, California, (1965-68). He then returned to teach at MIT.

Baltimore's area of research was in animal cancers. He discovered that some viruses are composed mainly of ribonucleic acid (RNA) and can transfer their genetic information to deoxyribonucleic acid (DNA). This DNA in turn, alters the hereditary pattern of the cell infected by the virus into a cancer cell. He went on to show that the virus causing vesicular stoma titis, reproduced itself through the action of an enzyme that copies RNA by a process that does not involve DNA. In 1970, he tested two cancer viruses to discover if they did anything similar. He found that both contained an enzyme that made DNA copies of the viral RNA, thereby reversing the common pattern of molecular biology, i.e. that genetic information always passes from DNA to RNA. For this substantial research Baltimore received a third share of the 1975 Nobel Prize for Physiology or Medicine.

In 1990, he became president of Rockefeller University. Some 18 months later in a controversial dispute, he resigned. However, he remained a member of the university faculty. He is un-married.

Renato Dulbecco was born in Catanzaro, Italy on February 22,1914. He received his MD from Turin University in 1936 and began teaching there. In 1947 he left for the US and Indiana University, followed by the California Institute of Technology (1949-63). He was a fellow at the Salk Institute for Biological Studies in La Jolla (1963-72), returning in 1977 as a research professor after 5 years as a director of the Imperial Cancer Research in London.

He pioneered the growing of animal viruses in culture in the 1950s and later investigated how certain viruses gain control of the cells they infect. He showed that the polyoma virus, which produces tumours in mice, inserts its DNA into the DNA of the host cell.

The cell then undergoes transformation into a cancer cell, reproducing the viral DNA along with its own and producing more cancer cells. He later suggested that human cancers could be caused by similar reproduction of foreign DNA fragments. For his research Dulbecco was awarded a third share of the 1975 Nobel Prize for Physiology or Medicine.
He is married with two children.

Howard **Martin Temin** was born in Philadelphia, Pa. US, on December 10, 1934. Born into a middle class Jewish family Tumin obtained his PhD from the California Institute of Technology where Dulbecco was his teacher, in 1959. Whilst working on his thesis he investigated how the Rous Sarcoma virus causes cancer in animals. One particular stumbling block was that the viruses main ingredient, ribonucleic acid (RNA) could not infect the cell if the synthesis of deoxyribonucleic acid (DNA) was halted.

It was Temin who, in 1965, suggested that somehow the virus turned its RNA into DNA, redirecting the reproductive activity of the cell and turning it into a cancer cell. That cell would then produce this DNA together with its own DNA, thus producing more cancer cells. His critics claimed that this thesis contradicted the laws of molecular biology, i.e. that genetic information always passed from DNA to RNA and not the reverse.

In 1970, Temin was proven correct and in 1975 was awarded a third share of the Nobel Prize for Physiology or Medicine. He is married with two daughters.

ECONOMICS

TJALLING KOOPMANS (1910-1985)
and
LEONID KANTOROVICH (1912-1986)

"for their contributions to the theory of optimum allocation of resources"

Tjalling Charles Koopmans was born in Graveland, Netherlands on August 28, 1910. He was educated in mathematics and physics at Utrecht and Leiden universities, obtaining his PhD in economics from Leiden in 1936. In 1940, he was in the US working for the British Merchant Mission during WW2. His work was concerned with the selection of shipping routes that would minimize the total cost of transporting required quantities of goods from locations in the US to certain destinations in the UK.

He demonstrated that the result was obtainable by the straightforward solution of a system of equations involving the costs of the materials at their source and the cost of shipping them by alternative routes. He also devised a mathematical model of the problem to show the required equations.

In 1944 Koopmans joined the Cowles Commission for research in Economics at Chicago University and there he extended his technique to a wide variety of economic problems. In 1955 the commission relocated to Yale University and he was appointed professor of economics at Yale. Probably his most important publication was *Three Essays on the State of Economic Science* (1957). Koopmans, now a US citizen, was awarded a half share of the 1975 Nobel Prize for Economics, for his work on activity analysis. He died in New Haven, Conn. on February 26, 1985. He was married with three children.

Leonid Vitalyevich Kantorovich was born in St. Petersburg, Russia on January 19, 1912. He was educated at Leningrad State University, where he received his PhD at the age of 18. He was a professor there in 1934, a position he held right through WW2 until 1960. From 1961 to 1971 he was head of the mathematics department of the USSR Academy of Sciences, before switching to head the government research department of the Institute of National Economic Planning (1971-76). Although Jewish he never experienced any anti-Semitic problems and in 1964 was elected to the Academy of Sciences of the Soviet Union. In 1965 he was awarded the Lenin Prize.

He was a world expert on the .rational utilization of scarce resources and their optimal allocation. He pioneered the method of linear programming, as a part of economic planning. He went to develop the concept known as resolving multipliers, in a country where critical analysis of Soviet economic policy differed from his ideas of practical economics. He maintained that the Soviet Union failed to achieve top economic growth because of failure to invest. His several publications include, *The Best Use of Economic Resources* (1959). In 1975 Kantorovich was awarded a half share of the Nobel Prize for Economics. He died in Russia on April 7,1986. He was married with two children.

PEACE

ANDREY SAKHAROV (1921-1989)

Andrey **Dmitriyevich Sakharov** was born Moscow, Russia on May 21, 1921. The son of a physicist, Andrey won a doctorate when he was 26 and became a full member of the Soviet Academy of Sciences by the age of 32. By this time he had spent several years working with Igor Tamm (qv) who was awarded the Nobel Prize for Physics in 1958. He was a theoretical physicist who enjoyed the luxuries and honours heaped upon him. In 1961, he protested against Khrushchev's plan to test a 100-megaton hydrogen bomb designed to show the world how strong the USSR was. It was the time of the Cuban crisis and President Kennedy was sabre rattling.

Sakharov feared the effects of a widespread radioactive fallout. Three years later he was mobilizing opposition to the later discredited biologist, T.D. Lysenko's doctrines of racial purity. In 1968 he published his essay, *Progress, Coexistence and Intellectual Freedom*, that called for the nuclear arms race to end and predicted how communist and capitalist systems should merge into a form of democratic socialism. In 1971 he married the human rights activist, Yelena Bonner.

The couple became increasingly at odds with the Soviet government, and speaking out against repression. He denounced the Soviet adventure into Afghanistan and called for a world wide boycott of the Moscow Olympic Games. In 1980, he was stripped of his honours and banished to the city of Gorky. In 1986 he was released and the government allowed the couple to return to Moscow. In April 1989 Sakharov was elected to the People's Congress and had his honours restored. He died a few months later in Moscow on December 14, 1989. In 1975 he was awarded the Nobel Peace Prize for his work on human rights and civil liberties.

1976

Death of Chairman Mao • Jimmy Carter is US President • Legionnaire's disease named • Concorde begins regular passenger service • Amnesty for Spanish political prisoners • German campaigner Ulrike Meinhof commits suicide in prison • J.M.Roberts, *History of the World* • Noam Chomsky, *Reflections on Langauge* • Barry Humphries, *Housewife-Superstar* • Films: *Network, All the President's Men, Face to Face, Taxi Driver* • R.K. Narayan, *The Painter of Signs* • Agatha Christie, René Cassin, Paul Robeson, Chou En-lie, General Montgomery, Max Ernst, Howard Hughes, Fritz Lang, Man Ray, Andre Malraux, Lee J Cobb, Max Ernst, Benjamin Britten die.

LITERATURE

SAUL BELLOW (1915-)

Saul Bellow was born in Lachine, Montreal, Canada on June 10,1915. His Russian Jewish parents brought him up in a Yiddish speaking household. Shortly after his birth, his parents moved to Montreal and there he received his early education. When he was nine the family moved to Chicago and Bellow later attended Chicago University and Northwestern University, from where he graduated with a BS in 1937. He then combined writing and teaching at Princeton, Minnesota, New York, Bard and Chicago universities.

His first novel was, *Dangling Man* (1944) a story in diary form about a man awaiting call-up into the army. It received mixed reviews but resulted in a Guggenheim scholarship, that in 1948, allowed Bellow to travel to Paris and Rome. *The Victim* (1947) is a study of the relationship between a Jew and Gentile who become each other's victim.

It was *The Adventures of Augie March* (1953) that brought him to the attention of a wide readership.

He was awarded the National Book Award of 1954. *Henderson the Rain King* (1959) continued the picaresque style about an eccentric millionaire in Africa. His list of novels is most impressive and includes *Hertzog* (1964) and the 1965 National Book Award, *Humboldt's Gift* (1975) and the Pulitzer Prize. In 1976 came the ultimate recognition, the Nobel Prize for Literature; **"for the human understanding and subtle analysis of contemporary culture that are combined in his work"**

Bellow often writes about Chicago, which he once claimed is the product of corruption, cynicism and confusion. This is brilliantly depicted in *Dean's December* (1982). His range of style often stretches from the sublime to the absurd but he is always original, as just two of his 1980s books, *More Die of Heartbreak* (1987) and *The Bellarosa Connection* (1989) demonstrate. He married for a fifth time in 1989. His bride, formerly one of his students when he was teaching at Chicago University, was 31; Saul Bellow was 74. He became a father in 2000 aged 85.

CHEMISTRY

WILLIAM LIPSCOMB (1919-)

William Nunn Lipscomb, Jr was born in Cleveland, US, on December 9, 1919. He graduated from Kentucky University in 1941 and received his PhD in 1946 from the California Institute of Technology. Then, between 1942 to 1946, he worked as a physical chemist in the Office of Science Research and Development. He then became assistant professor at Minnesota University leaving in 1959 as chief of the physical chemistry department. 1962-65 saw him as professor of chemistry at Harvard University.

His scientific development work was in the field of developing X-ray techniques. In particular his work resulted in the ability to map the molecular structures of numerous boron hydride compounds, known as boranes, and their derivatives. This resulted in the award of the 1976 Nobel Prize for Chemistry; **"for his studies on the structure of boranes illuminating problems of chemical bonding"**

He wrote, *Boron Hydrides* (1963) and *Nuclear Magnetic Resonance Studies of Boron and Related Compounds* (1969). He is un-married

PHYSICS

BURTON RICHTER (1931-)
and
SAMUEL TING (1936-)

"for their pioneering work in the discovery of a heavy elementary particle of a new kind"

Burton Richter was born in Brooklyn, New York, US, on March 22, 1931, into a traditional Jewish family. Having received his PhD from the Massachusetts Institute of Technology in 1956, he was appointed a professor at Stanford University, California. There he started experiments to confirm the validity of quantum electrodynamics at short distances.

From 1982 he has been associated with the Stanford Linear Accelerator Centre, he is now the director. In 1973, he completed the construction of the Stanford Positron-Electron Asymmetric Ring, a colliding beam accelerator. This allowed Richter to discover a new subatomic particle that became known as the J-particle; the first of a newly discovered group of massive, long-lived mesons. For this work Richter received a half share of the 1976 Nobel Prize for Physics.

He is married with two children

Samuel Chao Chung Ting was born in Ann Arbor, Mich. US, on January 17,1936. At the time of his birth his father, a Chinese college professor, was studying in the US. Samuel was raised in China and Taiwan and at the age of 20, returned to the US. There he attended Michigan University in the town of his birth and from where he received his doctorate in 1962. For a short while he taught at Columbia University, before working at a nuclear facility in Hamburg, Germany. In 1969, he was a professor at the Massachusetts Institute of Technology in Cambridge.

In 1974, he conducted experiments at the Brookhaven National Laboratory at Upton, Long Island where he discovered a new subatomic particle called, the psi-particle. Independent of Richter's discovery, this particle, thought to be composed of a charmed quark and its antiquark, led to a significant expansion and refinement of the quark model. For his work Ting was awarded with a half share of the 1976 Nobel Prize for Physics.

He has been married twice and has three children.

PHYSIOLOGY or MEDICINE

BARUCH BLUMBERG (1925-)
and
DANIEL GAJDUSEK (1923-)

"for their discoveries concerning new mechanisms for the origin and dissemination of infectious diseases"

Baruch Samuel Blumberg was born in New York, US, on July 28, 1925. He was born into a Jewish family who recognised the importance of education. In 1945 he graduated from Union College, Schenectady, New York. With looks that resembled a prizefighter, rather than a research professor, he went on to get an MD from Columbia University in 1951 and a PhD from Oxford University in 1957.

Thus, academically equipped, he joined the Clinical Research Institute for Cancer Research. During the 1960s and 70s, Blumberg was professor of medicine and genetics at Pennsylvania University. His research work led him to create a test for hepatitis viruses in donated blood and, in turn, an experimental vaccine against the disease.

In 1963, he discovered in the blood serum of an Australian Aborigine, an antigen that he determined, in 1967, to be part of a virus that causes hepatitis B, the most severe form of hepatitis. The discovery of this so-called Australian antigen, which causes the body to produce antibody responses to the virus, made it possible to screen blood donors for possible hepatitis B transmission. Further research showed that the body's development of antibody against the Australian antigen, was protective against further infection with the virus itself. For his work Blumberg was awarded a half share of the 1976 Nobel Prize for Physiology or Medicine.

In 1982 a safe and effective vaccine, utilizing Australian antigen, became commercially available. In May 1999, NASA chose Blumberg to lead a hunt through the heavens for signs of extraterrestrial life. He also heads the new Astro-biology Institute. He is married to an artist and they have four children.

Daniel Carleton Gajdusek was born in Yonkers, New York, US, on September 9, 1923. He graduated from Rochester University, NY, in 1943 and received a PhD from Harvard University in 1946. He was a Fellow in pediatrics and infectious diseases, at Harvard between 1949 and 52. It was in 1955, whilst a visiting investigator at the Institute of Medical Research in Melbourne, Australia, that he began the work for which he would later be honoured.

Gajdusek provided the first medical description of a unique central nervous disorder that appeared to only occur amongst the Fore people of New Guinea. It was known to them as *kuru* (trembling). Gajdusek lived among the Fore, he studied their language and culture and performed autopsies on *Kuru* victims.

He came to the conclusion that the disease was transmitted in the ritualistic eating of the brains of the deceased.   Gajdusek, head of the laboratories for virological and neurological research at the National Institutes of Health, theorised that the delayed onset of the disease could be attributed to a virus capable of extremely slow action or, perhaps, having the ability to remain dormant for years.

This study proved to have significant implications for research into the causes of multiple sclerosis, Parkinson's disease and other little-understood degenerative neurological disorders. The work resulted in Gajdusek being awarded a half share of the 1976 Nobel Prize for Physiology or Medicine. He is un-married. In 1997 he was sentenced to 30 years in prison in the US for sexually abusing young boys. On appeal, all but 18 months was suspended. He has been sued by one of his victims for $2.2 million.

ECONOMICS

MILTON FRIEDMAN (1912-)

Milton Friedman was born in Brooklyn, New York, US, on July 31, 1912. Educated at the universities of Rutgers and Chicago, he received his PhD, in 1946, from Columbia University. He then joined the staff of Chicago University. Friedman, a leading advocate of monetarism, expounded his right-wing economic theories in *Capitalism and Freedom* (1962). This work, and subsequent writings, influenced economic trends in the US and, during the 1980s , in the UK where the then prime minister, Margaret Thatcher, adopted his ideas and made him her guru.

His advice was partially responsible for the great recession of the late 1980s, with continued repercussions into the 1990s. In 1976, he was awarded the Nobel Prize for Economics. **"for his achievements in the fields of consumption analysis, monetary history and theory and for his demonstration of the complexity of stabilization policy"**
His autobiography, *Free to Choose* was published in 1979.

In 1996, the US finally dropped Friedman's philosophy on economic policy. At a lecture given in 1973 he said, in answer to a question, ' There is no such thing as a free lunch '. Friedman is married to an economist.

PEACE

MAIREAD CORRIGAN (1944-)
and
BETTY WILLIAMS (1943-)

Mairead Corrigan was born in Belfast, Northern Ireland in 1944. A Roman Catholic secretary working in Belfast, she founded, together with Protestant Betty Williams, the Northern Island Peace Movement. She began by organising peace petitions in the face of increasing sectarian violence. She and Williams started, in 1976, what became a mass movement known as 'Community of the Peace People'. In 1976, she shared the Nobel Peace Prize.

Two years later the show was over, the movement disbanded, the violence continuing.

Betty Williams was born in Belfast, Northern Island, on May 22,1943. A Protestant office worker who witnessed sectarian violence, she began circulating leaflets in Protestant areas calling for an end to violence. She came into contact with Mairead Corrigan and the two women set up, in 1976, what became known as 'The Community for Peace People'.

The world media hyped it up, uncaring that neither the leaders of the Protestant grouping, in the shape of Reverend Paisley, or the Nationalists in the shape of the IRA would take any notice.

The award of the Nobel Peace Prize for 1976 was part of the misunderstanding of the on-going Northern Island question. Indeed the 'community' broke up, amidst rancour, two years later. The two woman became estranged and Betty Williams moved to Florida, US. Despite the granting of two further Peace Prizes in 1998, violence from both sides continues. She is married with two children.

1977

US resumes executions after 10 year pause • Steve Bilko murdered by South African police • Anwar Sadat, President of Egypt, visits Israel and addresses the Knesset • First AIDS victims die • 'Pompidou Centre opens in Paris • Films; *Annie Hall, Star Wars, Julia, The Late Show, Padre Padrone* • J.K.Galbraith, *The Age of Anxiety* • Robert Coover, *The Public Burning,* Kamala Markandaya, *The Golden Honeycomb* • Anthony Eden, Vladimir Nabokov, Maria Callas, Julius 'Groucho' Marx, Sir Michael Balcon, Marc Bolan, Zero Mostel, Bing Crosby and Charles Chaplin die.

LITERATURE

VICENTE ALEIXANDRE (1898-1984)

Vicente Aleixandre was born in Seville, Spain, on April 26,1898. The son of a railway engineer, he studied law and business management and taught commercial law between 1920-22. In 1925 he became seriously ill and, whilst convalescing, began writing poetry.

Strongly influenced by the Surrealist technique, his first book of poetry, *Destruction or Love,* written in a free style, was published in 1935 and promptly banned by the Fascists, when they took over Spain. The ban lasted from 1936 to 1944, despite the fact that the book was awarded the National Prize for Literature. In 1944, he wrote, *Shadow of Paradise* followed in 1954 by, *History of the Heart.*

His 1962 offering, *In a Vast Domain*, deals with time, death and solidarity. His style changed with his later poetry to a metaphysical image. In his 1968 *Poems of Consummation,* he again explores the philosophy of death. The same theme occurs in *Dialogues of Insight.*(1974). Previously, in 1958, he wrote a book of prose about his fellow writers: *The Meetings.* Aleixandre was awarded the 1977 Nobel Prize for Literature; **"for a creative poetic writing which illuminates man's condition in the cosmos and in present-day society, at the same time representing the great renewal of the traditions of Spanish poetry between the wars"**

He died in Madrid on December 14, 1984. He never married.

CHEMISTRY

ILYA PRIGOGINE (1917-)

Ilya Prigogine was born in Moscow, Russia, on January 25th 1917. Taken to Belgium when a child, he was educated at the Free University in Brussels from where, in 1942, he received his PhD. There, he served as a professor from 1947 to 1962, at which time he became director of the International Institute of Physics and Chemistry at Solvay, Belgium.

From 1967, he was director of the Centre for Statistical Mechanics and Thermodynamics at Texas University in Austin. Here, his theoretical work extended the research of Lars Onsager. Prigogine developed the thermodynamic methods of understanding irreversible processes; this was in addition to the classical reversible reactions that were meant to result in states of equilibrium.

Prigogine was awarded the 1977 Nobel Prize for Chemistry; **"for his contributions to non-equilibrium thermodynamics, particularly the theory of dissipative structures"**

He is married.

PHYSICS

PHILIP ANDERSON (1923-), NEVILL MOTT (1905-)
and
JOHN VAN VLECK (1899-1980)

"for their fundamental theoretical investigations of the electronic structure of magnetic and disordered systems"

Philip Warren Anderson was born Indiana, US, on December 13, 1923. Educated at Harvard University, from where in 1949, he received a PhD, he went to work for the Bell Telephone Laboratories in Murray Hill, NJ.

He left for England and Cambridge University in 1967 and stayed, as professor of theoretical physics, until 1975. Then he re-crossed the Atlantic to teach at Princeton University. His research was mainly in solid-state physics, thus making possible the development of inexpensive electronic switching and memory devices in computers. He was awarded a third share of the 1977 Nobel Prize for Physics.

In 1982, he received the National Medal of Science. Among his writings are, *Concepts of Solids* (1963) and *Basic Notions of Condensed Matter Physics* (1984). His wife is a painter.

Nevill Francis Mott was born in Leeds, England, on September 30, 1905. Educated at Cambridge University, where he studied mathematics, he became a lecturer at Manchester University in 1929.

In 1933, he was professor of theoretical physics at Bristol University. Whilst he retained a lifelong interest in nuclear physics, his interest centred upon the study of metals, semiconductors, and photographic emulsion. This interest later extended to electrical conduction in noncrystalline solids.

In 1938, he devised the theoretical description of the effect that light has on a photographic emulsion at the atomic level. He was appointed director of the Henry Wills Physical Laboratories at Bristol in 1948. In 1954, Mott was Cavendish Professor of experimental physics at Cambridge University, until his retirement in 1971. Whilst at Cambridge, Mott introduced formulas that described the transitions of certain substances, between electrically conductive states and insulating states.

Knighted in 1962, Mott was awarded a third share of the 1977 Nobel Prize for Physics. He is married with two daughters.

John Hasbrouck Van Vleck was born in Middletown, Conn. US, on March 13, 1899. He was educated at the universities of Wisconsin, Madison and Harvard, from where in 1922 he received a PhD. He then taught at Wisconsin University, from 1928 to 1934. Then back to Harvard, where he eventually became chairman of the physics department, (1945-49), head of engineering and applied physics (1951-57) and between 1951 to 69, Hollis Professor of mathematics and natural philosophy.

During the early 1930s, Van Vleck developed the first fully articulated quantum mechanical theory of magnetism. He was later the main exponent of the ligand field theory of molecular bonding. He also made important contributions in the study of the spectra of free molecules, of paramagnetic reaction. Amongst his publications are, *Quantum Principles and Line Spectra* (1926) and *The Theory of Electric and Magnetic Susceptibilities* (1932).

Awarded a third share of the 1977 Nobel Prize for Physics, Van Vleck died in Cambridge, Mass. on October 27, 1980. When he was awarded the Nobel prize, Van Vleck had been married for over 50 years.

PHYSIOLOGY or MEDICINE

ROSALYN YALOW (1921-), ROGER GUILLEMIN (1924-)
and
ANDREW SCHALLY (1926-)

"for their discoveries concerning the peptide hormone production of the brain"

Rosalyn Sussman Yalow was born in New York, US. on July 19, 1921. She was born into a rabbinical family who prized education, especially in women on the basis that an educated man wanted an educated partner. She graduated in 1941 from Hunter College, NY. and received her PhD from Illinois University in 1945.

She became a consultant in nuclear physics and in 1947 joined the Bronx Veterans Administration Hospital. In 1950, she was appointed physicist and assistant chief of the radioisotope service. She now began investigating various medical applications of radioactive isotopes. Combining methods from radioisotope tracing and immunology, Yalow developed RIA. This proved to be a very sensitive and simple method for measuring minute concentrations of biological and pharmacological substances in blood. Using RIA, she studied insulin concentration in the blood of diabetics; this led to hundreds of other applications. In 1976, she became the first woman to be awarded the Albert Lasker Prize for basic medical research. A year later was awarded a third share of the Nobel Prize for Physiology or Medicine; **"for the development of radioimmunoassays of peptide hormones"**

She is married with two children.

Roger Charles Louis Guillemin was born in Dijon, France on January 11, 1924. Educated at the universities of Dijon, Lyon and Montreal he went on to teach at the Baylor College of Medicine in Houston, Texas, (1953-1970); save for a period 1960-63, when he taught at the Collège de France in Paris . From 1970, he was a resident fellow and research professor at the Salk Institute for Biological Studies in California. He became a US citizen in 1963.

He is noted for achieving the isolation of the first hypothalamic hormone to be discovered. TRH, the isolation and synthesis of somatostatin; a hypothalamic hormone that regulates activities of the pituitary gland and the pancreas.

He also discovered a new class of hormonal substances called endorphin. Guillemin in 1977, was awarded a third share of the Nobel Prize for Physiology or Medicine. He is married with six children.

Andrew Victor Schally was born in Wilno, Poland on November 30, 1926. He received his early education in Poland. As a Jew he was fortunate in being able to leave, together with his family, in 1939. He was educated at London University and worked for three years at the National Institute for Medical Research in London.

He graduated from McGill University Montreal with a PhD in biochemistry in 1955 and then spent 1957 to 1962, at the Baylor University in Houston. In 1967 he was a professor at the Tulane University School of Medicine. He became a US citizen in 1962.

Schally was involved with the work on formulating the synthesis of TRH and awarded a third share of the 1977 Nobel Prize for Physiology or Medicine. He is married but without children.

ECONOMICS

BERTIL OHLIN (1899-1979)
and
JAMES MEADE (1907-1995)

"For their path breaking contribution to the theory of international trade and international capital movements"

Bertil Gotthard Ohlin was born in Klippan, Sweden on August 3, 1979. He was educated at Lund and Stockholm universities. He developed an early interest in international trade and wrote a thesis on the subject in 1922. He then studied at Oxford University, followed by a stint at Harvard University. In 1924 he obtained a PhD from Stockholm University and a year later was appointed a professor at Copenhagen University. In 1930 he returned to Stockholm.

Ohlin then began an on-going dialogue with John Maynard Keynes, over Keynes' belief that Germany couldn't pay war reparations. In 1933, Ohlins became internationally known with his publication, *Interregional and International Trade.* He became head of the Swedish Liberal Party (1944-67) and a member of the Riksdag between 1938 and 1970. He was minister of commerce 1944-5.

He was awarded a half share of the 1977 Nobel Prize for Economics; . He died in Valadalen on August 3, 1979. He never married.

James Edward Meade was born in Swanage, Dorset, England on June 23, 1907. After graduating from Oxford University, with a first class honours degree, Meade spent a post-graduate year at Cambridge (1930-31). Regarded as a leftist economist, because of his admiration of Keynes, he served as a war economist during WW2 and became the leading economist to the post-war Labour government (1946-47).

He was professor of economics at the London School of Economics (LSE) between 1947 to 57 and at Cambridge (1957-68).

His publications include, *The Theory of International Economics*, made up of *The Balance of Payments* in 1951 and *Trade and Welfare* in1955. He provided a detailed analysis of the welfare effects of trade regulations, as well as trade discrimination and effective protection.

He was awarded a co-share of the 1977 Nobel Prize for Economics. He died in 1995 and was married with four children and seven grandchildren.

PEACE

AMNESTY INTERNATIONAL

Amnesty International's logo is a burning candle wrapped in barbed wire. This dramatic symbol reflects the work done. Amnesty, founded in London on May 28, 1961, through the efforts of Peter Beneson, a lawyer who had defended political prisoners in Hungary, South Africa and Spain. He now sought to establish an international agency for the protection of human rights. The organisation now has some 200,000 members in some 100 countries. Amnesty publicizes government wrongdoing in newsletters and annual reports. They are no respecters of persons and do not hesitate to criticize. Amnesty was awarded the 1977 Nobel Prize for Peace.

1978

Birth of the first 'test tube' baby • Camp David Agreement • First camera with automatic focus • David Hare, *Plenty* • Films: *The Deer Hunter*, *Midnight Express*, *The Chant of Jimmy Blacksmith*, *The Driver*, *Days of Heaven* • Isaac Bashevis Singer, *Shosha* • William Wharton, *Birdy* • Ian McEwan, *The Cement Garden* • Hugh MacDiarmid, *Complete Poems 1920-1976* • Harold Abrahams, Hubert Humphrey, Jomo Kenyatta and Golda Meir die.

LITERATURE

ISAAC BASHEVIS SINGER (1904-1991)

Isaac Bashevis Singer was born in Radzymin, Poland, when it was still part of the Russian Empire, on July 14, 1904. The son of a rabbi, he was educated at the Tachemoni Rabbinical Seminary in Warsaw.

Instead of following in his father's footsteps, Isaac got himself a job as a proofreader and translator for, *Literashe Bleter* a literary magazine. It was his older brother, Israel, an aspiring writer, who lured Isaac away from a rabbinical calling and led the way to a life of writing.

In 1935, Israel decided to seek his fortune in America and left. Disliking the way things were going for the Jews next door in Germany, and missing his brother, Isaac decided to leave his wife and son and follow Israel to the US. Later, his wife and child had a hellish life in Poland before eventually getting to Palestine, via Russia.

With his marriage dissolved, Singer married Alma Haimann, a

shopworker, in 1940. He obtained a post on the *Jewish Daily Forward,* but it wasn't until the death of Israel, whom Isaac regarded as a surrogate father, that he found the urge to write novels. With his wife working and his job undemanding, Singer worked in virtual isolation until the mid-1950s, when Saul Bellow (qv) discovered him. Singer, who wrote in Yiddish and was translated by his nephew or his friend Elizabeth Shub, now began establishing himself as a major literary figure. His work appeared in magazines as varied as *Playboy* and the *New Yorker.*

His books of short stories give the reader an insight into the vanished world of pre-war Jewish life in Poland. He pulled no punches and his description of Jewish life, showing its obsession with sex, dreams and ritual slaughter, did not go down well. A vegetarian, he was accused of equating the Holocaust with animal slaughter when he said, "all men are Nazis with respect to animals" Singer refused to be blinded to people's shortcomings and that included Jews, as he shows in his writings. Among his most important novels are *The Family Moskat* (1950), *The Magician of Lublin* (1960), *The Slave* (1962), *The Manor* (1967), *The Estate* (1969), *Enemies, a Love Story* (1972), *Shosha* (1978) and *The Penitent* (1983). He was awarded the 1978 Nobel Prize for Literature; **"for his impassioned narrative art which, with roots in a Polish-Jewish cultural tradition, brings universal human conditions to life"**

During his life Singer received many honours and titles. He once wrote , "A belief in God is as necessary as sex" He died of a stroke in Surfside, Florida on July 24, 1991. In 1998 his final novel was published. *Shadows on the Hudson* started life in 1957 as a serial in an American Yiddish newspaper. It is a powerful investigation of pre-war life in Warsaw that comes to post-war New York, in the shape of a Wall Street investment consultant.

CHEMISTRY

PETER MITCHELL (1920-1992)

Peter Dennis Mitchell was born in Mitcham, Surrey, England, on September 29, 1920. Educated at Queens College, Taunton and Jesus College, Cambridge, from where he received a BA in 1943 and a PhD in 1950. He was a University Demonstrator at Cambridge (1950-55), director of biochemical research at Edinburgh University (1955-63) and director of research at Glynn Research Institute (1964-86). Here Mitchell continued the work he started at Edinburgh.

The central idea of his photosynthesis and oxidation theory, first started as a tentative hypothesis in the scientific journal, *Nature* in 1961. Mitchell's idea was that energy stored at the organelle membrane, did exactly the work attributed to the supposed chemical intermediary. His theory was greeted by a great deal of professional skepticism. His untiring work resulted in the acknowledgment that the formulating of the chemiosmatic theory, explained the mechanisms by which energy is generated in the mitochondria of living cells. For this work Mitchell was awarded the 1978 Nobel Prize for Chemistry; **"for his contribution to the understanding of biological energy transfer through the formulation of the chemiosmotic theory"**

He received the Copely Medal from the Royal Society in 1981. He died in Bodmin, Cornwall on April 10, 1992. He was married twice and had a daughter and three sons.

PHYSICS

ARNO PENZIAS (1933-), ROBERT WILSON (1936-)

"for their discovery of cosmic microwave background radiation"

and
PETER KAPITZA (1894-1984)

Arno Allan Penzias was born in Munich, Germany on April 26, 1933. It was no place for a new- born Jewish baby. Several years passed before his parents were able to settle, in 1939, in America. Penzias was educated at the City College of New York and in 1962, received his PhD in physics from Columbia University.

He joined the Bell Telephone Laboratories in Holmdel, NJ. and there, he and Robert Wilson, began monitoring radio emissions from a ring of gas that surrounds the Milky Way galaxy. The two scientists were much surprised to discover a uniform static in the background they identified as a residual thermal energy, that spread throughout the universe.

It is now universally agreed that this background stems from the original explosion of billions of years ago and from which our universe was created. Their work has become known as the 'big bang' theory of creation. In 1976, Penzias became director of Bell Radio Research and in 1981, was vice-president of research at Bell Laboratories. He was awarded a third share of the 1978 Nobel Prize for Physics. He is married with children.

Robert Woodrow Wilson was born in Houston, Texas, US, on January 10, 1936. Educated at Rice University, Houston and the California Institute of Technology in Pasadena, from where in 1962 he received a PhD

He then began working at the Bell Telephone Laboratories (1963-1976) where he met Arno Penzias. The two scientists detected an unusual background radiation that seemed to permeate the cosmos uniformly and indicated a temperature of 3K. They concluded that this radiation appeared to be a remnant of the big bang, the primordial explosion of billions of years ago and from which the universe originated. He went on to contribute to many scientific journals on such subjects as background-temperature measurements, and millimetre-wave measurements of interstellar molecules. He was awarded a third share of the 1978 Nobel Prize for Physics. He is married with children.

Pyotr **Leonidovich Kapitza** was born in Kronshtadt, Russia on June 26, 1894. His mother was Jewish and his father a Russian Army general. Educated at the Petrograd Polytechnical Institute he remained there as a lecturer until 1921.

The influenza outbreak, following WW1, enveloped Kapitza's wife and two children, they died in 1921. He then took off for England and Cambridge University to work with Ernest Rutherford (qv).

He was appointed assistant director of magnetic research at the Cavendish Laboratory in 1924. There he designed equipment that achieved a magnetic field of 500,000 gauss, not exceeded in strength until 1956. In 1925, Kapitza was made a fellow of Trinity College, Cambridge and in 1929 was elected a fellow of the Royal Society, a distinct honour for a foreigner.

In 1934 he returned to Russia for a symposium. There he was arrested, his passport confiscated, by order of Stalin. A year later, he was appointed director of the Institute of Physical Problems of the Soviet Academy of Sciences in Moscow.

His area of research was in low temperature physics and he discovered superfluidity in helium ll, while investigating its heat-conduction qualities. In 1939, he built apparatus to produce large quantities of liquid oxygen for the Russian steel industry to use during WW2. For his scientific achievements during the 1930s and 40s, Kapitza in 1945, was awarded the title of Hero of Socialist Labour, the Soviet Union's highest civilian award. In 1946 he refused to work on the nuclear weapon programme and as a result fell out with Stalin. He was dismissed from his post at the Institute for Physical Problems and spent several years at his country house where he conducted research on ball lightning.

Following the death of Stalin in 1953, Kapitza was restored to his original post in 1955 and stayed until his death   He was an outspoken advocate of free scientific thought and in the 1960s was one of the Soviet scientists who was active in the Pugwash movement, a series of international conferences aimed at channelling scientific research into peaceful purposes. In 1978 he was awarded a third share of the Nobel Prize for Physics; **"for his basic inventions and discoveries in the area of low-temperature physics"**

He died in Moscow on April 8, 1984. He was married with two sons.

PHYSIOLOGY or MEDICINE

DANIEL NATHANS (1928-), HAMILTON SMITH (1931-)
and
WERNER ARBER (1929-)

"for the discovery of restriction enzymes and their application to problems of molecular genetics"

Daniel Nathans was born in Wilmington, Delaware, US, on October 30, 1928. The son of a Russian-Jewish immigrant, Nathans was educated at the University of Delaware and Washington University, St.Louis, from where he gained a medical degree in 1954. His subsequent research work ran in tandem with his work as professor of microbiology at John Hopkins University, Baltimore (1962-72).

Nathans used the restriction enzyme, isolated from the bacterium *Haemophilias influenzae* by Hamilton Smith, and investigated the structure of the DNA of the Simian virus 40, the simplest virus known to produce cancerous tumours.

Nathan's achievement, the creation of a genetic map of a virus, prepared the ground for the first application of the new enzymes that resulted in identifying the molecular basis of cancer. In 1978, Nathans was awarded a third share of the Nobel Prize for Physiology or Medicine. Nathans is now one of the leading microbiologists in the world. In 1956 he married Joanne Gomberg, they have three sons.

Hamilton Othanel Smith was born in New York, US, on August 23,1931. He graduated from the University of California in 1952 and received a medical degree from John Hopkins University in 1956. He was on the staff of Michigan University in 1962, and in 1967, returned to John Hopkins becoming professor of microbiology in 1973.

His studies revealed the first of what came to be called type ll restriction enzymes , whose predictable behaviour made them valuable tools in the study of DNA structure and in recombinant DNA technology. He was awarded a third share of the 1978 Nobel Prize for Physiology or Medicine, for his discovery of a new class of restriction enzymes, that recognize specific sequences of nucleotides in a molecule of DNA, and cleave the molecule at a particular point.

He is married with four sons and a daughter.

Werner Arber was born in Granichen, Switzerland, on June 3,1929. He studied at the Swiss Federal Institute of Technology in Zurich and Geneva University. Between 1960 and 1970 he taught at Geneva then, as professor of microbiology, at Basel University. During the late 1950s and early 1960s, he took the original work of Salvador Luria (qv) and extended it.

Arbor's research concentrated on the action of protective enzymes present in bacteria, modifying the DNA of the infecting virus. He was awarded a third share of the 1978 Nobel Prize for Physiology or Medicine.

He is married with two daughters.

ECONOMICS

HERBERT SMITH (1916-)

Herbert Alexander Simon Smith, was born in Milwaukee, US, on June 15, 1916. He graduated from Chicago University in 1936, gaining a PhD in 1943. After holding various posts in political science he became, in 1949, professor of administration and psychology at Carnegie-Mellon University, Pittsburgh. He later became professor of computer science there. He became known for his work on the theory of corporate decision taking, known as ' behaviourism'. It is layed out in his book, *Administrative Behaviour* (1947).

He tried to replace the highly simplified classical approach to economic modelling and its idea of decision taking. Crucial to the primary motivating factor was to keep risk factors to a minimum. Smith was awarded the 1978 Nobel Prize for Economics; **"for his contributions in a large number of fields including psychology, mathematics, statistics, and operations research, all of which he synthesized in a key theory within economic organizations"**

He later became increasingly involved in the attempt to create artificial intelligence by computer technology. He is married with three children.

PEACE

MENACHERN BEGIN (1913-1992)
and
ANWAR SADAT (1918-1981)

"for their efforts resulting in a peace treaty between Israel and Egypt"

Menachem **Wolfovitch Begin** was born in Brest-Litovsk, Russia on August 16,1913, and grew up in an orthodox Jewish household. It was in the atmosphere anti-Semitic Poland, that doubtless shaped his future life. His father instilled within him an enthusiasm for the establishment of a Jewish homeland. In 1935, Begin received a law degree from Warsaw University.

In 1938, he was leader of the Polish branch of the Zionist youth movement known as Betar. When the Germans invaded Poland in 1939, Begin escaped to Vilnius where the Soviets deported him to Siberia. A year later in 1941, he was released and allowed to join the Polish army in exile and posted to Palestine.

On his release from the Polish army, Begin joined the Irgun Zvai Leumi, an organization pledged to remove the British Mandate from Palestine and to create a Jewish state by any means possible. Following WW2, and the decimation of his family in the Holocaust, Begin became active in the war against British forces stationed in Palestine.

Following the establishment of the State of Israel in 1948, Begin founded the right-wing Herut Party and became its leader. In 1973, Herut merged with other parties to form the Likud Front, a right-wing nationalist party. In 1977, he was prime minister in a coalition government that sought an accommodation with Egypt. Through the imagination of Anwar Sadat, these efforts resulted in the Camp David Accords of 1978 . This brought peace between the two countries and has led to further peace initiatives, albeit the later Likud governments lacked the will of Begin in furthering the peace process.

In 1978, Begin was awarded a co-share of the Nobel Peace Prize, for his efforts in the resulting peace accords. In 1982 Begin chose to invade Lebanon, but the campaign did not turn out the way he had planned. He claimed it would take just 72 hours, in the event it took three years and Israel still occupies a large part of the South. The failure of this campaign led to Begin's resignation. He died in Tel-Aviv on March 9, 1992, a broken and depressed man who appeared to take little comfort in the fact that it was his original efforts that had got the peace process under way. He was married with two daughters and a son.

Muhammad **Anwar el-Sadat** was born in Mit Abu al-Kum, Egypt, on December 25,1918. He graduated from the Cairo Military Academy in 1938, and spent WW2 plotting to expel the British from Egypt, albeit with help from the Germans.

In 1942, the British arrested him but he escaped. In 1950 he joined Gamal Nasser's Free Officers organisation and took part in their coup against the King in 1952. He later supported Nasser in his bid to become president in 1956, and he subsequently held several high offices. He was vice-president when, in September 1970, Nasser died. Sadat was then elected president on October 15th.

It was in the arena of foreign affairs that Sadat came into his own. He played the USSR off against the USA, and vice versa, to such good effect that he was in an excellent position to join up with Syria and invade Israel in October 1973, during Yom Kippur. The war over, and some Egyptian territory reclaimed from the 1967 war, Sadat was on a high. He now worked towards peace and in November 1977 made his historic visit to Israel and addressed their parliament (Knesset). He caught the imagination of the world.

A series of intense negotiation began, continued and culminating in the Camp David Accord. It resulted in his being awarded a co-share of the 1978 Nobel Prize for Peace. His popularity in the West was not sustained in the Arab world. Opposition to the treaty and a downturn in the economic conditions in Egypt, resulted in the rise of Muslim extremism. It led to his being murdered, whilst reveiwing a miltary parade in Cairo, that was comemerating the 1973 Israeli-Arab war. It was October 6, 1981. He published his autobiography, *In Search of Identity* in 1978. Sadat was married with two sons and five daughters.

The third person involved with the success at Camp David was US President Jimmy Carter. In an article in *The New York Times* of October 11, 1998 it was stated that had Carter been nominated, by the deadline for such matters, he would have shared the prize.

1979

Revolution in Iran • USSR invades Afghanistan • Major accident at the Three-Mile Island Nuclear Power station in Pennsylvania, US • Medical confirmation that cigarette smoking causes cancer • Alban Berg, *Lulu* • Christopher Lasch, *The Culture of Narcissism* • Judy Chicago, *The Dinner Party* • Films; *Aliens, Manhattan, The Tin Drum, Kramer versus Kramer* • William Golding, *Darkness Visible* • Norman Mailer, *The Executioner's Song* • Bernard Malamud, *Dubin's Lives* • V.S. Naipaul, *A Bend in the River* • Philip Roth, *The Ghost Writer* • Bernice Rubens, *Spring Sonata* • John Wayne, Mary Pickford, Gracie Fields, Charlie Mingus, S.J.Perelman, Richard Rodgers, Al Capp, Jean Monnet, die.

LITERATURE

ODYSSEUS ELYTIS (1911-1996)

Odysseus Elytis was born in Iraklion, Crete, on November 2, 1911. His family was in the soap business and named Alepoudhelis. Elytis disliked the business, and the name and became Elytis. He studied law at Athens University but left to write poetry with a Surrealist flavour. He was strongly influenced by George Seferis (qv) who was the 1963 Nobel Laureate. His book, *Orientations* (1940), is a collection of his works at that time.

When Germany arrived to occupy Greece in 1941, Elytis was in Albania, fighting with a anti-fascist resistance group against the Italian occupiers. His, *Heroic and Elegiac Song for the Lost Second Lieutenant of the Albanian Campaign,* was regarded as the anthem to the cause of freedom.

Following the war, he returned home and nothing was heard from him for the next fifteen years. In 1959, he published *The Axion Esti,* a long poem in the Walt Whitman mode. Following the Greek colonel's coup of 1967, Elytis went to live in Paris. His later books include *The Sovereign Sun* (1971) and *The Stepchildren* (1974).

He was awarded the 1979 Nobel Prize for Literature; **"for his poetry, which, against the background of Greek tradition, depicts with sensuous strength and intellectual clear-sightedness modern man's struggle for freedom and creativeness"**
He died in Athens on March 19,1996. He never married. This was the first Nobel Prize awarded to a Greek.

CHEMISTRY

HERBERT BROWN (1912-)
and
GEORGE WITTIG (1897-1987)

"for their development of the use of boron-and phosphorus-containing compounds, respectively, into important reagents in organic synthesis"

Herbert Charles Brown was born Herbert Brovarnik in London, England, on May22, 1912. His Ukranian-Jewish parents decided to leave London and, by the age of two, Herbert was playing with his toys in a Chicago apartment. Despite financial hardships, Herbert made it to Chicago University from where, in 1938, he received his PhD.

He then taught at Wayne State University in Detroit until 1947. At that time he became professor of organic chemistry at Indiana's Purdue University. Brown, who has been the recipient of many awards and a member of the most important associations, reached the pinnacle of his career in 1979, when he was co-awarded the Nobel Prize for Chemistry;

His work had a revolutionary impact on the world of chemistry and considerable beneficial effects for humanity. In particular his work with borohydrides that led to the development of an important new class of inorganic reagents. His discovery of the organoboranes revealed an array of powerful and versatile reagents. His publications include, *Hydroboration* (1962) and *Organic Synthesis via Boranes* (1975).

He is married.

Georg Wittig was born in Berlin, Germany on June 16, 1897. He graduated from Marburg University in 1923 and received his PhD in 1926. He remained at Marburg as a university lecturer in chemistry until 1932. He worked at several universities during the Hitler regime culminating at Heidelberg University where, in 1965, he became Emeritus Professor.

His sphere of research involved carbanions, negatively charred organic species. He discovered a class of compounds called ylids, mediating a particular type of reaction that became known as 'Wittig reactions'. For his discovery, he was awarded a co-share of the 1979 Nobel Prize for Chemistry.

He died in Heidelberg on August 26, 1987. He never married.

PHYSICS

STEVEN WEINBERG (1933-), SHELDON GLASHOW (1932-)
and
ABDUS SALEM (1926-)

"for their contributions to the theory of the unified weak and electromagnetic interaction between elementary particles, including inter alia, the prediction of the weak neutral current"

Steven Weinberg was born in New York, US, on May 3,1933. He was a pupil at the Bronx High School of Science and there, in 1950, he met Sheldon Glashow, who like himself were the sons of immigrant Jewish parents. Weinberg went on to Cornell University and later spent a year in Copenhagen, at the Nordic Institute for Theoretical Atomic Physics. Then, in 1957, he obtained his PhD from Princeton University.

He researched at Columbia University before joining the staff at the University of California in 1960, switching to Harvard University in 1973 and Austin's University of Texas in 1983. He was awarded a third share of the 1979 Nobel Prize for Physics.

His research was in the field of formulating a theory that explains the known facts of the electromagnetic together with weak interactions.

He is married with a child.

Sheldon Lee Glashow was born in New York, US, on December 5, 1932. He graduated from Cornell University in 1954. In 1955, he received his MA and in 1959, a PhD, both from Harvard University. Following periods of teaching at Stanford (1961) and the University of California at Berkeley (1961-66), he returned to Harvard as a professor. A member of the National Academy of Science, he is a successful researcher in the field of nuclear physics.

For his work in the development of the 'electroweak theory', Glashow received the award of a third of the 1979 Nobel Prize for Physics. This theory marries two of the basic interactions of nature, electromagnetism and the weak nuclear force, into a single gauge theory. At Harvard, Glashow was Higgins Professor of Physics in 1979 and the Mellon Professor of Sciences in 1988.

He is married with four children.

Abdus Salam was born in Jhang Maghiana, Punjab, India on January 29, 1926. He was educated at Government College, Lahore and in 1952, received his PhD in mathematics and physics from Lahore. Between 1951-54, he was Professor of Mathematics at Lahore University, before going to Cambridge University as a lecturer in mathematics. In 1957, he was professor of theoretical physics at the Imperial College of Science and Technology in London. In 1964 he was a director of the International Centre for Theoretical Physics at Trieste, Italy.

He was awarded a third share of the 1979 Nobel Prize for Physics for his work in formulating a theory for encompassing both the electromagnetic interaction and the so-called weak interaction of elementary particles. Salam was the first Pakistani to be awarded a Nobel Prize. He is un-married.

PHYSIOLOGY or MEDICINE

ALLAN CORMACK (1924-1998)
and
GODFREY NEWBOLD (1919-)

"for the development of computer assisted tomography"

Allan MacLeod Cormack was born in Johannesburg, South Africa, on February 23, 1924. He graduated from Cape Town University in 1944, and then followed with advanced studies at Cape Town and Cambridge Universities. Between 1950 and 56, he was a lecturer at Cape Town University and, following a year's research fellowship at Harvard University, became assistant professor of physics at Tufts University.

At Tufts, his research centred upon the interaction of subatomic particles. He became a full professor in 1964 and chairman of the department from 1968 to 1976. He retired in 1980 and became a member of the American Academy of Arts and Sciences. A US citizen from 1966, he had established in the 1970s, the mathematical and physical foundations of computerized scanning.

He was awarded a half share of the 1979 Nobel Prize for Physiology or Medicine for his work on tomography. It is interesting to note that Cormack, unusually, never earned a doctorate degree in any field of science. He died on May 7, 1998 in Winchester, Mass. He was married with three children.

Godfrey Newbold Hounsfield was born in Newark, Notts. England on August 28, 1919. He was educated at City and Guilds College and Faraday House College, London. During WW2, he was in the Royal Air Force and working on radar and electrons. In 1951 he joined the research staff of EMI Ltd and led a design team that built the first all-transistor computer in the UK. In 1972 he was head of the medical systems research department.

He, independently of Cormack, developed computer -assisted tomography (CAT). This enables detailed X-ray pictures of 'slices' of the human body to be produced. He was awarded a half share of the 1979 Nobel Prize for Physiology or Medicine and knighted in 1981. He is un-married.

ECONOMICS

ARTHUR LEWIS (1915-1991)
and
THEODORE SCHULTZ (1902-)

"For their pioneering research into economic development research with particular consideration of the problems of developing countries"

William Arthur Lewis was born in Castries, St. Lucia, British West Indies on January 23,1915. He was educated at the London School of Economics (LSE), having won a government scholarship. He graduated in 1937 and later received a PhD in economics. He was a lecturer at LSE from 1938-47, professor of economics at Manchester University (1947-58), principal of University College, West Indies (1959-62), and professor of Princeton University between 1963 and 1983. He served as economic advisor to commercial companies and to several governments especially in Africa, Asia and the Caribbean.

He helped to establish the Caribbean Development Bank, for which service he was knighted in 1963. He was awarded a half share of the 1979 Nobel Prize for Economics

He wrote several important books including, *The Principles of Economic Planning* (1949), *The Theory of Economic Growth* (1955), *Tropical Development 1880-1913*(1971) and *Racial Conflict and Economic Development* (1985).

He died in Bridgetown, Barbados on June 15, 1991. He was married with two children.

Theodore **William Schultz** was born in Arlington, SD, US, on April 30,1902. He was educated at South Dakota State College and awarded a PhD from Wisconsin University in 1930. He taught at Iowa State College (1930-43), and was head of the economics department of Chicago University 1946-61). His view of economic development was based on the notion that agricultural development was a prior indispensable condition of industrialization. He caused quite an upraising of eyebrows, with his suggestion that human resources should be treated in the same way as financial resources; both producing profit from investment.

Amongst his many publications are, *Agriculture in an Unstable Economy* (1945), *The Economic Value of Education* (1963), *Investment in Human Capital* (1971) and *Investing in People: The Economics of population Quality* (1981). He was awarded a co-share of the 1979 Nobel Prize for Economics. He is married with three children.

PEACE

MOTHER TERESA (1910-1997)

Mother **Teresa of Calcutta, was born Agnes Gonxha Bojaxhiu** in what is now Skopje, Macedonia, on August 27,1910. She was the daughter of an Albanian grocer. She went to Ireland in 1928 to join the Institute of the Blessed Virgin Mary. Six weeks later she sailed for India to work as a teacher. She later requested permission to work among the poor of Calcutta. Having studied nursing, she moved into the slum areas where she organized clinics and dispensed medical treatment. She became an Indian citizen and created her own Catholic order, although her Indian nuns wore the sari as their habit. Her Missionaries of Charity later built a leper colony in Asanol, India called Shanti Nagar or Twon of peace.

In 1963, the Indian government awarded her the Padmashri or Lord of the Lotus, for her services to the Indian people. In 1971, she was awarded the first Pope John XXlll Peace Prize. By the time she received the 1979 Nobel Prize for Peace, Mother Teresa's Missionaries of Charity had 1,000 nuns operating in some 60 centres in Calcutta and 200 worldwide. She died in 1997. In 1999 Vatican officials, considering possible sainthood, have expressed concern that she did too little to treat the sick and accepted money from dubious sources including Duvalier, the ex-dictator of Haiti. It was alleged by Christopher Hitchings, in his book, *The Missionary Position* (1995) 'all efforts to discover what she did with the enormous sums of money given to her in gifts by individuals and institutions were sidetracked.' In addition her nursing methods have been heavily criticised.

She accepted a $1.25 million donation from Charles Keating who was later jailed for swindling small savers in a crooked savings and loan scam. Mother Teresa went to court to plea on his behalf. It was suggested to her by the DA that she should return the money. The suggestion was ignored.

1980

Iran-Iraq war starts • Archbishop Romero shot dead whilst celebrating mass in US backed San Salvador • Sony Walkman launched • Britain becomes net exporter of oil • A gene is transferred from one mouse to another • Films; *My Brilliant Career, Raging Bull, Last Metro, Ordinary People, Coal Miner's Daughter, Atlantic City, All That Jazz* • Anthony Burgess, *Earthly Powers* • A.N.Wilson, *The Healing Art* • John Kennedy Toole, *A Confederacy of Dunces* • Cecil Beaton, Graham Sutherland, Oskar Kokoschka, Erich Fromm, Jesse Owens, Jean-Paul Sartre, Alfred Hitchcock, President Tito, Romain Gary, Harold Clurman, Sir Ludwig Guttman, Henry Miller, C.P. Snow, Lewis Milestone, Peter Sellars, Mae West and John Lennon die.

LITERATURE

CZESLOW MILOSZ (1911-)

Czeslow Milosz was born in Sateiniai, Lithuania, Russia on June 30,1911. He was educated at Vilnius University. He published his first book of verse, *Poem of Frozen Time* in 1922, at which time he was a committed socialist and leader of a group of poets named Catastrophist, because of their predictions of impending world disaster.

During the German occupation of Poland in WW2, Milosz was most active in the Resistance and continued to write poetry including, *Invincible Song* (1942). In 1945 he published, *Rescue*, one of the first books to be published in Communist Poland. For his efforts he was rewarded with a government post in the foreign office.

He served as cultural attache in Washington and followed with a stint as first secretary for cultural affairs. In 1951, he applied for political asylum in France and nine years later changed his mind and did the same thing in Washington. He worked teaching at the University of California and became a US citizen in 1970.

His collection of essays, *The Captive Mina* (1953), is probably his best known work. Others of note include, *The Poetic Treatise* (1957), his autobiography, *Native Realm* (1959) and his novel, *The Seizure of Power* (1955). He was awarded the 1980 Nobel Prize for Literature, **"who with uncompromising clear-sightedness voices man's exposed condition in a world of severe conflicts"**

Although he won the Neustadt International Prize for Literature in 1978, by and large, by that time, any great importance he might of had as a literary figure, was well behind him. He never married.

CHEMISTRY

PAUL BERG (1926-), WALTER GILBERT (1932-)
and
FREDERICK SANGER (1918-)

"for their contributions concerning the determination of base sequences in nucleic acids"

Paul Berg was born in New York, US, to Russian Jewish parents, on June 30,1926. He was educated at Pennsylvania State University from where he graduated. He later obtained a PhD from Western Reserve University. Further studies took him to Copenhagen, before he returned home to take up the appointment as assistant professor of microbiology at Washington University, St Louis (1954-59). He went on to become professor of biochemistry at Stanford University and later chairman of the department (1969-74). He served in the US Navy during WW2.

Berg was responsible for devising a method for introducing 'foreign genes' into bacteria, thereby causing bacteria to produce proteins from the new gene. This type of genetic engineering was of great importance, paving the way for biochemical synthesis of insulin and interferon and enabling antiviral activity to be released by cells in response to virus infection. For this work Berg was awarded a third share of the 1980 Nobel Prize for Chemistry; **"for his fundamental studies of the biochemistry of nucleic acids, with particular regard to recombinant-DNA"**

He married Mildred Levy in 1947, they have a son.

Walter Gilbert was born in Boston, US, on March 21, 1932. The grandson of a rabbi, Gilbert was educated at Harvard University, from where he gained a BA in 1953, followed by an MA the following year. Thus armed, he went to England where he worked for his PhD at Cambridge University achieving his goal in 1957. Returning to the US, he joined the staff at Harvard University and gradually climbed the teaching ladder, becoming professor of microbiology (1969-1972). His chosen field of research lay in DNA and in 1972 he became American Cancer Society Professor of Molecular Biology.

He received a third share of the 1980 Nobel Prize for Chemistry; for his development of a method for determining the sequence of nucleotide links in the chainlike molecules of nucleic acids. In 1979, Gilbert joined a group of scientists and businessmen to form Biogen, a commercial genetic-engineering research corporation.

He is married to the poet Celia Gilbert; they have two children.

Frederick Sanger was born in Rendcombe, Glos. England on August 13, 1918. He was educated at St John's College, Cambridge, where, in 1932, he earned a doctorate in biochemistry. His original research lay in deducing the sequence of amino acids and for this work Sanger was awarded a share of the 1958 Nobel Prize for Chemistry.

He later turned his attention to the structure of nucleic acids and working on RNA and DNA. Using a highly original combination of radioactive labelling, gel electrophoresis, and selective enzymes he was able, by 1977, to deduce the full sequence of bases in the DNA. He was awarded a third share of the 1980 Nobel Prize for Chemistry, for his work that has given new, surprising and detailed knowledge of both proteins and genes

Sanger is only the fourth person ever to be awarded a second Nobel Prize. He was named a Companion of Honour in 1981 and made a member of the British Order of Merit in 1986. He married Margaret Howe in 1940 they have two sons and a daughter. His hobby is given as ' messing about in boats'

PHYSICS

JAMES CRONIN (1931-)
and
VAL FITCH (1923-)

"for the discovery of violations of fundamental symmetry principles in the decay of neutral K-mesons"

James Watson Cronin was born in Chicago, US, on September 29,1931. He graduated from Southern Methodist University in Dallas and received his PhD from Chicago University in 1955. In 1958, he was a professor at Princeton University and in 1971, professor of physics at Chicago. In 1964, he conducted an experiment that implied that reversing the direction of time would not precisely reverse the course of certain reactions of subatomic particles.

Prior to the experiment by Cronin and Fitch, it had long been held that particle interaction should be indifferent to the direction of time. In 1980 Cronin received a co-share of the Nobel Prize for Physics for this work. He is married with two daughters and a son.

Val Logsdon Fitch was born in Merriman, Neb. US, on March 10,1923. Originally trained as a chemist, he switched to physics. Whilst in the US Army, during WW2, he worked on the Manhattan Project at Los Alamos under Ernest Titterton, a British physicist. He graduated from McGill University, Montreal with a BA in electrical engineering in 1948 and gained a PhD in physics from Columbia University in 1954.

He became Cyrus Fogg Brackett Professor of Physics at Princeton University in 1976. For his work, in tandem with Cronin, on the particle interaction that disproved the existing theory carried out in 1964, he was awarded a co-share of the 1980 Nobel Prize for Physics.

His first wife, with whom he had two sons, died in 1972. He re-married in 1976 and has three stepchildren. He is a member of the American Physical Society, the American Academy of Arts and Sciences and the National Academy of Sciences.

PHYSIOLOGY or MEDICINE

JEAN DAUSSET (1916-), GEORGE SNELL (1903-1996)
and
BARUJ BENACERRAF (1920-)

"for their discoveries concerning genetically determined structures on the cell surface that regulate immunological reactions"

Jean-Baptiste-Gabriel-Joachim Dausset was born in Toulouse, France on October 19, 1916. His education was interrupted by WW2 which Dausset spent with the Free French Forces. The war over, he returned to his medical studies and in 1945 received his degree from Paris University. Between 1958 and 1977, he was professor of immunohematology at Paris University and from 1977, was professor of experimental medicine at the Collège de France.

In investigating the immunological reactions of patients who had received many blood transfusions, Dausset correctly hypothesized that a specific genetic variation among people accounted for different levels of reaction. He went on to demonstrate the existence of a gene complex that he designated HLA (human leucocyte A complex). He was awarded a third share of the 1980 Nobel Prize for Physiology or Medicine; **"for his studies of the genetic basis of immunological reaction"**

In 1963 he married Rose Mayoral from Madrid. They have two children. His hobby is modern plastic art. Following the receipt of the Nobel Prize, Dausset has created in Paris, the Human Polymorphism Study Centre and has set-up an intensive international collaboration to establish a genetic map of the human genome.

George **Davis Snell** was born in Bradford, Mass. US, on December 19,1903. He graduated from Dartmouth College in 1926 and received a DsC. from Harvard University in 1930. Between 1931-33 he was researching at Texas University and in 1935 he joined the staff of the Jackson Laboratory in Bar Harbor, Maine, with whom he remained until his retirement in 1969.

In the circumstances it must have come as a considerable surprise to Snell to be awarded a third share of the 1980 Nobel Prize for Physiology or Medicine; in recognition of the part he played in the identification of the H-2 gene complex. Snell died in 1996. He was married with three sons. His hobbies were playing tennis and skiing.

Baruj **Benacerraf** was born in Caracas, Venezuela, on October 29,1920. His family originated from Jewish-European stock and Baruj from the age of five, was brought up in Paris. In 1940 he was in the US and Columbia University, graduating in 1942. He became a naturalized US citizen in 1943 and received an MD from Queen's General Hospital, New York, in 1945.

Between 1946-48 he served in the US Army. Following a year of research at Columbia and six years at the Hopital Broussais in Paris, he returned to the US and New York University School of Medicine. Between 1968-70 he was chief of the immunologic laboratory of the National Institute of Allergy and Infectious Diseases, National Institutes of Health.

From 1970 he held the Fabian Chair of Comparative Pathology at Harvard University. He was awarded a third share of the 1980 Nobel Prize for Physiology or Medicine; **"for his work leading to the discovery the immune-response genes that regulate immunology in organ transplants and the prevent infection that leads to the rejection of transplanted organs"**

In 1943 he met and married Annette Dreyfus, a French refugee. They met at Columbia University.

ECONOMICS

LAWRENCE KLEIN (1920-)

Lawrence Robert Klein was born in Omaha, Neb. US, on September 14,1920. His grandparents were Jewish emigres from Europe. He graduated from the University of California in 1942 and received a PhD from the Massachusetts Institute of Technology in 1944. Between 1944-47 he did research in econometrics at Chicago University. He then spent two years on the staff of the National Bureau of Economic Research. He worked at Oxford University for four years dealing with statistical inference. Upon his return to the US he joined the University of Pennsylvania. In 1960 he was in Japan at Osaka University working on a joint model building project.

His researches have produced detailed accounts of economic changes. He was awarded the 1980 Nobel Prize for Economics; **"for the creation of econometric models and the application to the analysis of economic fluctuations and economic policies"**

Klein also developed the Link Project, which incorporates data from a wide area and does multiple forecasts based upon political and economic policies. He has written much upon his subject including, *An Economic Forecasting Model* (1967). He is married with three daughters and a son.

PEACE

ADOLFO PEREZ ESQUIVEL (1931-)

Adolfo Perez Esquivel was born In Buenos Aires, Argentine on November 26,1931. The son of a fisherman, Adolfo trained as an architect and became famous as a sculptor before becoming a champion of human rights. He was a professor of fine arts at the Argentine National School of Fine Arts in 1968, when he resigned to lead Peace and Justice as secretary-general. He tried to tread a middle path between the extremists of both left and right and earned the enmity of both.

In particular, he spoke for the thousands who disappeared during the military junta's reign of terror. He was arrested in 1977, and held without charge for over a year, during which time he was subjected to torture. In 1980 he was awarded the Nobel Peace Prize; **"for his work as champion of human rights and non-violent reform in Latin-America"**

He never married.

1981

Ronald Reagan 39th President of US • Martial Law in Poland • France has Socialist governement and high speed trains • US confirms the existence of the AIDS virus • Neil Dunn, *Steaming* **• Harvey Fierstein,** *Torch Song Trilogy* **• Films:** *Chariots of Fire, Reds, Mephisto* **• Muriel Spark,** *Loitering with Intent* **• Paul Theroux,** *The Mosquito Coast* **• Salman Rushdie,** *Midnight's Children* **• Moshe Dayan, Samuel Barber, Paddy Chayefsky, Abel Gance, Anwar Sadat and Moshe Dayan die.**

LITERATURE

ELIAS CANETTI (1905-1994)

Elias Canetti was born in Rustschuk, Bulgaria, on July 25,1905. The first language he spoke was Ladino. This is peculiar to Sephardic Jews and reflected his descent from Spanish Jewry. Indeed his first language was Spanish his second French and he wrote in German. He spent his formative years, following his father's death in 1913, moving between Switzerland, Germany, Austria and England. In 1927 he was part of the mob responsible for the protest burning of the Justizpalast in Vienna. He was there studying at Vienna University and from where, in 1929, he received a doctorate in chemistry.

In 1935 he published, *Auto-da-Fe*. As well as an observation of mass behaviour it was also a warning about the rise of totalitarianism. In 1938 he settled in England. He wrote much including, *Crowds and Power* (1960).

He also wrote imaginative plays including, *The Wedding* (1932), *Comedy of Vanity* (1950) and *The Numbered* (1964). His autobiographies, *The Tongue Set Free* (1977) and *Torch in my Ear* (1980) explain the origins and reasons for his work.

He was awarded the 1981 Nobel Prize for Literature; **"for writings marked by a broad outlook, a wealth of ideas and artistic power and for his works that explore the emotions of crowds and the position of the individual at odds with society around him"**

He died in 1994. He was married but had no children.

CHEMISTRY

KENICHI FUKUI (1918-)
and
ROALD HOFFMANN (1937-)

"for their theories, developed independently, concerning the course of chemical reactions"

Kenichi Fukui was born in Nara, Japan, on October 4,1918, the eldest of three sons. Originally interested in engineering Fuku took little interest in chemistry until he was at Kyoto University. During WW2 he worked for the Army Fuel Laboratory. He received his PhD in 1948 and was professor of chemistry at Kyoto from 1951. His area of research was the investigation of the mechanisms of chemical reactions.

He was awarded a co-share of the 1981 Nobel Prize for Chemistry; **"for obtaining interaction results in the formation of a new, occupied orbital that has properties intermediate between those of occupied and unoccupied orbitals"**

Fukui designated these labile orbitals "frontier orbitals" and provided examples of their significance in reactions that produced important classes of organic compounds. He died in Kyoto on January 9, 1998, he was un-married.

Roald Hoffmann was born in Zloczow, Poland, on July 18,1937. Although only a child of four when the Germans invaded Poland he was Jewish, and sent, with his family to a German labour camp. By a miracle he survived because, following the execution of his father for attempting to escape, his mother smuggled Roald out of the camp to be hidden by a sympathetic Christian family until the Russian Red Army liberated Poland and he, and a few of his surviving family, were able in 1949, to emigrate to relatives in the US.

He studied at Columbia and Harvard universities and received a BA from the former and an MA from the latter. He obtained his PhD in 1962 from Harvard, spent three years there researching before joining the staff of Cornell University where he was professor of chemistry (1968-74). His research work is considerable, a primary focus being on molecular orbital calculations and adjacent activities. He was awarded a co-share of the 1981 Nobel Prize for Chemistry; **"for his work in the use of synthesis of the complicated molecule of vitamin B12."**

Hoffman, a member of the US National Academy of Sciences stated in 1997, that ' the cloning of sheep by genetic engineering raises ethical questions'. His most recent publication, *The Same and Not the Same* seeks to enjoin the scientific world into the wider arena. Between 1986 and 88 he was involved with a TV series called, 'The World of Chemistry', it is a 26 half hour episodic event. Married, he now considers himself a poet.

PHYSICS

NICHOLAS BLOEMBERGEN (1920-), ARTHUR SCHAWLOW (1921-)

"for their contribution to the development of laser photography"

and
KAI SIEGBAHN (1918-)

Nicholas Bloembergen was born in Dordrecht, Netherlands on March 11, 1920. Educated at Utrecht University, from where he received his BA and MA, he went on to the US and undertook further study from Harvard before returning to Holland and obtaining his PhD from Leiden University in 1948. He returned to the US, becoming a citizen in 1958 and professor of chemistry at Harvard in 1980.

His involvement with lasers and masers allowed Bloembergen to provide the specifications for an improved version that has resulted in the widely used microwave amplifier. He developed laser spectroscopy which allows high-precision observations of atomic structure. His laser spectroscopic investigations led him to formulate nonlinear optics.

He was awarded a third share of the 1981 Nobel Prize for Physics. He is married with two children.

Arthur Leonard Schawlow was born in Mount Vernon, New York State, US, on May 5, 1921. As a child he moved with his family to Canada. He was educated at Toronto University obtaining his PhD in 1949.

In the same year he joined Charles Townes(qv) team at Columbia University where Townes was conducting the maser-laser project.

Townes and Schawlow in 1955 wrote , *Microwave Spectroscopy*. Scawlow was later a visiting professor at Columbia before moving to Stanford University.

In 1981 he received a third share of the Nobel prize for Physics, for investigating phenomena that are detectable only with the use of lasers. He is married with three children.

Kai Manne Borje Siegbahn was born in Lund, Sweden on April 20, 1918. The son of Karl Siegbahn, who received the Nobel Prize for Physics in 1924, Kai was educated at Stockholm and received his PhD in physics in 1944. In 1951 he was appointed professor at the Royal Institute of Technology in Stockholm and in 1954 he was at Uppsala University.

Siegbahn's area of research was electron spectroscopy for chemical analysis (ESCA) that depends on a fundamental phenomenon, the photoelectric effect, which is the emission of electrons that occurs when electromagnetic radiation strikes a material. It resulted in Siegbahn being awarded a third share of the 1981 Nobel Prize for Physics; **"for formulating the principles underlying ESCA and for refining the instruments used in carrying it out"**

During the 1970s, ESCA was adopted all over the world for analysing materials, including the particles in polluted air and the surfaces of solid catalysts used in petroleum refining. He is married with three children.

PHYSIOLOGY or MEDICINE

DAVID HUBEL (1926-), ROGER SPERRY (1913-1994)
and
TORSTEN WIESEL (1924-)

David Hunter Hubel was born in Windsor, Ontario ,Canada on February 27,1926. He was educated at McGill University, Montreal from where he received a BA in 1947 and a MA in 1951. He became a US citizen in 1953.

In 1959 he was on the staff of the Harvard Medical School. In 1965 he was professor of physiology. His area of research was the investigation of brain function and he, together with Wiesel, collaborated on discoveries concerning information in the visual system.

Hubel was awarded a third share of the 1981 Nobel Prize for Physiology or Medicine; **"for outstanding achievements in the analysis of the flow of nerve impulses from the retina to the sensory and motor centres of the brain"**
He is un-married.

Roger Wolcott Sperry was born in Hartford, Conn; US, on August 20, 1913. He received a BA in English, a masters in psychology and a PhD in zoology from Chicago University in 1941. He was part of the teaching staff from 1946 to 1954, at which time he moved to the California Institute of Technology as professor of psycho- biology.

Sperry was awarded a third share of the 1981 Nobel Prize for Physiology or Medicine; **"for his study of functional specialization in the cerebal hemispheres. The surgical and experimental techniques developed by Sperry begining in the late 1940s laid the groundwork for constructing a 'map' of mental processes"**

He later became a student of psychology. He was un-married when he died on April 17, 1994 in Pasadena, CA.

Torsten Nils Wiesel was born in Uppsala, Sweden on June 3, 1924. He received a medical degree from the Karolinska Institute in Stockholm in 1954 and remained there as an instructor in physiology. He then accepted a research appointment from the John Hopkins University Medical School in Baltimore and there he began his association with Hubel. In 1959 they both moved to Harvard University and in 1974 Wiesel was the Robert Winthrop Professor of Neurobiology.

He was awarded a third share of the 1981 Nobel Prize for Physiology or Medicine for the work he did, together with Hubel of the **"structural and functional details of the visual cortex, located in the occipital lobes of the cerebrum"**

Wiesel has remained a Swedish citizen. He has been married twice and has a child.

ECONOMICS

JAMES TOBIN (1918-)

James Tobin was born in Champaign, Ill. US, on March 5, 1918. He was educated at and graduated from Harvard University in 1940. During WW2, he was an officer in the US Navy and served on the destroyer USS Kearney. During this time he met up with Herman Wouk who would later use him as a character in his book, *The Caine Mutiny*.

The war over, Tobin returned to Harvard and obtained a PhD in Economics and in 1950, joined the staff of Yale University becoming professor of economics in 1957. Between 1949-50 he was at Cambridge University working in the department of applied economics.

Tobin strongly extended the usefulness of Keynes' economic analysis by greatly clarifying issues like, risk, portfolio management, as well as the role of financial markets in conveying information concerning underlaying conditions.

He was awarded the 1981 Nobel Prize for Economics ; **"for his analysis of financial markets and their relations to expenditure decisions, employment, production and prices"**

His many publications include, *The American Business Creed* (1961), *National Economy Policy* (1966) and *The New Economics One Decade Older*(1974). He is married with four children.

PEACE

The United Nations Office of the High Commissioner for Refugess

UNHCR has its offices in Geneva, Switzerland and was established by the UN General Assembly on January 1, 1951. It exists to provide legal and political protection for refugees and until they are able to acquire nationality in new countries of residence.

In 1954 and 1981 UNHCR has been awarded the Nobel Peace Prize.

1982

UK-Argentine war over the Falkland/Maldive Islands • Israel invades Lebanon • 20,000 British women protest at having US Cruise missiles at Greenham Common • Compact Discs (CD) players go on sale • Caryl Churchill, *Top Girls,* Michael Frayn, *Noises Off* • Films: *Gandhi, E.T., Tootsie, Fanny and Alexander, Fitzcarraldo* • Saul Bellow, *The Dean's December,* Anita Brookner, *Providence,* Thomas Keneally, *Schindler's Ark,* Alice Walker, *The Color Purple* • Ben Nicholson, Thelonious Monk, Rainer Fassbinder, Dame Marie Rambert, Grace Kelly, Pierre Mendes-France, Jaques Tati, Leonid Brezhnev and Artur Rubenstein die.

LITERATURE

GABRIEL GARCIA MARQUEZ (1928-)

Gabriel Garcia Marquez was born in Aractaca, Columbia, on March 6, 1928. Although his parents were poverty stricken, Gabriel took all the opportunities that came his way and studied law and journalism at the National University of Columbia and at Cartagena University. He began his career as a journalist in 1948. In the 1950s and 60s he worked for the Cuban news agency, La Presna in Columbia, Havana and New York. In the early 1970s, he was working as a screenwriter, journalist and publicist in Mexico City. In the early 1980s, restrictions on his travel in Columbia and the US were imposed because of his left-wing politics.

Several magazine articles and short stories appeared regularly from the 1940s onwards. A

book of short stories appeared in 1962 under the title, *No One Writes to the Colonel and other Stories*.

One Hundred Years of Solitude was a full length novel, published in 1967 which tells of the history of Macondo and its founders, the Buendia family. This story of Columnian history is probably his best known novel.

Other novels of note include, *Eyes of a Blue Dog* (1972), *The Autumn of the Patriarch* (1975), *Chronicle of a Death Foretold* (1981), *Love in the Time of Cholera*(1985) and *General in His Labyrinth* published in 1989 is a fictional account of the Latin-American hero Simon Bolivar during the final months of his life.

Garcia Marquez was awarded the 1982 Nobel Prize for Literature; **"for his novels and short stories, in which the fantastic and the realistic are combined in a richly composed world of imagination, reflecting a continent's life and conflicts. A central figure in the so-called magical realism movement in Latin-American literature"**

He is un-married.

CHEMISTRY

AARON KLUG (1926-)

Aaron **Klug** was born in Lithuania on August 11, 1926. When he was three his parents, anxious to escape rampant anti-Semitism, emigrated to South Africa. He was educated at the University of the Witwatersrand with the original intention of studying medicine; but he switched courses and took his degree in science. He then went to Cape Town University to do a doctorate in crystallography. However, he cut the course short, picked up an MA and took off for Trinity College, Cambridge , where he completed his PhD in 1953.

He won a research fellowship to Birbeck College. London University, to study viruses connected with the use of tobacco. In 1962 he returned to Cambridge and the Medical Research Council, becoming head of the structural studies branch in 1978. His biological discoveries were in the field of crystallographic electron technique development. His subsequent methods have been widely used to study proteins and viruses. He was awarded the 1982 Nobel Prize for Chemistry: **"for his development of crystallographic electron microscopy and his structural elucidation of biologically important nuclei acid-protein complexes and for his investigations of the three-dimensional structure of viruses and other particles that are combinations of nucleic acids and proteins"**

He was knighted in 1988 and awarded the Order of Merit. He was President of the Royal Society in 1996. He is married with two sons.

PHYSICS

KENNETH WILSON (1936-)

Kenneth Geddes Wilson was born in Waltham, Mass, US, on June 8, 1936. He graduated from Harvard University in 1956 and received a PhD from the California Institute of Technology. He spent a year with the European Council for Nuclear Research and was then appointed assistant professor at Cornell University in 1963. There he was later professor of physics (1971-88) switching to Ohio State University in 1988.

His research work provided, inter alia, a mathematical strategy for dealing with effects that involve neighbouring atoms or molecules as well as those that influence a specimen of material large enough to be observed experimentally. He was awarded the 1982 Nobel Prize for Physics; **"for his theory for critical phenomena in connection with phase transitions"**

His later work included his development of a general procedure for constructing improved theories concerning the transformations of matter called continuous, or second-order, phase transitions. Wilson is married.

PHYSIOLOGY or MEDICINE

SUNE BERGSTROM (1916-), BENGT SAMUELSSON (1934-)
and
JOHN VANE (1927-)

"for their discoveries concerning prostaglandins and related biologically active substances"

Sune Karl Bergstrom was born in Stockholm, Sweden on January 10, 1916. He was educated at the Karolinska Institute, Stockholm from where he was awarded, in 1944, doctorates in both medicine and biochemistry. Following research fellowships at Columbia University and Basel University, Bergstrom returned to Sweden to become professor of chemistry at Lund University. In 1958 he returned to the Karolinska Institute where, in 1963, he was head of the medical school. He became rector in 1969 until his retirement in 1977.

His area of research, which continued after his retirement, was in the area of biochemical compounds that influence blood pressure, body temperature, allergic reactions, and other physiological phenomena in mammals. Bergstrom was awarded a third share of the 1982 Nobel Prize for Physiology or Medicine; **"for being the first to demonstrate the existence of more than one compound and to determine the elemental compositions of two of them"** He is un-married

Bengt Ingemar Samuelsson was born in Halmstad, Sweden on May 21, 1934. Educated at Lund University, from where he graduated, he continued at the Karolinska Institute, Stockholm where he received a PhD in biochemistry in 1960 and a PhD in Medicine in 1961. He remained at the Karolinska Institute and eventually succeeded Bergstrom as head of the medical department.

His area of research was in the isolation, identification and analysis of many prostaglandins and resulted in his being awarded a third share of the 1982 Nobel Prize for Physiology or Medicine; **"for being the first to describe the process of prostaglandin formation"**

Prostaglandins are biochemical compounds that influence the blood pressure, body temperature, allergic reactions, and other physiological phenomena in mammals. He was the first person to describe the process of prostagland in formation.

He is married.

John Robert Vane was born in Tardebigg, Worcs, England, on March 29, 1927. He graduated from Birmingham University and in 1953 earned a PhD from Oxford University. He taught for two years at Yale University before returning to England to join the Institute of Basic Medical Sciences at London University. In 1973 he was research director of the Wellcome Research Laboratories in Beckenham.

Vane's area of research was also in the formation of prostagladins and resulted in the award of a third share of the 1982 Nobel Prize for Physiology or Medicine; **"for demonstrating that aspirin inhibits the formation of prostaglandins associated with pain, fever, and inflammation, Vane provided a physiological rationale for the effectiveness of the world's most widely used drug"**

Vane is married with two children.

In particular, his research into the physiological rationale for the effectiveness of the world's most widely used drug (aspirin) has given a new lease of life for its use. In 1986 Vane founded the William Harvey Research Institute which funds cardiovascular research. He was knighted in 1984.

ECONOMICS

GEORGE STIGLER (1911-1991)

George Joseph Stigler was born in Renton, Wash; US, on January 17, 1911. He graduated from Washington University in 1931, took a business degree at Northwestern University in1932 and a PhD in economics at Chicago University in 1938. There followed numerous appointments at numerous teaching establishments that ranged from 1936 to 1981.

Among his contributions in the field of economics was his study of economic information and his study of public regulation; here he concluded that at best it has little influence and that it is usually detrimental to consumer interests. His publications include; *The Theory of Price* (1946), *Essays in the History of Economic Thought* (1965), *The Citizen and the State (*1975) and *The Economist as Preacher and Other Essays* (1982).

Stigler was awarded the 1982 Nobel Prize for Economics; **"for his seminal studies of industrial structures, functioning of markets and causes and effects of public regulation"**

His autobiography appeared in 1988 under the title, *Memories of an Unregulated Economist.* He died of a heart attack in Chicago on December 1,1991. Married with three sons, he was proud of the fact that, unlike many economists, he jumped on no bandwagons and pursued his independent line without fear or favour. A man of considerable charm he demanded the highest standards of his students.

PEACE

ALVA MYRDAL (1902-1986)
and
ALFONSO GARCIA ROBLES (1911-1991)

Alva Reimer Myrdal was born in Uppsala, Sweden on January 31,1902. She was educated at the universities of Uppsala, Stockholm and Geneva. A proponent of child welfare and equal rights for women, she became director of the United Nation's Department of Social Welfare (1949-50) and followed as director of UNESCO. Elected to the Swedish parliament in 1962 she served as the Swedish representative on the UN Disarmament Committee (1962-73).

She played a prominent part in the international peace movement and was honoured by the receipt of the West German Peace Prize in 1970, the Albert Einstein Peace Prize in 1980 and the Jawaharial Nehru Award for International Understanding in 1981.

She was awarded a co-share of the 1982 Nobel Prize for Peace.

A prolific writer her publications include, *The Game of Disarmament: How the United States and Russia Run the Arms Race*(1976). She died in Ersta, near Stockholm on February 1,1986. She never married.

Alfonso Garcia Robles was born in Zamora, Mexico on March 20, 1911. He studied law at universities in Mexico, Paris and Amsterdam. He joined the Mexican foreign service and rose to become director-general in the Mexican Ministry of Foreign Affairs. He served for several years at the United Nations Secretariat.

Whilst serving as ambassador to Brazil, he first met with talk concerning nuclear armaments. Following the Cuban Missile Crisis of 1962, Garcia Robles persuaded the Mexican government to support a policy of excluding nuclear weapons from Latin America. This resulted in the Treaty of Tlatelolco (1967). This committed 22 nations of Latin America to bar nuclear weapons from their lands.

He was awarded a co-share of the 1982 Nobel Peace Prize for his work in the field of Nuclear Disarmament. He died in Mexico City on September 2, 1991. He never married.

1983

US invades Grenada • USSR shoots down Korean 747 jet • IBM produce personal computer with built-in hard disc • Britain deploys Cruise Missiles • First US woman astronaut in space • Robert Creeley, *Collected Poems 1945-1975* • Films: *King of Comedy, Educating Rita, Cross Creek* • Howard Jacobson, *Coming from Behind* • J.M. Coetzee, *Life and Times of Michael K* • Arthur Koestler, William Walton, Rebecca West, Kenneth Clark, Niklaus Pevsner, Harry James, George Cukor, Luis Bunuel and Joan Miro die.

LITERATURE

WILLIAM GOLDING (1911-1993)

William Gerald Golding was born St.Columb Minor, Cornwall, UK, on September 19, 1911. He was educated at Marlborough Grammar School, where his father was a teacher, and Brasenose College, Oxford. He graduated in 1935 and worked in small theatre companies and as a teacher. He joined the Royal Navy in 1940, took part in several sea battles until 1944 when he was given command of a rocket-launching boat during the invasion of Normandy, France in 1944.

After the war he returned to his teaching job at Bishop Wordsworth School in Salisbury and stayed until 1961. His first published novel was *Lord of the Flies* (1954) as a film in 1963 and 1990. It aroused much interest. *The Inheritors* (1955) is set in the last days of Neanderthal man and is most violent. *Pincher Martin* (1956) is a study of greed and self-delusion. Other novels include, *The Spire* (1964), *Darkness Visible* (1979) and the sea-faring trilogy, *To The Ends of the Earth* (1980-1989) and *Fire Down Below* (1989).

He was awarded the 1983 Nobel Prize for Literature; **"for his novels which, with the perspicuity of realistic narrative art and the diversity and universality of myth, illuminate the human condition in the world of to-day"**

Golding was knighted in 1988. He died in Falmouth, Cornwall on June 19, 1993. He was married with a son and daughter. Golding once defined the theme of his most famous work, *Lord of the Flies* as "grief, sheer grief, grief, grief grief."

CHEMISTRY

HENRY TAUBE (1915-)

Henry **Taube** was born in Neudorf, Sask. Canada on November 30, 1915. He was educated at Saskatchewan University and the University of California at Berkeley. He became a US citizen in 1942 and taught variously at Cornell, Chicago and Stanford universities.

In the late 1940s Taube carried out a series of experiments with isotopes in order to show that in water solution, the ions of metals form chemical bonds with several molecules of water and that the stability and geometric arrangement of the resulting hydrates vary widely.

Taube was able to show that in an intermediate stage of reaction, a chemical bond must form between one of the ions and a ligand that is still bonded to the other. This ligand acts as a temporary bridge between the two ions and its bond to the original ion can later break in such a way as to effect, indirectly, the electron transfer that completes the reaction.

Taube was awarded the 1983 Nobel Prize for Chemistry; **"for his work on the mechanisms of electron transfer reactions, especially in metal complexes and for findings that have been applied in selecting metallic compounds for use as catalysts, pigments and superconductors and in understanding the function of metal ions as constituents of certain enzymes"**
Taube never married.

PHYSICS

SUBRAHMANYAN CHANDRASEKHAR (1910-1995)
and
WILLIAM FOWLER (1911-)

Subrahmanyan **Chandrasekhar** was born in Lahore, India on October 19, 1910. He was the nephew of Sir Chanrasekhra Venkata Raman who won the Nobel Prize for Physics in 1930. He was educated at Presidency College, Madras University, and Trinity College, Cambridge. By the early 1930s scientists believed that after converting all of their hydrogen to helium, stars lose energy and contract under the influence of their own gravity. These are known as white dwarf stars and contract to about the size of Earth. Chandrasekhar would determine that a star having a mass more than 1.44 times that of the Sun does not form a white dwarf but instead continues to collapse, later becoming a neutron star. An even more massive star continues to collapse and becomes a black hole.

He joined the staff of Chicago University becoming professor of physics in 1952. He became a US citizen a year later. He did important work on energy transfer by radiation in stellar atmospheres and convection on the solar surface. He was awarded the Gold Medal of the Royal Astronomical Society in 1953, the Royal Medal of the Royal Society in 1962 . He was awarded a co-share of the 1983 Nobel Prize for Physics; **"for his theoretical studies of the physical processes of importance to the structure and evolution of the stars"**

Among his publications are, *Principles of Stellar Dynamics* (1942), *Radiative Transfer* (1950) and *Truth and Beauty: Aesthetics and Motivations in Science (*1987).

William Alfred Fowler was born in Pittsburgh, US, on August 9, 1911. He was educated at the California Institute of Technology from where in 1936 he received his PhD The co-award of the 1983 Nobel Prize for Physics; **"for his theoretical and experimental studies of the nuclear reactions of importance in the formation of the chemical elements in the universe"**

His role in formulating a widely accepted theory of element generation stemmed from the work he did in the 1950s with Fred Hoyle and Margaret and Geoffrey Burbidge that suggested that in stellar evolution, elements are synthesized progressively from light elements to heavy ones. Following his work on radio astronomy Fowler worked on relativistic effects on quasars and pulsars and studied subatomic particles released during nuclear reactions.

He was awarded the Barnard Medal in 1965 and the Vetlesen Prize in 1973.

He is married with two daughters.

PHYSIOLOGY or MEDICINE

BARBARA McCLINTOCK (1902-1992)

Barbara McClintock was born in Hartford, Conn; US, on June 16,1902. The daughter of a doctor, she studied plant genetics at Cornell University and received her doctorate in botany in 1927. She went on to spend more than 50 years at Carnegie's Cold Spring Harbor (NY) Laboratory. By observing and experimenting with variations of maize, she discovered that genetic information does not stand still.

She then isolated two control elements in genetic material and discovered they moved and their change of position affected the behaviour of neighbouring genes. She went on to suggest that these transposable elements were responsible for the diversity in cells during an organism's development.

It was many years until the importance of her research was recognized. Subsequently, it has been seen as pioneering work that has increased the knowledge of genetic function in a dramatic way. Barbara McClintock was awarded the 1983 Nobel Prize for Physiology or Medicine; **"for her discovery of mobile genetic elements"** and regarded as one of the most important figures in the history of genetics.

She would spend long hours alone in her laboratory, gave no lectures and refused to publish the results of her work. She feared no-one would take them seriously. When in the 1970s molecular biologists confirmed the existence of transposable genetic elements or; "jumping genes" Barbara was hailed as a scientific visionary. In 1933 she received a Guggenheim Fellowship and worked at the Kaiser Wilhelm Institute in Berlin. It was the time of Adolf Hitler and Barbara returned to the US. It was difficult for a woman to get a university appointment and she received many refusals.

She died in Huntingdon, New York on September 2, 1992. She never married.

ECONOMICS

GERARD DEBREVU (1921-)

G**erard Debreu** was born in Calais, France on July 4, 1921. He was educated at École Normale Supérieure. He was later educated at Paris University from where he received his DSc in 1956. He joined a Chicago based foundation that later moved to Yale University (1950-1959)

His monograph, *Theory of Values: An Axiomatic Analysis of Economic Equilibrium* appeared in 1959.

Debreu went on to develop methods that would analyse factors and influence equilibrium. He became professor of economics and mathematics at the University of California in 1962, and a US citizen in 1975. In 1970 he became a Fellow of the American Academy of Arts and Sciences. In 1972 he was an Overseas Fellow of Churchill College, Cambridge University.

He was awarded the 1983 Nobel Prize for Economics. **"For having incorporated new analytical methods into economic theory and for his rigorous reformulation of the theory of general equilibrium"**

In 1976 he was awarded the Chevalier de la Légion d'honneur. He is married with two daughters.

PEACE

LECH WALESA (1943-)

Lech Walesa was born in Popowo, Poland on September 29,1943. The son of a carpenter, Lech went to the local primary school followed by some years at a technical school. He worked as an electrician at the Lenin Shipyard at Gdansk (1966-76) before becoming a trade union leader. He was sacked in 1976 for leading a strike.

In 1980 he was re-instated at which time he held a meeting and declared a strike of workers against rising prices and poor conditions. It led to the creation of the Solidarity cause or free trade unions. The results were not lost in the world of the Roman Catholic church who saw an opportunity that might bring down the Communist government.

Walesa was jailed by General Jaruzelski in December 1981 and released in November 1982. He was awarded the 1983 Nobel Peace Prize and granted a personal audience with the Polish born Pope, John Paul ll. In 1989 he negotiated a an agreement with Jaruzelski that resulted in a coalition government. In 1990 Walesa became president of Poland. A short period later his sometimes abrupt and dictatorial manner caused critics to accuse him of aiming to become a dictator. He thereafter was forced to come to an accommodation with the prime minister, Hanna Suchocka in 1992-93.

He is married.

1984

Miners strike in Britain • IRA bombs British government • Indira Gandhi assassinated • President Reagan wins landslide victory • Dr Alec Jeffreys invents 'genetic fingerprinting' • Woman gives birth to a previously frozen fertilized embryo • Philip Glass Opera, *Akhnaten* **• Films:** *Passage to India; Paris, Texas; Amadeus:* **• Samuel Beckett,** *Collected Poems 1930-78* **• J.G.Ballard,** *Empire of the Sun* **• Iain Banks,** *The Wasp Factory* **• Martin Amis,** *Money* **• Anita Brookner,** *Hotel du Lac* **• Gore Vidal,** *Lincoln* **• Mary Wesley,** *The Camomile Lawn* **• Count Basie, John Betjeman, Joseph Losey, Lillian Hellman, Carl Foreman, Richard Burton and Francois Truffaut die.**

LITERATURE

JAROSLAV SEIFERT (1901-1986)

Jaroslav Seifert was born in Prague, Czechoslovakia, on September 23, 1901. He was born into a working class family living in a poor part of Prague. He made his living as a journalist from 1950 although he worked as a poet from 1920 when he published, *City in Tears*. He was an ardent Communist who expected great things from the Revolution. He gradually became disenchanted so culminating with his leaving the Party in 1929.

Aspects of life in his homeland became the principal subjects of his poetry, *Switch Off the Lights* (1938) tells of the Munich agreement which dismissed Czechoslovakia into the hands of Germany. *Clothed in Light* (1940) tells of Prague during the occupation. *The Helmet of Clay* (1945) explores the Prague uprising of 1945. In 1966 he was named 'Poet of the Nation' and in 1968 he was imprisoned briefly for his condemnation of the Soviet invasion of Czechoslovakia.

He was awarded the 1984 Nobel Prize for Literature; **"for his poetry which endowed with freshness, sensuality and rich inventiveness provides a liberating image of the indomitable spirit and versatility of man"**

He died in Prague on January 10, 1986. He was un-married.

CHEMISTRY

BRUCE MERRIFIELD (1921-)

Robert **Bruce Merrifield** was born in Fort Worth, Texas, US, on July 15, 1921. He was educated at the University of California and graduated in 1943. He later returned to UCLA and obtained his PhD in 1949. He then joined the Rockefeller Institute for Medical Research in New York where he remained.

During the 1950s and 60s, he developed the notion that the key to the synthesis of polypeptide was the anchoring of the first amino acid to an insoluble solid. Other amino acids could then be joined, one by one, to the fixed terminus. It later proved to be highly efficient and of great assistance for research on hormones, enzymes, the commercial manufacture of insulin and later of interferon.

Merrifield was awarded the 1984 Nobel Prize for Chemistry; **"for his development of methodology for chemical synthesis on a solid matrix"**

Later his development of a simple and ingenious method for synthesizing chains of amino acids in any predetermined order was of great assistance in the field of bio-chemistry.

Merrifield is married with six children.

PHYSICS

CARLO RUBBIA (1934-)
and
SIMON van der MEER (1925-)

"for their decisive contributions to the large project, which led to the discovery of the field particles W and Z, communicators of weak interaction"

Carlo **Rubbia** was born in Gorizia, Italy, on March 31, 1934. He was educated at the Normal School of Pisa and Pisa University from where, in 1957, he received a PhD. He stayed on to teach for two years before joining Columbia University on a research fellowship. He later returned to Italy and joined Rome University in 1960. In 1962 he became professor of physics at the European Centre for Nuclear Research (cern) in Geneva. In 1970 he was appointed professor of physics at Harvard University and for a long period divided his time between Harvard and CERN.

Rubbia's main claim to scientific fame was confirming the validity of the Weinberg-Salam (qv) theories of the 1970s, that the weak force and electromagnetism are different manifestations of a single basic kind of physical interaction. He went on to propose that the large synchrotron at

CERN be modified, so that beams of accelerated protons and antiprotons could be made to collide head-on, thus releasing energies great enough for the weak bosons to materialize.

In 1983 experiments with the colliding-beam apparatus proved that the *W* and *Z* particles are indeed produced and have particles that agree with the theoretical predictions. Rubbia was awarded a co-share of the 1984 Nobel Prize for Physics;   He is married with two children.

Simon van der Meer was born in The Hague, Netherlands, on November 24, 1925. He graduated from the Higher Technical School in Delft and joined the Phillips Company. He later received a degree in physical engineering from Delft University. In 1956 he joined the staff of the European Organization for Nuclear Research (cern) where he remained.

Manipulation of the beams required to accelerate protons required an effective way for keeping the particles from scattering out of the proper path and hitting the walls of the tube. Van der Meer devised a mechanism that would monitor the particle scattering at a particular point on the ring and trigger a device opposite of the ring to modify the electric fields in such a way as to keep the particles on course.

For his work in this important field, Van der Meer was awarded a co-share of the 1984 Nobel Prize for Physics;   He   is   married   with   two children.

PHYSIOLOGY or MEDICINE

NIELS JERNE (1911-1994), GEORGES KOHLER (1946-)
and
CESAR MILSTEIN (1926-)

"for theories concerning the specificity in development and control of the immune system and the discovery of the principle for production of monoclonal antibodies"

Niels Kai Jerne was born in London, England, on December 23, 1911. His parents were Danish and the family returned to Denmark shortly after Niels' birth. He was educated at and graduated from Leiden University and in 1951 received a medical degree from Copenhagen University.   Between 1956 and 1962 he was chief medical officer of the World Health Organization.

During the 1960s he taught at Geneva and Pittsburgh universities and was professor of experimental therapy at Goethe University in Frankfurt. He helped to found the Basel Institute for Immunology and was the director between 1969 and 1980. After teaching for a year at the Pasteur Institute in Paris he retired.

Jerne was the first to suggest the way in which antibodies are produced in order to match the invading bodies or antigens. He offered a comprehensive theory of the development of the immune system as a whole and in 1974 presented the 'network theory' in which he detailed the complex system of interactions whereby the immune system is activated to respond to and counteract disease and then is shutdown when not required.

He was awarded a third share of the 1984 Nobel Prize for Physiology or Medicine. He died in 1994. He was married.

Georges Kohler was born in Munich, Germany on April 17,1946. He obtained his PhD in biology in 1974 from Freiburg University. Between 1974-76 he worked with Cesar Milstein at the molecular research laboratory of The Medical Research Council in Cambridge, UK.

In 1975 they discovered the technique for producing monoclonal antibodies that were pure, uniform and highly sensitive substances used in diagnosing and fighting a number of diseases. Kohler went on to work at the Basel Institute of Immunology (1976-84). In 1985, he became a director of the Max Planck Institute of Immune Biology in Freiburg.

He was awarded a third share of the 1984 Nobel Prize for Physiology or Medicine. He is un-married.

Cesar Milstein was born in Bahia Blanca, Argentine, on October 8, 1926. His Jewish parents had earlier left Europe to escape on-going anti-Semitism. Cesar was a schoolboy when through reading the works of Louis Pasteur he became interested in science. Educated at Buenos Aires University he voyaged to England and Cambridge University from where in 1960 he received a PhD He returned to the Argentine and the National Institute of Microbiology in Buenos Aires (1957-63). Thereafter he was a member of the Medical Research Council's Laboratory of Molecular Biology and held dual Argentine and British citizenship.

The research he undertook into the fusion of short-lived, highly specific lymphocytes or antibody producing cells, with the cells of a myeloma, a type of tumour that can be made to reproduce indefinitely. The resulting hybrid cells retained the two desired properties, i.e. they perpetuated themselves, providing potentially unlimited amounts of any desired antibody. As a result Milsteain was awarded a third share of the 1984 Nobel Prize for Physiology or Medicine;

Milstein is married.

ECONOMICS

RICHARD STONE (1913-1991)

John **Richard Nicholas Stone** was born in London, England, on August 30, 1913. He originally studied law, whilst at Cambridge University until coming under the influence of Keynes. It resulted to his switching to economics and a degree in 1935. During WW2 he was employed at the Central Statistical Office and served in government.

Post war, he was appointed director of applied economics at Cambridge, remaining until 1955 when he became professor of finance and accounting at Cambridge University, Emeritus from 1980.

In 1941 Stone adopted a method of an accounting model that could be used to track economic activities nationally. In the 1950s, he created what in effect was a national bookeeping system and adopted by the British government. He was knighted in 1978. He later worked with the United Nations. He was awarded the 1984 Nobel Prize for Economics. **"For having made fundamental contributions to the development of systems of national accounts and hence greatly improved the basis for empirical economic analysis"**

Amongst his writings were, *Input-Output and National Accounts* (1961) and *Mathematical Models of the Economy and Other Essays* (1970). He died in Cambridge on December 6, 1991. He was married three times and had one daughter.

PEACE

DESMOND TUTU (1931-)

Desmond **Mpilo Tutu** was born in Klerksdorp, South Africa on October 7 1931. His parents were of Xhosa and Twasana stock and Desmond was educated at South African mission schools, where his father was a teacher. He wanted to become a doctor but there was insufficient money available for him to take the course, instead, in 1954, he became a teacher. He resigned in 1957 took himself unto the church and became ordained as an Anglican priest in 1961. He became a lecturer in a Johannesburg seminary until in the 1960s he moved to London, England.

There he obtained an MA from King's College, London. Between 1972 and 1975 he was assistant director for the World Council of Churches. He then returned to South Africa where he was appointed dean of Johannesburg (1975-76). In 1978, he accepted the appointment as the general secretary of the South African Council of Churches and was leading spokesman for the rights of black South Africans. He propagated the use of non-violence as a way of protest against apartheid and he influenced countries to apply economic pressures against his government.

A collection of his lectures was published in 1982 under the title of *The Divine Intention*. In 1983 *Hope and Suffering,* a collection of his sermons were published. In 1985 Tutu was installed as the Anglican Bishop of Johannesburg and in 1986 he was elected to be archbishop of Capetown.

In 1984 he was awarded the Nobel Peace Prize; **"for his role in the opposition to apartheid in South Africa"**

Following the free elections of the early 1990s, resulting in Nelson Mandela becoming the country's first black president, Desmond Tutu became head of the Truth and Reconciliation unit that has heard all about the wrongdoings committed during the apartheid years.

1985

Rainbow Warrior sunk in New Zealand by French Secret Service • First mixed marriage celebrated in South Africa • Race riots in Tottenham, London • Hole detected in the ozone layer over Antarctica • Christopher Hampton, *Les Dangereuses* • Jurgen Habermas, *The Philosophical Discourse of Modernity* • Stephen Spender, *Collected Poems* • Allen Ginsberg, *Collected Poems 1947-1980* • Films: *Out of Africa, Kiss of the Spider Woman, Ran, Witness* • Margaret Atwood, *The Handmaid's Tale* • Keri Hulme, *The Bone People* • John Mortimer, *Paradise Postponed* • Jeanette Winterson, *Oranges Are Not the Only Fruit* • Phil Silvers, Simone Signoret, Eugene Ormandy, Marc Chagall, Laura Ashley, Philip Larkin and Robert Graves die.

LITERATURE

CLAUDE SIMON (1913-)

Claude Eugene Henri Simon was born in Tananarive, Madagascar on October 10, 1913. He was the only son of a French cavalry officer killed in WW1 and was subsequently raised by his mother in Perpignan. Following studies in Paris, Oxford and Cambridge, Simon emerged as a worldly traveller ready to fight in WW2. He was captured by the Germans in May 1940 but escaped to join the French Resistance. During this time he completed his first novel, *The Trickster* (1945). The war over Simon settled in the south of France and cultivated his vineyards.

By the use of the novel, he defined his objects and as such was given the collective of, 'new novel'. He wrote *The Wind* (1957) with this purpose in mind. In 1947 he wrote *The Taut Rope* about the Spanish civil war.

A cycle of four novels written between 1958 and 1967 constitute a cycle containing re-occurring characters and themes.   Critics consider *The Flanders Road* (1960) the most important of these. Later works include *The Battle of Pharsalus*

(1969) and *Triptych* (1973).

He was awarded the 1985 Nobel Prize for Literature; **"who in his novel combines the poet's and the painter's awareness of time in the depiction of the human condition"**

His style lacks all punctuation and often has sentences of a 1,000 words. However, his novels remain most readable despite their seeming chaos. He is un-married.

CHEMISTRY

HERBERT HAUPTMAN (1917-)
and
JEROME KARLE (1918-)

"for their outstanding achievements in the development of direct methods for the determination of crystal structures"

Herbert Aaron Hauptman was born in New York, US, on February 14, 1917. The son of European-Jewish immigrants, he was educated at City College of New York. There he met Jerome Karle when they both graduated in 1937. Hauptman went on to Columbia University to study mathematics and once again met up with Karle. They decided to collaborate on the study of crystal structures.

Although Hauptman became a professor of biophysics at the State University of New York in 1973, he continued his collaborative research and invented mathematical equations to describe the way numerous spots appear on photographic film as a result of a crystal diffraction of X-rays. His work meant it was possible to understand the location of atoms within the crystal molecules, enabling them to be pinpointed following an analysis of the intensity of the spots.

For some years his work and ideas was neglected but gradually crystallographers began using these theories to determine the three -dimensional structure of many thousands of small biological molecules, including those of antibiotics, hormones and vitamins. It resulted in Hauptman receiving a co-share of the 1985 Nobel Prize for Chemistry. He is married with two daughters.

Jerome Karle was born in New York, US, on June 18, 1918. He received his PhD in physical chemistry from Michigan University in 1943. He joined the Manhattan Project in 1943-4 and in the latter part of 1944 joined the Naval Research Laboratory; in 1967 he was the chief scientist for research on the structure of matter.

Following WW2, he was joined by Hauptmann and the two began the study of crystal structures. Before the two scientists had created their molecular equation method, it took some two years to deduce the structure of a simple biological molecule.

In the 1980s, using powerful computers to perform the complex calculations demanded by the new method, the job took two or three days. He devised mathematical equations to describe the arrangements of numerous spots that appear on photographic film as a result of a crystal's diffraction of X-rays.

For his efforts in the project Karle was awarded a co-share of the 1985 Nobel Prize for Chemistry. Jerome Karle is married.

PHYSICS

KLAUS von KLITZING (1943-)

Klaus von Klitzing was born in Sroda, that was part of German occupied Poland, on June 28, 1943. At the end of WW2, his parents managed to evade the liberating Red Army and get to West Germany. There Klaus attended the Technical University of Brunswick, graduating in 1969. He received from Wurzburg University in 1972 a PhD in physics and by 1980 was a professor of physics at the technical department of Munich University. In 1985 he became director of the Max Planck Institute for Solid State Physics in Stuttgart.

His field of research was in the arena of demonstrating that electrical resistance occurs in very precise resistants by using the Hall Effect. This effect denotes the voltage that develops between the edges of a thin current, carrying ribbon placed between the poles of a strong magnet. The ratio of this voltage to the current is called the Hall resistance.

Further research caused Klitzing to eventually define the mathematical ratio between the motion of an electron in the innermost orbit around an atomic nucleus to the speed of light. The significance of this 1980 discovery was immediately recognised and allowed other scientists to study the conducting properties of electronic components with amazing precision.

He was awarded the 1985 Nobel Prize for Physics; **"for the discovery of the quantized Hall effect"** He is un-married.

PHYSIOLOGY or MEDICINE

MICHAEL BROWN (1941-)
and
JOSEPH GOLDSTEIN (1940-)

"for their discoveries concerning the regulation of cholestrol metabolism"

Michael Stuart Brown was born in New York, US, on April 13, 1941. He came from an East European-Jewish family who originally came to the US to escape persecution. He graduated from the University of Pennsylvania and obtained his MD from the university's medical school in 1966. Whilst working as an intern at the Boston General Hospital he met Joseph Goldstein. Between 1968 and 1971, the two conducted research at the National Institute for Health and later, at Southampton Medical School at Dallas, Texas.

They investigated the genetic factors that are the reason for high levels of cholesterol in the blood-stream. They were able to determine a genetic defect in patients and a deficiency in cell receptors for low-density lipoprotein (LDL), the primary cholesterol carrying particles. The two later collaborated in developing drugs in order to lower high levels of cholesterol. From 1977 Brown was director of the centre for Genetic Diseases in Dallas. He was awarded a co-share of the 1985 Nobel Prize for Physiology or Medicine. Brown is married with two daughters.

Joseph Leonard Goldstein was born in Sumner, SC, US, on April 18, 1940. He came from a similar Jewish family background to that of his collaborator, Michael Brown. He received his BS degree from Washington University in Lexington, Virginia. Four years later, he gained his medical degree from the Southwestern Medical School in Dallas, Texas and later taught there.

1968-72, Goldstein was conducting research at the National Institutes of Health; studying genetically predisposing factors that causes the accumulation of blood cholesterol in people prone to heart attacks.

In 1976 Goldstein was professor of medicine and molecular genetics at the University of Texas Health Science Centre at Dallas.

In 1985 Goldstein was awarded a co-share of the Nobel Prize for Physiology or Medicine for his part in the explanation of the process of cholesterol metabolism in the human body. Goldstein is un-married.

ECONOMICS

FRANCO MODIGLIANI (1918-)

Franco **Modigliani** was born in Rome, Italy on June 18, 1918. The son of a Jewish physician, Franco studied law until 1939 when, to escape increasing anti-Semitism, he left Italy for the US. There he studied economics at the New School for Social Research, in New York, receiving his Ph.D in 1944. He later taught at several US universities until, in 1962, he was appointed professor of economics at the Massachusetts Institute of Technology.

He pioneered various aspects of economic theory and in 1985 received the Nobel Prize for Economics; **"for his pioneering analysis of saving and of financial markets"**

Mogdigliani also did important research on financial markets, particulalry on the respective effects that a company's financial structure and its future earning potential have on the market value of its stock. His analysis of personal savings, he termed it, the life-cycle theory, and expalined that individuals built up a store of wealth during their working days for the purpose of utilisation during old age. This process has subsequently been the foundation of pension planning.

He is married with a son.

PEACE

INTERNATIONAL PHYSICIANS for the PREVENTION of NUCLEAR WAR

This is an international organisation of doctors who are opposed to the nuclear arms race and who seek to educate the public on the catastrophic medical consequences that would result from a nuclear war. It was founded in 1980 and led by prominent Soviet and US physicians under the leadership of Bernard Lown and Yevgeny Chazov.

The orgainisation promotes research on the medical, psychological and biospheric effects a nuclear war would have. It was awarded the 1985 Nobel Peace Prize. At this time it had the support of 135,000 members covering 41 countries. Of this number some 30,000 were in the US and some 60,000 in the USSR.

1986

US bombs Tripoli • Chernobyl nuclear power accident • State of Emergency declared in South Africa • NSPCC reports a doubling over one year of child sex abuse in the UK • The first 'laptop' computer introduced in the US • US space shuttle *Challenger* explodes on lift off • Return of Halley's Comet • Lucien Freud, *Painter and Model* • *The Independent* launched in UK • Films: *Jean de Florette, Hannah and Her Sisters, Platoon* • Kingsley Amis, *The Old Devils* • Christine Brooke-Rose, *Xorandor* • Vikram Seth, *The Golden Gate* • Christopher Isherwood, Joseph Beuys, Simone de Beauvoir, Jorge Luis Borges, Otto Preminger, Alan Lerner, Benny Goodman, Marcel Dassault, Bernard Malamud, Elisabeth Bergner, Emanuel Shinwell, Henry Moore and Harold Macmillan die.

LITERATURE

WOLE SOYINKA (1934-)

Wole Soyinka, was born Akinwande Oluwole Soyinka in Abeokuta, Nigeria on July 13, 1934. A member of the Yoruba tribe, he was educated at Government College and Ibadan University College. He later graduated in English from Leeds University, UK. He returned to Nigeria and founded the national theatre. The Orisun Theatre produced his play, *A Dance of the Forests* in 1960 to mark Nigerian independence celebrations. His play, *The Lion and the Jewel* published in 1963, is in a light vein and mocking of westernized schoolteachers. His duo of plays concerning Brother Jero as in *The Trials of Brother Jero* (1960) and *Jero's Metamorphosis* (1972) were critical of up-start churches.

His first novel, *The Interpreters* (1965) concerns the uncertainties of young intellectuals. His next novel, *Season of Atomy* (1973) didn't fare as well. His play, originally written in 1965 and entitled, *Madmen and Specialists* was produced in the US in 1979 under the title of, *Madmen Scientists.*

During the Biafran war of the late 1960s, Soyinka supported the Biafrans in their struggle for independence from Nigeria. He was jailed for two years. *The Man Diea* (1972) is an account of his ordeals. He published his autobiography, *Ake: The Years of Childhood* in 1981.

In 1986 Soyinka became the first black African to be awarded the Nobel Prize for Literature; **"who in a wide cultural perspective and with poetic overtones fashions the drama of existence"**

He is now professor of comparative literature and head of the department of dramatic arts at Emory University, Atlanta and un-married. In October 1998, after 4 years in exile, Soyinka made a speech to a university audience in Nigeria which he started by saying, "I shall not be brief as I have

---

carried a lot on my mind these past years. I intend to be discursive" He concluded by telling his cheering audience that following years of cruel military rule, democracy was around the corner.

In London, Soyinka in December 1998, took part in a march organised by Amnesty International called to protest against the ex Chilean dictator, Pinochett.

CHEMISTRY

DUDLEY HERSCHBACH (1932-), YUAN LEE (1936-)
and
JOHN POLYANI (1929-)

"for their contributions concerning the dynamics of chemical elementary processes"

Dudley Robert Herschbach was born in San Jose, Calif; US, on June 18, 1932. He was educated at Stanford University from where he obtained a BS and MS. He then went to Harvard University and obtained his PhD in chemical physics in 1958. Between 1959 to 1963 he taught at the University of California before switching to Harvard University where he was professor of science.

For his research in the field of chemical reactions, he applied a technique that was already popular in elementary particle physics; molecular beam scattering. He went on to invent what became known as the "crossed molecular beam technique" This brought together, at supersonic speeds, beams of molecules. It meant that a detailed molecule by molecule examination of the chemical reaction event.

He was awarded a third share of the 1986 Nobel Prize for Chemistry. Herschbach is married with two daughters.

Yuan Tseh Lee was born in Hsin-chu, Taiwan on November 29, 1936. He was educated in Taiwan and received a PhD from the University of California in 1965. Before teaching at Chicago University (1968-1974), he did postdoctoral work at the universities of Harvard and Berkeley. He became a US citizen in 1974.

His field of research was in further developing the work of Herschbach. This resulted in the study of larger and more complex molecules.

As a result he was awarded a third share of the 1986 Nobel Prize for Chemistry; **"for his role in the development of chemical-reaction dynamics"** He is married with two sons and a daughter.

John Charles Polanyi was born in Berlin, Germany on January 23, 1929. His family were expatriate Hungarians and his father a noted chemist. The family left Germany when Hitler and the Nazis took over. He was educated in England and obtained his PhD from Manchester University in 1952 and a doctorate in science in 1964. He developed his research programme at the National Research Council of Canada in 1952 and began teaching at Toronto University in 1956 becoming professor of chemistry in 1974.

Polanyi developed a technique that is known as infrared chemiluminescence. This is based on the observation that molecules, when excited, emit infrared light. By means of spectroscopic analysis of the changes in emitted light that take place during a chemical reaction, Polanyi was able to trace the exchange of chemical bonds. This technique helped to detail the disposal of excess energy that occurs during a process of chemical reaction.

His work resulted in his being awarded a third share of the 1986 Nobel Prize for Chemistry. He is married with a son and daughter.

PHYSICS

GERD BINNIG (1947-), HEINRICH ROHRER (1933-)

"for their design of the scanning tunnelling microscope"

and
ERNST RUSKA (1906-1988)

Gerd Binnig was born in Frankfurt am Main, Germany, on July 20, 1947. Educated locally, he received a PhD from Frankfurt University in 1978. He then joined the IBM Research Laboratory in Zurich. There he met Rohrer. Both scientists then worked on the design and structure of the first scanning tunnelling microscope (STM). This instrument produces images of the surfaces of conducting or semi-conducting materials so finely, that individual atoms can clearly be identified.

Quantum mechanical effects cause an electric current to pass between the fine tip of the STM's tungsten probe and the surface being investigated. The tip of the probe is only one tenth-billion of a metre or the width of an atom.

Binnig was awarded a co-share of half the 1986 Nobel Prize for Physics. He is married with a son and daughter.

Heinrich Rohrer was born in Switzerland, on June 6, 1933. He was educated at the Swiss Federal Institute of Technology from where in 1960 he received a PhD. He joined IBM Research Laboratory in Zurich and there met up and worked with Binnig. Thereafter, he worked with Binnig on the invention of the scanning tunnelling microscope and in 1986 received the other half of half of the Nobel Prize for Physics.

He is married with two daughters.

Ernst August Friedrich Ruska was born in Heidelberg, Germany on December 25, 1906. He was educated at Munich University between 1925-27 before going to the Technical Department of Berlin University. He there began his studies that would lead to his invention of the electron microscope. It had been long established that electrons have the properties of waves some 100,000 times shorter than those of light waves.

Ruska took the view that if electrons could be focussed on an object in the same manner as light then, at extremely high magnifications the electrons would produce far greater detail than conventional instruments.

He invented his first electron microscope in 1933. Hitler praised his work and Ruska was given every opportunity to build improved instruments . Ruska joined Siemens (who would later establish factories within concentration camps using slave labour) and developed the first commercial electron microscope in 1939. He continued with Siemens throughout WW2, leaving in 1955 to become director of the Institute for Electron Microscopy of the Fritz Haber Institute, resigning in 1972.

He was awarded a half of the 1986 Nobel Prize for Physics; **"for his fundamental work in electron optics, and for the design of the first electron microscope"** and died in Berlin on May 25,1988.

He was un-married.

PHYSIOLOGY or MEDICINE

STANLEY COHEN (1922-)
and
RITA LEVI-MONTCINI (1909-)

"for their discoveries of growth factors"

Stanley Cohen was born in Brooklyn, New York, on November 17, 1922. He was educated at Brooklyn College where in 1943 he received a BA. At Michigan University in 1948 he obtained PhD.

He joined up with Rita Levi-Montcini at Washington University, St Louis in 1952 as a researcher.

His area of research was the nerve growth factor and he eventually discovered a cell within this factor, which he termed epidermal growth factor (EGF). It was later shown that EGF influences a range of developmental events in the body.

He also discovered the mechanisms by which EGF is taken into and acts upon individual cells. In 1967 he was appointed professor of biochemistry at Vanderbilt University, Nashville. He was awarded a half share of the 1986 Nobel Prize for Physiology or Medicine: **"for his researches on substances produced in the body in the body that influence the development of nerve and skin tissues"** He is un-married.

Rita Levi-Montcini was born in Turin, Italy on April 22, 1909. One of a pair of twins with an older brother and sister, born to Jewish parents. She studied medicine at Turin University, where she remained after obtaining her MD, to research the effects of peripheral tissues on nerve cell growth. Her work was interrupted when the Germans occupied Italy (1943-45), driving her into hiding. Post-war she resumed her work in Turin.

In 1947 she accepted a post at Washington University, St Louis, to study with the eminent zoologist Dr. Hamburger, then working on the growth of nerve tissues in chicken embryos. They worked together to discover that a nerve growth implanted into chicken embryos produced a nerve growth factor (NGF). Stanley Cohen now took the place of Hamburger. They went on to discover a bodily substance that stimulates and influences the growth of nerve cells.

Levi-Montcini was awarded a co-share of the 1986 Nobel Prize for Physiology or Medicine; **"for discovery of a bodily substance that stimulates and influences the growth of nerve cells"**

In 1961 she established a research medical laboratory in Rome and thereafter travelled constantly back and forth between Italy and the US. She holds joint citizenship and talks openly about her life in her autobiography, *In Praise of Imperfection* (1988). She never married.

ECONOMICS

JAMES BUCHANAN (1919-)

James Mcgill Buchanan was born in Murfreesboro, Tenn; US, on October 2, 1919. He was educated at Tennessee State College, from he obtained a BS in 1940. Tennessee University produced an MA in 1941 and, following 5 years in the US Navy, he received a PhD from Chicago University (1948). He taught at a number of universities from 1950 to 1969. Between 1969 and 1983 he was professor of economics at Virginia Polytechnic Institute before transferring to Fairfax University, VA.

His arena of economic discovery was the development of what became known as ' the public choice theory' this was a unique method of analysing economic and political decision making. He wrote a large number of books including, *The Calculus of Consent: Logical Foundations of Constitutional Democracy* (1962), *The Demand and Supply of Public Goods* (1968) and *The Political Legacy of Lord Keynes* (1977).

He was awarded the 1986 Nobel Prize in Economic Sciences **"for his development of the contractual and constitutional bases for the theory of economic and political decision-making"**

He is married but has no children.

PEACE

ELIE WIESEL (1928-)

Elie Wiesel was born in Sighet, Romania on September 30, 1928. The large Jewish population was not deported to the death camps until the latter part of 1944. Not that this made any difference; there were very few survivors. Elie was fifteen when he and his large family were divided up on arrival at Auschwitz, Poland. Elie, fit for work, went one way; his family, either too old or too young, another. He never saw them again. He was later taken to Buchenwald to work as a slave labourer, there his father was murdered.

He has spent his life making sure the world never forgets the Holocaust. Following liberation and the end of WW2, he settled in France and studied at the Sorbonne in Paris. He became a journalist and worked on French and Israeli newspapers. In 1956 he went to the US and in 1963 became an American citizen. Elie Wiesel was a professor at City College, New York and in 1976 became professor of humanities at Boston College. His first book, written in Yiddish, was the result of urging by novelist Francois Mauriac *And the World Has Remained Silent* (1956) is part autobiographical and deals with a young lad's spiritual reaction to Auschwitz.

His books generally appear to ask 'why?'; Why was the Holocaust allowed to happen?. In 1962 he wrote, *The Town Beyond the Wall* which examines apathy. *A Beggar in Jerusalem* (1968) deals with the philosophical questions attached to man killing man. *Souls on Fire* (1972) and *The Testament* are Hasidic tales. Wiesel has lectured all over the world and whilst the core of his message concerns the Holocaust, he uses this horror as a basis on which to condemn all violence, oppression and racial bigotry. He was awarded the 1986 Nobel Peace Prize. In 1996 he published part one of his memoirs, *All Rivers Run to the Sea.* This covers the period 1928-1969. In May 1996, at the Cannes Film Festival, a 90 minute documentary film on the life of Elie Wiesel was shown in the 'Director's Fortnight' section. Directed by the Hungarian, Judit Elek, it is an emotional tour-de-force. He is un-married.

1987

Ronald Reagan accepts full responsibility over the Iran-Contra scandal but doesn't resign • A great storm sweeps over south-east England • Russian leader Mikhail Gorbachev criticises Joseph Stalin for political errors • World population of 5 billion is double the level of 1950 • Allan Bloom, *Closing of the American Mind* • First glass-fibre optic cable laid across the Atlantic Ocean • Simon Schama, *The Embarrassment of Riches* • Caryl Churchill, *Serious Money* • Films: *Pelle the Conqueror, Wings of Desire, The Last Emperor, The Dead* • Toni Morrison, *Beloved* • Tom Woolfe, *The Bonfire of the Vanities* • Ian McEwan, *The Child in Time* • Liberace, Danny Kaye, Primo Levi, Andres Segovia, Jascha Heifetz, Fred Astaire, Jean Anouilh, Jacqueline du Pre and James Baldwin die.

LITERATURE

JOSEPH BRODSKY (1940-1996)

Joseph Brodsky, was born, Iosip Aleksandrovich, in Leningrad, Russia on May 24, 1940. He was the only son of Jewish parents and it was they who instilled in him a love of books and writing. He left school at 15 and worked first in an armaments factory, then in a morgue. Whenever he had spare time he wrote poetry. Following the publication of four poems in an anthology, Brodsky became recognized as a new voice in Russian poetry. However, his poetry was not popular with everyone and it certainly wasn't politically correct. He was 24 when he was sentenced to five years imprisonment for 'parasitism'.

The state claimed he wasn't working and wasn't a registered member of the Writer's Union. Brodsky claimed to be a individualist and during his trial the following Kafkaesque dialogue took place.

Prosecutor: What is your occupation?
Brodsky: I am a poet
Prosecutor: Who included you in the list of poets?
Brodsky: Who included me in the list of human beings?

He served eighteen months in prison and spent the time reading the works of many poets, including WH. Auden; an episode that changed his life. Of particular significance was Auden's elegy to WB Yeats, written in 1939.

Follow poet, follow right
To the bottom of the night,
With your unconstraining voice.
In the prison of his days,
Teach the free man how to praise.

Brodsky began developing his mind, and his imagination, developing his lifelong optimism concerning good art and good actions. He once said, "evil, especially political evil, is always a bad stylist" He learnt to speak and write English and started a correspondence with Auden. In June 1972 he was expelled from the Soviet Union with a one-way ticket to Tel Aviv via Vienna, where he met and stayed with Auden.

Selected Poems was published in 1973. He later moved to the US and held visiting professorships at Michigan and Columbia universities. He received an honorary doctorate from Yale and in 1981 received a grant from the MacArthur Foundation. His parents tried to leave Russia, but to no avail, and Joseph was not allowed to return for his mother's funeral.

He recalls this event in his moving essay, *In a Room and a Half*. It tells the story of growing up in a tiny apartment in war-torn Russia. In 1986 he published, *Less Than One: Selected Essays*. This book, and his accumulated poetry, resulted in the 1987 award of the Nobel Prize for Literature; **"for an all-embracing authorship, imbued with clarity of thought and poetic intensity"**

He was only 55 when he died on January 28, 1996. He was a heavy drinker and a chain smoker who continued the habit despite having open-heart surgery in 1979 and two subsequent heart attacks. His somewhat bizarre lifestyle often reflected his work. Probably one of the greatest poets of the century, his last two works were published posthumously in October 1996; *On Grief and Reason: Essays by Joseph Brodsky* and his final collection of poems; *So Forth*. Brodsky once declared; 'literature started with poetry'

CHEMISTRY

DONALD CRAM (1919-), CHARLES PEDERSON (1904-1989)
and
JEAN-MARIE LEHR (1939-)

"for their development and use of molecules with structure-specific interactions of high selectivity"

Donald James Cram was born in Chester,Vt; US, on April 22, 1919. He was educated at Rollins College, Fla; and Nebraska University. He received his PhD in organic chemistry from Harvard University in 1947. He joined the staff of the University of California in LA in the same year and became a full professor there in 1956. Pederson had done the ground breaking work on the two dimensional organic compounds that are able to recognize and selectively combine with the ions of certain metal elements.

Cram, for his part, synthesized molecules that took this chemistry into three dimensions, creating a selection of differently shaped molecules that could interact selectively with other chemicals because of their complimentary three-dimensional structures. He was awarded a third share of the 1987 Nobel Prize for Chemistry. He has been twice married.

Charles John Pederson was born in Pusan, Korea on October 3, 1904. He had a Norwegian father and a Korean mother and was educated locally and in the US at Dayton University in Ohio, from where he graduated. His masters degree came from the Massachusetts Institute of Technology in 1926. He took a job as a research chemist with du Pont de Nemours and Co; and remained for 42 years.

In the 1960s, Pederson synthesized a group of compounds that he named crown ethers for their structure, i.e. a loose, flexible ring of carbon atoms punctuated at regular intervals with oxygen atoms. By varying the size of the rings, Pederson found that crown ethers could bind the ions of certain metal elements at the centre.

His experiments were expounded by Cram and Lehr but it was Pederson who showed them the way. He was awarded a third share of the 1987 Nobel Prize for Chemistry. He died in Salem, New York on October 26, 1989. He was married.

Jean-Marie Lehr was born in Rosheim, France on September 30, 1939. He was educated at Strasbourg University from where in 1963, he received a PhD in chemistry. In 1970 he became a professor of chemistry at Louis Pasteur University and from 1979 was also a professor at the Còllege de France in Paris. Lehn expounded on Pederson's work in creating crown ethers, by creating a molecule that combines with the chemical acetylcholine, an important neurotransmitter in the brain.

His work raised the possibility of creating totally artificial enzymes that would have characteristics superior to their natural counterparts in the human body. He too was awarded a third share of the 1987 Nobel Prize for Chemistry. He is married with two sons.

PHYSICS

ALEX MULLER (1927-)
and
GEORG BEDNORZ (1950-)

"For their important breakthrough in the discovery of superconductivity in ceramic materials"

Karl Alexander Muller was born in Basel, Switzerland, on April 20, 1927. Having received his PhD from the Swiss Federal Institute of Technology in 1958, he joined the IBM Zurich Research Laboratory, where he eventually headed the physics department becoming an IBM fellow in 1982.

He was a specialist in the ceramic compounds known as oxides and began experimenting in the early 1980s with substances that would become superconductive, so conducting electricity with no resistance at higher temperatures than had ever been reached. In 1986 he was able to reach superconductivity, in a recently constructed barium-lanthanum - copper oxide at a temperature of 35K (-238° C), some 12K higher than previously known.

This discovery started a wave of renewed superconductivity experiments by scientists worldwide, now using oxides, and within a year temperatures around 100K had been reached. Muller was awarded a co-share of the 1987 Nobel Prize for Physics. It is possible that superconductivity can achieve temperatures high enough for the generation and transmission of electric power, with important economic implications.

He is married with a son.

Johannes Georg Bednorz was born in Germany on May 16, 1950. He was educated at Munster University and received his PhD from the Swiss Federal Institute of Technology at Zurich in 1982. He joined the IBM Zurich Research Laboratory where he worked under Muller whilst he was experimenting superconductivity.

The two men worked together thereafter in their joint discovery of superconductivity in certain substances, particularly ceramic materials, at temperatures higher than had previously been thought possible.

It was Bendorz who was the experimenter in charge of the actual making and testing of the oxides As a result, Bendorz received a co-share of the 1987 Nobel Prize for Physics. He is married.

PHYSIOLOGY or MEDICINE

SUSUMU TONEGAWA (1939-)

Susumu Tonegawa was born in Nagoya, Japan on September 5, 1939. He was educated at Kyôto University from where, in 1963, he received his BSc degree. He earned a PhD in biology from the University of California at San Diego in 1969. Between 1971 and 1981 he was a member of the Basel Institute for Immunology. In 1981 he was at the Massachusetts Institute of Technology.

His area of research was the immune system. He was to be able explain how the immune system can produce the vast variety of antibodies required to immobilize the different microbes and antigens that from time to time invade the body.

Various antibodies bind to, or attack, a specific type of antigen or particular specie of microbe. Tonegawa was able to prove, following a series of experiments, that around 1,000 pieces of genetic material in the antibody manufacturing part of the B lymphocyte can be shuffled or recombined into different sequences. The resulting variations means the production of some 1,000,000,000 different types of antibodies, each specific to a different antigen.

As a result, Tonegawa was awarded the 1987 Nobel Prize for Physiology or Medicine; **"for his discovery of the genetic principle for generation of antibody diversity"** as well as for his fundamental discoveries concerning the body's production of antibodies. He has been twice married.

ECONOMICS

ROBERT SOLOW (1924-)

Robert **Merton Solow** was born in Brooklyn, New York, US, on August 23,1924. The son of Jewish immigrants from Eastern Europe, he served in the US Army between 1942 and 45. He was educated at Harvard University from where he received his BA (1947), MA (1949) and PhD in 1951. He began a teaching career at the Massachusetts Institute of Technology in 1949 becoming a full professor in 1958.

In the 1950s Solow developed a mathematical model that demonstrated the relative contributions of various factors to producing and sustaining economic growth. His work resulted in governments channelling funds into technological research to encourage economic growth. He showed, that contrary to traditional economic thinking, that the rate of technological progress is actually more important than capital accumulation.

He claimed that greater efficiency and productivity that result from qualitative improvements such as new machines and improved human skills, are more important than strictly quantitive investments that result in a greater number of machines and factories.

As a result Solow was awarded the 1987 Nobel Prize for Economics, **"for his contributions to the theory of economic growth"**

He is married with children.

PEACE

SANCHEZ ARIAS (1941-)

Oscar **Arias Sánchez** was born in Heredia, Costa Rica, on September 13, 1941. Born into a wealthy coffee-growing family in Costa Rica, he was educated at Costa Rica University, where he studied economics and earned a PhD from Essex University in England. In the 1960s, he began working for the left-wing National Liberation Party (PLN) and in 1972 he was appointed minister of planning in the government of José Figueres staying until 1977. He was elected secretary-general of the PLN and in 1986, won the general election to become president of Costa Rica.

As president, he took measures to cope with his country's heavy foreign debts as well as other economic problems. However, his main concern was in trying to restore peace and political stability in Central America.

Critical of the Sandinista government of Nicaragua, he wouldn't allow the Contras to operate from Costa Rica, much to the chagrin of the US, who supported the right-wing Contras. In February 1987, he proposed a regional peace plan for Central American countries that would set a date for cease-fires between governments and rebels, ensure an amnesty for political prisoners and a schedule for free and democratic elections.

Arias and the leaders of Guatemala, El Salvador, Honduras and Nicaragua signed this plan in August 1987. In October he was awarded the 1987 Nobel Prize for Peace; **"in recognition of his efforts to achieve the beginnings of peace in the region"**

He is un-married

1988

USSR withdraws from Afghanistan • Ethnic violence in Azerbaijan • Mikhail Gorbachev elected President of USSR • Benazir Bhutto becomes Prime Minister of Pakistan • The Holy Shroud of Turin proves to date from 14th century • Philip Larkin, *Collected Poems* **• Stephen Hawkins,** *A Brief History of Time* **• Films;** *A Fish Called Wanda, Au Revoir Les Enfants, Legend of the Holy Drinker* **• Peter Carey,** *Oscar and Lucinda* **• Salman Rushdie,** *The Satanic Verses* **• Elaine Feinstein,** *Mother's Daughter* **• Ove Arup, Aantal Dorati, Richard Feynman, Alan Paton and Pietro Annigoni die**

LITERATURE

NAGUIB MAHFOUZ (1911-)

Naguib Mahfouz was born in Cairo, Egypt on December 11, 1911. The son of a civil servant, he attended Cairo University before going to work in the cultural section of the civil service from 1934 and until he retired in 1971. His early novels are set in ancient Egypt but by the time he wrote his major works he had turned to describing modern Egypt. The three novels that comprise *The Cairo Trilogy* is his best known work and describes life in Cairo from WW1 to the overthrow of King Farouk in 1952.

Other novels deal with social change as it affects women and political prisoners. *Children of Gebelawi* was banned because of its argumentative religious theme. Other novels include, *The Thief and the Dogs* (1961), *The Beggar* (1965), and *Mirimar* (1967). He wrote some 30 screenplays, short stories and several plays.

He was awarded the 1988 Nobel Prize for Literature; **"who, through works rich in nuance-now clear-sightedly realistic, now evocatively ambiguous- has formed an Arabian narrative that applies to all mankind"** He now became the first Arabic writer to be so honoured.

He is un-married.

CHEMISTRY

JOHANN DEISENHOFER (1943-), ROBERT HUBER (1937-)
and
HARTMUT MICHEL (1948-)

"for the determination of the three-dimensional structure of a photosynthetic reaction centre"

Johann Deisenhofer was born in Zusamaltheim, Germany on September 30, 1943. He received his PhD from the Max Planck Institute for Biochemistry in Martinsried in 1974. There he conducted research until 1987, when he joined the staff at the Howard Highes Medical Institute in Dallas, US. He, together with Huber and Michel, began studying the structure of a protein complex found in certain photo synthetic bacteria. This protein termed, photo-synthetic reaction centre, was found to play a crucial role in initiating a simple type of photosynthesis.

Between 1982 and 1985 the three scientists used X-ray crystallography to determine the exact arrangement of the more than 10,000 atoms that make-up the protein complex. Deisenhofer was awarded a third share of the 1988 Nobel Prize for Chemistry. He was married in 1989.

Robert Huber was born in Munich, Germany on February 20, 1937. He was educated at the Munich technical University, from where, in 1960, he received his PhD In 1972 he joined the staff of the Max Planck Institute for Biochemistry; there he met up with Deisenhofer and Michel and three men worked on the structure of a protein complex.

Huber, an internationally recognized expert in the use of X-ray diffraction to determine the atomic structure of complex molecules such as proteins. His work led to the complex photosynthetic reaction centre that is essential to photosynthesis in certain bacteria. In 1988 Huber received a third share of the Nobel Prize for Chemistry. He is married with four children.

Hartmut Michel was born in Ludwigsburg, Germany on July 18, 1948. He received a PhD from Wúrzburg University in 1977 and then trod the well worn path to the Max Planck Institute for Biochemistry in Martinsried, where he found Deisenhofer and Huber. They were eventually successful in determining the three-dimensional structure of a four-protein complex, called a photo synthetic reaction centre.

It was Michel's preliminary work, done in the period from 1978 to 1982, that showed the way for the three scientists future joint research.

For his part in this work Michel received the remaining third share of the 1988 Nobel Prize for Chemistry. He is married with a child.

PHYSICS

LEON LEDERMAN (1922-), MELVIN SCHWARTZ (1932-)
and
JACK STEINBERGER (1921-)

"for the neutrino beam method and the demonstration of the doublet structure of the leptons through the discovery of the muon neutrino"

Leon Max Lederman was born in New York, US: on July 15, 1922. He was educated at the City College of New York, from where, in 1943, he graduated with a BS. He went on to Columbia University obtaining a PhD in 1951. In 1958 he was a full professor at Columbia before transferring to the Fermi National Accelerator Laboratory in Batavia, Ill. there he was the director from 1979-89.

Lederman, together with fellow researchers from Columbia; Schwartz and Steinberger, researched the uses of neutrons and between 1960-62 collaborated at the Brookhaven National Laboratory on Long Island, New York. They established that the neutrons that produced muon were in fact previously unknown and were a distinct type of neutrinos which they named, muon neutrinos. As a result Lederman received a third share of the 1988 Nobel Prize for Physics.

The high energy neutrino beams, that their researches produced, have since become a basic tool in the study of subatomic particles and nuclear forces . The use of such beams has made possible the study of radioactive decay processes involving the weak nuclear forces in nature.

He has been married twice with three children.

Melvin Schwartz was born in New York, US: on November 2, 1932. He received his PhD from Columbia University in 1958 and remained there, teaching from 1958 to 1966. He then went to Stanford University as professor of physics and stayed until 1983. During this time he was president of Digital Pathways, Inc a company he founded to design computer-security systems.

Part of the team concerned with neutrinos-subatomic particles, that have no electric charge and virtually no mass, it was Schwartz who suggested that the three researchers devise a way to increase the statistical probability of neutrino interactions, by producing a beam consisting of hundreds of billions of neutrinos and sending a beam through a detector of solid matter. The bombardment produced a stream of different particles which then passed through a steel barrier 44 feet thick (13.4m) that filtered out all other particles except neutrinos. Thus the three physicists discovered a new type of neutrino, which came to be known as the muon neutrino. Schwartz was awarded a third share of the 1988 Nobel Prize for Physics. He is married.

Jack Steinberger was born in Bad Kissingen, Germany on May 25, 1921. Jewish, like his two fellow scientists, his education was interrupted by being forced to leave Germany in 1934, because of anti-Jewish laws. He immigrated to the US, and Chicago. In 1948 he received his PhD from Chicago University. Between 1950 and 1971 he was professor of physics at Columbia University, New York and, from 1968, was a physicist at the European Organization for Nuclear Research (CERN) in Geneva.

In the early 1960s, Steinberger and his two colleagues, devised a landmark experiment in particle physics using the accelerator at the Brookhaven National Labortory, N.Y. The three scientists obtained the first laboratory-made stream of neutrinos and in the process discovered a new type of neutrino they called a ' muon neutrino'.

As a result, Steinberger was awarded a third share of the 1988 Nobel Prize for Physics. What the three men achieved meant that the use of such beams made possible the study of radioactive-decay processes involving the weak nuclear force, or weak interaction, one of the four fundamental forces in nature. He has been twice married with four children.

PHYSIOLOGY or MEDICINE

JAMES BLACK (1924-), GERTRUDE ELION (1918-)
and
GEORGE HITCHINGS (1905-)

"for their discoveries of important principles for drug treatment"

James Whyte Black was born in Uddington, Scotland on June 14, 1924. He received an MD from St.Andrews University in 1946 and spent the next ten years teaching at various universities before joining Imperial Chemical Industries in 1958. In 1964, he was head of biological research at Smith Kline & French Laboratories. In 1978, he was director of therapeutic research at Wellcome Research Laboratories. In 1981 he received a knighthood.

His research work was on the interactions between, certain cell receptors in the body, and chemicals in the bloodstream that attach to them. He was looking for a drug that would relieve angina. It was already known that beta receptors in the heart muscle, when stimulated by the hormones epinephrine and norepinephrine, cause the heartbeat to quicken and increase the strength of the heart's contractions. Black developed a drug that would block the beta receptor sites. The resulting inhibition of the hormone's excitatory effects reduced the heart's demand for oxygen and thus reduce anginal pain. Other beta blocking agents were sunsequently developed to deal with other heart conditions.

Black later used a similar approach to develop drugs that would treat stomach and duodenal ulcers, which are largely caused by oversecretion of gastric acids. He developed a drug that could block histamine receptors that stimulate the secretion of gastric acid in the stomach.

He was awarded a third share of the 1988 Nobel Prize for Physiology or Medicine; "for his development of two important drugs, propanolol and cimetidine" He is married with a daughter.

Gertrude Belle Elion was born in New York, on January 23, 1918. She was the daughter of immigrant Jewish-Russian parents. Her parents explained to their teeage daughter that educated men wanted educated wives. She soaked up knowledge and discovered a preference for science. Accordingly she obtained a scholarship to Hunter College.

Watching her grandfather dying from stomach cancer gave her the urge to become a biochemist. She graduated in 1937 only to find a lack of money, combined with being a woman, made it difficult to obtain a place to study for a PhD, important in the pursuance of her chosen career.

A series of incidents affected her. She was forced to become a secretary in order to live. Then her fiancé died. She spent the next seven years grieving her lost love and doing all sorts of jobs to accumalate sufficient money to pay the fees demanded by New York University.

WW2 helped her. The war caused a labour drain and, male chemists being in short supply, research laboratories turned to women. Gertrude Elion got a job with Burroughs Wellcome, a British company, in a research laboratory in Tuckahoe, New York. She and a colleague, George Hitchings, did radical research that resulted in developing drugs that interuppted the life cycles of abnormal cells leaving healthy cells intact.

At night she studied for a doctorate at Brooklyn Polytechnic Institute. However, two years into her course, the Dean decided he wanted Elion to leave her job and become a full time student. She refused and was subsequently dismissed from the Institute. A short while later, in 1950, and without a doctorate, she became responsible for two major cancer treatments. One was purine compound that interfered with the formation of leukemia cells. Although her discovery required further investigation, childhood leukemia could be cured in 80% of all cases as a direct result of Elion's work. The second was a drug called Imuran used to prevent rejection following kidney transplants.

In 1968 Hitchings retired and Gertrude Elion was appointed head of the Department of Experimental Therapy for Burroughs Wellcome. She spent as much time as possible researching an anti-virus drug. She achieved her ambition with the discovery of a drug called Zovirax which is effective against herpes, shingles and chicken pox. Billion dollar sales resulted from this discovery. Elion retired in 1983 but continued working as a consultant. Her previous research work was instrumental in producing a drug named Azidothymidine, now used to treat patients with AIDS virus. On October 17, 1988 she heard she had been awarded a third share of the 1988 Nobel Prize for Physiology or Medicine; "for her work demonstrating the differences in nucleic acid metabolism between healthy and diseased cells"

In 1991 she became the first woman to be elected to the National Inventors' Hall of Fame; and she still hasn't obtained her doctorate.

George Herbert Hitchings was born in Hoquiam, Wash: US, on April 18, 1905. He received his BA and MA from Washington University and obtained a PhD in biochemistry from Harvard University in 1933. He then taught at Harvard University until 1939. In 1942 he joined the Burroughs Wellcome Laboratories and stayed until his retirement in 1968.

Here he spent some 40 years working with Gertrude Elion. His most important find was the drug Allopurinol, and an important treatment for gout.

Other drugs that Hitchings worked on include pyrimethamine, an antimalarial agent; trimethoprim; a treatment for urinary and tract infections; and acyclovir; the first effective treatment for viral herpes

He was awarded a third share of the 1988 Nobel Prize for Physiology or Medicine. Hitchings died on February 27, 1998 whilst living in Chapel Hill, NC. He was married with two children

ECONOMICS

MAURICE ALLAIS (1911-)

Maurice Allais was born in Paris, France on May 31,1911. He studied economics at the École Polytechnique and then at the École Nationalle Supérieure des Mines de Paris. In 1937 he was working for the state-owned mining administration. In 1944, he became professor of economics at the National Superior School of Mines. He was an artillery officer in the French Alpine Army during WW2. In 1977 he was named an officer of the Legion of Honour.

His principal works, two large studies published in the 1940s, in which he examines the workings of state-owned monopolies, and lays the theoretical foundation for determining the prices of these monopolies' products or services in such a way as to offer maximum economic efficiency, whilst still providing social benefits. His ideas became a guiding force for planning state enterprises in terms of prices rather than by direct regulation. His work was particularly important in view of the growth of state-owned monopolies in the economies of western Europe following WW2.

Allais was awarded the 1988 Nobel Prize for Economics; **"for his pioneering contributions to the theory of markets and efficient utilization of resources"**

He never married

PEACE

UN PEACEKEEPING FORCES

The United Nations in their attempts to promote harmonious interaction among the countries of the world sometimes uses peacekeeping forces to halt fighting in or between various countries.
Such situations are becoming most frequent with UN Peacekeeping Forces being used in East Timor in September 1999.

1989

Nelson Mandela makes first public statement in 25 years • George Bush and Mikhail Gorbachev declare end of Cold War • Collapse of Communism in Eastern Europe • Researchers identify the gene responsible for cystic fibrosis • Films: *Cinema Paradiso, When Harry met Sally, My Left Foot, Driving Miss Daisy* • Martin Amis, *London Fields* • Zazuo Ishiguro, *The Remains of the Day* • James Kelman, *A Disaffection* • Robert Nye, *The Memoirs of Lord Byron* • A.J. Ayer, Laurence Olivier, Irving Berlin, Samuel Beckett, Felix Topolski, Vladimir Horowitz, Nicolae Ceausescu and Lennox Berkeley die.

LITERATURE

CAMILO JOSE CELA (1916-)

Camilo José Cela Trulock was born in Iria Flavia, Spain, on May 11, 1916. He was educated at Madrid University. His first novel, written during the Spanish Civil War whilst fighting for Franco's Fascist army, was *Pascual Duarte*. His next was *The Hive* (1951), an innovative and perceptive story of postwar Madrid that cemented Cela's popular reputation.

His work is described as skilful with colourful descriptions and deep powers of observation. This is especially shown in his travel books, based on his journeys through rural Spain and South America. His most noted are, *Journey to the Alcarria* (1948), *From the Mino to the Bidasoa* (1952), *Jews, Moors and Christians* (1956). He also wrote essays, poetry and plays and became a member of the Spanish Academy in 1957.

In 1955 he settled in Majorca and founded the literary review, *Papeles de Son Armadans* (1956-79). In 1968, his multivolume *Diccionario secreto* began appearing. In 1989 he was awarded the Nobel Prize for Literature; **"for a rich and intensive prose, which with restrained compassion forms a challenging vision of**

man's vulnerability"

Cela is considered to have revitalized Spanish literature. He never married.

CHEMISTRY

SIDNEY ALTMAN (1939-)
and
THOMAS CECH (1947-)

"for their discovery of catalytic properties of RNA"

Sidney Altman was born in Montreal, Canada, on May 7, 1939. His family came from Eastern Europe to escape anti-Semitic persecution. Altman received his BS in physics from the Massachusetts Institute of Technology in 1960 and his PhD from Colorado University in biophysics in 1967. He was a molecular biology fellow at Harvard University between 1967-69 and at Cambridge University 1969-70. He became a full professor at Yale University in 1980, department chairman 1983-85 and dean between 1985-89.

Working independently, Altman, during his researches into RNA factors, discovered that RNA could have active enzymatic functions. This new knowledge opened fresh areas of scientific research and prompted scientists to re-think their theories of how life first began on Earth. It was originally believed that enzymatic activity belonged to the area of protein molecules- Altman showed a different way.

As a result of his findings he was awarded a half share of the 1989 Nobel Prize for Chemistry. He is married with two children.

Thomas Robert Cech was born in Chicago, US: on December 8, 1947. He was educated at Grinnel College in Iowa and received his BA in 1970. He received his PhD in chemistry, from the University of California, Berkeley in 1975, before becoming an Institute Fellow at Massachusetts Institute of Technology (1975-77). He became a full professor at Colorado University in 1980.

Cech was the first person to show that an RNA molecule could catalyse a chemical reaction and he published his findings in 1982. Altman however, had earlier strongly pointed the way to such a conclusion and in 1983 demonstrated how it was achieved.

For his work on the resulting discovery, Cech was awarded a half share of the 1989 Nobel Prize for Chemistry. He is married with two daughters.

2 years ago

PHYSICS

HANS DEHMELT (1922-), WOLFGANG PAUL (1913-)

"for the development of the ion trap technique"

and
NORMAN RAMSAY (1915-)

Hans Georg Dehmelt was born in Gölitz, Germany on September 9,1922. During WW2 , he was a soldier in Hitler's army from 1940 and until he was captured by US troops in 1945. He later resumed his studies at Göttingen University and received a PhD in physics in 1950. He was in the US in 1952 teaching at Washington University; becoming a full professor there in 1961 and receiving US citizenship.

In 1955 he developed what became known as the Penning trap. This can confine electrons and ions in a small space for long periods of time in relative isolation. This opened the way for the precise measurement of key properties of electrons. In the 1970s, Dehmelt used this trap to measure an electron's magnetic movement to an accuracy of four parts in a trillion; the most precise measurement of the time.

As a result he was awarded half of one half (quarter) of the 1989 Nobel Prize for Physics. He has been married twice and has a child.

Wolfgang Paul was born in Lorenzkirch, Germany on August 10, 1913. He was educated at Munich and Berlin Institutes and received a PhD in physics from Berlin Technical University in 1939. A member of the Nazi party, Paul was a lecturer at Göttingen University during WW2 becoming a full professor in 1950. From 1952 he was at Bonn University.

During the 1950s he developed the Paul Trap which used a radio-frequency current to maintain an alternating electric field that isolates and confines charged particles and atoms in a small place. It allowed physicists to study atomic properties and test physical theories with high degrees of precision.

In 1989 Paul received half of one half of the Nobel Prize for Physics. He is twice married with four children.

Norman Foster Ramsey was born in Washington, DC, US: on August 27,1915. He was educated at Columbia University from where he received a PhD in physics in 1940. He also received a DSc from Cambridge University in 1954. Then followed a spell of teaching at various US universities including Harvard where, in 1966, he became Higgins Professor of Physics.

Ramsey, in 1949, perfected a method in order to study the structure of atoms by sending them through two separate oscillating electromagnetic fields. This meant that important data, concerning the structure and behaviour of atoms, was achieved. His work laid the foundation for the modern cesium atomic clock which sets present time functions.

Ramsey was awarded one half of the 1989 Nobel Prize for Physics; **"for the invention of the separated oscillatory fields method and its use in the hydrogen maser and other atomic clocks"**

He is twice married with seven children.

PHYSIOLOGY or MEDICINE

MICHAEL BISHOP (1936-)
and
HAROLD VARMUS (1939-)

"for their discovery of the cellular origin of retro-viral oncogenes"

John Michael Bishop was born in York, Pa. US: on February 22, 1936. He graduated from Gettysburg College and received an MD from Harvard Medical School in 1962. Following a spell as an intern, he became a researcher in virology at the National Institutes of Health at Bethesda. In 1972 he was a professor at the University of California Medical Centre in San Francisco.

In 1970 Bishop joined Varmus to test the idea that healthy body cells contain dormant viral oncogenes that when triggered cause cancer. They worked with the known cause of cancer in chickens known as the Rous sarcoma virus.

They went on to discover that within healthy cells there was evidence of the cancer causing genes. Their investigive work appears to be common to all forms of cancer and provided inv aluable information for cancer research. By 1989 scientists all over the world, had identified more than 40 genes having cancer-causing potential in animals. Bishop was awarded a half share of the 1989 Nobel Prize for Physiology or Medicine. He is married with two sons.

Harold Elliot Varmus was born in Oceanside, NY; US, on December 18,1939. He graduated from Amherst College, Mass. with a BA in 1961, received an MA in 1962 from Harvard University and an MD in 1966 from Columbia University. He met Bishop at the University of California and the two collaborated on genes known as oncogenes that ordinarilly control cellular growth and division. However, if they are picked up by infecting viruses or affected by chemical carcinogens, they can be rendered capable of causing cancer.

Their research in the mid-1970s, superseeded a theory that cancer is caused by viral genes, distinct from a cell's normal genetic material that lays dormant in body cells until activated by carcinogens. Varmus was awarded a co-share of the 1989 Nobel Prize for Physiology or Medicine. He is married with two sons.

ECONOMICS

TRYGVE HAAVELMO (1911-)

Trygve Magnus Haavelmo was born in Skedsmo, Norway, on December 13,1911. Following the outbreak of WW2 he left Norway for the US and delivered his doctoral dissertation, 'The Probability Approach to Econometrics' at Harvard University in 1941. In 1945 he was Commercial Attache at the Norwegian Embassy in Washington, DC.

During the earlier 1940s Haavelmo worked at Chicago University. He returned to Norway in 1947. For the next year he was at the Ministry of Finance in Oslo. He joined Oslo University retiring in 1979 as professor emeritus.

Haavelmo's statistical techniques made it possible for the development of econometric models that predict how a change in one aspect of the economy might well affect others. As a result, his econometrics made possible the predictions regarding the course of national economics, so allowing governments to formulate more accurate policies concerning economic policies.

He was awarded the 1989 Nobel Prize for Economics; **"for his clarification of the probability theory foundation of econmetrics and his analyses of simultaneous economic structures"**

He never married.

PEACE

THE DALAI LAMA (1935-)

The title of 'Dalai Lama' for the head of Tibetan Buddhists was first used in 1391. The title has continued uninteruppted until the 14th in line, Bstan-dzin-rgya-mtsho, was enthroned in 1940. He was 5 years old at the time. In 1959 he and 100,000 followers fled to India following their revolt against their Chinese rulers who had invaded the country in 1950. The Dalai Lama set up a government-in-exile in the Himalayan Mountains in a town called Dharmsala.

He was awarded the 1989 Nobel Peace Prize; **"in recognition of his non-violent campaign to end Chinese domination of Tibet"** The Dalai Lama has spent most of the subsequent decade traveling the world and pleading his course.

1990

German re-unification • Margaret Thatcher resigns • David Dinkins becomes first black mayor of New York • First human gene experiment • Wembley concert to celebrate the release of Nelson Mandela • Damian Hirst, *My Way* • Karl Popper, *A World of Propensities* • Derek Walcott, *Omeros* • Nadine Gordimer, *My Son's Story* • Hanif Kureishi, *The Buddha of Suburbia* • Mordecai Richler, *Solomon Gursky Was Here* • Films; *Jesus of Montreal, Cinema Paradiso, Goodfellas, My Left foot* • Greta Garbo, A.J.P. Taylor, Bruno Kreisky, Armand Hammer, Paulette Goddard, Alberto Moravia, Bruno Bettelheim, Berthold Lubetkin, Leonard Bernstein and Aaron Copland die.

LITERATURE

OCTAVIO PAZ (1914-1998)

Octavio Paz was born in Mexico City, Mexico, on March 31, 1914. His family was financially ruined during the Mexican Civil War and Octavio grew up in poor circumstances. He was educated as a Roman Catholic school and at Mexico University. He decided to become a writer and published his first book of poetry, *Forest Moon,* in 1933. In 1937 Paz visited Spain and supported the Government forces during the Spanish Civil War. The result of his Spanish experience was *Beneath Your Clear Shadow and Other Poems.* He journeyed onto Paris where Surrealism had a strong

and on-going influence upon him.

Back home in Mexico, Paz founded and edited several literary magazines. These included, *Taller* in 1939 and *The Prodigal Son* in 1943. In the 1970s he founded his final magazine, *Plural*. His major poetic works are *They Shall Not Pass!* (1937), *Freedom Under Parole* (1949, *Eagle of Sun?* (1951), and *The Sun Stone* (1957).

In 1946 he entered the Mexican diplomatic corps and served in various capacities all over the world. Between 1962 to 1968, he was Mexican ambassador to India. He resigned from the corps in 1968 as a protest against Mexico's brutal treatment of student radicals.

Paz was awarded the 1990 Nobel Prize for Literature; **"for impassioned writing with wide horizons, characterized by sensuous intelligence and human integrity"** He was un-married.

Paz died in Mexico City on April 19, 1998. He constantly warned governments to treat their people as individuals and not as tools.

CHEMISTRY

ELIAS COREY (1928-)

Elias James Corey was born in Methuen, Mass; US, on July 12, 1928. He studied at the Massachusetts Institute of Technology where he received a BS in 1948 and a PhD in 1951. He went on to become professor of chemistry at Harvard University in 1959.

There, together with his group of graduate students, Corey synthesized around 100 molecules found only in nature. Thus he was able to produce a group of drugs known as synthetic prostaglandins; a group of hormone type compounds used to treat infertility and, in some cases, induce labour.

Corey was awarded the 1990 Nobel Prize for Chemistry; **"for his development of the theory and methodology of organic synthesis"**

In the retrosynthetic analysis that he developed, chemists start with the target molecule and work backwards, carefully analysing its structure and dissecting it piece by piece. By systematically breaking key chemical bonds that join the major components of the target molecule, it is possible to arrive at a set of simple predecessors. These can then be reassembled into the target molecule, in the simplest manner, thereby making synthesis faster, cheaper and more efficient.

Corey is married with three children.

PHYSICS

RICHARD TAYLOR (1929-), JEROME FRIEDMAN (1930-)
and
HENRY KENDALL (1926-)

"for their pioneering investigations concerning deep inelastic scattering of electrons on protons and bound neutrons , which have been of essential importance for the development of the quark model in particle physics"

Richard Edward Taylor was born in Medicine Hat, Canada, on November 2, 1929. He was educated at Alberta University from where he received his BA in 1950 and his masters in 1952. He went to the US and Stanford University, from where he received his PhD in physics in 1962.

Between 1962 and 1968 he was on the staff of Stanford Linear Accelerator Centre. There he met up with Friedman and Kendall. All three worked on a series of experiments that eventually confirmed the hypothesis that protons and neutrons are made up of quarks. Taylor went on to become as associate professor at Stanford in 1968 and a full professor two years later. He was awarded a third share of the 1990 Nobel Prize for Physics. He is married.

Jerome Isaac Friedman was born in Chicago, US, on March 28, 1930. He was born into a middle-class Jewish family who placed education as a top priority. As a result, Friedman was educated at Chicago University from where he received a PhD in 1958. A teacher and researcher, he began his teaching career at the Massachusetts Institute of Technology in 1960, becoming a full professor in 1967 and head of the physics department in 1983.

His research career started whilst he was at Chicago and continued later at Stanford University. Here he met up with Taylor and Kendall. They carried on where Murray Gell-Man (qv) left off, confirming Gell-Man's hypothesis of 1964 regarding the existence of fundamental particles, known as quarks.

They used a particle accelerator to direct a beam of high energy electrons at target protons and neutrons. They found that the manner in which the electrons scattered from the targets indicated that both protons and neutrons are composed of hard, electrically charged, point-like particles. For his part Friedman was awarded a third share of the 1990 Nobel Prize for Physics.

He is married with four children.

Henry Way Kendall was born in Boston, Mass, US, on December 9, 1926. He was educated at Amherst College, from where he obtained a BA in 1950 and at the Massachusetts Institute of Technology (MIT), from where he received a PhD in physics in 1955. He stayed on as a US National Science Foundation Fellow and between 1956-1961 taught and researched at Stanford University. He returned to MIT in 1961 becoming a full professor in 1967.

Kendall, together with Taylor and Friedman, worked at the Stanford Linear Accelerator Centre from 1967-73. There, they confirmed the existence of the quarks first hypothesized by Gell-Mann in 1964. Kendall, for his part, was awarded a third share of the 1990 Nobel Prize for Physics.

He is un-married.

PHYSIOLOGY or MEDICINE

JOSEPH MURRAY (1919-)
and
DONNALL THOMAS (1920-)

"for their discoveries concerning organ and cell transplantations in the treatment of human disease"

Joseph Edward Murray was born in Milford, Mass; US, on April 1, 1919. He was educated at Holy Cross College, Worcester, Mass; from where in 1940 he received a BA. From Harvard Medical School he received a medical degree in 1943. He undertook his surgical residency at Bingham Hospital, Boston. Between 1964 and 1986 he was chief plastic surgeon at Brigham and between 1972 and 1985, he was chief plastic surgeon at the Children's Hospital Medical Centre in Boston. In 1970 he became professor of surgery at Harvard Medical School.

During WW2, whilst grafting skin on wounded soldiers, he noticed that grafts were only compatible between identical twins. Believing that such might also be the case for transplanted internal organs as well, he experimented with kidney transplants in dogs. In 1954 he performed a kidney transplant for a person whose genetically identical twin, volunteered to donate a kidney.

The recipient survived for a number of years. Murray continued to search for ways of suppressing a patient's immune system in order to keep it from rejecting genetically foreign parts. With the use of immunosuppresive drugs, he performed in 1962, the first successful kidney transplant using a kidney donated from a donor unrelated to the patient. Later, Murray was successful at transplanting a kidney from a cadaver. He was awarded a half share of the 1990 Nobel Prize for Physiology or Medicine. He is married with six children.

Edward **Donnall Thomas** was born in Mart, Texas, US, on March 15, 1920. He was educated at Texas University, from where he obtained a BA in 1941 and an MA in 1943. From Harvard University Medical School he received an MD in 1946. Between 1953 and 1963 he was a professor of medicine at Columbia University College of Physicians and Surgeons. Thereafter he was at the Washington School of Medicine in Seattle.

Thomas's field of research was in haematology, cancer research, irradiation biology and biochemistry. He was awarded a half share of the 1990 Nobel Prize for Physiology or Medicine for his work in transplanting bone marrow from one person to another; an achievement related to the cure of those with leukemia and other blood cancers and blood diseases. He is married with three children.

ECONOMICS

HARRY MARKOWITZ (1927-), MERTON MILLER (1923-)
and
WILLIAM SHARPE (1934-)

"for their pioneering work in the theory of financial economics"

Harry **Markowitz** was born in Chicago, Ill; US, on August 24, 1927, the son of middle-class Jewish parents He was educated at Chicago University where he received a BA in Philosophy in 1947, an MA in 1950 and a Ph.D in 1954.

He then joined the staff of Rand Corp; Santa Monica, 1952-60, and 1961-63. It was here he met up with Sharpe, who would later base his research on Markowitz's work. Between 1963-68 he was with Consolidated Analysis Centres, Santa Monica;. California University, LA, 1968-69. Arbitrage Management Company, New York, 1969-72 and IBM Research Centre, before joining New York University as professor of finance.

Markowitz researched what became known as 'the portfolio theory'. This sought to prove that a diversified portfolio, that mixed assets, could be practical. His techniques for measuring risk, associated with various assets, and his techniques for mixing assets later became routine investment methods. He was awarded a third share of the 1990 Nobel Memorial Prize in Economic Science and credited with developing a computer language called 'Simscript', used to write economic-analysis programmes. He is unmarried.

Merton **Howard Miller** was born in Boston, Mass: US, on May 16, 1923. He was educated at Harvard University, from where in 1944, he received a BA. He then worked at the US Treasury Department before graduating from Johns Hopkins University with a PhD in 1952. He taught at the Carnegie Institute of Technology until 1961 when he became a professor of finance at Chicago University's Graduate School of Business Administration.

Miller was part of the Modigliani-Miller theorem. Modigliani was awarded the Nobel Prize in 1985 and the theorem explains the relationship between a company's capital asset structure and dividend policy and its market value and cost of capital; the theorem demonstrated how a manufacturing company funds its activities is less important than the profitability of those activities. Miller, who received a third share of the 1990 Nobel Memorial Prize for Economic Sciences, was recognised as one of the most important developers of theoretical and empirical analysis in the field of corporate finance.   He is twice married with three children.

William **Forsyth Sharpe** was born in Cambridge, Mass;US, on June 16, 1934. He was educated at California University, LA, from where he received his Ph.D in economics in 1961. He was influenced by Markowitz, when the two met at the Rand Corp; (1957-61). Subsequently Sharpe taught economics at Washington University, Seattle, (1961-68) and at Stanford University from 1970 and until he retired to run his own investment consultant company.

Sharpe's research produced the ' capital asset pricing model'. A financial model that explains how security prices reflect risks and potential returns. His theory stressed how the market pricing of risky assets enables them to fit into an investor's portfolio because they can be made to blend with less risky investments. He was awarded a third share of the 1990 Nobel Memorial Prize for Economic Sciences. He is married with two children.

MIKHAIL GORBACHEV (1931-)

Mikhail **Sergeyevich Gorbachev** was born in Privolye, USSR, on March 2, 1931. The son of Russian peasants, Mikhail was educated in the Soviet system in south-west Russia and in 1946 joined the Young Communist League. He spent the next four years driving a combine harvestor on a state owned farm. In 1952 he was at Moscow University studying law. He graduated with a law degree and joined the Communist Party.in 1971. He was a candidate member of the Poliburo in 1979 and a full member the following year.

Graduaally Gorbachev rose up the polictical ladder until, on March 11, 1985, he was elected by the Politburo to be general secretary of the ruling Communist Party . At that time he was the youngest member of the Politburo. He set about consolidating his personal power and developing rapid growth of a stagnant economic situation. To this end he called for technological modernization and increased productivity.

In 1987 he recognized that the changes he had intiated had failed to produce results. He then began deep reforms of the Soviet economic and political system. This new policy became known as, *glasnost* or openess. It meant that a major cultural thaw then took place that allowed the media to become critical of all sections of Russian society.

The Stalinist era was examined and then repudiated. A period of *perestroika* or restructuring was undertaken. There were free elections and polictical parties of all colours emerged. A limited free market was established and trappings of capitalist methods encouraged.

In foreign affairs the world breathed easier as the cold war subsided and warmer relations developed both polically and by trade. Gorbachev now turned his attention to Afghanistan and ordered the withdrawal of Soviet troops. He didn't however have everything his own way. There was objection from the Communist Party to his policies with the result that a new method of government was developed and the Congress of the Peoples Deputies elected.

Gorbachev envisaged a reforming Communist Party would lead the way throuout Eastern Europe. However, as democratically non-Communist governments were elected in East Germany, Poland, Hungary and Czechslovakia took place, the writing for the USSR was on the wall. Withdrawals of Soviet troops from Warsaw Pact countries took place and in 1990 the Congress abolished the Communist Party's constitutionally guaranteed monoply of political power in the Soviet Union. Gorbachev was awarded the 1990 Nobel Peace Prize **for his striking achievements in international relations.**

Events didn't proceed as Gorbachev might have hoped and when the Russian government under Yeltsin, agreed to from a new commonwealth he resigned as president of the Soviet Union. It was December 25, 1991. The great revolution had lasted just over 74 years.

On September 20, 1999 Raisa Gorbachev died. Her husband was heartbroken; his sweetheart from his college days would no longer be constantly at his side. He has a daughter.

1991

Yugoslavia breaks up • USSR breaks up • Apartheid ends in South Africa • The preserved body of a man, plus artifax, dating from c. 3,300 BC, discovered in Italian Alps • Norman Foster, Stanstead Airport, Essex, England • Ariel Dorfman, *Death and the Maiden* • Films; *Thelma and Louise, Silence of the Lambs, Barton Fink,* • Norman Mailer, *Harlot's Ghost* • Ben Okri, *The Famished Road* • Harold Brodkey, *The Runaway Soul* • Robert Maxwell, Stan Getz, Margot Fonteyn, Serge Gainsbourg, Graham Greene, Oliver Messiaen, Henry Shapiro, Joe Papp, Yves Montand, Natalie Ginzburg, Angus Wilson die.

LITERATURE

NADINE GORDIMER (1923-)

Nadine Gordimer was born in Springs, Transvaal, South Africa, on November 20, 1923. The daughter of a Jewish watchmaker who had immigrated from Lithuania, she was educated at Witwatersrand University. She didn't stay to graduate. From the age of nine she had developed a love for writing. By the time she was fifteen she had a short story published in *Forum*. Her first book, *The Soft Voice of the Serpent* , published in 1952 was a collection of short stories. A year later she published a novel; *The Lying Day* concerned the tension of apartheid. *A World of Strangers* was published in 1958 and banned by the government. Two further novels, *The Late Bourgeois World* (1966) and *Burgher's Daughter* (1979) suffered a similar fate.

In 1974 she won the Booker McConnell prize with *The Conservationist.* Her books are an indictment of the frustrations and stupidity of the apartheid regime as well as the cruelty used by the police in enforcing it. Gordimer refused to leave South Africa permanently, despite her life at times being in danger. During short trips abroad she exposed the racist regime. In 1971 she taught at Columbia University in New York. In 1987 she wrote, *A Sport of Nature* about her experience of being Jewish. In 1991 Nadine Gordimer won the Nobel Prize for Literature; **"who through her magnificent epic writing has-in the words of Alfred Nobel-been of very great benefit to humanity"**

Not only was she the first woman to win this coveted prize for twenty-five years, she had the bizarre experience of, on the one hand, having her books banned by the South African government and, on the other, being publicly praised by the country's president for ' this exceptional achievement , which is also an honour to South Africa'. That statement was the more hypocritical by de Klerk, because Gordimer was co-founder of the Congress of South African writers , 98% of whose members were black and supported the Arts and Culture wing of the ANC. In 1996 she published *Writing and Being.* Nadine Gordimer is married with two children.

CHEMISTRY

RICHARD ERNST (1933-)

Richard **Robert Ernst** was born in Winterhur, Switzerland, on August 14, 1933. He received a BA in chemistry and a Ph.D in physical chemistry from Eidgenössische Technische Hochschule in Zurich. From 1963 to 1968 he worked as a research chemist in Palo Alto, Calif; in 1966 Ernst discovered the sensitivity of NMR techniques could be increased by replacing the slow, sweeping radio waves usually used in NMR spectroscopy with short, intense pulses. His discovery allowed analysis of a great number of nuclei and smaller amounts of materials.

In 1968 Ernst returned home to teach at his alma mater. He was assistant professor in 1970 and full professor in 1976. His next important contribution to NMR spectroscopy was a technique that allowed a high-resolution, two dimesional study of very large molcules. He refined the process and scientists were able to determine the three dimensional structure of organic and inorganic compounds and of biological macromolecules such as proteins. He was awarded the 1991 Nobel Prize for Chemistry; **"for his contribution to the development of the methodology of high resolution nuclear magnetic resonance (NMR) spectroscopy"**

Richard Ernst is married with three children.

PHYSICS

PIERRE de GENNES (1932-)

Pierre-Gilles **de Gennes** was born in Paris, France on October 24, 1932. The son of a physician, Gennes studied at the École Normale Supérieure and was later employed as an engineer at the French Atomic Energy Commission (1955-61). He was then a professor at Paris University (1961-71) and professor at the Collège de France from 1971. de Gennes field of research from the 1960s focussed on crystals, both organic and inorganic, with related studies and analyses of other materials. Here he tried to determine their molecular behaviour in ordered and disordered states.

He was awarded the 1991 Nobel Prize for Physics; **"for discovering that methods developed for studying order phenomena in simple systems can be generalized to more complex forms of matter, in particular to liquid crystals and polymers"** de Gennes has been described by several judges, as "the Isaac Newton of our time" in having successfully applied mathematics to generalized explanations of several different physical phenomena.

He is un-married.

PHYSIOLOGY or MEDICINE

ERWIN NEHER (1944-)
and
BERT SAKMANN (1942-)

"for their discoveries concerning the function of single ion channels in cells"

Erwin Neher was born in Landsberg, Germany, on March 20, 1944. He was educated at the Technical University in Munich from where he received a degree in physics. He worked for his masters degree at Wisconsin University in the US, before returning to Germany and the Max Planck Institute for Psychiatry in Munich for postgraduate work, (1968-72).

He received a PhD from the Technical University of Munich. He first conceived the idea of the patch-clamp technique whilst preparing for his doctoral thesis. In 1972, Neher was at Göttingen University and two years later he began his association with Sakmann. Although Neher moved to the Washington University in Seattle the collaboration continued. In 1976 both men presented their patch-clamp findings at a scientific gathering in 1976. Neher returned to the Max Planck Institute in Göttingen in 1976 and in 1983 was made director of the institute's membrane biophysics department. He was awarded a half share of the 1991 Nobel Prize for Physiology or Medicine.

Erwin Neher is married with three sons and two daughters.

Bert Sakmann was born in Stuttgart, Germany on June 12, 1942. Between 1969 to 1970 Sakmann was working as a research assistant in the department of neurophysiology at the Max Planck Institute for Psychiatry. He then continued his postdoctoral studies at University College, London. He was a British Council fellow in the department of biophysics prior to receiving his PhD from Göttingen University in 1974. Working together with Nether, he conclusively established the existence of characteristic sets of ion channels in cell membranes; some of which permit the flow of only positive ions, while others pass only negatively charged ions.

They went on to examine a wide range of cellular functions, eventually discovering the role that ion channels play in such diseases as diabetes, cystic fibrosis, epilepsy, certain cardiovascular diseases and types of neuromuscular disorders. These discoveries enabled the development of new and specific drug therapies. In 1979 Sakmann became research associate in the Max Planck Institute's membrane biology group. In 1983 he was head of the group and two years later was director of the Institute's department of cell physiology. He was awarded a half share of the 1991 Nobel Prize for Physiology or Medicine.

He is un-married.

ECONOMICS

RONALD COASE (1910-)

Ronald Harry Coase was born in Willesden, London on December 29, 1910. He was educated at the London School of Economics (LSE) and received a Bachelor of Commerce degree in 1932; During WW2, he served in the Central Statistical Office of the War Cabinet. In 1951 he was awarded a PhD in economics. He taught at the LSE from 1932-1951, followed by Buffalo University, N.Y. 1951-58, Virginia University, Charlottesville, 1958-64 and Chicago University from 1964. There he became professor of economics at the law school, taught at the Graduate School of Business and edited the *Journal of Law and Economics* between 1964-1982.

Coase did pioneering works on the manner in which transaction costs annd property rights affect business and society. In his most famous paper, *The Problem of Social Cost* (1960), he challenges the class togic of prohibiting behaviour that damages others. His work was a call to legal scholars to pay attention to the importance of an efficient marketplace and a preference for negotiation rather than litigation.

The Royal Swedish Academy of Sciences cited Coase for this research also for ' pioneering the study of how property rights are distributed among individuals by law, contract, and regulations, showing that this determines how economic decisions are made and whether they will succeed '

Coase was awarded the 1991 Nobel Memorial Prize for Economic Sciences. **"for his discovery and clarification of the significance of transaction costs and property rights for the institutional structure and functioning of the economy"**

He never married.

PEACE

DAW SAN SUU KYI (1945-)

Daw San Suu Kyi was born in Burma on June 19, 1945. She was the daughter of Burmese nationalist leader who had fought the Japanese during their occupation of Burma in WW2. In 1960 Suu Kyi left Burma for Britain and Oxford Universty. She married Michael Aris, who died in 1999, and settled in England. Although she had two children she returned to Burma in 1988 to take care of her sick mother.

Whilst in Burma, she became involved in politics, becoming a leader and general-secretary of the National League for Democracy. In 1989, she was put under house arrest by the military regime. Her party won the Burma elections of May 1990, by a substantial margin but the military dictatorship refused to give up power. As a result Suu Kyi, has been forced to remain under house arrest and isolation. She was awarded the Nobel Peace Prize in 1991. In the meantime the world powers refuse to give Burma the assistance the majority of the people need to overpower an evil regime.

In 1999, the fascist Burmese military junta, backed by the US, refused to allow Aung San Suu Kyi an unrestricted exit visa to visit her dying husband in England. For years the authorities have been trying to get her to leave Burma but Aung San, knowing she would never be allowed to return, has stayed. The military junta continues to terrorise Burma and the G8 countries continue to do business despite calls for a an embargo. To-day Daw San Suu Kyi is internationally recognised as the real leader of Burma and a very brave person.

1992

Clinton wins US Presidential election • Tories win fourth consecutive election • 58 people die in Los Angeles rioting after white police are acquitted of beating black motorist • First woman speaker for British Parliament • Lloyd's of London lose £2 billion in one year's trading • Polytechnics in Britain become universities • Church of England allow women priests • Films; *Howard's End, The Player, Malcolm X, Orlando, Strictly Ballroom, The Story of Qiu Ju* **• John Guare,** *Six Degrees of Separation* **• Toni Morrison,** *Jazz* **• Michael Ondaatje,** *The English Patient* **• Barry Unsworth,** *Sacred Hunger* **• Menachem Begin, Isaac Asimov, Satyajit Ray, Francis Bacon, Marlene Dietrich and Willy Brandt die.**

LITERATURE

DEREK WALCOTT (1930-)

Derek Alton Walcott was born in Castries, Saint Lucia, on January 23, 1930. Of mixed Black, Dutch and English descent, Derek was educated at St Mary's College, St Lucia and at the West Indies University in Jamaica. He has taught at schools in Grenada and St Lucia, and written poetry and articles for magazines in Trinidad and Jamaica. He also wrote plays and these began to be produced in St Lucia in 1950. Between 1958-59 he studied theatre in New York and lived thereafter in Trinidad and the US and teaching in part at Boston University.

Walcott is probably best known for his poetry starting with, *Green Night: Poems 1948-1960* (1962). It is typical of his early poetry and is a celebration of the natural beauty of the West Indies. This is also the feature of further poetry; *Selected Poems* (1964), *The Castaway* (1965) and *The Gulf* (1969). *Another Life* (1973) is an autobiographical poem of book length. In *Sea Grapes* (1976) and *The Star-Apple Kingdom* (1979) his style is more economical and tense as he attempts to examine the situation of being a Black writer in America. *Collected Poems, 1948-1984* was published in 1986.

He has written some 30 plays, the best known of which are *Dream on Monkey Mountain* produced in 1967, *Ti-Jean and His Brothers* (1958) and *Pantomime* (1978).

He was awarded the 1992 Nobel Prize for Literature; **"for a poetic oeuvre of great luminosity, sustained by a historical vision, the outcome of a multicultural commitment"**

Derek Walcott is un-married.

CHEMISTRY

RUDOLPH MARCUS (1923-)

Rudolph A Marcus was born in Montreal, Canada on July 21, 1923. His parents were Jewish immigrants from Europe. Marcus was educated at McGill University in Montreal from where in 1946, he received his PhD.

From 1951 he began work at the Polytechnic Institute of Brooklyn, New York (1951-64). He followed with a period at Illinois University (1964-78). He joined the California Institute of Technology in 1978.

During the 1950s, Marcus began investigating electron-transfer reactions. He published a number of scientific papers on the subject, between 1956 and 65, before concluding that subtle changes occur in the molecular structure of the reactants and the solvent molecules around them. He went on to establish that the relationship between the driving force of an electron-transfer and the reaction's rate is described by a parabola.

Scientists were for a long time most sceptical of his conclusions but in the 1980s, they were confirmed. It resulted in Marcus being awarded the 1992 Nobel Prize for Chemistry; **"for his contributions to the theory of electron transfer reactions in chemical systems"**

He is un-married.

PHYSICS

GEORGES CHARPAK (1924-)

Georges Charpak was born in Poland on August 1, 1924. In 1931 his family moved from Poland to Paris. During WW2, Charpak fought in the French Resistance until 1943, when he was imprisoned by the Vichy French. In 1944 he was handed over to the Germans and sent to Dachau Concentration Camp. There he remained until the camp was liberated in 1945.

He became a French citizen and earned a PhD in 1955, from the Collège de France in Paris where he worked in the laboratory of Frédéric Joliot-Curie. In 1959 he joined the staff of CERN (European Organization for Nuclear Research) in Geneva. In 1984 he became Joliot-Curie professor at the School of Advanced Studies in Physics and Chemistry in Paris. In 1985 he was made a member of

the French Academy of Sciences.

In 1968 Charpak built the first multiwire proportional chamber. Unlike earlier detectors, the multiwire chamber recorded up to a million tracks per second, sending data directly to a computer for analysis. The speed and precision of the multiwire chamber revolutionized high energy physics. By the 1990s such detectors were at the heart of almost every experiment in particle physics. Charpak was awarded the 1992 Nobel Prize for Physics; **"for his invention and development of particle detectors, in particular the multiwire proportional chamber"**

PHYSIOLOGY or MEDICINE

EDMOND FISCHER (1920-)
and
EDWIN KREBS (1918-)

"for their discoveries concerning reversible protein phosphorylation as a biological regulatory mechanism"

Edmond H.Fischer was born in Shanghai, China on April 6, 1920. The son of Swiss parents, Edmond was educated at Geneva University from where he received a PhD in 1947. He stayed on, conducting research, until 1953 at which time he left for the US and Washington University in Seattle. Becoming a full professor in 1961.

Here he met Krebs. The two men made their discoveries in the mid-1950s, while studying reversible phosphorylation or the attachment or detachment of phosphate groups to cell proteins. They were the first to purify and characterize one of the enzymes involved in the process of phosphorylation.

They also discovered the enzymes that catalyse the attachment and detachment of phosphate groups. These are known as protein kinases and phosphates. In the years that have followed these essential discoveries, scientists have been able to identify many other enzymes that regulate specific processes in cells, leading to explanations of the mechanisms controlling basic activities in all living cells. Fischer was awarded a co-share of the 1992 Nobel Prize for Physiology or Medicine.

Edmond Fischer is twice married with three children.

Edwin G. Krebs was born in Lansing, Iowa, US, on June 6, 1918. Krebs received a medical degree from Washington University, St Louis in 1943. From 1946 to 1948 he did research there under the biochemists, Carl and Gerty Cori (qv). In 1968 he was at California University at Davis before returning to Washington University in 1977.

During the 1950s, he and Fischer began investigating the processes by which muscle cells obtain energy from glycogen; the form in which the body stores sugar. The Coris had previously shown that cells use an enzyme called phosphorylates to release glucose from glycogen. Krebs and Fischer showed that phosphorylase could be converted from an inactive to an active form by the addition of a phosphate group taken from the compound adenosine triphosphate.

The enzymes that catalyse this process are termed kinases. They also demonstrated that phosphorylase is inactivated by the removal of a phosphate group, catalysed by enzymes called phosphatases. Mulfunctions in protein phosphorylation have been implicated in the case of diabetes, cancer, and Alzheimer's disease.

Krebs was awarded a co-share of the 1992 Nobel Prize for Physiology or Medicine. He is married with three children.

ECONOMICS

GARY BECKER (1930-)

Gary Stanley Becker was born in Pottsville, Pa; US, on December 2, 1930. The son of middle class Jewish parents, Becker was educated at Princeton University and Chicago University, from where he obtained a PhD in 1955. He stayed on at Chicago to teach economics until1957, when he moved to Columbia University. He later returned to Chicago University where he was appointed professor of economics and sociology, a postion he held until 1983.

The core of his theoretical writings, is the presumption that rational economic choice, which governs the majority of human behaviour, is based on self-interest. His 1957 book *Economics of Discrimination,* examines race preferences in the labour place. In *Human Captial* (1964), he claims that a person's investment in education is on a par with a company investing in machinery.

In 1981 he published, *A Treatise on Family,* comparing a household with a factory. His conclusions regarding the role of women, were taken on board by the feminist movement of the 1980s. Becker has also written in the same analytical mould on drug addiction and criminal behaviour. He was awarded the 1992 Nobel Memorial Prize in Economic Sciences; **"for having extended the domain of microeconomic analysis to a wide range of human behaviour and interaction, including nonmarket behaviour"**

He twice married and has two daughters and two stepsons.

PEACE

RIGOBERTA MENCHU (1959-)

Rigoberta Menchú was born in Guatemala in 1959. Her father was the leader of a peasant organization opposed to Guatemala's miltary dictatorship and murdered whilst protesting at human-rights abuses by the military. Her younger brother was kidnapped, tortured and burned to death by a military death squad in 1979. In 1980, her mother was kidnapped, raped, mutilated and murdered by governement soldiers.

Menchú fled to Mexico in 1981, and there she was cared for by members of a liberal Roman Catholic group. She joined international efforts to force the Guatemalan government to stop its brutal counterinsurgency campaigns (supported by the American CIA) against Indian peasants.   She became a skilled public speaker and organizer, in the course of her work, and gained international prominence in 1983, with her widely translated book, *I, Rigoberta Menchú.*

Here she tells the story of her impoversished youth and recounts the horrors of the torture and murder of her father, brother and mother. She was awarded the 1992 Nobel Peace Prize for her continuing efforts to achieve social justice and mutual reconciliation in Guatemala.

However, years later it has transpired that Menchu's life story is not as it originally appears. For her childhood exploitation we should now read ' a private Catholic boarding school'. Landlord brutality would appear to be a feud between her rich father and his in-laws. It would be nice to think that Ms Menchu has shared her Nobel good fortune with her less fortunate brethren.

1993

Presidents Bush and Yeltsin sign nuclear arms pact • Israel and Vatican establish ties • IBM losses $4.97 billion; largest corporate loss ever • 72 people die in Texas cult fire • Key cancer gene identified • Films; *Schindler's List, The Piano, The Age of Innocence, In the Name of the Father, Farewell My Concubine, Three Colours: Blue,* **• Roddy Doyle,** *Paddy Clarke Ha Ha Ha* **• E. Annie Proulx,** *The Shipping News* **• Vikram Seth,** *A Suitable Boy* **• Arthur Ashe, Sammy Cahn, Federico Fellini, Art Hodes, Alexander Dubcek, Elizabeth Frink, William Golding and Freya Stark die.**

LITERATURE

TONI MORRISON (1931-)

Toni Morrison (Chloe Anthony Wofford) was born in Lorain, Ohio, US, on February 18, 1931. She grew up in Midwest America and educated at Howard University, Washington DC from where she graduated with a BA in 1953. She gained an MA from Cornell University, New York, in 1955. She spent two years teaching at Texas Southern University, followed by Howard University, where she stayed until 1964. In 1965 she became a fiction editor.

Her first book, *The Bluest Eye* (1970), is a novel of initiation about a young Black girl obsessed by the need to have blue eyes. Her next novel, *Sula* (1973), concerns the circumstances surrounding living in a community. *Song of Solomon* (1977) is about a man searching for his identity. It brought Morrison to the attention of the American reading public. *Tar Baby* (1981) was critically acclaimed as was her 1987 novel, *Beloved* .

Toni Morrison's use of fantasy in a poetic way allows her stories to have a rich and strong style. She was awarded the 1993 Nobel Prize for Literature; **"who in novels characterized by visionary force and poetic import, gives life to an essential aspect of American reality"**

She published her novel, *Paradise* in 1998. Toni Morrison is un-married.

CHEMISTRY

KARY MULLIS (1944-)
and
MICHAEL SMITH (1932-)

Kary Banks Mullis was born in Northern Carolina, US, in 1944. He obtained a PhD in biochemistry from the University of California in 1973. In 1986, he published a paper explaining how short, specific sequences of DNA can be rapidly replicated many times. To perform the PCR technique, the double-stranded target DNA is first denatured by being raised to a high degree of temperature and so produce single strands of DNA. Two very short sequences of artificial single-stranded DNA are then attached to the template DNA.

The single stranded DNA, known as, oligonucleotides, are then attached to the template DNA and repeated many times , giving rise to a massive amplification of the target DNA. In 1993 Mullis was co-awarded the Nobel Prize for Chemistry: **"for his invention of the polymerase chain reaction (PCR) method"**

Married to Cynthia and now divorced with two sons, Mullis now spends his time writing and living with Jennifer in a log cabin.

Michael Smith was born in Blackpool, England on April 26, 1932. Educated locally and at Manchester University, he obtained a PhD in 1956. Shortly after, he was awarded a fellowship with the British Columbia Research Council in Canada. Here he studied the chemical effects of DNA and RNA fragments. In 1960, and now married with three children, Smith moved to the Institute for Enzyme Research at the University of Wisconsin. There he worked on the synthesis of ribo-oligonucleotides, a most challenging aspect nucleic acid chemistry.

Then a year later he accepted a post with the Fisheries Research Board of Canada Laboratory in Vancouver, learning about marine biology.

In 1966, supported by an award from the Medical Research Council of Canada, he was able to become a faculty member of the Department of Biochemistry. In 1986, he founded a new interdisciplinary institute, the Biotechnology Laboratory at the University of British Columbia.

In 1993, he was awarded a co-share of the Nobel Prize for Physics; **"for his fundamental contributions to the establishment of oligonucleiotide-based, site directed mutagenesis and its development for protein studies"**

He looks forward to spending less time with admin work leaving time for sailing and skiing.

PHYSICS

RUSSELL HULSE (1950-)
and
JOSEPH TAYLOR (1941-)

"for the discovery of a new type of pulsar, a discovery that has opened up new possibilities for the study of gravitation"

Russell Alan Hulse was born in New York, US on November 28, 1950. Due to a lack of finance his college choice was most limited. He subsequently went to Cooper Union and received a degree in physics in 1970. Then he went to the University of Massachusetts in Amherst, where he did his thesis on radio astronomy and for which he received a PhD. This was followed by his spending 1975-77 at the National Radio Astronomy Observatory in Charlottesville, Virginia.

He joined the Princeton University Plasma Physics Laboratory in 1977, where he developed new computer codes modelling the behaviour of impurity ions in the high temperature plasmas of controlled thermonuclear fusion devices. From this beginning, grew the multi-species impurity transport code. His work was awarded with the co-award of the 1993 Nobel Prize for Physics.

He is un-married. His hobbies include photography, bird watching, target shooting, canoeing, skiing and much else.

Joseph Hooton Taylor, Jr was born in Philadelphia, US, on March 29, 1941. He comes from a family of Quakers who can trace their arrival in America back to the days of the Pilgrim Fathers. As a result he was educated at Quaker institutions such as Haverford College.

He received a PhD from Harvard University, following his thesis on radio astronomy. He has subsequently been associated and working at the University of Massachusetts and at Princeton University. He subsequently received a co-share of the 1993 Nobel Prize for Physics for his work connected with the understanding of signal processing techniques that was most important in understanding pulsars.

He is married

PHYSIOLOGY or MEDICINE

RICHARD ROBERTS (1943-)
and
PHILLIP SHARP (1944-)

"for their discoveries of split genes"

Richard Roberts was born in Derby, England in 1943. Following his education at City of Bath School he was eventually accepted at Sheffield University. In 1965 he graduated in chemistry. He received his PhD from Sheffield following which he accepted a post at Harvard University in 1969.

He spent much time in the realm of the acronyms of the time; DNA, RNA, ATP, UDP and much else. He was involved in the work of sequencing a RNA, that was involved in bacterial cell wall biosynthesis, going on to discover a new method of successful sequencing.

In 1972 Roberts moved to Cold Spring Harbor to work with Jim Watson. There he worked to make preparations on Endonuclease R, an enzyme thought to be able to cleave DNA into specific pieces. This investigative work, plus his work on Adenovirus-2 mRNAs, resulted in a half share of the 1993 Nobel Prize for Physiology or Medicine.

In 1992, he moved to a private laboratory making research reagents, in particular, restriction enzymes. There, he is now joint Research Director. He is most insistent that the structure of the molecules they work with must be known if they are to understand how they function. Roberts is married with four children. He now, in 1999, uses his Nobel status to advertise Hovis bread for a TV advertisement.

Phillip Sharp was born in 1944 in Kentucky, US. His family were farmers and Sharp spent his early years on the farm. Education was local to begin with, eventually progressing to Union College in eastern Kentucky. He continued onto the University of Illinois, where his doctoral thesis dealt primarily with the description of DNA as a polymer, using statistical and physical theories.

In 1969 he received a post-doctoral position at the California Institute of Technology where his work was investigating research in molecular biology. He used the hetero duplex method and electron microscopy to study the structure of plasmids of the sex factors and drug resistant factors of bacteria. He was particularly interested in how sex factor plasmids acquired genomic sequences from the bacterial chromosome.

Sharp later spent a year at Cold Spring Harbor Laboratory where he, and others, used hybridization techniques to map sequences in the simian virus 40 genome that were expressed as stable RNAs in both infected cells and oncogenic cells transformed by this virus. In 1974 he accepted a post under Salvador Luria (qv) at Centre for Cancer Research at the Massachusetts Institute of Technology.

More, and intensive, research followed which resulted in the find that the nuclei of cells productively infected by adenovirus contained abundant sets of viral RNAs which were not transported to the cytoplasm. Sharp's work resulted in a co-share of the 1993 Nobel Prize for Physiology or Medicine.

He became director of MIT in 1985 and resigned in 1991 to become Head of the Biology Department. However, since 1978, Sharp has been part of a biotech company in Switzerland known as Biogen Inc. He is married with three daughters and his career publications exceed 250.

ECONOMICS

ROBERT FOGEL (1926-)
and
DOUGLASS NORTH (1920-)

"for turning the theoretical and statistical tools of modern economics on the historical past"

Robert Fogel was born in New York, US in 1926, the son of a working class Jewish family. Following a local education, Fogel later obtained a PhD from John Hopkins University in 1963.

Until 1975, he taught at Chicago University at which time he switched to Harvard University. In 1981 he once again returned to Chicago, this time as director of the Centre for Population Economics.

Fogel is identified with two particular issues. His 1964 book which argued that the spread of the railroad, was not as important to the opening of the American West as had previously been the case. He argued that the rivers and canals would have done the job just as well and at considerably lower cost. His second book, *Time on the Cross*, written with Stanley Engerman was published in 1974. Here he argues that slavery had been far more profitable than previously thought. His message brought wide criticisms asserting that the authors were endorsing slavery.

It forced Fogel to later publish a four volume study called, *Without Consent or Contract,* in which he forcefully argues that slavery ended not because it was economically inefficient but because it was morally repugnant.

Fogel was able to bring quantitative methods to economic history and for empirical work that ignored the blackboard. The co-award of the 1993 Nobel Prize for Economics was greeted with enthusiasm by his colleagues for describing events as 'cliometrics'. Fogel is married with two sons.

Douglass North was born in Cambridge, Mass, US, in 1920. As an undergraduate at the University of California, Berkeley, he was considered a Marxist. Service during WW2 in the merchant marine and later, nine months service as a government photographer, chronicling the farm life of California, persuaded North to become an Economist.

His books, *The Rise of the Western World* (1971) and *Structure and Change in Economic History*, clearly establish the role institutional change, especially property rights, could be expected to play in a rigorous theory of economic development. In 1968, North wrote a paper on ocean shipping in which he shows that organizational changes played a greater role in increasing productivity than did technical change.

This feature of North's work was specifically mentioned when he was awarded a co-share of the 1993 Nobel Prize for Economics.

North, has been a professor at Washington University, St. Louis since 1982. He has been married twice and has three sons.

PEACE

NELSON MANDELA (1918-)
and
FREDERIK de KLERK (1936-)

"for their attempts to establish democracy and racial harmony in South Africa"

Nelson Rolihlahia Mandela was born in Transkei, South Africa on July 25,1918. His father was Chief Henry Mandela of the Tembu Tribe. Nelson was educated at the University College of Fort Hare and Witwatersrand University, Capetown from where he graduated in law in 1942.

In 1944 Mandela joined the African National Congress (ANC) and in 1948, began his resistance to the ruling National Party's apartheid policy.

He went on trial for treason and acquitted in 1961. By this time the ANC was banned and Mandela advocated the setting up of a military wing. In 1961 was formed Umkhonto we Sizwe. In 1962 Mandela was arrested for taking part in an illegal organization and sentenced to five years hard labour. A year later and he was again on trial, accused of attempting to overthrow the government by force. On June 12, 1964 Mandela, and others, were sentenced to life imprisonment

Between 1964 and 1982, he was incarcerated on Robben Island, off Cape Town. He was later transferred to the mainland and Pollsmoor Prison. During his years in prison Mandela became the conscience of the world. His reputation grew and became widely accepted as the voice of Black South Africa. He became the symbol of a growing resistance to apartheid. This movement gathered strength with Mandela constantly refusing to compromise his political beliefs to obtain his release.

On February 18, 1990, Mandela was released. It caught the imagination of the world. Apartheid was doomed. In 1991, at the first National Conference of the ANC held inside South Africa, Mandela was elected President of the ANC. In 1993 Mandela, together with Frederik de Klerk, was awarded the Nobel Peace Prize.

In May 1994, the first national election was held in which all races, including Blacks, could vote. The result was an overwhelming victory for the ANC. Thereafter Mandela became President of South Africa. He stood down in 1999. During his presidency, tourism has increased by leaps and bounds, law and order is a vital issue and the Blacks are desperately trying to play catch-up. However, it is expected that time will gradually increase the economic and living standards of those who have suffered for so long.

Mandela married Winnie Madikizela in 1958; they divorced in 1995. In 1998 Mandela married Graca Machel. At the time Mandela and de Klerk were awarded the Peace Prize they were barely on speaking terms.

Frederik **William de Klerk** was born on March 18, 1936 in Johannesburg, South Africa. His father was Senator Jan de Klerk, a leading politician who later became a cabinet minister in a right-wing government. Frederik's brother however, was a liberal journalist and one of the founders of the Democratic Party.

De Klerk graduated with a law degree from Potchefstroom University in 1958 and thereafter practised law in Vereeniging, Transvaal. In 1972 he was elected to Parliament as a National Party member. In 1978 he was appointed Minister of Posts and Telecommunications. As time proceeded he held numerous governmental posts culminating on December 1, 1986, as leader of the House of Assembly.

De Klerk was a supporter of apartheid and as such, was elected leader of the national Party in 1989 becoming President in 1989. In his inaugural speech he called for a non-racist country. He lifted the ban on the ANC and in response to overwhelming international demand, released Nelson Mandela (qv).

He now likes to take pride that it was by his efforts that apartheid ended and that he was responsible for the new constitution that created the principle of 'one person, one vote'.

He has attended the Truth and Reconciliation hearings, that Bishop Desmond Tutu set up, but has failed to show true regret for the past. Many atrocities were carried out during his presidency for which satisfactory answers have not been provided.

Professor Jonathan Gluckman, the South African born pathologist, sent to de Klerk direct, his findings that proved that police were murdering and torturing suspects. de Klerk refused to intervene and the police killings continued.

In the face of international hostility to apartheid, and the mass opposition of many countries of the world, as well as the continual baring of South Africa in world sporting events, it wasn't unsurprising that de Klerk acted as he did. He was awarded a co-share of the 1993 Nobel Prize for Peace. Once married with three children, he is now retired from politics and divorced. His ex-wife, an ardent supporter of apartheid, could not tolerate Mandela and his colleagues being in the same vicinity as her. His autobiography, *The Last Trek, A New Beginning,* was published in 1999.

1994

IRA mortar bombs hit Heathrow Airport • Muslims and Croats agree on Bosnia Federation • Half a million die in Rwanda civil war • Channel Tunnel opened by the Queen and President Mitterrand • 50th Anniversary of D-Day • US Institute of Health announces key to cancer found • 900 die in Baltic Sea ferry disaster • UK launches National Lottery • Paul Touvier, first Frenchman found guilty for crimes against humanity gets life imprisonment • US invades Haiti • Norway wins Winter Olympics • Earth survives near-miss with an asteroid • Israel withdraws from Gaza Strip-Arafat returns to Palestine • Nelson Mandela becomes President of South Africa • Israel and Jordan end state of war • Norway says 'no' to EU • Diana Rigg, *Medea* • Li Zhisui, *The Private Life of Chairman Mao* • James Waller, *The Bridges of Madison County* • John Gray, *Men are From Mars, Women are From Venus* • Films: *Pulp Fiction, Bullets over Broadway, The Shawshank Redemption, Chungking Express, Four Weddings and a Funeral* • Matt Busby, Brian Johnston, Telly Savalas, Melina Mercouri, Eugene Ionesco, Richard Nixon, Aryton Senna, Lindsay Anderson, Jacqueline Kennedy, John Smith, Billy Wright, Jean Borota, Bernard Delfont, John Osborne, Dinah Shore, Burt Lancaster, Joseph Cotten, Fernando Rey and Cab Calloway die.

LITERATURE

KENZABURO OE (1935-)

Kenzaburo Oe was born in 1935 in Shikoku, Japan. It was a village life and no-one from Oe's family had ever left the village in the valley. He was six, when Japan embarked on its' militaristic adventures that left its mark on every nook and cranny in feudal Japan, with the Emperor considered both a God and monarch. His mother and grandmother were the village storytellers and Oe was brought up on his nation's myths and history.

Japan's defeat in 1945 brought enormous change, even in remote village areas. Now the schools taught democracy. This was something Oe could well appreciate; so much so he decided Tokyo was the place for him. He was eighteen when he arrived in the capital. The following year he enrolled in the French Literature department of Tokyo University. His studies there and his introduction to the French Renaissance period in general and François Rabelais in particular, it was the impetus Oe needed to start writing.

In 1957 he won the Akutagawa Award for his short story, *The Catch*. His first novel, *Bud-Nipping, Lamb Shooting,* (1958) tells the tragic story of how war tears apart a rural life. In *The*

Youth Who Came Late (1961) Oe portrays Tokyo student life under US occupation. In 1964 he wrote, *A Personal Matter.* Here he tells the story of living with a mentally handicapped child-his son, Hikari. *The Silent Cry* (1967) is a work that joins up myths and history in a contemporary age.

In *Letters to My Sweet Bygone Years* (1987), Oe tells of a young man who, banking on his cosmology and world view of Dantes, strives, but fails, to establish a cultural base in the forest.

In his trilogy, *Until the Saviour Gets Socked* (1993), *Vacillating* (1994) and *On The Great Day* (1995), Oe ends one stage of his life.

He was awarded the 1994 Nobel Prize for Literature; **"who with poetic force creates an imagined world where life and myth condense to form a disconcerting picture of the human predicament to-day"** . He is married with a child.

CHEMISTRY

GEORGE OLAH (1927-)

George Olah was born on May 22, 1927 in Budapest, Hungary. His father a middle-class lawyer. Olah was educated at a school run by a Roman Catholic order. He graduated, survived the chaos of war and began studying chemistry at the Technical University of Budapest. He was particularly interested in organic chemistry. He became an assistant to Professor Geza Zemplen on a no fee basis. Zemplen had a reputation for partying, events that continued for days.

Olah attempted to research fluorine containing carbohydrates, but this was frowned upon. Olah persisted and Zemplen eventually gave in. Materials were hard to come by in post war Hungary but Olah got by. Hungarian education was now modelled on the Soviet style with research institutes established under the auspices of the Academy of Sciences. There Olah was able to join a small research group. In 1956, a right-wing revolt led to many thousands of citizens leaving for the West. They included Olah, his wife and son.

They journeyed to London and relatives of his wife. From there they moved to Montreal, Canada where his mother-in-law lived. Olah was offered a position with Dow Chemicals in Sarnia, Ontario. During the late fifties he worked on stable carbocations that led to the Friedel-Crafts type manufacture of etylbenzene for styrene production.

In 1965 he was invited to join Western Reserve University in Cleveland, Ohio as a professor of chemistry. 12 years later and the family moved to California where Olah became in charge of the Chemical Research department of the University of Southern California in Los Angeles.

Olah was awarded the 1994 Nobel Prize for Chemistry; **"for his contribution to carbocation chemistry"** He is married with two sons.

PHYSICS

BERTRAM BROCKHOUSE (1918-)
and
CLIFFORD SHULL (1915-)

Bertram Neville Brockhouse was born on July 15, 1918 in Alberta, Canada. In 1926 the family moved to Vancouver. Educated at King George High School, Vancouver until 1935 when the family moved to Chicago, he attended classes at night, at Central YMCA College, and worked by day, repairing and building radios.

In 1938 the family returned to Vancouver. During WW2 he served in the Royal Canadian Navy servicing ASDIC equipment at a shore base. Armed with a grant, he joined the University of British Columbia and enrolled to study physics and mathematics. After obtaining his BA, Brockhouse joined the Low Temperature Laboratory at Toronto University. There, his thesis subject was a contribution to the Solid State physics involving experiments at both high and low temperatures.

In 1950 he obtained his PhD. He joined the Dominion Government Establishment at Chalk River and in 1951, he was involved with experiments concerning the scattering of neutrons by highly absorbing elements. The apparatus involved was later used on slow neutron spectroscopy eventually creating the 'spin wave' on a microscopic basis.

In 1962 he was appointed professor of physics at McMaster University in Hamilton, Ontario. There he used the neutron diffractometer, and other equipment, for continuing experimentation in neutron spectroscopy. During the 1970s, he explored various factors in general physics although he was often hampered by bouts of ill-health. In 1994 he was co- awarded the Nobel Prize for Physics; **"for the development of neutron spectroscopy"**

He is married with several children.

Clifford Shull was born on September 23, 1915 in Pittsburgh, US. Educated locally and at the Carnegie Institute of Technology he reached New York University in 1937. From there in 1941 he received his PhD. Part of his research programme was the work done on the neutron interactions with various materials. He joined the research laboratory of the Texas Company at Beacon, NY. There he studied the microstructures of catalysts using gas adsorption and X-ray diffraction. Other fields of investigation included diffraction processes, crystallography and solid state physics.

In 1955 he joined the faculty of Massachusetts Institute of Technology. There he continued his work using neutron radiation from a reactor in many fields; until his retirement in 1986. He was awarded a co-share of the 1994 Nobel Prize for Physics; **"for the development of the neutron diffraction technique"** He is married with three sons

PHYSIOLOGY or MEDICINE

ALFRED GILMAN (1941-)
and
MARTIN RODBELL (1925-1998)

"for their discovery of G-proteins and the role of these proteins in signal transduction in cells"

Alfred Gilman was born in 1941 in New Haven, Conn. US. In 1955 he was sent to boarding school at the Taft School, Watertown, Conn. Thereafter he was at Yale University studying biochemistry. He left for Case Western Reserve University in 1962. There he did experimental work in molecular biology as it applied to the nervous system.

He concentrated on clonal cell lines and genetic approaches. In 1971, he became assistant professor of pharmacology at the University of Virginia in Charlottesville. His continuing research with the advent of ligand binding assays for receptors. In 1981 he became professor of pharmacology at Dallas University. In 1994 Gilman was co-awarded the Nobel Prize for Physiology or Medicine.

He is married with two daughters and a son.

Martin Rodbell was born on December 1, 1925 in Baltimore, US. Educated locally, he graduated from Baltimore City College and joined John Hopkins University in 1943. Following service in the US Navy, during WW2, Rodbell later explained how, as a Jew, he would rather have been fighting Germans than Japanese. He returned to John Hopkins where he became attracted to French literature and became an avid reader of contemporary French writers.

His father wanted him to study medicine but he preferred the course on biological sciences. Eventually he settled on biochemistry and left for the University of Washington in Seattle. In 1954, he obtained his PhD in biochemistry and left Seattle for Urbana, becoming part of the Chemistry department at the University of Illinois. There he researched the biosynthesis of chloramphenicol, an antibiotic, the molecule of which contained a nitro group appended to its benzene ring and two chlorides in the aliphatic side chain.

Later, using a newly developed 'fingerprinting' method, he established that some five different proteins were present in human chylomicrons. Years later these five proteins proved to have very significant roles in diseases involving lipoprotein. In 1960, he was granted a fellowship at the Free University of Brussels in order to study cell biology embryology. Upon his return, Rodbell joined the Institute of Arthritis and Metabolic Diseases working to discover whether lipoprotein lipases was synthesized and released from fat cells.

He discovered that collagenase rapidly digested the tissue matrix, releasing fat cells. As fat cells float to the surface of the incubation medium, it was possible to separate and purify these cells from the mostly vascular cells in adipose tissue. The procedure adopted by Rodbell later changed the course of this type of research.

Between 1981 and 83 he was professor of biology at Geneva University where he carried out research on the structure and function of glucagon. In 1994 he received a co-share of the Nobel Prize for Physiology or Medicine.

He married Barbara Ledermann whose Dutch parents perished in Auschwitz. They had four children. Rodbell died in 1998.

ECONOMICS

JOHN HARSANYI (1920-), JOHN NASH (1928-)
and
REINHARD SELTEN (1930-)

"for their pioneering analyses of equlibria in the theory of non-co-operative games"

John **Harsanyi** was born on May 29, 1920 in Budapest, Hungary. Although Jewish, Harsanyi was educated at the Lutheran Gymnasium in Budapest. He graduated in 1937 winning the first prize for mathematics. Until Germany occupied Hungary in March 1944, Harsanyi was serving in a labour unit. In November 1944 the Germans decided to deport the labour unit to an Austrian concentration camp. Just before the train left Budapest railway station, Harsanyi escaped and sought refuge with a Jesuit priest he knew and lived out the war in the cellar of a monastery.

The war over, he re-enrolled at Budapest University. As he already had a credit for pre war studies in pharmacy he was able to obtain his PhD in 1947. In April 1950 he and the lady who would become his wife, illegally left Hungary. They eventually surfaced in Australia in December of that same year.

His English was poor and his degree unrecognized and he spent most of the next three years working in a factory. In the evenings he took courses in economics at Sydney University. At the end of 1953 he received an MA. In 1954 he was appointed a lecturer in economics at Queensland University in Brisbane. In 1956 he was awarded a Rockefeller Fellowship to Stanford University from where he received a PhD in economics.

In 1958 the couple returned to Australia and the Australian National University in Canberra. Then came an appointment as professor of economics at Wayne State University in Detroit. In 1964 he transferred to the University of California in Berkeley. His research in game-theoretic problems, that started in 1950-53, now became re-established. It had originated with the four published papers on co-operative and non-cooperative games now known as the Nash Equilibria.

This work gradually extended to games without transferable utility. In 1994, he received the Nobel Prize for Economic Sciences. He has written much including, *Rational Behaviour and Bargaining Equilibrium in Games and Soc* (1977), *Essays on Ethics, Social Behaviour and Scientific Explanation* (1976) and *Papers in Game Theory* (1982). Harsanyi is married with a son.

John **Nash, Jr** was born on June 13,1928 in Bluefield, WV. US. Education was a series of local schools. Graduating from high school, he joined Carnegie Technical in Pittsburgh, studying chemical engineering. He graduated with a BS and MS. Then came Princeton University and an eventual PhD. From 1951 to 1959 he was on the faculty of M.I.T.

During this period he solved a classical problem relating to differential geometry. That was the problem to prove the isometric embeddability of abstract Riemannian manifolds. He then underwent a series of mentally related illnesses that meant protracted stays in hospitals. He later carried on where John von Neumann left off in the field of 'zero-sum' games.

Ferociously competitive, Nash sailed through all problems until, in his mid-twenties, he went through a series of homosexual adventures, fathered an illegitimate child and telling Chicago University he couldn't accept their offer of a job because he had just been appointed Emperor of Antarctica.

After some 20 years in and out of hospitals, schizophrenia was diagnosed. Helped by Princeton University, Nash slowly recovered. For his research work, he was awarded a third share of the 1994 Nobel Prize for Economic Sciences.

He is still working as a scientist and is married.

Reinhard **Selten** was born on October 10, 1930 in Breslau, Germany. Selten was baptized because his Jewish father feared for his safety. In the event he grew up in the Nazi society, working at menial jobs with little or no schooling. He survived the war, although his father died in 1942. The remaining family moved to Austria and there in Melsungen, Selten went to high school. To get to and from school meant a three and a half hour walk. He put the time to good use by creating and solving problems of elementary geometry and algebra.

Between 1951 and 1957 he studied mathematics at Frankfurt University and received a BA. He found he was becoming more and more interested in game theory and economics. His later master's thesis and later still his PhD thesis, had the aim of axiomatizing a value for e-person games in extensive form. It meant seeing the perfectness of a problem at an early stage.

For ten years from 1957, he was a research assistant to Heinz Sauermann, an economist at the University of Frankfurt am Main. Selten received his PhD in mathematics in 1961 and took part in a game theory conference held at Princeton University. There followed in 1965 a game theory workshop in Jerusalem, when game theory was still a small field. It was from this time that he met and co-operated with John Harsanyi (qv)

He was appointed a full professor of economics at the Free University of Berlin in 1969 and stayed until 1972 at which time he moved to Bielefeld University. Here he continued his experimental research on game theory and it's application to industrial organization. He spent 12 years at Bielefeld, with time off to attend conferences and give lectures at the University of California at Berkeley. In 1984 he moved to Bonn University. In 1994 he was awarded a Nobel Prize for Economic Sciences. He is married, without children. In 1991 both husband and wife discovered they had diabetes. As a result

Frau Selten has had both legs amputated and is approaching blindness.

PEACE

YASIR ARAFAT (1929-), SHIMON PERES (1923-)
and
YITZHAK RABIN (1922-1995)

Mohammed Abad Arouf Arafat was born in 1929 in Jerusalem, Palestine. Following a general education he went to Cairo University to study civil engineering. He interrupted his education to take part in the fighting that followed the declaration of the State of Israel. He joined the Palestinian forces fighting with the grand mufti of Jerusalem. Following the war he returned to university and later graduated with a degree.

In 1956 he served with the Egyptian Army during the Suez campaign. The following year he founded the commando group, Al Fatah. Then, between 1957-65, he worked for a construction group in Kuwait. However, during this period he repeatedly led fedayeen raids deep into Israeli territory.

In 1964, he linked Al Fatah with similar groups in the PLO, becoming chairman of that organization in 1968. From then on he changed the focus of PLO from pan-Arabism to Palestinian national aspirations. After the Arab League recognized the PLO as the sole representative of Palestine Arabs in 1974, he worked to achieve international recognition. To this end he became the first non-governmental representative to address a plenary session of the General Assembly of the UN. He began shedding his image of a terrorist in favour of that as a moderate statesman. In 1988 he proclaimed and independent Palestinian state and recognized the right of Israel to exist; thus meeting the US condition for substantive dialogue with the PLO.

The world was startled when on September 13, 1993, Prime Minister Rabin of Israel and Arafat agreed to the signing of a peace accord that called for Israel and the PLO to recognize each other and for Palestinian self-rule in the Gaza Strip and parts of the West Bank including Jericho. This became effective in May 1994. For his efforts to create peace in the area Arafat was awarded a share of the 1994 Nobel Peace Prize. Arafat is now President of the Palestinian National Authority. He is married with a child.

Shimon Peres was born in 1923 in Poland. As a child he emigrated with his family to Palestine in 1934. There he studied at the Ben Shemen Agricultural School. He became a founder member of Kibbutz Alumot in the Jordan Valley. During the War of Independence, Peres, a protégée of prime minster Ben-Gurion, became responsible for arms purchases and recruitment. In 1949 he headed the procurement delegation to the US.

He became director general of the Ministry of Defence between 1953-59. Since 1959 he has been a member of the Knesset, the Israeli parliament. At various times he has been deputy minister of defence, minister of immigrant absorption, minister of transport and communications, minister of information. He was minister of defence, 1974-77, during which time he was responsible for the daring Entebbe Airport rescue operation that caught the imagination of the world.

Between 1984-86 he was prime minster of a National Unity Government and between 1986-88, was minister of foreign affairs. Between 1988-90, he was leader of the opposition in the Knesset. In 1990 he left office over differences on peace talks with the Palestinians. He continued to lead the Labour Party until February 1992 when he lost in party elections to Yitzhak Rabin (qv).

When Labour won the general election of June 1992, Peres became foreign minister. In September 1993, he signed an historic peace agreement between Israel the PLO. It paved the way for limited self-rule in Israeli-occupied territories. For his part in the peace talks Peres was awarded a share of the 1994 Nobel Peace Prize.

He is married with two sons and a daughter. He became Prime Minister following the assassination of Rabin (qv) in 1995. He failed to win the general election of 1996 and there followed three years of Likud rule in what became to be known as the 'nothing years'.

Yitzhak Rabin was born on March 1, 1922 in Jerusalem, Palestine. He studied at the Kadouri Agricultural College, an institution peculiar to Jewish Palestine where pupils and teachers were on first name terms and agreed on the curriculum. He graduated with distinction. Whilst still at college, where his aim was to become a farmer, he was persuaded to join the Jewish Settlement Police being set-up by the British. His military career began during WW2, when he was part of a unit that included British and Australian troops, who invaded Lebanon, then under the control of Vichy France. Then he joined the 'Palmach' an elite unit of the Haganah. During the War of Independence (1948-49) he commanded the Harel Brigade deployed on the Jerusalem front.

The war over, he spent the next 20 years with the Israel Defence Force (IDF) as OC Northern Command (1956-59), as Chief of Operations and Deputy Chief of Staff (1959-64) and Chief of Staff (1964-68) which included the 'Six Day War', although he was overshadowed by the personality and exciting figure of Moshe Dayan.

On January 1,1968, he retired from the army becoming Israeli ambassador to the US. After five years he returned to Israel to become active in the Labour Party and a member of the Knesset. Under Golda Meir in 1974, Rabin was appointed minister of labour. A few months later he had succeeded Meir to become Prime Minister and leader of the Party. Following defeat in the next general election by Likud, under Begin(qv), Rabin's party was in opposition.

He led the Labour Party to victory in the 1992 general election and became Prime Minister. In 1993 , following secret negotiations, Rabin agreed to the signing of an historic peace accord with Arafat(qv) and the PLO. TV viewers, watching the scene from the lawns of the White House in Washington, held their breath as Arafat held out his hand to Rabin. There was a moments hesitation before the two men shook hands and everyone cheered. This agreement paved the way for further peace talks.

In 1994 Rabin shared the Nobel Peace Prize for his contribution to Middle East peace. On November 4, 1995, Rabin having just addressed a large peace rally, was murdered by a Jewish man, a student of religion. Rabin was married with children.

In June 1948, Menachem Begin (qv), leader of the Irgun Zvai Leumi, reneged on an agreement with the new Israeli government. The *Altalena* was bringing a shipload of arms to Israel but only for the use of some 800 members of the Irgun who were on board. This was during the first Israeli-Arab truce and Ben-Gurion refused to countenance the idea of any independent army. In the event there was a pitched battle in front of the hotels where UN observers were staying.

The insurgents were fighting in the grounds of the Ritz Hotel when a young Israeli officer threw a hand grenade at them from out of an upper floor window. That ended the fighting. The officer was Yitzhak Rabin. The event was never forgotten or forgiven by Israeli right-wingers.

1995

Earthquake devastates Kobe • 50th anniversary of the Holocaust • Mir and Discovery rendevous in space • Prime Minister Rabin assassinated •University of California confirms McDonald major contributor to poor health • Water found on Mars • Russia invades Chechnya • Chirac becomes French President • Ozone hole over Antarctica widens • 500 killed in India train crash • US man given 25 years for stealing a slice of pizza • French nuclear tests in Pacific • Alfred Dreyfus officially absolved • Martin Amis, *The Information* **• Bill Gates,** *The Road Ahead* **• Stephen King,** *Rose Madder* **• Films:** *Secrets and Lies, Trainspotting, Seven, The Usual Suspects, Braveheart, Leaving Las Vegas, Dead Man Walking, The Client, Underground, The Madness of King George, The Bait, Cyclo* **• Harold Wilson, Joe Slovo, Ginger Rogers, Ken Saro-Wiwa, Louis Malle, Ida Lupino, Robert Bolt and Gerald Durrell die.**

LITERATURE

SEAMUS HEANEY (1939-)

Seamus Heaney was born on April 18, 1939 in County Derry, Northern Island. His father owned a small farm and was a cattle dealer. At twelve, Seamus won a scholarship to St. Columb's College, a Catholic boarding school in Derry. He later became a student at Queen's University, Belfast. Here he studied languages and began writing poetry. He became a teacher in Belfast and published *North*. His poetic line was pure Anglo-Saxon, later it would become Mediterranean.

He became a member of the 'Northern School' of Irish poets and writers and in the mid-1960s he began to be noticed. In 1970-71, he was a visiting lecturer at the University of California at Berkeley and upon his return to Ireland, he resigned from Queen's in order to work full time as a poet and free-lance writer. That period over, he became a lecturer at Carysfort

College until 1982, when he spent long periods at Harvard University. Here, in 1984, Heaney was named Bolyston Professor of Rhetoric and Oratory. In 1989, he was elected for a five year period to be Professor of Poetry at Oxford University.

His best known poetry includes, *Death of a Naturalist* (1966), *Door into the Dark* (1969), *Selected Poems, 1965-1975* (1980), *Station Island* (1984), *The Haw Lantern* (1987) and *Seeing Things* (1991). His essays include *Preoccupations: Selected Prose, 1968-1978* (1980), *The Government of the Tongue* (1988), *A Collection of Critical Essays* (1993) and *The Redress of Poetry: Oxford Lectures* (1995) In 1991 he wrote a drama, *The Cure at Troy. A Version of Sophocles' Philoctetes,*

He also wrote a number of critical studies. In 1995 Heaney was awarded the Nobel Prize for Literature; **"for works of lyrical beauty and ethical depth, which exalt everyday miracles and the living past"**

His latest book, *Opened Ground: Poems 1966-1996* was published in 1998. He has lived in Dublin for the past thirty years and most concerned about 'the troubles'. On December 2nd 1999 he was most uplifted when the Northern Island political parties put the past behind them and agreed to share power in Stormont. He is married with three children.

CHEMISTRY

PAUL CRUTZEN (1933-), MARIO MOLINA (1943-)
and
SHERWOOD ROWLAND (1927-)

"for their work in atmospheric chemistry, particularly the formation and decomposition of ozone"

Paul Crutzen was born on December 3, 1933 in Amsterdam, Holland. His early education was largely interrupted by WW2. He eventually reached a middle technical school to train as a civil engineer and later worked for the Bridge Construction Bureau in Amsterdam. In July 1959 Paul, and his family moved to Stockholm and started an alternative career training in the field of meteorology.

In 1963 he was an MS. His work caused him to be recognised as a pure theoretician. In 1965, he began to develop a numerical model of the oxygen allotrope distribution in the stratosphere, mesosphere and lower thermosphere. It resulted in his becoming interested in the photochemistry of atmospheric ozone. It derived in his receiving a third share of the 1995 Nobel Prize for Chemistry, .

Between 1977-80, he was director of research at the National Centre of Atmospheric Research in Boulder, Colorado.

He is married with two daughters.

Mario **Molina** was born on March 19, 1943 in Mexico City, Mexico. His father was a lawyer who also taught law. Mario was educated in Mexico City until, at the age of eleven, he was sent to a boarding school in Switzerland. In 1960 he joined the National University of Mexico. In 1972 he obtained a PhD in physical chemistry from the University of California at Berkeley.

Together with Sherwood Rowland (qv) he developed the 'CFC-ozone depletion theory' their investigations resulted in the world being informed of the great threat CFC's in the atmosphere meant to the Earth's stratospheric ozone layer. In 1975, he was appointed a member of the faculty at the University of California. In 1982 he was at the Molecular Physics and Chemistry Section at the Jet Propulsion Laboratory. Here he conducted experiments in the circumstances of the depletion of ozone over Antarctica.

In 1989, he moved to the Massachusetts Institute of Technology where he continued his researches on global atmospheric chemistry. In respect of his work, Molina was awarded a third share of the 1995 Nobel Prize for Chemistry.

Following his retirement from chemistry matters, Molina served as Mexican ambassador to Ethiopia, Australia and the Philippines. He is married with a son.

Sherwood **Rowland** was born on June 28, 1927 in Delaware, Ohio, US. His father was a university professor and his son's education, both elementary and high school was received at the town's public schools.

He graduated from high school in 1943 and joined Ohio Wesleyan University. He then joined the chemistry department of Chicago University. From there in 1952, he obtained his PhD and joined Princeton University as an instructor in the chemistry department.

In 1956, he was assistant professor at Kansas University which had facilities in radio-chemistry. In 1964, he was at the University of California as professor of chemistry. There he was involved in 'hot atom chemistry', funded by NASA. In 1970 he became interested in atmospheric matters and from 1973 he controlled a research group that has done much to alert the world to the great danger society is causing to the ozone layers. In 1995 Rowland was awarded a third share of the Nobel Prize for Chemistry. He is married with a child.

PHYSICS

MARTIN PERLS (1927-)
and
FREDERICK REINES (1918-1998)

Martin Perl was born in 1927 in New York, US. His parents went to the US to escape the endemic anti-Semitism of Poland. Martin grew up in middle class New York and went to good local public schools. Following graduating from Madison High School in 1942, Martin enrolled in the Polytechnic Institute of Brooklyn to study chemical engineering.

His studies were interrupted by his joining the United States Merchant Marine for the latter part of WW2. The war over, he re-joined the Polytechnic and received his degree in chemical engineering in 1948.

He joined the General Electric Company (GEC) working as a chemical engineer in the electron tube division. Having to know about how electron vacuum tubes worked, he took a course at Union College, Schenectady, on atomic physics and advanced calculus. There his tutor explained the difference in physics to chemistry and thereafter Perls would become a physicist.

He joined the doctoral course at Columbia University in 1950 and five years later was awarded his PhD. He joined the University of Michigan and worked in bubble chamber physics with Donald Glaser (qv). In 1957 he decided to go it alone and, having obtained research funds from Washington, he and a colleague, Lawrence Jones, set up their own laboratory.

The eventual result was the award of a co-share of the 1995 Nobel Prize for Physics; **"for the discovery of the tau lepton"**

A lepton is a fundamental particle that does not interact strongly with other particles. There are several different types of lepton of which tau is one. Perl is un-married.

Frederick Reines was born on March 16, 1918 in Patterson, NJ. US. Reines parents had also emigrated to the US from Eastern Europe, to escape the violent anti-Semitism then existing. The youngest in a family of four meant there were always books around the house, especially as his sister was studying medicine and his brothers the law. A student at Union Hill High School, he graduated and joined Stevens Institute of Technology.

He received a degree in engineering in 1939 and a master of science degree in mathematical physics in 1941. He then switched to New York University to work on his doctoral thesis. Before he could complete this work he was recruited to work under Richard Feynman (qv) at Los Alamos's theoretical division of the Manhattan Project. Here he worked for 15 years. In 1958 he was a delegate to the Atoms for Peace conference in Geneva.

In 1959 he became professor of physics at the Case Institute of Technology in Cleveland, Ohio. Here, during his seven year tenure, he built up a group working on various studies of physical experiments that culminated in an experiment in a South African gold mine that produced the first observation of the neutrinos produced in the atmosphere by cosmic rays.

This area of research continued at the University of California at Irvine, where Reines became the founding dean of the School of Physical Services. He stayed until 1974 at which time he returned to full time research. He switched to proton decay investigation and a programme of reactor neutrino experiments.   In 1995 he was awarded a co-share of the Nobel Prize for Physics: **"for the detection of the neutrino"**

An excellent opera singer from his university days his interest in music lasted until his death on August 26, 1998. Reines who died whilst living in California, was married with a son and daughter.

PHYSIOLOGY or MEDICINE

EDWARD LEWIS (1918-), CHRISTIANE VOLLARD (1942-)
and
ERIC WIESCHAUS (1947-)

"for their discoveries concerning the genetic control of early embryonic development"

Edward Lewis was born on May 20, 1918 in Wilkes-Barre, Pen: US. Educated locally, he went on to Minnesota University from where, in 1939, he received a BA. In 1942 he obtained a PhD from the California Institute of Technology. During WW2 he was an officer in the United States Army Air Force and worked as a meteorologist and oceanographer in the Pacific war.

In 1947-48 he was a Rockefeller Foundation Fellow at Cambridge University. At divers times throughout the fifties, sixties, seventies and eighties, Lewis held various professorial posts at California Institute of Technology.

His work in the field of genetics is world known, not least through his large output of text papers. In 1990 he was awarded the National Medal of Science. He was awarded a third share of the 1995 Nobel Prize for Physiology or Medicine.

He is married to an artist and has three children.

Christiane Nusslein-Volhard was born on October 20, 1942 in Frankfurt, Germany. Her father was an architect who practised throughout the Hitler regime. She attended Frankfurt University and soon became interested in biology. She worked extensively on DNA and RNA-DNA hybridisation and developed a method for large scale purification of very clean RNA polymerase.

She was later involved in isolating RNA polymerase binding sites from fd Phage. Later she concentrated on advance genetic experimentation. In 1995 she was awarded a third share of the Nobel Prize for Physiology or Medicine. She is un-married.

Eric Wieschaus was born on June 8, 1947 in South Bend, Indiana, US. As a child in a Catholic family he was educated at Catholic schools, following the family move to Birmingham, Alabama when Eric was six years old.

He was later educated at Notre Dame where he became active against US involvement in Vietnam. He switched to Yale University in order to study biology. Following his PhD, Wieschaus spent some time in Switzerland working and experimenting. In particular he made germ line mosaics using *K10* and mitotic recombination.

In 1978 he had a job with the European Molecular Biology Laboratory in Heidelberg, Germany. In 1981 he moved to Princeton University where he teaches genetics at undergraduate level. His ongoing experimental work included carrying out large scale mutagenetic screens for maternal effect mutants.

The loci identified by these screens, allowed Drosophila oogenesis to come to rival embro genesis as an ideal system for studying patterning. Much of his current work centres on genes controlling cell shape changes during gastrulation. In 1995 he received a third share of the Nobel Prize for Physiology or Medicine.

He is married with three daughters. He is most interested in music and is an amateur artist of some distinction.

ECONOMICS

ROBERT LUCAS (1937-)

Robert E. Lucas was born in 1937 in Yakima, Washington, US. Educated at local schools he graduated from Roosevelt High School. He won a scholarship to Chicago University in order to take an arts degree. He then obtained a Woodrow Wilson Doctoral Fellowship which took him to the University of California and a history programme. The emphasis developed on economic history and finishing the course by switching back to Chicago University.

He joined the faculty of Carnegie-Mellon University, and stayed for some years. Here he began

theoretical work on the decisions of business firms to invest in physical capital and improved technology. He was much influenced by Milton Friedman (qv) and his beliefs on economic and political matters.

In 1974 he joined the faculty of Chicago University where he presently serves. In 1995 Lucas was awarded the Nobel Memorial Prize for Economics: **"for having developed and applied the hypothesis of rational expectations, and thereby having transformed macroeconomic analyses and deepened our understanding of economic policy"**

In 1959 he married Rita Cohen, they divorced in 1982. They have two sons.

PEACE

JOSEPH ROTBLAT (1908-)
and
THE PUGWASH MOVEMENT

Joseph Rotblat was born on November 4, 1908 in Warsaw, Poland. Too poor to go to secondary school he received an MA from the Free University of Poland in 1932 by attending free night school. He followed with a PhD in physics from Warsaw University in 1938. Increasing anti-Semitism was just one reason for leaving Poland in 1939. Another was the offer of a post at Liverpool University.

Between 1939 and 1944, he worked on the creation of an atom bomb; both at Liverpool and Los Alamos, US. Following the dropping of the bomb on Japan that ended WW2; Rotblat, together with such luminaries as Einstein and Bertrand Russell, became increasingly concerned that atomic weaponry would become the basis of the 'cold war'. Their pleas to government were ignored.

In 1957, Rotblat organized a conference of like-minded scientists in a remote Canadian village on the coast of Nova Scotia, called Pugwash. Thus was one of the great movements of the second half of the 20th Century born. Pugwash members, with Rotblat at their head, warned the world of the dangers of unchecked nuclear manufacture and testing. He also warned of the possible dangers from some types of civil nuclear reactors. He scorned French nuclear testing in the Pacific and influenced the eventual ban on testing.

In 1950 Rotblat was appointed professor of physics at St. Bartholomew's Hospital Medical College in London, part of London University, and stayed until 1976. He is now Emeritus. Between 1978 and 1988 he was chairman of the British Pugwash Group. Since 1988 onwards he is president of the Pugwash Conferences on Science and World Affairs. Awarded the CBE in 1965 he was knighted in 1998.

He was awarded the Albert Einstein Peace Prize in 1992 and the Nobel Peace Prize in 1995. In a radio programme he said how he knew he was nominated for the award but that John Major was also nominated and he thought Major would got the award. In the event the right wing of the Conservative Party were most upset at the award going to Rotblat who they regarded as a 'fellow traveller' of the Communist Party.

Pugwash Conferences are a series of meetings where scientists from many countries discuss problems of nuclear weapons and world security. The first conference was held in 1957 at Pugwash, Nova Scotia, Canada and subsequent conferences have been held in Russia, UK, Yugoslavia, India, US, Czechoslovakia, Romania and Sweden.

The chief concern of Pugwash is to bring together leading scholars from many countries in order to discuss ways of reducing armaments and reduce the arms race. Another activity, is to examine the social responsibility of scientists to economic development and population growth as well as environmental destruction. Pugwash was co-awarded the 1995 Nobel Peace Prize.

1996

John Howard wins Australian general election • World-wide ban on British beef • Boris Yeltsin re-elected President of Russia • Many Israelis killed in suicide bombings • TWA 747 explodes in US killing 228 • Swiss banks open books on Holocaust accounts • Taleeban take control of Afghanistan • Bill Clinton re-elected US President • Divers find palace of Cleopatra • Benjamin Netanyahu wins Israeli general election • Stonehenge judged to be 5,000 years old • children massacred at Dunblane school • 34 die in Tasmania shooting • Gary Aldrich, *Unlimited Access* **• Anonymous,** *Primary Colours* **• Graham Swift,** *Last Orders* **• Films:** *The English Patient, Shine, Fargo, The Eighth Day, Michael Collins, Kolya, The People vs Larry Flynt* **• ex-President Mitterrand, Gene Kelly, Ella Fitzgerald, Andreas Papandreou, Marcel Carné, Michael Bentine, William Rushton, Laurens van der Post, Ronnie Scott, Dorothy Lamour, Frank Whittle and Marcello Mastroianni die.**

LITERATURE

WISLAWA SZYMBORSKA (1923-)

Wislawa Szymborska was born on July 2, 1923 in Kornik, Poland. Her father an agronomist, her mother a housewife. In 1931 the family moved to Cracow. Between 1945 to 48 she studied Polish literature and sociology at Jagiellonian University.

She began writing poetry whilst at university and, in March 1945, whilst the war was still on-going she wrote her poem *I am Looking for a Word* . This was published in the daily, 'Dzicnnik Polski' whilst the Red Army was racing to liberate Poland.

During 1953-81, she worked as the poetry editor on the Cracow literary weekly, 'Zycie Literackie'. It also enabled her to have her essays, entitled, *Lektury nadobowiazkowe*, published. She has published some 16 books of poetry that have been translated into many languages. In

addition she translates French poetry.

In 1991 she received the Goethe Prize and in 1996 the Nobel Prize for Literature; **"for poetry that with ironic precision allows the historical and biological context to come to light in fragments of human reality"**

Wislawa Szymborska is divorced. Her latest book is *Poems New and Collected; 1957-1997.*

CHEMISTRY

ROBERT CURL (1933-), HAROLD KROTO (1939-)
and
RICHARD SMALLEY (1943-)

"for their discovery of fullerenes"

Robert Curl was born on August 23, 1933 in Alice, Texas, US. His father was a Methodist minister who, because of his work, was constantly on the move, with the result that Robert lived in a series of small Texas towns. Following a assortment of local public schools, Curl received his later education at Rice Institute. Here he was most fortunate to be instructed in chemistry by teachers who inspired him. He later went to the University of California at Berkeley from where he received a PhD.

He obtained a position at Harvard University where he worked on developing a method for measuring barriers to internal rotation using microwave spectroscopy. He received an offer of an assistant professorship from Rice Institute which he accepted in 1958 and where he can still be found.

He spent much time studying the spectra of free radicals and other aspects of physical chemistry. In 1996 he was awarded a third share of the Nobel Prize for Chemistry for his contribution for the discovery of fullerenes.

He married a fellow student from Berkeley.

Harold Kroto was born on October 7, 1939 in Wisbech, Cambs. England. His parents originated from East Germany and changed their name from Krotoschiner to Kroto. His Jewish father left Germany in 1937 via Holland, for England where he was interned on the Isle of Man as an enemy alien when WW2 started.

The family moved to Bolton in Lancashire where his father had set up a small business. Although funds were scarce, they managed to have their son educated at Bolton School. He left for Sheffield University that was considered at the time to have the best chemistry department in the UK.

In 1961 he obtained a BSc and in 1964 a PhD. Thus armed he left for Canada and the National Research Council in Ottawa. In 1965 Kroto discovered a singlet-singlet electronic transition of the NCN radical and worked on pyridine. This was followed by a spell on microwave spectroscopy.

In 1967 he returned to England and Sussex University. By 1970, he had carried out research on the electronic spectroscopy of gas phase free radicals and rotational microwave spectroscopy. In 1991, he was awarded a Royal Society Research Professorship that allowed him to concentrate on research.

In 1995 he inaugurated the Vega Science Trust in order to produce educational films for television presentation. In 1996 he was awarded a third share of the Nobel Prize for Chemistry.

Married with two sons, his advice to his students is never give up and try not to let anyone down. A keen tennis player and member of Amnesty International, Kroto was knighted in 1997.

Richard Smalley was born on June 6, 1943 in Akron, Ohio, US. When he was three, the family moved to Kansas City and an expensive neighbourhood. Richard was educated in the public school system, culminating in the local high school, Southwest High.

He spent two years at Hope College in Holland, Michigan, where he concentrated on chemistry. Then came Michigan University at Ann Arbor, from where he graduated in 1965 with a BS degree in chemistry. He then spent two years working for Shell Oil at their polypropylene manufacturing plant in Woodbury, NJ.

In 1968, he was admitted to Princeton University from where he later obtained his PhD. In 1973, he began postdoctoral studies at Chicago University. It was a time when tunable dye lasers were beginning to transform molecular spectroscopy. Further experimental work followed, involving low rotational temperatures for a polyatomic molecule in a supersonic beam.

In 1976 he transferred to Rice University, Texas as assistant professor of chemistry. Here he set up a free jet machine in order to use pulsed dye lasers in the ultraviolet, in order to study ordinary molecules in depth. His work resulted in the award of a third share of the 1996 Nobel Prize for Chemistry. Smalley is married with a son.

PHYSICS

DAVID LEE (1931-), DOUGLAS OSHEROFF (1945-)
and
ROBERT RICHARDSON (1937-

"for their discovery of superfluidity in helium-3"

David Lee was born on January 20, 1931 in Rye, NY, US. His grandparents were immigrant Jews who emanated from Lithuania. He graduated from the high school in Rye and went on to Harvard University. Following an early interest in cosmology he studied a course in physics.

He graduated from Harvard in 1952 and joined the US Army in time for the final stages of the Korean War. After two years he was released and joined the University of Connecticut. Here he stayed for eighteen months, during which time he concentrated on experimental physics, to which end he built an ionization gauge control for an accelerator. Having completed his masters he joined the PhD programme at Yale University in 1955.

He obtained his PhD in 1959 and joined the faculty of Cornell University where he is now professor of physics. Following his work on superfluids, that resulted in Helium-3, Lee was awarded a third share of the 1996 Nobel Prize for Physics.

Married with two sons, his interests are climbing and hiking in mountains, sailing and cooking.

Douglas Osheroff was born in 1945 in Aberdeen, Washington, US. His father, a doctor, was the son of Jewish immigrants from Russia. His mother the daughter of a Lutheran minister. At high school Douglas excelled at physics and chemistry and as a result, he enrolled at the California Institute of Technology, (Caltech)

Here he found the going hard, especially in the field of mathematics, however, over a three year period he gradually improved. Years later, when Caltech was offering a teaching post, he told the board he hadn't had a very illustrious career as an undergraduate. To this the interviewing chairman remarked, "That's OK Doug, we are not hiring you to be an undergraduate"

In his senior year at Caltech, he joined a group working in the low temperature laboratory. This work influenced his decision to go into solid state physics consequently he joined Cornell University's graduate school. In 1972, he joined Bell Telephone Laboratories and he and his recent wife moved to New Jersey. Here he became part of the Department of Solid State and Low Temperature Research. His later research resulted in discovering antiferromagnet resonance in nuclear spin ordered solid 3He.

After fifteen years at Bell, Osheroff moved to Stanford University. Here he continued with his experimental work. Between 1993-96, he had the Physics Department chair. For his work on superfluiditys, resulting in helium-3, Osheroff was awarded a third share of the 1996 • Nobel Prize for Physics.

Robert Coleman Richardson was born on June 26, 1937 in Georgetown, Washington, DC. US. During his early years his father was away serving in the US Army. In 1954 he entered the Virginia Polytechnic Institute. Here he switched from chemistry to physics because of his colour blindness. He later obtained his PhD from Duke University.

In 1966 he received an invitation to join the staff at the Laboratory of Atomic and Solid State Physics of Cornell University. He has remained there ever since. His work in the field of low temperature physics was rewarded by the award of a third share of the 1996 Nobel Prize for Physics.

He is married with two daughters.

PHYSIOLOGY or MEDICINE

PETER DOHERTY (1940-)
and
ROLF ZINKERNAGEL (1944-)

"for their discoveries concerning the specificity of the cell immune defence"

Peter Doherty was born on October 15, 1940 in Brisbane, Australia. His family had left England for Australia around the middle of the 19th century. Following a local education he enrolled at Queensland University from where, in 1962, he received a BSc in veterinary medicine. Following his masters at Queensland in 1966, Doherty joined Edinburgh University in Scotland from where, in 1970, he obtained his PhD.

He spent a year as senior scientific officer at the Moredun Research Institute in Edinburgh, following which, he returned home as a Research Fellow in the Microbiology department of the John Curtin School of Medical research at the Australian National University at Canberra.

Here he studied the pathogenesis of Semliki Forest virus infection in mice, before switching to the lymphocytic choriomeningitis virus model. He also met up with Rolf Zinkernagel (qv) who was a visiting fellow.

The two men spent time working together on the 'single T cell receptor altered self' hypothesis. Doherty travelled much, giving his lecture to some 20 institutions where the world's most important members of the immunology establishment worked and lived. The principle place was the US. Now, for the first time, they became aware of the work being done in Australia. Their ideas contradicted the accepted US model for the role of immune response genes and reversed the perception of the existing transplantation system. His listeners heard him with a mixture of unbelieving and anger.

In 1982 Doherty was appointed professor and head of the department at the Australian National

University, he stayed until 1988 at which time he joined the University of Tennessee in Memphis. Between 1988 and 1992, he was chairman of the immunology department at St .Jude Research Hospital. From 1992 to the present, he is Adjunct professor in the Department of Pathology and Pediatrics at the university's College of Medicine.

In 1987, he became a Fellow of the Royal Society and in 1996 was awarded a co-share of the Nobel Prize for Physiology or Medicine. He is married with two sons and has an abiding love of Australian Rules Football.

Rolf Zinkernagel was born on January 6, 1944 in Basel, Switzerland. His father was a scientist, his mother a laboratory technician. He was educated in Basel, at the Mathematisch-Naturwissenschaftliches Gymnasium, followed by Basel University's Medical department. (1962-68). He received his MD from Basel in 1970.

Between 1971 and 73, he was a Postdoctoral Fellow at the Institute of Biochemistry at Lausanne University. Here he learned about immunology, immuno-chemistry and the frustrations of experimental work. It was here that Rolf became interested in the potential of immune responses to disease. He was now married to an eye doctor and has two children. His efforts to find a suitable institution to pursue his new career was essential. He applied to many possible places in England, US and Australia.

The result was that he was offered a position with the Department of Microbiology in Canberra, Australia, providing he had his own salary. Fortunately, his post-doctoral fellowship from the Swiss Foundation for Biomedical Fellowships allowed him 32,000 SF for two years.

In 1973 the family arrived in Canberra. Here he worked on cell-mediated immunity against salmonella and listeria, and to learn more about the role of cell-mediated versus antibody-dependant immune effector mechanisms, in these infectious disease models. Here he met Peter Docherty (qv). In 1975 he obtained his PhD from Canberra.

In 1976 he left Australia and joined the Department of Immunopathology at the Research Institute of Scripps Clinic at La Jolla, California. He stayed until 1979. Here he continued studying cell-mediated immunity. In 1979, Rolf and the family returned to Switzerland and the Department of Pathology at Zurich University Hospital, as an assistant professor. In 1988 he became a full professor and in 1992, head of the Institute of Experimental Immunology.

He was awarded a co-share of the 1996 Nobel Prize for Physiology or Medicine for his work on the cell-immune system.

ECONOMICS

JAMES MIRRLEES (1936-)
and
WILLIAM VICKREY (1914-1996)

"for their fundamental contributions to the economic theory of incentives under asymmetric information"

James Mirrlees was born in 1936 in Galloway, Scotland. His father was a bank teller. Educated at local schools, he later won a scholarship to Edinburgh University. At 21 he won a scholarship to Cambridge and Trinity College.

After several false starts Mirrlees decided upon a career in economics. He embarked on a three year PhD course. He took time off to work with Nicholas Kaldor who at that time was working on a paper on growth. Further time was taken for a project in India. Upon his return he received a teaching fellowship at Trinity. His thesis was finally completed in 1963, entitled, *Optimum Accumulation Under Uncertainty.*

In 1968 he was appointed professor of economics at Oxford University. In 1995 he was back at Cambridge and Trinity College. In 1996 he was awarded a co-share of the Nobel Memorial Prize for Economics. He is married with two daughters.

William Vickrey was born in 1914 in Victoria, BC, Canada. His elementary and secondary education was in Europe and the US. He graduated from Phillips Andover Academy in 1931 and received a BS in mathematics from Yale University in 1935. He received an MA degree from Columbia University (1935-37) and then went to work for the National Resources Planning Board at the US Treasury .

During WW2, Vickrey, a member of The Religious Society of Friends, decided to become a conscientious objector. In 1946 he began a teaching career at Columbia University as a lecturer in economics. He was awarded a PhD in 1948, following his dissertation, *Agenda for Progressive Taxation.* He became a full professor in 1958 and chairman of the department from 1964 to 1967 retiring as professor emeritus in 1982.

He was a member of the Shoup mission, that developed a full system for revising Japan's tax system. He later became a consultant in the US, overseas and with the United Nations. He wrote much, consisting of eight books and hundreds of articles and notes. He was awarded a co-share of the 1996 Nobel Memorial Prize for Economics for his work connected to asymmetric information.

He died in October 1996 whilst living in Hastings-on-Hudson, New York. He married in 1951.

PEACE

JOSÉ RAMOS-HORTA (1949-)
and
CARLOS BELO (1948-)

José Ramos-Horta was born on December 26, 1949 in Dili, East Timor. Following training as a lawyer, he became a Fellow at St. Anthony's College, Oxford University specialising in International Relations. His father was a Portugese national who was deported to East Timor by the fascist dictator, Antonio Salazar

Ramos-Horta studied law in the US and later returned to East Timor whilst it was still a colony of Portugal. Working for independence, he was exiled to Mozambique in 1970. He returned to East Timor in 1972.

In 1975, following the withdrawal of Portugal, East Timor became an independent nation and Ramos-Horta became Minister of External Relations and Information, in the first provisional government of East Timor. Nine days later Indonesia, with the backing of the US, invaded East Timor and once again Ramos-Horta was an exile.

He eventually settled in Sydney, Australia, becoming a professor at the University of New South Wales. However, he continued speaking out against the violence being used by the occupying Indonesian military. Through his efforts, the UN in 1999, organised a free vote to decide whether the population wanted to be independent or ruled from Jakarta. In the event nearly 80% of the voters decided on independence. At once the pro Indonesia militia set the country alight and upwards of 150,000 have fled to avoid the violence.

In 1996 Ramos-Horta was awarded a co-share of the Nobel Peace Prize. He has been the Permanent Representative to the UN for the East Timorese independence movement since 1975.

Carlos Filipe Ximenes Belo was born on February 3, 1948 in Wailacama, East Timor. In 1983 he was ordained a bishop and became spiritual leader of an area that is overwhelmingly Catholic. Therein lies the present problem. Indonesia, who rules East Timor with a rod of iron is overwhelmingly Muslim.

The government has organised several attempts on Belo's life, but he is still around to organise resistance to Indonesian repression. This resistance has resulted in the UN holding a general election in East Timor with the result, that East Timor has decided on independence and awaits the Indonesian Parliament to ratify the East Timorese decisions.

For his efforts Carlos Belo was co-awarded 1996 Nobel Peace Prize. During 1999 the UN, on the initiative of Belo and others, held a general election to determine the question of East Timor's autonomy. In the event there was an overwhelming in favour of independence. The Indonesian government promoted an armed resistance and members of the UN, as well as the general population, were killed, wounded and persuaded to leave the country. Carlos Belo was evacuated during the September disturbances and succeeded in getting to the UN in New York, where he has persuaded the UN to create a force to stop the bloodshed. The United Force arrived on September 18, 1999 seemingly too late to save the country from destruction and the loss of much life.

On December 1st 1999 Belo returned to East Timor and a heroes welcome.

1997

Princess Diana of Wales killed • 'Tiger Woods youngest player ever to win US Masters • Tony Blair wins UK general election • Blair apologises for Irish famine • Britain returns Hong Kong to China, US refuses a total ban on landmines • Oasis, *D'You Know What I Mean?* • Arundhati Roy, *The God of Small Things* • Frank McCourt, *Angela's Ashes* • John Grisham, *The Partner* • Films: *Nil By Mouth, Men in Black, The Full Monty, Hana-Bi, Titanic, As Good as it Gets, LA Confidential, Netherlands,* • Mother Teresa, Deng Xiaoping, Versace, John Denver, James Stewart, Stephane Grappelli, Fred Zimmerman, Allen Ginsberg, Robert Mitchum, George Solti and Isaiah Berlin die.

LITERATURE

DARIO FO (1926-)

Dario Fo was born on March 24, 1926 in Leggiuno-Sangiamo, Italy. His first theatrical experience was to collaborate on satirical revues for small cabarets and theatres. Following his marriage to the actress Franca Rame, they founded the Campagnia Dario-Fo-Franca in 1959. This, together with their humorous TV shows, made them most famous. In 1968 they joined the Communist Party and set-up the acting group, Nuova Scena. They toured poor cities, factories, parks and gymnasiums.

His plays included the *Accidental Death of an Anarchist* (1974), *We Can't Pay? We Won't Pay!* (1974) . *Comic Mystery*, is a solo piece based on medieval mystery plays but with a topical contemporary content that changes with each audience. Fo has written, in total, some 70 plays. In May 1984, whilst appearing in a theatre in Argentina, fascists and right-wing Catholic organisations threw hand grenade containing tear gas whilst the police stood by and made no attempt to interfere.

In August 1984, following an invitation from Joe Papp the New York theatrical producer, Fo and his group were refused entry into the US for a second time. In November 1985 they were granted a six day entry visa, following the decision by Alexander Cohen to stage the *Accidental Death of an Anarchist* on New York's Broadway. In May 1986, Fo received a normal entry visa following an invitation from Harvard University who performed *Mistero Buffo.*

In July 1995, Fo was struck by cerebral ischaemia and loses 80% of his sight. A year later he is much recovered and tours Denmark, Italy and by the end of 1996 he is cured. Fo was awarded the 1997 Nobel Prize for Literature; **"who emulates the jesters of the Middle Ages in scourging authority and upholding the dignity of the downtrodden"**

His work has been produced in the theatres of over 50 countries.

CHEMISTRY

JOHN WALKER (1941-), PAUL BOYER (1918-)

"for their elucidation of the enzymatic mechanism underlying the synthesis of adenosine triphosphate"

and
JENS SKOU (1918-)

John Walker was born on January 7,1941 in Halifax, Yorks, England. He was educated at Rastrick Grammar School, followed by St. Catherine's College, Oxford, from where he received a BA in chemistry in 1964. In 1969, he obtained his PhD from Oxford University, following a research period on peptide antibiotics. He spent 1969 to 1971 at the School of Pharmacy at Wisconsin University and then from 1971 to 1974 at the Institut Pasteur in Paris.

He then joined the Protein and Nucleic Acid Chemistry division at the Medical Research Council's Laboratory of Molecular Biology at Cambridge University. He went for a three months trial in June 1974. He is still there. His research work includes the analysing of G4 proteins and mitochondria, using direct methods. In 1978, he applied protein chemical methods to membrane proteins and later began a structural study of the ATP syntheses from bovine heart mitochondria.

His on-going research work led directly to a share of the 1997 Nobel Prize for Chemistry. He subsequently received a quarter share of the prize money. He is married with two daughters. In 1995 he was elected a Fellow of the Royal Society.

Paul Boyer was born on July 31,1918 in Provo, Utah, US. Educated at local schools he graduated at sixteen from Provo High School. He then joined the Brigham Young University, working off times as a waiter at a local hotel. He joined the biochemistry department of Wisconsin University in Madison, funded by a scholarship from Wisconsin Alumni Research Foundation.

He obtained his PhD in 1943, at which time he became engaged on war work at Stanford University, working on blood plasma proteins for treatment of battlefield shock. The war over, he accepted an offer as an assistant professor at the University of Minnesota. Here officialdom took over in the shape of a draft board who decided that Boyer was required by the US Navy. After a year working in his private laboratory at the Naval Medical Research Institute at Bethesda, he was discharged and returned to civilian life.

He received a Guggenheim Fellowship in 1955, which took him to Sweden and Stockholm University. In 1963 he was at the University of California, Los Angeles (UCLA) and on-going research which proved disappointing. In 1965, he was director of the Molecular Biology Institute at UCLA. Here his research was more rewarding and in 1971, he was able to recognise the first main postulate of what was to become the binding change mechanism for ATP synthesis.

During the decades that followed, the principles so far discovered were expanded, explored and promoted. In 1997, he was awarded a share of the Nobel Prize for Chemistry and a quarter share of the prize money. He is married with children and a declared atheist.

Jens Skou was born on October 8, 1918 in Lemvig, Denmark. He was the son of a wealthy timber and coal merchant. When he was twelve years old his father died and three years later Jens was at boarding school in Haslev in Zealand. He graduated and decided to study medicine at Copenhagen University. He took the usual seven year course and received his medical degree in 1944.

During WW2 Denmark was occupied by Germany and freedom of speech became impossible. The population became most anti-German, and gradually took upon itself acts of sabotage. Following his appointment as a doctor, Skou became an intern at a hospital in Northern Denmark. His work there prompted him to prepare a thesis on local anaesthetics. In 1947 he was at Aarhus University working on his doctoral thesis. To make ends meet Skou, in 1949, took a job as a locum doctor. It changed his political outlook from conservative to social democrat and the belief that a free health service is essential.

His doctoral paper was published in 1957. Now he turned from local anaesthetics to active transport of cations; an ion in an electrolyte which carries a positive charge. The work that followed meant the discovery of the first molecular pump in cells. Powered by ATP molecular pumps, are protein molecules that transport ions, or electrically charged atoms, via cell membranes. Skou discovered sodium potassium in ATPase, a special enzyme that functions as such a pump by degrading ATP and using the released energy to power the transport process.

Skou was awarded a half share of the 1997 Nobel Prize for Chemistry: **"for the first discovery** of an ion transporting enzyme" He also received half of the prize money. He is married with two daughters. Now retired, he enjoys fly-fishing; when the weather is right.

PHYSICS

STEVEN CHU (1948-), CLAUDE COHEN-TANNOUDJI (1933-)
and
WILLIAM PHILLIPS (1948-)

"for their development of methods to cool and trap atoms with laser light"

Steven Chu was born in 1948 in St Louis, US. In 1950 the family moved to Garden City, New York. His father had come to the US in 1943 in order to attend the Massachusetts Institute of Technology. At the time of Steven's birth, his father was teaching at Washington University. Education was the most important feature in the Chu family doctrines and Steven was destined to become 'the academic black sheep', in a family that boasted six members awarded three MDs, four PhDs plus a law degree.

Following his graduation from Garden City High, he was accepted by Rochester University. Later, hoping to become a theoretical physicist, he applied for entry to the University of California at Berkeley. He began in the autumn of 1970. In 1978 he was offered a job as assistant professor at Berkeley, he refused, feeling he should have a much wider experience of the academic world.

He joined Bell Laboratories and never returned to Berkeley. At Bell he wrote a paper reviewing the current status of x-ray microscopy, began as an experiment on energy transfer in ruby. He also spent time and effort planning an experiment on the optical spectroscopy of positroniums; considered the most basic of all atoms. The Management at Bell considered he was ruining his career by trying an impossible experiment and two years later they advised on abandonment. Chu however insisted on continuing, and two years later succeeded, having obtained one of the most accurate measurements of quantum electrodynamic corrections to an atomic system.

In 1983 he became head of the Quantum Electronics Research Department, a branch of Bells, at Holmdel, NJ. By now his research interests had widened and he was using picosecond laser techniques to look at excitons as a potential system for observing metal-insulator transitions. With this equipment, he accidentally discovered a counter-intuitive pulse-propagation effect. It was while he was developing the electron spectrometer that he began thinking about the idea of trapping atoms with light. A number of experiments were carried out, with the result that laser cooling made it all possible. In 1987 he joined Stanford University. Although he continued with his experimental work in laser cooling and trapping of atoms, he later turned to polymer physics and biology. A year on and he was able to manipulate individual DNA molecules by attaching micron-sized polystyrene spheres, by means of optical tweezers, to the ends of the molecule.

He had been at Stanford for 10 years when it was announced that he had been awarded a third share of the 1997 Nobel Prize for Physics. Steven Chu is un-married.

Claude Cohen-Tannoudji was born on April 1, 1933 in Constantine, Algeria. His family arrived in Algiers in the 16th century having fled from Spain during the Inquisition. His forebears refused to submit to baptism preferring to remain Jewish. In 1870, Algerian Jews obtained French citizenship. The arrival of the US Army in Algeria in 1942, prevented the Vichy authorities from shipping Algerian Jews to France and then onto the death camps.

Claude completed his primary and secondary education in Algiers and then went to Paris and the Ecole Normale Supérieure. Following his graduation, Claude served in the French Army for over two years. Part of his service included being in a scientific department studying the upper atmosphere with rockets releasing sodium clouds at the sunset. By looking at the fluorescence light, re-emitted by the sodium atoms excited by the sunlight, it was possible to measure the variations with the altitude of various parameters, such as the wind velocity or temperature.

At the beginning of 1960, he entered the French National Centre for Scientific Research in order to achieve a PhD. This he obtained some three years later at which time he began teaching at Paris University. His main area of research was understanding atom-photon interactions in the high intensity limit where perturbative treatments are not valid. This atom + photons system, became known as 'dressed atom'

The dressed atom approach has also been very useful in the optical arena. Spontaneous emission plays an important role as a damping mechanism and as a source of fluorescence photons. In 1973, he was appointed a professor at the Collège de France. In the early 1980s he began a series of lectures on radiative forces in which he stressed the importance of dressed atoms. Interested in the work being done by Steven Chu (qv) Cohen-Tannoudji, following investigation of quantum interference effect velocity selective, was able to demonstrate a new cooling scheme with no lower limit.

In 1997 he was awarded a third share of the Nobel Prize for Physics. Married in 1958 the couple had three children. In 1993 their eldest child, Alain died at the age of 34. At the Nobel award ceremony Claude Cohen-Tannoudji dedicated his Nobel Lecture to the memory of Alain.

William Phillips was born on November 5, 1948 in Wilkes-Barre, Penn. US. His educated parents inculcated in their children a love of reading. In 1966, Phillips joined the college his parents had attended, Juniata College. Following his graduation he applied to join the Massachusetts Institute of Technology. In 1970 he married and began at MIT.

For his doctoral thesis he measured the magic moment of the proton in H20- it is still the best available. He then studied the collisions of laser-excited atoms. He was awarded a Chaim Weizmann fellowship to work on projects of his own choosing at MIT, for a further two years.   In 1976 he obtained his PhD.   In 1978 he joined the National Institute of Standards and Technology.

Here he explored ways of improving measurement capabilities and pursuing laser cooling opportunities. He was awarded a third share of the 1997 Nobel Prize for Physics. He is married with two daughters.

PHYSIOLOGY or MEDICINE

STANLEY PRUSINER (1942-)

Stanley Prusiner was born on May 28, 1942 in Des Moines, Iowa, US. His grandfather was part of the great immigration wave that arrived in the US in the latter half of the 19th century in order to escape Russian anti-Semitism. At the time of his birth, Stanley's father was in the US Navy and the family moved to Cincinnati, Ohio. WW2 over, his father practised as an architect.

Educated locally and at Walnut Hills High School, he was accepted by the University of Pennsylvania in order to study chemistry. He later transferred to the university's medical school, where he undertook a variety of co-related research. This included the study of the surface fluorescence of brown adipose tissue in Syrian golden hamsters, as they rose from hibernation. This resulted in his finding large changes in the fluorescence of brown fat during non-shivering thermogenetics.

He spent 1968-1974 at the University of California at San Francisco; first as an intern and then a Residency in Neurology. During this time he studied glutaminases in *E. coli*. And also investigated Creutzfeldt-Jakob disease (CJD) In 1974, he was appointed an assistant professor of neurology. He has remained at San Francisco, where he is now professor of biochemistry.

His research into the cause of viruses led him to investigate the sedimentation behaviour of the scrapie agent. Although funding for his research often caused problems and some delays Prusiner pushed on with his investigations. He published an article in early 1982, in which he uses the term 'prion' when describing his work hitherto on scrapie and CJD. The term prion is derived from -protein and infectious. Many poured scorn on his findings but Prusiner's analysis of the situation was eventually proven correct and prions have gained wide acceptance among scientists.

He has received a number of awards, including one from the American Academy of Neurology; Potamkin Prize for Alzheimer's Disease Research in 1991. The Albert Lisker Award for Basic Medical Research, 1994, the Keio International Award for Medical Science, Keio University, Tokyo, 1996, plus many more culminating in the highest award possible the 1997 Nobel Prize for Physiology or Medicine; **"for his discovery of Prions- a new biological principle of infection"**

Prusiner is married with two daughters

ECONOMICS

ROBERT MERTON (1944-)
and
MYRON SCHOLES (1941-)

"for a new method to determine the value of derivatives"

Robert **Merton** was born on July 31, 1944 in New York, US. His father was professor of sociology at Columbia University. He grew up in Hastings-on-Hudson, a commuting suburb, where he received his early education. In 1966 he obtained a BS from Columbia University in engineering mathematics. He received his MS in applied mathematics from the California Institute of Technology in 1967 and a PhD from Massachusetts Institute in Technology in economics in 1970.

Thus equipped, he became a research assistant at the Massachusetts Institute of Technology followed by a stint as an instructor at the department of economics. In 1988- onwards he is professor of business administration at Harvard University.

His field of research includes periods investigating and creating. These included a central modelling theme and continuous time stochastic processes. Then he developed dynamic models of optimal lifetime consumption, portfolio selection, equilibrium asset pricing and contingent-claim pricing. He was awarded a co-share of the 1997 Nobel Memorial Prize for Economics. He is married with three children.

Myron **Scholes** was born on July 1,1941 in Timmins, Ontario, Canada. He was ten when the family moved south to Hamilton. Educated locally, he decided to enroll in McMaster University in Hamilton. He graduated in 1962 and went on the Chicago University where he worked for his PhD.

He became an assistant professor at Massachusetts Institute of Technology and there met Robert Merton. He then returned to Chicago University and the Graduate Business School. Here he studied the effects of the taxation of dividends on the prices of securities, capital structure issues and the effects of taxes on the optimal liquidation of assets.

Between 1973-80, he was involved with the Centre for Research in Security Prices and this led to the development of large research data files of daily security prices. In 1983, he left Chicago for Stanford University, where he studied and wrote about pension planning. He reduced his time at Stanford and joined Salomon Brothers Inc. as managing director and joint head of its fixed-income-derivative sales and trading group. In 1997 he was co-awarded the Nobel Memorial Prize for Economics.

He is married with two daughters and has a passion for golf and skiing.

PEACE

THE INTERNATIONAL CAMPAIGN TO BAN LANDMINES (ICBL)
and
JODY WILLIAMS (1950-)

The International Campaign to Ban Landmines is defined as a flexible network of organisations that share common objectives. These came together in October 1992 and their campaign calls for an international ban on the use, production, stockpiling and transfer of antipersonnel landmines, for increased international resources for humanitarian mine clearance, and increased international resources for mine victim assistance programmes.

To-day this network represents over 1,000 human rights groups in some 60 countries. Probably the most famous supporter was HRH Princess Diana who was killed in Paris. The publicity she generated was enormous, unfortunately little more than lip service has resulted and with the NATO offensive against Serbia in 1999, the amount of bomb clearance required is greater than that needed in 1992.

The paradox is that in the same year the organization was awarded the Nobel Peace Prize, the country in which the movement started and where the movement works from, viz, America, refuses to ban the manufacture and use of landmines and refused to sign and ratify the convention held in Ottawa in December 1997 and signed by more than 120 countries.

Jody Williams was born on October 9, 1950 in the US, and is the founding co-ordinator of the International Campaign to Ban Landmines. She has supervised the growth of ICBL to 1,000 non-governmental organisations in more than sixty countries. She is totally dedicated in her efforts to outlaw the manufacture and employment of landmines and anti personnel mines.

She has been the driving force behind the conferences held in Oslo 1997 and Ottawa 1997.

She has a Master's Degree in International Relations from the John Hopkins School of Advanced International Studies and a BA from Vermont University in Burlington. Prior to founding the ICBL, Williams worked for some 10 years building public awareness of US policy in Central America and how the CIA exploited right wing organisations to destabilise legitimate governments as in Chile, El Salvador and others

If she can persuade the US government to come aboard her present campaign it would mean the beginning of the end.

1998

President Clinton denies he had sex with Monica Lewinski • President Clinton admits he had sex with Monica Lewinski • Helmut Kohl defeated in German general election • US fighter jet causes cable car crash in Italy • Royal Navy gives command of warships to women • Space probe finds water on the Moon • Viagra in general use • Israeli transsexual wins European song contest • Longest suspension bridge in Europe opened by Queen Margrethe of Denmark • Over a hundred killed in German train crash • Bombing of US African embassies leaves 257 dead • Swissair flight crashes, 229 die • Pinochet of Chile accused of mass murder is held under house arrest in England • Pakistan gets A-Bomb • David Hare, *The Blue Room* • Julian Barnes, *England, England* • Ian McEwan, *Amsterdam* • Patrick McCabe, *Breakfast on Pluto*, Films: *The General: Festen: Character: Henry Fool: Lock, Stock and Two Smoking Barrels: Eternity and a Day: La Classe de Neige: La Vita e Bella : Good Will Hunting:* • Banda Hastings, Frank Muir, Enoch Powell, Frank Sinatra, Linda McCartney, Roy Rogers, Maurice Schumann, Lloyd Bridges, Dr Spock, Barry Goldwater, Akira Kurosawa die.

LITERATURE

JOSÉ SARAMAGO (1922-)

José Saramago was born in 1922 in a small village north of Lisbon, Portugal. A need of money halted his advanced educational studies and he trained instead as a mechanic. He then tried various jobs in various departments of the civil service before switching to the world of newspapers and publishing. He worked for one publishing house for twelve years and then became assistant editor for the *Diário de Noticias*. The political unrest in Portugal in 1975 forced him to resign his position.

In 1969 he joined the then illegal Communist Party. Between 1975 and 80, he earned a living as a translator, until his literary efforts began coming to fruition and he could live by his writings. His work covered poetry, prose, essays, drama and stories. He was 60, before he achieved a major success. In 1977, he published *Manual of painting and calligraphy: a novel*. The basic theme is the heart of a painter as well as a writer. To some extent it is autobiographical, embracing love, ethics and the time of 1974 when the Portugese dictator, Salazar was forced to retire.

In 1982 his novel, *Baltasar and Blimunda* was published. It is a rich and multifaceted story that embraces a historical and individual perspective. Another of Saramago's important efforts is, *The year of the death of Ricardo Reis* published in 1984, that tells the tale of the events that took place in Lisbon

426

in 1936 during the dictatorship. *A history of the seige of Lisbon* was published in 1989 and is in effect a novel within a novel. In 1995 he published *Blindness*: *a novel* . Here he explores in an imaginative way a capriciousness that is otherwise engaging.

His latest work is, *All the Names,* and deals with a minor official in a registration office that is of metaphysical dimensions. His style is considered idiosyncratic and he resembles someone who is constantly searching for an obscurity he doesn't quite recognise. In 1992 he moved to the Canary Islands.

In 1998 he was awarded the Nobel Prize for Literature **"who with parables sustained by imagination, compassion and irony continually enables us once again to apprehend an illusory reality"** He is un-married.

CHEMISTRY

WALTER KOHN (1923-)
and
JOHN POPLE (1925-)

Walter Kohn was born in Vienna, Austria on March 9, 1923. Following the arrival of Hitler in 1938, Kohn, a Jew, was fortunate to leave Austria for Canada and the US. Following service in the Canadian Infantry Corps, 1944-45, Kohn worked for his BA degree in Mathematics and Physics at Toronto University. The same university awarded him an MA in Applied Mathematics and from Harvard University, he obtained a PhD in Physics in 1948.

He became an instructor at Harvard's physics department and stayed until 1950. Between 1950 and 1960 he was at Carnegie-Mellon University, Pittsburgh, Penn. starting as an assistant and leaving as a full professor. He was a professor in the Physics Department of UCSD, San Diego between 1960 and 79, leaving to take up an appointment at UCSB, Santa Barbara as the director of the Institute of Theoretical Physics until 1984, at which time he became a professor of physics at the same establishment and where he still works as emeritus and research professor.

Kohn is a condensed matter theorist, who efforts have resulted in an understanding of the electronic structure of materials. He has played a leading role in the development of the density functional theory, something that has caused scientists to take a radical reappraisal to the electronic structure of atoms, molecules and solid materials in physics, chemistry and material science.

His work in the field of superconductors has been of the utmost importance. He received a co-share of the 1998 Nobel Prize for Chemistry; **"for his development of the density-functional theory"**

Although his work has been in the field of quantum chemistry and a relative newcomer to a branch of chemistry, there has been an enormous theoretical and computational development the consequence of which is revolutionising the whole of chemistry.

John Pople was born in 1925 at Burnham-on-Sea, England. In 1951 he obtained a PhD from Cambridge University. In 1964 he took up an appointment as professor of chemical physics at Carnegie-Mellon University in Pittsburgh, where he first met up with Walter Kohn. Pople later became professor of chemistry at Northwestern University in Illinois, where he presently works.

Pople is one of the two scientists most prominent in the new field of quantum chemistry and to Pople goes the distinction of having developed the entire quantum-chemical methodology now used in various branches of chemistry. His work developing computational methods makes it possible to study theoretically molecules, their properties and how they act together in chemical reactions. His methods are based on the fundamental laws of quantum mechanics.

A computer is fed with details of a molecule or a chemical reaction and the result is a description of the properties of that molecule. In order to make his make his computational technics accessible to researchers, he designed a special computer programme known as Gaussian.

Pople was awarded a co-share of the 1998 Nobel Prize for Chemistry; **"for his development of computational methods in quantum chemistry"**

PHYSICS

ROBERT LAUGHLIN (1950-), HORST STÖRMER (1949-)
and
DANIEL TSUI (1939-)

"for their discovery of a new form of quantum fluid with fractionally charged excitations"

Robert Laughlin was born in 1950 in Visalia, CA. US. He obtained his PhD in Physics from the Massachusetts Institute of Technology in Cambridge. His research is mainly in high-temperature superconductivity theory. It includes the use of condensed matter lattice gauge theories and the use of quasi particles that carry fractional quantum numbers.

During the early 1980s, Laughlin worked researching the quantum Hall effect. This has to do with the behaviour of electrons in a magnetic field at the interface between two semiconductors. In his paper of 1983, he explains a phenomenon discovered by Stömer and Tsui the previous year.

Laughlin showed, by theoretical analysis, that the electrons in a powerful magnetic field can condense to form a kind of 'quantum fluid' related to the quantum fluids that occur in superconductivity and in liquid helium. What is so important for researchers, is that events in a drop of quantum fluid can afford more profound insights into the general inner structure and dynamics of matter.

Edwin Hall, in 1879, was still a student, when he discovered an unexpected phenomenon. He

428

found that if a thin gold plate is placed in a magnetic field at right angles to its surface, an electric potential, flowing along the plate can cause a potential drop at right angles both to the current and magnetic field. This is better known as 'the Hall effect'

Laughlin was awarded a third share of the 1998 Nobel Prize for Physics. He is now a professor of physics at Stanford University in California.

Horst Stömer was born in 1949 in Frankfurt-Main, Germany. He obtained a PhD in physics from Stuttgart University, Germany in 1977. He went to work for Bell Laboratories and spent 20 years becoming during 1992-97, director of the Physical Research Laboratory. In 1998 he joined Columbia University, New York. He and Daniel Ysui worked in the area of condensed matter with the emphasis on semiconductors.

His advanced work on 'the hall effect' and the interaction of many electrons rather that the property of any individual particle is at the origin of his observations. The associate theory is challenging and at the front of to-days efforts to understand complex multi particle systems.

For his work on the project Stömer was awarded a third share of the 1998 Nobel Prize for Physics.

Daniel Tsui was born in 1939 in Henan, China. He came to the US in 1958 in order to enter Augustana College, Rock Island Ill. He obtained his PhD from Chicago University in 1967. Between 1968 and 1982 he was a technical staff member of Bell Laboratories in New Jersey. Then in 1982 he became a professor of physics in the electrical engineering section of Princeton University, NJ. He still works there.

Tsui and Stömer worked together in 1982, at which time they discovered the fractional quantum hall effect. This led to Laughlin's finding that the electrons in a powerful magnetic field can form quantum fluid, in which parts of an electrons can be identified.

Tsui was awarded a third share of the 1998 Nobel Prize for Physics. He is married.

The research work resulting in the Nobel Prize is of the greatest importance. Their contributions have led to a breakthrough in our understanding of quantum physics and to the development of new theoretical concepts of significance in many branches of modern physics.

PHYSIOLOGY or MEDICINE

ROBERT FURCHGOTT (1916-), LOUIS IGNARRO (1941-)
and
FERID MURAD (1936-)

"for their discoveries concerning nitric oxide as a signalling molecule in the cardiovascular system"

Robert Furchgott was born on June 4, 1916 in Charleston, South Carolina, US. He received a BA in chemistry from the University of North Carolina in 1937 and a PhD from Northwestern University in Biochemistry in 1940.

Between 1956 and 1988, he was a professor in the pharmacology department of State University of New York. His field of research was the study of drugs on blood vessels that often achieved contradictory results. The same drug would sometimes cause a contraction and other times a dilation. Furchgott speculated if perhaps, the variation might depend on whether the surface cells inside the blood vessels were intact or damaged.

In 1980, he demonstrated in an ingenious experiment, that acetylcholine dilated blood vessels only if the endothelium was intact. He concluded that blood vessels are dilated because the endothelial cells produce an unknown signal molecule that makes vascular smooth muscle cells relax. He termed this signal molecule, EDRF, the endothelium-derived relaxing factor. His findings led to a search to identify the factor.

For his work in identifying the problem Furchgott received a third share of the 1998 Nobel Prize for Physiology or Medicine.

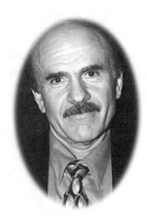

Louis Ignarro was born on May 31, 1941 in Brooklyn , New York. US. In 1962 he obtained his BA in pharmacy from Columbia University, New York. In 1966 he received his PhD in pharmacology from the University of Minnesota.

Between 1979 and 1985, he was professor of pharmacology at Minnesota; in 1985, he was doing the same job at UCLA school of medicine in LA, CA. He is still working there.

Ignarro discovered in 1977 how nitroglycerin and related vasodilating compounds act and found that they release nitric oxide (NO). This relaxes smooth muscle cells. He was intrigued by the concept that a gas could regulate important cellular functions and speculated that endogenous factors, such as hormones, might also act through NO. However, there was no experimental evidence to support this idea at that time. That would come later.

For his input into the overall picture, Ignarro was awarded a third share of the Nobel Prize for Physiology or Medicine.

Ferid **Murad** was born on September 14, 1936 in Whiting, Indiana, US. At Western Reserve University, school of medicine, Cleveland, Ohio, between 1958-65, Murad obtained an MD and a PhD. Following appointments at a number of important universities, he is presently at the Department of Integrative Biology, Pharmacology and Physiology at Texas University Medical School, Houston.

Murad's field of research was in the hunt for EDRF's chemical type. He performed a brilliant series of analysis that concluded, independently of anyone else in 1986, that EDRF was identical to NO. The problem posed by Furchgott was thus solved. When the two scientists presented their findings at a conference held in July 1986 it evoked an avalanche of research in many laboratories around the world. This was the first discovery that a gas can act as a signal molecule in the organism.

For his part part in the story, Murad received a third share of the 1998 Nobel Prize for Physiology or Medicine.

Alfred Nobel who invented dynamite, in which nitroglycerin plays an important part and nitric oxide also, was advised by his doctor to take nitroglycerin for his heart pain. Nobel refused stating it would cause headaches. He wrote in a letter; 'it is ironical that I am now ordered by my physician to eat nitroglycerin' It had been known for many years that this treatment has beneficial effects against chest pain. However, it would take a 100 years until it was expounded that nitroglycerine acts by releasing nitric oxide gas.

ECONOMICS

AMARTYA SEN (1933-)

Amartya **Sen** was born on November 3,1933 in Bengal, India. He was educated at Vishwa Bharati and he graduated from Presidency College, Calcutta in 1953 with a BA in economics.
He then went to England and Cambridge University, from where he obtained a PhD in 1956.

He returned to India and until 1958, was professor of economics at Jadavpur University, Calcutta. He returned to Cambridge and for six years was a Fellow at Trinity College. He then spent eight years as professor of economics at Delhi University. Between 1971 and 1977, he was a professor at the London School of Economics. 1977-81, he was at Nuffield College, Oxford, then he spent the next seven years as Drummond Professor of Political Theory at Oxford University.

He then switched to the US, becoming Professor of Economics and Philosophy at Harvard University, 1987-1998. In 1998 he was appointed Master of Trinity College, Cambridge. His area of work has been broad and most varied. He has written much including, *On Economic Inequality*, *On Ethics and Economics* and *Poverty and Famines*. His research activities include collective choices and social welfare, as well as economic variations in different countries and amongst different groups. He has also done a considerable amount of research identifying the causes of poverty.

His work resulted in the award of the 1998 Nobel Memorial Prize for Economics. **"for his several key contributions to the research on fundamental problems in welfare economics"**

PEACE

JOHN HUME (1937-)
and
DAVID TRIMBLE (1944-)

John Hume was born on January 18, 1937 in Londonderry, N. Ireland, UK. He was educated at St. Columb's College, Derry and St. Patrick's College, Maynooth from where he obtained an MA. He has been leader of the Social Democratic and Labour Party (SDLP) since 1983 and an MP from 1979.

He is one of the three Northern Island MEPs. and holds honorary doctorates from several US universities. He published *Personal Views on Politics, Peace and Reconciliation in Ireland* in 1996.

One of the most important figures in the 'Good Friday' agreement, John Hume has been a tireless worker for a peaceful solution to Northern Ireland's troubles. As a result, he was awarded a co-share of the 1998 Nobel Peace Prize: **"John Hume has throughout been the clearest and most consistent of Northern Island's political leaders in his work for a peaceful solution"**

Married with two sons and three daughters he has wide interests and lives in Derry. He and Trimble each received about £300,000.

David William Trimble was born on October 15, 1944 in Bangor, Northern Ireland, UK. He was educated at Bangor Grammar School and Queen's University, Belfast from where he obtained an LLB. In 1977 he was a senior lecturer at the Faculty of Law, Queen's University.

In May 1990 he became an MP and in 1995 was elected Leader of the Ulster Unionist Party. In 1998 he became First Minister of the Northern Island Assembly and appointed a Privy Counsellor.

A key player in the peace talks that led directly to the 'Good Friday' peace accord of 1998, he has found it most difficult to persuade his colleagues to vote for the presented package. Only the enormous support of the ordinary citizens of the Province for peace has persuaded Ulster Unionist doubters to take part. However, subsequent events, in particular decommissioning of IRA weaponry, has seen the proposed Assembly's date set back. It remains to be seen if Trimble is sufficient a leader to persuade his followers to leave aside the question of decommissioning, on the basis that the IRA having weapons is quite meaningless if they are not used.

In the meantime Trimble accepted the co-award of the 1998 Nobel Prize for Peace; **"awarded for showing great political courage when, at a critical stage of the process, he advocated solutions which led to the peace agreement"**

He is married with two sons and two daughters and enjoys music and reading.

1999

Barok wins Israeli general election for Labour • Italy's 'trial of the century' and Andreotti is found 'not guilty' • France jails Papon for 10 years • East Timor chooses independence, Indonesia surrenders East Timor to the UN • NATO wages an air-war against defenceless Yugoslavia: Many civilians killed • US is only NATO country using the death penalty • Millions hit by Indian cyclone • Kansas in the US refuses to teach Darwin's theory of evolution in their schools • Military junta takes over Pakistan and is dismissed from British Commonwealth • Northern Island forms a joint sharing Assembly • Hundreds of thousands of people all over the world protest at the actions of WTO when they met at Seattle, US. • Films: *Agnes Brown, Run Lola Run, Shakespeare in Love, Star Wars, Notting Hill,* • JM Coetzee, *Disgrace* • Andrew O'Hagan, *Our Fathers* • Ahdaf Soueif, *The Map of Love* • Anita Desai, *Fasting, Feasting* •   Lionel Bart, King Hussein, Stanley Kubrick, Yehudi Menuhin, Anthony Newley, Dirk Bogarde died.

LITERATURE

GÜNTER GRASS (1927-)

Günter Grass was born in1927 in Danzig-Langfuhr, Poland. His parents were Polish-German. In 1939 Hitler invaded Poland and the area in which Günter lived was once again deemed to be part of Germany, having been declared a 'free city' by the League of Nations following WW1. It is now, once again, part of Poland and known as Gdañsk. Grass was called up for service in the German army during WW2. He was taken prisoner by American forces and held until the early part of 1946. Upon his release he found work as a farm labourer, then as a miner. Using his savings, he went to Düsseldorf and Berlin and studied art. The result was that he was able to make a small living as a sculptor, graphic artist and writer in Paris and then Berlin.

In 1955 Grass became a member of the socially critical Gruppe 47 (Grass describes the Gruppe in his book, *The Meeting at Telgte*). His first book of poetry was published in 1956 and his first play produced in 1957. In 1959 came his international debut with the publication of *The Tin Drum*. Later a feature film. It is a satirical panorama of German behaviour and customs during the first half of the 20th century. It was the first part of what became known as the Danzig Trilogy, the others being, *Cat and Mouse* and *Dog Years*.

In the 1960s he allied himself with the Social Democrat party and its' leader, Willy Brandt. He wrote much about post-war Germany and he pleaded for a Germany free from fanaticism and totalitarian ideologies as expressed in *The Plebeians Rehearse the Uprising.*

The Flounder and *The Rat,* reflect Grass' interest in the Peace and Environmental Movements. An excellent graphic artist he has often been responsible for his book covers. In *My Century* (1999) he presents the history of the past century, year by year, from a personal point of view.

Much admired by writers of the calibre of Garcia Màrquez, Gordimer and Oe, Grass has been awarded the 1999 Nobel Prize for Literature, **"whose frolicsome black fables portray the forgotten face of history"**

In his novel *Dog (1965)* Grass writes, "While God was still at school, in the heavenly playground he came up with the idea of creating the world, together with his schoolmate, the talented little Devil"

CHEMISTRY

AHMED ZEWAIL (1946-)

Ahmed Zewail was born in Egypt on February 26, 1946. He was educated at Alexandria University, from where he obtained his BA and MA degrees before emigrating to the US. In 1974 he obtained a PhD from Pennsylvania University. He then went to the University of California at Berkeley as an IBM research fellow. In 1976 he was on the teaching staff at Caltech. In 1982 he became a full professor.

In 1990 the Linus Pauling (q.v.) Chair at Caltech was founded and Zewail became its first occupant. His pioneering investigation of the fundamental chemical reactions, using ultra-short laser flashes, on the time scale on which the reactions actually occur, Professor Zewail's contributions have brought about a revolution in chemistry and other sciences because this method of investigation can be used to understand and predict important reactions.

He was awarded the 1999 Nobel Prize for Chemistry; **"for his studies of the transition states of chemical reactions using femosecond spectroscopy"**

Zewail's financial reward is 7.9 million SEK. He is married to a physician and has four children. He lives in San Marino, California and has dual Egyptian and US nationality.

PHYSICS

GERARDUS T' HOOFT (1946-)
and
MARTINUS VELTMAN (1931-)

"for elucidating the quantum structure of electroweak interactions in physics"

Gerardus't Hooft was born in 1946 in Den Helder, Netherlands. In 1972 he obtained his PhD from Utrecht University where he has been Professor of Physics since 1977. Hooft in 1969 joined Veltman, his Nobel partner. He was 22 and had written a first, brief dissertation on high energy physics. His job was to help in the search for a method of renormalizing non-abelian gauge theories.

T'Hooft succeeded beyond all expectations and in 1971 published two articles that represented an important breakthrough in the on-going research programme. With the aid of Veltman's computer programme, t'Hooft's partial results were now verified and together they worked out a calculation method in detail. The non-abelian gauge theory of electro-weak interaction became a functioning theoretic situation and it was possible, as it had been 20 years previously for quantum electrodynamics, to commence performing precise calculations.

It all led to t'Hooft receiving a half share of the 1999 Nobel Prize for Physics and a half share of the prize of $970,000. He has been a member of the Dutch Academy of Sciences since 1982. He is married to a doctor who works as an anaesthetist; they have two daughters.

Martinus Veltman was born in 1931 in the Netherlands and in 1963 obtained a PhD from Utrecht University. Then, until 1981, he was professor of physics at Utrecht. He later switched to the University of Michigan at Ann Arbor. He is now retired.

He and t'Hooft were awarded the 1999 Nobel Prize for Physics for having placed particle theory physics on a firmer mathematical foundation. They showed in particular, how the theory may be used for precise calculations of physical quantities. Experiments at accelerator laboratories in Europe and the US have recently confirmed many of the calculated results. In 1993 Veltman received the High Energy and Particle Physics Prize from the European Physical Society for his work in renormalizing gauge theories.

He is without doubt the leading developer of gauge theories. He focuses on field theoretic aspects of gauge theories and their applications to elementary particle physics, radiative corrections in the Standard Model, the Higgs sector of the Standard Model and its implications for phenomenology and the new physics beyond the Standard Model, and vacuum structure of field theories. He shared the $970,000 awarded by the Nobel Foundation as part of the 1999 Nobel Prize.

PHYSIOLOGY or MEDICINE

GÜNTER BLOBEL (1936-)

Günter Blobel was born on May 21, 1936 in Waltersdorf, Germany. He obtained a PhD in Oncolgy in 1967 and then went to live and work in the US. Since 1969 he has been associated with the Rockefeller University in New York and is presently a professor there.

Now an American citizen, he has pioneered studies of how proteins find their directions inside living cells. He discovered that they contain signals that appear to act as postal codes, showing where in the cell they should go. His discoveries have pinpointed some genetic diseases caused by misplacement of proteins. These include cystic fibrosis as well as the early development of kidney stones.

He found signalling systems that have turned out to be universal covering as they do animal, plant and yeast cells. His work has resulted in developing more effective methods of using cells as protein establishments. In 1999 he was awarded the Nobel Prize for Physiology or Medicine; **"for the discovery that proteins have intrusive signals that govern their transport and localization in the cell"**

Dr Blobel is a founder member of Friends of Dresden and has said he will use part of the Nobel Prize money of 7.9 million Swedish Kroner, he has received, in rebuilding the town's synagogue, destroyed during the Nazi regime and the city's Frauenkirche, destroyed by Allied bombing during WW2.

ECONOMICS

ROBERT MUNDELL (1932-)

Robert Mundell was born in Canada in 1932. He was an undergraduate at the University of British Columbia and did post-graduate work at the London School of Economics. In 1956 he obtained a PhD from M.I.T, his thesis was on international capital movements. He has been a professor at several places, including, during the period of 1966 to 1971, at the University of Chicago where he was professor of economics. However, he has had an on-going affiliation with Columbia University, New York since 1974.

Mundell has been an advisor to a number of international organizations which include the UN, the IMF, the World Bank, the European Union, as well as governments in North and South America and Europe. Known as 'father of the Euro' his ideas laid the foundations for European economic and monetary union. Mundell's research, some of it dating back 40 years, is at the heart of teaching in international macroeconomics and is still enormously macroeconomics and is still enormously relevant to decision-makers.

He has long been considered a contender for the ultimate reward in world economics for his efforts on financial policies . It therefore came as no surprise that Robert Mundell was awarded the 1999 Nobel Memorial Prize for Economics; **"for his analysis of monetary and fiscal policy under different exchange rate regime"**

He received a cash prize of $970,000.

PEACE

MÉDECINS san FRONTIÉRES

Médecins san Frontiéres has been awarded the 1999 Nobel Peace Prize for **"its pioneering humanitarian work on several continents"** The organization was set up by doctors in France in 1971, its main principle being that all disaster victims have a right to receive professional assistance as quickly and efficiently as possible. The prize, worth £593,000, is awarded to an organisation rather than an individual; the first time since 1988. For MsF the prize could be an embarrassment. They pride themselves on keeping their distance from officialdom.

Considered the most glamourous and independent of aid organizations, it came about when it was founded by Dr Bernard Kouchner and three others; all veterans of the famous 1969 French student revolt that nearly toppled the French government. Their determination was to operate their radical movement without bothering about diplomatic niceties or sovereignty.

Recruits, who number some 2,000 a year and come from all over the world, must pledge to work independently of political and religious authority. They operate in 80 countries and continue the spirit of their founders. As proof of their clout; in 1991, with only a few days notice, they flew 57 aircraft with 2,000 tonnes of supplies into Eastern Turkey, ignoring the protests of the Turkish government, in order to save the Kurds following their exodus from Iraq post the Gulf War.

ALPHABETICAL ORDER
(the year quoted refers to when the prize was awarded)

Addams, J-1931
Adrian, E-1932
Agnon S-1966
Alder, K-1950
Alfvén, H-1970
Allais, M-1988
Altman, S-1989
Alvarez, L-1968
Anderson, C-1936
Anderson, P-1977
Andric, I-1961
Anfinsen,C-1972
Angell, N-1933
Appleton, E-1947
Arafat, A-1994
Arber, W-1978
Arias
Sanchez,O-1987
Armand, R-1901
Arnoldson, K-1908
Arrhenius, S-1903
Arrow, K-1972
Asser,T-1911
Aston, F-1922
Asturias, M-1967
Axelrod, J-1970

Baeyer, A-1905
Bajar, F-1908
Balch, E-1946
Baltimore, D-1975
Banting, F-1923
Barany, R-1914
Bardeen, J-1956
Barkla, C-1917
Barton, D-1969

Basov, N-1964
Beadle, G-1958
Becker, G-1992
Beckett, S-1969
Becquerel, A-1903
Bednorz, J-1987
Beernaert, A-1909
Begin, M-1978
Behring, E-1901
Békésy, G-1961
Bellow, S-1976
Belo, C-1996
Benavente y Mar-
tinez, J-1922
Benacerraf, B-1980
Berg, P-1980
Berguis, F-1931
Bergson, H-1927
Bergstrom, S-1982
Bethe, H-1967
Binnig, G-1986
Bishop, J-1989
Bjornstjerne, B-1903
Black, J-1988
Blackett, P-1948
Bloch, F-1952
Bloch, K-1964
Bloembergen,
N-1981
Blumberg, B-1976
Böll, H-1972
Bohr, N-1922
Bohr, A-1975
Borlaug, N-1970
Born, M-1954
Bordet, J-1919

Bothe, W-1954
Bourgeois, L-1920
Bovet, D-1957
Boyer, P-1997
Boyd-Orr, J-1949
Bragg, WH-1915
Bragg, WL-1915
Brandt, W-1971
Branting, K-1921
Brattain, W-1956
Braun, K-1909
Briand, A-1926
Bridgeman, P-1946
Brockhouse, B-1994
Brodsky, J-1987
Broglie, L-1929
Brown, H-1979
Brown, M-1985
Buchanan, J-1986
Buchner, E-1907
Buck, P-1938
Buisson, F-1927
Bunche, R-1950
Bunin, I-1933
Burnet, M-1960
Butenandt, A-1939
Butler, N-1931

Calvin, M-1961
Camus, A-1957
Canetti, E-1981
Carducci, G-1906
Carrel, A-1912
Cassin, R-1968
Cech, T-1989
Cecil, E-1937

Cela, C-1989
Chadwick, J-1935
Chain, E-1945
Chamberlain, J-1925
Chamberlain,
O-1959
Chandrase-Khar,
S-1983
Charpak, G-1992
Chu, S-1997
Cherenkov, P-1958
Churchill, W-1953
Claude, A-1974
Coase, R-1991
Cockcroft, J-1951
Cohen-
Tannoudji,C-1997
Compton, A-1927
Cooper, L-1972
Cori, C-1947
Cori, G-1947
Cormack, A-1979
Cornforth, J-1975
Corey, E-1990
Corrigan, M-1976
Cournard, A-1956
Cram, D-1987
Crutzen, ?-1995
Curie, M-1903/1911
Curie, P-1903
Curl, R-1996

Dalai Lama-1989
Dalen, N-1912
Dale, H-1936
Dam, C-1943

Dausset, J-1980
Daws, C-1925
Debreu, G-1983
Debye, P-1936
de Duve, C-1974
Deisenhofer, J-1988
Dehmelt, H-1989
Delbruck, M-1969
Deledda, G-1926
Diels, O-1950
Dirac, P-1933
Doherty, P-1996
Doisy, E-1943
Domagk, G-1939
Dulbecco, R-1975
Ducommun, E-1902
Dunant, J-1901
Du Vigneaud, V-1955

Eccles, J-1963
Echegaray y
Eizaquirre, J-1904
Edelman, G-1972
Egas Moniz, A-1949
Ehrlich, P-1908
Eigen, M-1967
Eijkman, C-1929
Einstein, A-1921
Einthoven, W-1924
Elion, G-1988
Eliot, T-1948
Elytis, O-1979
Enders, J-1954
Erlanger, J-1944
Ernst, R-1991
Esaki, L-1973
Estournelles, de Con-
stant-1909
Eucken, R-1908
Euler, U-1970

Faulkner, W-1949
Fermi, E-1938
Feynman, R-1965
Fibiger, J-1926
Finsen, N-1903
Fischer, E-1902
Fischer, E-1973
Fischer, E-1992
Fischer, H-1930
Fitch, V-1980
Fleming, A-1945
Florey, H-1945
Flory, P-1974
Fo, D-1997
Forssmann, W-1956
Fogel, R-1993
Fowler, W-1983
France, A-1921
Franck, J-1925
Frank, I-1958
Fried, A-1911
Friedman, J-1990
Friedman, M-1976
Frisch, R-1969
Fukui, K-1981
Furchgott, R-1998

Gabor, D-1971
Gajdusek, D-1976
Galsworthy, J-1932
Garcia-Robbs,
A-1982
Garcia Marquez,
G-1982
Gasser, H-1944
Gell-Mann, M-1969
Gennes, P-1991
Giaever, I-1973
Giauque, W-1949
Gide, A-1947

Gilbert, W-1980
Gilman, A-1994
Gjellerup, K-1917
Glaser, D-1960
Glashow, S-1979
Gobat, C-1902
Golding, W-198
Goldstein, J-1985
Golgi, C-1906
Gorbachev, M-1990
Gordimer, N-1991
Granit, R-1967
Grignard, V-1912
Guillaume, C-1920
Guillemin, R-1977
Gullstrand, A-1911

Haavelmo, T-1989
Haber, F-1918
Hahn, O-1944
Hammarskjold,
D-1961
Hamsun, K-1920
Harden, A-1929
Hartline, H-1967
Hassel, O-1969
Hauptmann, G-1912
Hauptman, H-1985
Haworth, W-1937
Hayek von, F-1974
Heaney, S-1995
Heidenstam, V-1916
Heisenberg, W-1932
Hemingway, E-1954
Hench, P-1950
Henderson, A-1934
Hershey, A-1969
Herz, G-1925
Herzberg, G-1971
Hess, V-1936

Hess, W-1949
Hesse, H-1946
Hewish, A-1974
Hevesy, G-1943
Heymans, C-1938
Heyrovsky, Y-1959
Heyse, P-1910
Hicks, J-1972
Hill, A-1922
Hinshelwood,
C-1956
Hitchings, G-1988
Hodgkin, A-1963
Hodgkin, D-1964
Holley, R-1968
Hopkins, F-1929
Houssey, B-1947
Huber, R-1988
Hoffmann, R-1981
Hofstadter, R-1961
Hubel, D-1981
Huggins, C-1966
Hull, C-1945
Hulse, R-1993
Hume, J-1998
Huxley, A-1963

Ignarro, L-1998
International Com-
mittee of the Red
Cross-1917/1963
International Peace
Bureau-1910
Institute of Interna-
tional Law-1904

Jacob, F-1965
Jensen, J-1944
Jensen, J-1963
Jerne, N-1984

Jiménel, J-1956
Johnson, E-1974
Joliot-Curie, F-1935
Joliot-Curie, I-1935
Josephson, B-1973
Jouhaux, L-1951

Karlfeldt, E-1931
Kamerlingh-Onnes,
H-1913
Kantorovich, L-1975
Kapitza, P-1978
Karle, J-1985
Karrer, P-1937
Kastler, A-1966
Katz, B-1970
Kawabata, J-1968
Kellog, F-1929
Kendall, E-1950
Kendall, H-1990
Kendrew, J-1962
Kenzaburo, O-1968
Khorana, H-1968
King-Martin Luther,
1964
Kipling, R-1907
Kissinger, H-1973
Klein, L-1980
de Klerk, F-1993
Klitzing, K-1985
Klug, A-1982
Koch, R-1905
Kocher, E-1909
Kohler, G-1984
Kohn, W-1998
Koopmans, T-1975
Kornberg, A-1959
Kossel, A-1910
Krebs, E-1992
Krebs, H-1953

Krogh, A-1920
Kroto, H-1996
Kuhn, R-1938
Kusch, P-1955
Kuznets, S-1971

Lafontaine, H-1913
Lagerkvist, P-1951
Lagerlof, S-1909
Lamb, W-1955
Landau, L-1962
Landsteiner, K-1930
Lange, C-1921
Langmuir, I-1932
Laue, M-1914
Laughlin, R-1998
Laveran, C-1907
Lawrence, E-1939
Laxness, H-1955
Lederberg, J-1958
Lederman, L-1988
Lee, D-1996
Lee, T-1957
Lee, Y-1986
Leger, A-1960
Lehr, J-1987
Lelour, L-1970
Lenard, P-1904
Leontief, W-1973
Levi-Montalcini,
R-1986
Lewis, A-1979
Lewis, E-1995
Lewis, S-1930
Libby, W-1960
Lipmann, F-1953
Lippmann, G-1908
Lipscomb, W-1976
Loewi, O-1936
Lorenz, K-1973

Lorentz, H-1902
Luria, S-1969
Luthuli, A-1960
Lwoff, A-1965

MacBride, S-1974
Macleon, J-1923
Maeterlinck, M-1911
Mahfouz, N-1988
Mandela, N-1993
Mann, T-1929
Marconi, M-1909
Marcus, R-1992
Markowitz, H-1990
Marous, R-1992
Marshall, G-1953
Martin, A-1952
Martin du Gard,
R-1937
Martinson, H-1974
Mauriac, F-1952
Mayer, M-1963
McMillan, E-1951
Meade, J-1977
Menchin, R-1992
Merrifield, R-1984
Metchnikoff, E-1908
Meyerhof, O-1922
Michel, H-1988
Michelson, A-1907
Miller, M-1990
Millikan, R-1923
Milosz, C-1980
Mistral, G-1945
Mitchell, P-1978
Milstein, C-1984
Modigliani, F-1985
Moissan, H-1906
Molina, M-1995
Mommsen, T-1902

Moneta, E-1907
Moore, S-1972
Morrison, T-1993
Mössbauer, R-1961
Mott, J-1946
Mott, N-1977
Mottelson, B-1975
Muller, H-1946
Muller, K-1987
Muller, P-1948
Mulliken, R-1966
Murad, F-1998
Mullis, K-1993
Murray, J-1990
Myrdal, A-1912
Myrdal, G-1974

Nansey, F-1922
Nathans, D-1978
Natta, G-1963
Neel, L-1970
Neher, E-1991
Nernst, W-1920
Neruda, P-1971
Newbold, G-1979
Nicolle, C-1928
Niremberg, M-1968
Noel-Baker, P-1959
Norrish, R-1967
North, D-1993
Northrop, J-1946

Ochoa, S-1959
Ohlin, B-1977
Olah, G-1994
O'Neill, E-1936
Onsanger, L-1968
Osheroff, D-1996
Ossretçky, C-1935
Ostwald, W-1909

Palade, G-1974
Pasternak, B-1958
Paul, W-1989
Pauli, W-1945
Pauling, L-1954/1962
Pavlov, I-1904
Paz, O-1990
Pearson, L-1957
Pedersen, C-1987
Penzias, A-1978
Peres, S-1994
Perls, M-1995
Perez Esquivel, A-1980
Perrin, J-1926
Perutz, M-1962
Phillips, W-1997
Planck, M-1918
Pirandello, L-1934
Pire, D-1958
Polanyi, J-1986
Polpe, J-1998
Pontoppidan, H-1917
Porter, G-1967
Porter, R-1972
Powell, C-1950
Pregl, F-1923
Prelog, V-1975
Prigogine, I-1977
Prochorov, A-1964
Prusiner, S-1997
Pugwash Committee-1995
Purcell, E-1952

Quasimodo, S-1959

Rabi, I-1944
Rabin, I-1994

Rainwater, J-1975
Ramon y Cajal, S-1906
Ramos-Horta, J-1996
Ramsey, N-1989
Ramsey, W-1904
Rayleigh, J-1904
Reichstein, T-1950
Reines, F-1995
Renault, L-1907
Rene, F-1901
Reymont, W-1924
Richards, D-1956
Richards, T-1914
Richardson, R-1996
Richardson, O-1928
Richet, C-1913
Richter, B-1976
Robbins, F-1954
Roberts, R-1993
Robinson, R-1947
Rodbell, M-1994
Roentgen, W-1901
Rohrer, H-1986
Rolland, R-1915
Roosevelt, T-1906
Root, E-1912
Ross, R-1902
Rotblat, J-1995
Rous, P-1966
Rubbia, C-1984
Ruska, E-1986
Rowland, S-1995
Russell, B-1950
Rutherford, E-1908
Ruzicka, L-1939
Ryle, M-1974

Saavedra Lamos,

C-1936
Sabatier, P-1912
Sachs, N-1966
Sadat, A-1978
Sakharov, A-1975
Sakman, B-1991
Salam, A-1979
Samuelson, P-1970
Samuelsson, B-1982
Sanger, F-1958/1980
Saramago, J-1998
Sartre, J-P,-1964
Sato, E-1974
Schally, A-1977
Schawlow, A-1981
Schrieffer, J-1972
Schrödringer, E-1933
Schultz, T-1979
Schwartz, M-1988
Schweitzer, A-1952
Schwinger, J-1965
Seaborg, G-1951
Seferiades, G-1963
Segré, E-1959
Seifert, J-1984
Semenov, N-1956
Sharpe, W-1990
Shaw, G-1925
Sherrington, C-1932
Shockley, W-1956
Sholokhov, M-1965
Shull, C-1994
Siegbahn, K-1924
Siegbahn, K-1981
Sienkiewicz, H-1905
Sillanpaa, F-1939
Simon, C-1985
Simon, H-1978
Singer, I-1978
Skou, J-1997

Smalley, R-1996
Smith, H-1978
Smith, M-1993
Snell, G-1980
Soddy, F-1921
Söderblom, N-1930
Solow, R-1987
Solzhenitzyn, A-1970
Soyinka, W-1986
Spemann, H-1933
Sperry, R-1981
Spitteler, C-1919
Stanley, W-1946
Stark, J-1919
Stein, W-1972
Steinbeck, J-1962
Steinberger, J-1988
Stern, O-1943
Stigler, G-1982
Stone, R-1984
Stormer, H-1998
Stresemann, G-1926
Sully, P-1901
Sumner, J-1946
Sutherland, E-1971
Suttner, B-1905
Suu Kyi, D-1991
Svedberg, T-1926
Szent-Gyorgyi, A-1937
Szymborska, W-1996

Tagore, R-1913
Tamm, I-1958
Tatum, E-1958
Taube, H-1983
Taylor, J-1993
Taylor, R-1990
Temin, H-1975

Theiler, M-1951
Theorell, H-1955
Tho, Le Duc, 1973
Thomas, E-1990
Thomson, G-1937
Tinbergen, J-1969
Tinbergen, N-1973
Ting, S-1976
Tiselius, A-1948
Tobin, J-1981
Todd, A-1957
Tomonega, S-1965
Tonegawa, S-1987
Townes, C-1964
Trimble, D-1998
Tsui, D-1998
Tutu, D-1984

Undset, S-1928
Urey, H-1934

Van't Hoff, J-1901
Van de Meer, S-1984
Vane, J-1982
Van Vleck, J-1977
Varmus, H-1989
Virtanen, A-1945
Volhard, E-1995

Walcott, D-1992
Walker, P-1997
Wallach, O-1910
Werner, A-1913
White, P-1973
Wieland, H-1927
Wilkinson, G-1973
Willstätter, R-1915
Windaus, A-1928
Wittig, G-1979
Woodward, R-1965

Yalow, R-1977
Yang, C-1957
Yeats, W-1923
Yukawa, H-1949

Zeeman, P-1902
Zernike, F-1953
Ziegler, K-1963
Zinkernagel, R-1996
Zsigmondy, R-1925

COUNTRY of BIRTH
(the year quoted refers to when the prize was awarded)

ARGENTINE
Saavedra, C-1936
Houssay, B-1947
Esquivel, A-1980
Milstein, C-1984

AUSTRIA
Fried, A-1911
Barany, R-1914
Pregl, F-1923
Zsigmondy, R-1925
Wagner-Jauregg, J-1927
Landsteiner, K-1930
Schrodinger, E-1933
Hess, V-1936
Kuhn, R-1938
Pauli, W-1945
Perutz, M-1962
von Frisch, K-1973
Lorenz, K-1973
von Hayek, F-1974

AUSTRALIA
Florey, H-1945
Burnet, F-1960
Eccles, J-1963
Prokhorov, A-1964
Cornforth, J-1975
Doherty, P-1996

BELGIUM
Beernaert, A-1909
Maeterlinck, M-1911
Lafontaine, H-1913
Bordet, J-1919

Heymans, C-1938
Pire, D-1958
Claude, A-1974

BRAZIL
Medawar, P-1960

BULGARIA
Canetti, E-1981

BURMA
Kyi, D-1991

CANADA
Banting, F-1923
Giauque, W-1949
Pearson, L-1957
Huggins, C-1966
Hubel, D-1981
Taube, H-1983
Altman, S-1989
Taylor, R-1990
Marcus, R-1992
Brockhouse, B-1994
Vickrey, W-1996

CHILE
Mistral, G-1945
Neruda, P-1971

CHINA
Brattain, W-1956
Lee, T-1957
Yang, C-1957
Fischer, E-1992

COLUMBIA
Marquez, G-1982

COSTA RICA
Sanchez, O-1987

CZECHSLOVAKIA
von Sutner, B-1905
Cori, C-1947
Cori, G-1947
Heyrovsky, Y-1959
Seifert, J-1984

DENMARK
Finsen, N-1903
Bajer, F-1908
Gjellerup, K-1917
Pontoppidan, H-1917
Krogh, A-1920
Bohr, N-1922
Fibiger, J-1926
Undset, S-1928
Dam, C-1943
Jensen, J-1944
Bohr, A-1975

EAST TIMOR
Ramos-Horta, J-1996

EGYPT
Hodgkin, D-1964
el-Sadat, M-1978
Mahfouz, N-1988

FINLAND
Sillanpaa, F-1939

Virtanen, A-1945
Granit, R-1967

FRANCE
Prudhomme,S-1901
Passey, F, -1901
Curie, P-1903
Becquerel, A-1903
Mistral, F-1904
Moissan, H-1906
Laveran, C-1907
Renault, L-1907
Estournelles, P-1909
Grignard, V-1912
Sabatier, P-1912
Carrel, A-1912
Werner, A-1913
Richet, C-1913
Rolland, R-1915
Guillaume, C-1920
Bourgeois, L-1920
France, A-1921
Perrin, J-1926
Briand, A-1926
Bergson, H-1927
Buisson, F-1927
Nicolle, C-1928
Broglie, L-1929
Curie, I-1935
Joliot-Curie, JF-1935
du Gard, R-1937
Gide, A-1947
Jouhaux, L-1951
Mauriac, F-1952
Cournand, A-1956
Camus, A-1957

Perse, SJ-1960
Sartre, JP-1964
Jacob, F-1965
Lwoof, AM-1965
Monod, J-1965
Kastler, A-1966
Cassin, R-1968
Leloir, L-1970
Neel, L-1970
MacBride, S-1974
Guillemin, R-1977
Dausset, J-1980
Debrevu, G-1983
Simon, C-1985
Lehn, JM-1987
Allais, M-1988
de Gennes, PG-1991

GERMANY
Roentgen, W-1901
von Behring, E-1901
Mommsen, C-1902
Fischer,E-1902
von Baeyer, A-1905
Koch, R-1905
Buchner, E-1907
Michelson, A-1907
Eucken, R-1908
Ehrlich, P-1908
Braun, K-1909
von Heyse, P-1910
Wallach, O-1910
Kossel, A-1910
Wien, W-1911
Hauptmann, G-1912
Laue, M-1914
Willstatter, R-1915
Haber, F-1918
Planck, M-1918
Stark, J-1919

Nernst, W-1920
Einstein,A-1921
Meyerhof, O-1922
Franck, J-1925
Hertz, G-1925
Stresemann, G-1926
Wieland, H-1927
Quidde, L-1927
Windaus, A-1928
Mann, T-1929
Euler-Chelpin,
H-1929
Fischer, H-1930
Bosch, K-1931
Bergius, F-1931
Warburg, O-1931
Heisenberg, W-1932
Speman, H-1935
von Ossietzky,
C-1935
Loewi, O-1936
Butenandt, A-1939
Domagk, G-1939
Stern, O-1943
Hahn, O-1944
Chain, E-1945
Hesse, H-1946
Diels, O-1950
Alder, K-1950
Schweitzer, A-1952
Staudinger, H-1953
Lipmann, F-1953
Krebs, H-1953
Born, M-1954
Bothe, W-1954
Kusch, P-1955
Forssmann, W-1956
Mossbauer, R-1961
Ziegler, K-1963
Mayer, M-1963

Jensen, J-1963
Bloch, K-1964
Lynen, F-1964
Sachs, N-1966
Eigen, Manfred-1967
Bethe, H-1967
Delbruck, M-1969
Katz, B-1970
Herzberg, G-1971
Brandt, W-1971
Boll, H-1972
Fischer, E-1973
Kissinger, H-1973
Penzias, A-1978
Wittig, G-1979
Kohler, G-1984
Polanyi, J-1986
Binnig, G-1986
Ruska, E-1986
Bednorz, J-1987
Deisenhofer, J-1988
Huber, R-1988
Michel, H-1988
Steinberger, J-1988
Dehment, H-1989
Paul, W-1989
Neher, E-1991
Sakmann, B-1991
Selten, R-1994
Volhard, C-1995

GREECE
Elytis, O-1979

GUATEMALA
Asturias, M-1967
Mechu, R-1992

HUNGARY
Lenard, P-1905

von Nagyrapolt,
A-1937
von Hevesy, G-1943
von Bekesy, G-1961
Wigner, E-1963
Gabor, D-1971
Olah, G-1994
Harsanyi, J-1994

ICELAND
Laxness, H-1955

INDIA
Ross, R-1902
Tagore, R-1913
Raman, C-1930
Khorana, H-1968
Salam, A,-1979
Chandrasekhar,
S-1983

ITALY
Carducci, G-1906
Golgi, C-1906
Moneta, E-1907
Marconi, G-1909
Deledda, G-1926
Pirandello, L-1934
Fermi, E-1938
Quasimodo, S-1959
Segre, E-1959
Natta, G-1963
Luria, S-1969
Montale, E-1975
Dulbecco, R-1975
Rubbia, C-1984
Modigliani, F-1985
Levi-Montcini,
R-1986

JAPAN
Yukawa, H-1949
Tomonaga, S-1965
Kawabata, Y-1968
Esaki, L-1973
Sato, E-1974
Fukui, K-1981
Tonegawa, S-1987
Oe, K-1994

KOREA
Pederson, C-1987

LATVIA
Ostwald, C-1909

LITHUANIA
Klug, A-1982

LUXEMBOURG
Lippmann, G-1908

MACEDONIA
Mother Teresa-1979

MEXICO
Robles, A-1982
Paz, O-1990
Molina, M-1995

NETHERLANDS
Van't Hoff, J-1901
Lorentz, H-1902
Zeeman, P-1902
van der Waals, J-1910
Asser, T-1911
Kamerlingh, O-1913
Einthoven, W-1924
Eijkman, C-1929
Debye, P-1936
Zernike, F-1953
Tinbergen, J-1969
Tinbergen, N-1973
Koopmans, T-1975
B l o e m b e r g e n, N-1981
van der Meer, S-1984
Crutzen, P-1995

NEW ZEALAND
Wilkins, M-1962

NIGERIA
Soyinka, W-1986

NORWAY
Bjornson, B-1903
Hamsun, K-1920
Lange, C-1921
Nansen, F-1922
Onsager, L-1968
Hassel, O-1969
Frisch, R-1969
Giaever, I-1973
Haavelmo, T-1989

PALESTINE
Arafat, Y-1994
Rabin, Y-1994

POLAND
Curie, M-1903 and 1911
Sienkiewicz, H-1905
Reymont, W-1924
Rabi, I-1944
Reichstein, T-1950
Agnon, S-1966
Schally, A-1977
Singer, IB-1978
Hoffmann, R-1981
Walesa, L-1983
von Klitzing, K-1985
Charpak, G-1992
Peres, S-1994
Rotblat, J-1995
Szymborska, W-1996

PORTUGAL
Moniz, A-1949

RHODESIA
Luthuli, A-1960

ROMANIA
Palade, G-1974
Wiesel, E-1986

RUSSIA
Pavlov, I-1904
Mechnikov, I-1908
Bunin, I-1933
Karrer, P-1937
Waksman, S-1952
Semenov, N-1956
Pasternak, B-1958
Cherenkov, P-1958
Frank, I-1958
Tamm, I-1958
Landau, L-1962
Basov, N-1964
Sholokhov, M-1965
Solzhenitsyn, A-1970
Kuznets, S-1971
Leontief, W-1973
Kantorovich-L-1975
Sakharov, A-1975
Prigogine, I-1977
Kapitsa, P-1978

Begin, M-1978
Milosz, C-1980
Brodsky, J-1987
Gorbachev, M-1990

SAINT LUCIA,WI
Lewis, A-1979
Walcott, D-1992

SOUTH AFRICA
Theiler, M-1951
Cormack, A-1979
Tutu, D-1984
Gordimer, N-1991
Mandela, N-1993
de Klerk, F-1993

SPAIN
Echegaray y Eizaaguirre, J-1904
Ramon, S-1906
Benavente, J-1922
Jimenez, J-1956
Ochoa, S-1959
Cela, C-1989
Aleixandre, V-1977

SWEDEN
Arrhenius, S-1903
Arnoldson, K-1908
Lagerlof, S-1909
Gullstrand, A-1911
Dalen, N-1912
von Heidenstam, V-1916
Branting, K-1921
Siegbahn, K-1924
Svedberg, T-1926
Soderblom, N-1930
Karlfeldt, E-1931

Tiselius, A-1948
Lagerkvist, P-1951
Theorell, A-1955
Hammarskjold, D-1961
Alfven, H-1970
Euler-Chelpin, U-1970
Johnson, E-1974
Martinson, H-1974
Myrdal, G-1974
Ohlin, B-1977
Siegbahn, K-1981
Wiesel, T-1981
Bergstrom, S-1982
Samuelson, B-1982
Myrdal, A-1982

SWITZERLAND
Dunant, J-1901
Ducommun, E-1902
Gobat, C-1902
Kocher, E-1909
Spitteler, C-1919
Muller, P-1948
Hess, W-1949
Bloch, F-1952
Bovet, D-1957
Arber, W-1978
Rohrer, H-1986
Muller, K-1987
Ernst, R-1991
Zinkernagel, R-1996

TAIWAN
Lee, Y-1986

TIBET
The Dalai Lama-1989

TURKEY
Seferiades, G-1963

UNITED KINGDOM
Cremer, W-1903
Ramsay, W-1904
Rayleigh, J-1904
Thomson, J-1906
Kipling, R-1907
Rutherford, E-1908
Bragg,WH-1915
Bragg, WL-1915
Barkla, C-1917
Soddy,F-1921
Aston, F-1922
Hill, A-1922
Yeats, W-1923
Macleod, J-1923
Shaw, GB-1925
Chamberlain, J-1925
Wilson, C-1927
Richardson, O-1928
Harden, A-1929
Hopkins, F-1929
Galsworthy, J-1932
Sherrington, C-1932
Adrian, E-1932
Dirac, P-1933
Angell, N-1933
Henderson, A-1934
Chadwick, J-1935
Dale, H-1936
Haworth, W-1937
Thomson, G-1937
Cecil, E-1937
Fleming, A-1945
Robinson, R-1947
Appleton, E-1947
Blackett, P-1948

Boyd-Orr, J-1949
Russell, B-1950
Powell, C-1950
Cockcroft, J-1951
Walton, E-1951
Martin, A-1952
Synge, R-1952
Churchill, W-1953
Hinshelwood, C-1956
Shockley, W-1956
Todd, A-1957
Sanger, F-1958
Noel-Baker, N-1959
Kendrew, J-1962
Crick, F-1962
Hodgkin, A-1963
Huxley, A-1963
Norrish, R-1967
Porter, G-1967
Beckett, S-1969
Barton, D-1969
Porter, R-1972
Hicks, J-1972
White, P-1973
Wilkinson, G-1973
Josephson, B-1973
Hewish, A-1974
Ryle, M-1974
de Duve, C-1974
Corrigan, M-1976
Williams, B-1976
Mott, N-1977
Meade, J-1977
Mitchell, P-1978
Brown, H-1979
Hounsfield, G-1979
Sanger, F-1980
Vane, J-1982
Golding, W-1983

Jerne, N-1984
Stone, R-1984
Black, J-1988
Coase, R-1991
Smith, M-1993
Roberts, R-1993
Heaney, S-1995
Kroto, H-1996
Mirrlees, J-1996

UNITED STATES OF AMERICA
Roosevelt, T-1906
Root, E-1912
Richards, T-1914
Wilson, W-1919
Millikan, R-1923
Dawes, C-1925
Compton, A-1927
Kellog, F-1929
Lewis, S-1930
Addams, J-1931
Butler, N-1931
Langmuir, I-1932
Morgan, T-1933
Urey, H-1934
Minot, G-1934
Murphy, W-1934
Whipple, G-1934
O'Neill, E-1936
Anderson, C-1936
Davisson, C-1937
Buck, P-1938
Lawrence, E-1939
Doisy, E-1943
Erlanger, J-1944
Gasser, H-1944
Hull, C-1945
Northrop, J-1946
Sumner, J-1946

Stanley, W-1946
Bridgman, P-1946
Muller, H-1946
Mott, J-1946
Balch, E-1946
Eliot, TS-1948
Faulkner, W-1949
Hench, P-1950
Kendall, E-1950
Bunche, R-1950
Seaborg, G-1951
McMillan, E-1951
Purcell, E-1952
Marshall, G-1953
Hemingway, E-1954
Pauling, L-1954 and 1962
Enders, J-1954
Weller, T-1954
Robbins, F-1954
du Vigneaud, V-1955
Lamb, W-1955
Bardeen, J-1956
Richards, D-1956
Beadle, G-1958
Lederberg, J-1958
Tatum, E-1958
Chamberlain, O-1959
Kornberg, A-1959
Libby, W-1960
Glaser, D-1960
Calvin, M-1961
Hofstadter, R-1961
Steinbeck, J-1962
Watson, J-1962
Townes, C-1964
Luther King, M-1964
Woodward, R-1965
Schwinger, J-1965

Feynman, R-1965
Mulliken, R-1966
Rous, F-1966
Hartline, H-1967
Wald, G-1967
Alvarez, L-1968
Holley, R-1968
Nirenberg, M-1968
Gell-Mann, M-1969
Hershey, A-1969
Axelrod, J-1970
Samuelson, P-1970
Borlaug, N-1970
Sutherland, E-1971
Moore, S-1972
Stein, W-1972
Anfinsen, C-1972
Bardeen, J-1972
Cooper, L-1972
Schrieffer, J-1972
Edelma, G-1972
Arrow, K-1972
Flory, P-1974
Mottelson, B-1975
Rainwater, L-1975
Baltimore, D-1975
Temin, H-1975
Bellow, S-1976
Lipscomb, W-1976
Richter, B-1976
Ting, S-1976
Blumberg, B-1976
Gajdusek, D-1976
Friedman, M-1976
Anderson, P-1977
van Vleck, J-1977
Yalow, R-1977
Wilson, R-1978
Nathans, D-1978
Smith, H-1978

Smith, H-1978
Weinberg, S-1979
Glashow, S-1979
Schultz, T-1979
Berg, P-1980
Gilbert, W-1980
Cronin, J-1980
Fitch, V-1980
Snell, G-1980
Klein, L-1980
Schawlow, A-1981
Sperry, R-1981
Tobin, J-1981
Wilson, K-1982
Stigler, G-1982
Fowler, W-1983
McClintock, B-1983
Merrifield, B-1984
Hauptman, H-1985
Karle, J-1985
Brown, M-1985
Goldstein, J-1985
Herschbach, D-1986
Cohen, S-1986
Buchanan, J-1986
Cram, D-1987
Solow, R-1987
Lederman, L-1988
Schwartz, M-1988
Elion, G-1988
Hitchings, G-1988
Cech, T-1989
Ramsey, N-1989
Bishop, J-1989
Varmus, H-1989
Corey, E-1990
Friedman, J-1990
Kendall, H-1990
Murray, J-1990
Donnall, T-1990

Markowitz, H-1990
Miller, M-1990
Sharpe, W-1990
Krebs, E-1992
Becker, G-1992
Morrison, T-1993
Mullis, K-1993
Hulse, R-1993
Taylor, J-1993
Sharp, P-1993
Fogel, R-1993
North, D-1993
Shull, C-1994
Gilman, A-1994
Rodbell, M-1994
Nash, J-1994
Rowland, S-1995
Perls, M-1995
Reines, F-1995
Lewis, E-1995
Wieschaus, E-1995
Lucas, R-1995
Curl, R-1996
Smalley, R-1996
Lee, D-1996
Osheroff, D-1996
Richardson, R-1996

VENEZUELA
Benacerraf, B-1980

VIETNAM
Theo, Le Duc-1973

YUGOSOLAVIA
Ruzicka, L-1939
Andric, I-1961
Prelog, V-1975

LITERATURE

Agnon, S-1966
Aleixandre, V-1977
Andric, I-1961
Armand, R-1901
Asturias, M-1967

Beckett, S-1969
Bellow, S-1976
Benaventa, J-1922
Bergson, H-1927
Bjornstjerne, B-1903
Boll, H-1972
Brodsky, J-1987
Buck, P-1938
Bunin, A-1933

Canetti, E-1981
Camus, A-1957
Carducci, G-1906
Cela, C-1989
Churchill, W-1953

Deledda, G-1926

Echegaray   y
Eizaguirre, J-1904
Eliot, T-1948
Elytis, O-1979
Eucken, R-1908

Faulkner, W-1949
Fo, D-1997
France, A-1921

Galsworthy, J-1932
Garcia-Marquez,
G-1982
Gide, A-1947

Gjellerup, K-1917
Golding, W-1983
Gordimer, N-1991

Hamsun, K-1920
Hauptmann, G-1912
Heaney, S-1995
Heidenstam, V-1916
Hemingway, E-1954
Hesse, H-1946
Heyse, P-1910

Karlfeldt, E-1931
Kawabata, J-1968
Kenzaburo, O-1994
Kipling, R-1907

Jensen, J-1944
Jimenel, J-1956
Johnson, E-1974

LagerKvist, P-1951
Lagerlof, S-1909
Laxness, H-1955
Leger, A-1960
Lewis, S-1930

Maeterlinck, M-1911
Mahfouz, N-1988
Mann, T-1929
Martin   du   Gard,
R-1937
Martinson, H-1974
Mauriac, F-1952
Milosz, C-1980
Mistral, G-1945
Mommsen, T-1902
Morrison, T-1993

Neruda, P-1971

O'Neill, E-1936

Pasternak, B-1958
Paz, O-1990
Pirandello, L-1934
Pontoppidan, H-1917

Quasimodo, S-1959

Rene, F-1901
Reymont, W-1924
Rolland, R-1915
Russell, B-1950

Sachs, N-1966
Saramago, J-1998
Sartre, JP-1964
Seferiades, G-1963
Seifert, J-1984
Shaw, GB-1925
Sholokhov, M-1965
Sienkiewicz, H-1905
Sillanpaa, F-1939
Simon, C-1985
Singer, I-1978
S o l z h e n i t z y n ,
A-1970
Soyinka, W-1986
Spitteler, C-1919
Steinbeck, J-1962
Sully, P-1901
Szymborska, W-1996

Tagore, R-1913

Undset, S-1928

Walcott, D-1992
White, P-1973

Yeats, W-1923

CHEMISTRY

Alder, K-1950
Altman, S-1989
Anfinsen, C-1972
Arrhenius, S-1903
Aston, F-1922

Baeyer, A-1905
Barton, D-1969
Berg, P-1920
Berguis, F-1931
Bosch, K-1931
Boyer, P-1997
Brown, H-1979
Buchner, E-1907
Butenandt, A-1939

Calvin, M-1961
Cech, T-1989
Corey, E-1990
Cornforth, J-1975
Cram, D-1987
Crutzen, -1995
Curie, M-1911
Curl,   -1996

Debye, P-1936
Deisenhofer, J-1988
Diels, O-1950
Du Vigneaud, V-1955

Eigen, M-1967
Ernst, R-1991

Fischer, E-1902
Fischer, E-1993
Fischer, H-1930

Flory, P-1974
Fukui, K-1981

Giauque, W-1949
Gilbert, W-1980
Grignard, V-1912

Haber, F-1918
Hahn, O-1944
Harden, A-1929
Hassel, O-1969
Hauptman, H-1985
Haworth, W-1937
Herzberg, G-1971
Hevesy, G-1943
Heyrovsky, Y-1959
H i n s h e l w o o d ,
C-1956
Hodgkin, D-1964
Hoffmann, R-1981
Huber, R-1988

Joliot-Curie, F-1935
Joliot-Curie, I-1935

Karle, J-1985
Karrier, P-1937
Kendrew, J-1962
Klug, A-1982
Kohn, W-1998
Kroto, -1996
Kuhn, R-1938

Langmuir, I-1932
Lee, Y-1986
Lehr, JM-1987
Lelour, L-1970
Libby, W-1960
Lipscomb, W-1976

Marcus, R-1992
Marous, R-1992
Martin, A-1952
McMillan, E-1951
Merrifield, R-1984
Michel, H-1988
Mitchell, P-1978
Moissan, H-1906
Molina, -1995
Moore, S-1972
Mulliken, R-1966
Mullis, K-1993

Natta, G-1963
Nernst, W-1920
Norrish, R-1967
Northrop, J-1946

Olah, -1994
Onsanger, L-1968
Ostwald, W-1909

Pauling, L-1954
Pedersen, C-1987
Perutz, M-1962
Pregl, F-1923
Prelog,V-1975
Prigogine, I-1977
Polanyi, J-1986
Pople, J-1998
Porter, G-1967

Ramsay, W-1904
Richards, T-1914
Robinson, R-1947
Rowland, -1995
Rutherford, E-1908
Ruzicka, L-1939

Sabatier, P-1912

Sanger, F-1958
Sanger, F-1980
Seaborg, G-1951
Semenov, N-1956
Skou, J-1997
Smalley, -1996
Smith, M-1993
Soddy, F-1921
Stanley, W-1946
Stein, W-1972
Sumner, J-1946
Svedberg, T-1926

Taube, H-1983
Tiselius, A-1948
Todd, A-1957

Urey, H-1934

Van't Hoff, J-1901
Virtanen, A-1945

Walker, -1997
Wallach, O-1910
Werner, A-1913
Wieland, H-1927
Wilkinson, G-1973
Willstatter, R-1915
Windaus, A-1928
Wittig, G-1979
Woodward, R-1965

Ziegler, K-1963
Zsigmondy, R-1925

PHYSICS

Alfven, H-1970
Alvarez, L-1968
Anderson, C-1936

Anderson, P-1977
Appleton, E-1947

Bardeen, J-1956
Barkla, C-1917
Basov, N-1964
Becquerel, A-1903
Bednorz, J-1987
Bethe, H-1967
Binnig, G-1986
Blackett, P-1948
Bloch, F-1952
Bloembergen,
N-1981
Bohr, N-1922
Bohr, A-1975
Born, M-1954
Bothe, W-1954
Bragg, WH-1915
Bragg, WL-1915
Brattain, W-1956

Braun, K-1909
Bridgman, P-1946
Brockhouse, -1994
Broglie, L-1929

Chadwick, J-1935
C h a m b e r l a i n ,
O-1959
C h a n d r a s e - K h a r,
S-1983
Charpak, G-1992
Cherenkov, P-1958
Chu, S-1997
Cockcroft, J-1951
C o h e n - T a n n o n d j i,
-1997
Compton, A-1927
Cooper, L-1972

Cronin, J-1980
Curie, M-1903
Curie, P-1903

Dalen, N-1912
Dehmelt, H-1989
Dirac, P-1933

Einstein, A-1921
Esaki, L-1973

Fermi, E-1938
Feynman, R-1965
Fitch, V-1980
Fowler, W-1983
Franck, J-1925
Frank, I-1958
Friedman, J-1990

Gabor, D-1971
Gell-Mann, M-1969
Gennes, P-1991
Giaever, I-1973
Glaser, D-1960
Glashow, S-1979
Guillaume, C-1920

Heisenberg, W-1932
Herz, G-1925
Hess, V-1936
Hewish, A-1974
Hofstadter, R-1961
Hulse, R-1993

Jensen, J-1963
Josephson, B-1973

Kamerlingh-Onnes, H-1913
Kapitza, P-1978

Kastler, A-1966
Kendall, H-1990
Klitzing, K-1985
Kusch, P-1955

Lamb, W-1955
Landau, L-1962
Laue, M-1914
Laughlin -1998
Lawrence, E-1939
Lederman, L-1988
Lee, D-1996
Lee, T-1957
Lenard, P-1904
Lippmann, G-1908
Lorentz, H-1902

Marconi, M-1909
Mayer, M-1963
Michelson, A-1907
Millikan, R-1923
Mossbauer, R-1961
Mott, N-1977
Mottelson, B-1975
Muller, K-1987

Neel, L-1970

Osheroff, D-1996

Paul, W-1989
Pauli, W-1945
Penziar, A-1978
Perl, -1995
Perrin, J-1926
Phillips, -1997
Planck, M-1918
Procherov, A-1964
Powell, C-1950
Purcell, E-1952

Rabi, I-1944
Rainwater, J-1975
Ramsey, N-1989
Rayleigh, J-1904
Richardson, O-1928
Richardson, -1996
Reines, -1995
Richter, B-1976
Roentgen, W-1901
Rohrer, H-1986
Rubbia, C-1984
Ruska, E-1986
Ryle, M-1974

Salam, A-1979
Schawlow, A-1981
Schrodinger, E-1933
Schrieffer, J-1972
Schwinger, J-1965
Schwartz, 1988
Segre, E-1959
Shockley, W-1956
Shull, -1994
Siegbahn, K-1924
Siegbahn, K-1981
Stark, J-1919
Steinberger, J-1988
Stern, O-1943
Stormer, -1998

Tamm, I-1958
Taylor, J-1993
Taylor, R-1990
Thomson, G-1937
Ting, S-1976
Tomonaga, S-1965
Townes, C-1964
Tsui, -1998

Van de Meer, S-1984

Van Vleck, J-1977

Waals, J-1910
Walton, E-1951
Weinberg, S-1979
Wien, W-1911
Wigner, E-1963
Wilson, C-1927
Wilson, K-1983
Wilson, R-1978

Yang, C-1957
Yukawa, H-1949

Zeeman, P-1902
Zernike, F-1953

PHYSIOLOGY or MEDICINE

Adrian, E-1932
Arber, W-1978
Axelrod, J-1970

Baltimore, D-1975
Banting, F-1923
Barany, R-1914
Beadle, G-1958
Behring, E-1901
Békésy, G-1961
Benacerraf, B-1980
Bergstrom, S-1982
Bishop, J-1989
Black, J-1988
Bloch, K-1964
Blumberg, B-1976
Bordet, J-1919
Bovet, D-1957
Brown, M-1985
Burnet, M-1960

Carrel, A-1912
Chain, E-1945
Claude, A-1974
Cohen, S-1986
Cori, C-1947
Cori, G-1947
Cormack, A-1979
Cournard, A-1956
Crick, F-1962

Dale, H-1936
Dam, C-1943
Dausset, J-1980
Delbruck, M-1969
de Duve, C-1974
Doisy, E-1943
Doherty, P-1996
Domagk, G-1939
Dulbecco, R-1975

Eccles, J-1963
Edelman, G-1972
Egas Moniz, A-1949
Ehrlich, P-1908
Eijkman, C-1929
Einthoven, W-1924
Elion, G-1988
Enders, J-1954
Erlanger, J-1944
Euler, U-1970

Fibiger, J-1926
Finsen, N-1903
Fischer, E-1992
Fleming, A-1945
Florey, H-1945
Forssmann, W-1956
Furchgott, R-1998

Gajdusek, D-1976

Gasser, H-1944
Gilman, A-1994
Goldstein, J-1985
Golgi, C-1906
Granit, R-1967
Guillemin, R-1977
Gullstrand, A-1911

Hartline, H-1967
Hershey, A-1969
Hench, P-1950
Heymans, C-1938
Hess, W-1949
Hill, A-1922
Hitchings, G-1988
Hodgkin, A-1963
Holley, R-1968
Hopkins, F-1929
Houssay, B-1947
Hubel, D-1981
Huggins, C-1966
Huxley, A-1963

Ignarro, I-1998

Jacob, F-1965
Jerne, N-1984

Katz, B-1970
Kendall, E-1950
Khorana, H-1968
Koch, R-1905
Kocher, E-1909
Kohler, G-1984
Kornberg, A-1959
Kossel, A-1910
Krebs, E-1992
Krebs, H-1953
Krogh, A-1920

Landsteiner, K-1930
Laveran, C-1907
Lederberg, J-1958
Levi-Montalcini,
R-1986
Lewis, E-1995
Lipmann, F-1953
Loewi, O-1936
Lorenz, K-1973
Luria, S-1969
Lwoff, A-1965

Macleod, J-1923
Metchnikoff, E-1908
Meyerhof, O-1922
Milstein, C-1984
Muller, H-1946
Muller, P-1948
Murad, F-1998
Murray, J-1990

Nathans, D-1978
Neher, E-1991
Newbold, G-1979
Nicolle, C-1928
Nirenberg, M-1968

Ochoa, S-1959

Palade, G-1974
Pavlov, I-1904
Porter, R-1972
Prusiner, S-1997

Ramon y Cajal,
S-1906
Reichstein, T-1950
Richards, D-1956
Richet, C-1913
Robbins, F-1954

Roberts, R-1993
Rodbell, M-1994
Ross, R-1902
Rous, P-1966

Sakman, B-1991
Samuelsson, B-1982
Schally, A-1977
Sherrington, C-1932
Smith, H-1978
Snell, G-1980
Spemann, H-1933
Sperry, R-1981
Sutherland, E-1971
Szent-Györgyi,
A-1937

Tatum, E-1958
Temin, H-1975
Theiler, M-1951
Theorell, H-1955
Thomas, E-1990
Tinbergen, N-1973
Tonegawa, S-1987

Vane, J-1982
Varmus, H-1989
Vollhard, C-1995

Wagner, J-1927
Waksman, S-1952
Wald, G-1967
Warburg, O-1931
Watson, J-1962
Weller, T-1954
Whipple, G-1934
Wiesel, T-1981
Wieschaus, E-1995
Wilkins, M-1962

Yalow, R-1977

Zinkernagel, R-1996

ECONOMICS

Allais, M-1988
Arrow, K-1972

Becker, G-1992
Buchanan, J-1986

Coase, R-1991

Debreu, G-1983

Fogel, R-1933

Friedman, M-1976
Frisch, R-1969

Haavelmo, T-1989
Harsanyi, J-1994
von Hayek, F-1974
Hicks, J-1972

Kantorovich, L-1975
Klein, L-1980
Koopmans, T-1975
Kuznets, S-1971

Leontief, W-1973
Lewis, A-1979
Lucas, R-1995

Markowitz, H-1990
Meade, J-1977
Merton, R-1997
Miller, M-1990
Mirrlees, J-1996

Modigliani, F-1985
Myrdal, G-1974

Nash, J-1994
North, D-1993

Ohlin, B-1977

Samuelson, P-1970
Scholes, M-1997
Schultz, T-1979
Seltern, R-1994
Sen, A-1998
Sharpe, W-1990
Simon, H-1978
Solow, R-1987
Stigler, G-1982
Stone, R-1984

Tinbergen, J-1969
Tobin, J-1981

Vickerey, W-1996

PEACE PRIZE

Addams, J-1931
Amnesty
International-1977
Angell, N-1933
Arnoldson, K-1908
Arias Sanchez,
O-1987
Arafat, A-1994
Asser, T-1911
Aung Son Suu Kyi-
1991

Bajer, F-1908
Balch, E-1946

Beernaert, A-1909
Begin, M-1978
Belo, ?-1996
Borlaug, N-1970
Bourgeois, L-1920
Boyd-Orr, J-1949
Brandt, W-1971
Briand, A-1926
Branting, K-1921
Buisson, F-1927
Butler, N-1931
Bunche, R-1950

Cassin, R-1968
Cecil, E-1937
Chamberlain, J-1925
Corrigan, M-1976
Cremer, W-1903

Dalai Lama- 1989
Dawes, C-1925
Ducommun, E-1902
Dunant, J-1901

Estournelles de
Constant-1909

Fried, A-1911

Garcia-Robbs,
A-1982
Gobat, C-1902
Gorbachev, M-1990

Hammarskjöld,
D-1961
Henderson, A-1934
Hull, C-1945
Hume, J-1998

Institute of
International
Law-1904
International Peace
Bureau-1910
International
Committee of the
Red Cross-
1917/1963

Jouhaux, L-1951

Kellog, F-1929
King, Martin L-1964
Kissinger, H-1973
de Klerk, F-1993

La Fontaine, H-1913
Lange, C-1921
Luthuli, A-1960

MacBride, S-1974
Mandela, N-1993
Marshall, G-1953
Menchu, R-1992
Moneta, E-1907
Mott, J-1946
Myrdal, A-1982

Nansen, F-1922
Noel-Baker, P-1959

Ossietçky, C-1935

Pauling,L-1962
Pearson, L-1957
Peres, S-1994
Perez Esquivel,
A-1980
Pire, D-1958

Pugwash
Committee-1995

Rabin, I-1994
Ramos-Horta-1996
Renault, L-1907
Roosevelt, T-1906
Root, E-1912
Rotblat, J-1995

Saavedra, C-1936
Sadat, A-1978
Sakharov, A-1975
Sato, E-1974
Schweitzer, A-1952
Söderblom, N-1930
Stresemann, G-1926
Suttner, B-1905

Tho, Le Duc,-1973
Trimble, D-1998
Tutu, D-1984

Wafesa, L-1983
Wiesel, E-1986
Williams, J-1997
Wilson, W-1919

Notes

Notes

Notes

Notes

Notes

Notes

Notes

Notes

C.1

R 920 SYM	Symons, Alan		
	AUTHOR		
Nobel laureates, 1901-2000			$35.00
3043039000806	TITLE		

Date	Per	Teachers Name	Room